From Social Butterfly to Engaged Citizen

From Social Butterfly to Engaged Citizen

Urban Informatics, Social Media, Ubiquitous Computing, and Mobile Technology to Support Citizen Engagement

edited by Marcus Foth, Laura Forlano, Christine Satchell, and Martin Gibbs

epilogue by Judith Donath

The MIT Press
Cambridge, Massachusetts
London, England

For information about special quantity discounts, please e-mail special_sales@mitpress.mit.edu

This book was set in Stone Sans and Stone Serif by Toppan Best-set Premedia Limited. Printed and bound in the United States of America.

Library of Congress Cataloging-in-Publication Data

From social butterfly to engaged citizen : urban informatics, social media, ubiquitous computing, and mobile technology to support citizen engagement / edited by Marcus Foth . . . [et al.] ; epilogue by Judith Donath.
    p.   cm.
Includes bibliographical references and index.
ISBN 978-0-262-01651-3 (hardcover : alk. paper)
1. Ubiquitous computing. 2. Social media. 3. Political participation. I. Foth, Marcus. II. Title.
QA76.5915.F76   2012
302.23'1—dc22

                                                              2011011450

10 9 8 7 6 5 4 3 2 1

Contents

Preface

Marcus Foth, Laura Forlano, Christine Satchell, and Martin Gibbs

This book offers a pathbreaking collection of research and theory about the emerging field of urban informatics; its form provides a material artifact that intervenes in the digital realms of communities, cities, and spaces around the world from Finland to the United States, Australia, Korea, and Bangladesh. Over the past decade, ubiquitous computing, social media, and mobile technologies have become integral parts of our social lives and work practices, as well as shaping the way we make sense of our cultures and engage as citizens. This book contributes to better understanding the opportunities and challenges provided by the tools, interfaces, methods, and practices of social and mobile technology that enable participation and engagement.

The following chapters illustrate how Web 2.0 applications such as blogs, wikis, video, and photo-sharing sites as well as social networking systems offer an arguably more open, collaborative, personalizable, and therefore more participatory Internet experience than what has previously been possible. Giving rise to a culture of participation, an increasing number of these social applications are now available on mobile phones, where they take advantage of device-specific features such as sensors, location, and context awareness. The scholars, commentators, and practitioners in this book critically examine a range of applications of social and mobile technology such as social networking, mobile interaction, wikis, twitter, blogging, virtual worlds, shared displays, and urban screens, and their role in fostering community activism, civic engagement, and cultural citizenship.

As a material artifact, the book signifies the coming together of an international group of academics and practitioners from a diverse range of disciplines such as computing and engineering, social sciences, design, digital media, and human–computer interaction. In some cases, contributors' connection to the book has developed over the course of a few months through electronic exchanges; for others, it is the result of participation in one of two workshops that preceded the editorial work on this book. The first workshop was titled "Digital Cities 6: Concepts, Methods, and Systems of Urban Informatics" and took place in June 2009 at Pennsylvania State University in University Park, as part of the Fourth International Conference on Communities and Technologies (C&T 2009). About a month later, in July 2009, an Australian Research Council Human Communication Science Network (ARC HCSNet) workshop, titled "From Social Butterfly to Urban Citizen," took place at Queensland University of Technology in Brisbane.

First and foremost, this book is about engagement with communities, cities, and spaces through the use of digital tools, applications, and devices. The majority of people on the planet now live in cities, and even in the developing world, mobile phones are now considered to be one of the primary modes of communication. The question of how to harness these technologies for the purpose of engagement is critical. We examine the topic of engagement through the lens of five different themes, which frame the main sections of the book. These are: Theories of Engagement, Civic Engagement, Creative Engagement, Technologies of Engagement, and Design Engagement. This introductory section will give a brief overview of the topics, issues, and themes covered in each section. Additionally, the specific chapters will be described in more detail in the individual section forewords.

Theories of Engagement

What theories and methods are appropriate for understanding the research questions emerging in the field of urban informatics? In this section, authors outline competing theories that have been used to analyze the complex sociotechnical configurations that are abundant in the field of urban informatics. Understanding these nuances, much less designing for them, is a challenging endeavor.

Theoretically, urban informatics research has moved beyond simplistic proclamations of "anytime, anywhere" access to data, information, and networks toward the integration of technologies into meaningful cultural practices contextualized in specific communities, cities, and spaces. From this perspective, the city is spatially constituted as a hybrid that merges digital and physical worlds into a new urban form whose technological and material edges are seemingly invisible without close analysis. At the same time, with the growing use of mobile phones, the city is temporally reorganized according to fluid time rather than fixed, clock time. Similarly, the aesthetic properties of cities are transforming with respect to bodily senses such as sight, touch, and sound. Methodologically, there is a need for experimentation with new combinations of methods in order to capture and analyze data from people, technologies, and environments.

As Dourish and Satchell argue in chapter 2, these changing understandings and social norms offer opportunities for designers to rethink how social technologies might be reframed and embedded with an ideology of a "socially conscious urban citizen." Whether driven by individual need, compelling applications, or the design of particular technologies or services, mobile technologies offer the potential for emergent forms of engagement with colocated people, objects, and environments. How can urban informatics support and enable a new urban citizenship?

Civic and Civil Engagement

In this section, authors turn to complementary realms of civic engagement around issues of food, gardening, climate change, citizen science, and activism. These kinds of civic engagement may take the form of publicly displaying information on urban screens and encouraging the participation of passersby, using technology to monitor the use of natural resources for a community, or enabling citizens to collect information about the environments around them. Underlying these different modes of engagement are competing sets of assumptions about the purpose of technology as well as about the nature of the human condition—assumptions drawing on a wide range of disciplines that contribute to the field of urban informatics. For example, what level of participation constitutes civic engagement? How do technologies incorporate the role of users? How are they appropriated, used, and codeveloped for the purposes of civil engagement in ways that have not been anticipated by the designers themselves?

In recent years, food, the environment, and sustainability have been at the forefront of political agendas and, as a result, have been taken up by scholars and practitioners in the field of urban informatics. One of the strengths of urban informatics research is its focus on the nuanced cultural practices of people and on how these practices are enhanced or constrained by technologies. This focus distinguishes the field from the scientific and economic models of sustainability, which, to a great extent, overlook the role of individuals. Specifically, emergent forms of organizing enabled by technology have great potential to contribute to healthier and more sustainable cultural practices.

Creative Engagement

How can technologies help us engage creatively with our families, our communities, our surroundings, and ourselves? This section looks at the narratives, soundscapes, media, and social interactions that make up life in urban centers around the world, including New York, Dubai, Beijing, Dhaka (Bangladesh), Melbourne, Sydney, and Aalborg (Denmark). While a plethora of location-based mobile applications have been introduced over the past decade, the majority are concerned with facilitating seamless mobility, navigation, and connectivity. The contributors to this section articulate the value of hyperlocal new media art projects that challenge the overriding assumptions embedded in the field of urban computing.

Rather than approaching the role of mobile technologies from the perspective of efficiency and productivity, these authors consider the value of play, culture, and lived experience. According to the chapter on poor Bangladeshi urban youth by Wong and Ling (chapter 15), technology is valued not for its utility but for its role as a "social machine." While at the individual level, the mobile phone occupies a key role for communicating with others, it also enables communication with interactive and digital objects such as street signs and bus stops as well as augmented reality and urban screens. In chapter 13, Kirwan and Travis describe such an ambient urban ecosystem in their analysis of "urban media" in three cities.

As devices and data move from bodies to buildings, what stories will cities tell about and to their inhabitants? How might this data—gathered from a host of wireless sensors, cameras, and networked computers—be visualized and displayed? Who will be able to participate in its creation, modification, and markup? How can we ensure that the value of play, wandering, and spontaneity is reinforced as the sentient city awakens circuit by circuit, grid by grid?

Technologies of Engagement

How do the technologies and tools of the sentient city allow us to develop new methods for understanding ourselves, our relationships, and social networks as well as the spaces, cities, and zones that we inhabit? Besides developing theoretical constructs, researchers in the field of urban informatics must also use the technologies they study in order to devise new research methods. From combining ethnographic and observational data gathered at the ground level to analyzing the flows of digital traffic in networked urban spaces, the authors in this section describe new ways of using GPS, RFID, Bluetooth, social networks, and wireless hotspots as well as the technological agendas of the Korean u-city, or ubiquitous city.

Methodological innovations have great value for advancing the field of urban informatics. While social scientists are typically trained to master only one method—for example, qualitative or quantitative research—scholars in other disciplines such as computer science or design have a greater opportunity to blend a variety of methods. This combination of techniques is vital in emergent research areas in which little is known about the subject yet the opportunities for data gathering are wide and underexplored.

Should researchers in urban informatics conduct interviews, build applications, deploy networks, or use some combination of these activities? How should they do this and in what order? By analyzing the technological details of ongoing projects, is it possible to develop better and more focused plans for research and interventions in urban environments? It is becoming more and more clear that researchers in the field of urban informatics must not only strive to develop hybrid sociotechnical (and spatial) theoretical concepts but also gain competency in a wide range of methods in order to do justice to their research subjects. It is this challenge as well as the excitement of designing new ways of knowing that makes urban informatics such a promising and engaging topic for study.

Design Engagement

Design research approaches and interventions offer a valuable way of learning about and informing the development of sentient cities. In this section, authors explore a range of design interventions in urban settings including the introduction of interaction portals and robots as well as the use of personas, charettes, and other design research techniques in order to prompt the design of mobile offices and residential dwellings. As mentioned above, design researchers have the flexibility of integrating a wide range of concepts and methods into a human-centered, iterative, agile, and interdisciplinary approach. For example, ethnography and qualitative research are often combined with highly visual activities such as mapping, prototyping, scenario planning, and personas. As design has moved from the aesthetics of graphics and usability of interfaces to creation of services and modeling of organizations and systems, it has become even more valuable to the study of urban informatics.

When understood at the level of systems, sentient cities are amenable to an Actor Network Theory (ANT) approach to evaluating the roles and interactions of people, technologies, and the built environment. As DiSalvo and Lukens argue, a "nonanthropocentric" approach is useful to grapple with the role of robots in allowing participants to see and sense the city. In addition to augmenting human awareness of the built environment, technology mediates copresence and awareness among people in public spaces through mobile social network applications such as Foursquare and interactive urban screens. As designers of spaces, technologies, and activities become more deeply engaged in the future lives of cities, it is likely that design approaches will allow us to better articulate and visualize the complex nature of sociotechnical and spatial relations.

Conclusion

Editing a book in an emerging area such as urban informatics is a challenging but exciting process. It is an exercise in attempting to draw boundaries around a field that may not yet exist. The themes, topics, and authors included in this volume are slices of a broad range of academic disciplines, theoretical traditions, and geographies around the world. While our work will sit side by side on the pages of the book, it is unlikely that we will all ever be in the same room. As many of the following chapters illustrate, urban informatics is characterized by a distinctly physical, material, and spatial relationship to technology and sociocultural practices. In the case of this book, its materiality is symbolic of a complex arrangement of social relations, technologies, and spaces.

The editors and authors of this book share a passion for understanding how people are increasingly bound up in complex sociotechnical relations in our communities, cities, and spaces as well as a fundamental concern that the technologies embedded in our everyday social lives should also enable us to engage critically, civically, and deeply with the current problems of the world. To achieve this, it is necessary to develop new concepts, theories, and methods suitable for understanding the relationships between people, technologies, and environments in concert with one another.

Hybrid theories and mixed methods offer great potential for enhancing the understanding of research subjects in the area of urban informatics. Yet, while concepts such as sociotechnical assemblages can help to steer scholars away from overly technodeterministic language, it is desirable to go much further in specifying related concepts and theories. And, while most of us would agree that sentient cities are deeply sociotechnical, it is still necessary to "zoom in," so to speak, on the exact relationship that one is studying rather than continuing to be mired in the messy and mind-boggling details. Are you mainly concerned with people? With technologies? With places? A greater and deeper focus on the core actors that you seek to understand—while keeping the overarching communicative ecology of urban informatics in mind—will greatly increase the scope, reach, impact, and value of the research. Furthermore, and in tandem with the need for a wide range of concepts that articulate the sentient city, urban informaticians are forever the inventors of new methodologies for conceiving of projects, gathering various types of data, and analyzing that data. For many of us, using the technologies we study in our daily lives as well as in research settings will allow these methods to emerge and bring great value to our research.

Our work is made significantly more challenging by the fact that our research subject is moving quickly as social norms and technologies are continually changing. At the same time, a great sense of opportunity, innovation, collaboration, and risk taking is associated with the emergence of new fields of research. It would be too difficult to forge such a path alone, and thus we are both grateful and fortunate to have included the work of so many of our colleagues around the world. Like butterflies themselves, we believe that the research presented in this book will travel across great distances and pollinate minds, universities, and academic disciplines.

Acknowledgments

As we move from a postindustrial to a digital society, our increasing need to be in contact with each other has escalated to the point where the idea of connectivity becomes one of the defining features of global cultures. The mobile artifact, for example, has transcended its initial functionality as a communications device to become a defining symbol of what it means to be a participating member of society in the early twenty-first century.

To date, much of our personal engagement with technology has been to facilitate social interactions. Yet recent technological developments provide additional functionalities that enhance the possibility for other sorts of constructive engagement. For example, not only can we find the quickest way to get across town to meet our friends, but we can also establish the most environmentally sustainable route to our destination. We believe that just as mobile phones, and more recently, social networking sites have created new spaces for social interactions, so too can new technologies be enhanced with capabilities to provide users with the opportunity for ethically driven interactions.

We would like to thank all those involved in supporting our exploration of how new and innovative advances can help transform the user from a "social butterfly" to an "engaged citizen." We are extremely grateful to the MIT Press for publishing this book, and would specifically like to thank our editor, Douglas Sery, for his insights, patience, and guidance through the process. The additional support from MIT Press staff—including Katie Helke, Elizabeth Judd, Sandra Minkkinen, and Pamela Quick—has also been invaluable.

In addition, we would like to thank John M. Carroll, who, as the chair of the Fourth International Conference on Communities and Technologies 2009, shared a vision that acted as one of the precursors to our book. To Clio Andris, who presented the keynote address at the "Digital Cities 6" workshop held on June 25, 2009, in conjunction with C&T 2009, as well as Carlo Ratti, you both exemplify the possibilities for technology to radically invigorate urban centers—thank you.

Many thanks go to the Human Communication Science Network (HCSNet) funded by the Australian Research Council, specifically Robert Dale, Chris Cassidy, and Lawrence Cavedon, who supported our workshop "From Social Butterfly to Urban Citizen," held at Queensland University of Technology in Brisbane on July 13–14, 2009. Along with "Digital Cities 6," that workshop served as one of the main incubators for this book. Of course, our keynote speaker—Adam Greenfield (founder of Urbanscale and author of *Everyware* and *The City Is Here for You to Use*)—deserves copious praise for his inspiring exploration of the potential utopian and dystopian outcomes of the digitization of urban spaces. His attendance was made possible by a generous sponsorship from the Queensland Research Lab of National ICT Australia (NICTA).

We are honored to have five renowned researchers write the section forewords, distilling the core ideas of the book and providing an intellectually rich commentary in the context of the particular theme of their section. Therefore, for their insights, we would like to thank Phoebe Sengers (Theory), Yvonne Rogers (Civic), Gary Marsden (Creative), Atau Tanaka (Technology), and Mark Blythe (Design).

We would also like to thank our colleagues who have been so generous, sharing their time and knowledge with us. These include the staff and students of the Urban Informatics Research Lab at Queensland University of Technology, especially Julie-Anne Edwards and Gretchen Coombs, as well as the Interaction Design Group at the University of Melbourne. In addition to the authors of book chapters themselves, the following colleagues acted as external reviewers who provided invaluable comments and feedback. The standard of critiques you provided was superb and played an integral part in shaping the book. The noble act of reviewing is greatly appreciated and we hope to reciprocate over time!

Marcus Foth, Laura Forlano, Christine Satchell, and Martin Gibbs

External Reviewers

• Matthew Allen, Department of Internet Studies, Curtin University of Technology, Australia
• Nicola Bidwell, James Cook University, Australia
• Axel Bruns, ARC Centre of Excellence for Creative Industries and Innovation, Queensland University of Technology, Australia
• Keith Cheverst, Computing Department, Lancaster University, UK
• Barbara Crow, Faculty of Liberal Arts & Professional Studies, York University, Canada
• Ali Dada, SAP Research, Switzerland
• Peter Dalsgaard, Information and Media Studies, Aarhus University, Denmark
• Ernest Edmonds, Faculty of Engineering and Information Technology, University of Technology, Sydney, Australia
• Ingrid Erickson, Social Science Research Council, Brooklyn, NY, U.S.

- Víctor M. González, Centro de Innovación, Investigación y Desarrollo en Ingeniería y Tecnología, Universidad Autónoma de Nuevo León, Mexico
- Elizabeth Goodman, iSchool, University of California, Berkeley, U.S.
- Connor Graham, Computing Department, Lancaster University, UK
- Mariann Hardey, Sociology, University of York, UK
- Tuck Leong, Information and Media Studies, Aarhus University, Denmark
- Jennifer Mankoff, Human-Computer Interaction Institute, Carnegie Mellon University, U.S.
- Mark McGuire, Department of Design Studies, University of Otago, NZ
- Denise Meredyth, Institute for Social Research, Swinburne University of Technology, Australia
- Anna Meroni, Politecnico di Milano, Italy
- Justin O'Connor, Creative Industries Faculty, Queensland University of Technology, Australia
- Nancy Odendaal, African Centre for Cities, University of Cape Town, South Africa
- Ismael Peña-López, School of Law and Political Science, Open University of Catalonia, Spain
- Ricky Robinson, National ICT Australia (NICTA), Australia
- Mark Rouncefield, Computing Department, Lancaster University, UK
- Mark Shepard, School of Architecture and Planning, State University of New York at Buffalo, U.S.
- Sushmita Subramanian, People and Practices Research, Intel Corp., U.S.
- Nick Taylor, Computing Department, Lancaster University, UK
- Martin Tomitsch, Faculty of Architecture, Design & Planning, University of Sydney, Australia
- Anthony Townsend, Director of Technology Development, Institute for the Future, U.S.
- Greg Wadley, Department of Information Systems, University of Melbourne, Australia
- Katharine S. Willis, Locating Media, University of Siegen, Germany
- Brit Ross Winthereik, IT University of Copenhagen, Denmark

I Theories of Engagement

Foreword

Phoebe Sengers

What is "design theory" when it comes to contemporary urban informatics? More specifically, what is design theory with respect to a topic whose community includes media theorists, technologists, policy analysts, interaction designers, and more? Centrally, it is hybrid. What is notable in the following chapters is how discussions of technologies, of people's reactions to technologies in their everyday lives, and of politics are seamlessly interwoven. These domains are not interlinked but interfused; the conversation moves without skipping a beat from one to the other and back again. Technology, society, politics, design; these are not simply co-constructed, but to some degree indistinguishable. One cannot talk of one, it seems, without speaking of the others.

In chapter 1, for example, Martijn de Waal demonstrates how specific framings of urban ubiquitous media reveal and replay particular longer-standing visions of the city as a political domain. He traces three such "technourban imaginaries." The first is a notion of city as infrastructure, rooted around an individualist ideology. The second is a liberal vision of the city as an information system where self-interested individuals can pursue their own goals while, at the same time, code becomes law. The third is a view of the city as a community, hosting encounters among "familiar strangers." Each political orientation to the city lends itself to, and is reinforced by, a particular strand of urban informatics research.

In chapter 2, Paul Dourish and Christine Satchell turn to social media, one of the components of the urban informatics vision. Common frames for social media include, on the one hand, emphasis on the democratic aspects of self-expression, and, on the other, concerns about the privacy implications of a generation publishing information about itself publically, permanently, and apparently haphazardly. Dourish and Satchell turn these individualist frames upside down by looking at the moral economy of social media—that is, moral and ethical aspects of how information is produced and exchanged. They identify four key attributes of social media from this perspective: (1) reciprocality—social media are experienced not only individually but collectively; (2) responsiveness—participation involves a temporal dimension; (3) responsibility—

moral pressures and expectations lie behind participation; and (4) rejection—the need for attention to exclusions and absences. They suggest that understanding the political dimensions of social media requires envisioning participants not just as authors and audiences of social media but in terms of publics constituted through the act of publication.

In chapter 3, Gillian Fuller and Ross Harley return us to the ubiquitous city, and particularly to the new power relations constructed through "smooth" (i.e., transparent) mobility and wireless connectivity, or, as they put it, "a new type of environment in which vision (paradoxically) recedes and everyday experience is increasingly structured by way of proxemics and exchange of information over radio waves." An invisible infrastructure of wireless dataveillance overlays the city, seducing us through its ease of access. "Touchless" technologies, they argue, actually expand the range of touch, leading to a "dance between what is perceived, what is known, and what is registered." Citizenship, Fuller and Harley argue, in the wireless city becomes unaware.

In chapter 4, Kurt Iveson focuses on the governance practices of the ubiquitous city, specifically those predicated on "Web 2.0" ideas of communication from citizens to government. He identifies specific ideologies of the city that implicitly underlie different technological interventions around graffiti and its governance: discipline, or the use of technologies to identify and sort those who break the rules of the community; responsibilization, which involves citizens themselves in identifying and reporting illegal acts or in other activities to improve their quality of life; and politicization, which encourages debate and discussion among citizens about the objectives of policy and seeks to enroll people and practices currently left out. The conclusion of this analysis is that participation is not enough to guarantee that technologies will truly be progressive; it may involve citizens collecting information on behalf of authorities rather than themselves taking part in the political constitution of their city.

From these chapters as a whole emerges a vision of the technosociopolitics of the wireless city. On the one hand, technologies enact visions of what the city could or should be that have longer histories than the ubiquitous technologies themselves. As the technologies are implemented, they reinforce these imagined urbanisms and shift them from the sphere of the imagined to the real. This is why it is necessary in evaluating urban technologies to consider the politics both of technology and of the city. At the same time, everyday actions and life around these technologies are more complex, more nuanced, more emergent than the agendas imagined for them can reflect. Design theory therefore calls for attention to both the stratifications brought through these visions-made-code and the slippage between those visions and the complexities of social action.

1 The Ideas and Ideals in Urban Media

Martijn de Waal

Over the last decade a new set of media, technologies, software, and cultural practices has emerged that changes how we experience the city and shape our urban culture. They range from the mobile phone to GPS navigation; from iPhone apps to "smart" systems that optimize traffic circulation; from listening to an alternative soundtrack on an mp3 player to using a smart phone to locate friends or nearby sites that matches one's interests.

There is no single name or discourse for these technologies. Labels range from "ubiquitous computing" to "locative media," from "ambient intelligence" to "the Internet of things," and from "the sentient city" to "urban informatics."[1] Nor do these technologies have a single point of origin or trajectory of deployment—although many do have their genesis in military research programs.[2] Some are rolled out by government agencies that want to bring order to and control urban space. Others are marketed by profit-driven telecommunication companies trying to provide their customers with personalized services. Sometimes community workers take up the technology, hoping it can enhance mutual understanding between different cultural groups. There are even artists who work with these very technologies to critique their role in promoting a consumer based society or bringing about a "society of control." And then there are the actual users of the technologies that often appropriate them in slightly different ways than intended by their designers or marketers.

What all these urban media—the catchall term that I will use in this chapter—have in common is that they no longer adhere to the anything-anytime-anywhere-new-media paradigm of the 1990s.[3] Rather, they are centered on location-sensing capacities and aim to intervene in or add to a specific here-and-now. Their exact interventions differ, but as the examples given above show, urban media are making deep inroads on a diverse range of activities of place making—be they the top-down deployment by government agencies or the bottom-up appropriation by urbanites in their everyday life.[4]

In relation to the main theme of this book—the opportunity and challenges for social participation and engagement—two different ways of theorizing urban media urge themselves on us. One would be to focus on the affordances of urban media and what these could mean for civic life.[5] The main question then would be, How does the utilization of these urban media—as the outcome of an intricate process of design and appropriation—reshape our urban society?

In this chapter, however, I would like to turn that question more or less around. Rather than looking at the way technology reshapes urban culture, I want to investigate how ideas and ideals about the city also reshape technology. What role do our ideas of what a city should be play in the design and appropriation of urban media?

Technological and Urban Imaginaries

The shaping and appropriation of technology in relation to society represents a complex process that involves many different actors—from designers to government policymakers and investors, as well as users—all of whom have their own preferences and interests. The material characteristics of the technologies themselves factor into this relationship as well. Here I want to point to one specific yet important element in these complex assemblages: the performative role of what I will call the urban-technological imaginary.

As Anne Galloway has convincingly shown in her. "A Brief History of the Future of Urban Computing and Locative Media" (2008), it is impossible to reduce the introduction of new technologies to a single idea by a single actor or institution that is rationally rolled out, step by step. Galloway points to different "forums for negotiating" that play a part in deciding "what we want and what we don't want," among which she numbers open markets, institutional regulation (courts, government agencies, NGOs), special-interest groups, and grassroots activism.

In this negotiating process, Galloway explains, expectations play a very important part. Differing visions on technology—deliberately utopian or dystopian—are uttered in this process, and these may become performative. These visions, hopes, and fears—rational or irrational, fact based or emotionally appealing—may directly affect government policy decisions, design criteria, investment by venture capitalists, people's stances toward a new product, and so on. Similarly, Flichy has called these performative expectations the "technological imaginary" (Flichy 1999; Marvin 1988).

In the field of urban development we find similar "imaginaries" at work. Is not the whole history of urban planning—from Ebenezer Howard's Garden Cities to Disney's gated community, Celebration, in Florida or Korea's "smart and sustainable city," Songdo—a history of (sometimes misguided) attempts to turn imaginary urban utopias into forms and volumes, bricks and mortar? "Urban imaginaries," writes Jude Bloomfield (2006, 46), "focus on sensory and emotional experience and practices, on the imprint of collective memory on imagining how the city could be, on the different, often conflicting social constructions of the city's future."

In the development of urban media the technological imaginary and the urban imaginary come together to form a technourban imaginary. Central issues in the debates in which the technourban discussions are shaped include: What exactly is a city? How do we expect it to function? Who has which rights? How should we as citizens—with all our differences—live together in an urban society? How can we use technology to realize these ideas? Or how do new technologies jeopardize these ideals?

More formally, the technourban imaginary is shaped around both ideas of what a city is (Is a city primarily a bunch of infrastructure or should it be understood essentially as a community?) as well as around urban ideals (What kind of community do we want the city to be; how and to whose advantage should the infrastructure be managed?). Technourban imaginaries often combine these two framings in a particular approach of what a city should be.

These particular technourban imaginaries play a role in the design of many urban media technologies. Sometimes they are made explicit in the discussion around their implementation. At other times they are left implicit. Often they relate to particular disciplinary framings of technology and society, and they almost always build on (or explicitly want to counter) historical framings of urban culture. In the rest of this chapter I would like to bring out a few of these technourban imaginaries at work in the design and appropriation of urban media and investigate how they relate to participation and citizen engagement.

U-City

The first technourban imagination I want to discuss here can be found in a design approach called "u-City." This term—short for "ubiquitous city"—has been coined by the Korean government in an attempt to promote an industry around the design of "smart cities." The central idea is that urban computing should make urban life more comfortable, efficient, and easier to manage. The focus is on systems of smart traffic management, or smart objects such as tires that give off warnings when the pressure is too low. Another interest is the development of personalized services like receiving a message when your children have arrived safely at school. Hwang (2009) calls this idea "The City as a Service."

We see similar promises in other discourses on ubiquitous computing, uttered at conferences, through advertising, and in professional publications, where new technologies are brought to the market to either increase efficiency or help personalize the city through friend finders or recommendation systems. The goal is to put people in control of their surroundings. Ubiquitous computing, it is argued, will create "seamless experiences" where computers operate calmly in the background.[6]

This particular way of understanding the city can be linked to a historic modernist idea of urban technology in which the city is envisioned as a collection of efficiently managed, ever-improving technological infrastructures whose successive rollout will bring us a better life. In their book *Splintering Urbanism* (2001), Stephen Graham and Simon Marvin trace this idea back to the mid-nineteenth century and connect it with the scientific positivism of that era. Dazzling new technologies like electricity or more mundane ones such as sewer systems would lead the way to a better life. Ambitious municipalities, they write, wanted their cities to be a "blaze of light," "rearing out of the darkness of the surrounding non-electrified regions" (p.46).[7]

These discussions on the benefits of the new infrastructures were held in concert with the first debates on the ills of the modern industrial metropolises that gave birth to the discipline of urban planning. This new professional field hoped to solve social problems like slumming, bad hygienic conditions, and the threat of social revolt by the emerging underclass by bringing a new unitary spatial order to the city. How exactly that was to be carried out varied according to which urban imaginary these planners subscribed to. Ebenezer Howard envisioned garden cities with a cooperative political and economic structure, whereas Baron Haussmann wanted to bring order to the existing city with his broad boulevards that simultaneously were to increase hygiene as well as the authorities' ability to assert military control over the masses.

At the same time, and on an important point, the u-city discourse of the twenty-first century also differs from the modernist infrastructural movement of the nineteenth century. Stephen Graham and Simon Marvin point out that in the modern industrial city, the ideals were universal access to infrastructure networks such as the electrical grid or the road system. These infrastructure networks integrated all citizens into the same technological system on the same level. Perhaps the most important aspect of Haussmann's urban imaginary, they state, was the idea to use infrastructural interventions to create a unitary city.

At the beginning of the twenty-first century, utilities and infrastructure are no longer seen as public services equally accessible by all, or as integrators that hold all the smaller elements together in a bigger system. Rather they are seen as marketable commodities sold to specific consumer groups. The modernist unitary ideal has given way to a post-Fordist and neoliberal one. For instance, a "smart toll road" will adapt its pricing scheme to demand: the busier the traffic, the higher the toll.

Such technological systems might make the city more efficient and tailored to individuals, yet these systems also address their users very differently. Whereas the modern infrastructure addresses its users as equal citizens, these personalized infrastructural services address them as "individual customers." This could create new forms of inequality. Graham (2005) speaks of an emergence of "Software Sorted Geographies" and Lieven De Cauter (2004) warns of the emergence of a "Capsular Society." Such developments could even create a shift in the relations between citizens and the city. Do people still see themselves as citizens—with all the rights and duties involved? Or are they starting to think of themselves as customers, which sets up a different relationship between the "customer" and the owner of the system as well as between users themselves?[8]

Although this critique is valuable, driving it to extremes also risks overlooking opportunities that dynamic pricing systems and flexible services may allow for civic engagement. The problem that Graham and Marvin have diagnosed is not so much the technology itself, but the urban imaginary of a neoliberal city of services. Yet couldn't these same infrastructural technologies also be deployed in the service of other urban imaginaries—for instance, an environmentally sustainable city?

Take for instance the Smart Cities project at the MIT Media Lab. The way the city is framed is again as a collective of infrastructures: "Buildings and cities can usefully be compared to living bodies. They have skeleton and skin systems that provide shelter and protection to their inhabitants, metabolic systems that process inputs of materials and energy to support daily life, and now artificial nervous systems consisting of sensors, networks, and ubiquitously embedded computational capacity."[9] Yet here the application of ubiquitous computing is applied to making the city environmentally sustainable. The project includes a design for a new city car that can be rented through a dynamic pricing system. Popular routes and times of day are more expensive than other times and routes. The goal here is not to maximize profit or to provide exclusive services to the rich, but rather to allocate scarce resources such as natural resources and mobility as efficiently as possible.

Urban Flaneurs and Situationists

The second technourban imaginary that I want to discuss here is one often found in the world of locative media art (Tuters and Varnelis 2006). In this imaginary, two old urban tropes play an important role: Walter Benjamin's flaneur and Guy Debord's Situationist International movement.

Over the last decade, many artists and designers have criticized the commercial applications of urban media, such as those based on the ideal of the u-city. They point out that the urban-technological imaginary of a personalized city tailored to one's private preferences, while blocking out undesired places or people, endangers some of the essences of their own urban ideal: a city in which play, serendipity, and curiosity play an important role.

On the centennial celebration of the Futurist Manifesto, American researcher Eric Paulos published the "Manifesto of Open Disruption and Participation" (2009), which made the case for such a conceptualization of urban culture: "We claim that the successful ubiquitous computing tools, the ones we really want to cohabitate with, will be those that incorporate the full range of life experiences. We want our tools to sing of not just productivity but of our love of curiosity, the joy of wonderment, and the freshness of the unknown." In the domain of locative media art[10] we have seen a number of experiments that match Paulos's call and have turned the urban imaginary of efficiency and personalization inside out. The project *You Are Not Here—A Dislocative Tourism Agency,* for instance, lets its participants experience the city space in an extended way. In this project a map of Baghdad is projected on the city grid of New York and participants are invited to make their way to a number of "Baghdad tourist spots" through the streets of New York. When they arrive at the corresponding location in Manhattan, they will find a sticker with a phone number. When dialed, they will hear a story about Baghdad.

The recent interest in "psychogeographic" artist interventions like this one is also apparent in art festivals that have emerged over the last few years, such as the Conflux festival in New York that wants to investigate "everyday urban life through emerging artistic, technological and social practice. . . . Over the course of the long weekend the sidewalks are literally transformed into a mobile laboratory for creative action. With tools ranging from traditional paper maps to high-tech mobile devices, artists present walking tours, public installations and interactive performance."[11]

As Dimitris Charitos, Olga Paraskevopoulou, and Charalampos Rizopoulos (2008) have pointed out, projects like "You Are Not Here" clearly reflect the ideals of the 1950s–1960s Situationist International. This group of artists, writers, and architects centered around Guy Debord worked to counter the rationalist city models tailored to the consumerist logic of the "society of spectacle" with an approach centered on subjective experiences of the city, including areas and experiences marginalized in the dominant way of thinking about urban culture.[12]

Williams, Robles, and Dourish (2009) have pointed out that the Parisian poet Baudelaire and the German philosopher Walter Benjamin also form an important source of inspiration for many urban media practitioners. Here the image of the "flaneur" is often invoked as the "solitary and thoughtful stroller" that wanders around the city casting his glance at the turbulence of the crowds, picking up its idiosyncrasies as seeds for his own thoughts and feelings. Or as Kracauer has put it: "To the flaneur the sight of the city were like dreams to a hashish smoker" (quoted in McQuire 2008, 42). Williams, Robles, and Dourish (2009) note a similarity between this fin de siècle mode of being and a design approach encouraged by Paulos and Beckman, who write: "We marvel at mundane everyday experiences and objects that evoke mystery, doubt, and uncertainty. . . . How can we design technology to support such wonderment?" (quoted in Williams, Robles, and Dourish 2009, 7)?

Although a design approach based on the principles of wonder, surprise, confusion, or dislocation may indeed enrich the experience of the city, it is not without its critics. Williams and colleagues (2009) find the position of the flaneur too detached. One wonders from a safe distance about urban phenomena, but the flaneur is never really engaged or called into action. Flanerie "privilege[s] passive voyeurism and imagination tending towards illusion. The alternate mobilities, inhabitations and appropriations alive in the city (homelessness and immigration, among other things) are left for examination by someone else" (Williams, Robles, and Dourish 2009, 7). Kazys Varnelis (2009) has attacked the rise of interest in Situationism on similar grounds by suggesting "Situationism's fatal flaw is that . . . its goal was always to valorize individual experience over the collective." There is thus a fine line of which designers working from this approach should be aware. While indeed locative media could aim to provide alternative experiences in the city, there is also the issue of how to truly engage the user.

The City as an Operating System

The third technourban imaginary I would like to bring out makes use of a metaphor in which the city is compared with computer systems. Here, the city is understood as an "operating system" or an "information processing system." This approach to cities understands them as complex systems in which the city mainly functions as a marketplace where people exchange goods, information, and cultural practices.[13]

Agency is usually located at the level of the individual who is driven by his or her own goals and desires, yet on an aggregate level particular customs, legal codes, or institutions may emerge over time, thus hardening specific practices and power relations in stone, law, or today, software code. Once emerged, these same customs, codes, or institutions may enable or restrain future actions and goals of urbanites.[14] They form the kernel of a civil society, so to speak.

Although the metaphor of the operating system itself is new, this way of framing the city also has its roots in earlier debates on urban culture. It is for instance related to the thoughts of Chicago School researcher Louis Wirth. In the late 1930s, in his influential article "Urbanism as a Way of Life" (1938), he laid out how the density of the city leads to cultural specialization, a spatial segregation of lifestyles, and a breakdown of rigid social structures.

Now, critics claim, a new urban operating system is on the rise. Wirth's OS was based on a combination of high density and the spatial proximity of different groups of urbanites who, for the most part, remain strangers to each other. The "urban OS" of our time is written in software code, can sense individual actions in real time, and can aggregate these into data that can be used to actuate all sorts of actions. This, Anthony Townsend (2000, p5) claims, changes the metabolism of urban life. For instance, through the mobile phone "decision-making and management of everyday life is increasingly decentralized," which means that the city system becomes "more complex and less predictable." Townsend call this new complex system the "real-time city" "in which system conditions can be monitored and reacted to instantaneously [and at a distance]."

This idea of the city lies behind much of the work of MIT's SENSEable City Lab. In many projects, the labs make use of the tracking affordances of urban media, tracing the whereabouts of people, city buses, or other objects throughout the city. This data is fed into a system that aggregates this information in real time and can be used in different contexts. For instance, public transport could be adjusted to real-time movements of people in the city. Here the city is conceived as an operating system that—through various real-time sensor networks—generates all sorts of (aggregated) data streams. One of the goals of urban media designers is then to build relevant services—for either consumers or citizens—that make use of and build on these real-time data streams.

In the future these developments may lead to semantic knowledge bases. In an article on the SENSEable City WikiCity project, the researchers project a future in which you can ask your urban informatics device questions like "what is the best place—with regard to my current location, weather forecast, environmental conditions and other factors—to fly a kite today" (Calabrese, Kloeckl, and Ratti 2009)?

Now that may seem like a somewhat trivial affair, but of course this depends on the sort of questions you might use to personalize the city. Change the questions, and this approach may even empower new groups. Over the last few years, reports have surfaced about African farmers who receive market prices at different locations for their produce by SMS and so are able to negotiate better prices. Small shopkeepers—again in Africa—order their supplies by SMS rather than driving to bigger cities, or use the phone to schedule appointments with clients. People who work in the informal or semiformal economies can organize their life and their use of the city more efficiently and increase their knowledge of social processes and market conditions.

The City as a Commons

A fourth technourban imaginary frames the city as a commons—a set of resources that belong to the collective of citizens. Technology is then brought in to provide tools for citizens to collectively take care of their city. Examples are the use of wikis to allow for collective planning exercises (see Schuilenburg and De Jong 2006), or the use of reputation systems that allow for trust in collective action with unknown others (see Rheingold 2002).

Artist Usman Haque's installation *Natural Fuse* is an interesting example that both illustrates and questions this approach. Participants in *Natural Fuse* receive a flower box equipped with watering equipment as well as with a bottle of vinegar. They also receive an electrical appliance such as a lamp, radio, or fan. The flower boxes and electrical appliances are linked to each other and (via the Internet) to the similar sets belonging to other users.

The central idea is that the CO_2 digestion of the plants in the network offsets the CO_2 emissions caused by the use of the electrical appliances. If all the participants in the network use less energy than their plants compensate for, the system will water the plants and they will grow. However, if all users in the system consume more energy than can be compensated for, the system will start to kill plants by releasing the vinegar in the soil of the plants.

This means that if individuals use too much energy, other people's plants will be killed. On the other hand, if they choose to conserve energy, that means someone else in the system may make use of the CO_2-absorption capacities of their plants, allowing others to temporarily use more energy. A switch on the set illustrates this choice. Users can set their system to "selfish" and thus consume more energy than they offset with their plants, or they can set the switch to "selfless."

Natural Fuse thus turns the energy management into a commons—a space and resource shared by and accessible to all participants. The idea of the commons is based on the old British custom of the communal pasture where all herdsmen in the community were allowed to graze their cattle.

However, the collective management of a commons runs at a great risk. It will only work if participants are willing to cooperate and allow for mutual accommodation. If participants only follow their own rational self-interest, the commons risks overgrazing. As Garrett Hardin (1968) has written, "The rational herdsman concludes that the only sensible course for him to pursue is to add another animal to his herd. And another. . . . Therein is the tragedy. Each man is locked into a system that compels him to increase his herd without limit—in a world that is limited."

Can we thus conceive of an urban media system that promotes the collective well-being? Could we conceive of some sort of peer-to-peer governance model that could prevent overuse of scarce resources?

This is (as I have demonstrated elsewhere) the question that *Natural Fuse* addresses; it illustrates the opportunities of an "urban energy commons" as well as the problem of the tragedy that bears the same name. It challenges our thinking about the viability of a networked urban commons. Yet it does not provide any definite answers: Would creating awareness through direct feedback mechanisms about the impact of rational selfish behavior be able to prevent it? Or would we instead need complex reputation systems? Or perhaps sentient bookkeeping systems in which our allotted ratios are kept or traded? Can we do this through peer-to-peer technologies, or do we need central institutions that act as trusted third parties (De Waal 2009a)?

The City as a Community of Strangers

The next technourban imaginary that I would like to bring out is the idea of the city as a community of strangers. Since the rise of the modern industrial metropolis, theorists such as Simmel, Sennett, Jacobs, and Lofland have pointed out that the main characteristic of urban life is to be surrounded by strangers who will remain strangers. Yet at the same time, one has to share resources and live together with these strangers and relate to their differences in some way or other (Simmel 1969; Sennett 1969; Lofland 1973; Jacobs [1961] 2000; McQuire 2008).

Both Jacobs and Lofland have demonstrated how the working of the city streets can build trust between strangers. In *The Death and Life of Great American Cities,* Jacobs describes how out of the many trivial repeated interactions of everyday life, a sense of trust between strangers is built up over time. Waiting together at the bus stop, exchanging small talk in the corner store, it is these kinds of interactions through which people become "familiar strangers" to each other. Jacobs states that "the sum of such casual, public contact at a local level . . . is a feeling for the public identity of people, a web of public respect and trust and a resource in time of personal or neighborhood need" (p. 67).

Jacobs has been critiqued for a nostalgic take on her cozy West Village city life, whereas such mechanisms in the city at large were thought to be impossible to maintain. Social geographers and urban sociologists such as Blokland and Ray (2008) have convincingly shown that such public familiarity is indeed a lot harder to find today than a few decades ago (also see Blokland 2005). Urbanites have become more mobile and their patterns of daily life are less synchronous, decreasing their opportunities for repeated interaction.

In the domain of urban media there is, however, a large interest in remediating or translating the idea of public familiarity with the help of digital media. In a way social networks like Twitter and MySpace do allow a sense of public familiarity even though one is not in the same place or same time. On the other hand, it could be argued that such networks are mainly made up of people who already know each other and thus does not do much for the building up of public familiarity—even though it is technically possible to "follow" or "befriend" strangers based on a geographic location.

Perhaps one of the best-known examples that builds on this idea of public familiarity is the project "Familiar Strangers" and the *Jabberwocky* application that came out of it. Jabberwocky is a mobile phone application that allows users to see if any familiar strangers are around—people that one has encountered before at other times and places. The designers of Jabberwocky hope that in this way a sense of feeling at home or even trust and solidarity can be promoted: "We believe that the extensions to this relationship using small personal wireless objects and applications on existing mobile phones can allow individuals to more acutely gauge their social relationship to people, places and the crowds around them over time. We also believe that such tools are capable of encouraging community solidarity, even transitory solidarity" (Paulos and Goodman 2004, 3).

The City as a Public Sphere

The last technourban imaginary I would like to discuss is the idea of the city as an active public sphere. This imaginary too departs from the notion that the city consists of strangers who must live together: the focus is now on how the city allows them to be confronted with each other, to exchange ideas, and to debate the future of the city. Often this ideal is juxtaposed with the suburban ideal of homogeneity. Urban citizens among others, Richard Sennett claims, should not retreat to their comfort zones, but instead should embrace the complexities, differences, and conflicts that urban life brings about (Sennett 1970, 1977, 1990, 2001).

Over the last decade we have seen many urban media projects that in one way or another seem to answer Sennett's call (albeit sometimes indirectly). There is for instance a whole range of geoannotation projects that allow citizens to mark up urban space with their own ideas, histories, or thoughts. Often the hope is expressed that these projects will lead to an exchange of insights.

In an article in the 2006 *Leonardo Electronic Almanac*, Lily Shirvanee expects that the sharing of experiences through locative media could lead to what she has called "social viscosity." The stories collected could work as crystallization points for (imagined) communities or starting points for processes of exchange, deliberation, or contestation. Shirvanee suggests that "this viscosity of space is perceived as a bond that may exist not only between people with established relationships who can find each other 'on the street' in a mobile context, but also between strangers, thereby inspiring a new community and, possibly, creating the potential for a more democratized public space."

An example is the project *Textales* that uses an urban screen to bring about a site for contestation in the city. The initiators organized workshops in which participants were asked to make pictures of political issues that affected life in their neighborhood—such as housing inequity. These pictures were shown on an urban screen in the neighborhood and passersby could comment on the pictures by sending a text message that would be displayed on the screen. In an article on the project Annay and Strohecker (2009) directly refer to theories on democracy and deliberation and hope that a project like *Textales* can help to form "issue publics" around particular concerns in which a "collective epistemology" might arise "that helps us to consider our own viewpoints and those of our fellow citizens."

Conclusion

I have now shown six technourban imaginaries at work in both the design and appropriation of urban media. This list is not meant to exhaustive. Rather I wanted to bring out a number of different and sometimes conflicting perspectives on what the city should be and how technology is thought to bring that ideal about. I wanted to show that whereas we often focus on the impact of technology on urban culture, the reverse is also true. Many urban media are purposely designed to remediate traditional ideas about urban culture.

Also, the neat categorization I have made here serves an analytic purpose only. Several of these technourban imaginaries could be combined. In fact, it could be argued that projects whose main focus can be reduced to a single framing of what a city is are often problematic. For instance, advocates of the city as a set of personalized infrastructures might miss important points about the fact that a city is also a community and thus contributes to the balkanization of urban culture.

Similarly, many art projects that do address the city as a (political) community have their own critics. Many of these projects are noncommittal. Their duration is often short, their audience is a small self-selected crowd, and only seldom is there follow-up that might turn these art projects into a more sustainable addition to the experience of the city. Could they be integrated in the infrastructure of the city in a more durable way? In short, designers of urban media would do best to address several framings of the city at once. This criticism—although important—does not mean that these art projects are meaningless. What many of them at least do well is tease out the techno-urban imaginaries at work in the shaping of urban media. These can be valuable contributions to the general debate.

Only by bringing out these often-implicit urban ideals can we engage in the discussion of how these urban media can best serve society. That is what I have tried to do here. By highlighting the urban ideas and ideals at work in discussions on urban media, I hope to show that the process in which these technologies are designed and appropriated is an open one. And even though one or two of these urban-technological imaginaries may dominate the debate and design of new services, there are also alternatives.

Notes

This contribution builds on and elaborates some of my earlier work on this theme, especially De Waal 2009b. I also build on the notion of latent ideals in urban media as described in Williams, Robles, and Dourish 2009.

1. See for instance Galloway 2008 for an extensive list of different labels.

2. An important impetus for the development of urban media was the decision of the U.S. military in 2000 to make an unscrambled version of the GPS system available to the general public. From then on, the signal has been accurate enough to pinpoint users of GPS devices on street level rather than somewhere in a neighborhood. Many Location Based Media now make use of this location-sensing technology.

3. This shift from "placelessness" to "situatedness" has been theorized by Tuters and Varnelis 2006, Varnelis 2008, as well as Shepard and Greenfield 2007. On a formal level, Mark Tuters and Kazys Varnelis (2006, http://networkedpublics.org/locative_media/beyond_locative_media) have pointed out two main characteristic affordances of what they call "locative media" that enable this shift from "placelessness" to "situatedness." One is the capacity to annotate places, "virtually tagging the world." The other affordance has a phenomenological quality that enables "tracing the action of the subject in the world."

4. As Lefebvre has shown, the experience of place is always a negotiation between the physical top-down design and ordering of space by governments, architects and developers, and the personal trajectory of its inhabitants—their history, memories, and symbolic interpretations of the space. Urban media can thus be understood as an extra layer somewhere between Lefebvre's top-down representation of space and his bottom-up representational space.

5. Hutchby (2001) has defined affordances as the "functional and relational aspects which frame while not determining the possibilities for agentic action in relation to an object. In this way technologies can be understood as artefacts which may be both shaped by and shaping of the practices humans use in interaction with, around and through them." The term *affordances* "stress[es] that the range of possibilities for interpretation and action is nowhere near as open for either 'writers' or 'readers' as the technology as text metaphor implies. . . . We have to accept that technological artefacts do not amount simply to what their users make of them; what is made of them is accomplished in the interface between human aims and the artefact's affordances" (p. 450).

6. Mark Weiser's influential article "The Computer of the 21st Century" (1991) and his publication co-authored with Seely Brown, *Designing Calm Technology* (1995), are often referred to in this debate. See also Anne Galloway's (2008, 113) take on the history of ubicomp, in which she explains how "the desire to have computing so seamlessly and efficiently embedded in our daily lives is grounded in a profoundly utopian vision connected to cultural and historical notions of technological 'progress.'" At the same time she argues that Weiser's claim has often been misunderstood. Although he argues for an "invisible" technology, he also stresses the importance of seamful experiences.

7. Graham and Marvin (2001) connect this positivist outlook on urban infrastructures with broader social developments. For instance, the urban reform movement inspired by this idea "was led by sanitarians, engineers, urban planners, and the growing middle class" and they "equated the efficiency of infrastructural systems with the quality of the entire civilization" (p. 44). The regulation of water for instance played an important part. The scientific discovery of bacteria and the privatization of bodily hygiene played was important for the ideas about the sanitized, hygienic city, and the emergence of underground waterducts.

8. See also my earlier contribution about this debate (De Waal 2009b).

9. William Mitchell, *Welcome!*, http://cities.media.mit.edu/.

10. The term "locative media" started to surface around 2003 as a label for art projects that used location-based technologies such as GPS receivers. Genealogies of locative media often trace the term to an artistic workshop organized in 2003 by Marc Tuters and Karlis Kalnins together with the RICX Media Centre in Latvia (see http://locative.x-i.net for a description of the workshop). The phrase "locative media" was initially invoked to demarcate this technological art practice from two other fields. The first was the artistic practice of "net.art" that focused on the placeless experience of cyberspace through the computer terminal. Locative media art was to break down the barrier between the physical world and a virtual world. It aimed to use technology to connect the database world of the Internet with the experience of real places. Second, the term "locative

media" claimed the use of these technologies for art practice rather than for commercial services that had started to develop under the name of "location-based services."

11. See the Conflux website, "About," http://confluxfestival.org/2009/about/.

12. Others also point out links with Constant's infrastructural urban utopia New Babylon or Archigram's advocacy for using technology to empower people to shape their own urban infrastructure (McQuire 2008). Similarly, the experimental interest of locative media art can also be linked to the vocabulary of 1960s architects such as Team Ten, who "were the first to seek a kind of town planning and architecture that could bring about pleasure, uncertainty, relaxation . . . and even disorder" (Rouillard 2007, 17).

13. See for example Anthony Townsend (2009, xxiii): "In the pre-electronic era, face-to-face proximity and the clustering of functions was the most efficient means of replicating, transmitting and searching for information in social and economic networks. Over time, new tools augmented this function, but in a sense the city itself is our original greatest information technology."

14. This vision is brought forward in De Landa 2006.

References

Annay, Mike, and Carol Strohecker. 2009. TexTales: Creating interative forums with urban publics. In M. Foth, ed., *Handbook of Research on Urban Informatics: The Practice and Promise of the Real-Time City*. Hershey, PA: IGI Global.

Blokland, Talja. 2005. *Goeie buren houden zich op d'r eigen*. The Hague: Dr. Gradus Hendriks-stichting Den Haag.

Blokland, Talja, and Douglas Ray. 2008. The end of urbanism: How the changing spatial structure of cities affected its social capital potentials. In T. Blokland and M. Savage, eds., *Networked Urbanism: Social Capital in the City*. Burlington, VT: Ashgate.

Bloomfield, Jude. 2006. Researching the urban imaginary: Resisting the erasure of places. In F. Bianchini, ed., *Urban Mindscapes of Europe*. New York:Editions Rodopi.

Calabrese, Francesco, Kristian Kloeckl, and Carlo Ratti. 2009. WikiCity real-time location-sensitive tools for the city. In M. Foth, ed., *Handbook of Research on Urban Informatics: The Practice and Promise of the Real-Time City*. Hershey, PA: IGI Global.

Charitos, Dimitris, Olga Paraskevopoulou, and Charalampos Rizopoulos. 2008. Location-specific art practices that challenge the traditional conception of mapping. *Artnodes* 8.

De Cauter, Lieven. 2004. *De capsulaire beschaving. Over de stad in het tijdperk van de angst*. Rotterdam: NAi Publishers.

De Landa, Manuel. 2006. *A New Philosophy of Society*. New York: Continuum International Publishing Group.

De Sola Pool, I. 1973. Public opinion. In I. de Sola Pool, F. Frey, N. Schramm, N. Maccoby, and E. B. Parker, eds., *Handbook of Communication*. Chicago: Rand McNally.

De Waal, Martijn. 2009a. *Three Philosophical Questions about the "Sentient City"—A Response to the Exhibition towardthe Sentient City*. New York: Architectural League of New York.

De Waal, Martijn. 2009b. The urban ideals of location-based media. In H. Tsui and N. Ford, eds., *Cities of Desire: An Urban Culture Exchange between Vienna and Hong Kong*. Vienna: City Transit Publisher.

Flichy, Patrice. 1999. The construction of new digital media. *New Media & Society* 1 (1): 33–39.

Galloway, Ann. 2008. "A Brief History of the Future of Urban Computing and Locative Media." Ottawa: Faculty of Graduate Studies and Research, Department of Sociology and Anthropology, Carleton University.

Graham, Stephen. 2005. Software-sorted geographies. *Progress in Human Geography* 29 (5): 562–580.

Graham, Stephen, and Simon Marvin. 2001. *Splintering Urbanism: Networked Infrastructures, Technological Mobilities and the Urban Condition*. London: Routledge.

Hardin, Garrett. 1968. The tragedy of the commons. *Science* 162 (3859):1243–1248.

Hutchby, Ian. 2001. Technologies, texts and affordances. *Sociology* 35 (2): 441–456.

Hwang, Jong–Sung. 2009. U-city: The next paradigm of urban development. In M. Foth, ed., *Handbook of Research on Urban Informatics: The Practice and Promise of the Real-Time City*. Hershey, PA: IGI Global.

Jacobs, Jane. [1961] 2000. *The Death and Life of Great American Cities*. London: Pimlico.

Lofland, Lyn. 1973. *A World of Strangers: Order and Action in Urban Public Space*. New York: Basic Books.

Marvin, Carolyn. 1988. *When Old Technologies Were New: Thinking about Electric Communications in the Late Nineteenth Century*. New York: Oxford University Press.

McQuire, Scott. 2008. *The Media City: Media Architecture and Urban Space*. Thousand Oaks, CA: Sage.

Paulos, Eric. 2009. Manifesto of open disruption and participation. In E. Paulos, ed., *Paulos.net*.

Paulos, Eric, and Elizabeth Goodman. 2004. The familiar stranger: Anxiety, comfort and play in public places. In *Proceedings of CHI*. New York: ACM Press.

Price, Vincent. 1992. *Public Opinion*. Thousand Oaks, CA: Sage.

Rheingold, Howard. 2002. *Smart Mobs: The Next Social Revolution*. Cambridge, MA: Perseus.

Rouillard, Dominique. 2007. The invention of urban interactivity. *Anomalie digital_arts* 6. Interactive Cities: 3-17.

Schuilenburg, Marc, and Alex De Jong. 2006. *Mediapolis*. Rotterdam: 010 Publishers.

Sennett, Richard. 1969. *Classic Essays on the Culture of Cities*. New York: Appleton-Century-Crofts.

Sennett, Richard. 1970. *The Uses of Disorder: Personal Identity and City Life*. New York: Norton.

Sennett, Richard. 1977. *The Fall of Public Man*. New York: Knopf.

Sennett, Richard. 1990. *The Conscience of the Eye: The Design and Social Life of Cities*. New York: Knopf.

Sennett, Richard. 2001. A flexible city of strangers. *Monde Diplomatique*, February.

Shepard, Mark, and Adam Greenfield. 2007. Urban computing and its discontents. In M. Shepard, O. Khan, and T. Scholz, eds., *Architecture and Situated Technologies Pamphlets*. New York: Architectural League of New York.

Shirvanee, Lily. 2006. Locative viscosity: Traces of social histories in public space. *Leonardo Electronic Almanac* 3. http://leoalmanac.org/journal/vol_14/lea_v14_n03-04/toc.asp.

Simmel, Georg. 1969. The metropolis and mental life. In Richard Sennett, ed., *Classic Essays on the Culture of Cities*. New York: Appleton-Century-Crofts.

Townsend, Anthony. 2000. Life in the real-time city: Mobile telephones and urban metabolism. *Journal of Urban Technology* 7 (2): 85–104.

Townsend, Anthony. 2009. Foreword. In M. Foth, ed., *Handbook of Research on Urban Informatics: The Practice and Promise of the Real-Time City*. Hershey, PA: IGI Global.

Tuters, Marc, and Kazys Varnelis. 2006. Beyond locative media: Giving shape to the Internet of things. *Leonardo* 39 (4): 357–363.

Varnelis, Kazys. 2008. *Networked Publics*. Cambridge, MA: MIT Press.

Varnelis, Kazys. 2009. Against Situationism. *varnelis.net*.

Weiser, Mark. 1991. The computer of the 21st century. *Scientific American*, September, 94–100.

Weiser, Mark, and John Seely Brown. 1995. *Designing Calm Technology*. Palo Alto, CA: Xerox Parc.

Williams, Amanda, Erica Robles, and Paul Dourish. 2009. Urbane-ing the city: Examining and refining the assumptions behind urban informatics. In M. Foth, ed., *Handbook of Research on Urban Informatics: The Practice and Promise of the Real-Time City*. Hershey, PA: IGI Global.

Wirth, Louis. 1938. Urbanism as a way of life. *American Journal of Sociology* 44 (1): 1–24.

2 The Moral Economy of Social Media

Paul Dourish and Christine Satchell

Technologies such as social networking sites and microblogging applications are tightly enough coupled to conventional mass media that it is instructive to examine them from a media perspective. Such an orientation draws our attention away from the details of interaction with particular applications and more to the forms of public enacted through participation with digital social media. We draw on a series of studies to illustrate the moral and social character of participation in social media, and suggest that the emergence of new publics in social media may provide a useful approach to analysis of digital media ecologies.

In the growing focus on networked information systems as part of a broader pattern of engagements between people, publics, and audiences, we have witnessed the emergence of "social media"—digital systems through which people engage in social relations of many sorts. Examples of technologies that fall under this broad umbrella are social networking sites, social virtual realities, blogging and microblogging, always-on mobile communication, and systems for sharing media and user-generated content. At their heart they focus not just on individuals but also on collectives and on connecting people together—they are, in that sense, social. Similarly, they are media in the traditional sense of interaction mediated by representational forms, but also in the more informal sense that they live alongside "traditional media"—print, images, film, TV, radio, and so on—as a source of information and a site of engagement. Arguably, then, the understanding of social media—their uses and consequences—reaches beyond traditional questions of usability and lies more in the area of sociality and engagement.

As users of social media are well aware, however, conventions and norms of behavior adapted from everyday life often map poorly into the online domain. When using social media sites such as Facebook, Flickr, YouTube, and Twitter, the metaphors that they use to link people together—"friends," "followers," "fans," "contacts," and so on—are only the loosest guide (if any) to online behavior; instead, social media, as new sites of interaction, are places where new behaviors emerge. Our primary topic here considers the dilemmas and responsibilities of online life in social media—the

tensions of being connected or disconnected, the quandaries over accepting or rejecting connection requests, the difficulties of crafting identity for fluid audiences, and
the dynamics of interaction. We argue it is in these troubles that we see the novelties
of social media emerge.

In this chapter we take a high-level view of social media, focusing not on specific
applications, domains, websites, or technologies, but on the forms of engagement that
social media engender. This is not to suggest that all social media are the same, or
even that everyone's experience with any particular medium or technology is the
same. However, we argue common issues arise that characterize social media in a broad
sense, and provide a different analytic perspective than we would gain from looking
at particular systems or applications. We do not take the perspective that social life
merely happens "within" such systems, or that social life "shapes" such systems, but
rather that these systems provide a site for the production of social and cultural reality.
In other words, media are always already social and the engagement with, in, and
through media of all sorts is a thoroughly social phenomenon.

Accordingly, in this chapter, we examine two phenomena concurrently: social life
seen through the lens of social media, and social media seen through the lens of social
life. In particular, we want to understand the ways that a set of broad phenomena
concerning forms of participation in social life is articulated in the domain of social
media. As a conceptual entry point, we use the notion of the "moral economy" as a
means to open up the domain of inquiry.

We first discuss the notion of the "moral economy" as it has been used by a number
of social theorists, and then identify a particular set of conceptual concerns that we
suggest link it to the phenomena of social networking in general. We then discuss a
series of examples drawn from a range of studies to elaborate and ground this conceptual framework in empirical data. This leads us to a broader consideration of audiences and publics in social media that, we suggest, holds important lessons for how
we treat social media analytically.

The Moral Economy

We regard social media as novel sites for the expression of age-old problems. Accordingly, the framework we bring to it is one that has been developed by scholars of other
aspects of social life.

Different scholars have used the term *moral economy* in slightly different ways. One
early and classic account of the moral economy is that of historian E. P. Thompson
in his influential paper, "The Moral Economy of the English Crowd in the Eighteenth
Century" (1971). Thompson examines accounts of a number of food riots that
"erupted" in English towns and villages throughout the eighteenth century. Both
contemporary and historical accounts of these riots depict them as outbreaks of

irrational violence on the part of turbulent mobs, a view that denies the rioters any conscious historical or political agency. Thompson argues instead for the crowds as engaged in rationally motivated defense of traditional values in the emergence of modern market capitalism. In Thompson's analysis, the violence of the riots was not an instinctive response spurred by hunger, but instead was rooted in outrage over price gouging by bakers and others in the face of scarcity. The rioters, Thompson suggests, were not motivated by hunger, greed, or the desire for free bread; rather, they expected bakers to respect the social contract by which their primary responsibility was toward their fellow townspeople. Appropriate compensation for their labor was due in this context; price gouging, by contrast, was a symptom of the erosion of social relations by the logic of the market and the primacy of profit. The conflict between these motivations and principles for the organization of economic arrangements underwrote the violent incidents.

Thompson's notion of the "moral economy" focuses on the moral and ethical considerations that underwrite and surround economic activity. In her studies of the social organization of scientific enterprises, Lorraine Daston (1995) provides a somewhat different account. Unpacking the "moral economy of science," Daston argues that scientific practice is not simply compatible with but dependent on an underlying social structure that is suffused with moral values—commitments to collectivity, objectivity, mobility, and applicability, among others. In contrast to the norms of scientific communities famously outlined by Merton, Daston's moral economy is foundational to the content as well as the practice of science—to its objects and to the objectivities with which they are produced. Here, then, the "economy" reaches beyond commercial exchange to encompass a wider social framework of collective engagement with acts of production, consumption, and regulation.

Daston's expansive use of the term *economy* to encompass a wider range of social structures is reminiscent of Baudrillard's ([1970] 1988) exploration of the way economic models of production and consumption come to dominate the experience of everyday life. Baudrillard does not employ the term *moral economy* and yet it is implicitly present in his exploration of, in the first instance, the expansion of the disciplines of industrial capitalism to consumption as well as production, and, in the second, their encroachment on leisure activities as well as working activities. He talks of the "ethics of pressured performance"—the dynamics of "efficiency" that come to dominate everyday life, expressed in the need to cram every moment of a vacation with appropriately engaging activities, the pressure to be conversant with popular culture motifs, the moral imperative to fill leisure time with hobbies and amateur pursuits, and, by contrast, the scorn and shame often associated with "wasted time."

Taking these three views together, then, we can identify a set of common themes that ground our use of the notion of moral economy. The central idea that we want to explore is the moral and ethical dimension of systems of production, consumption, and reciprocal exchange. We see these as extending beyond the sphere of traditional economic life, focusing more generally on an economic reading of everyday actions—most particularly, here, the patterns of social relations embodied in social media. At the center of this lie the problems of reciprocality, responsiveness, responsibility, and rejection. How do activities in social media engender reciprocal social responsibilities? What forms of responsiveness are expected? What opportunities for rejection do they open up?

These are not new problems, of course; they are issues that attend all communication media. The pressures associated with media responsiveness are demonstrated in studies of the temporalities of electronic mail exchange (Tyler and Tang 2003) as well as those that figure "availability for interaction" as a central consideration in both face-to-face and electronically mediated environments (e.g., Avrahami, Fussell, and Hudson 2008; Fogarty, Hudson, and Lai 2004) However, the rapid uptake of new communication technologies and the spread of new forms of social media (such as social networking websites) create new pressures and contexts in which these questions come to the fore.

In a much-cited paper that anticipated the application of metaphors of political and cultural economy to social media, Taylor and Harper (2002) draw on Marcel Mauss's anthropological studies of the "gift economy" as a way of understanding text messaging on mobile phones (Mauss [1950] 1990). Mauss had studied cultural settings characterized by the exchange of goods through gifting rather than through market capitalism, and Taylor and Harper suggest that similar practices are at work in both how gifts are given and how media objects are valued. However, an important aspect of Mauss's analysis is missing from Harper and Taylor's account. Through the example of the potlatch, Mauss draws attention to the status achieved through gift giving—a demonstration not so much of conspicuous consumption as of conspicuous generosity. As Mauss notes, the expectations of reciprocity in gift giving lead inevitably to a breakdown where the generosity of a gift, or the splendor of a public feast, can no longer be matched. Mauss's gift economy, then, is not purely altruistic; it is a form of status display, a status battle that can be won or lost. Thus, inherent in the gift is the specter of the failure to match it; gifting is seen in a broader context of extended exchange and reciprocal responsibilities. Our concern here is with this movement from "gift" to "gift economy" implied by the iteration of interactions over time.

Conceptual Framework

In applying the concept of moral economy to the phenomena of social media, we begin by setting out the conceptual resources that we think each term offers. We will begin here by exploring in a little more detail what we mean by social media, and what it implies to take that particular perspective. We will then detail some particular concerns that arise from adopting the perspective of the moral economy.

Social Media

Although we opened this chapter with an informal account of what we mean by social media, it is useful to draw attention to some particularly salient concerns that arise when we take this perspective. By focusing on "social media" rather than on specific technologies or on concepts such as social networking or community, particular considerations are brought into view.

The first—consonant with a concern with moral economy—includes considerations of production and consumption. Theories of media arising from, say, the Frankfurt school (e.g., Adorno 1991) or the Birmingham school (e.g., Warner 2002) have developed different positions on the nature of media forms as expressions of—or sites for contests over—ideology, power, and control. Although this is not our primary topic here, we are certainly concerned with the force of normative behavior in and around social media. More generally, though, by invoking these kinds of perspectives, our goal is to think of media in terms of the conjoined production and consumption of media objects and events—whether those are SMS messages, Facebook groups, Twitter "tweets," YouTube videos and comments, Flickr photographs and tags, MySpace pages, or e-mail messages. To the extent that these are brought forth explicitly for others, and viewed, processed, reproduced, and commented on by others, we find the metaphor of production and consumption useful.

The second concern that the perspective raises is on forms of participation. Thinking in terms of media rather than simply technologies, and then acknowledging the ways media are shaped by forms of social engagement, focuses attention on the forms and degrees of participation in which people engage around media. In particular, for us, we think of media in terms of *ecologies* of participation—the differential, collective uptake of different media concurrently, and the ways they are employed in concert rather than separately and individually. The abstracted focus on media emphasizes diversity. Different users will tend to have very different configurations and ecologies of media in terms of their forms of participation.

Similarly, this stands in contradistinction to the unifying, essentializing, and homogenizing tendencies associated with studies of "community." Rather than focus on "community" as an object or an outcome, we want instead to think about the practices of mediated engagement through which individuals enact social relationships. For example, when one considers a social network site such as Facebook, Friendster, Orkut, or LinkedIn, questions of "community" are immediately thrown into question. One person's Facebook status updates are immediately visible to everyone linked to them, for instance, but yet, since everyone has a different set of links, everyone's page of "latest updates" is unique. How, then, does a focus on "community" apply? Later, we will suggest that Michael Warner's work on "publics" provides some useful intellectual leverage. For the moment, we simply note that our focus is on observable media interactions rather than on the more abstract notion of community.

Moral Economy

If we take the notion of moral economy as our high-level framework, what series of issues does it raise for the experience of social media? An orientation toward moral economies directs us to think of patterns of exchange, moral pressures, and their ethical interpretations. For our purposes here, though, we identify a series of themes that connect the experience of social media to the broader arguments of reciprocality, responsiveness, responsibility, and rejection. These are not entirely independent categories—each shapes and frames the others. However, they serve as a set of orienting ideas through which we will be able to unpack specific examples.

Reciprocality[1] identifies a fundamental concern that the experience of social media is at once an individual and a collective experience. People participate together, and that togetherness or collective engagement requires some kind of alignment between their expectations, their performances, and their actions. Part of the effort associated with social media is the effort of developing this sense of the reciprocal engagements that it supports; learning "how things work around here," and crafting a personal presence that aligns with others. Even within a single medium, these may differ widely; there are different clusters of behavior associated with any system as it gets adopted and appropriated by different groups, and indeed, patterns of engagement and the norms of online behavior change and evolve over time. The central idea here, though, is that people are connected through their engagements; they mutually condition the experience of social media for each other in direct and distanciated ways, and the alignments of actions and interests produce collective behaviors that contextualize individual actions.

Responsiveness draws attention to the temporal organization of actions in social media. Actions in social media play out over time, and take on their own temporalities that in turn shape individual participation. Blog posts, tweets on Twitter, updates on social networking sites, SMS text messaging, and e-mail, for instance, all have temporal dimensions. Although each of us might have a different set of expectations about the temporal organization of each in our own lives, the fact that we do associate temporalities with them at all—thinking of some as slow and stately, some as fast-paced blips, some as fleeting, and some as deep. Different social media tend to find their way into our own private media ecologies in different ways, but a central concern arises in the matching of temporalities between people—how responsive people are, when they might be expected to see actions, when they might be expected to respond to them, how often they might be expected to be present or visible, and so forth. Responsiveness speaks to the temporalities of collective engagement with social media.

Responsibility identifies the moral pressures that lie behind participation and engagement with social media. Clearly, one does not hold a responsibility to media but rather to each other, expressed through such media. However, the fundamental concern here is that social media set expectations—that if one has a blog, one should post to it regularly, or that if one follows someone on Twitter, one should keep on top of the recent updates. The moral and ethical dimension of this responsibility is manifested in at least two ways: first, as a moral pressure that expresses itself primarily as a lack or a failure (the failure to update the blog as often as one should, or the sense that things are being missed in the Twitter stream), and second, as a form of social sanction—that is, something that offers to others the possibility to criticize, upbraid, or comment on one's failure to live up to expectations.

Finally, here, by introducing a notion of *rejection*, we acknowledge the importance of exclusion and absence in the social settings that social media create. An absence may be as remarkable as a presence, and rejection—whether the exclusion of individuals in a particular media form, or someone's refusal to participate altogether—are part and parcel of the experience (Satchell and Dourish 2009). The dynamics of social media as a whole mean that the "center of mass" may shift and change—from one form to another, from one site to another, from one application to another, or, more likely, in ever-shifting configurations of multiple media. If, from the perspective of the moral economy, participation in social media is a form of participation in collective social relations, then it follows that social media also provide the basis for forms of nonparticipation, exclusion, segregation, separateness, and isolation—intentionally or otherwise. Indeed, the very idea that different social media have different target audiences or user classes, or that they lend themselves to forms of use that are connected to specific, different social groups, directly invokes a form of separation as well as a form of collectivity.

A crucial aspect of what we are exploring is social behavior produced in virtual public, and the classic work of Erving Goffman (1959, 1963) is clearly relevant. Goffman's detailed and insightful studies of face-to-face conduct and public behavior turn on the importance of managing "face" and the distinction between the forms of interaction and social display that take place between the different roles people play—such as between the "front-stage" behavior of professors meeting with students, and their "back-stage" conversations behind closed doors. Goffman explores the range of pressures on conformance to norms in public, and the practices by which identity pressures are managed. However, while his work remains crucially important in online environments, there is more going on here. Goffman largely takes "public" for granted, and indeed, although in many of the cases he explores there are significant social, economic, and geographic conditions on participation, his assumptions are not unwarranted. In the online world, though, "public" is more complicated. The public cannot be taken for granted, because the public is not well understood, and "public behavior" is itself in question. Publics are being constituted through action in social media, and the question of what might be public, what might be private, what might occupy some transitional space, and how that transitional space is to be defined and determined—these questions are all under definition and debate. In fact, the critical question here is how the moral economy of social media—the social relations being enacted and developed through them—are generative of a notion of "public." We return to this question after considering some empirical evidence.

Watching Social Media Happen

Having painted the theoretical backdrop, we now want to discuss some specific cases of social media use. The experiences we discuss in this section are drawn from a range of studies conducted over the last few years, including some data gathered specifically for this investigation. We first drew on a three-year investigation of young peoples' use of mobile phones. Thirty-five technologically competent users, eighteen to thirty years old, living in Melbourne, Australia, participated. A second study focused in more detail on the experiences of four people using mobile blogging software in support of their efforts to stop smoking (Graham et al. 2007). We supplemented these with an investigation specific to the issues outlined here, which included eleven people, aged twenty-six to forty-one, one student, eight professionals and two full-time parents, using several different technologies, and both users and nonusers of social media tools. In all cases, open-ended interviews were conducted and grounded theory techniques were used to analyze the data. However, given the mix of studies, we do not present these as ethnographic or quasi-ethnographic accounts of media culture; rather, we present them as illustrative examples that allow us to see how some of the concepts we have discussed above play out in practice.

The Production of Acceptable Personas

Social media create opportunities to present oneself to others. Unsurprisingly, issues also arise over the question of how one wants to be presented, and to whom. When social media participants involve groups from many different spheres of life—work colleagues, professional acquaintances, neighbors, friends, family, and strangers—the problems of crafting an appropriate persona may become especially acute. This is reflected in the privacy settings associated with many social media technologies, which allow others to be grouped or categorized, yet these explicit articulations rarely capture the nuance and complexity of ongoing social relationships.

This may be experienced as positive or negative—for some, the ease of having everyone in one place outweighs the problems of collapsing social worlds. However, complex social pressures attend the mixing of people across social media. Several of our participants noted recurring difficulties turning down a work-related request on social sites: "You can't say no to a work colleague can you? And that is the worst thing. Once you say yes to them you need to think about what you write on Facebook" (Chloe, thirty-three, primary school teacher).

The difficulty crafting appropriate personas was vividly demonstrated in a study that followed four participants' attempts to give up smoking with the aid of a mobile-phone-based blogging software. The problems arose when people did not stop smoking and felt the twin moral pressures—to engage with others through the system but also to show themselves as successful "quitters." Fleur, a thirty-two-year-old research associate, commented, "I've got a reason to not use the technology anymore because I'm still smoking. Blogging—why would I want to share this with the world?" The sense that, through social media, an image of oneself is presented to the world brings with it considerations of what that "self" should be.

The Perils of Disconnection

The mobile-phone study highlighted that connectivity provided mobile-phone users with a sense of reassurance; however, with this comes the consequence of vulnerability due to unwanted calls. Users tried to protect themselves against this seemingly contradictory dynamic of openness versus isolation. Essentially, the mobile phone created conflicted users who tried to balance the need for connectivity with the desire to be, at times, uncontactable.

A participant in this study, Maria, twenty-seven, described how the very act of turning her phone off—a decision meant to provide a brief respite from day-to-day responsibilities—had created the need for discourses of justification in regard to why she had failed in her responsibility to be connected. The act of turning her mobile phone off to enhance the "back-to-nature" experience of a two-day hiking trip in the Blue Mountains, just outside Sydney, Australia, resulted in her mother and sister filing a missing persons report because her phone had been switched off for nearly forty-eight hours. This example also raises questions about the problems of voluntary—if temporary—nonparticipation in social media, and the customs and habits that we acquire when we expect others to be available to us. What is at issue here is not that the phone was turned off, but that it was so unusual that this happened; after all, the problem that gave rise to the alert when Maria was missing was not simply that her location was unknown (it would have taken a good deal longer to determine this), but rather that the usually instantaneous contact could not be established. What it attests to is that it is no easy individual decision to render oneself unavailable via any tool, technological or not; it implies something about how one is engaged with others. Again, this is not to tell a story of "a world out of control" but simply to underscore the way that presence and participation create new interpretive frames within which absence is read (and vice versa).

Social Network Manicuring

Among users of social networking sites in particular, the intricacies of navigating the tricky new social conundrums thrown up by Facebook interactions were commonly discussed. These included maintaining a dedication to the site, deciding how and when to deflect an unwanted friendship request, the need to "manicure" one's network by defriending, the possibility that a digital friendship "cull" might spill into a real-world encounter, reading the cultural signifiers of loose-tie and close-tie refriending, and the "colliding-worlds" syndrome.

The fundamental issue that runs through all of these conundrums is the fact that social media are not independent sites of interaction, but rather reflect and connect with offline activities. It is not simply that real-life relationships are reflected in online activity; more than this, people discussed the expectation that one must join up in order to maintain real-life and digital relationships. This was true even for people who don't use social media—in fact, for them the moral pressures are particularly clear: "I'm getting friend invitations (via email) even though I'm not on Facebook. I'm not even using it, but my friends are still imposing it on me" (Sharam, thirty-five, consultant).

After they had joined up, participants discovered that a defining feature of social networking sites is the amount of time one has to devote to being a contributing member of one's network. Commitment and timeliness are key components, but so is the simple degree to which one must actively maintain a presence. One participant pointedly commented, "Facebook is like one massively, high maintenance friend, that you have to sit down and talk to every single day if they are going to have any real relevance in your life" (Leroy, thirty-eight, fashion designer). The pressure to be appropriately responsive is evidenced by the guilt reported by seven participants for not being more present: "It can take me weeks to comment on a friend's wedding picture, or status update, but I do feel vindicated because Facebook is banned at my work and people know that, so at least I have a reason" (Natalie, twenty-six, sales). For this participant, then, the issue is not simply their responsiveness but rather the impression it gives—the importance that "people know" there is a reason. The moral imperatives that govern appropriate participation become visible in these expressions of regret and anxiety.

Not paying close and regular attention could even lead to social discord: "A person I know ignored a mate's friendship request (because he had not logged on to see it). Then they bumped into each other and it created bad blood through misunderstanding and bad communication" (Leroy).

The vital importance of having each socially significant person in your life appearing as a thumbnail picture on your site, and yours on theirs, was summed up by Alex, thirty-five, a part-time production assistant: "By not saying yes to a friendship request, I'm deleting them as a friend." Even nonusers suffer from the perils of rejecting friendship invitations: "I'm still in the awkward position of being perceived as rude by my lack of response" (Sharam).

On the other hand, defriending may be seen as a way of discouraging friendships, and the digital world has presented a soft option for removing unwanted acquaintances. One participant noted, "It's a great way of shedding friends, and who needs to add them at this stage in our life?" (Christie, thirty-six, computer scientist).

Attempts to keep networks intimate and civilized resulted in the practice of "friendship culls." Yet attempts to keep one's digital network perfectly manicured could lead to awkward face-to-face situations: "I had a run-in with a friend that I had culled—she confronted me, in person, at a party. So if you do cull people, you have to be accountable. . . . It's your face. It's Facebook!" (Vivien, thirty, editor).

Naturally, whenever there is defriending, the act of refriending may occur. Changes in the status of close-tie (especially romantic) relationships were often closely observed by others on the network. The majority of our participants reported that they followed the ups and downs of their friends' dating adventures via their changing status with the other person. Again, the bleeding of online and offline interactions is a key concern—questioning the easy dismissal of social media interaction as inherently inauthentic, but drawing attention to the active processes by which different forms of interaction are articulated.

Responsiveness in Phatic Communication

The Facebook "poke" is an example of a communication exchange in which the very act of interacting or sharing information transcends its content. The emphasis is on maintaining social bonds rather than transmitting a message. This is often referred to as "phatic communication" (Fiske 1990). As in everyday life, these seemingly trivial phatic exchanges are very important in reassuring connectedness and are genuinely valued within relationships (Gibbs et al. 2005). Arguably, much communication through social media is phatic, but in some cases, such as "pokes," it is explicitly so since no other communication is involved.

Smith (2008) studied the online social networking activities of eight participants for two weeks, through a diary study and online observation, followed by an interview. Smith found that the exchange of the Facebook "poke" was a widely adopted practice. One of the motives that participants gave for this was a feeling of obligation. Several participants explained that one of the main reasons they reply to individuals is solely to be polite and they are consciously aware of this fact; as one person put it, "If I just ignored it I [would] take that as being rude." One's responsibility to others required reciprocation, a marker of shared participation. While the poke is light on information, it's heavy on social meaning.

Civic and Political Participation

Media connect people and events. By thinking less in terms of social applications and more in terms of social media, we see them as points of connection, and hence as linked to activities and events outside themselves. Social networking sites are not islands; they are enmeshed in a larger world of people and events. Recently this has been demonstrated most clearly in coordinated campaigns organized around political and world events, which generate not only groups and discussions, but coordinated status updates where people use their status to reproduce position statements and express solidarity around issues of concern. Prominent examples of late have included debate about reform in U.S. healthcare, responses to the disputed 2009 Iranian election, and the 2007 Burmese antidemocracy actions.

For our Australian study participants, one particularly notable case was the occasion of Prime Minister Kevin Rudd's February 2008 apology to the "stolen generation"—the generation of Aboriginal children forcibly removed from their families, as recently as the 1960s. Rudd had promised an apology as a campaign pledge and issued it shortly after taking office, an occasion that caused large crowds to gather in public spaces to watch the live broadcast and was the source of a major outpouring of public emotion. The event was mirrored on Facebook; thousands of people changed their status to "is sorry," which itself became a news story (Kent 2008).

Again, issues of responsiveness and responsibility are central here. Participation in online activism creates pressures to respond; arguably, it is more visible and more persistent than participation in a public meeting and more firmly entwined with everyday life. The effectiveness of such mechanisms lies not least in their pressures toward conformity; the balance lies in the way those pressures are exerted through friends and colleagues rather than through strangers—yet a form of broader solidarity is simultaneous engendered. It is a connection, if not with the public, then with a public.

Audiences and Publics

As these examples illustrate, when we look at social media through the lens of moral economies, the issues that come to the fore are pressures of participation and the framing of personas and identities. However, as we have noted, these questions are made more complicated in social media by the vexing problem of precisely with whom one participates and to whom one presents oneself. Goffman (1963) talks of behavior in public places, and yet these spaces are not quite public in Goffman's sense. The "audience" in social media is not the general public, but neither is it generally a specific individual. Indeed, one of the characteristics of many social media (and one reason some avoid them) is the "public" performance of "private" communication to a collection of witnesses that is somewhat unknown. Questions of "privacy" and of "audience" consequently arise, but answers are unsatisfying because the concepts do not apply well.

In the area of media studies, Michael Warner (2002) has drawn attention to the importance of understanding "publics" rather than, or in addition to, a conventional notion of audience. Warner's elaboration of publics is grounded in traditional mass media, although they have particular resonance in the domain of user-generated content and social media online, and the concept provides some analytic purchase on the topics discussed in this chapter.

The essence of the notion of a "public" lies in contrast with a traditional notion of audience. The idea of "audience" essentially encapsulates a relationship between an author and the consumers of some media object, such as a piece of writing, an image, or a film. An audience is an imaginary relation—that is, the relation that it describes exists primarily in the imagination of the author who pictures an audience as part of the process of production. Like audience, public is an imaginary relationship, but instead of a relation between producer and consumers of media objects, a public is a relation among consumers. The essence of the public is a moment of recognition; it lies in the idea that "this was made for people like me." It is in that formulation of "people like me," as inspired by, indexed by, and grounded by a particular media form, media object, or set of media objects, that the public comes into being. It is a putative relationship, then, between me (as a media consumer) and the "people like me"—a group that may never previously have been imagined or formulated as a unit until the occasion of recognition.

Warner details several important properties of publics that can be related to digital and social media (Lindtner et al. 2009), and two are particularly relevant here. The first is that, as we outlined above, a public is a "relation amongst strangers" (Warner 2002, 74). The second is that a public is "the social space constituted by the reflexive circulation of discourse" (2002, 90). Circulation of media objects and patterns of mediated interaction—update, transmission, retransmission, transformation—and reflection on that circulation—the explicit and self-conscious examination of media practices and one's relationship to them—are constitutive of publics in Warner's formulation.

Warner's alternative approach provides a useful perspective on a number of issues that arise when examining social media use. We will focus on three: communication, community, and privacy.

First, Warner's approach, by focusing on publics as relations that emerge from acts of recognition and interpellation, turns our attention away from communication toward participation as the essential activity of social media. What drives social media are the forms of collective participation and the consequent relations among people that are enabled, rather than specific communicative acts or the transmission of messages. Instrumental accounts of social media use, focusing on communication rather than participation, are left somewhat bereft here. For example, a recent report received considerable coverage in both online and traditional media for its conclusion that Twitter posts contain largely "Pointless Babble" (Pear Analytics 2009). The analysis proceeded from the assumption that the "value" of microblogging lay in the dissemination of news and information (messages of "pass-along value"), which might be in danger of being drowned out by other messages. By thinking not in terms of author and audience, but rather in terms of the public induced by acts of participation and recognition, we may be able to retheorize the practices of social media without making them dependent on an instrumental account of communication.

Similarly, it provides us with a different view than that of "community," which is often a starting point for thinking about participation and engagement through information technology. The term *community* has no stable definition in these studies (nor would we necessarily want it to have), but is conventionally invoked for a sense of mutual interests, common purpose, and collectivity at different scales. However, a notion of community, we would argue, obscures as much as it reveals, for at least three reasons. The first is that it is a somewhat homogenizing notion, placing uniformity ahead of diversity; the second is that it focuses on outcomes rather than processes, and frames the community as a stable entity rather than something dynamically produced and reproduced; the third is that it looks out with the individual to understand how people come together. By turning our attention to the formation of public as an imaginary, and understanding its production within the active engagement with circulating discourse, Warner provides a useful alternative that encompasses diversity, difference, and resistance within a frame of collective action.

Finally, the notion of a public as constituted through media participation—and more broadly, the idea of the moral economy as a way to understand participation in social media—reframes traditional discussions of privacy. If we focus on communication and the transmission of messages, then privacy is thought of as the types of messages transmitted or the people to whom they might be transmitted. By thinking about social media in terms of participation and publics, we are offered a view of privacy that centers on accountability and forms of public life—the shaping of discourse and engagement (Troshynski, Lee, and Dourish 2008). Here, privacy is not so much about protecting and sequestering information; instead, it is a way of acting socially and participating in social life.

We have argued that the notion of "moral economy" offers a useful perspective on engagement with social media. What it provides is a way of thinking about social media not as tools for instrumental action but as a means of participating in social life—ways of engaging with others that entail reciprocal responsibilities and forms of social sanction that manifest themselves as moral and emotional pressures. This leads to a need to be able to theorize the collectives within which these engagements take place. Warner's work offers an opportunity to do this while maintaining a focus on the performative aspects of media engagement. It supports a notion of social media as a site of authentic social engagement. Importantly, we are not arguing for authentic social engagement *rather than* "pointless babble," to use the terms of the Pear Analytics report we cited earlier. Rather, what we are pointing to is authentic social engagement *through* pointless babble; the same sort of "pointless babble" and seemingly inconsequential banter that is the foundation of much day-to-day interaction. These interactions are consequential inasmuch as they constitute a circulation of discourse within which publics emerge and identities are enacted.

The moral economy of social media evidences forms of social participation—responsibility, responsiveness, reciprocality, and rejection—as they manifest themselves in people's talk about social media, provide us with prima facie evidence that some sort of social collective exists within which norms can be established. Warner's account of publics begins to unpack how these collectives arise, and turns particular attention to the circulations of media objects as a central element in these processes.

More broadly, though, the applicability of Warner's model underscores the value of an approach that focuses on a media analysis rather than a usability analysis. Two elements are key here—first, a collective view that emphasizes the ecology of media tools (rather than focusing on individual applications, websites, or systems), and second, a view of social acts conducted with and through contemporary technologies, which is in contrast to a focus on the technologies in and of themselves.

Conclusion

Social digital systems of various sorts—social networking sites, photo-sharing applications, communication and messaging technologies, microblogging, and so on—have undeniably become aspects of the fabric of everyday life in many societies. They are aspects of how political campaigns are organized; they are part of the economy of mass media, from news outlets to celebrity agents; outages are major press stories. They continue to evolve, and traditional human-computer interaction (HCI) concerns—design and evaluation, functionality and fitness, usability and access—will continue to be important considerations into the future.

In this chapter we have suggested that it may also be useful to take a complementary approach, and to think about what media analysis might have to tell us about the emergence of cultural and social forms mediated by these technologies. So, rather than understanding some contemporary interaction issues in terms of the use of tools, we have advocated an alternative approach that frames the issues as participation in media and media cultures. We have turned to two conceptual frameworks to do this at different levels—the notion of the moral economy to highlight the ethical complexities, emotional fabric, and emergent norms governing appropriate participation in mediated collectivities, and a conceptualization of publics that turns attention to questions of identity and practice in the circulation of mediated discourse.

Popular accounts of social media portray them either as inherently frivolous or as sites of authentic social engagement. In our analysis, we have attempted to examine precisely what this social engagement might comprise. We take the moral considerations that people evince as evidence of substantive engagement on some level; the questions this opens up concern the processes by which these substantive engagements emerge and develop.

Acknowledgments

This work was supported in part by the U.S. National Science Foundation under awards 083860, 0838499, and 0917401. It was also supported by a Linkage Grant provided by the Australian Research Council: "Swarms in Urban Villages: New Media Design to Augment Social Networks of Residents in Inner City Developments" (LP0776341).

Note

1. *Reciprocity*, in communication media, generally points to an even-handed bidirectionality—"if I can see you, you can see me." We have something different in mind here—the property of engendering mutual and reciprocal social implications.

References

Adorno, T. 1991. *The Culture Industry*. London: Routledge.

Avrahami, D., S. Fussell, and S. Hudson. 2008. IM waiting: Timing and responsiveness in semi-synchronous communication. In *Proceedings of the ACM Conference on Computer Supported Cooperative Work,* San Diego, CA, 285–294. New York: ACM.

Baudrillard, J. [1970] 1988. *The Consumer Society: Myths and Structures*. London: Sage.

Daston, L. 1995. The moral economy of science. *Osiris* 10:2–24.

Fiske, J. 1990. *Introduction to Communication Studies*. New York: Routledge.

Fogarty, J., S. E. Hudson, and J. Lai. 2004. Examining the robustness of sensor-based statistical models of human interruptibility. In *Proceedings of the SIGCHI Conference on Human Factors in Computing Systems,* Vienna, 207–214. New York: ACM.

Gibbs, M., F. Vetere, M. Bunyan, and S. Howard. 2005. SynchroMate: A phatic technology for mediating intimacy. In *Proceedings of the Conference on Designing for User eXperiences*, San Francisco. New York: AIGA.

Goffman, E. 1959. *The Presentation of Self in Everyday Life*. Garden City, NY: Doubleday Anchor.

Goffman, E. 1963. *Behavior in Public Places: Notes on the Social Organization of Gatherings*. New York: Free Press.

Graham, C., C. Satchell, M. Rouncefield, J. Balmford, and P. Benda. 2007. Lessons from failure: Re-conceiving blogging as personal change support. In *Proceedings of the Conference on Designing for User eXxperiences,* Chicago, 2–17. New York: ACM.

Kent, M. 2008. Writing for a cause: E-activism gives politics a new face. *The Melbourne Age*, February 24.

Lindtner, S., J. Chen, G. Hayes, and P. Dourish. 2009. Towards a framework of publics. *LUCI Working Paper*. Irvine: University of California.

Mauss, M. [1950] 1990. *The Gift: The Form and Reason for Exchange in Archaic Societies*. London: Routledge.

Pear Analytics. 2009. Twitter Study—August 2009. http://www.pearanalytics.com/wp-content/uploads/2009/08/Twitter-Study-August-2009.pdf.

Satchell, C., and P. Dourish. 2009. Beyond the user: Use and non-use in HCI. In *Proceedings of the 21st Annual Conference of the Australian Computer-Human Interaction Special Interest Group*, Melbourne, 9–16. New York: ACM.

Smith, J. 2008. A Poke Is Worth a Thousand Words: Social Networking and Phatic Interactions. Unpublished honors dissertation, Department of Information Systems, University of Melbourne.

Taylor, A., and R. Harper. 2002. Age-old practices in the "New World": A study of gift-giving between teenage mobile phone users. In *Proceedings of the SIGCHI Conference on Human Factors in Computing Systems*, Minneapolis, 439–446. New York: ACM.

Thompson, E. P. 1971. The moral economy of the English crowd in the eighteenth century. *Past & Present* 50:76–136.

Troshynski, E., C. Lee, and P. Dourish. 2008. Accountabilities of presence: Reframing location-based systems. In *Proceedings of the 26th Annual SIGCHI Conference on Human Factors in Computing Systems*, Florence, 487–496. New York: ACM.

Tyler, J., and J. Tang. 2003. When can I expect an email response? A study of rhythms in email usage. In *Proceedings of the European Conference on Computer Supported Cooperative Work ECSCW 2003*, Helsinki, 239–258. Heidelberg: Springer.

Warner, M. 2002. *Publics and Counterpublics*. Cambridge, MA: Zone Books.

3 The Protocological Surround: Reconceptualizing Radio and Architecture in the Wireless City

Gillian Fuller and Ross Harley

Moving within an architectural surround, a person fashions an evolving matrix, an architectural surround not entirely of her own making.
—Arakawa and Gins 2002, 40

Sensual Integration in the Mobile Wireless City

This chapter proceeds from an assumption that the widespread introduction of wireless devices into the urban environment involves the formation of new relationships between bodies and practices of power. Here we want to initiate some discussion around the ontological and sociological implications of ubiquitous networks, especially as they pertain to an engagement with mobility and wireless technologies.

With the increasing prevalence of WiFi, RFID, Bluetooth, and other novel radio technologies, a new kind of electromagnetic space is becoming integral to the life and shape of the urban environment. We are not so much concerned with the history of radio broadcasting as we are with redeployment of radio across urban environments in novel and unexpected ways. The contemporary electromagnetic spaces discussed in this chapter now occupy the banal and increasingly pervasive geometries of super-distributed control—a barely discernible "surround" that inaugurates a new politics of ubiquity.

Following Arakawa and Gins (2002, 39), we propose that the "characteristic features for an immensely large architectural surround such as a city will be everything that makes it a city, including those bustling or ambling through it." Increasingly this surround is becoming informationalized, involving the dispersal of processing power into the everyday environment—what Adam Greenfield (2006) terms "everyware information processing." It forms part of a protocological ensemble that enables the automatic opening of doors, the registering of identity data, or the enabling of credit card transactions, telephone calls, and access to toll roads to happen (apparently) seamlessly. This increasingly pervasive surround harnesses "all of the power of a densely networked environment, but refining its perceptible signs until they disappear into the things we do everyday" (Greenfield 2006, 26). Surrounded by an electromagnetic spectrum thick with information, the technologized atmosphere has drafted the body into the service of the urban infrastructure.

This chapter is an attempt to reconceptualize radio and architecture in contemporary urban environments, and to consider some of the emergent architectural and protocological surrounds—sometimes "not entirely of our own making" (Arakawa and Gins 2002, 40). We ask how this evolving interpenetration of architectural surfaces, bodies, signals, and waves (utilized by the mobile devices that guide and track a wide range of constantly moving human bodies and material objects) can be seen to create new kinds of social engagement and "forces of relationality."

This interpenetration occurs in two ways. First, communicating devices are in the business of exchanging information (and not meaning), and thus operate under the nonrepresentational governance of protocol. Second, the negotiability of semantic systems gives way to the nonnegotiability of code. As Alexander Galloway (2006, xiii) puts it, "Protocol is a circuit not a sentence." Moreover, the increasing integration of mobile bodies within multisensate urban infrastructures (visible and invisible, tactile and contactless) requires a body that moves in certain ways and at certain times in order for the whole to be able to function. City, device, and body become prosthetically interrelated, part of a greater assemblage of mobile organizations (Terranova 2004; Galloway 2006; Manning 2007).

The much vaunted "freedom" offered by wirelessness is enabled by achieving what appears to be the total ubiquity of body-network relations. Always on and always connected, wireless technologies offer considerable freedom of movement by collapsing previously disparate spatial locations of labor (home, office, etc.) into the mobile space of flows we now occupy (Castells 1996). What holds us in place is not the disciplinary fantasy or the architectural backdrop of modernity. Today our bodies are held in place by a dynamic architecture that is enabled in part by the novel use of radio spectrum and wireless communication. The move from disciplinary to control societies has been understood (see Deleuze 2006 and Foucault 1996) in terms of the breakdown of one form of confinement into another "mechanism of control as rigorous as the harshest confinement" (Deleuze 2006, 178). Here we want to explore how the "protocological surround" enabled by wireless technologies invokes a different power relation—irreducible to the logic of surveillance or control, but based instead on conditions of "smooth" mobility and wireless connectivity.

This chapter explores how ubiquitous wireless technologies recalibrate the experience of urban spatiality. We propose that these new forms of situated computing cannot be understood outside of specific modes of social engagement, and that this is best framed in terms of a reconsideration of the interplay between radio, urbanism, and architecture.

The relationships between architecture, movement, and the city have long been discussed in terms of regimes of vision—for instance, the panoramas of railways, the idea of the cinematic city, or framing devices of all kinds. Anne Friedberg (2006, 242) wonders whether there is "a new logic to vision as our windows, frames, screens are ever more fractured and virtually multiplied? Which technologies will break through the frame and have us climb out through the virtual window?" Eric Gordon has argued that radio "reframed" the modern city by dint of its inherently networked architecture, which broke the enframing regime of vision through the foregrounding of scale. Transmission towers strung together new connections that were beyond the horizon— "out of sight." The urban imaginings invoked by radio's invisible connections and increasingly active air (Sloterdijk 2009) were made concrete in the aesthetics of a nascent mobile modernism in which electrical, telegraphic, and radio transmission towers rose up to harness the invisible power of the air. The broadcasting of audio via radio waves also saw the inauguration of new soundscapes that challenge the dominance of visuality in the urban realm. The "invisible empire of the air" was made visible through an acoustic aesthetic that "prioritised connectivity over isolation and mobility over stagnation" (Gordon 2005, 265). This invisible relational dynamic remains crucial to the role wireless networks play in media change today. Adrian Mackenzie (2008) asserts that with wireless networks "connectivity, intermittent, unstable and uneven as it often is, lodges in many of the overlaps, overflows and outgrowths badged as convergence, mobile media, and pervasive or ubiquitous computing."

The new deployment of low-powered radio generates an intimacy that strangely may not always be felt directly on the body, but that nevertheless affects the body's ability to act. That is, we may not perceive the invisible radio waves of the electromagnetic spectrum and may not feel the constant touch of machines registering our details, but they invariably affect how we move. In a sense, this dance between what is perceived, what is known, and what is registered provides the experiential foundations of everyday life.

The potential spatial and social implications of new ubiquitous infrastructures have been noted by a number of researchers. Anthony Townsend (2007, 396) reminds us that the "pervasive deployment of telecommunications networks was one of the defining characteristics of the 20th century city in the developed world." As the twenty-first century sees the pervasive deployment of new location-aware computing and telecommunications that is reshaping the geography of many sociospatial activities, "urban form has responded to the new spatial freedoms allowed by pervasive telecommunications" (p. 396).

Dodge and Kitchin similarly argue that pervasive computing and the rendering of everyday objects into smart objects represent a major new regime, but from their perspective it is one of *recording* (after the previous regimes of writing and the printing press). Mundane and routine, this embedding of computing power into our everyday lives will constitute new pervasive "sociospatial archives" capable of recording details about all the places a mobilized individual has been. They situate this as part of the historical shift from surveillance to what they call *sousveillance*—"the internal counter to external surveillance" (Dodge and Kitchin 2007, 432). Under the pretext of efficiency of movement, congestion reduction, or discourses of security, this new regime of recording is not top down, but rather inside out and bottom up.

Echoing the work of Thrift (2008), Dodge and Kitchin frame their studies of mobilized pervasive computing in terms of trying to capture "the outlines of a world just coming in to existence, one which is based on continuous calculation at each and every point along each and every line of movement" (quoted in Dodge and Kitchin 2007, 432). They highlight the shift from watching (surveillance) to recording of "capta"—that is, those "units of data that have been selected and harvested from the sum of all potential data" and typically derived from the use of swipe cards, the logging of computers, the tracking of vehicles by way of onboard locational devices, and so on (Dodge and Kitchin 2005, 854). These automated networks "produce particular and new sociospatial formations" and so far do not fill out the whole space of the city (Dodge and Kitchin 2007, 434). The question remains to what extent ubiquitous computing will create novel sociospatial effects that may include the creation of "a mobile panopticon (as opposed to the partial oligopticon)" of the urban metropolis (Dodge and Kitchin 2007, 436).

Loaded with our various radio-enabled peripherals (mobile phones, key fobs, e-tags, contactless smart cards, and other remote keyless systems), our senses are becoming more diffuse yet more interconnected. We beep unknowingly, register data, upload personal information, download encryption signals, or transmit passwords and identity codes. Our senses now engage with peripherals and systems of "dataveillance" that have become essential to traversing urban networks and architectures—and these devices are themselves increasingly integrated into the hard- and software of the city. We experience this in the form of tollbooths, automated door sentry systems, RFID gantries, and cell towers, to name but a few of these new topological constants that trace and record (and in some instances block) our every move. One's becoming is "becoming networked," "becoming relational." To be actualized, presence must be partial—situated and sensate, cybernetically sensitive to feedback within the system (Terranova 2004).

The prosthetic devices we are referring to here reach out and touch other devices (without ever actually touching them) across a scale that can no longer be contained by "frames." These sensing devices activate both near and far, light and heavy, untethered and encumbered to "an empire of functions" (Thrift 2008, 9) in which antennas and algorithms reorganize contemporary practices of experience. An "awareness of the network"—an ever-present possibility of another connection—has now become built into everyday experience. In the process, these sensing devices are folded into the network; they are integrated into the city and into the "cloud of electromagnetic radiation that bathes us in information" (Varnelis 2008).

Radio on

This process occurs in physical realms that some scholars call "hertzian space": the space of radio signals in everyday environments. To understand this in more detail, we need to turn to a discussion of radio's genealogy and transformation into a new procedural system for the construction of contemporary spaces.

Some recognition of the history of radio can help us contextualize developments over the last decade or so of ubiquitous media. In terms of the presence of the electromagnetic spectrum, radio is part of the late nineteenth-century scientific discoveries. Since the mid-1880s when the German physicist Heinrich Hertz identified what we now call radio waves, technologists have been concerned with practical issues to do with "what kind of device it would take to modulate and detect such waves and how far they would travel" (De Sola Pool 1990, 25). Wave-based and invisible, radio had a significant social impact and was quickly brought within legislative and regulatory frameworks that sought to minimize the impact of interference among a swelling number of transmissions. The regulation of airwaves and spectrum was from the very outset a hot political topic: "Interference by broadcasters with one another quickly became so severe that the industry appealed to the U.S. government to set up some system of licensing so that radio stations could be alone in their segment of the spectrum" (De Sola Pool 1990, 26). It was not until the mid-1980s that low-powered radio devices (operating at certain frequencies in a very limited part of the spectrum) were deregulated and opened up for unlicensed use.

Radio is the technical apparatus of hertzian space—the atmosphere of electromagnetic radiation that surrounds us in information and the space that makes panoptical technologies (but not regimes of vision) obsolete. As Eric Gordon's work demonstrates, early responses to radio (and its electromagnetic invisibility) in New York illustrate how the separate fields of radio and architecture have changed—for example, where they have come from, how they have previously been theorized, and particularly in relation to networked technologies of the past. Light, sound, and data all ride the electromagnetic forces that are now infusing the gravitational forces of classical and [post]modernist architecture. How is this new use of the spectrum clashing with, flowing alongside, and resisting the other noncorporeal forces of power that are warping and folding the fabric of urban experience? Anthony Dunne (2005, 101) puts it this way. Radio,

meaning part of the electromagnetic spectrum, is fundamental to electronics. Objects not only "dematerialise" into software in response to miniaturisation and replacement by services, but also literally dematerialise into radiation. . . . Whereas cyberspace is a metaphor that spatialises what happens in computers distributed around the world, radio space is actual and physical, even though our senses detect only a tiny part of it.

Simply put, we are concerned with looking at how bodies are becoming bound to the fabric of the city through the invisible, silent, and sometimes unregulated waves of radio. We want to trace its connection to the emergent logic of touch that appears around "contactless technologies" enabled by electromagnetic fields using technical procedures drawn from the fields of radio and radar engineering (Finkenzeller 2003, 7). In recent years, automatic identification procedures have transformed distribution logistics, service industries, and material flow systems. Their evolution from barcode and optical character recognition to silicon chips has ushered in a range of electronic data-carrying devices that allow for the contactless transfer of information between the device and its reader. Because of the procedures used for the transfer of power and data, contactless ID systems are called radio frequency identification (or RFID) systems.

While RFID technologies are increasingly prevalent, they are not without controversy. Bruce Sterling's (2009) long-running "Arphid Watch" blog contains a good summary of one persistent objection: "Many aspects of RFID interaction are fundamentally invisible; as users we experience two objects communicating through the 'magic' of radio waves. This invisibility is also key to the controversial aspects of RFID technology; once RFID antennas are hidden inside products or in environments, they can be invoked or initiated without explicit knowledge or permission."

This invisibility requires a new conceptualization that is not based on visuality, but rather, is founded on distributive principles that deal in waves, frequencies, and modulations. For us, the protocols of radio offer a crucial way to understand emergent networks of ubiquity. A number of authors have discussed very similar issues in publications that have sought to make a contribution to what might be termed "new media urbanism" (Graham and Marvin 1996; Townsend 2001, 2007; McCullough 2007; Zook and Graham 2007). As this issue has developed as a topic, it has become clear that the reality of an invisible technological unboundedness is far more complex and differentiated than many proponents of ubiquitous or pervasive computing acknowledge.

We might also usefully recall Lewis Mumford's (1938, 239) prescient studies of invisible infrastructures such as sewage and communication systems, which can be viewed in the same manner: "Beneath the visible city, an invisible city grows apace: a buried city of water pipes and sewers and gas mains and electric cables and steam pipes and telephone wires." More recently, Stephen Graham raised many of the issues discussed in this chapter in his book *Telecommunications and the City* (1996).

Ubiquitous media and the changing social relationships that frame their use can also be seen as providing another variable geometry of everyday urban environments. As Crang, Crosbie, and Graham (2006, 2552) argue, these changes present "opportunities for restructuring the time-space dynamics of everyday lives, service supply regimes, and the broader time-space patterns of urban development. The dynamic and relational geographies of such transitions reconstitute cities as key spatial pivots within telescoping scalar relations, operating at near instantaneous speeds, from the scale of the body to the transnational." They posit a "multispeed urban landscape" that structures urban areas in an uneven, accelerated, and differentiated fashion. The urban morphology, which has been affected by new communication technologies, is also in a process of "unevenly reconfiguring the logistical time-space practices of everyday urban life" (Crang, Crosbie, and Graham 2006, 2554).

As McCullogh (2007, 389) puts it, although the "dematerialized and tunneling effects of global communication certainly exist, the local integration and tuning of crossovers between these and preexisting infrastructures also becomes an important competitive advantage for a city." In response to Castells, McCullough argues that "not all is flow in the space of flows . . . the flows of people, goods, and information require fixed channels, switches, and fittings to become most effective" (p. 390). As can be witnessed with many location-based services (such as RFID, onboard navigation systems, intelligent transportation systems, and the like) attest, the issue of control or "access" within the use of such technologies is different depending on the technology used and where you use it.

There are a number of different technological systems that employ spread-spectrum radio technology to create these new mobile architectures associated with ad hoc networks, personal area networks, and wireless systems such as Bluetooth, RFID, and WiFi. The 802.11 family of over-the-air modulation techniques (commonly known as WiFi) was first released in 1997. WiFi is a particular type of unlicensed spread-spectrum technology made available by the deregulation of certain radio frequencies for unlicensed use in 1985. Confined to a narrow part of the spectrum, this technical standard allows devices to operate on the 2.4 GHz band without a license. Although initially conceived as a small experimental project, wireless local area network devices based on the international 802.11 standard became popular as a nonregulated use of the radio spectrum. WiFi allows for a range of wireless network practices to emerge that are based on a set of global standards of interoperability. It is because of this technical standard that WiFi networks have become so popular as a connective and enabling technology, "free as the air" (despite the fact that many networks are closed or only available via credit card).

Within the space constraints of this chapter, a short mention of what privacy means and how it is affected in relation to issues of freedom and control is warranted. Beyond the obvious issues to do with who has access to the network and the personal data that may be present, there are also new questions concerning the potential for wireless technologies to create a mobile panopticon. Dodge and Kitchin (2007, 236) point to a number of concerns that pertain to the embedding and interconnecting of RFID-type devices into the everyday environment:

This location information will be generated at a fine spatial resolution, pinpointed to (potentially) within a few millimetres through pattern recognition, wireless triangulation to fixed sensor nets, and GPS, and will be dynamically collected so that the precise path of an individual can be recalled. All manner of things will "know" where they are at all times, while many other "dumb" objects will be routinely "chipped" using RFID . . . technologies, making them instantly locatable on demand. Such rich capta will have the effect of opening up new time-space queries that were previously impossible.

The layers of radio communication operate at a series of scales, from long-distance high-powered radio signals to low-powered near-field signals. They form part of the creation of a machine-readable world that captures, stores, and exchanges vast amounts of highly granular personal data about mobile bodies, objects, transactions, and territorial units in urban environments. Across a variety of different technical protocols, layers, and devices, automatic identification and tracking of devices by readers operate in an apparently seamless fashion. A high density of private information is packaged, processed, and recognized by a number of quite different technical systems, each of which has its own parameters and ability to share personal data it collects and records. This new kind of machine communication is defining an emergent architectural matrix that is both background and foreground—a new type of "protocological surround."

Protocol is by nature "indifferent to the content of information" that it enables, publishes, and distributes (Galloway 2006, xvi). We do not use the term *protocological surround* metaphorically. Thus a protocological surround is a requisite condition for the type of *sousveillance* that Dodge and Kitchin discuss, inasmuch as it describes a network of material actions and processes and the way that protocols are layered, stratified, sometimes "blatantly hierarchical" (Galloway 2006, xvi). This type of protocol also highlights the regulated nature of information flows across multiple scales.

This protocological surround should not be confused with an enclosure, because it is as fragmented and dynamic as the bodies with which it coheres. An enclosure is merely one term in a semantic myriad of "surrounds," which includes a variety of perspectival terms (like foreground, background, middle ground, periphery), navigational terms (such as path, enabling, blockage), volumetric terms (such as full and empty), as well as a host of other "atmospheric surrounds" (like clear, polluted, spooky, or tense). Thus the surround is as open as it is closed.

Operating under these wireless protocols, large and small devices constantly exchange data, creating new infospatial formations that are perpetually shifting, impermanent, and flexible. The scale of this protocological operation is more personal, domestic, and intimate. It is often related to the movements of our bodies in their own idiosyncratic quotidian movements. This flexible movement partly defines the protocological surround: it is a type of machine chatter that creates an enormous amount of background "conversation" we hardly ever hear, let alone see.

Machine recognition is largely achieved today through a technological ensemble that utilizes the radio spectrum in ways that confound traditional understandings of radio. Miniature transponders are embedded in an increasing array of everyday objects, which are typically "read" by data capture devices (known as "interrogators" or "readers"). An interrogator typically "contains a radio frequency module (transmitter and receiver), a control unit and a coupling element to the transponder. . . . Many readers are fitted with an additional interface to enable them to forward the data received to another system (PC, robot control system, etc.)" (Finkenzeller 2003, 7). The old conceptual models of broadcast radio and the regulatory practices of government are no longer appropriate to describe or understand the present plethora of radio-based identification systems that are shaping the new topologies we are exploring.

For this reason, this broader reconceptualization of radio cannot be reduced to the increased use of two-way functionality. The multiplicity of today's radio has little to do with the singularity of "the radio" that we have come to associate primarily with AM or FM radio stations. New radio technologies such as WiFi, Bluetooth, and RFID show us how some of these potentialities are being realized. The liveness and invisible aesthetics of classical radio also have little to do with the rapid evolution of the new urban surrounds that are emerging out of these contemporary technological and social formations. Most importantly in the context of this discussion, they draw our attention to the changing relationship between bodies and spaces. For Parisi and Terranova, "what bodies are thought to be" is "a matter of an historically specific organisation of forces bought into being by capital and discursive investments" (cited in Clough 2007, 16). With this in mind, then how is the disciplinary body as "organism/self/ subject" that was enclosed within the multiple architectures of the Foucauldian "great confinement" reorganized by what we might call the "enforced mobility" of the "great connection" (in which material walls and optical regimes reconfigure as wireless channels and hot spots built out of air and numbers)?

Following the work of Nigel Thrift and others, we can say that these new systems we are describing are reordering life through new nonrepresentational systems of classification, mediation, and measurement—a "qualculated" world of continuous and ubiquitous calculation (Thrift 2008, 102). The qualculated body is one that is endlessly varying, in constant oscillation. It moves through the city as a mobile body. As Brian Massumi (2002, 4) succinctly puts it, "When a body is in motion, it does not coincide with itself. It coincides with its own transition: its own variation." Thus movement, the relentless flow of bodies and bits, becomes fundamental to thinking through both space and bodies; in other words, movement is "nothing but affects and local movements" (Parisi and Terranova 2000).

As Mackenzie (2008) notes, wireless networks operate through what he calls "prepositionality"; in other words, they govern and express spatiotemporal relations like "at," "in," "with," "by," "between," "near," and so on: "Because of their prepositional power to connect subjects and actions, wireless networks act conjunctively, they conjoin circumstances, events, persons and things." This prepositional relationship is transductive, pragmatically stitching the potentials of semantics into an ongoing experience of the city; it is also in a sense "governmental" and anticipatory, not only preceding the "thing," the "noun," and so forth, but in so doing, determines spatiotemporal relations. There is a big difference between being "in" range and being "out" of range in a wireless world.

Wireless technologies thus hold the multiple surfaces of bodies in an evolving matrix that controls a person's experience of the city. And digital cities, with all their baroque foldings and multiple surfaces (each sensing each other and creating a riot of beeps, alternating lights, and intelligent passages), are about experience. Wirelessness structures experience and does not construct stable objects or static space. In a dematerializing (i.e., radio/wireless) city, the quality of experience becomes paramount, increasingly measured by how mobile one can be. The experience of the city is where many of the prime forces of power operate. As Deleuze (2006, 70) explains Foucault's concept of power, "We can conceive of a necessarily open list of variables expressing a relation between forces or power relations, constituting actions upon actions: to incite, to induce, to seduce, to make easy or difficult, to enlarge or limit, to make more or less probable and so on."

But here in the radio city, power itself is made ubiquitous, soliciting its subjects by way of speed and convenience. No stopping, no waiting—no resistance, in all senses of the phrase. In other words, power makes things smooth by taking away the friction that previously slowed down the body and its associated disciplinary information (what are now its multiple datasets stored across interconnected networks of business and governmentality).

Wireless Regimes and the Lightness of Touch

Under these new conditions, our understanding of touch needs to move from the intimate and localized sensation of body on body (in whatever form that body may take) to a type of haptic engineering in which touch (as a sense) is extended over larger and more public spaces. Following Manning (2007, 156), for us, touch is a prosthetic gesture: "Touch is a prosthesis through which our bodies make contact. Touch is the manner in which I navigate from a subject position (an imagined stability) to an in-betweenness where the line between you and me becomes blurred. To touch is to become posthuman."

Touch is extending its sensory range as more surfaces are becoming touchable, "thresholding" us increasingly into the logistical drives of architecture. Along with this transformation, our descriptions of tactile sensations such as "soft," "hard," "hold," "push," "grasp," and so on will also change in meanings (Thrift 2008, 103). True to the locative sense of the contemporary urban condition, we don't "touch" so much as we move *in* or *out* of touch. In terms of a cybernetic sense of targeting, we stay "in range" of the machines we couple and exchange data with.

The increase of tactile surfaces available for connectivity is tantamount to an increase in the multiple prostheses available to produce certain types of relations and certain types of data. Following Bruno Latour's "Parliament of Things" (Latour 1993), we could say that our prostheses have voices in the datascape. Or as Bratton and Jeremijenko (2009) note, as objects become "alive" and give voice to information, they gain a public voice in our mobile civic lives. We are touched by machines that touch each other, and in so doing create new intensities of force.

When we speak of people navigating a city, of scanning and being scanned, it is important not to monumentalize the nature of control society. From our present perspective, this is not a Big Brother style patdown from a broadcast radio imaginary. Instead, we would like to suggest that our daily navigations through these radio-enabled networks are much more modulated than this. For the touch we are dealing with is, on the whole, a light and intimate touch that often happens in the background of other complex negotiations with the city/architecture. As Manning (2007, vx) affirms, "I reach out to touch you in order to invent a relation that will in turn, invent me." As we sign up for various plans and attach various wireless prosthetics to our already thoroughly layered skin/phone/car/subway assemblages, we reach out to institutions of transit, information, and architecture in a loaded "handshake." The compulsory exchange of personal data has never been so easy or seemingly painless—for those who comply at least. The topology of this "surround," however, is riddled with power relations.

Once locked into this grid of the "urban sensible," we flex and move within a constant surround of touch in which one threshold folds into another (apparently seamlessly). Bodies and machines generate and radiate electromagnetic waves in infinite compositions. However, as is often the case, the decentering of bodies and subsequent deinstitutionalization results in an ever-tighter integration into a modulated system of control that is both public and pervasive. Thus we are touched by the machine.

But what is it that is touched? Certainly it is a touch that extends beyond the skin. Touch is not just concerned with the literal laying on of hands—though in the ubiquitous city that also occurs with greater and greater frequency. For instance, at the airport, the security officer's latex-gloved hands runs over your breasts and along the inner leg, as if the clinical semiotic of the glove miraculously desexes the body and eradicates a lifetime of taboos associated with intimate and uninvited touch by strangers. Of course if we have read the governmental fine print on our boarding pass, we have "consented." To gain the "right" to travel, we submit to the surrounding processes that form part of our conditions of movement. Or as Erin Manning (2007, xxii) says, "to touch is not simply to put the organs in contact with the world. Touch foregrounds the senses as machinic assemblages." This is precisely a form of touching without touching; or in the terms of RFID technologies, it is a form of "contactless contact."

In an increasingly seamless world of ubiquitous computing and low-powered radio transmissions, there are no more hard-line borders. There are just intersecting thresholds of intensity. While the recognizable architectural thresholds of window, door, and entrance continue to be invoked in the construction of contemporary space, ubiquitous radio identification systems add a significant number of background thresholds into the equation. Often unnoticed (or at least not foregrounded in an obvious, visible fashion), these transmissions between transponders and radio frequency readers have become pervasive in the background architecture of contemporary urban life. We are in touch with a highly variegated system of tracking and identification without being in direct contact with the surface of objects or places.

This "contactless contact" is one of the key characteristics of low-powered radio and miniaturized ubiquitous modulation-demodulation procedures. The digital communication systems that facilitate the transfer of data are brought about by a series of intimate transmissions and signal decodings that are achieved by way of electromagnetic waves in the radio spectrum. This contactless transfer of data between the data-carrying device and its reader constitutes a new set of spatial and material protocols that give shape to the ubiquitous city.

Paul Virilio (1995, 36) believes "the centre is no where—the circumference is everywhere at once." From outer space to inner space, it has all been colonized and integrated precisely because everything is now so converged and connected. Of course, this is not always a good thing, as Vilem Flusser (2002, 20) has noted: "An omnipresent dialogue is just as dangerous as an omnipresent discourse."

Engagement and Contact in the Wireless Surround

What kind of sensuous regime is in operation when contact is not felt, noise is not heard, and vision is conducted without optic techniques? When engagement is prosthetic? It remains for us to ask how citizens can engage with power under these new conditions of mobility and connectivity. As we have shown, many of the transactions and interrelations that make up the new architectural topology we are concerned with here occur outside the field of vision—we might even say "under the radar." The contactless contact we are describing assumes a body that does not itself need to be aware of the network.

The wireless body is connected, linked in, and fully operationalized—and yet mostly it is unable to perceive the network and its own conditions of existence. The protocological surround of the wireless city, this "everyware," operates at the scale of the body and at the scale of architecture. Despite this, we tend to engage with the city in a disengaged fashion, and within a barely perceptible protocological surround.

Under such conditions, the notion of citizen with all its incumbent rights is modulated back into the space of flows (in the same way that any other material object in this mobility system is). Here we might highlight the transformation of civil society to logistical society and ask what kind of engaged citizen we might imagine if citizenry isn't even really aware of its engagement anymore.

The logic of access, control, tracking, and supply-chain management grants unique identifiers by way of radio waves that define new shapes for the city. They promise synchronization, anticollision protocols, and "automatic" identification on the fly. Signal, spectrum, coding, and modulation procedures fold into haptic relations and new possibilities of touch. Even when you're not touching something you're touching something. This is what happens when networks go mobile—they have to graft on to you in a new way. There's a contact of some sort, even if it is "contactless contact." Within the parameters of the new control society, we need to focus on the politics of touch. Politics and aesthetics have moved off the body (without organs) and shifted elsewhere. The sources of control happen within the realm of touch, and we need to think about this in terms of the politics of these new conditions.

We have highlighted the pernicious ubiquity of radio frequencies in everyday accessories of mobility: the car key, e-tag, bus card, and money cards that give us access (or not) to networks of data, objects, mobility, and highways. These diagrammatics and aesthetics refer to the ways we enter physical and data portals, pass through the threshold, open the door, enter the passenger section, and so on. A number of thematics emerge: the inadvertence of the network; the ineluctable nature of data transfer; distributed processing; compulsory dialog in the background of the ubiquitous city. These machinic communications are largely unseen, unknown, but not unfelt. This thresholding activity is happening all around us and all the time. It is registered on bodies with the intensity of the communication handshake. And still, the lightness of touch and the intimacy of radio we are invoking here are highly charged. It is almost a sexual intimacy that emerges between you and the things in your pocket that can be "read" by a machine. All of these things are associated with closeness, personalization, the touching of the senses, or the penetration of a vibration that literally goes inside your body. Following David Bissell (2010), we would say vibration is "not an intermediary force that is exerted by or forms a presence between more-or-less powerful objects. Rather the event of vibration as a process generates the very effect of different materialities whilst on the move."

The topological constancies we are invoking here do not privilege the visual, but instead focus on how that coding and modulation happens over a complex invisible assemblage. A new understanding of the wireless city is not about mapping the urban panorama; it is about mapping the "protocological surround" that allows us to understand how the complex interplay of bodies, spaces, and data interconnect to form new geographies and architectures.

The topological formation we are describing is also what we might call "membranic." If classical radio is largely concerned with analog wave and modulation procedures, digital modulation procedures invoke a concatenation of low-powered and spread-spectrum signals, coding, and transcoding. Wireless architecture is thus also about negotiating and understanding the different channels, "membranes," and thresholds that we are folded into. In this sense there are multiple variations on the "wireless body" and the "wireless city," which is why architecture and urbanism need to attend to this new topology. Hence we can say that the skin of architecture—what we have been calling the "protocological surround"—is digitally modulated. It oscillates across a spectrum of code signal that organizes the body and architectural space in a variety of ways.

Under such conditions, the "freedom" implied by wirelessness comes at a cost. The total ubiquity of body-network relations actually constrains freedom of movement as much as it appears to allow it. In the emergent wireless city, we are increasingly enmeshed in the informational loops of feedback and emergence that modulate boundaries between bodies and objects/spaces of all sorts. The wireless city is organized into differential degrees of speed and intensity that invoke new technosocial relationships between embodiment and information, between bodies and borders.

In this seamless world of ubiquitous computing there are no more borders, only thresholds of intensity where the ambient reality of life in the city is formed through prosthetic desire for mobile momentum and easier connections; where our wireless lives (that seemingly free us in space) only bind us tighter to a digitally modulated geography of the air.

References

Arakawa, and Madeline Gins. 2002. *Architectural Body*. Tuscaloosa: University of Alabama Press.

Bissell, David. 2010. Vibrating materialities: Mobility-body-technology relations. Area: *Journal of the Royal Geographical Society* (with the Institute of British Geographers) 43 (4): 479–486.

Bratton, Benjamin, and Natalie Jeremijenko. 2009. *Suspicious Images, Latent Interfaces*. New York: Architectural League of New York.

Castells, Manuel. 1996. *The Rise of the Network Society*. Oxford: Blackwell.

Clough, Patricia. 2007. *The Affective Turn: Theorizing the Social*. Durham, NC: Duke University Press.

Crang, Michael, Tracie Crosbie, and Steven Graham. 2006. Variable geometries of connection: Urban digital divides and the uses of information technology. *Urban Studies* (Edinburgh, Scotland) 43 (13): 2551–2570.

Deleuze, Giles. 2006. *Foucault*. Minneapolis: University of Minnesota Press.

de Sola Pool, Ithiel 1990. *Technologies without Boundaries: On Telecommunications in a Global Age.* Cambridge, MA: Harvard University Press.

Dodge, Martin, and Rob Kitchin. 2007. Outlines of a world coming into existence: Pervasive computing and the ethics of forgetting. *Environment and Planning B: Planning & Design* 34:431–445.

Dunne, Anthony. 2005. *Hertzian Tales.* Cambridge, MA: MIT Press.

Finkenzeller, K. 2003. *RFID Handbook: Fundamentals and Applications in Contactless Smart Cards and Identification.* New York: Wiley.

Foucault, Michel. 1996. Seminar of 17 March 1976. Trans. David Macey. In *Society Must Be Defended.* New York: Picador.

Friedberg, Anne. 2006. *The Virtual Window: From Alberti to Microsoft.* Cambridge, MA: MIT Press.

Flusser, Vilem. 2002. *Writings.* Minneaopolis: University of Minnesota Press.

Galloway, Alexander. 2006. *Protocol: How Control Exists after Decentralization.* Cambridge, MA: MIT Press.

Gordon, Eric. 2005. Toward a networked urbanism: Hugh Ferriss, Rockefeller Center, and the "Invisible Empire of the Air." *Space and Culture* 8:247–268.

Graham, Stephen, and Marvin, Simon. 1996. *Telecommunications and the City: Electronic Spaces, Urban Places.* London: Routledge.

Greenfield, Adam. 2006. *Everyware: The Dawning Age of Ubiquitous Computing.* Berkeley, CA: New Riders Publishing.

Latour, Bruno. 1993. *We Have Never Been Modern.* Cambridge, MA: Harvard University Press.

Mackenzie, Adrian. 2008. Wirelessness as experience of transition. *fibreculture 13.* http://journal.fibreculture.org/issue13/issue13_mackenzie.html.

Manning, Erin. 2007. *The Politics of Touch.* Minneapolis: University of Minnesota Press.

Massumi, Brian. 2002. *Parables for the Virtual: Movement, Affect, Sensation.* Durham, NC: Duke University Press.

McCullough, Malcolm. 2007. New media urbanism: Grounding ambient information technology. *Environment and Planning B: Planning & Design* 34:383–395.

Mumford, Lewis. 1938. *The Culture of Cities.* New York: Harcourt, Brace.

Parisi, Luciana, and Tiziana Terranova. 2000. Heat-death, emergence and control in genetic engineering and artificial life. *Ctheory.* http://www.ctheory.net/articles.aspx?id=127.

Sloterdijk, Peter. 2009. *Terror from the Air.* New York: Semiotexte.

Sterling, Bruce. 2009. *Arphid Watch.* http://www.wired.com/beyond_the_beyond/category/arphid-watch/.

Terranova, Tiziana. 2004. *Network Culture: Politics for the Information Age.* London: Pluto.

Thrift, Nigel. 2008. *Non-Representational Theory.* London: Routledge.

Townsend, Anthony. 2001. The Internet and the rise of the new network cities, 1969–1999. *Environment and Planning B: Planning & Design* 28:39–58.

Townsend, Anthony. 2007. Seoul: Birth of a broadband metropolis. *Environment and Planning B: Planning & Design* 34:396–413.

Varnelis, Kazys. 2008. Architecture for hertzian space. http://www.varnelis.net/articles/architecture_for_hertzian_space.

Virilio, Paul. 1995. *The Art of the Motor.* Minneapolis: University of Minnesota Press.

4 Mobile Media and the Strategies of Urban Citizenship: Control, Responsibilization, Politicization

Kurt Iveson

In cities around the world a range of experiments are under way to explore the new possibilities mobile media technologies might offer for urban governance. Many of these experiments involve establishing new channels of information from urban authorities to urban inhabitants in the hope that city life can be made better by providing people with useful information where and when they need it. In such efforts, government and commercial information is made available on the World Wide Web, and the networked and location-aware attributes of mobile media devices are enlisted to enable people to access this information while they are on the go. But experiments are also underway that seek to enhance the flow of information in the other direction, from urban inhabitants to urban authorities. Here, efforts are underway to extend the participatory practices and cultures associated with social media and Web 2.0 to urban governance by helping people to engage with one another and with urban authorities as citizens.

As these experiments gather momentum, it is important that we establish clear frameworks to inform their development and evaluate their performance. This is not only a matter of predicting and evaluating the "successes" and "failures" of experiments with mobile media and networked sensing according to established aims and objectives. It is also a matter of considering their wider implications by critically reflecting on the aims, objectives, and assumptions of different applications of mobile media in the realm of urban governance. Such critical reflections and frameworks are beginning to emerge, offered by scholars and activists coming from a range of disciplinary backgrounds including urban geography and sociology, cultural studies, human–computer interaction, urban planning, and legal studies (see Crang and Graham 2007; Galloway 2004; Greenfield and Shepard 2007; Kang and Kuff 2005; Paulos, Honicky, and Hooker 2009; Williams, Robles, and Dourish 2009).

In this chapter I draw on recent debates about the changing nature of urban governance and citizenship in order to identify and evaluate different ways of using social and mobile media as tools for citizen engagement in urban governance. The central claim of the chapter is that the forms of participation and engagement enabled by mobile media can be put to use for very different purposes, not all of which will necessarily result in a more empowered citizenry. As such, participation and engagement are neither progressive nor oppressive, neither just nor unjust. The crucial evaluative question for mobile media applications in the field of urban governance is not so much "Do they facilitate citizen participation and engagement?", but rather, "What is the vision of the good citizen and the good city that they seek to enact?"

The chapter proceeds in four steps. First, I describe three applications of social and mobile media in a particular field of urban policy—graffiti. My purpose here is to show some different ways the roles of citizens armed with smartphones have been scripted in the contentious field of graffiti policy. What model of citizenship and engagement informs these different applications? To answer this question, the next section of the chapter considers these three applications through the lens of recent discussions about urban governance and citizenship in contemporary cities. I argue that these three applications nicely illustrate three different ways that social and mobile media can be mobilized in urban governance: control, responsibilization, and politicization. The third section of the chapter elaborates on these three concepts and considers their relationship to each other. Finally, the chapter concludes with a discussion of participation, politics, and the good city. I argue that participation does not equal empowerment, although empowerment will certainly involve participation.

Mobile Media, Citizen Engagement, and the "Graffiti Problem"

Applications of mobile media concerned with the place of graffiti in the urban environment provide us with an excellent window onto the wider debates about participation, urban governance, and citizen engagement that are the subject of this chapter. Graffiti is a feature of city life that polarizes urban populations. Urban authorities in many cities devote significant resources to eradicating illegal graffiti on the grounds that graffiti detracts from urban quality of life (Iveson 2010). On the other hand, there are those that argue that (good) graffiti can make a significant contribution to urban aesthetics and creativity (Iveson 2009; Burnham 2010). On the surface these disagreements about the place of graffiti in urban life and the nature of "the graffiti problem" may appear to be only matters of aesthetic taste. But in fact such disagreements tend to become the very stuff of urban politics and citizenship. Disagreements over issues like graffiti are underpinned by competing visions of the good city, and they inevitably come to be expressed through competing efforts to realize these visions in reality. These efforts to shape and order cities make use of a variety of different techniques and technologies of urban governance. This is precisely how mobile media technologies come to be enmeshed in urban governance and politics—their affordances and possibilities are explored in the service of different visions of the good city. Applications of these technologies are developed to solve problems that have been framed with reference to one or another vision of the good city and the good citizen. So, let's take a look at some examples of how the kinds of citizen engagement afforded by mobile media (in combination with other sensing technologies) have been put to work in order to solve "the graffiti problem."

First, consider the *graffiti-e-nose*, a device that has been developed as a new weapon in the "war on graffiti." Developed by the E-Nose Company based in Sydney, Australia, the graffiti-e-nose is an odor-sensing device that can detect aerosol paint fumes at a distance of 45 meters. On detecting these fumes, the device then sends real-time alerts to security agencies via SMS.[1] The odor-sensor technologies on the graffiti-e-nose were first developed by NASA, and then adapted for use against graffiti by its university-based inventors who have now established a consortium to commercialize e-nose technologies for further security and military purposes. The graffiti-e-nose is designed to address the limitations of conventional CCTV for graffiti prevention, which at best offers a visual deterrent and an after-the-fact documentation of graffiti that might assist in convicting a graffiti writer who has been apprehended. New surveillance technologies such as the graffiti-e-nose promise to assist with the "real-time" detection and apprehension of graffiti writers by helping authorities catch graffiti writers in the act. Since its development, the graffiti-e-nose has been picked up by several local authorities and urban infrastructure providers across four capital cities in Australia, and is attracting positive press coverage internationally.

Citizens Connect is my second example of the use of mobile media technologies in addressing the graffiti problem. Citizens Connect is a Boston-based service designed to help citizens connect to their local government. The key feature of Citizens Connect is an iPhone application, which enables users to log requests for urban maintenance with the city. So, for instance, if a citizen comes across a piece of graffiti or a hole in the road, they can take a geotagged photo of the offending graffiti or hole and then submit this photo directly to the city's maintenance team via their iPhone (see figure 4.1). According to the City of Boston, "The Citizens Connect iPhone app is part of Mayor Menino's and the City of Boston's strategy for Citizen-to-City transactions called Citizens Connect. The Citizens Connect iPhone app is targeted at enlisting Boston residents and visitors to gather information about the physical state of the city."[2] In one sense, there is nothing radically new here. A concerned citizen has always been able to take note of the offending graffiti and call the city from a landline at a later time (many cities including Boston have established graffiti hotlines for precisely this purpose)—they might even have written a letter! The point of Citizens Connect is that citizens armed with smartphones might be more likely to connect with the city if this can be done on-the-go and in real time with little inconvenience and investment of precious time. With Citizens Connect, then, the city is hoping new technology can help create more conducive conditions for what it calls "citizen sourcing," and thereby bring government closer to the citizen.

Figure 4.1
User interface for Citizens Connect iPhone application. *Source*: www.cityofboston.gov.

Unlike the graffiti-e-nose, which is a stealth technology designed to work on behalf of citizens, Citizens Connect is designed to involve citizens directly in taking responsibility for urban governance. Indeed, Citizens Connect has been cited as one example of how mobile computing technologies might be deployed to enhance urban life through facilitating citizen participation in urban governance, to the mutual benefit of both municipal authorities and citizens (Hirshberg 2009). For authorities, citizens can be enlisted as eyes and ears on the street. For citizens, direct channels of communication with authorities are enabled, and (hopefully) this will also make those authorities more responsive and accountable to their citizens.

Third, consider the *ReFace* project organized by Perth art collective ololo in collaboration with production company WBMC. From a technical perspective, this project is quite similar to Citizens Connect. For ReFace, citizens armed with digital cameras and smartphones were similarly asked to take geotagged pictures of graffiti and submit

Figure 4.2
ReFace Projection, Perth. *Source*: Jerrem Lynch (jerrem.com).

them to a web address. But the purpose of this citizen participation was quite different. Pictures were uploaded to an interactive online gallery on the ReFace website and
could be viewed (and sorted by artist, location, or photographer) and rated by members
of the public. In April 2009, during the City of Perth's International Arts Festival, the
top-rated images were projected onto the walls of prominent buildings in the city at
night, using "Projector Bombing" technologies pioneered by the Graffiti Research Lab
(see figure 4.2). Audience members that night also had a chance to participate in real-
time laser tagging and digital painting activities. The purpose of ReFace was described
in the following manner on the project website:

Watch bare city walls transform into vibrant public art sites as curated galleries of stick-ups,
stencils and freehand Street Art are projected on buildings across town as part of the Perth International Arts Festival's *ReFace* project.

As the city throbs with an influx of nocturnal visitors, *ReFace* investigates whether public
perception changes when the artwork is impermanent, providing street artists with a legal means
to get their work shown on some of the most notorious walls in Perth.[3]

As Jerrem, one of the members of the Graffiti Research Lab (Australia) involved in ReFace noted, "It's interesting how people react to the non destructive copies of real world 'vandalism.'"[4]

Making Cities Better? Models of Citizen Engagement in Graffiti-e-nose, Citizens Connect, and ReFace

Each of these three uses of mobile media claims to make the city better by working with its citizens. But how should we critically evaluate these claims? Clearly, these three examples are informed by quite different visions of the good city and the place of graffiti within it. And they also involve quite different visions of citizen engagement and the good citizen. We can turn to recent debates about the nature of urban citizenship to help us think through the important differences. As we will see, these three applications of mobile media are illustrative of three quite different models of urban governance and citizenship.

The concept of citizenship refers to "a bundle of entitlements and obligations which constitute individuals as fully fledged members of a socio-political community, providing them with access to scarce resources" (Turner 1994, i). The study of citizenship brings into focus the rules and norms by which members of a political community are identified and governed. Of course, in a *democratic* political community, participation is simultaneously an entitlement and an obligation of membership as a citizen: "Citizenship in a democracy consists in the participation of citizens in the ways in which their conduct is governed by the exercise of political power in any system or practice of governance. Citizens participate by 'having a say' and 'negotiating' how power is exercised and who exercises it" (Tully 1999, 170). I will return to this double-edged nature of participation shortly. First, however, I want to elaborate on the *urban* dimensions of citizenship.

Recent years have witnessed a rekindling of interest in the city as a site and subject of citizenship (see Holston and Appadurai 1999; Isin 1999, 2002; Iveson 2007; Staeheli 2003; Varsanyi 2006). This renewed focus on the relationship between cities and citizenship is indicative of a growing recognition that questions of citizenship are no longer (if they ever were) settled exclusively at the scale of the nation-state. Even as the nation-state remains crucial to the setting of the juridical or formal dimensions of citizenship (such as nationality and immigration rules), the more substantive matter of how we live together and govern our conduct as citizens is often worked out in the context of everyday urban interactions and contestations.[5]

Of course, the question of how we live together as citizens in cities is contested. Crudely, we can divide the kinds of disagreement that emerge among citizens into two categories. First, citizens disagree about how to respond to issues and problems of agreed importance. Here, citizens may contest the merits of different policy solutions to problems, which are identified by various governing institutions. But the scope of disagreement over urban citizenship also has a broader dimension. Second, citizens may also disagree about *how they conduct their disagreement.* Here, citizens may contest the rules that define who has the right to be heard *as a citizen* and who does not, and/or they may contest the rules and norms about how citizens should properly engage in political debate (Rancière 1999). James Tully (1999) has applied the analogy of the "game" to these different aspects of disagreement over citizenship. As he puts it, "The study of any game will involve, first, the analysis of the rules in accordance with which the game is routinely played and the techniques of government or relations of power that hold them in place. Second, it will involve the 'strategies of freedom' in which some participants refuse to be governed in this way, dispute and seek to modify the rules, and thus think and act differently to some extent" (p. 167).

Using this analogy, we might say the first kind of disagreement identified above is conducted within the existing rules of the game, while the second kind of disagreement is about the very rules of the game.

Because of these disagreements, configurations of citizenship have been subject to change across time and space. Different configurations of citizenship rules and norms become entrenched in particular times and places, only to be challenged and modified through politics along the two axes identified above. These politics are often highly charged, precisely because different configurations of urban citizenship (or ways of "playing the game") work to privilege certain people and certain interests over others. Power is exercised through the normalization, institutionalization, and contestation of different configurations of citizenship. Indeed, the pursuit of social control can be thought of as the effort to stabilize a particular configuration of urban citizenship. Attempts to challenge these configurations by changing the "rules of the game" have variously been referred to as exercises in "insurgent" (Holston 1998) or "dissident" (Sparks 1997) citizenship.

So, with this brief discussion of urban citizenship in mind, let's return to our three examples in the field of graffiti policy. What different configurations of urban citizenship are privileged by our three different applications of mobile media and networked sensing to the graffiti problem?

The graffiti-e-nose is premised on the notion that the interests of the city and its citizens can be advanced through the identification, apprehension, and punishment of those who write graffiti. Here, technology is envisaged as a new "weapon" in the "war on graffiti," which is being waged by urban authorities on behalf of a beleaguered citizenry said to be sick and tired of the damage caused by vandalism (Iveson 2010). Graffiti is a problem to be solved, and the graffiti-e-nose is offered as a new technological solution. This approach rests on a categorical distinction between the good citizens and the graffiti writers. Those who write graffiti are the targets—by breaking the law and violating someone else's claim to property ownership, they are considered *antisocial*. The graffiti-e-nose is designed to enlist sensing technology and mobile media on behalf of property owners both to prevent and to punish this antisocial behavior.

Citizens Connect embodies a related but slightly different configuration of urban citizenship. Certainly, it too is premised on the dominant conception of the "graffiti problem," where graffiti is a problem to be eradicated, and citizens are imagined to be locked in a conflict (often described as a "war") with antisocial graffiti writers. But the solution offered by Citizens Connect scripts a different role for the good citizen. Rather than being a passive victim on whose behalf urban authorities act, in Citizens Connect the good citizen is imagined as an active, participating partner in urban governance. The iPhone application is designed to facilitate this participation. As Boston officials put it, the citizen is "enlisted" in the maintenance of good urban order. By downloading the application for his or her iPhone, taking a picture of graffiti, and submitting it to city authorities, the good citizen exercises responsibility for their neighborhood in partnership with the state.

In their conceptions of urban citizenship, I would argue that the graffiti-e-nose and Citizens Connect are examples of the use of mobile media applications to advance neoliberal projects for urban governance and citizenship. While neoliberal approaches to urban governance continue to unfold in different ways across time and space (Peck and Tickell 2002), it is nonetheless possible to sketch some shared characteristics of these emerging "neoliberalisms." In many areas of urban and social policy, we have seen the introduction of privatization, marketization, consumerization, and securitization, with governments "steering" and regulating rather than "rowing" and providing (Rose 2000b, 324). All this is informed by skepticism about the capacity of political action through the state to bring about the good of individuals and communities. The best regulatory mechanism for social activity is thought to be the market, which encourages autonomous actors to size up the available information and make informed choices about what is good for them. The state has been reconceived as "merely one partner in government, facilitating, enabling, stimulating, shaping, inciting the self-governing activities of a multitude of dispersed entities—associations, firms, communities, individuals—who would take onto themselves many of the powers, and the responsibilities previously annexed by 'the state'" (Rose 2000a, 96). Individuals, families, organizations, communities, and entire cities are said to know what is best for themselves, not government—they must find a way to be autonomous in a competitive world, and they must take responsibility for pursuing their own best interests. Of course, this does not mean the complete withdrawal of "the state," but a recasting of its role. The state simultaneously "rolls back" its involvement from some areas of social provision, and "rolls out" a set of incentives and assistance packages designed to encourage the formation of these autonomous and responsible citizens who are capable of governing themselves (Peck and Tickell 2002).

Newly emerging measures in the domain of law and order are firmly enmeshed in this neoliberal policy agenda. Urban order is to be achieved by urging and enabling citizens and communities to "take upon themselves the responsibility for the security of their property and their persons" (Rose 2000b, 327). Government through responsibility is as dominant here as in other dimensions of social and economic policy. How is this to be achieved? According to sociologist Mitchell Dean (2002), government in the service of good order becomes a matter of both:

• Punishing those who refuse to take responsibility for themselves, who have rejected the opportunities provided for them to take their place in the community and thereby constitute a threat to civility and good order
• Assisting those individuals and associations who are willing to take responsibility for their own security and the civility of their community, through partnership and the provision of "opportunity"

Drawing on this analysis of neoliberal urban governance, we can label these two governance strategies as *control* and *responsibilization*.

The graffiti-e-nose and Citizens Connect are good examples of how property owners and citizens equipped with mobile media are being mobilized in neoliberal urban governance strategies. In the case of the graffiti-e-nose, mobile media devices are connected with networked sensors in a technology that seeks to *control* graffiti by capturing and punishing "antisocial" graffiti writers who have failed to take their place in the community. In Citizens Connect, mobile media devices equipped with Web 2.0 applications are enlisted to assist individuals in taking *responsibility* for their own communities. In both cases, the discourse of "community" is central—its ties, bonds, and values become the very means by which neoliberal government seeks to achieve urban order (Rose 2000b, 329). Some years ago, Stanley Cohen (1985, 116) noted this emerging centrality of the discourse of "community": "It would be difficult to exaggerate how this ideology—or more accurately, this single word—has come to dominate Western crime-control discourse in the last few decades." In the cases of the graffiti-e-nose and Citizens Connect, then, the forms of citizen engagement enabled by mobile media are put to work "in the name of good citizenship, public order and the control or elimination of criminality, delinquency and anti-social conduct" (Rose 2000b, 324).

However, we must not succumb to the tendency to see these neoliberal strategies of social control as all powerful or beyond contestation (Larner 2003). As noted earlier, dominant configurations of citizenship never have things all their own way. This is certainly true of neoliberalism, as neoliberal ideologies compete with others to shape the strategies of urban governance. Giving citizens more responsibility for their own governance, helping them to take charge of their own destiny, is a risky strategy. There is always the chance that citizens might deploy their autonomy in unpredictable ways. As Nancy Fraser (2003, 165) has pointed out in her discussion of neoliberalism, we should not be too quick to "reduce its autonomy-fostering orientation to a normalizing regimentation." Neoliberalism is far from a cohesive program, and is prone to all sorts of "internal fissions and contradictions" (O'Malley 1998). Most importantly for our discussion here, the techniques and technologies developed in the service of neoliberal governance efforts are by no means guaranteed to work, nor are their applications exclusively bound to neoliberal projects. "Autonomous," "responsible" citizens might mobilize these very same techniques and technologies for alternative ends. To return to the language used earlier, they might try to change the "rules of the game." Indeed, O'Malley (2009, 277) notes that "many features of neoliberalism were fought for by both the political left and right. . . . Responsibilization owes at least some of its nature and impetus to politically left demands to take back control from the state and expertise—even if the result has not always been as intended."

This is why ReFace is significant. Unlike both the graffiti-e-nose and Citizens Connect, the aim of ReFace is not to offer a new "solution" to the "graffiti problem." Rather, it seeks to *redefine* the very nature of the graffiti problem, which is to be solved by provoking a debate about the place of graffiti in the city. Here, systems and processes for participation are not designed to enlist the citizenry in the ongoing war on graffiti, they are instead designed to engage citizens in debate and dialog about the aims and objectives of graffiti policy. ReFace thereby contests the notion that graffiti is nothing but antisocial behavior by focusing on its artistic and provocative qualities. It even invites citizens to see their own art and writing projected on walls in the city, if only temporarily. Here, we see social and mobile media used not so much in the service of control or responsibilization, but in the service of *politicization*. My use of the term *politicization* here is based on the particular understanding of the political discussed above, as a kind of practice that disrupts existing norms and rules of citizenship. As Tully (1999, 170) puts it, "Politics is the type of game in which the framework—the rules of the game—can come up for deliberation and amendment in the course of the game" (see also Rancière 1999; Iveson 2009). ReFace is an example of politicization in action, as "insurgent" or "dissident" citizens use it to make the claim that graffiti and graffiti writers (not to mention graffiti lovers) might actually have a proper place in the city (as both a physical environment and a political community). Citizen engagement is not premised on playing by the rules of the game in the "war on graffiti" as it is with the graffiti-e-nose and Citizens Connect.

Mobile Media, Urban Governance, and Citizenship: Control, Responsibilization, Politicization

Drawing on the analysis above, let me now consolidate this basic typology of different uses of social and mobile media technologies for urban governance and citizen

Table 4.1
Strategies of control, responsibilization, politicization

Strategy	Purpose	Associated uses of mobile media
Control	Securing the city on behalf of "good citizens" through the identification and containment of "antisocial" urban inhabitants who are either unable or unwilling to be part of the city	Surveillance, identification, and sorting of populations and activities
Responsibilization	Assisting urban citizens in taking responsibility for their own quality of life through the good governance of their selves and their communities	Provision of better information to inform/shape choice in context, consultation of citizens about predefined policy options, new lines of communication between citizens and urban authorities
Politicization	Claiming of new "rights to the city" by contesting the rules and norms of belonging, in order to include people/practices that have no proper place in the city	"Making the invisible visible," harnessing autonomy to network with other participants in political projects, forging displacements through interruptions to everyday routines and arrangements of space

engagement. I have argued that we can distinguish between three families of governance strategies, which make use of the possibilities of mobile media (table 4.1).

Now, it is important to note that this typology (like all typologies) is quite crude, and is offered only as a heuristic device. The messy reality of urban life and the rapid mutation of technology have a happy habit of exceeding such attempts at containment and categorization! Indeed, the distinctions between the different purposes, characteristics, and applications I have sketched in table 4.1 are not nearly so neatly differentiated in practice.

For instance, there is a very fine line between the use of mobile media and networked sensors in the service of politicization and their use in the service of control because *both* of these citizenship strategies involve "making the invisible visible" (Iveson 2007, 213–218). Being seen (and heard) is a fundamental condition of making political claims and participating in political life as a citizen. Furthermore, the politicization of an issue frequently involves efforts to expose something previously hidden to wider public attention. As Sandercock (2003, 224) puts it, insurgent urban politics involves "making the hitherto invisible visible" in order to "also make it discussable." But visibility is also a tool of control. Indeed, the history of efforts to control the city is a history of efforts to render people and practices visible to the "eye of power" (De Certeau 1984; Foucault 1980). Given that "making the invisible visible" is frequently used to describe the aspirations of applications in the burgeoning field of urban informatics,[6] then clearly different applications of mobile media are going to be caught up in a highly fraught politics of visibility (Crang and Graham 2007; see also Barnes 2009). Think of our three examples above, each of which mobilizes mobile media and networked sensors to make graffiti more visible but for quite different purposes. ReFace seeks to contest and politicize urban places by haunting them with visual projections of their hidden potential to be surfaces for graffiti. But the graffiti-e-nose seeks to expose graffiti writers to security agencies, and the images collected through Citizens Connect can be used to map the activity of individual graffiti writers to assist with their prosecution. Beyond these considerations of graffiti, Nathan Eagle's (2009) work on slum mapping in Nairobi also illustrates this tension between visibility for politicization and visibility for control. He has used data provided by mobile-phone companies to map the extent of slum populations and the times and locations of economic activities. Such efforts to make slum populations visible are absolutely crucial to facilitating the political claims of slum dwellers for rights to the city because this information can be used by government to better target services to slum populations (Appadurai 2001). As such, "making the invisible visible" is a valuable tool for politicization. On the other hand, if the current administration were replaced by a more repressive regime, the same map could be used to direct the bulldozers for the kinds of slum-clearance operations that we have witnessed in other parts of sub-Saharan Africa (Davis 2004). In other words, "making the invisible visible" could also be put to work for controlling urban slum dwellers who were previously "off the radar."

Similarly, there is also a fine line between responsibilization and politicization: the facilitation of participation/collaboration through mobile media may look quite similar even if the purposes are quite distinct. We saw that this was the case with the Citizens Connect and ReFace applications. We could further illustrate this with some consideration of Web 2.0 applications such as user-generated review pages. Armed with networked mobile media devices, we might be able to access information about restaurants that has been provided by previous patrons or government inspection agencies. If we are in an unfamiliar neighborhood looking for something to eat, this could be very handy indeed (Greenfield and Shepard 2007). Such an application of mobile media is designed to enable us to make better market choices as individuals by accessing information, and as such is a fairly straightforward example of responsibilization. But the very same applications could be modified to help us share information about the labor practices of different restaurants, or the sustainability of the produce they use to produce their food. Connected as they are to collective efforts to change the nature of urban life, these applications might be considered examples of politicization, which make the invisible visible. In the United States and United Kingdom, for example, so-called CarrotMobbers deploy the "carrot" of consumer buying rather than the "stick" of boycotting (or bad publicity) to encourage ethical business by using the networking capabilities of mobile media devices to assemble crowds at establishments that have embraced ethical and sustainable business practices (Taylor 2008).

Finally, we should also note that the uses of different mobile media applications for citizenship would inevitably escape their intentions. In this chapter, I have focused mainly on the intentions of the examples under consideration in order to construct my typology. But we can well imagine how these intentions might fail to be met. Perhaps the aspirations of the graffiti-e-nose for stealth surveillance (whereby it senses graffiti writers but remains invisible to them) will come unstuck thanks to politicians seeking to promote their use of the device in the media. And surely a picture of the closely guarded device will eventually find its way onto the Internet. Perhaps the aspirations of Citizens Connect will not be met because the kinds of people who like to complain to the Boston authorities about graffiti are not the kinds of people who carry iPhones. And perhaps the effect of projecting virtual graffiti in order to ReFace a wall will only reinforce for some people the destructive nature of "real" graffiti.

Mobile Technologies and Citizen Engagement: Participation ≠ Empowerment (but Empowerment = Participation)

Let us now return to the question posed at the beginning of this chapter: How should we evaluate the impact of experiments that seek to use social and mobile media technologies to help people engage with one another and with urban authorities as *citizens*?

The analysis I have offered in this chapter suggests that there is no single answer to this question. I have argued that different applications of social and mobile media technologies will have different impacts on urban life, depending on the model of governance and the strategies of citizenship they embody. For those of us who want to make the city more democratic, the challenge is to identify and exploit the possibilities of social and mobile media for the politicization of existing exclusions and inequalities. I hope that I have demonstrated in this chapter that the concept of urban citizenship provides a useful conceptual tool through which we can approach this task.

In conclusion, one of the most important implications of the control-responsibilization-politicization framework I have advanced here is this—if a mobile media application deployed in the service of urban governance is participatory and engages citizens, this does not make it inherently progressive or empowering. Or, to put it another way, empowerment must involve participation, but the reverse is not necessarily true. The active participation of citizens in the gathering and analysis of digital data about their own activities and the cities they inhabit does not necessarily signal the emergence of a *politics* of the good city. Rather, such participation may well be bound up with projects of neoliberal urban governance through control and respon-sibilization. As Greenfield and Shepard (2007) have observed, some visions of partici-pation embedded in urban informatics technologies position the citizen as little more than a collector or provider of information on behalf of urban authorities. We there-fore need to ask critical questions about the kinds of participation that are enabled by applications of mobile devices and their associated visions of the city. Are we partici-pating in enacting someone else's vision of the good city? Or are we participating in struggles to make the game of urban citizenship more just?

Notes

1. www.e-nose.info/documents/E-Nose_security.pdf.

2. http://www.cityofboston.gov/mis/apps/iphone.asp.

3. http://reface.abc.net.au. Ololo and WBMC received funding from the Australian Broadcasting Corporation, ScreenWest, and the Department of Culture and the Arts (Western Australia) for this project. A documentary about ReFace project can be found at http://vimeo.com/6029672.

4. http://www.grlaustralia.com.

5. This is particularly so in an age of globalization. While it is frequently observed that globaliza-tion is challenging the dominance of the nation-state as the site of citizenship (King and Kendall 2004), this only reinforces the significance of the city for citizenship. As Isin (1999, 13) has observed, "Cities, particularly global cities, have become political spaces where the concentration of different groups and their identities are intertwined with the articulation of various claims to citizenship rights."

6. Dan Hill has described this term as "ubiquitous" and even "massively over-used" in the field, even as he still finds it useful (see his entries at www.cityofsound.com on October 11 and 13, 2009).

References

Appadurai, A. 2001. Deep democracy: Urban governmentality and the horizon of politics. *Environment and Urbanization* 13:23–43.

Barnes, S. 2009. Sydney Sidetracks: Listening in to "history where it happened" using the ABC's television and radio archives. Paper presented at the Australia and New Zealand Communications Association conference "Communication, Creativity and Global Citizenship," Brisbane, July. http://www.cpe.qut.edu.au/conferences/2009/anzca/proceedings/Barns_ANZCA09.pdf.

Burnham, S. 2010. The call and response of street art and the city. *City* 14 (1–2): 133–139.

Cohen, S. 1985. *Visions of Social Control: Crime, Punishment, and Classification.* Oxford: Blackwell.

Crang, M., and S. Graham. 2007. Sentient cities: Ambient intelligence and the politics of urban space. *Information Communication and Society* 10 (6): 789–817.

Davis, M. 2004. Planet of slums. *New Left Review* 26: 5–34.

Dean, M. 2002. Liberal government and authoritarianism. *Economy and Society* 31 (1): 37–61.

De Certeau, M. 1984. *The Practice of Everyday Life*. Berkeley: University of California Press.

Eagle, N. 2009. Engineering a common good: Fair use of aggregated, anonymized behavioral data. Paper presented at the "Engaging Data Forum," MIT, Boston, October 12. http://senseable.mit .edu/engagingdata/program.html.

Foucault, M. 1980. The eye of power. In C. Gordon, *Power/Knowledge: Selected Interviews and Other Writings, 1972–1977*. Brighton, Sussex: Harvester Press.

Fraser, N. 2003. From discipline to flexibilization? Rereading Foucault in the shadow of globalization. *Constellations* (Oxford, England) 10 (2): 160–171.

Galloway, A. 2004. Intimations of everyday life. *Cultural Studies* 18 (2–3): 384–408.

Greenfield, A., and M. Shepard. 2007. *Urban Computing and Its Discontents*. New York: Architectural League of New York.

Hirshberg, P. 2009. Keynote address presented at the "Engaging Data Forum," MIT, Boston, October 12. http://senseable.mit.edu/engagingdata/program.html.

Holston, J. 1998. Spaces of insurgent citizenship. In L. Sandercock, ed., *Making the Invisible Visible: A Multicultural Planning History*. Berkeley: University of California Press.

Holston, J., and A. Appadurai, eds. 1999. *Cities and Citizenship*. Durham, NC: Duke University Press.

Isin, E., ed. 1999. *Democracy, Citizenship and the Global City*. London: Routledge.

Isin, E. 2002. *Being Political: Genealogies of Citizenship*. Minneapolis: University of Minnesota Press.

Iveson, K. 2007. *Publics and the City*. Oxford: Blackwell.

Iveson, K. 2009. War is over (if you want it): A new approach to the graffiti problem. *Australian Planner* 46 (4): 22–31.

Iveson, K. 2010. The wars on graffiti and the new military urbanism. *City* 14 (1–2): 112–131.

Kang, J., and D. Kuff. 2005. Pervasive computing: Embedding the public sphere. *Washington and Lee Law Review* 62 (1): 93–147.

King, R., and G. Kendall. 2004. *The State, Democracy and Globalization*. Basingstoke: Palgrave.

Larner, W. 2003. Neoliberalism? *Environment and Planning D: Society & Space* 21 (5): 509–512.

O'Malley, P. 1998. Indigenous governance. In M. Dean and B. Hindess, eds., *Governing Australia: Studies in Contemporary Rationalities of Government*. Melbourne: Cambridge University Press.

O'Malley, P. 2009. Responsibilization. In A. Wakefield and J. Fleming, eds., *The SAGE Dictionary of Policing*. London: Sage.

Paulos, E., R. J. Honicky, and B. Hooker. 2009. Citizen science: Enabling participatory urbanism. In M. Foth, ed., *Handbook of Research on Urban Informatics: The Practice and Promise of the Real-Time City*. Hershey, PA: IGI Global.

Peck, J., and A. Tickell. 2002. Neoliberalizing space. *Antipode* 34 (3): 380–404.

Rancière, J. 1999. *Disagreement: Politics and Philosophy*. Trans. J. Rose. Minneapolis: University of Minnesota Press.

Rose, N. 2000a. Governing cities, governing citizens. In E. Isin, ed., *Democracy, Citizenship and the Global City*, 95–109. London: Routledge.

Rose, N. 2000b. Government and control. *British Journal of Criminology* 40 (2): 321–339.

Sandercock, L. 2003. *Cosmopolis II: Mongrel Cities in the 21st Century*. London: Continuum.

Sparks, H. 1997. Dissident citizenship. *Hypatia* 12 (4): 71–110.

Staeheli, L. 2003. Introduction: Cities and citizenship. *Urban Geography* 24 (2): 97–102.

Taylor, T. 2008. Meet the CarrotMob. *The Guardian*, September 18.

Tully, J. 1999. The agonic freedom of citizens. *Economy and Society* 28 (2): 161–182.

Turner, B. S. 1994. General commentary. In B. S. Turner and P. Hamilton, eds., *Citizenship: Critical Concepts*. London: Routledge.

Varsanyi, M. W. 2006. Interrogating "urban citizenship" vis-à-vis undocumented migration. *Citizenship Studies* 10 (2): 229–249.

Williams, A., E. Robles, and P. Dourish. 2009. Urbane-ing the city: Examining and refining the assumptions behind urban informatics. In M. Foth, ed., *Handbook of Research on Urban Informatics: The Practice and Promise of the Real-Time City*, 1–20. Hershey, PA: IGI Global.

II Civic Engagement

Foreword

Yvonne Rogers

Along with over half a million people across the globe, I was a victim of the "Ash Cloud." I was stranded on another continent—no way of getting home with all planes grounded. The Icelandic volcano had erupted and spread its ash plume menacingly across Northern European skies. It was the last day of the ACM Human Factors Conference in Computing Systems 2010 (CHI) in Atlanta, and as laptops, iPhones, and newly acquired iPads were switched on the first thing in the morning, it dawned on many of us that we were facing a crisis. What were 200+ Brits, Swedes, Danes, French, Irish, Germans, Swiss, and other nationalities—scheduled to return to or fly via London, Paris, or Copenhagen that day—going to do? How were we going to survive? Where would we stay? Did we have enough money? What were we to do if no planes were allowed to fly for weeks and even months as some news reports predicted?

Social networking went into overdrive—both face to face and online. Many planned and unplanned meetings took place in cafés, hotel lobbies, restaurants, and bars. And much posting, commenting, and updating occurred. Only then did I truly appreciate the power and comfort of Facebook and Twitter—their ability to bring together a loosely connected group of people who had been thrown together so they could share their concerns, anxieties, advice, and help. Being a self-confessed nonuser of either, I suddenly felt a bit of an outsider as my colleagues, students, and fellow conference attendees all sat glued to their screens, updating, commiserating, and joking about the "puff-puff," the "plume," and being "stuck in the USA." I even resorted occasionally to over-the-shoulder surfing to see just how much I was missing of the online action.

Within hours most had sorted themselves out using various grassroots tactics. The tweets and postings were highly supportive and informative. It was fascinating to track where people ended up. The Swedes stayed at the Hyatt, the Germans went off to a good-value hotel in midtown, a Nottingham/London crowd escaped to a resort in the countryside, some ex-pat Canadians slunk home to Toronto, and one Brit even went to Las Vegas to visit his relatives. Several groups emerged on Facebook with postings such as "chi2010 and stuck in America," and the official twitter stream became,

"#CHIstuck2010." Beki Grinter (http://beki70.wordpress.com/) kindly compiled all the disparate sources of emerging reports, help being offered, and so on into a unified blog and stated, "It was because there were people who ended up stuck in Atlanta that I had written a blog post, a way to disseminate information about Atlanta. So, I was already beginning to explore the social media in crisis space. But largely as a matter of trying to be helpful." A number of organizational initiatives were also set up shortly afterward—the CHI conference organizers and Georgia Tech faculty offered free accommodations, food, and so on to those in need.

It was civic engagement in action—on an individual, group, country, organizational, and government level. Never before had I witnessed so much camaraderie on such a scale. This experience also illustrates what Fiorella de Cindio and Christian Peraboni describe in chapter 6 as the two main forms of participation: grassroots and institutional. Whereas CHIstuck was about crisis management, De Cindio and Peraboni write about Italian citizenship, discussing the challenges of trying to integrate top-down with bottom-up approaches. The authors ask if organizations can piggyback on local people's efforts to help them address their concerns (e.g., improving cycle lanes) rather than working as separate entities. If so, what are the challenges of doing so?

An alternative approach to using the double act "Facebook and Twitter" is to develop particular tools customized to the activity at hand. In chapter 8, Tad Hirsch describes three such tools designed specifically for activists—that is, loosely coordinated groups wanting to mobilize and share information as a way of confronting injustice. Security, privacy, and the need for accuracy are considered key. Tools provided for different kinds of activist activities include mobile texting with map visualization, sophisticated group management, and video sharing and commenting.

An important part of civic engagement that has become widely accepted is blogging—both amateur and professional. During the Ash Cloud experience, many commented on the impact of the volcano on the environment, even noting how the amount of CO_2 the volcano produced was less than the amount saved by the hundreds of thousands of flights canceled over the six-day no-fly period. There was also much coverage of the farmers in Kenya who were suffering when tons of roses had to be destroyed while planes were grounded and therefore unable to deliver their goods.

Whether to buy Kenyan green beans in Europe or the United States is an example many of us use when considering the dilemma of food sustainability: we may reduce carbon emissions by only buying locally produced vegetables but the Kenyan farmers will suffer if we choose not to eat their beans. Swap roses for beans? We may feel good that we bought locally grown daffodils and that there were far fewer carbon emissions during Ash Cloud week, but thousands of Kenyan farmers had to go hungry as a consequence.

Food culture and sustainability is the topic of chapter 5, by Jaz Hee-jeong Choi and Eli Blevis. They argue that "change is necessary in how we live our daily lives" in terms of how we imagine, produce, prepare, and consume food. Much political, academic, and journalistic discussion of food sustainability has been about supply chains and the reduction of carbon emissions. Choi and Blevis extend this chain of thought literally onto the chopping board by making us consider aspects of food preparation and consumption in new ways. They also suggest the need to consider the challenges of "change" at many levels, from individual to global, transcending our traditional comfort zones of disciplines, domains, and boundaries.

In chapter 7, Jonas Fritsch and Martin Brynskov present a new framework for considering behavioral change—specifically for reducing carbon emissions in the city of Aarhus, Denmark, which has set the goal of being CO_2 neutral by 2030. They describe how engagement, affect, and information can be manipulated when designing new "urban interfaces" to engage civic discourse on reducing their carbon footprint. One of the projects they describe that used this framework is "CO2nfession/CO2mittment." Besides having a great name, the installation consisted of a booth where people were encouraged to enter and confess their CO_2 sins, such as driving excessively or eating reindeer steaks. These were recorded and then relayed onto public screens located in the city, such as bus shelters. Talk about throwing good ol' Catholic guilt into the mix and seeing what happens!

Chapter 10, by Eric Paulos, describes a series of mobile and ubiquitous applications developed to provide real-time air-quality data on mobiles and other gadgets. Their provocative example is of a t-shirt that measures and expresses air quality to passersby, by letting them know if the air around the wearer is bad. The project aimed to increase awareness and discussion in the community.

Finally, Bjorn Nansen, Jon M. Pearce, and Wally Smith use a shock story at the beginning of chapter 9 to illustrate the extremes people will go to when they feel passionate about sustainability. They describe an example of "water rage" reported in the Australian news in 2007: A man watering his front lawn in Sydney was accused by a passerby of wasting water. The man reacted by turning his hose on the passerby, who in turn retaliated by punching and kicking the man, who then later died of a heart attack. The man was actually entitled to water his garden on that particular day even though hose bans were in place for other days. Water use in Australia clearly is a very serious matter. The chapter describes the SmartGardenWatering project that provides expert advice on how to be more efficient with water use when gardening. For example, the software tool developed suggests decreasing the frequency of watering and increasing the duration of watering in order to have a lush garden. The authors hope next to enable a community of gardeners in Melbourne to share their tips, successes, and workarounds.

This part of the book offers much food for thought for technology developers, political activists, organizations, and the general public to better understand and decide how to care for the environment. Social networking, sharing/aggregation, and dissemination tools are key to this process. But as these technologies become more pervasive, questions arise about inclusion: how can we enable *nonusers* (through their own choice or for other reasons) who want to be active members of their community to not feel left out? Connecting those who now communicate primarily through online social networking with those who still prefer to use older channels of communication and dissemination may become an increasing challenge.

When the Ash Cloud cleared, I returned home safe and sound. But I still haven't signed up for Facebook or Twitter!

5 Advancing Design for Sustainable Food Cultures

Jaz Hee-jeong Choi and Eli Blevis

Our paper, "HCI & Sustainable Food Culture: A Design Framework for Engagement," presented at the 2010 NordiCHI conference, introduced a design framework for understanding engagement between people and sustainable food cultures (Choi and Blevis 2010). Our goal for this chapter is to expand our notion of this design framework and the program of research it implies. Throughout the chapter we make reference to the aforementioned conference proceedings paper. Restating the design framework and its motivations serves the dual purpose of making this chapter self-contained and of recording the framework in a more substantially archival form. We also provide additional examples to consider how the framework may be applied. Finally, we reflect on the effectiveness of the framework itself. Our examples are not intended to be universal, but rather very "ultimate particular" (Nelson and Stolterman 2003) instances and illustrations targeted as the material of specific reflection that precedes broader claims. As such, the form of this chapter is best understood as part reflective, part design theory, and part photographic essay.

Assuring a sustainable future has become one of the main concerns for human-computer interaction (HCI) researchers in recent years (DiSalvo, Sengers, and Brynjarsdottir 2010). While *sustainability* as a term warrants multifold interpretations, recent years have seen a particular emphasis on environmental sustainability as "climate change" became part of the global political and social consciousness. One imminent consequence of global warming is related to food, the vital foundation of human sustenance (Food and Agriculture Organization of the United Nations 2008). Humans simply cannot exist without food intake. Essentially, sustainability in this sense is based on "securing" food: having access to stable availability and use of quality food (Food and Agriculture Organization of the United Nations 2010). However, current food production and consumption practices do not ensure food security for the future, but rather seriously threaten it (Food and Agriculture Organization of the United Nations 2008). One of causes indentified for this predicament is the widening divide between urban and rural environments. People living in urban environments—including urban, suburban, and periurban regions (all of which are generally referred to as urban/metropolitan/city in this chapter)—increasingly see food as objects of consumption or the "final products" to be consumed but with a declining awareness of the long and complex process of "creating" and "preparing" food. This situation has deteriorated with the unprecedented scale of urban growth in recent years, broadening the segregation between the rural and urban environments, and thereby further limiting knowledge about and access to fresh produce. Global urban population has been increasing rapidly, which suggests that availability of food resources in urban areas is also becoming increasingly scarce. The UN Population Fund (UNFPA 2007) predicts that urban populations will grow and reach 60 percent of the entire global population by 2030. Therefore, as seen in recent global economic and ecological turmoil, change is necessary in how we live our daily lives in order to create a positive outlook for global food security.

Now is a crucial time for HCI researchers to create actionable knowledge through identifying, testing, and building on technical opportunities that can be augmented and realized to cultivate urban food cultures that are environmentally, socially, and healthwise sustainable. In considering how to design such HCI experiences, we argue that the answer is "engagement": engagement across disciplines, engagement with and among users (and nonusers), and engagement for sustainability, or rather, "sustained usability." These three elements of engagement yield five facets (two perspectives and three domains) of the design framework:

• Engagement across disciplines: The perspective of transdisciplinarity—transcending disciplinarity and values orientation
• Engagement with and among users/nonusers: The domain of urban informatics at the intersection of people, place, and technology (Foth 2009)—participatory, context-aware, and interactive networks
• Engagement for sustained usability: The perspective of design—design criticism and critical design

While this framework may be generally applicable to any inquiry about or practice within a values-oriented design space, we intend to use it specifically to serve as a theoretical underpinning for our exploration of HCI design for sustainable food culture. Further, this framework is not intended to be complete. We hope to expand and refine it as a theoretical foundation and apply it to our study of sustainable food culture and ubiquitous technology (http://www.urbaninformatics.net/projects/food) as a matter of theoretically informed practice. Similarly, our practice will further inform this theoretical frame, making the development an iterative and incremental process. Our primary intention is therefore to initiate this process by defining the theoretical frame in the context of sustainable food cultures as a basis to apply to future study. Below is the summary of this framework:

1. *Engagement across disciplines: The perspective of transdisciplinarity—transcending disciplinarity and values orientation.* HCI has emerged as an evolving multidisciplinary domain of study (Carroll 2001). As DiSalvo, Sengers, and Brynjarsdottir (2001) argue, there is an opportunity and necessity to reconcile disciplinary divides through HCI design in order to create an environment where a sustainable future can be comprehensively examined and negotiated across scholarly disciplines, domains of research, and practices. Movements such as *Take a Bite out of Climate Change* (www.takeabite. cc) highlight the confluence of domains germane to sustainability, thereby reasserting the need for creating a broader, holistic understanding of current issues in food culture. Transdisciplinarity as a principle or approach provides a conceptual means to achieve such an understanding through integrative research (Blevis and Stolterman 2008; Lawrence and Després 2004). While similar integrative research approaches such as multi- and interdisciplinarity are based fundamentally on the segregation of disciplines by means of *comparing* and *combining*, transdisciplinary research focuses on *transcending* disciplinarity by focusing on goals that emerge from an emphasis on values and issues as well as ontological and epistemological perspectives. Transdisciplinarity is thus "at once between the disciplines, across the different disciplines, and beyond all discipline" (Nicolescu 2002, 44). Given the diverse roles both food and technology play in people's lives around the world, designing HCI for urban food sustainability must seek ways to utilize ubiquitous technology's flexibility in scale of application (for example, on the continuum of individual/collective, private/public, and local/global) to improve the health, social, and environmental bottom lines of everyday human-food interaction at the intersection of people, place, and technology. Transdisciplinarity for food sustainability research is an essential perspective because it provides dialogic knowledge development that can tackle real-life problems that are inherently multifaceted.

2. *Engagement with and among users/nonusers: The domain of urban informatics at the intersection of people, place, and technology—participatory, context-aware, and interactive networks.* There has been an emphasis on participatory/DIY culture (Hartley 1999; Jenkins et al. 2006) as a prominent characteristic of contemporary society in which significant economic, sociocultural, and technological transformations arise from large-scale consensual participation of individuals enabled by everyday communication networks such as the mobile phone and the Internet. Crowd-sourcing services, as notably explained by Shirky (2008), illustrate this phenomenon. Services such as urbanspoon (www.urbanspoon.com) and Foursquare (www.foursqaure.com) are prominent examples and function as repositories of crowd-sourced information and recommendations for restaurants, coffee shops, and general places of interest based on urban location. This apparent shift in people's mode and motivation for participation shows that a usable and efficient HCI design to bring about changes needs to be innately

supportive and persuasive in guiding users' actions rather than exerting control or coercion. The design must then be scalable in context awareness—from macro- and microcontexts (or contextual elements)—and adaptive to provide the optimal solution for the given overall (or chosen as the most significant) context. Steel's (2008) observation on the relationship between urban development and food shows that in urban environments, "Food shapes cities, and through them, it moulds us" and the city is thus "partly shaped by food" (p. 322). Therefore the opportunity network technology offers for cultivating sustainable urban food culture is essentially twofold: first, assistance in understanding and navigating through the food layer of the given place, and second, encouraging sustainable food practices, which in turn shape the city. Building a food culture to ensure a more sustainable future is thus an iterative and evolutionary process involving interactions among people, place, and technology. The use of interactive technologies and networks to scaffold access to information and social mechanisms of awareness and community is likely to be mission critical to sustainable food practices, and to preparation for and adaptation to the changing conditions of food production and culture that are increasingly induced by climate change.

3. *Engagement for sustained usability: The perspective of design—design criticism and critical design.* Though technologies provide useful ways to help cultivate sustainable food culture from the individual to the global level, they are also part of the broader contemporary influences shaping the natural ecology. For the "sustainability of" an HCI design for sustainable food culture, the design must also incorporate anticipation of the technology's sociocultural, health, and environmental impact. To achieve this, a continual examination of a technology's effectiveness is an imperative part of the overall development of the technology. Within the rich field of design theory, one idea that has particular relevance to sustainability issues is the notion of design criticism and critical design as complementary activities that are necessary companions in design processes. Design criticism refers to what is needed to understand and interpret present ways of being, while critical design refers to what is needed to ensure that our actions lead to ways of being for a sustainable future (Blevis 2007). Because critical design is perceived in the absence of a complete understanding of present ways of being, design criticism (strategic) and critical design (tactical) are interdependent and coevolving.

We expect to take this bivalent approach as we apply our framework to our future work on our project "Eat, Cook, Grow: Ubiquitous Technology for Sustainable Food Culture in the City." Sustained usability must equally involve, first, looking for and applying design criticism to various forms of the design of ubiquitous technologies for sustainable food culture that we may uncover by observation or from secondary sources, and second, suggesting the design of new forms of interactivity that inspire sustainable food practices, while still preserving the joy of urban experiences.

In what follows in this chapter, we present a small sample of photographic records of experiences of one of the authors, which reflect three key issues in the current sustainable food domain: (1) the context of food cultures, (2) farmers' markets, and (3) food production. These issues can and should be discussed in relation to all three elements of the framework outlined above. For purposes of this chapter, we present each example as a corresponding case to each of the framework elements, respectively: (1) engagement across disciplines, (2) engagement with and among users/nonusers, and (3) engagement for sustained usability.

The Context of Food Cultures: Engagement across Disciplines

The contexts of food culture vary widely from one place to another. Figures 5.1–5.3 illustrate this variety based only on a small sample of the experiences of one of the contributors. Even a short self-analysis in the form of a photo essay such as this shows a personal food culture spanning diverse social and geographic contexts that include a domestic environment, restaurant, and garden across two continents. Whether it is a continent or a small kitchen in one's own house, each place has its own

Figure 5.1
New York City Cantonese-style Chinese restaurant.

Figure 5.2
Hot pot at home, Midwestern United States.

atmosphere and rules of engagement for each entity that constitutes the place in its current form. Figure 5.1 shows a Chinese restaurant meal with friends in New York City. Figure 5.2 shows a Chinese hot pot meal prepared at home with friends. Figure 5.3 shows a restaurant meal with family in Beijing.

Some of the key transdisciplinary elements of the images collected together in figures 5.1–5.3 include (1) multicultural aspect of urban life, which is becoming increasingly prominent in metropolises around the world; (2) restaurant culture as a form of social interaction—here in celebration of reunion; (3) the sociological issues of a home-cooking dinner party (in contrast to a restaurant experience), especially in terms of participatory culture enacted through the preparation of the meal—the hot pot meal pictured is surely one of the most participatory forms of sharing a meal; (4) the political issues connected to the abundance of food supply and the consumerism of restaurant cultures; (5) the absence of any form of digital technology, virtual social networking, or any manner of virtual or online world collaboration with the scenes at hand. Each of these elements also consists of multiple disciplinary aspects for interpretation.

Figure 5.3
Restaurant, Beijing.

Food that has been prepared and presented for consumption (as seen in the preceding images) represents complex physiological and cultural compounds that are intricately and dynamically interrelated. Douglas (1997, 44) emphasizes that the meaning of a meal is construed by repeated analogies: "Each meal carries something of the meaning of the other meals, each meal is a structured social event which structures others." Designing for technological artifacts to encourage sustainable food practices of users therefore requires an understanding of the complex, continued development of such analogies and what opportunities exist for technological means to bring about appropriate and effective changes for individual users as well as the society as a whole. The situations presented in the preceding images require understandings that vary from deep cultural understanding or situated behavioral sensitivity to different cultural contexts (otherwise referred to as "cultural intelligence" or CQ; see Earley and Ang 2003 and Earley and Mosakowski 2004), to awareness of individual dietary requirements in order to create a positive experience of organizing and participating in the given dining experience. Transdisciplinary research provides a useful means to reconcile such multiple domains of consideration.

Farmers' Markets: Engagement with and among Users/Nonusers

Figure 5.4 shows a scene from a farmers' market in Indiana. Farmers' markets have being growing in number in many places around the world. The U.S. Department of Agriculture (USDA 2010) reports a 16 percent increase in farmers' markets around the United States in 2010 alone, representing an increase of approximately 248 percent since 1994. This growth demonstrates increasing engagement between farmers' markets and people as consumers and providers of goods and services. Figure 5.4 presents multiple layers of such people, five of whom stand out. In the foreground a young urban resident with a baseball cap contemplates the wares; also in the foreground a young Amish woman leans to see if she has made a sale; in the middle

Figure 5.4
Farmers' market scene, Indiana.

ground an older Amish man waits for customers; a little farther away a young Amish man sits on the table, resting from spending a long time on his feet; and in the background a customer is walking by, yawning. Interspersed among these layers are vegetables, tables, canopy tents, and pickup trucks. The pickup trucks contrast with the traditional Amish clothing. A closer look at the boxes used to transport vegetables reveals that the produce comes from Tennessee, a few hundred miles to the south of Indiana, raising the question of whether the produce and economy of the market can be described as "local." This notion requires a significant—particularly ethical—examination because another box is marked California, a state more than two thousand miles to the west of Indiana. The images suggest that there may be a disparity between the consumers' assumptions and the vendors' practices at the markets.

As Guthrie and colleagues (2006) assert, we have, at a global level, transitioned from the first industrial era, which involved resource extraction and money, to the new era of resource conservation and values; this shift in emphasis from *synthetic* to *authentic* food is the basis of what is called the "real food revolution." The growth of farmers' markets can be interpreted as an affirmation of this revolutionary process, the "post-productivist" era "in which consumers are increasingly concerned with issues of food safety, food quality, and the association of their food with lifestyles which embrace ecological, ethical and community awareness" (Holloway and Kneafsey 2000, 297). As such, consumers at farmers' markets have an overriding expectation for produce to be fresh, organic, and locally sourced, and for activities that occur at the marketplace to contribute to the economic and social capital of the community (Holloway and Kneafsey 2000). The ability to ask the vendor about the origins of the goods in the market is enabled because the vendor is supposedly also the producer; this is one of the key sustainable practices supported by the concept of the farmers' market. However, in the scene portrayed in figure 5.4, the boxes labeled with distant origins limit faith in this potential.

In most current farmers' markets around the world, people and place are of critical importance apropos of engagement. Engagement by means of technology is an opportunity space in which systems can be devised to allow vendors to certify the origins, organic credentials, and safety of their food offerings, which then allows customers to be assured of the same. The idyllic nature of the farmers' market is also an opportunity for the city to promote itself by means of advertising its local charm through the use of online media, including social media. Though the physical-world interactivity of the farmers' markets does not rely on virtual-world artifacts at the moment, this situation could change in the near future. For example, network technologies and social media could be used to promote local farmers' markets, and online carbon calculators could be devised to help consumers understand and vendors certify the potentially positive sustainability and environmental impacts of favoring the farmers' market as a distribution mechanism over larger commercial enterprises. Thus designing for engagement with users and nonusers refers to the use of technologies, and more importantly, the access and use of certain information and knowledge. Because knowledge and information can be explicit to certain groups of people and tacit to others, technological bridging in this context must be established between and among various sociocultural individuals or clusters (as conveyed by layers of people in figure 5.4).

Food Production: Engagement for Sustained Usability

Figures 5.5–5.7 illustrate three related contexts of growing food. Figure 5.5 shows the last farm in Fremont, California. The farm is surrounded on all sides by upscale suburban development; the land is valued for its location but is currently used to support a vegetable stand. The owner believes that he is being socially responsible by holding out against developers who would repurpose this land promptly, given the opportunity, and by offering produce that has been grown without the use of pesticides. Figure 5.6 shows a public display advertising a microscale business consultancy targeted at teaching clients individualized permaculture techniques to grow

Figure 5.5
The last farm in Fremont, California.

Figure 5.6
Food-growing consultancy, Midwest.

food for themselves. Figure 5.7 shows the harvesting of a winter garden in the presence of substantial snowfall at a semiurban residence in a small Midwestern American college town.

As previously mentioned, the growth in farmers' markets affirms there is an increasing demand among citizens for more ethical, ecological, and alternative solutions for their consumption needs. The overarching point here is that the existing profit-driven economic system upheld by hegemonic corporate entities is detrimental to sustainable futures, and thus it is necessary for individual community members to take part in changing the situation. This approach also poses a new microsocial dimension to the more macropolitical "Plan of Implementation" proposed by the Johannesburg World Summit for Sustainable Development in 2003: a call for development of a global framework for "promoting social and economic development within the carrying capacity of ecosystems by de-linking economic growth from environmental degradation" (Jégou and Manzini 2008). The consumer-driven microsocial approach departs from the "old-fashioned" resistance movements reified as protests and boycotts; instead it "plays with market forces" (Jégou and Manzini 2008, 21). Having the agency of individuals at the center of social and economic actions

Figure 5.7
Suburban winter garden, Midwest.

allows for fundamental and sustained changes in society in a more democratic and participatory manner.

As anthropologist Margaret Mead notably said, "Never doubt that a small group of thoughtful, committed citizens can change the world; indeed, it is the only thing that ever has." Digital technologies can offer accessible and effective means to raise awareness of various ideologies and discourses as well as to prompt more sustainable behaviors in the domain of food production and consumption. Network technologies may also be deeply implicated as a facilitative tool to connect individuals and communities, which in turn can convert "a small group" into "larger networks of actors" that can realize ecological prosperity. As such, designing technologies for sustainable food cultures must be open and adaptive to individual users' needs and desires in order to encourage, accommodate, and sustain changes in behaviors and ideologies within the context of coevolutionary social changes. As discussed earlier, design criticism/critical design framework (Blevis et al. 2007) may provide an ongoing design and evaluation tool that maintains the given technology's relevance, usefulness, and attractiveness to the user and thus strategically and tactically ensures its sustained use. In the case of contexts, as conveyed in figures 5.5–5.7, existing technologies can link the apparently disconnected scenarios by raising awareness of current affairs in producing food (local farms and food industry), allowing access to knowledge of growing food (food-growing consultancy and education), and assisting in the pragmatic application and sharing of the knowledge gained (backyard/community gardening). With advances in ubiquitous technologies, opportunities for effective sustained use are increasing.

Reflection and Future Directions

We have introduced a framework for understanding design in the context of sustainable food cultures. The framework consists of three elements, namely (1) engagement across disciplines, (2) engagement with and among users/nonusers, and (3) engagement for sustained usability. We have then applied the framework to three distinct and contrasting exemplars, which reflect three key issues in the current sustainable food domain: (1) the context of food cultures, (2) farmers' markets, and (3) food production. Taken together, the framework and exemplars yield a fairly complex morass of issues and concerns. This complexity is probably intrinsic to the nature of the problem at hand, namely sustainable food cultures.

In our future research, starting with "Eat, Cook, Grow: Ubiquitous Technology for Sustainable Food Culture in the City," we intend to apply the framework to still more examples. In so doing, we hope to refine this framework, untangle the complex web of issues connected to sustainable food cultures, and suggest conceptual systems— particularly those involving the materials of network technologies—that can foster more sustainable food cultures and practices in the future. This chapter describes the hopeful beginning of a journey—a broad framing of how we intend to look at issues of food culture to address sustainability concerns and encourage participation of people in creating more environmentally, socially, and healthwise sustainable food cultures in the future.

References

Blevis, Eli. 2007. Sustainable interaction design: Invention & disposal, renewal & reuse. In Mary Beth Rosson and David Gilmore, eds. *Proceedings of the SIGCHI Conference on Human Factors in Computing Systems.* San Jose, CA: ACM.

Blevis, Eli, Lim Youn-kyung, David Roedl, and Erik Stolterman. 2007. Using design critique as research to link sustainability and interactive technologies. In Douglas Schuler, ed. *Proceedings of the 2nd International Conference on Online Communities and Social Computing*, 22–31. Berlin: Springer Verlag.

Blevis, Eli, and Erik Stolterman. 2008. The confluence of interaction design & design: From disciplinary to transdisciplinary perspectives. Paper presented at the Design Research Society Biennial Conference, Sheffield, UK, July 16–19.

Choi, J. H.-j., and E. Blevis. 2010. *HCI & Sustainable Food Culture: A Design Framework for Engagement*. In Ebba Þóra Hvannberg and Marta Kristín Lárusdóttir, eds. *Proceedings of the 6th Nordic Conference on Human-Computer Interaction: Extending Boundaries*, Reykjavik, Iceland, October 16–20,112–117. New York: ACM.

Carroll, John M. 2001. *The Evolution of Human-Computer Interaction*. informIT 2001. http://www.informit.com/articles/article.aspx?p=24103.

DiSalvo, Carl, Phoebe Sengers, and Hronn Brynjarsdottir. 2010. Mapping the landscape of sustainable HCI. In Proceedings of the 28th International Conference on Human Factors in Computing Systems, Atlanta.New York: ACM.

Douglas, Mary. 1997. Deciphering a meal. In C. Counihan and P. Van Esterik, eds., *Food and Culture: A Reader*, 36–54. New York: Routledge.

Earley, P. Christopher, and Soon Ang. 2003. *Cultural Intelligence: Individual Interactions across Cultures*. Stanford, CA: Stanford University Press. http://gateway.library.qut.edu.au/login?url=http://library.books24x7.com/library.asp?%5eB&bookid=7343.

Earley, P. Christopher, and Elaine Mosakowski. 2004. Cultural intelligence. *Harvard Business Review* 82 (10): 139–146.

Food and Agriculture Organizataion of the United Nations. 2008. *Climate Change, Water and Food Security*. ftp://ftp.fao.org/docrep/fao/010/i0142e/i0142e07.pdf.

Food and Agriculture Organization of the United Nations. 2010. *FAQ: What Is Meant by Food Security?* http://www.fao.org/spfs/about-spfs/frequently-asked-questions-spfs/en/.

Foth, Marcus. 2009. *Handbook of Research on Urban Informatics: The Practice and Promise of the Real-Time City*. Hershey, PA: Information Science Reference.

Guthrie, John, Anna Guthrie, Rob Lawson, and Alan Cameron. 2006. Farmers' markets: The small business counter-revolution in food production and retailing. *British Food Journal* 108 (7): 560.

Hartley, John. 1999. *Uses of Television*. London: Routledge.

Holloway, L., and M. Kneafsey. 2000. Reading the space of the framers' market: A case study from the United Kingdom. *Sociologia Ruralis* 40 (3): 285–299.

Jégou, François, and Ezio Manzini, eds. 2008. *Collaborative Services: Social Innovation and Design for Sustainability*. Milan: Edizioni POLI.design.

Jenkins, Henry, Katie Clinton, Ravi Purushotma, Alice J. Robinson, and Margarate Weigel. 2006. *Confronting the Challenges of Participatory Culture: Media Education for the 21st Century*. http://www.digitallearning.macfound.org/site/c.enJLKQNlFiG/b.2108773/apps/nl/content2.asp?content_id=%7BCD911571-0240-4714-A93B-1D0C07C7B6C1%7D&notoc=1.

Lawrence, Roderick J., and Carole Després. 2004. Futures of transdisciplinarity. *Futures* 36 (4): 397–405.

Nelson, H. G., and E. Stolterman. 2003. *The Design Way: Intentional Change in an Unpredictable World: Foundations and Fundamentals of Design Competence.* Englewood Cliffs, N.J.: Educational Technology Publications.

Nicolescu, Basarab. 2002. *Manifesto of Transdisciplinarity.* Trans. K.-C. Voss. Albany, NY: State University of New York Press.

Shirky, Clay. 2008. *Here Comes Everybody: The Power of Organizing without Organizations.* New York: Penguin Press.

Steel, Carolyn. 2008. *Hungry City: How Food Shapes Our Lives.* London: Vintage.

UNFPA. 2007. *State of World Population 2007: Unleashing the Potential of Urban Growth.* Ed. U. N. P. Fund. New York: United Nations Population Fund.

USDA. 2010. *Farmers Market Growth: 1994–2010.* http://www.ams.usda.gov/AMSv1.0/ams .fetchTemplateData.do?template=TemplateS&navID=WholesaleandFarmersMarkets&leftNav =WholesaleandFarmersMarkets&page=WFMFarmersMarketGrowth&description=Farmers%20 Market%20Growth&acct=frmrdirmkt.

6 Building Digital Participation Hives: Toward a Local Public Sphere

Fiorella De Cindio and Cristian Peraboni

The so-called Web 2.0 has been an incubator for a number of initiatives and for several social networking sites that collect citizens' remarks and suggestions on the state of public spaces, on the quality of public services, and on public officials' activities, and that include facilities to enable participants' aggregation around civic causes. All these initiatives encourage basic civic engagement, but the way they are designed and managed hampers their evolution toward higher levels of citizen involvement in (online) deliberative processes. This study analyzes some Web 2.0 civic websites and identifies three key design factors that hinder the growth of civic participation toward more significant levels. It goes on to propose design guidelines for online social interaction systems that—alongside existing grassroots spaces—act as hives to collect and coalesce "civic" pollen (information, reported problems, ideas, opinions, participants) from various web sources into trustworthy online participation environments that foster deliberation.

Introduction

From its very origin, the Internet has afforded a communication, collaboration, and participation platform with strong potential for giving citizens voice and for increasing democracy (Rheingold 1991; Blumler and Coleman 2001; Mossberger, Tolbert, and McNeal 2008; Schuler 2008). In the 1980s and 1990s, free nets and community and civic networks (Schuler 1996; Venkatesh 2003) represented a significant effort to involve citizens in public affairs. They proved to be excellent environments for collecting civic intelligence (Schuler 2001), for supporting the development of people's projects (De Cindio 2004), for designing (online) public services (De Cindio, Peraboni, and Ripamonti 2007), and for promoting public dialog among citizens and between citizens and local institutions (Ranerup 2000; De Cindio and Schuler 2007). However, they had little impact on public discourse and on decision-making processes, mainly because of their inadequacy in supporting effective deliberation (De Cindio and Schuler 2007).

Currently, years after those early efforts, the Web 2.0 phenomenon (O'Reilly 2005) is rediscovering the participatory and social dimension of the Net. The opportunities offered by Web 2.0 have enabled new kinds of online communities and several other types of online social interactions—for example, blogs (Keren 2006) and social networks (Boyd and Ellison 2007). These online spaces have allowed citizens' committees around the world to debate or to organize protests, petitions, and other forms of civic activism, as well as to collect citizens' remarks and suggestions. Joichi Ito (2005) calls these phenomena, based on many-to-many conversations, "Emergent Democracy." The same rationale is behind initiatives like the Personal Democracy Forum (http://personaldemocracy.com/). These Web 2.0 social interaction environments, often the result of grassroots and unstructured initiatives, are usually characterized by a significant number of participants.

On the other hand, in recent years, several projects have aimed to explore the potential of e-participation and e-deliberation environments (see for example Tambouris, Kalampokis, and Tarabanis 2008; OECD 2001). Unlike Web 2.0 initiatives, these projects have often been promoted by (mainly local) public institutions that adopt a top-down approach. According to the Recommendation Rec (2001)19 of the (EU Committee of Ministers 2001, 3), they assign "major importance to communication between public authorities and citizens and encourage local leaders to give emphasis to citizens' participation and careful consideration to their demands and expectations, so as to provide an appropriate response to the needs which they express." These initiatives, indeed, attempt to use technology to open new channels for participation in the democratic process, thus enabling citizens to connect with one another or with their elected representatives and government. Specifically, the e-deliberation environments pursue the stated goal of providing specific tools to support public debate among (groups of) citizens and public bodies in order to find solutions to specific problems. Examples of this kind of online experiment include support for parliamentary action (Coleman 2004; Macintosh et al. 2007), policymaking (Macintosh 2004; Coglianese 2003), consultation through portals (Honor Fagan et al. 2006), online deliberative polling (Luskin, Fishkin, and Iyengar 2004), the online political engagement of young people (Loader 2007), and so forth. However, although these experiments have reported some positive findings about the potential for deliberative outcomes (see for example Macnaughton 2004; Handler et al. 2008; Winkler 2007), the structured, institutional form of participation often yields a low number of participants.

These two different forms of participation (unstructured, grassroots, and voluntary versus structured and institutional) are characterized by different interaction models, methods, and tools. Integrating them is one of the main challenges today. Is it possible to reconcile the technological and participation approaches typical of online communities, of social networks, and of social applications generally, where large numbers of people are involved and mobilized, with the e-participation and e-deliberation environments created by public institutions to support citizen involvement in decision-making processes? Which online spaces and technologies should these (local) public institutions provide to finalize citizens' voluntary engagement in creating a (local) public sphere (Habermas 1996) that is effective in meeting the challenges the community has to face?

Reconciling the bottom-up and the top-down approaches means finding ways to draw the mass of active people scattered across the web to online places designed for civic purposes. This is akin to acting as the beekeeper who creates a hive to support bees' social organization, so that they can fly around and pick pollen but then have a safe place to deposit it and produce their precious honey. Even if this process is mainly driven by institutional, social, and political factors, technology may act as the enabler, facilitating the merger or, if the technology is not appropriately designed, hindering it (Riley 2005). This chapter discusses the interplay between some seemingly technological features or options and the resulting social structure of the online social environments thus created. Rooted in fifteen years of experience at the Civic Informatics Laboratory (LIC) of the University of Milan, it draws on the work of managing the Milan Community Network (RCM) and promoting several related projects to foster civic engagement and public dialog.

This background is used to analyze, in the following section, the policies and social structures that characterize Web 2.0 social interaction environments and to identify three main causes that hinder the evolution of participation toward higher levels of citizen involvement in (online) deliberative processes. On this basis, the third section discusses issues that need to be considered when designing civic hives—that is, trustworthy, participatory, and deliberative environments that create space suitable for gathering outside participatory input into more structured, formal, and institutional forms of citizen involvement. Finally, the last section draws some conclusions and outlines the direction of future work.

Analyzing Participation in Web 2.0 Civic Initiatives

As Habermas states (1996, 360), the public sphere "cannot be conceived as an institution," but as "a network for communicating information and points of view" that "coalesce into bundles of topically specified public opinions." Thanks to its characteristics, the Internet—particularly Web 2.0—can play a positive role in making the public sphere more inclusive, collaborative, and interactive.

Indeed, the web now hosts several initiatives that reflect significant attempts to promote active citizenship. However, if we consider Habermas's characterization of the public sphere above, it can be seen that most of these initiatives only support the creation of "a network for communicating information and points of view" but fail to enable the creation of a shared space for ideas to bloom through public dialog.

This section surveys some of these "2.0 civic initiatives," ordered from weaker to richer levels of involvement. Their analysis provides a basis for identifying issues to address when designing online environments with the capacity to promote the rise of a mature public sphere.

A Survey of Paradigmatic Web 2.0 Civic Initiatives

At the bottom, we find websites that have been set up to enhance the transparency of public processes—for instance, by publishing the archives of government bodies. Examples include VEdemo for the Venice municipal council and holyrood.tv for the Scottish Parliament. TheyWorkForYou.com in the United Kingdom repackages public information about MPs' activities so citizens can monitor their representatives' behavior. Similar initiatives have been carried out in other countries: TheyWorkForYou.co.nz in New Zealand, OpenAustralia.org in Australia, KildareStreet.com in Ireland, and OpenParlamento.it in Italy. Although one might quite reasonably consider these sites broadcast communication from institutions to citizens, they are often labeled Web 2.0. This is the case with VEdemo, for example, which appears in the Web 2.0 section of the municipality's website.

One step up, we find sites that enhance the delivery of information from public institutions to citizens through the use of interactive tools, such as maps. One example is ChicagoCrime.org, where public data on local crime are georeferenced on a map of the city. Another is ARGOS, the Automatic and Remote Grand Canal Observation System, in the Web 2.0 section of the City of Venice website, which combines images collected by sensors along the Canal Grande with a map of the city to provide information about shipping traffic density and to monitor illegal activity. Although these initiatives provide better information on public issues, they do not promote any active role for citizens. They can be considered a precondition for active participation.

Citizens become content providers in so-called social rating websites set up for the purpose of providing feedback:

• *On the state of public spaces* FixMyStreet.com in the United Kingdom and the Internet Reporting Information System (IRIS) in Venice are good examples of sites that allow citizens to use a map to report problems for local government to fix.

• *On the quality of public services* An interesting example is the PatientOpinion.org. uk website, which allows patients to comment, review, and rate the healthcare services they have received.

• *On the activity of public officials* RateMyCop.com and RateMyTeachers.com are the most frequently cited initiatives of this type. Their purpose is to give to citizens a place to voice their opinion on public officials who have affected their lives.

• *On other citizens' behavior* These sites aim to foster the public shaming of "bad citizens" so as to raise awareness about a problem. For example, MyBikeLane.com and

Caughtya.org act as online "halls of shame" that expose cars illegally parked, respectively, in bike lanes and in handicapped parking spaces.

An example of deeper involvement is PeerToPatent.org, where the U.S. Patent Office asks citizens to collaborate in assessing pending patents. Citizens thus help public officials make proper decisions by providing information.

These initiatives call on citizens to provide their knowledge of public issues so institutions can easily gather information that would otherwise be dispersed or difficult to access and collect. This way, citizens help local government enhance public services and spaces, and they contribute to the monitoring of public officials. However, such sites also encourage a passive attitude to solving the problems citizens help identify, since it is someone else—namely some public institution—that has to take care of the problems. The implicit claim is: "Fixing the problem in *my* street is *your* problem."

We might interpret this situation through the classification by the report *Citizens as Partners: Information, Consultation and Public Participation in Policy-Making* (OECD 2001), which identifies three progressive levels of collaboration between citizens and public institutions:

1. *The information level* Public institutions (i) are committed to providing citizens with all needed information completely and promptly; moreover, they (ii) should also commit to accepting and publishing comments on this information and on other materials provided by individuals or groups of citizens.[1]
2. *The listening level* Public institutions are committed to listening to citizens' opinions before making decisions.
3. *The involvement level* Public institutions are committed to involving citizens in the decision-making process.

This classification sheds light on the level of participation guaranteed by the various initiatives. The first group—holyrood.tv, TheyWorkForYou.com, and ChicagoCrime.org—stays at level (1i): the easy availability of public information can be seen a precondition for participation.

In the second group—FixMyStreet.com, MyBikeLane.com, PatientOpinion.org, RateMyCop.com, and RateMyTeachers.com—the public information space is enriched with content provided by citizens, corresponding to level (1ii). If the public institution involved considers the information collected through these sites before acting, the second level of participation is in some way achieved. However, it is worth noting that not even this is assured: it all depends on what relationship the site owner has established with the government body to which citizens' remarks are to be referred. For example, this is the case with FixMyStreet.com, owned by MySociety.org ("a non-profit based on a charity"), which has established agreements with several municipalities in the United Kingdom. It is also the case of the IRIS site in Venice, of course, since this is managed by the municipality itself. On the other hand, in some cases there may be no such relationship (e.g., with MyBikeLane.com or with sites for rating teachers).

The PeerToPatent.org initiative is one of the few cases in which citizens have an actual impact on the decision-making process, since the information citizens provide influences it. However, the initiative does not aim to involve citizens in the decision. Rather, it restricts citizen participation to the preliminary phase of the decision-making process, involving the public only in providing information relevant to a U.S. Patent Office decision to grant or refuse a patent application. Although significant, citizens' contribution stops at level (1ii).

Three Factors That Shape the Hives

Summarizing the points discussed above, we can conclude that these initiatives—often promoted with the Web 2.0 label to suggest active citizen participation—actually provide support only for gathering and sharing information. There is neither a conscious effort to listen to citizens' opinions on a certain policy, as might occur in a public forum (online) or through consultation (online), nor are citizens involved in the decision-making process. The participation promoted under the Web 2.0 label is quantitatively significant, but of low quality. Several factors may underlie this outcome, including actual power relations, the true political will to promote citizen involvement, and others of a similar nature. However, in addition to these, certain more or less technical factors also affect participation. An analysis of these factors follows. It, in turn, forms the basis for drafting the guidelines in the next section on growth conditions for participation hives. The guidelines attempt to address issues of both participant quantity and participation quality.

The first factor concerns *participant identification*. To facilitate participation, nearly all such sites adopt a weak authentication policy, in the typical blog style: registration on the site is often not required and, even when it is, participants need only provide a username (or *nickname*) and, perhaps, an e-mail address, which is only actually checked in a few cases. In some cases it is "suggested" that people register using their first and last names, but the vast majority conforms to common habit and does not follow the suggestion. As a result, posts are signed by nickname, making them de facto anonymous. This happens on RateMyTeachers.com, where teachers are listed by name but the students who evaluate them disappear behind nicknames. Similarly, one can ask government to solve a problem on FixMyStreet.com using a fake identity. Anonymity may be acceptable when rating a movie, as on www.imdb.com. Nicknames are also used on eBay, for instance, to identify buyers and sellers, but here a strong reputation policy prevents the risks associated with anonymity. Anonymity does not foster the rise of the sense of mutual trust that should inspire sites set up for civic purposes: a public dialog on relevant civic issues with a group of digital ghosts is neither gratifying nor stimulating.

A second factor involves the *ownership* of the site. This raises two issues. The first is the relationship between the website owner and the authorities in charge of the service being critiqued or of the territory being discussed. The second is whether public officials have made any commitment to consider comments or to address problems. Most of the Web 2.0 civic initiatives studied here have been conducted outside any institutional umbrella and are managed by independent organizations. In several cases, ownership is not completely clear (typically, the "About Us" section is hidden, cryptic, or even missing). Nor is there a *participatory contract*—that is, a reciprocal commitment among the promoter of the initiative, its participants, and the public institution of reference. In fact, the connection set up with (local) administration(s) is seldom openly and clearly declared, and, when it is, it states no definite commitment to consider and solve the problems.

One of the best cases is FixMyStreet.com, owned by MySociety. From a list provided on the website (www.fixmystreet.com/reports), one can infer which public administrations have agreed to hear problems reported in posts on the FixMyStreet website. However, the commitment undertaken by these councils is quite vague. The site says: "[The problems] are reported to the relevant council by mail. The council can then resolve the problem the way they normally would. Alternatively, you can discuss the problem on the website with others, and then together lobby to fix it, or fix it directly yourselves." So there is no actual commitment by the councils to solve the problems, but on the website citizens can see lists of "new problems," "recently fixed," "old fixed," "older problems," and many "old problems, state unknown" (see, for instance, the Birmingham City Council).

The situation worsens when the initiative (such as MyBikeLane.com and Caugthya. org) is independently promoted by (groups of) citizens with no connection to a public institution. Conversely, more tangible impact on the quality of public spaces and services is guaranteed when the site for collecting people's remarks is directly managed by local government, as in the case of Venice's IRIS system. As figure 6.1 shows, citizens can see the status of each remark (rightmost column): "received" (*Ricevuta*), "assigned" (*In carico*), or "closed" (*Chiusa*), although some problems are closed with no solution. However, citizens who have provided input have also delegated the municipality to solve it.

The final issue we want to analyze concerns the *technical solutions* that underpin participation in the websites considered above. Although we believe that technology is not the key factor in success, it nevertheless plays a substantial role in shaping participation. Specifically, it is worth noting that the above-mentioned sites pay scant attention to fostering dialog among participants. They let citizens post opinions but do not promote peer-to-peer discussions. Comments are often optional add-ons to the posts (as in Caughtya.org and MyBikeLane.com) or to the problem reported (as in FixMyStreet.com and the Iris project). In some cases, comments are not even allowed

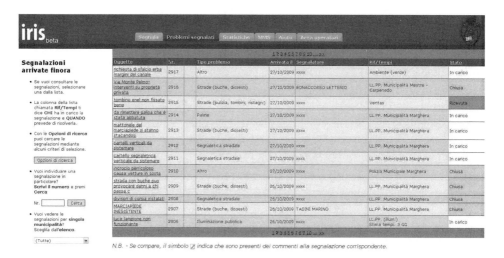

N.B. - Se compare, il simbolo ☑ indica che sono presenti dei commenti alla segnalazione corrispondente.

Figure 6.1
The list of the problems reported on the IRIS website.

(e.g., on PatientOpinion.org.uk and RateMyTeachers.com). As a result, comments, when present, remain isolated remarks rather than exchanged opinions.

Similar considerations emerge from our analysis of social networking websites. Facebook has no a specific civic "social object" but hosts several grassroots citizens' initiatives. Authentication is weak and fake identities are increasingly frequent. It is owned by a private company with no connection with any public institution, but registered members can create a cause, recruit other people into that cause, and raise money directly through the cause. Change.org is a social network that explicitly aims at enabling and supporting civil society action. In addition to supporting existing causes, its members can open a new petition or sign existing petitions. Participants have to register but, again, the registration policy is weak and ownership is in private hands here, too.

These social networks help raise awareness of "important" causes. They may have tangible impact when a very large number of subscribers are achieved through very simple actions: seconding a cause, signing a petition. However, this may be too simple. One click does not promote knowledgeable participation or actual civic engagement.

Building a Participation *Hive*: Conditions for Growing Participation

The three issues that emerge from the above analysis are relevant when planning online social interactive systems designed to foster greater civic participation. Erected alongside existing grassroots spaces, such systems can act as hives to collect and coalesce civic pollen (information, reported problems, ideas, opinions, and participants) from various web sources into a trusted online participation environment that supports deliberation. Designing such civic hives means creating "spaces for human communication and interaction" (Winograd 1997, 156) and requires a "better understanding of the features and functions of the social aspects of the systems" (Handler et al. 2008, 66), coupled with the technological knowledge needed to develop simple, straightforward solutions.

In discussing these issues, this section makes reference to four e-participation case studies set up with the openDCN software platform (De Cindio, Peraboni, and Sonnante 2008b). The development of this software platform springs from the realization, discussed above, that technology is not the key factor in success but nevertheless can play a substantial role in shaping e-participation. For this reason, although existing software would be easy to reuse, it is often unsuited to the task because it has been designed for a (slightly) different purpose and for a different audience. This was our original reason for undertaking the development of openDCN, which embeds the experience accumulated at the Civic Informatics Laboratory while managing the Milan Community Network and several related initiatives.

The following section gives a brief overview of the openDCN software platform and the case studies used for subsequent discussion of three issues: *participant identification*, *platform ownership*, and *support for effective public dialog*.

Four E-Participation Case Studies on openDCN

openDCN is a software platform developed to support online participation and deliberation. Its name—where DCN stands for Deliberative Community Networks (De Cindio, De Marco, and Grew 2007)—stresses the belief (De Cindio and Schuler 2007), supported by empirical evidence (De Cindio and Peraboni 2009), that online deliberation needs to rely on a solid community. Therefore, openDCN provides tools for managing two main spaces:

• A *community space* is designed to foster public dialog on civic issues, as the basis for establishing a climate of mutual trust among participants, for sharing civic intelligence, and for promoting civic engagement. This mutual trust is not a prerequisite of the system, but needs to be cultivated during the participatory experience as the fruit of dialog and cooperation among participants. It can be facilitated by certain sociotechnical design choices, which are dealt with below.

• A *deliberative space* aims to finalize online interactions so as to extend them toward the decision-making process.

The two spaces need each other and should not be seen as separate environments. Rather, they are different dimensions that intersect to create the whole participatory space within which the weight of each dimension may vary to match the characteristics of any e-participation initiative. Each space is "animated" by software tools that support a variety of online social interactions. Such features include tools for

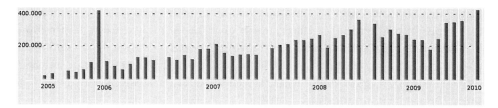

Figure 6.2
The trend of page views of ComunaliMilano2006 and partecipaMi.

asynchronous as well as synchronous interaction, tools for gathering the opinions of a large number of citizens (consultations as well as petitions), blogs, event calendars, and the like. As of this writing, openDCN consists of five tools (*CityMap, Informed Discussion, Regulated Meeting, Certified Citizen Consultation,* and *Agenda*). For the purposes of this chapter, we discuss some details of two of them below.

Efforts to develop openDCN have been driven by the need to carry out the e-participation initiatives that represent the case studies used in the following discussion.

partecipaMi

The partecipaMi platform has been up and running since January 2007, managed with an early prototype of openDCN. It represents the evolution of a website—ComunaliMilano2006—that was set up to foster dialog between candidates and electors on the occasion of the Milan municipal election (for more details, see De Cindio, De Marco, and Ripamonti 2007; De Cindio, Di Loreto, and Peraboni 2009). The continued growth in the number of registered members (as of February 21, 2010, there were 2,940), a solid number of monthly page views (figure 6.2), the increasing participation of elected representatives, and a couple of significant episodes—one discussed in De Cindio, Di Loreto, and Peraboni 2009, the others below—indicate that partecipaMi is increasingly taking on the role of significant online public square for the city. It is seen as a natural outgrowth of the RCM Milan Community Network, overcoming the latter's characteristic BBS style.

e21 for Digital Citizenship

The most intense software development for the platform openDCN took place within the "e21 for the Development of Digital Citizenship in Agenda 21" project, aimed at supporting the well-known Local Agenda 21 participatory process with a suite of integrated software tools. As part of e21, openDCN was tested in a large field experiment that involved ten different municipalities in Lombardy (a region in northern Italy), whose outcome was presented in De Cindio and Peraboni 2009.

Figure 6.3
The Sicurezza Stradale homepage.

Sicurezza Stradale

The openDCN system was then used to run *Sicurezza Stradale* (or "Road Safety"), an initiative that grew out of partecipaMi and is in some ways analogous to FixMyStreet. com. The initiative is jointly promoted by Ciclobby—a nonprofit organization that advocates using bicycles to get around the city—and by the RCM Foundation. The Sicurezza Stradale website uses *community space* to enable citizens to report places of danger on a map (figure 6.3). Each recommendation consists of a flag on the map associated with a message describing the situation and proposing possible solutions. Other participants can add comments. A discussion forum, where more general issues are debated (e.g., the difficult relationships among bikers, motorcyclists, and pedestrians), complements the flagged map. This "Road Safety Forum" is the online counterpart of an institutional committee set up by the City Council to study how to improve traffic in the city. It sees the participation of the city alderman in charge of traffic issues, of several members of the city council, and of representatives of nonprofit organizations, as well as of individual citizens concerned with this issue.

E-Learning Community Space and Deliberative Process

openDCN was also used to set up an e-learning environment for the "Virtual Communities" class at the University of Milan. In this case, behind a discussion area hosted in *community space*, which teachers and students use to engage one another and to share course materials, the online environment is enriched with a deliberative process for assessing the class, which consists of two anonymous questionnaires before the exam (run with the certified consultation tool) and of an open discussion after the exam between students and teachers that is based on the results of the previous steps.

These four field experiments afford a basis for argumentation in the following sections.

Identifying Participants

As detailed above, one key factor in the design of effective online participation has to do with people's online identity (or identities) and with their interplay vis-à-vis offline identities. We have witnessed a weak style of identification gain footing on the web: comments typically do not require a registration and are often anonymous (as in blogs). Our long-standing experience running RCM suggests that, in order to create a trustworthy environment that encourages government officials and representatives to undertake online dialog with citizens, this weak form of identification must be forsaken for an online identity that should, insofar as possible, reflect citizens' offline identity (De Cindio, Ripamonti, and Di Loreto 2008). If citizens hope for a public answer from someone with an official role who appears online with her/his actual identity, they will have to do the same: to "show their face" and accept the responsibility of participating with their actual identity.

The partecipaMi and Sicurezza Stradale initiatives adopt the same approach that has distinguished RCM from the outset: registered participants are invited to provide a free-text résumé (a personal profile) and a picture of themselves to increase mutual acquaintance and foster a sense of community. Let us note that this is precisely the same approach applied by numerous social networks (Facebook, LinkedIn, etc.). However, while RCM was strict in requiring registration, partecipaMi and Sicurezza Stradale follow the current web custom and allow a weaker form of authentication. As on blogs, comments in community space can be posted even by unregistered users. Nevertheless, and this is a significant difference, people have to give their first and family names in any case. They are also asked to provide an e-mail address, to which a verification message is sent. Unconfirmed messages are tagged with an "email not verified" warning. These choices, of course, do not prevent anyone from using a fake identity, but they do ensure that it is intentional behavior. However, registration is required to access higher degrees of participation such as taking part in a citizens' consultation. The community manager acts as the facilitator of a more inclusive participation: he prods unregistered participants who contribute often to become registered participants, so they can not only to comment but also open new discussions. Moreover, to increase participants' visibility as community members, the community manager encourages registered users to complete their profiles.

These choices have never been questioned and we have never been given any reason to believe that anyone has been discouraged from participating because of them. On the contrary, several public officials have explicitly stated a greater willingness to participate in online public dialog and to consider people's comments precisely because citizens write in under their actual identities—certified by the registration policy and reinforced by the community—thus taking responsibility for what they write. We got the same advice from members of the municipalities involved in the e21 project.

However, there are situations in which participants' privacy is worth protecting. This may be the case with public consultations, discussions about sensitive issues, or public assessments of officials that could boomerang on participants, as with assessments of teachers by students or of police officers by citizens. In all these cases, there is a mismatch between the need for a strict authentication policy (so that, e.g., only the students who have actually taken a class can rate the teacher) and the need to adopt secrecy techniques to protect participants' personal data.

Unlike RateMyTeachers.com, which supports fully anonymous comments with no guarantee of students' identities, when we used the openDCN system to assess the Virtual Communities class (and its teachers), we designed the authentication policy of the evaluation process in such a way that only students registered for the course were eligible participants. The protection of students' identities is guaranteed by combining completely anonymous polling with a public discussion. The anonymous polling is run with the certified consultation tool, which embeds an e-voting protocol (Bruschi, Poletti, and Rosti 2002). In the public discussion, after exams have been graded, nonanonymous students and teachers analyze any issues that emerged from the questionnaires. While the participation in the anonymous questionnaires was numerically good (more than 80 percent of the students attending the class, either physically or remotely, answered), only a few students participated in the online public discussion. Aside from the number of participants, the nature of the messages revealed how hard it is for students to talk openly about teachers and with teachers. To overcome this problem, in the upcoming class, we will use a technique to anonymize student accounts during discussion.

These examples show the need for a variety of authentication and identification strategies. Weaker levels of participation require weaker responsibility. Higher degrees of participation require higher responsibility. Participating by adding a comment to a post is different from being involved in a decision-making process. The technology can and must balance strong authentication with flexible, personal-data protection policies.

Ownership: Participatory Contracts and Role of Third Parties

To set up effective participation environments, two related key factors need to be addressed: (1) the need for a "participatory contract" that establishes the mutual commitment between the institution and its citizens, perhaps mediated by a third party that would typically act as promoter of the initiative, and (2) the potential role of such a third party.

When the public-dialog website is directly promoted and managed by a government organization (as, for example, in the case of the IRIS system run by the Venetian municipality or PeerToPatent.org run by the U.S. Patent Office), part of the organization's job is to define and clarify its commitment toward those who participate in the initiative. We note that in neither of the cases mentioned is this at all clear. Even if the contract were clear, directly managing the public dialog is not necessarily the easiest solution. As a matter of fact, it may be critical for a government organization to host a discussion in which citizens strongly criticize it or some of its key officials. We know of several such cases. A trusted third party, acting as intermediary between the government organization and citizens, may help avoid such problems.

For instance, this is the role played by MySociety in promoting and managing FixMyStreet.com, as well as by the RCM Foundation in partecipaMi and Sicurezza Stradale. Both are nonprofit organizations and their fundamental role is:

• To establish a relationship with government organizations of reference (i.e., several borough, district, city, and county councils, in MySociety's case, and Milan's mayor and City Council, in RCM's case)
• To define the commitment the government organization has made to take action on the basis of what happens online and specify what government requires from citizens in terms of authentication, identification, and fairness
• To guarantee, finally, that commitments undertaken are fulfilled by all the social actors

It is worth noting that the commitment may be weak, as in the case of FixMyStreet, where the local councils merely agree to receive citizens' suggestions. Examples of participatory contracts explicitly taken by government organizations can be drawn from the e21 project, where three different patterns emerged (De Cindio and Peraboni 2009). These participatory contracts are binding in different ways. However, in our experience, what really counts is that the commitment, whatever it is, be made clear to all participants and then fulfilled. This is precisely the guarantor role for which a trusted third party is needed.

One Milan City Council member's recent posting in the "Citizenships and Democracy" forum (http://www.partecipami.it/?q=node/7903) illustrates how significant the role played by a trusted third party can be:

The discussion started by Claudio Edossi about the Ecopass[2] policy, which has involved several City Council members, both from the majority and from the opposition coalition, highlights the growing importance of the role played by partecipaMi (and by the RCM Foundation): it represents a "no-parties' land," a place where councilors feel free to take part in a political discussion while thinking of the city's actual interests, regardless of belonging to a political party or of the parties' balance of power. . . . This situation might seem paradoxical, but it should sound a political alarm: the results and the impact of the Ecopass policy—which is the only new structural measure to reduce traffic and pollution in an Italian metropolitan area—**are being discussed neither in the city government meetings nor in city council meetings: council members and city managers discuss it on partecipaMi!** (bold in original)

Supporting Effective Public Dialog

As observed earlier in this chapter, the absence of dialog in the Web 2.0 civic initiatives is one of the most significant hindrances to establishing a climate of mutual trust among participants.

The openDCN system provides two main dialog tools designed to involve a large number of people (ordinary citizens, as well as politicians and public administrators) who cannot be assumed to be familiar with online interaction. To reduce the barriers to participation in online public forums, both tools include specific features for fostering an effective public dialog (De Cindio, Peraboni, and Sonnante 2008a).

The first feature concerns how messages are displayed in a discussion thread, improving the *interactivity* (Winkler 2007) of the discussion itself. To overcome the display limitations of classic online forums and blogs, indented threads of messages are shown so as to ensure participants remain aware of the discussion context. When someone wants to read a message, a simple JavaScript opens the body of the message (and then closes it) within the same webpage that hosts the message list. This solution helps citizens visualize the nesting of posts and replies at a glance. It also enables people to choose, if need be, the right position for their own post.

The second feature aims to improve the *rationality* (Winkler 2007) of the discussion by providing an organized visualization of information resources (documents, links, videos, etc.). Every discussion has an information space that gathers all the materials attached to single posts or directly uploaded by participants. Subsequent participants view the discussion and its information materials on a single page. This helps encourage participants to support their arguments "by appropriate and reasonably accurate factual claims" (Fishkin and Luskin 2005, 285).

The third feature imports a trait typical of social rating environments: it allows citizens to express their degree of agreement and to flag posts or information materials as relevant. This feature enables people to express agreement or disagreement without forcing them to write a post, thus providing (technological) support for what Edward (2006) calls different *styles of citizenship*: one "stronger," more active, and another, apparently "weaker."

Ultimately, what matters even more than technical features is that a social structure suited to preserving *fair dialog* among participants be created (De Cindio et al. 2003). In all the online civic sites we manage, a so-called Galateo (or "netiquette principles") is codified and prominently published in the homepage menu bar. The Galateo defines a set of standards and specific rules for online behavior that, above and beyond mere netiquette, on the one hand, and national laws on the other, should guarantee fair dialog in a welcoming environment where everyone can feel at ease expressing her/his own ideas and opinions. The Galateo brings with it the need to choose a trusted person committed to making sure the Galateo is observed: this is the *community manager*. Rather then as a censor in charge of disapproving messages that fail to comply with the Galateo, she/he plays the role of the person who helps participants state their ideas in a fair and civil fashion. In particular, she/he supports public officials and members of local government who are often less familiar with communication in these online environments.

The technical features introduced in openDCN to support rational and interactive discussion, together with the tireless work of the community manager, help Sicurezza Stradale participants do something more than simply identify problems. Participants are implicitly and explicitly encouraged to provide documents to describe the problem and, when possible, to share and discuss the solutions they envision. As a result, roughly 50 percent of the advice include comments that reinforce the original post and, in some cases, a different opinion or solution is presented.

Conclusion

Web 2.0 has boosted several grassroots civic initiatives that promote citizen activism in an effort to assess and ameliorate public spaces and services, to monitor the activity of public officials, managers, and representatives, as well as to support people's civic participation generally. The increasing popularity of several social networks, along with the advent on these networks of applications for petitioning and for supporting civic causes, provides an additional online arena for bringing issues of public interest to the attention of a larger audience.

The Obama campaign was exemplary in stimulating, throughout the world, the realization that the sociopolitical arena has already radically changed because of the role the Internet plays as a platform for civic engagement. It is worth noting that this amounted to a sort of definitive demonstration, since experimental evidence had already been around for several years.

However, as seen above, these initiatives, though significant, still bear the hallmarks of low-quality participation. They limit citizens' contributions to the lower of the levels identified by the OECD. Moreover, awareness is growing that this huge partici-patory potential can be lost if the promises are not fulfilled (Osimo 2008; Osimo 2009). We believe that this risk is strongly related to how these initiatives are designed and managed. On the basis of our experience in creating and managing sustainable online civic environments, this chapter has analyzed certain key design factors that limit current grassroots initiatives. Where possible we have suggested design guidelines to overcome these limits.

While the value of setting up civic online communities (along the lines of early community networks) is shown by the field cases, we note that promoting the creation of a mature public sphere, one that can reinforce public dialog and foster citizen involvement, is primarily a task for government organizations. They are called on to provide trustworthy participatory and deliberative environments in which, thanks to proper design choices, people's recommendations and ideas can be gathered as a first step toward promoting deeper, structured, formal, and institutional forms of citizen involvement in deliberative processes. Instead of trying to reproduce the grassroots initiatives on their websites, the government organizations need to act alongside such initiatives—similar to the strategy of a beekeeper who builds a hive to support the bees' social organization, which, starting with picking pollen, leads to the production of honey. The beekeeper would make a mistake in constraining the bees' ability to fly around, but she/he has to expend effort to provide them the proper environment: the hives. This task can be accomplished in collaboration with third parties able to guarantee the proper relationship between citizens and government organizations.

The Obama administration, continuing from Obama's campaign, has been moving in this direction by setting up the Open Government Initiative (an umbrella for a number of innovative activities and efforts to increase public participation) that adopt Web 2.0 citizens' language. This initiative collects their input and, even more important, conveys the message that the government needs citizens' skills and collaboration. However, it reproduces the choices typical of the Web 2.0 initiatives that we have questioned above. Though it is not the only factor, of course, this can make participation more a promise than a reality (Sifry 2009).

We believe the challenge of building appropriate hives for civic participation is likely to evolve toward a public sphere where citizens participate in the decision-making process, which has a better chance of being successful at the local level. Although local issues may have extralocal aspects, at the local level, the interplay between the online dimension and the offline dimension is, by nature, easier.

Notes

1. It is worth noting that we have slightly improved the original classification by introducing point (ii), which allows citizens to view themselves as *advisers* rather than *users* of the public information, while officials begin to see citizens as resources rather than mere sources of criticism and protest.

2. Ecopass is the most important policy aimed at managing traffic and pollution in Milan. Like the *London Congestion Charge*, it taxes the most polluting vehicles.

References

Blumler, J. G., and S. Coleman. 2001. *Realising Democracy Online: A Civic Commons in Cyberspace.* London: IPPR.

Boyd, D. M., and N. B. Ellison. 2007. Social network sites: Definition, history, and scholarship. *Journal of Computer-Mediated Communication* 13 (1): 11.

Bruschi, D., G. Poletti, and E. Rosti. 2002. E-vote and PKI's: A need, a bliss or a curse? In D. Gritzalis, ed., *Secure Electronic Voting.* Norwell, Massachusetts: Kluwer Academic Publishers.

Coglianese, C. 2003. *E-rulemaking: Information Technology and Regulatory Policy.* Technical report. Cambridge, MA: Center for Business and Government, John F. Kennedy School of Government, Harvard University.

Coleman, S. 2004. Connecting parliament to the public via the Internet: Two case studies of online consultations. *Information Communication and Society* 7 (1): 1–22.

De Cindio, F., O. Gentile, P. Grew, and D. Redolfi. 2003. Community Networks: Rules of Behavior and Social Structure. *The Information Society Journal, Special Issue "ICTs and Community Networking,"* M. Venkatesh, ed., 19(5): 395-406.

De Cindio, F. 2004. The role of community networks in shaping the network society: Enabling people to develop their own projects. In D. Schuler and P. Day, eds., *Shaping the Network Society: The New Role of Civil Society in Cyberspace.* Cambridge, MA: MIT Press.

De Cindio, F., A. De Marco, and P. Grew. 2007. Deliberative community networks for local governance. *International Journal of Technology, Policy and Management* 7 (2): 108–121.

De Cindio, F., A. De Marco, and L. A. Ripamonti. 2007. Enriching community networks by supporting deliberation. In C. Steinfield, B. T. Pentland, M. Ackerman, and N. Contractor, eds., *Communities & Technology 2007*, 395–418. London: Springer Verlag.

De Cindio, F., I. Di Loreto, and C. Peraboni. 2009. Moments and modes for triggering civic participation at the urban level. In M. Foth, ed., *Handbook of Research on Urban Informatics: The Practice and Promise of the Real-Time City,* 97–113. Hershey, PA: IGI Global.

De Cindio, F., and C. Peraboni. 2009. Fostering e-participation at the urban level: Outcomes from a large field experiment. In A. Macintosh and E. Tambouris, eds., *Proceedings of the First Conference on eParticipation (ePart 2009)*, LNCS 5694, 112–124. Berlin: Springer Verlag.

De Cindio, F., C. Peraboni, and L. A. Ripamonti. 2007. Community networks as lead users in online public services design. *Journal of Community Informatics—Special Issue on Community Informatics and System Design* 3 (1).

De Cindio, F., C. Peraboni, and L. Sonnante. 2008a. Improving citizens' interactions in an e-deliberation environment. In P. Bottoni and S. Levialdi, eds., *Proceedings of the Working Conference on "Advanced Visual Interfaces—AVI2008,"* 486–487. New York: ACM Press.

De Cindio, F., C. Peraboni, and L. Sonnante. 2008b. A two-room e-deliberation environment. In D. Foster and D. Schuler, eds., *DIAC-2008/OD2008—Directions and Implications of Advanced Computing; Conference on Online Deliberation: Tools for Participation*. Berkeley: University of California.

De Cindio, F., L. A. Ripamonti, and I. Di Loreto. 2008. Interplay between the actual and the virtual in the Milan Community Network Experience. In A. Aurigi and F. De Cindio, eds., *Augmented Urban Spaces: Articulating the Physical and Electronic City*. Aldershot: Ashgate.

De Cindio, F., and D. Schuler. 2007. Deliberation and community networks: A strong link waiting to be forged. Paper presented at the *CIRN Conference 2007—Communities in Action*. Prato, November 5-7.

Edward, A. 2006. Online deliberative policy exercises and styles of citizenship: Issues of democratic design. Position paper presented at the *DEMOnet Workshop on eDeliberation Research*, Leeds, UK, October 16.

EU Committee of Ministers. 2001. Recommendation Rec(2001)19 of the Committee of Ministers to member states on the participation of citizens in local public life.

Fishkin, J. S., and R. C. Luskin. 2005. Experimenting with a democratic ideal: Deliberative polling and public opinion. *Acta Politica* 40: 284–298.

Habermas, J. 1996. *Between Facts and Norms*. Cambridge: Polity Press.

Handler, J., N. Shadbolt, W. Hall, T. Berners-Lee, and D. Weitzner. 2008. Web science: An interdisciplinary approach to understanding the web. *Communications of the ACM* 51 (7): 60–69.

Honor Fagan, G., D. R. Newman, P. McCusker, and M. Murray. 2006. *E-Consultation: Evaluating Appropriate Technologies and Processes for Citizens' Participation in Public Policy*. Final report of the e-Consultation Research Project. www.e-consultation.org.

Ito, J. 2005. Emergent democracy. In M. Ratcliffe and L. Lebkowsky, eds., *Extreme Democracy*. Lulu.com.

Keren, M. 2006. *Blogosphere: The New Political Arena*. Lanham, MD: Lexington Books.

Loader, B. D. 2007. *Young Citizens in the Digital Age: Political Engagement, Young People and New Media*. London: Routledge.

Luskin, R. C., J. S. Fishkin, and S. Iyengar. 2004. Considered opinions on US foreign policy: Face-to-face versus online deliberative polling. Paper presented at the International Communication Association Conference, New Orleans, May 27–31.

Macintosh, A. 2004. Characterizing e-participation in policy-making. In R.H. Sprague, ed., *Proceedings of the 37th Annual Hawaii International Conference on System Sciences*. Washington, DC: IEEE Computer Society.

Macintosh, A., N. Adams, A. Whyte, and J. Johnston. 2007. E-petitioning in the Scottish Parliament. In H. Chen, L. Brandt, V. Gregg, R. Traunmüller, S. Dawes, E. Hovy, A. Macintosh, and C. A. Larson, eds., *Integrated Series in Information Systems Digital Government—E-Government Research, Case Studies, and Implementation*. New York: Springer.

Macnaughton, G. 2004. *Seminar Report: eDemocracy.* Brussels: European Commission eGovernment Unit, February 12–13.

Mossberger, K., C. J. Tolbert, and R. S. McNeal. 2008. *Digital Citizenship: The Internet, Society, and Participation.* Cambridge, MA: MIT Press.

OECD. 2001. *Citizens as Partners: Information, Consultation and Public Participation in Policy-Making.* Paris: OECD Publishing.

O'Reilly, T. 2005. *What Is Web 2.0: Design Patterns and Business Models for the Next Generation of Software.* http://oreilly.com/web2/archive/what-is-web-20.html.

Osimo, D. 2008. *Web 2.0 in Government: Why and How?* JRC Scientific and Technical Reports. Seville: European Commission.

Osimo, D. 2009. Government 2.0: tra utopia e realismo. Invited talk at the workshop "Mettere i Governi davanti all'evidenza—Valutazione delle politiche, web 2.0 e competenza dei cittadini," University of Milan, October, 27, 2009. www.pubblica.org.

Ranerup, A. 2000. On-line discussion forums in a Swedish local government context. In M. Gurstain, ed., *Community Informatics: Enabling Communities with Information and Communication Technologies*, 359–379. London: Idea Group Publishing.

Rheingold, H. 1991. Electronic democracy: The great equalizer. *Whole Earth Review* (Summer): 4–8.

Riley, T. B. 2005. E-platform for citizens' engagement: A three-tier approach. In International Conference on Engaging Communities, Workshop on Platform for e-Participation, Brisbane, Queensland.

Schuler, D. 1996. *New Community Networks: Wired for Change.* Addison-Wesley.

Schuler, D. 2001. Cultivating society's civic intelligence: Patterns for a new "world brain." *Information Communication and Society* 4 (2).

Schuler, D. 2008. *Liberating Voices: A Pattern Language for Communication Revolution.* Cambridge, MA: MIT Press.

Sifry, M. 2009. The useful myth of the Obama campaign. Invited lecture at the First International School of Digital Transformation (SDT2009), Porto, Portugal, July 19–24.

Tambouris, E., E. Kalampokis, and K. Tarabanis. 2008. A survey of e-participation research projects in the European Union. *International Journal of Electronic Business* 6 (6).

Venkatesh, M., ed. 2003. Special issue on "ICTs and Community Networking." *Information Society Journal* 19 (5).

Winkler, R. 2007. Online deliberation: Towards a research framework for the assessment of online debates. In A. Avdic, K. Hedström, J. Rose, and A. Grönlund, eds., *Understanding eParticipation: Contemporary PhD eParticipation Studies in Europe*, 183–201. Örebrö: University Library.

Winograd, T. 1997. From computing machinery to interaction design. In P. Denning and R. Metcalfe, eds., *Beyond Calculation: The Next Fifty Years of Computing*, 142–162. Amsterdam: Springer Verlag.

7 Between Experience, Affect, and Information: Experimental Urban Interfaces in the Climate Change Debate

Jonas Fritsch and Martin Brynskov

The climate change debate provides an excellent example of a contentious issue that has become so overexposed that it is hard to say anything that will be heard or noticed. In 2009, Denmark saw an informational tsunami related to climate change, which climaxed in December with the UN Climate Summit in Copenhagen, COP15,[1] where a follow-up deal to the Kyoto Protocol[2] from 1997 was being sought. The discussions surrounding the event included elements of global political trends, national and commercial interests, and so many more factors that the process of "taking climate action"—whether you were for or against spending the resources—was (and still is) in itself so complex that it evaded many of the characteristics of a good news story except one: relevance.

Communicators and stakeholders have drawn on all genres to convey every angle imaginable on the topic of climate change, from classical print and broadcast news journalism to social media and artistic events to lobbyist lunches and political activism, all in the hope or expectation that they could be heard and make a difference. Today more than ever, efforts are directed at changing individual citizens' attitudes or habits, but it can be overwhelming for them to relate to the wealth of information, opinions, or advice ranging from the extremely concrete to the immensely abstract.

At the Center for Digital Urban Living[3] (DUL) at Aarhus University in Denmark, several projects have addressed the climate change debate through the development of experimental urban interfaces. Thus, they all focus on the *medium* rather than on the *content* of the debate (although we do not suggest that such a separation is trivial). The overall research trajectory has been to explore how these interfaces can support an engaged civic discourse on the issue of climate change in an open and innovative way.

In this chapter we analyze two interactive climate projects designed in Aarhus and point to some issues that we have identified to be central to designers and users of urban media and interfaces. The two projects are *Climate on the Wall* and *CO2nfession/CO2mmitment*. The analysis will be established through three different theoretical "lenses": *engagement*, *affect*, and *information*. Since the projects themselves are fairly easy to grasp and have been reported on elsewhere (and are documented on the web), we only present them briefly, although with enough detail to support the analysis. However, we expand the theoretical foundation of the two more experience-oriented of the three lenses—engagement and affect—since they are likely to be more unfamiliar to this book's readers.

We begin with a short survey of efforts in the field of interaction design to address ways to engage citizens in the climate change debate as users of interactive systems. Next we present engagement, affect, and information as theoretical concepts and perspectives grounding the analysis. The two projects are then described in a condensed manner, as are the methodological considerations of the data collection feeding into the analysis. Finally, we conclude with some observations about experimental urban interfaces in general, based on our experiences with these projects and framed by the theoretical lenses.

Related Work

The literature is rich with descriptions of and reflections on interactive systems designed to make people aware of climate change and to encourage them to reduce their energy consumption. The examples range from gamelike and ambient energy monitors for the home to ambient visualizations and interventions in public space. In this section, we present some of the underlying (ideological) tendencies in the fields of human-computer interaction (HCI) and interaction design and additionally give an overview of some of the practical projects undertaken in this domain. We sum up by tentatively giving our own position on designing experimental urban interfaces to make people engage with the climate change debate.

Designing Interactive Climate Relations

Blevis (2007) has introduced the notion of *Sustainable Interaction Design* (SID)— developed to define sustainability as a core semantics for interaction design. The definition serves as a lens through which design values, design methods, and designs themselves may be evaluated. Blevis (2007, 503) specifically highlights the "link between interactive technologies and the use of resources, both from the point of view of how interactive technologies can be used to promote more sustainable behaviors and—with more emphasis here—from the point of view of how sustainability can be applied as a critical lens to the design of interactive systems, themselves."

In a comprehensive survey, Goodman (2009) analyzes three environmental discourses in HCI: SID (mentioned earlier) as well as *Re-visioning Consumption* and *Citizen Sensing*. According to Goodman, SID is primarily concerned with motivating behavioral change in end users seen as consumers by providing them with new information about the products they consume. As such, it is the designer's role to influence technology consumers with information that motivates better decision making, by providing information, through visualizing resource consumption, or through persuasive applications such as games. Re-visioning Consumption deals with the way people enact beliefs about humans, technology, and the environment. The results are not design interventions but visions of how technology practices embody feelings toward nature. Finally, the Citizen Sensing research framework moves sensor-based environmental information systems from wilderness areas to cities, to visualize spatial variances in local levels of air pollution, noise pollution, or water pollution; these engage people as civic actors that need to protect themselves from pollution.

Pierce, Odom, and Blevis (2008) provide a comprehensive survey of interaction design for ecovisualizations, described as any interactive devices targeted at revealing energy use in order to promote sustainable behaviors or foster positive attitudes toward sustainable practices. They argue that it is essential for designers and interaction design researchers to work toward facilitating more sustainable ways of being in the world: "Across these fields, concern continues to grow with respect to how interactive technologies can be used (i) to better inform the choices people make in their everyday lives, (ii) influence the psychological and behavioural factors motivating these decisions and (iii) motivate positive behaviour or social change" (p. 1). Zapico, Turpeinen, and Brandt (2009) list a range of interactive projects under the rubric of "climate persuasive services" that are all directed toward changing behavior in favor of "low-carbon lifestyles." They consider mobile phones, pervasive sensors, and social media as key technological drivers for the development of climate persuasion applications.

The ideas presented so far relate to higher-level reflections and possible ideological considerations that apply to the designers, the design process, the final design product or environment, and its end users. In addition, an extensive range of interactive, climate related design projects have been carried out; we will briefly touch on a few to give a feel for the spectrum (for an in-depth overview, see Pierce, Odom, and Blevis 2008 as well as Zapico, Turpeinen, and Brandt 2009).

Many of the climate-related projects are located in the home. The *Watson* and the *Eco-Eye* are energy monitors that integrate direct and ambient real-time feedback on total energy consumption in a household. In the gaming genre, we find *Kill a Watt*, which lets you monitor energy resources in a way similar to computer games—with goals and different levels so you can improve your skills. The Interactive Institute in Stockholm[4] has carried out various interactive projects aimed at increasing energy awareness in the design research program *Static!*. Based on reflective and critical design, the researchers have sought answers to the question of how design can affect people's energy awareness and choices. Among the notable projects is the *Power-Aware Cord*, which is a redesigned power strip where the cord is designed to visualize energy— the more energy consumed, the more the cord is illuminated. Pierce, Odom, and Blevis (2008) have created the *Energy Challenge* interface where an EV (Eco-visualization) showed measurements of electricity and water consumption to encourage energy conservation behavior in a competition between dormitories at Oberlin College and Indiana University Bloomington.

Moving from the home out into urban space, the climate-related projects often take on an artistic character. DiSalvo et al. (2009) investigate how HCI researchers working on sustainability can benefit from understanding the discourses and practices of eco-logically engaged art. Among other projects, the authors present Tiffany Holme's *7000 Oaks and Counting*, a public animation that changes based on the amount of electricity consumed by a building, or dynamic carbon loads generated throughout the day. According to DiSalvo et al., this particular project's main focus is to foster dialog, and thus investigate public engagement with environmental matters through technology.

Other similar projects include *Nuage Vert*, a public installation in Helsinki made by the art group HeHe, where a laser light was projected onto the smokestacks of a local coal-based power station to illustrate the current levels of electricity consumption by local residents. On the verge of the home and urban space, applications like *PEIR* (Personal Environmental Impacts Report) let you track your carbon footprint on a mobile platform.

Summing Up

In DUL we have primarily been involved in the creation of climate projects in urban and public space. The projects have been aimed at creating awareness about the climate change debate, offering citizens—as users of interactive systems—invitations to participate in events where they could voice their opinions in an open and innova-tive way. Sometimes it was possible to learn something about consumption and sus-tainability, and sometimes the focus was more on establishing a relation between the theme and the person that would hopefully lead to a renewed engagement through dialog. This is an explicit move away from a narrower behaviorist approach (like the Watson or the Eco-Eye) that focuses on behavior change, toward an approach focusing on facilitating civic discourse—which may ultimately lead to behavior change (not unlike the ecoart approach in for example, 7000 Oaks and Counting or the reflective approach from the Power-Aware Cord). But the involvement and power relationships between citizens and authorities are seen differently. This is also evident in the fact that to a great extent, the important activities of the two DUL cases analyzed in this chapter are not necessarily happening within the interactive system, but rather outside or in connection to them. In that sense, these experimental urban interfaces can be characterized as open systems that structure a discourse around them, as opposed to more traditional (HCI-focused) systems where much of the action is contained within the system. The notion of "the debate" then becomes less monolithic, since the purpose of the systems is to allow the user-citizen to take part in a variety of conversations, which in turn emphasizes the collective aspect of citizenship. This is conceptually in line with work like *Projected Realities* by Gaver and Dunne (1999), which brings together collaborative technologies for the home and public space to form interactive channels of expression and communication that can be actively appropriated by the users.

It can be argued that the DUL climate projects presented in this chapter are closely related to the core values in SID as developed by Blevis (2007); they draw attention to climate change in a number of ways. However, it is arguable whether sustainability in itself has been a core value in the interactive design of the DUL projects. To more specifically qualify this discussion, we now offer a theoretical foundation for conceptualizing the projects presented, focusing on the tensions between engagement, affect, and information.

Theoretical Foundation and Relations

The theoretical framework presented in this chapter has been instrumental for validating the results of the design projects as well as for sketching directions for present and future design projects and trajectories. Following the different theoretical paths, we have created projects providing different means of engagement in order to affect people's participation in the climate debate through the informative use of interactive technologies. In doing so, we will show how the projects can be understood as experimental urban interfaces that create new experiential relations among people, content, situation, technology, and the environment—and among engagement, affect, and information.

Engagement

The literature on engagement as a qualified and distinct goal of design has emerged concurrently with the rise of the experience-oriented domain, as exemplified by McCarthy and Wright (2004). Increasingly, designing for living with digital technologies implies considerations of the experiential qualities that come into play to form our experience of the designed interactive environments. Working with experience-oriented design projects, a salient theme in DUL has been to explore the notion of what we have termed *engaging interaction*. In line with Dalsgaard 2009, Dalsgaard and Dindler 2009, and McCarthy and Wright 2004, we are inspired by pragmatist philosophy, particularly that of John Dewey, which offers an interesting perspective on exploring and experimenting with how situated interactive systems and installations may engage users in participation and inquiry.

When defining the notion of engagement based on these ideas, we heavily rely on Dalsgaard and Dindler, who, in their article "Peepholes as Means of Engagement in Interaction Design" (2009), argue for a pragmatist conceptualization of engagement to shed light on people's relation to interactive systems and the environments in which they exist. Dalsgaard and Dindler develop "an understanding of engagement as emergent and relational, constituted not only by the relation between a subject and an interactive artifact, but as a phenomenon that develops in the complex transactions between people, physico-spatial surroundings, socio-cultural practices, and technologies" (p. 2). Engagement can be said to unfold "in inquiry, the mutual process in which the user in an interactive environment encounters a problematic framing of her experience, motivating an exploration of the situation through interaction with the intended outcome of transforming the perceived practice" (p. 4).

Engagement in itself cannot be seen as an experiential quality since it resides on a higher level of abstraction and may be regarded as a "meta-quality that encompasses a number of experiential qualities" (Dalsgaard and Dindler 2009, 2). Engagement with interactive systems is fundamentally embedded in particular situations and cultural practices, and drawing on Berleant (1991), Dalsgaard and Dindler focus particularly on participation or participatory engagement and the reciprocal relation between a person and a system. Motivation (as the dynamics characterizing a person's activity and relations to the surroundings in concrete situations) and motives (denoting the long-term goals that have affected a person over extended periods) are seen as other constituents, this time drawing on cultural-historical theory. Together, these positions develop engagement as a relational phenomenon dependent on what people bring to a given situation in terms of motivation. The Deweyan concept of transaction captures the dynamics of how engagement unfolds in time through inquiry.

Moving from a theoretical argument to a more design-oriented realm, Dalsgaard and Dindler develop the notion of *means of engagement* to describe the particular constructs that are intentionally shaped through design to mediate our engagement in the world:

These means can take on many shapes; . . . we are interested primarily in the particular qualities of interactive systems that act as means of engagement. In our further discussion, we will thus limit our focus to interactive artifacts and environments and explore *means of engagement as the intentional constructs that are produced through design, which encompass or relate to the features of the situation that are relevant in conducting engagement.* (p. 5; our emphasis)

Affect

Whereas engagement as it has been presented so far can be said to focus on higher-level forms of experience seen as a more abstract "coming together" of experiential qualities, we will argue that it is possible to talk about engagement on a different experiential level as well using the concept of affect. As part of the experience-oriented approach in HCI and interaction design, specific attention has been granted to developing accounts of the experiences interactive systems have to offer on an emotional and affective level (see, e.g., Picard 1997; Norman 2005; Sengers et al. 2002; Boehner et al. 2005; also see Fritsch 2009 for a comprehensive review). Affect as a concept has been greatly influential in broadening the scope of both the theoretical foundations and practical design implications in interaction design and HCI, notably in the form of *affective computing* (Picard 1997) and *emotional design* (Norman 2005). However, Picard and Norman's attempt to structure, formalize, and represent emotions and affect as informational units has been challenged within the communities of HCI and interactions design. A range of researchers have advocated rethinking the concepts, arguing that emotions and affect are in the *interaction* between a user and a system, and not to be found in the code or hardware (see, e.g., Sengers et al. 2002 and Boehner et al. 2005).

In this section we introduce the notion of affect as developed by philosopher Brian Massumi. Massumi works in the intersection between art, architecture, and political and cultural theory. In his development of affect as a concept, Massumi (2002) directly addresses forms of lived experience when describing affect as a qualitatively different experiential dimension than that of emotions and feelings, which, he suggests, can be seen as personalized, or recognized affect. Massumi emphasizes that affect cannot be transferred directly from one object or person to another. Instead, it must be understood in processual and relational terms, as a dimension of every event. Starting from the notion of affective experience, Massumi provides a vocabulary for conceptualizing the *experiential fields* interactive systems have to offer in terms of events, microperceptual shock, capacitation/activation, and conditions of emergence and becoming.

Affective Experience

Massumi develops his notion of affect from the French philosopher Gilles Deleuze's reception of Spinoza's philosophy. Affect is defined in terms of the ability to "affect or be affected," which, according to Massumi (2009), places affect between the customary categories of subject and object. Instead of working with predetermined and static notions of the experiential, he stresses the importance of understanding the relations that occur in the middle of a field of experience. The focus is to describe and understand a relational event that plays out differently every time, taking up the past differently and creating new potentials for the future. The ability to affect and be affected is understood as two facets of the same and every event.

Drawing on Spinoza again, Massumi (2009, 1) states that "a power to affect and be affected governs a transition, where a body passes from one state of capacitation to a diminished or augmented state of capacitation." Central to this understanding is the heightening, for example, of a person's feeling of power to affect a given situation, which would entail an augmented state of capacitation or activation. The felt, affective quality of a given experience is that which characterizes the feeling of transition as the body moves from one power of existence to another. A body is defined by what capacities it carries from step to step, and the charge of affect is not something fixed.

When discussing more directly what causes changes in our experience of a given situation on an affective level, Massumi uses the Peircean concept of shock, which precedes every event. According to Massumi (2009, 3), affect is inseparable from the concept of shock, understood as "a change in focus, or a rustle at the periphery of vision that draws the gaze toward it. In every shift of attention, there is an interruption, a momentary cut in the mode of onward deployment of life." An onset of experience, which by nature is imperceptible, a microperception that is felt but not registered consciously leads to a recueing of our bodily powers of existence. According to Massumi (2009, 4), the world we live in is made up of these microperceptions, cutting in, cueing emergence, priming capacities. Not every tendency and capacity activated bears fruit in the meaning of becoming actualized, but everything leaves its trace:

The body, in this eventful re-beginning, carries tendencies reviving the past and already striving toward a future. In its commotion are capacities reactivating, being primed to play out, in a heightening or diminishing of their collective power of existence. The body figures here as a cut in the continuity of relation, filled with potential for re-relating, with a difference. *Microperceptual shock is like a re-cueing of our bodily powers of existence.* (p. 4; our emphasis)

A Massumian approach to describing the experiential fields offered by interactive environments needs to take into consideration how they might activate and capacitate bodies as they move into and through various affective experiences in interactive situations. The focus is on describing the relational complexity of the events forming and being formed by these affective experiences and microperceptual shocks. The initial, precognitive, affective experience also relates to the theory of engagement, feeding forward into more qualified experiences and feeding back through affective retroactivation in different situations. In the analysis, we describe how we have sought to design experiential fields using microperceptual shock in order to create events that result in an augmented capacitation in relation to the climate debate on different levels of engagement.

Information

It has often been the role of artists to frame an important issue in the public debate—through the use of microperceptual shocks—to stir debate or reflection. But the freedom of the artist and the tendency to shun high levels of exact information leave a design space to be explored: between *engagement* and *information*. In our designs, we have been mapping a design space that we often characterize by these two dimensions. Information is here to be understood in a casual manner as facts and chunks of conversation that matter to people, not bits or bandwidth in the formal sense.

The climate change issue is parallel to many other public discussions, and it should be debated in an informed way if it is to be of any substantial value. The frequency of populist, uninformed positions on both sides of the debate—either pro or contra climate action—is considerable. Moreover, there is a tension between style and rhetoric on the one hand and experience and engagement on the other. Something may be informative but perceived as dull and therefore irrelevant in the context of many activities in public/urban space. As a consequence, we have found the usual models of relationships between information and cognitive (over)load of less use. Although activities in public space exhibit characteristics found in heterogeneous nomadic work situations (e.g., Strauss et al. 1985), the blended casual-yet-intentional nature of many urban activities creates different requirements (for lack of a better word) for new urban interfaces. The interruptions are more social in nature and concern aspects like self-representation, shared play, and casual conversation rather than efficiency and conciseness (Brynskov et al. 2009).

Drawing on the theory outlined above, one might conceptualize this challenge as a general research question: What means of engagement will bring together the immediate, affective experience with a qualified, motivational exploration of a given informational content? Put differently: What strategies for affecting and engaging people in an urban setting have the potential for letting people connect to and provide informational content aimed at, in this particular context, increasing climate awareness? Moreover, what strategies motivate people to actively change their habits to reduce energy consumption or the like?

We want to be able to adjust the level of information balanced against the affectively engaging experience. Over time, we have informally used a "scale" of interactivity (ranging from least to most):

static → dynamic → reactive → interactive → participatory → communicative

Others exist, but we have found this granularity helpful in our vocabulary as designers as well as analysts.

Summing Up

Through the development of the concepts of engagement, affect, and information, we have built a theoretical foundation for exploring the interactive projects we present in the following section. Essential to this framework is the heterogeneity of the theoretical lenses presented, and their coming together in this particular context to describe the affective experience as well as the means of engagement aimed at getting people involved in the exchange of information in relation to climate change. Affect and engagement relate to each other in the account of the microperceptual, and motivational factors that form the experiential fields offered by the two interactive installations. The processual, transactional, but nontransmissional is key for conceptualizing the openness of the installations, creating the possibility of engaging interactions with the informational content. In the next section we present the two design cases before using the theoretical lenses to illustrate how the cases work on different experiential levels to engage people in the civic discourse on climate change.

Figure 7.1
Climate on the Wall (street view).

Case Projects

The City of Aarhus, Denmark, has a goal: it wants to be CO_2 neutral by 2030. To meet that challenge, the municipality needs to engage its citizens on an individual level to make a difference by reducing their emission of CO_2. This has led to an ambitious strategic venture aimed at addressing every citizen through various city initiatives. One was a large exhibition, *CO2030*, held in conjunction with the international Beyond Kyoto conference, which had more than 1,500 attendees and a list of prominent international keynote speakers.

The general purpose of the CO2030 exhibition was to create an opportunity for the citizens of Aarhus to meet up and get inspiration and good advice on how to decrease CO_2 emissions. To attract people to the exhibition and to put real citizen faces on the efforts for a better climate, DUL was invited to contribute to the exhibition.

Climate on the Wall

Climate on the Wall[5] functioned as an interactive generator of climate statements using *Ridehuset*—home to the CO2030 exhibition and a prominent building in the city center—as a backdrop. The installation used the Ridehuset facade as a display by means of projection technology involving two overlapping projectors placed in two temporary towers erected for the occasion.

On the facade, a number of words relating to carbon emissions and climate issues floated above the heads of passersby. Some of the words were emphasized to form a statement about climate change. As people approached or walked past, the words pulsated and attracted attention. If a person stopped, the word above the person would

Figure 7.2
CO2nfession/CO2mmitment (booth, camera, and outdoor screen).

grow and turn into a speech bubble. This word could now be dragged to a different part of the facade. In this way, people were able to create and manipulate sentences relating to climate change. The concept borrows from refrigerator magnets with words that can be arranged to form statements and sentences.

During the exhibition, the installation was only accessible at night due to the projections. It attracted considerable attention and engaged a variety of people in playful interaction with the facade. People started sharing thoughts on the climate situation, and in general the installation spurred many conversations about both the exhibition and the theme of carbon emission. People were easily attracted to the Climate on the Wall project, and the messages projected on the wall were mostly simple and straightforward.

CO2nfession/CO2mmitment

CO2nfession/CO2mmitment[6] was an advanced video installation developed by DUL in partnership with AFA JCDecaux and the Municipality of Aarhus. It put a face on the efforts for climate improvements and gave the citizens of Aarhus a voice to be heard—and seen—throughout the city.

The installation itself consisted of two parts: one inside the exhibition space (Ridehuset), and the other on information stands and bus stops throughout the city. In Ridehuset, people could enter a booth, where it was possible to confess one's climate sins (using too much water or electricity, eating too much red meat, driving too much, etc.) and to commit oneself to a more active fight for a better climate in Aarhus. In the booth, a number of props served as an inspiration to creatively convey the climate story people wanted to tell. A video recorded people's confessions/

commitments in the booth, which were shown as a live feed outside the booth to attract bystanders.

The video was edited the same day and distributed on the screens in the city. People at these screens could hear the sound of the videos by touching a sensor on the screens. The installation thus tried to render the fight for a better climate a personal and immediately relevant issue to the people of Aarhus, while at the same time attracting people to Ridehuset for the exhibition. During the exhibition, sixty-eight recordings were made and distributed around the city. Located in busy city locations, these screens showed edited versions of the videos 24/7 for four days.

A wide range of people used the installation, including people just visiting the exhibition who found it a good opportunity to get something off their chest to the city mayor. The videos recorded were extremely diverse, ranging from straightforward and simple confessions to complex animated narratives using the props in creative ways.

Data Collection and Preliminary Findings

The design, development, and use of the systems were documented in various ways. Since DUL has a heavy focus on design processes, the early stages were captured and documented with structured notes, pictures, and video in order to be able to go back and look at how, for example, various sources of inspiration played a role in the final results. The actual use and reception were captured by the same structured means, with the addition of user questionnaires, interviews with key stakeholders, and observations (of footfall, noticeable incidents, etc.). The quantitative data did not provide much insight into the topics this chapter explores: we have made these general observations when working with urban interventions (see, e.g., Brynskov et al. 2009).

Most users perceived the Climate on the Wall project very positively, describing it with adjectives like "fun," "exciting," "engaging," and "catchy." Most of them were seeing it for the first time, and they generally figured out how to use it by themselves, sparked by their (intentionally unavoidable) physical interaction with the wall and drawing on expectations from the speech-bubble metaphor. Some learned by looking at others, and only a very few never figured out how it worked.

As for CO2nfession/CO2mmitment, typical motives from those who entered the booth included curiosity and peer pressure; only one person mentioned wanting to bring more attention to the climate debate. As for the screens in the city, a number of people commented on their existence. Stories of people going to a certain screen to see themselves were reported, but also stories of people being surprised when suddenly seeing their friends appearing on the video screens. In general, although the screens created attention in the city, it nonetheless proved difficult to attract people to actively engage and explore the content of the videos. Two-thirds of the people interviewed had activated the sound using the "Press for sound" button, and most of them found the volume appropriate. However, few of them could actually remember the informational content of what was being said, either because the volume was not high enough to allow for comprehension, or because the content did not interest them enough to pay continuous attention.

Analysis of the Projects

On the basis of the presented theoretical foundation and the collected data, we now seek to explore how our projects function as new, situated, interactive technologies and urban interfaces. The following analysis is intended to illustrate the experiential complexity in designing for participation in civic discourse (in this case on climate change). The analysis will describe the various intentional and unintentional means of engagement, how the installations can be seen to offer particular affective experiences, and how this relates to uncovering and contributing to the production of informational content.

Engagement

We will argue that the two projects presented offer different means of engagement and thresholds of participation to make people engage in the civic discourse on climate change and explore the CO2030 exhibition space. Both Climate on the Wall and CO2nfession/C02mmitment can concurrently be seen as installations in their own right, as parts of the greater exhibition, as a way of engaging people in the interaction with the installations, and as a means for engaging people playfully in uncovering and contributing to the more "serious" content provided in the exhibition space.

Climate on the Wall playfully sought to "lure"—or invite with a low participation threshold—people into participating in the climate debate, hopefully to provide new insights and to spur reflections on-site on the part of the citizens engaged in the particular interactive situation. Whether this initial engagement might work as an inducement for long-term engagement leading to changing habits remains an open question. The concrete means of engagement used in the installation relate to the words fluttering around when you moved past the installation (spurring curiosity, grabbing attention); the playful, bodily interaction with the façade; and the choice of words related directly to the climate debate and everyday life of the people passing by—for example, using local geographic names or the name of the local soccer team ("AGF"). Climate on the Wall may be understood as an object of inquiry that invites material-semiotic experimentation and exploration in its own right (it is a new and alien intervention into the cityscape, after all), as well as a tool for inquiry and sense-making with regard to problematic situations beyond the immediate fascination and interaction with the installation. People usually did not try to write anything specific on the wall, but while the majority found it too hard to write anything that made sense, they commonly described the experience as fun. It was important for most users that they were active participants, which they described as giving them a greater feeling of engagement and involvement. The content presented on the facade offered ways of relating to, reflecting on, communicating, and socially debating carbon emission issues that hopefully lead to fruitful transactions in the civic discourse.

CO2nfession/CO2mmitment draws on well-known vox pop setups in its design, creating a high degree of recognizability ("fifteen minutes of fame") with the installation. Concrete means of engagement include the overall design of the booth, the props, and, more subtly, the fact that the installation offers people an opportunity to voice their opinions publicly all over the city. There were mixed reactions to the kind of communication facilitated by the interactive setup. While some felt that the personal exposure was warranted, or indeed needed, due to the urgency of the theme, others perceived the setup as negative, often because they did not find it interesting enough to engage. A great number of people who did not enter the booth did engage in conversation with the people (designers) operating the installation, explaining why they would not enter and voicing their opinions outside the booth. In general, the installation was found to encourage personal reflexivity and allowed people to enter into dialog with its values (Leong and Brynskov 2009). In the city, video and sound were used to attract attention, working fairly well for some, but also blending in with the rest of the urban noise and rhythm very quickly. Arguably, the sound part, which could be activated by touching a buttonlike area, was mostly used in an experimental way concerning the technological and interactive setup and not with respect to the content of the installation. The content of the installation was wholly created by the people interacting with it and therefore became a concrete sociocultural manifestation of engaged transactions and societal relations, often spurred by and leading to further inquiry.

Affect

When considering the two interactive installations from an affective point of view, there are notable differences in the experiential fields they offered. Climate on the Wall immediately and directly activated the users of the installation affectively through microperceptual shocks, offering cues for people to engage in an exploration of the interaction with and the content of the facade. The wall in itself attracted attention through its animations, which—via webcams—incorporated and expressed the movements and presence of passersby on the wall either passively (nonconsciously) or actively (through conscious interaction). These microshocks prime the experiential field, altering the basic relation to the way the physical space is perceived. The fact that your bodily presence affects the surroundings creates an affectively engaging interactive environment, differing from the traditional use of technology in the form of desktop computers as well as the normal way of being in urban space. The affective relation to the interactive system was changed due to the physical activation, in many cases leading people to wave, run, or jump around in front of Ridehuset, a behavior not normally associated with buildings and facades in the city. In this respect, Climate on the Wall spurred behavior that added a shock effect to the interaction with the installation, where the people interacting attracted more attention to the setup.

All these factors encourage people to actively explore the interactional setup and content, as well as giving them a chance to voice an opinion. Actually being able to conspicuously express your personal statements about climate issues in a public space might change the parameters for engaging in civic discourse. Admittedly, many of the conversations surrounding the installation were concerned with uncovering the technical setup and not the climate debate. However, the data collected also show how people perceived this style of reaching out to citizens as a way of giving them a platform for engagement on a larger (societal) scale and as a strong incentive to commit themselves in the climate debate.

CO2nfession/CO2mmitment needs to be approached differently from an affective point of view. The design of the installation does not aim to engage people immediately in the interaction like Climate on the Wall. However, because affect is part of every event, it is also possible to explore what kinds of affective experiences the installation facilitates. The installation offers a way for its users to become affectively engaged in the climate change debate through their participation in civic discourse. Climate change as a subject is loaded with so much tension that it is impossible to not be affected by it. At the same time the amount of information and the possible consequences can be so abstract and overwhelming that taking action becomes difficult. Inviting people to actively take part in the debate, by literally demanding they enter the confessional booth, sit down, and voice their opinion, can change their participation from passive to active, or even performative. In this way, you might argue that the installation in itself makes possible an activation of people's capacities, by allowing them to contribute their own content—but also by letting them explore the content of others. Examples show that people created affective ties with what they saw, sometimes recognizing their friends on the screens, which made them more curious as to what could be explored in the exhibition space as well as on other bus stops throughout the city. Others deliberately made recordings they later wanted to show friends and family in the city. Hence, this kind of setup might offer the potential for creating serendipitous encounters in the city through the deployment of experimental urban interfaces. CO2nfession/CO2mmitment's open, malleable infrastructure consists solely of people who have actually chosen to invest themselves in voicing their opinions and lived stories. The whole point of the system is to display people's stories in the city, thus creating a civic voice with a personal face that might then contribute to changing the affective experience of the civic discourse on climate change. Affectively speaking, CO2nfession/CO2mmitment also empowers people and changes the parameters for the way they might conceive something such as advertising in urban space. It becomes possible to imagine urban interfaces with a whole new potential for relating and contributing to the cityscape.

It is interesting how both projects challenge the way the affective experience of the cityscape is perceived. What is changed is the basic way in which people, in Adam Greenfield and Mark Shepard's (2007) words, perceive the built urban space due to the experiential fields offered by the plasticity of the digital and interactive interventions. In both cases, this facilitates the creation of new microperceptual shocks in order to get the attention of the passersby and offer them ways to engage in climate discussions.

Information

The tension between engagement and information has emerged as a pivotal challenge in our work with interactive media facades and other types of urban interventions. It seems that whenever the threshold for participation is low and the interaction forms are simple, engagement goes up. At the same time, the amount of information that can be mediated goes down. This section characterizes this phenomenon using the two cases as examples.

Climate on the Wall was conceptualized as a step up in information complexity from our earlier media facade designs (e.g., Aarhus by Light; Brynskov et al. 2009), which were abstract and biased sharply toward the playful. The speech bubbles lent themselves to both playful interaction and communication. Thus they ranked high on both interactivity (being "participatory"; see the scale mentioned in the previous "Information" section) and on information. However, there was a marked difference between the *perceived* usefulness as a communication tool (for creating short slogans) and its *actual* effectiveness when participants tried to write something. In short, it did not work. People could not casually engage for a few minutes and leave a statement behind for others to read and elaborate on. On the other hand, the interaction was fun, and the participants did not seem to care much that they could only fiddle with words rather than communicate. The conclusion for us has been that we have nudged closer to the ideal of engaging interaction *and* communication in public space by using an experimental urban interface, a media facade, but that many more experiments still have to be made in order to create urban interactive platforms with communicative qualities that are engaging.

CO2nfession/CO2mmitment is very different from Climate on the Wall in terms of both interaction and information. The interface is participatory but hardly experimental (talking to a video camera, watching a video with selective audio at a bus stop), and the amount of information that can be conveyed is much larger—participants can say and show whatever they want. Still, it can be argued that the wall and the booth and broadcast have about the same *effect*: some reflexivity on the part of the active participant (see Leong and Brynskov 2009) and a peripheral awareness that somebody wants us, the bystander, to think about climate change. Our interpretation is that the relationship between engagement and information is such that they balance out. If more informational detail were to be added in either system, it would be less accessible to an audience in a public space because the engagement threshold would be raised, which would require a larger interactional investment. Similarly, if the experience were to be made more engaging, it would be harder to integrate in casual urban activity patterns, thus closing the activity off. One solution—or dynamic—we would point to as a prerequisite to raising both the level of engagement and information is that of a specific genre of interface that was conventionalized (or crystallized in the activity theoretical sense) so that it would not be perceived as interfering with expected behavior in public space.

Discussion, Concluding Remarks, and Future Work

The projects presented in this chapter represent different takes on how to engage citizens in developing new relations to the climate change debate through particular interactive and participative situations drawing on well-established cultural practices and experimental uses of urban interfaces. A common key goal of the installations was to facilitate an open and participatory variety of conversations on climate change, to playfully lure people into voicing their own opinions, and to put a personal face on the somewhat abstract struggle for a better climate. This goal was pursued by taking the citizens' opinions seriously and by giving them an opportunity to become (more) conscious of their habits—doing so in public and urban settings has arguably led to reflection, discussion, and perhaps changes in the overall lifestyle of the involved participants.

The kinds of climate projects we in DUL have been developing do not match easily with the three trends of sustainable HCI presented in the related work above. There is only indirect information about products and sustainability and no direct visualization of energy consumption. Importantly, no normative or absolute guidelines come out of any of the projects; rather, they are aimed at activating people, engaging them in civic discourse to help find new answers to the challenges presented by the changing climate conditions—thus more indirectly improving sustainability through reflexivity.

In the analysis, however tentatively, it is possible to give a nuanced account of the projects through the theoretical lenses of engagement, affect, and information. The means of engagement utilized in the projects differ in important ways, as does the relation between engagement and information. The concept of affect provides a rich way to conceptualize the experiential fields offered by the designed interactive environments in terms of particular conditions of emergence for interaction and the notion of microperceptual shock. The dynamics of the analysis make it possible to move back and forth between concrete means of engagement in the design and the way these means are felt on an affective level. The affective experience might offer motivational cueings and capacitations for engaging with and contributing to the content of the installations. Seen as a whole, the theoretical foundation provides a rich way of conceptualizing the tensions between the design of an intuitively and immediately appealing and engaging system, and the design of a system that engages users in a thorough exploration of the informational content provided as part of the interactional setup. The three perspectives are intended to fit a design process using a situational approach like the Design Space Explorer (Dalsgaard, Halskov, and Nielsen 2008). It is an ongoing design challenge to actually make these ends come together, especially when designing for urban or public settings that are mostly used for transit and short stays.

The empirical findings and the analysis underline the way people actively appropriate and make sense of the installations in multiple, unforeseen ways. The openness of the installations has proved to be an asset in engaging people creatively in playful interactions (Climate on the Wall) and modes of production and content making (CO2nfession/CO2mmitment). It remains an open question how and to what degree one should balance constrained and open-ended interactions in an urban or public environment. Nonetheless, as this chapter indicates, it can be an asset working with different thresholds and levels of engagement that create open-ended conditions of emergence that you neither can nor should try to fully control. The openness of the systems and their differing combinations of engagement, affect, and information provide different entry points into the climate debate.

Summing up, we argue that both the conceptual and practical design process leading to Climate on the Wall and CO2nfession/CO2mmitment, as well as the evaluative work done so far, have provided useful insights on how to increase the focus on content and information in the design of affectively engaging, interactive urban interfaces. In the future, we hope to pursue the goal of creating urban interfaces that engage people immediately in the interactive exploration of a given installation or content, while also actively affecting people's everyday lives in positive ways. In doing so, we will seek to map in greater detail the design space encompassing engagement, affect, and information.

Notes

1. http://en.cop15.dk/.

2. http://unfccc.int/kyoto_protocol/items/2830.php.

3. http://digitalurbanliving.dk.

4. http://www.tii.se/projects/static.

5. http://digitalurbanliving.dk/climate-on-the-wall.

6. http://digitalurbanliving.dk/co2nfession-co2mmitment.

References

Berleant, Arnold. 1991. *Art and Engagement*. Philadelphia: Temple University Press.

Blevis, Eli. 2007. Sustainable Interaction Design: Invention & disposal, renewal and reuse. In M. B. Rosson, .D. Gilmore, eds. *Proceedings of the SIGCHI Conference on Human Factors in Computing Systems* (San Jose, California, USA, April 28–May 03, 2007). CHI '07, 503–512. New York, NY: ACM Press.

Boehner, K., R. DePaula, P. Dourish, and P. Sengers. 2005. Affect: From information to interaction. In O. W. Bertelsen, N. O. Bouvin, P. G. Krogh, and M. Kyng, eds. *Proceedings of the 4th Decennial Conference on Critical Computing:* between sense and sensibility. August 20–24, 2005, Aarhus, Denmark. New York, NY: ACM Press.

Brynskov, M., P. Dalsgaard, T. Ebsen, J. Fritsch, K. Halskov, and R. Nielsen. 2009. Staging urban interactions with media facades. In T. Gross, ed. *Proceedings of Interact 2009*, 154–167. Berlin: Springer Verlag. http://www.aarhusbylight.dk/index-english.html.

Dalsgaard, P. 2009. Designing Engaging Interactive Experiences: A Pragmatist Perspective. PhD dissertation, Department of Information and Media Studies, Aarhus University.

Dalsgaard, P., and C. Dindler. 2009. Peepholes as means of engagement in interaction design. In T. Bratteig and B. Sevaldson, eds. *Online Proceedings of Nordes 2009: The Third Nordic Design Research Conference*, Oslo, Norway: UiO. http://ocs.sfu.ca/nordes/index.php/nordes/2009/paper/view/289

Dalsgaard, P., K. Halskov, and R. Nielsen. 2008. A design space explorer for media façades. In N. Bidwell, ed. *Proceedings of OZCHI 2008*, Cairns, Australia, December 8–12, 2008. New York, NY: ACM Press.

DiSalvo, C., K. Boehner, N. A. Knouf, and P. Sengers. 2009. Nourishing the ground for sustainable HCI: Considerations from ecologically engaged art. In D. R. Olsen Jr., and R. B. Arthur, eds. *Proceedings of CHI 2009*, 385–394.

Fritsch, Jonas. 2009. Understanding affective engagement as a resource in interaction design. In T. Bratteig. and B. Sevaldson, eds. *Online Proceedings of Nordes 2009: The Third Nordic Design Research Conference*, Oslo, Norway: UiO. http://ocs.sfu.ca/nordes/index.php/nordes/2009/paper/view/297.

Gaver, W., and A. Dunne. 1999. Projected realities: Conceptual design for cultural effect. In M. G. Williams. and M. W. Altom, eds. *Proceedings of the SIGCHI Conference on Human Factors in Computing Systems: The CHI Is the Limi,* 600–607. New York, NY: ACM Press.

Goodman, Elizabeth. 2009. Three environmental discourses in human-computer interaction. In D. R. Olsen Jr. and R. B. Arthur, eds. *Proceedings of CHI 2009*, 2535–2544. New York, NY: ACM Press.

Greenfield, Adam, and Mark Shepard. 2007. *Urban Computing and Its Discontents*. Architecture and Situated Technologies Pamphlet 1. New York: Architectural League of New York.

Leong, Tuck, and Martin Brynskov. 2009. CO2nfession: Engaging with values through urban conversations. In M. Foth, J. Kjeldskov, and J. Paay, J., eds. *Proceedings of OZCHI 2009*. New York, NY: ACM Press.

Massumi, Brian. 2002. *Parables for the Virtual: Movement, Affect, Sensation*. Durham, NC: Duke University Press.

Massumi, Brian. 2009. Of Microperception and Micropolitics. Interview with Brian Massumi by Joel McKim. In *Inflexions: A Journal for Research-Creation*, Vol. 3, "Micropolitics: Exploring Ethicoe-Aesthetics", October 2009. www.inflexions.org.

McCarthy, John C., and Peter Wright. 2004. *Technology as Experience*. Cambridge, MA: MIT Press.

Norman, Donald. 2005. *Emotional Design: Why We Love (or Hate) Everyday Things*. New York: Basic Books.

Picard, Rosalind W. 1997. *Affective Computing*. Cambridge, MA: MIT Press.

Pierce, J., W. Odom, and Eli Blevis. 2008. Energy aware dwelling: A critical survey of interaction design for eco-visualizations. In N. Bidwell, ed. *Proceedings of OZCHI 2008*, Cairns, Australia, December 8–12, 2008. New York, NY: ACM Press.

Sengers, P., R. Liesendahl, W. Magar, C. Seibert, B. Müller, T. Joachims, W. Geng, P. Mårtensson, and K. Höök. 2002. The enigmatics of affect. In B. Verplank and A. Sutcliffe, A., eds. Proceedings of DIS2002, London, 87–98. New York, NY: ACM Press.

Strauss, A., S. Fagerhaugh, B. Suczek, and C. Wiener. 1985. *Social Organization of Medical Work*. Chicago: University of Chicago Press.

Zapico, J. L., M. Turpeinen, and N. Brandt. 2009. Climate persuasive services: Changing behaviour towards low-carbon lifestyles. In S. Chatterjee and P. Dev, eds. *Proceedings of Persuasive '09*, Claremont, CA, New York, NY: ACM Press.

8 More Than Friends: Social and Mobile Media for Activist Organizations

Tad Hirsch

Political activists around the world have been quick to adopt social and mobile media for use in protests and mass mobilizations. In recent years, demonstrators in Moldova and Iran employed social networking sites like Facebook and the microblogging service Twitter to share their stories with international audiences (Mungiu-Pippidi and Munteanu 2009; Morozov 2009); the use of mobile-phone text messaging by protesters in Spain, the Philippines, and the United States has also been extensively reported and analyzed (for example, Castells 2007).

Scholarship has tended to focus on examples of activists appropriating commercial products and services to mobilize large groups of sympathizers, often in rapid response to egregious betrayals of the public trust. As these studies illustrate, broad mobile-phone adoption coupled with the easy social networking capabilities offered by so-called Web 2.0 technologies enable loosely coordinated groups of individuals to spontaneously mobilize and share information to confront injustice. Howard Rheingold (2002) has dubbed these collectives "smart mobs," a formulation that continues to hold sway.

Activists from Argentina to Zimbabwe have exploited the ease with which services like Facebook, YouTube, and Twitter enable spontaneous information sharing and collective action by large numbers of people. However, analysis that emphasizes street protest and mass mobilization risks overstating the importance of tactics that, in reality, constitute a relatively small component of activist practice. Street protest, for example, is most effective for easily understood issues with clear heroes and villains, where consensus already exists among a sufficient number of potential actors. As Shirky (2008) observes, successful demonstrations are predicated on large numbers of people already agreeing—at least tacitly—with the protest objectives. Without this consensus, demonstrations are sparsely attended, attract little media attention, and generally fail to inspire future action.

However, activist campaigns are often built around issues for which there is no widespread consensus or sympathy. Most activists are not able to mobilize large numbers of ordinary people in extraordinary acts of civic engagement or public dissent. Rather, campaigns are carried forward in increments through the persistent efforts of small groups whose members are deeply engaged with their cause and committed to each other. Accordingly, activism tends to be less concerned with particular mobilizations than with creating and nurturing movements. Central to this effort is the creation of activist organizations that marshal and direct resources, coordinate and amplify individual action, and provide mechanisms for collective decision making. Organizations provide members with a collective identity while simultaneously providing a focal point for outsiders including journalists, opponents, and new recruits. They are also of central importance in enabling social movements to endure over time (Melucci 1996).

When we look across the broader range of activities that make up activist practice, it becomes clear that technologies and services designed for explicitly commercial purposes are often not ideally suited for activist use. For example, they may not provide adequate security for activists working in particularly contentious climes, and they often impose conditions on the ownership and dissemination of data that are at odds with activists' need to repurpose and rebroadcast content across a variety of media and contexts. More broadly, the model of social relations that undergirds commercial services, which tends to emphasize relationships between autonomous individuals, may not mesh well with activists' emphasis on organizations and movements. Simply put, Facebook, Twitter, YouTube, and the like are not activist technologies (despite their appropriation by activists), and often do not mesh well with the complexities of real-world activism.

Accordingly, activists around the world have come to rely on a growing number of social and mobile media technologies that have been developed by and for activists. Although less well known, less widely used, and often less fully developed than their commercial counterparts, they provide features and address concerns that are of particular interest to activist communities. In so doing, they challenge assumptions that underpin the design of commercial services and broaden our understanding of what social and mobile media can be.

In this chapter, I argue that activist technology projects are distinct from commercial services in several ways. Activist social media projects proceed from a fundamentally different orientation toward social relations that privileges organizations and collective action over individuals and personal behavior. Accordingly, they have unique instrumental goals—that is, they are designed to meet needs and address problems that are different in both form and substance than those that motivate commercial design. Activist technology projects also embody a distinct set of values, meaning that they are shaped by a different set of concerns (or at least, a different weighting among competing concerns) than their commercial counterparts.

I will present three recent activist social media projects: Ushahidi, an incident-reporting system developed during Kenya's 2007 postelection violence; Crabgrass, a social networking software platform developed by an American radical technology collective; and the Hub, a video-sharing site developed by an international human rights advocacy organization. I have selected these examples because they demonstrate a range of activist activities and modes of social organization. Ushahidi, for example, began its life as an informal collaboration by a network of Kenyan bloggers; Crabgrass is a project by an engineering collective associated with radical leftist movements; the Hub is an offering by an established nongovernmental organization (NGO). These examples are also noteworthy for their similarities to well-known commercial services. Crabgrass and the Hub are roughly analogous to Facebook and YouTube, while Ushahidi combines elements of Twitter and Google Maps.

I describe the conditions surrounding each project's conception, detail the goals and values that influenced each design process, and highlight commonalities and differences between them. Finally, I consider how these examples relate to existing commercial social and mobile media services.

This chapter proceeds from the assertion that, because most of the current literature on activist use of social and mobile media focuses on what activists *can* do with commercial services, it tends to overlook what they *cannot* do. That is to say, analysts who study activist appropriation of services like Facebook and Twitter often miss the ways activist needs outstrip the capabilities that these services offer. I suggest that examining activist alternatives to commercial social and mobile media services provides valuable insights both into the technology design and into the nature of contemporary advocacy movements.

Ushahidi: Channeling Citizen Journalism for Crisis Reporting

The aftermath of Kenya's disputed 2007 presidential election saw an eruption of violence across the country, resulting in over 1,000 deaths and hundreds of thousands displaced. Concerned that official reports underestimated the extent of the unrest, several bloggers living both in Kenya and abroad created a website (http://www .ushahidi.com/) called Ushahidi—Swahili for "testimony"—to collect and visualize incident reports from Kenyan citizens. Their goal was to provide an accurate and unbiased account of the postelection unrest.

Ushahidi allowed citizens to report incidents of postelection violence by sending text messages from their mobile phones, which were displayed on an interactive map (figure 8.1). Ultimately, Ushahidi recorded nearly 140 incidents including riots, murders, and rapes. A number of events and incidents were also reported that promoted peace and reconciliation. While Ushahidi did not claim to provide a full accounting of all that happened across Kenya, the site documented many incidents that escaped coverage by the mainstream media. Subsequent analysis of media coverage found little geographic overlap between Ushahidi's coverage and the mainstream media (Meier and Brodock 2008).

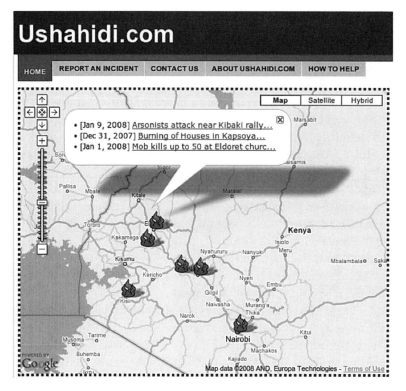

Figure 8.1
Ushahidi.com.

Since the elections, the Ushahidi team has made its software available to other NGOs under open-source licenses. It has been deployed to monitor elections in Mexico and India, medical supply shortages in Kenya, Uganda, Malawi, and Zambia, and attacks on immigrants in South Africa. Al Jazeera used it in its coverage of the January 2009 conflict in Gaza, and it was combined with FrontlineSMS—another open-source activist technology project—to monitor Afghan elections later that year. In December 2009, Ushahidi received a $1.4 million grant from the Omidyar Network that will enable the organization to continue software development and evangelism, as well as to establish a board of directors and offices in Kenya.

Ushahidi was not the first site to combine citizen journalism with map visualiza-tion; it was preceded by several noteworthy examples, including Jonathon Mendez and Greg Stoll's Katrina Information Map, which visualized eyewitness accounts of poststorm New Orleans (Singel 2005), and the *New York Times'* map visualization of readers' reports during a New York City transit workers' strike in 2005. However, Usha-hidi was unique in several respects. The use of text messaging for incident reporting provided an immediacy lacking in earlier efforts. While the Katrina Information Map, for example, relied on reports submitted via laptop and desktop computers often hours or days after events occurred, Ushahidi featured reports direct from the field.

Ushahidi's creators were also committed to data verification. Not content to rely solely on eyewitness accounts, they used government sources, NGO reports, and journalist accounts to verify the incident reports they received; each incident that appears on the Ushahidi site is marked with an icon indicating whether it has been confirmed by external sources.

This commitment to verifying the accuracy of crowdsourced data sets Ushahidi apart from other social media and citizen journalism platforms. Most commercial providers take the stance that their role is to provide a platform for their users; responsibility for the truth or falsehood of a particular piece of content lies with its author. While providers might exercise editorial control from time to time, as in cases of libel or defamation, such intervention is usually undertaken in response to a complaint or threatened legal action and is limited to editing or removing questionable content. It is rare for a commercial service provider to directly endorse particular bits of user-generated content as accurate, reliable, or valuable.

Ushahidi, in contrast, took an active role in monitoring and, where possible, verifying the accuracy of its users' posts. This reflects the context in which the site was developed, where much of the postelection violence was fueled by rumor and innuendo and there was the very real possibility that accounts appearing on the site could further inflame passions rather than help to calm them.

Ushahidi's commitment to accuracy and verifiability reflects a communication strategy that one finds in many activist campaigns. Because they promote marginalized interests in the face of powerful state and corporate opposition, activists often assume a heightened standard of credibility. Public statements that activists make are closely scrutinized; errors may be used to undermine their credibility. Some activists argue that the bar is higher for activist communications than it is for, say, mainstream media outlets or public relations professionals. An environmentalist that I interviewed in the course of this research put it succinctly: "As an activist, I don't have the luxury of lying." For example, if the *New York Times* makes a false claim in its reporting, it prints a correction the next day with little or no lasting damage to its credibility as an institution. If environmental activists, on the other hand, overstate the health impacts of emissions from a local paper mill, the mill owners may use the error to undermine the validity both of the activists' project and of the activists themselves, who may be branded as "radicals" or "crazies."

Crabgrass: Social Networking for Collectives

Crabgrass (http://crabgrass.riseup.net) is a social networking and collaboration platform for social movements and nonprofit organizations. It was initiated by Riseup

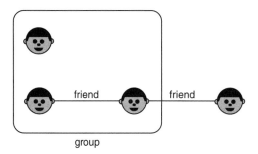

Figure 8.2
Personal social networking.

Labs, a Seattle-based radical technology collective that since 1999 has provided e-mail accounts, web hosting, and software development to activist organizations around the world. The project developed out of the collective's experience working with social movements, and its deep understanding of opportunities and limits that social networking and collaboration software offers for activists. While Riseup acknowledges that Facebook and Twitter are effective outreach tools because of their broad user base, the collective believes that these services are ill suited for internal communications and collaboration.

Crabgrass includes a number of features common to social networking and collaboration software, including the ability to make links and send messages between users. However, its orientation toward social movements has led to a number of design departures, including more nuanced group management, greater emphasis on privacy and security, and enhanced collaboration and decision-making tools.

Of these, the group-management features are the most significant and arise from a fundamental rethinking of the model of social relations that undergirds social media design.

Commercial services like Facebook and Twitter are oriented toward what we might call "personal social networking" (figure 8.2). These sites are designed to support lightweight connections between individuals. They are based on a relatively flat model of social relations in which connections between people are more or less equivalent—for example, Facebook users are "friends," not "best friends" or "casual acquaintances": LinkedIn users are "connections," not "employees" or "mentors."

Personal social networking is a simplistic model of social organization that trades complexity for ease of use. Connections are easily established and are maintained with little effort. (The are also relatively ephemeral, as evidenced by Burger King's 2009 promotion in which 233,906 Facebook users were defriended in exchange for free hamburgers (Pang 2009).) While the model's simplicity has no doubt contributed to social networking's rapid-fire growth, Crabgrass founders argue that it is insufficient

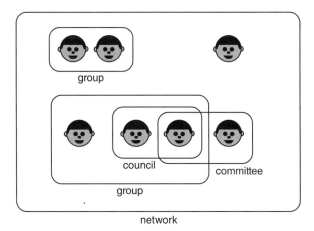

Figure 8.3
Collective social networking.

to capture the "complexity of relationships that activist organizations face in the real world."

Instead, Crabgrass takes what we might call a "collective social networking" approach in which the primary goal is communication and collaboration within and between groups. The central concept for Crabgrass is the "group," which represents a collection of people who are involved with each other on an ongoing basis. Starting from the premise that activist networks are centered on collectives rather than individuals, the designers have developed a nested model of social organization that recognizes hierarchy and supports several kinds of relationships between individuals and groups (figure 8.3). The software makes distinctions between "friends" and "peers," and also supports "committees" (subgroups), "councils" (subgroups with enhanced privileges), and "networks" (collections of groups that are collaborating together on a project). Each of these configurations comes with its own membership and privacy settings that allow individuals and groups to exert fine-grained control over the information they choose to share and with whom. Besides engaging in messaging, groups share media assets including audio and video files, and collaborate to create and edit documents, events, and task lists.

Crabgrass' orientation toward social movements has also led to a reordering of other design priorities. Like many other activist communication systems, Crabgrass privileges privacy and security concerns. For example, users and groups set their own policies governing information sharing, data are stored in an encrypted format, and the default configuration only accepts secure connections between servers and clients.

Crabgrass' voting features are also more supple than the simple "majority wins" tools found on many social media sites. Crabgrass users can create straw polls that allow users to individually rate various options under consideration; the platform also supports instant runoff elections that allow participants to rank options rather than simply choosing a single preference. Advocates for such "alternative voting" mechanisms argue that they are more democratic than simple majority voting because of the protections for minority viewpoints and the ability of users to express more nuanced opinions (Tideman 2006). That they are included in the Crabgrass platform reflects deep and abiding commitments on the part of the system's designers to democratic decision-making and egalitarian processes.

Finally, it is important to note that Crabgrass is offered as both a service and a software platform. Activists and organizations can create accounts on Riseup's servers to utilize Crabgrass' features, but are also encouraged to download the software and host their own services. Doing so enables an organization to maintain stricter control over its data, integrate Crabgrass into existing communication systems, and customize features as needed.

WITNESS Video Hub: Situating Human Rights Videos in an Activist Milieu

WITNESS is a U.S.-based nonprofit organization that promotes the use of video in human rights advocacy. Since its founding in 1988, the organization has provided video cameras to human rights groups, worked with advocacy organizations around the world to produce documentary videos, and distributed videos to journalists and politicians.

In the fall of 2007 WITNESS unveiled "The Hub" (http://hub.witness.org/), a website where individuals and organizations can upload and view human rights–related videos (figure 8.4). The Hub offers similar functionality to other video-sharing sites like YouTube or Dailymotion. Users can upload, view, and rate videos, and engage in discussion with other users by entering comments. WITNESS lists a number of additional features that are currently under development, including support for uploading and viewing videos from mobile phones.

While WITNESS continues to post its videos to a variety of video-sharing sites, the organization argues that the Hub provides an alternative communication channel that is better suited to activists' needs than its commercial counterparts for several reasons. First, the Hub places a premium on protecting the identities of users who post content to the site and of activists who may appear in videos. This is a primary concern in human rights video work, where activists can face imprisonment or worse at the hands of the authorities their work exposes. The Hub's commitment to security extends to the site's policies of not requiring users to provide personal information to the site and their commitment to "never share, sell or trade your personal information. Ever." The Hub also features online identity-protection tutorials and promotes the use of TOR, an open-source software tool that masks IP addresses, making it difficult to associate Internet traffic with specific computers or physical locations.

Figure 8.4
The Hub homepage.

Second, the Hub also differs from commercial sites in that it does not claim owner-ship of the videos that it hosts. Instead, videos are published under Creative Commons licenses that allow activists to repost, repurpose, and reuse videos in advocacy cam-paigns. Although not currently supported, the Hub intends to allow users to download videos so they can be shown in offline venues or reused in new advocacy video produc-tions. The Hub contrasts this with YouTube and other commercial services that own the content on their websites regardless of its provenance, which WITNESS says both limits activist ability to repurpose videos for advocacy and potentially leads to the dis-tasteful spectacle of private enterprise profiting from human rights abuse footage.

Third, the Hub's sole focus on human rights enables advocacy videos to be high-lighted in ways that are impossible on commercial services. The site's founders describe the experience of looking for human rights videos on YouTube as akin to "finding a needle in a haystack" (Jenkins 2008). The sheer volume of videos on commercial sites coupled with the tendency of those sites to feature videos based on popularity or aggregate ranking often has the effect of burying human rights videos under a mountain of pratfalls, music videos, and dancing babies. While YouTube has introduced a "nonprofits and activism" channel, it has quickly become a dumping ground for all manner of fringe movements and conspiracy theories.

Perhaps most importantly, from WITNESS' perspective, the Hub situates human rights videos in an activist milieu. Videos are categorized by issue (for example, "war crimes" or "child labor") and by country. The site contains blog entries and feature articles that highlight particular issues or campaigns, such as "the role of archives in human rights" or "Bhopal: 25 Years of Injustice." The Hub encourages users to join groups organized around various issues and suggests ways for viewers to become directly involved with human rights campaigns by, say, attending real-world events or donating to advocacy organizations. The Hub also offers online training to would-be video activists through a series of "Video Advocacy Guide" videos that instruct viewers on filming, editing, and distributing advocacy videos. These features represent an attempt to go beyond simply distributing human rights video via the web; they are aimed at providing activists with all the tools they need to use those videos in a variety of on- and offline advocacy campaigns.

Designing for Activist Organizations

Ushahidi, Crabgrass, and the Hub were all developed with activist organizations in mind. The use cases envisioned by their designers centered on collective action rather than individual behavior and assumed explicitly political objectives. This unique perspective yielded a distinct set of requirements and features. For instance, Crabgrass offers more sophisticated group management and decision-making capabilities than other social networking platforms, the Hub links video content to activist campaigns and organizations, and Ushahidi allows editors to vouch for the accuracy of users' submissions.

These projects also embody a set of values that reflect the activist communities from which they emerged. For instance, Crabgrass and the Hub privilege user privacy and data security—perennial concerns for activist technology design made more urgent by such well-publicized incidents as Chinese authorities' 2005 arrest of dissident Shi Tao based on information provided by Yahoo! and attempts by U.S. prosecutors in 2010 to charge WikiLeaks founder Julian Assange under the Espionage Act.

Activist designers are often explicit about the ways that ethical values shape their decisions. For example, both WITNESS and the Riseup collective raise concerns about commercialization of activist media. While some of this discussion is framed in instrumental terms (for instance, activists' need to distribute and reuse videos and software), both organizations include a moral dimension in their considerations. Riseup is openly anticorporate and lists a nonprofit orientation among the desirable features in choices it makes about software platforms. While perhaps less radical, WITNESS' discussion of commercial ownership is not limited to concerns about licensing and distribution; the organization also raises the distasteful possibility of commercial sites appearing to profit from human rights video. In explicitly acknowledging the ways that they deliberately encode ethical concerns into technology projects, these designers offer a template for what Friedman, Nussbaum, and others call "value-sensitive design" (Friedman 1996; Flanagan, Howe, and Nissenbaum 2008).

These projects' shared orientation and values do not imply a uniform or consistent set of features or requirements. Indeed, we can identify instances where decisions made by one project are at odds with those made by another. For example, one might suggest that the anonymity the Hub offers its users might allow for the sort of uncorroborated content that Ushahidi's creators were concerned could instigate a violent backlash in postelection Kenya. Recognizing these contradictions points to the importance that specificity plays as a value undergirding these projects. Each project presented here set out to address a narrowly defined need, for a narrowly defined audience. Ushahidi was developed to catalog incidences of postelection violence in Kenya; Crabgrass to facilitate collaboration across activist networks; the Hub to disseminate human rights videos. The specificity of purpose exhibited by these projects is contrasted with commercial services, which are generally designed to support a range of usages by as broad an audience as possible. YouTube, for example, facilitates virtually any type of video sharing; Facebook hosts an ever-expanding portfolio of applications.

This difference in scope is intimately tied to the institutional goals of the organization responsible for each project. YouTube's and Facebook's approaches are aligned with the fact that they are commercial services whose businesses depend on attracting large numbers of users. While the revenue streams for sites like Facebook, YouTube, and Twitter continue to be works in progress, evolving business models appear to be based on delivering advertisements to large numbers of users organized into such easily digestible market segments as geography and interests, and on enabling viral marketing campaigns that exploit insights about social network structure that are gained by conducting data analyses on users.

In contrast, activist organizations generally operate without profit-making considerations and do not necessarily depend on maintaining large constituencies. They can, in a sense, afford to be more specialized than commercial services. This is not to say that activist technology projects are immune from financial considerations; as I have shown elsewhere, they are absolutely influenced by the economic conditions under which they occur (Hirsch 2009a). However, the logics that drive funding decisions affecting activists and NGOs are different than in the commercial sector and are often more closely tied to notions of social impact than to aggregated numbers of users. In the cases described here, social impact is understood in terms of global networks of activist organizations.

Each project described in this chapter was undertaken by an organization that hoped to support other activists, often without direct financial compensation. Each required an activist organization to take on the development and day-to-day management of the project. In all three of the examples presented in the chapter, the design of an activist technology was accompanied by the simultaneous design of an activist organization to manage it. In the case of Ushahidi, a loosely connected network of bloggers coalesced into an NGO initially to take on the roles of developing software and vetting incident reports, and ultimately to evangelize the software to the global activist community, solicit funds, and direct further technical development. With the Hub, the development of a video-sharing site facilitated new relationships between an established organization and other advocacy groups, and required a new set of policies and additional staff responsibilities. Similarly, Crabgrass provides both a new hosting opportunity for the Riseup collective and a set of new organizing capabilities for the organizations that adopt it.

Designing technologies and services for adoption by organizations adds its own set of requirements to software development projects. In addition to thinking through end users' needs and experience, designers have to contend with the adopting organization's institutional goals, including the organization's ability to project its identity through the technology (what we might think of as "branding"), and the ability to act collectively in directing projects, coordinating action, and mobilizing resources. Solutions intended for uptake by organizations also often have to be customized and integrated with existing technical systems and organizational practices. This is a matter of both technology design and technology licensing. For example, Crabgrass offers flexible group-management tools that better reflect the complexities of activist social arrangements than popular social networking software. Because Crabgrass is available under open-source licenses that allow the software to be altered with little cost or restriction, an organization can choose which features meet its needs and can combine Crabgrass with other open-source software products. As a result, organizations can use Crabgrass to integrate group management and other social network features into customized platforms that present constituents with a seamless communication experience. Ushahidi's modular design and its open-source licensing similarly facilitate adoption by other organizations.

Having described activist projects as a distinct form of social media, let us now consider how activist social media relate to commercial services. As Pinch and Bijker

(1984) observe, there is often significant interplay between artifacts produced for different purposes; innovation is often a process of appropriating features developed by one social group for use by another. There is certainly a great deal of back-and-forth between activist and commercial media. For example, much of today's "citizen journalism" is an evolution of the Indymedia movement, and Twitter's creators have credited the activist TXTmob service as an important precursor (Hirsch 2009b). New services like TwitterMap (http://twittermap.tv/) and TwitterVision (http://beta .twittervision.com/) produce map visualizations of Twitter feeds, extending Ushahidi's core functionality. Facebook and other social media services' group-management capabilities continue to evolve in ways that echo Crabgrass' design. Activist media projects similarly borrow from commercial services. Crabgrass is a case in point—it was designed from the get-go as an activist response to the widespread adoption of popular social networking sites.

However, we should also recognize that activist technology projects proceed from an orientation and set of values that are at least partially incompatible with business requirements. For example, it would be difficult to imagine Facebook introducing privacy controls that prohibited the company from conducting social network analysis on its users. Indeed, incommensurability with business objectives is largely the point of activist technology design. Activist projects allow organizations to create communication channels that function independently of commercial offerings. While the need for such channels is often couched in terms of privacy and information security, it also reflects deeper issues in activist communication strategy. As activist groups engage social media to promote their causes, they often find themselves to be "small fish in a vast sea" (Clark 2007). Activist media tend to garner far less interest than other kinds of content on sites primarily used for entertainment. Even when activist messages do garner significant attention, organizations may be frustrated by the tenor of the discussion and the difficulties in translating viewership into committed action. As WITNESS' Sam Gregory puts it, activists' goals of "transforming a transitory audience into an engaged public" are at odds with the structure of commercial sites like YouTube (in Walker 2008). Gregory sees a greater value in disseminating human rights media among committed activists rather than using social media sites to reach largely disengaged audiences—despite their numbers. By enabling activist organizations to create separate discursive spaces for activist concerns, activist technology projects facilitate the creation of what Gregory calls "communities oriented towards action": groups of people who share commitments to one cause or another, and who are oriented toward translating those commitments into concrete action. In short, activist technology projects provide a material substrate that enables movements and organizations to create, nurture, and mobilize *constituencies*: collectives whose orientation toward collective action distinguishes them from the "users" that frequent commercial social media sites.

Conclusion

While commercial services like Facebook, YouTube, and Twitter have become important components of advocacy campaigns around the world, activist technology projects like Ushahidi, Crabgrass, and the WITNESS Video Hub help us see the limits of corporate media services for political activism. As we have seen, activist technology projects often proceed from different models of social organization than their commercial counterparts. Placing activism at the center of technology design highlights new requirements and leads to new features that are absent from tools designed to serve a more general audience. Activist media's unique context leads to innovative solutions that, in some instances, anticipate broader technical trends. Examining emerging practices in activist communities can thus provide a glimpse into one possible future for social and mobile media.

Activist design projects also tend to operate according to a different set of values than their commercial counterparts. While these values may at times be incommensurate with business objectives, looking closely at activist design projects can help us think critically about the assumptions and biases that underpin social media projects more generally. In particular, they help us understand the key role that institutional goals play in shaping social and mobile media technologies and environments, and the policies that govern their use.

References

Castells, M. 2007. *Mobile Communication and Society: A Global Perspective*. Cambridge, MA: MIT Press.

Clark, J. 2007. *Big Dreams, Small Screens: Online Video for Knowledge and Action*. Washington, DC: Center for Social Media, American University. http://www.centerforsocialmedia.org/resources/publications/bigdreams.

Flanagan, M., D. C. Howe, and H. Nissenbaum. 2008. Embodying values in technology: Theory and practice. In J. van den Hoven and J. Weckert, eds., *Information Technology and Moral Philosophy*. Cambridge: Cambridge University Press.

Friedman, B. 1996. Value-sensitive design. *Interactions* 3 (6): 16–23.

Hirsch, T. 2009a. Communities real and imagined: Designing a communication system for Zimbabwean activists. In *Proceedings of the 4th International Conference on Communities and Technologies*, June 25–27, University Park, PA., 71–76. New York: ACM.

Hirsch, T. 2009b. FEATURE: Learning from activists: Lessons for designers. *interactions* 16 (3): 31–33.

Jenkins, H. 2008. From Rodney King to Burma: An interview with Witness' Sam Gregory. *Confessions of an Aca-Fan: The Official Weblog of Henry Jenkins*. http://henryjenkins.org/2008/04/from_rodney_king_to_burma_an_i_1.html.

Meier, Patrick, and Kate Brodock. 2008. *Crisis Mapping Kenya's Election Violence: Comparing Mainstream News, Citizen Journalism and Ushahidi*. Cambridge, MA: Harvard Humanitarian Initiative (HHI), Harvard University. http://irevolution.wordpress.com/2008/10/23/mapping-kenyas-election-violence.

Melucci, A. 1996. *Challenging Codes: Collective Action in the Information Age*. Cambridge: Cambridge University Press.

Morozov, E. 2009. Iran: Downside to the "Twitter revolution." *Dissent* 56 (4): 10–14.

Mungiu-Pippidi, A., and I. Munteanu. 2009. Moldova's "Twitter revolution." *Journal of Democracy* 20 (3): 136–142.

Pang, K. 2009. Burger King drops "Whopper Sacrifice" Facebook Application. *Chicago Tribune*, January 16. http://archives.chicagotribune.com/2009/jan/16/business/chi-0116-talk-whopperjan16.

Pinch, T., and W. Bijker. 1984. The social construction of facts and artefacts: Or how the sociology of science and the sociology of technology might benefit each other. *Social Studies of Science* 14 (3): 339–441.

Rheingold, H. 2002. *Smart Mobs: The Next Social Revolution*. New York: Basic Books.

Shirky, C. 2008. *Here Comes Everybody: The Power of Organizing without Organizations*. New York: Penguin Press.

Singel, R. 2005. A disaster map "Wiki" is born. *Wired*, September 25. http://www.wired.com/software/coolapps/news/2005/09/68743.

Tideman, N. 2006. *Collective Decisions and Voting: The Potential for Public Choice*. Aldershot: Ashgate.

Walker, P. 2008. WITNESS: CCTV for the masses? *Innovations: Technology, Governance, Globalization* 3 (2): 61–65.

9 Gardening Online: A Tale of Suburban Informatics

Bjorn Nansen, Jon M. Pearce, and Wally Smith

Each object gathers around itself a different assembly of relevant parties. Each object triggers new occasions to passionately differ and dispute. Each object may also offer new ways of achieving closure without having to agree on much else. In other words, matters in dispute—taken as so many issues—bound all of us in ways that map out a public space profoundly different from what is usually recognized under the label of "the political."
—Bruno Latour (2005)

This chapter describes a project carried out by the authors to develop and evaluate an online application to help people in suburban Melbourne water their gardens more efficiently. Rather than being a conventional report of design and evaluation work, our intention here is to reflect on the deeper challenge that we encountered, and still face, around the introduction of interactive software into a private, yet increasingly politicized situation. The sense of politics that we have in mind is not the formal one of politicians, public debate, and decision making—important as these are. But rather, it is the kind of politics that gestures to a more informal and mundane form of citizenship. This form of civic participation includes cultural practices such as leisure and consumer activities (Burgess, Foth, and Klaebe 2006), and it acknowledges that such practices are reflected in and created through a "politics of things"—the uses and arrangements of everyday objects (Latour 2005). In this case, the affective and material practices of gardening, which are normally excluded from political processes, emerge as a site of expression for cultural citizenship. This kind of citizenship, we will argue, bears on the act of designing new technologies that seek entrance into established situations like gardening. We describe our project as a tale in "suburban informatics," because it attempted to use interactive software and social media to connect situated, ephemeral, and private suburban practice with more public, formalized, and enduring kinds of forums in the pursuit of civic participation.

To set the scene, we begin with a story of suburban "water rage." On Wednesday, October 30, 2007, a sixty-six-year-old man, Ken Proctor, was watering his front lawn in the Sydney suburb of Sylvania, when a passerby, Todd Munter, accused him of wasting water. Proctor turned his hose on Munter, who responded by punching and knocking Proctor to the ground before kicking him. Proctor suffered a heart attack and, despite Munter's attempts to resuscitate him, died a short time later. In early 2009, Munter was sentenced to three years and three months in prison for manslaughter. This story reminds us how everyday water use is becoming increasingly contested and politicized in Australia. Or rather, water is returning to its more usual politicized state, as the modern promise of an engineered and endless supply begins to falter (Strang 2004). As with many other affluent countries, persistent drought and looming climate change are severely straining the certainty of water flows. The normal politics of government has intervened in Australia with state-specific restrictions that limit watering to specified days and that outlaw some activities such as washing cars or watering lawns. These offer to bring a sense of fairness in water use, though ironically, Proctor was actually entitled under council restrictions to water with a hose on the day he was attacked and killed. What normal politics cannot change, immediately at least, are the norms and accepted practices of watering and their inscriptions in the technologies and material arrangements of gardening. Everyday water use—how it is consumed, used, and reused in the support of leisure activities, domestic routines, cleanliness, and private gardens—has now emerged as a critical arena for civic and environmental engagement.

The project we describe here was a collaboration with horticultural scientists who had been working on a longer project to study garden water needs and use. The horticultural project envisaged a lone gardener using a computer and mathematical model to plan and manage a suitable watering regime. However, subsequent design of the online application and evaluation of it in the field (or rather garden) has pointed us toward a different vision of garden watering and the ways it might be supported. In what follows we describe the thinking behind the original design, its reception by gardeners, and the design challenge that emerged. As already suggested, this challenge concerns the way garden watering is deeply embedded in the physical spaces, tools, and arrangements of the garden, as opposed to being an activity that follows directly from detached and deliberative decision making. This insight draws on the theories from the field of science and technology studies (STS), notably Actor-Network Theory (ANT), to see gardens and their watering as deeply localized and sociotechnical practices that are organized through a distributed arrangement of entities, including humans, plants, and technologies (Hitchings 2003; Latour 2005). This networked or relationally oriented approach directs our attention to theoretical and practical questions of changing garden watering practices, but it also directs us to broader questions about research methods and design work in collaborative projects, and to political questions about how to promote collective and sustainable action for ambitious civic goals. Thus, sociotechnical theory can help to address the contexts and outcomes of HCI research, design, and implementation. This is fundamentally about the inseparability of its social dimensions from its material and distributed forms. In this instance the influence of gardening norms, shared practices, and transfers of knowledge has pointed us toward the use of social networking technologies to enhance our software and for the possibility of a broader community engaging in water conservation.

In the next section, we describe how the project arose through a collaboration between horticulturalists and interaction designers, and outline the project's key aims. We then follow with a sketch of the first version of the application (called SmartGardenWatering, SGW 1.0), leading to a report of its reception by gardeners. Next we describe the theoretical impetus and design challenges for the development of a second version (SGW 2.0), which adopts some Web 2.0 technologies. In conclusion, we briefly reflect on how the application of ideas from STS to HCI can bring a practical understanding of emerging spaces and formations of community engagement, citizenship, and politics.

The Collaborative Research and Design Project

The motivation behind the SmartGardenWatering project was to provide expert, scientific advice to Melbourne gardeners about how to be more efficient in their gardens with water use. The project was initiated by two horticulturalists (Geoff Connellan and Peter May, Department of Resources and Land Management, University of Melbourne), who obtained funding from the Smart Water Fund (2009) in 2005 to generate research data on plant water requirements and to convey it in a meaningful way to the public. Connellan and May believed there was a paucity of knowledge in the general community about how much water plants needed. While they had the scientific knowledge and resources to gather further data through research, they realized that conveying this knowledge to the public in an effective manner would be a challenge. Hence, in 2005, they approached an author of this chapter to assist in producing software to communicate their water model and data. After two years of gathering data relating to plant water use, performance of mulches, soil moisturizing agents, and watering systems, they developed a mathematical model to determine a watering schedule for Melbourne gardeners. During the third year of the project (2008), two of the authors of this chapter explored how to represent this work in a way accessible to gardeners and the first version of the software program was launched. This was an interesting challenge. It required us to take a large amount of research data, horticultural expertise, and a formative water model to design software that would allow nonexperts to explore it, manipulate it, and learn from it.

It is instructive to think through one of the ways that the simulation software was designed to bring new knowledge to the gardener. The simulation model carries an in-built assumption (based on research) that the ideal depth of water to deliver to a garden at any one watering is 10 mm. As water soaks into the ground, it wets a considerable depth of soil; 10 mm of watering will soak through to a depth of about 200 mm. To apply much less than 10 mm of water (so less than 200 mm depth) risks encouraging shallow root growth. But more than 10 mm is likely to result in loss of water as it drains down below the top 200 mm of soil—this is where most of a plant's feeder roots are found. Hence the gardener needs to know (1) how long a watering system should run in order to deliver a 10 mm dose, given that the efficiency of application is not perfect due to a number of factors like runoff, absorption by mulch, possible loss due to wind, and so on, and (2) how frequently this 10 mm dose should be applied, given that some will transpire through the plant, some will evaporate, and some will drain through the soil. Based on the research done by the horticultural team, the software uses the above factors to determine the water schedule. It takes into account the flow rates of various common watering devices, the impact on efficiencies due to runoff, mulch and climate conditions, the evapotranspiration of various plants, and the impacts of different soil types. The calculation of the watering schedule has to take these parameters into account, as well as data about average rainfall and evaporation rates in the garden's location.

The design approach began in a traditional HCI manner of working closely with the horticultural experts, defining scenarios and user personas, and experimenting with possible screens with members of the target user group (Pearce, Murphy, and Smith 2008). An emerging aim was to produce a resource for general application that was fun to use and encouraged exploration of the scientific model of water consumption. Hence the project shifted from one of simply presenting scientific research data to the public, toward one of presenting an environment in which the public could confidently explore and experiment to produce a practical outcome (a watering schedule) as well as an educational outcome (to better understand how various factors affect garden water use). This shifting aim toward greater interaction and education was manageable only insofar as it could be agreed and accommodated by the various parties involved, which included the funding body, the scientists, the HCI designers, and users. Or, to put it another way, the direction was only viable if the network of actors did not break up under the translation of aims and meaning. Central to this, the software served as a focal point of the network around which the actors managed their various accountabilities to others (see Suchman, Trigg, and Blomberg 2002). Equally important in this emerging and shifting network around the project were the nonhuman "actants," including the software, plants, and watering technologies. This view of the project, then, emphasizes the deeply connected nature of research and design, which in Latourian terms is a political situation where an assembly of relevant parties and things gather around the design object. Rather than a simple process of finding out user needs and meeting them through design, this suggests a more complex picture that must accommodate multiple requirements, and in this case necessitated beginning with the more intractable and immutable water needs of plants before turning to the more mutable practices of people.

SmartGardenWatering.org.au

We named the software "SmartGardenWatering" (SGW 1.0), and this section now describes it. The SmartGardenWatering software is a Flash application that allows Melburnians to model their garden characteristics (size, area, plants, physical conditions, watering devices) and obtain a schedule for watering throughout the year, as well as advice on the performance of rainwater tanks. The user begins by entering the postcode of their home, after which they are informed of the average rainfall and soil type for that area. They then define one or more "zones." A zone is an area of the garden that is served by one watering system (e.g., a vegetable patch watered using a dripper, shrubs watered with a soaker hose, etc.). Next, users are taken to the main screen of the program that allows them to enter information about each garden zone using four horizontal "accordion-style" tabs: "plants," "conditions," "watering," and "schedule" (figure 9.1). These accordions slide up and down as the user clicks on them.

The "plants" tab allows users to describe what plants are contained in each zone by choosing from a "quick selection" of major plant groups, or from a more detailed

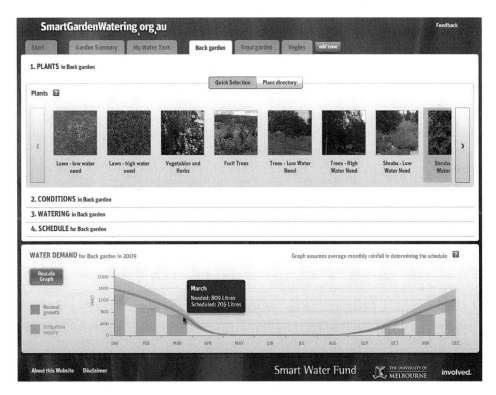

Figure 9.1
Main screen showing plant choice and demand graph.

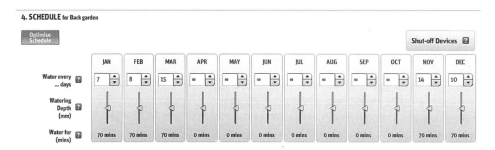

Figure 9.2
Schedule tab showing how frequency and duration of watering can be adjusted.

database of 1,500 plants (taken from the *Burnley Plant Directory* (Burnley 2009)). This immediately displays an animated line on the graph at the bottom of the screen (the solid line in figure 9.1). This represents the water demand of the garden throughout the year. From here on, this line updates in an animated fashion as changes are made to any settings in the program. The "conditions" tab presents choices relating to the physical conditions within that particular zone of the garden: area of the zone, an option to change soil type, density of planting, microclimate conditions, slope, and the type of mulch applied. The "watering" accordion presents a choice of watering devices (drip hoses, above or below mulch, soaker hoses, sprays, etc.). When a selection is made, blue bars appear on the graph showing the calculated schedule for each month of the year (these can been seen at the left and right ends of the graph in figure 9.1; one of them is highlighted with a rollover). It will be noticed that the bars sit just *below* the demand line displayed on the graph. The shaded band above and below the line indicates a region moving from *just surviving* to *lush garden growth* and the program aims to produce a schedule that errs on the conservative side of this region. If users wish, they may modify the schedule in the next tab.

The "schedule" tab allows manual adjustment of the watering schedule (figure 9.2). This may be required if the user wishes to have a particularly lush garden, or maybe notices an alert that warns of a violation of current watering restrictions. Such violations can often be resolved by decreasing the *frequency* of watering and increasing the *duration* (depth) of watering.

Finally, a "My water tank" tab at the top of the screen (figure 9.1) allows the user to explore how a water tank would perform if connected to one or more of the garden zones. The important parameters here are the tank capacity, the collection roof area, at what time of the year the tank is expected to be empty (or full), and to which zone(s) it is attached. The user is able to print out a summary of all the schedule information and water demands produced by the program.

Going into the Garden: The Reception of SGW 1.0

To evaluate the SGW 1.0 interface we conducted a field study of how gardeners go about watering their gardens, and how readily and how well they could use SGW 1.0. This stage of the research was timed to coincide with the public launch of version 1.0 of the SGW tool, with responses to be analyzed to feed the requirements for the development of a later version (SGW 2.0). The study involved twenty participants in Melbourne, with fieldwork interviews taking place during the late summer and early autumn of 2009, which was part of a significant period of drought. Participants were recruited through canvassing at the 2009 Melbourne International Garden and Flower Show; snowballing from other participants; contacts with community gardening groups; and through social networks of researchers. Despite a small sample size, the sampling strategy was designed to include a degree of variability in suburban location, garden type and age, gardening expertise, watering methods, sources, devices, and routines.

The method of the study began with a "garden tour." This involved the participants walking through their garden, talking through their watering techniques and approach, and often carrying out watering tasks. The researcher followed, observing acts of watering and photographing the garden arrangements. This was followed by a semistructured interview about watering approaches related to garden watering history; current routines, techniques, and timing of watering; devices used and interacted with in the act of watering the garden; and sources of knowledge about garden watering. This garden-tour method was employed in order to situate the research in the place where the object of study occurred, and thus to assist participants in the visual recognition and recall of the numerous idiosyncrasies of watering practices. Following the tour and interview, participants were given the URL of SGW to explore and with which to model their garden. After a week, a second interview in participants' homes was conducted to gather their feedback, experience with, and reflections on the software. Again, this interview took place in the location of practice, with the researcher sitting with the participant in front of the screen while the SGW program was navigated and discussed.

The interviews indicated some enthusiasm for the online application, while also turning up some fairly standard, and even expected, usability problems. For example, the initial zone-defining screen was found to be confusing, as was navigating the plant database and using the hand-watering calculation (see Pearce et al. 2009 for more information). But as indicated earlier, our aim in this chapter is not to review these findings in detail, most of which are fixable in principle and so somewhat uninteresting theoretically. What we are concerned with here is something more intangible: a deeper design problem that we inferred in this attempt to introduce online software into the world of gardening. This deeper challenge is less definite than a list of usability problems, and harder to articulate. Nevertheless, it is probably more influential in directing our design thinking, and so in the remainder of this section we will sketch the issues around it, and continue this into the following sections where we discuss a future version of the software. In essence, the deeper design challenge might be stated as the problem of how gardeners might connect the software to their personal garden watering practice *and* to the larger world of garden watering practices. A number of disparate observations underlie this sense of a design challenge.

One surprise in the study was the wide range of existing water minimization technologies and techniques adopted in private suburban gardens. Techniques included familiar things such as replacing plants and lawn with hardier types; putting mulch on the garden; installing "off-the-shelf" or commercial watering devices such as reticulated systems (drips placed under mulch), as well as tanks; and reusing gray water from inside the house ("gray water" is used broadly here to refer to any form of recycled domestic water). Also on show were the full range of watering devices, and most gardeners used a combination of types: reticulated systems, both automatic and manual; drip hoses, above or below mulch; soaker hoses; handheld hoses; sprays; and bucketing water. The more "low-tech" options remained the dominant modes in comparison to expensive and/or elaborate reticulated or automatic systems. But the range of techniques and technologies also included many DIY efforts to capture, store, and redirect water. DIY efforts were those that did not involve the purchase of a commercial solution, but were instead more vernacular and improvised techniques such as using bins, cutting holes in downpipes, and channeling water with extra PVC piping. Collectively, these strategies encompassed using less water, using water more efficiently, storing water, and reusing water. What the study suggested, for our sample at least, was that water use was very much bound up with idiosyncratic, hybrid, and subtle arrangements for garden watering. This challenged the scope or relevance of the tool, because inscribed in SGW 1.0 applicability, were simpler or quantifiable arrangements involving more orderly, measurable, or "programmable" watering technologies.

A central issue in the uptake of SGW 1.0, then, relates to the ease with which the tool can be integrated into or encompass the diversity of garden watering practices, technologies, and especially the more informal and often messy methods of watering developed by domestic gardeners. The interviews confirmed the expected finding that the tool is better accommodated within automated and reticular watering devices and systems. It was more difficult to integrate and so transform garden watering in relation to more improvised methods and devices—such as bucketing gray water on the garden—which is less predictable, often fleeting, and harder to quantify or model with a high degree of certainty. The representative of our sample is clearly an issue in presenting such a finding. But at a minimum, the study suggests that regardless of the increase or uptake of standardized, formal, and commercial systems for watering gardens, which are more efficient in their use of water, more informal and low-tech options will inevitably persist, even if only at the periphery of garden watering practices.

This important insight of the study about gardening, as a set of localized and sociotechnical practices, reflects well-developed theories in social and cultural research on technology in use. The significance and more general existence of such everyday formations beyond gardening have been described in cultural geography as "routine creativity" (Shove et al. 2007) and in media studies as "vernacular creativity" (Burgess 2006). Further, the picture of gardeners presented here echoes a number of recent ethnographic and qualitative analyses of water consumption and sustainability informed by ANT and STS (Allon and Sofoulis 2006; Head and Muir 2007; Sofoulis 2005; Van Vliet, Chappells, and Shove 2005). These studies amend approaches that locate their research, explanations, or solutions to water resource management and sustainability with either the individual and demand-side management (i.e., psychological determinants of behavior), *or* with the population and supply-side strategies (i.e., engineering solutions). Instead, the fundamental insight of this area of social science is that effective and sustainable strategies for reducing water consumption and for enabling community engagement do not lie simply with individuals and changing their attitudes, or with scientific knowledge or engineering new infrastructures. Rather, in acknowledging that individual action is informed (and constrained) by the material and technical dimensions of social life, this research suggests that solutions to reduce domestic and garden water use and increased engagement are to be found in more distributed "sociotechnical" and "intermediate" arrangements (Sofoulis 2005). These are situated between individual consumption and infrastructural provision, and can be achieved by bringing together the "distributed competencies" (Shove et al. 2007) of experts, systems of provision, water authorities, gardeners, and the materials or technologies they use to water their gardens. This acknowledges the value of localized knowledge and of vernacular sociotechnical garden watering practices, which are often too complex to be accommodated within the material limitations of a scientific model based on quantifiable data but can nevertheless operate in complementary ways in a shared project of water conservation.

This theory has important implications for and presents a challenge to HCI design: How to design "suburban informatics" that are able to integrate with existing and largely situated, idiosyncratic, and low-tech private suburban practices? One of ANT's contributions is to problematize the distinction between the social and the material. In thinking about gardening, then, we might see that material arrangements of the garden—the hoses, taps, drippers, plants, beds, paths—embody the sociality of gardening, its norms and accepted practices. Taking this further, it might be seen that the difficulty of SGW 1.0 in connecting with the idiosyncratic materiality of each garden is at once a problem of failing to connect with the social sphere of distributed but shared garden practice. In its current form, SGW 1.0 attempts to bring the authority of science to the consideration of gardeners. But in various ways, discussed in the next section, many of our gardeners did not submit to the authority of this expertise that had supposedly been delegated to a piece of software. Or we might say that the device brought an uncomfortable kind of social presence that was often not accepted because it did not connect with the social realm of gardening. Considerations of this sort led us to take the next version of the software toward a Web 2.0 or social media application. The thinking was that such an application might encourage a politics of things for civic engagement by building shared public platforms or networks for participation and exchanges that mobilize private practices, vernacular resourcefulness, and material affordances in relationships with water authorities, science, and other water users.

SmartGardenWatering 2.0

Some of the authors applied for and received further funding from the Smart Water Fund to extend the project through 2009–2010 to establish an online community of gardeners who could model their gardens and their watering needs, save and share their models, and communicate within an online gardening community. As part of this, the intention is to improve on the basic usability problems and also increase the flexibility of the tool to integrate with disparate water arrangements. Hence this extended project is focused on improving the software, as well as designing and establishing an online community. We also aim to validate the existing water model through field trials in which water use and garden conditions will be monitored in people's homes. We first describe some of the changes being made to the software, then outline the new Web 2.0 features being added. We refer to this new software as SGW 2.0.

To chip away at the deeper design challenge, we are attempting to identify specific aspects of the obstacles that block connection between the software and gardening practice. One of our aims in revising the program was to reduce its apparent complexity. We approached this task through several changes to the design, as well as changing the programming environment from Flash to XHTML and Javascript on top of a server-side web application and database. Many users told us that they wanted the program to tell them how long to water using a handheld hose. We have simplified the calculation to facilitate this. The schedule screen (figure 9.2) was quite off-putting to some. It was included to allow users to alter their schedule should they want a lusher garden than the program would allow—or maybe their installation of a water tank meant that they were not restricted by the water-restriction regulations. This screen has been removed and replaced with a smart calculation that simply calculates a dose as close as possible to the optimum dose of 10 mm (see figure 9.1). Access to the advanced plant database has been vastly improved to make exploring plants easier and more enjoyable.

A further effort to facilitate connection to gardening practice is in addressing some users' concerns that the program was not clever enough. These concerns tended to come from expert gardeners who used their knowledge to evaluate the accuracy of the recommendations rather than accept them at face value, and from others who realized that the schedule was based on average rainfall patterns and could not take into account recent rain events. To this end we are currently exploring the display of recent rainfall and evaporation measurements. We are carrying out research into the use of both desktop and mobile devices to indicate whether rain has fallen in the past few days in the user's suburb or if unusually high evaporation has occurred, and then advise whether to skip or add a watering based on these events.

The most significant changes to the new version are in the area of social networking. We aim to create a community of gardeners sharing ideas about how they are managing to keep their gardens thriving with minimum water use. Users are able to register within the program and save their modeled gardens to return to later and edit. In doing this, we seek to introduce Web 2.0's mode of interaction—play, socializing, display—for the purposes of engaging "users" in a form of civic participation in the project of domestic water conservation. The saved garden models are available to others who may wish to view them and learn from the way they have organized plants, used water tanks, constructed watering systems, and so on. They are accessible through a Google Maps interface and users will be encouraged to explore other gardens and rate them. An important part of an online community like this is to be able to share comments and even photos; however, this faces severe challenges such at the prohibitive cost of providing moderation. We have chosen to link to Facebook for this purpose and set up groups to encourage and support such interactions.

In taking these steps, we are attempting to move away from a model in which scientists pass a sanctioned form of knowledge about garden management to the public. We have become sensitive to the fact that gardens are special places and many gardeners will not readily accept, often for good reason, the authority of impersonally delivered scientific information and calculation. Through our software design, we express the belief that the means to share and exchange gardening practices will create a different kind of authority and legitimacy. Through its encounter with a public rather than an isolated individual, the site offers the potential to gather together the expert knowledge of science with the vernacular knowledge and routine creativity of gardeners.

Theoretical and Practical Implications for HCI Design

Having outlined our experience of SGW 1.0 and our thinking for SGW 2.0, we now offer more general reflections on the way we have approached the design of these artifacts. This brings us back to the chapter's opening discussion of how a recognition of distributed sociotechnical arrangements and contexts, informed by STS and ANT theory, might contribute to HCI design projects. The main question to be explored is: How might these sociological theories help us to locate our design projects within the emerging spaces and formations of community engagement, citizenship, and politics? This operates beyond traditional and formal sites of political expression to include more culturally inflected dimensions, such as affective, leisure, and consumer activities.

Our design intention is for SGW 2.0 to support what Burgess, Foth, and Klaebe (2006) describe as online communities of "episodic" or "occasional" publics. These are less institutionally organized or enduring spheres of public engagement, but instead emerge provisionally in new spaces and around nascent issues. As Burgess, Foth, and Klaebe (2006, 1) write, "new media opens up opportunities for the greater visibility and community-building potential of cultural citizenship's previously 'ephemeral' practices." SGW 2.0 allows for the ephemeral or invisible practices, and forms of technology use and engagement, in offline, backyard water conservation to be presented and shared online—with the desired effect of contributing to water sustainability as an aspect of everyday civic life. It thereby affords participatory forms of cultural engagement and citizenship in ways that complement new media with older and low-tech media. Inscribed in SGW 2.0 is an attempt to promote opportunities for communicating and sharing ideas, practices, and efforts to facilitate more emergent solutions for the future of water sustainability.

Drawing on ANT, such episodic and occasional publics need to be recognized as relationally organized and realized in materially distributed ways that are not confined to assemblies of humans, but include what Latour (2005) describes as a "parliament of things." Latour foregrounds the part played by nonhuman entities in political spaces, associations, and processes. Here materials present affordances that work to organize particular meanings, practices, and performances. This not only challenges the anthropocentrism of democratic processes, but also shows how many contemporary political and ecological disputes involve the representation and inclusion of nonhuman entities. This points to an ethical need to include or account for a broad constituency of people and objects within a particular assembly. Just as cultural citizenship questions what it means to participate and how people participate in a democracy, Latour questions who gets to participate in a political process. Who represents others? The present research reflects the significance of sociotechnical dimensions for culture and cultural citizenship as an expanded milieu of civic engagement. This is a more inclusive citizenship that brings nature and technologies into the participatory and representative space assemblies of humans.

Consider how the design approach taken here attempts to support the development of new relationships between nature (rainfall or the water requirements of plants); culture (expert knowledge, water providers, and regulators); technology (systems of provision and watering); and people (the symbolic and phenomenological dimensions of gardens). These are not seamless or fixed connections, but situated configurations that afford and constrain patterns of interaction. This establishes an unstable politics, characterized by uncertainties, antagonisms, and challenges to forms of participation. In the present context, the ephemeral and visible dimensions of participation in such networks raise questions for sustainability or cooperation as a critical aspect of water use in domestic gardens.

One important implication of this perspective for the SGW 2.0 project is the possibility of failure resulting from a "lack" of participation or even conflict. Failure to generate participation is the ever-present, and perhaps the greatest, danger facing every HCI project, though it is not easily expressed or addressed in the field's technical language. Failure to participate in SGW 2.0 reflects the debates around cultural economies of attention and the competing demands in everyday mediated life, where an exhaustive number of issues and objects clamor for attention. It presents problems for designing *for* participatory culture, where a certain kind of participation is introduced by online and social networks—one that privileges an ideal of continuous, active, and visible participation. This may not integrate with established forms of "offline" participation noted above around the vernacular creativity and use of analog technologies in private gardens. Such offline forms of participation, involving interactions with gardens and water in backyards, remain largely invisible, discontinuous, and disconnected from a broader public, and so may not be easily translated into other spheres or domains. Alternatively, the fear of antagonism and conflict rather than cooperation and engagement relates to the contested values around water use, as illustrated by the earlier story of "water rage." With something as politicized as water, there is a certain wariness to making oneself identifiable or visible in an online public.

Despite these social limits, in addition to the material limits of the software, it is hoped that a sociotechnical approach can promote collective and sustainable action. For this, the use of social media and "suburban informatics" is not envisaged as a design solution, but rather as contributing to an interactive and collaborative space that will encourage more participatory models of environmental engagement. It is also hoped this will support a community of broader constituents, accommodate competing knowledge and interests, and connect situated, ephemeral, and private suburban practice with more public, formalized, and enduring kinds of forums for the expression of cultural citizenship and a politics of things.

Conclusion

This chapter has discussed the design and reception of an application to assist people in using water more efficiently in their gardens; it has also elaborated on the design challenge for the ongoing development of this application through the use of social media technologies. As noted, the challenge of developing such an application to support gardeners in their watering directs our attention to a number of theoretical, practical, and political questions. These relate to garden watering as a localized and sociotechnical practice, which is organized through a distributed arrangement of human, natural, and technological entities, knowledge, and activities. Recognizing such distributed processes and configurations can contribute to a broader understanding of emerging spaces and formations of community engagement, citizenship, and politics. Yet, this also has implications for the value and efficacy of HCI design projects, such as SGW 2.0, as a form of "suburban informatics" directed toward supporting water conservation in domestic gardens.

References

Allon, Fiona, and Zoe Sofoulis. 2006. Everyday water: Cultures in transition. *Australian Geographer* 37:45–55.

Burgess, Jean. 2006. Hearing ordinary voices: Cultural studies, vernacular creativity and digital storytelling. *Continuum: Journal of Media & Cultural Studies* 20 (2): 201–214.

Burgess, Jean, Marcus Foth, and Helen Klaebe. 2006. Everyday creativity as civic engagement: A cultural citizenship view of new media. Paper presented at the Communications Policy & Research Forum, Sydney 25–26 September.

Burnley Plant Directory. 2009. http://www.land-environment.unimelb.edu.au/urbanhorticul ture/.

Connellan, Geoff, Peter May, and Liz Denman. 2008. Decision support tool to aid in the watering assessment of Melbourne household gardens. Paper presented at the Irrigation Australian Conference, Melbourne, May 20–22.

Head, Lesley, and Pat Muir. 2007. Changing cultures of water in eastern Australian backyard garden. *Social & Cultural Geography* 8 (6): 889–905.

Hitchings, Russell. 2003. People, plants and performance: On actor network theory and the material pleasures of the private garden. *Social & Cultural Geography* 4 (1): 99–113.

Latour, Bruno. 2005. From realpolitik to dingpolitik or how to make things public. In B. Latour and Peter Weibel, eds., *Making Things Public: Atmospheres of Democracy*, 14–41. Cambridge, MA: MIT Press.

Pearce, Jon, John Murphy, and Wally Smith. 2008. Supporting gardeners to plan domestic watering: A case study of designing an "everyday simulation." Paper presented at the OzCHI 2008 Conference, Cairns, Australia, December, 10–12.

Pearce, Jon, Wally Smith, Bjorn Nansen, and John Murphy. 2009. SmartGardenWatering: Experiences of using a garden watering simulation. In M. Foth, J. Kjeldskov, and J. Paay, eds., Proceedings of OZCHI 2009, 217–224.

Shove, Elizabeth, Matthew Watson, Martin Hand, and Jack Ingram. 2007. *The Design of Everyday Life*. New York: Berg.

Smart Water Fund. 2009. http://www.smartwater.com.au.

Sofoulis, Zoe. 2005. Big water, everyday water: A sociotechnical perspective. *Continuum: Journal of Media & Cultural Studies* 19:445–463.

Strang, Veronica. 2004. *The Meaning of Water*. Oxford: Berg.

Suchman, Lucy, Randall Trigg, and Jeannette Blomberg. 2002. Working artefacts: Ethnomethods of the prototype. *British Journal of Sociology* 53 (2): 163–179.

Van Vliet, Bas, Heather Chappells, and Elizabeth Shove. 2005. *Infrastructures of Consumption: Environmental Innovation in the Utility Industries*. London: Earthscan.

10 The Rise of the Expert Amateur: Citizen Science and Microvolunteerism

Eric Paulos, Sunyoung Kim, and Stacey Kuznetsov

If you cannot measure it you cannot improve it.
—Lord Kelvin (Preece et al. 1884)

Bureaucrats sometimes do not have the correct information, while citizens and users of resources do.
—Elinor Ostrom (1990), winner of the 2009 Nobel Prize in Economics

Manifesto

We are at an important technological inflection point. Most of our computing systems have been designed and built by professionally trained experts (i.e., computer scientists, engineers, and designers) for use in specific domains and to solve explicit problems. Documents often called "user manuals" traditionally prescribed the appropriate usage of these tools and implied an acceptable etiquette for interaction and experience. A fringe group of individuals, usually labeled "hackers" or "nerds," have challenged this producer-consumer model of technology by hacking novel hardware and software features to "improve" our research and products. A similar creative group of technicians called "artists" have redirected the techniques, tools, and tenets of accepted technological usage away from their typical manifestations in practicality and product. Over time the technological artifacts of these fringe groups and the support for their rhetoric have gained them a foothold in computing culture and eroded the established power discontinuities within the practice of computing research. We now expect our computing tools to be driven by an architecture of open participation and democracy that encourages users to add value to their tools and applications as they use them. Similarly, the bar for enabling the design of novel personal computing systems and "hardware remixes" has fallen to the point where many nonexperts and novices are readily embracing and creating fascinating and ingenious computing artifacts outside of our official and traditionally sanctioned academic and industrial research communities.

How have we as "expert" practitioners been influencing this discussion? By often constructing our practice around the design of technology for task-based and problem-solving applications, we have unintentionally established such work as the status quo for the human computing experience. We have failed in our duty to open up alternate forums for technology to express itself and touch our lives beyond productivity and efficiency. Blinded by our quest for "smart technologies," we have forgotten to contemplate the design of technologies to inspire us to be smarter, more curious (Paulos et al. 2008), and more inquisitive. We owe it to ourselves to rethink the impact we desire to have on this historic moment in computing culture. We must choose to engage with and perhaps lead a dialog that heralds an expansive new practice of designing to enable participation by experts and nonexperts alike.

We are experiencing the rise of the "expert amateur." We must change our mantra: "not just usability but usefulness and relevance to our world, its citizens, and our environment." We must design for the world and what matters. This means discussing our computing research alongside new keywords such as the economy, the environment, activism, poverty, healthcare, famine, agriculture, soil, food, homelessness, literacy, religion, and politics. We must design new models of participation and volunteerism. While traditional mechanisms for volunteering exist, most involve commitments on the order of hours (e.g., beach cleanup), days (e.g., Habitat for Humanity), months (e.g., Peace Corps), or years (e.g., national military service).

Microvolunteerism explores the newly emerging design territory for volunteering on the order of seconds—"I have forty-two seconds at this bus stop; how can I volunteer?" In this chapter we attempt to explore the research design territory and the potential for all of us to collaborate and benefit as a society from this cultural movement. Through the lens of a series of research projects and design interventions, we detail the challenges and opportunities for leveraging the power of citizens, low-cost sensing, and ubiquitous technologies to facilitate real, positive environmental change.

Environment, Technology, and Us

As computer scientists, engineers, and technologists we have a long history of problem solving. However, many of today's challenges—the problems that often matter most—can be classified as societal-scale "wicked problems" (Rittel and Webber 1973, 1974) where stakeholders have radically different views on the definition and explanation of the problem, the formulation and acceptability of possible solutions, as well as the meaning and permanence of "success." Wicked problems, such as environmental sustainability, are best approached through design research (Laurel 2003) where a range of provocations is often used in a loose, creative process focused more on problem making than on problem solving. This problem creation often reframes the issues and encourages innovation and nonincremental solutions that genuinely ameliorate key aspects of the original problem.

There is an ethical obligation for all of us to address issues of concern to humans, our society, and the environment. Encouragingly, a plethora of human-computer interaction (HCI) practitioners have confronted societal issues such as environmental sustainability by reappropriating traditional HCI techniques. As HCI researchers and designers, we may lack the technical proficiency to innovate novel battery technologies, energy-saving lighting, or a hydrogen vehicle transportation infrastructure. However, we do have the ability to draw on a wide range of tremendously valuable skills involving computing practices focused on culture, society, gaming, persuasion, emotion, play, interaction, and so on. We are also proficient at designing novel research methodologies to approach and study such problems. It is this range of creative strategies that is essential to finding solutions to societal level problems such as environmental sustainability. While considerable foundational research has emerged at this intersection of design research, HCI, and the environment (Dourish 2010, Blevis 2007; DiSalvo et al. 2009; DiSalvo, Sengers, and Brynjarsdóttir 2010; Foth et al. 2008; Woodruff et al. 2008; Woodruff and Mankoff 2009), we are still very much at the inception of ideals and principles for this movement. Unlike previous approaches to complex problems, we are rapidly entering an era of a hyperparticipatory culture. Where in the 1960s the challenge of sending humans to the moon and returning them safely was ultimately solved by the brave scientists and engineers of the day, solutions to current human challenges such as those surrounding environmental issues will ultimately include highly collaborative and participatory approaches. Innovations involving not only scientists, but more importantly, everyday citizens and nonexperts are crucial. One cultural methodology we can impart across our technological practices as well as personal technologies like mobile phones to foster this participatory culture, is that of citizen science (Beck, Giddens, and Lash 1994; Irwin 1995; Corburn 2005).

In this chapter we outline a framework for operationalizing citizen science practices that engage us across a range of personal and public digital technologies. We narrate a series of investigative insights and research developments within the scope of participatory practices involving a range of technologies beyond mobile phones and cultural engagements. We are hopeful that this work will inspire further research regarding human health and environmental issues by empowering everyday people to learn, understand, act, improve, and broaden their awareness of the environment and improve the health and well-being of humans and our world.

Citizen Science

The concept of nonexpert citizens collecting scientific data has existed for well over a hundred years (LeBaron 2006). However, a renewed manifestation of citizen science has emerged, invigorated by the recent introduction of open development platforms for sensor-rich mobile phones, demonstrations of the power of crowdsourcing, and the cultural adoption of participatory practices to research, build, and study systems that allow everyday people to act as "citizen scientists" in collecting, sharing, educating, raising awareness, and solving problems across our landscapes and ecosystems. This new, technologically enabled cultural practice often refocuses our landscapes as living laboratories where citizens play a new and active role in sharing, reporting, and interpreting, personally collected data to help facilitate scientific research. These efforts are aimed at exposing the dynamic interactions between people and the natural ecosystems and improving overall human health and well-being. This data-collection practice augments traditional scientific data-sampling techniques by introducing an important new actor, everyday nonexpert citizens with sensor-equipped mobile phones. This new approach has the potential to radically change and expand the model of how scientific research is conducted.

Citizen science (Irwin 1995) builds on a large body of related projects that enable citizens to act as agents of change. There is a long history of such movements from grassroots neighborhood watch campaigns to political revolutions. One of the better known movements is the National Audubon Society's Christmas Bird Count (CBC), where a census of birds in the Western Hemisphere has been performed annually by citizens since 1900 (LeBaron 2006). More recently, the immense public interest in such collective movements has been attested by the success of online approaches such as SETI@Home (Anderson et al. 2002); citizen-sensing strategies such as "The Great World Wide Star Count," an international event that encourages everyone to go outside, look skyward after dark, and report the count of stars they see (in effect measuring light pollution) (Ward et al. 2008); and "Project BudBurst," where people submit time-stamped images of when flowers in their city bloom (in effect a phenological study of climate and pollen counts) (Meymaris et al. 2008). There are also many examples of citizen science projects that have outpaced traditional science. For example, Operation Moonwatch (McCray 2008), a citizen-driven effort started by Fred Whipple in 1956 to train people to spot human-made satellites, had established well over 200 teams in locations around the world by the surprise October 1957 launch of Sputnik. As a result, for the opening months of the Space Age, members of Operation Moonwatch were the only organized worldwide network that was prepared to spot and help track satellites.

More recently, technology-driven models for participatory sensing have emerged (Burke et al. 2006; Campbell et al. 2008; Paulos, Honicky, and Hooker 2009). Our research hypothesis is that this new usage model for participatory sensing will lead to important contributions to four primary long-term research goals:

1. Improve the science literacy of everyday citizens through active participation in basic scientific data collection and use of scientific principles (Jenkins 1999; Brossard, Lewenstein, and Bonney 2005).
2. Provide professional scientists and stakeholders with access to richer, finer-grain data sets for modeling, analyzing, and advancing both fundamental and applied knowledge regarding people and ecosystems (Jasanoff 2003; Petersen 1984).

3. Develop new usage models and experiences for the mobile-phone and ubiquitous computing technologies as tools for promoting transparency and enabling grassroots participation in local community and civic government policymaking.

4. Create greater public awareness and understanding of the relationships between humans and the natural environment, particularly with regard to sustainability and environmental issues.

Our research leverages the power of crowdsourcing, the recent open-development platforms of mobile phones, and the cultural adoption of participatory practices to research, build, and study systems that allow everyday people to act as "citizen scientists" in collecting, sharing, educating, raising awareness, and solving problems across neighborhoods, cities, and nations. Our research positions citizens as a central, driving element for collecting, reporting, interpreting, and collectively improving our health and the health of our natural environment. In our proposal we outline a research plan that leverages the synergy across four enabling technological and cultural themes:

1. Increasing sensor integration into mobile phones

2. The rise of the expert amateur and do-it-yourself (DIY) culture specifically in terms of the making of novel, personalized technology (Kuznetsov and Paulos 2010b)

3. Open mobile-phone development APIs coupled with "app store"–style mobile distribution mechanisms

4. The cultural rise of technologically leveraged grassroots participatory models and crowdsourcing techniques for community and societal change

We frame these emerging citizen-authored sensor datasets and the social practices evolving around them using our vocabulary: collect, express, share, and change. We outline the challenges to operationalizing each of these four elements of citizen science.

Collect   Why and how will people be motivated to participate in collecting data? How and what type of data will be collected? When will samples be taken? How will problems of sensor accuracy, drift, and calibration be addressed? What are the reasonable sets of sensors to use? Which sensors are best for individuals? Policymakers? Scientists? What environmental and human conditions make sense to measure? Where should the sensors be mounted and in what contexts and positions are they best sampled? What sample frequency is best suited to each sensor, user, and context? How will novel hardware be integrated into mobile platforms by nonexperts? What will be the overall user experience of collecting sensor data? To what degree is it automatic versus user controlled? Is it collected by people, places, or a hybrid?

Express   How will issues of "sensor legibility" be expressed such as sensor range, accuracy, norms, drift, and calibration? How will the collected data be experienced? On an individual's personal mobile phone? In a public space or shared signage? In the home, office, transit, or automobile? Which ranges of expressive techniques are best suited to individuals? Social groups? Neighborhoods? Cities? States? Nations? To what degree is the data scientifically expressed with numbers and raw values? Interpreted and abstracted? Viewed as ambient information? How are sensor norms decided? How are time, trends, gradients, and averages represented? Over what time ranges and resolutions? What are appropriate techniques to interact with the data and in which contexts? How do different expressive techniques (visual, tactile, audio, etc.) inspire more persuasion, curiosity, awareness, education, sensor literacy, indifference, individual behavioral change, or the desire to act for societal-level change?

Share   How will collected data be shared? Which data standards, protocols, and formats should be adopted and/or expanded? How will privacy be addressed? What techniques will be used to ensure that the data is trustworthy and valid? What practices of fair use, reuse, and individual ownership will be appropriate? How will data be archived, preserved, and authenticated? How can data best be shared with nonexperts, community leaders, scientists, health organizations, urban planners, civic government, decision and policymakers, local nongovernment organizations (NGOs), local industry, and activists groups?

Change   What tools and techniques will facilitate the most productive debate and ultimate positive social benefit? How will people use the data to argue for and against various hypotheses? How will data be compared? Can we "design for doubt" such that individuals interpreting the data address the range of potential underlying possibilities for sensor failures and user errors, both accidental and malicious in intent? What tools or frameworks best encourage active participation and the development of real solutions to human and environmental problems using these novel citizen science datasets and the issues they reveal?

In the remainder of the chapter we confront a subset of these research questions and highlight a range of insights and results in this territory.

Sensor Stories

Over the past several years we have conducted a wide range of studies into human and environmental health and well-being using novel mobile and DIY sensing technologies and techniques. The successes and challenges of individual efforts across several projects are discussed below. We explore this design space through three sensing domains:

Mobile sensors   Integration of environmental sensing with mobile-phone technology
Movable sensors   Low-cost, stand-alone environmental sensors designed to be placed and moved in and across public spaces (not attached or integrated into a mobile phone)

Fixed sensors   Indoor and domestic environmental sensing designed to measure and share indoor air quality and similar environmental factors

We conclude with some open challenges and forward envisionings of such technologies and practices in our near future. Our story begins with human health and air quality.

Human Health and Air Quality

The World Health Organization reports that two million people die each year from the effects of air pollution, twice the number of deaths from automobile accidents (World Health Organization 2006). Direct causes of air pollution–related deaths include aggravated asthma, bronchitis, emphysema, lung and heart diseases, respiratory allergies, visual impairment, and even sudden infant death syndrome (SIDS) (Klonoff-Cohen, Lam, and Lewis 2005). In cities, automobile exhaust alone can contribute to as much as 95 percent of all CO emissions (U.S. Environmental Protection Agency 2007). Recent studies have also revealed that 97 percent of European citizens living in urban areas are exposed to pollution levels that exceed EU limits (European Union 2004). Current sparse sensing strategies do little to capture the dynamic variability arising from urban microclimates, daily automobile traffic patterns, human activity, and smaller industries. Are we to believe that the park, subway exit, underground parking lot, building atrium, bus stop, and roadway median are all equivalent environmental places? In general, the individual citizen has very little direct awareness of the air quality they encounter daily and almost no public forum to debate strategies for change. Several recent projects have explored citizen measurement of air quality such as Hooker's Pollution e-Sign (Hooker et al. 2007); Preemptive Media's AIR (Areas Immediate Reading) mobile device (Costa, Schulte, and Singer 2008); *Proboscis'* *Snout* (Social Tapestries 2007); Millecevic's Neighborhood Satellites (Milicevic 2007); the Everyday Learning Lab's Smoke Rings (Foley-Fisher and Strohecker 2005); Jeremijenko's (2005) Feral Robotic Dogs; EQUATOR's e-science project, which included extensive carbon monoxide samples taken by people across several streets in London (Milton and Steed 2007); and bike-based mobile air-quality sensing by Cambridge Mobile Urban Sensing (CamMobSens) (Kanjo and Landshoff 2007).

Ergo: Air Quality On the Go

One of our first research probes, *Ergo* (Paulos, Honicky, and Goodman 2007) developed in 2006, involved studying the experience of receiving air-quality data on a mobile platform while on the go. Ergo was a simple SMS system that allowed anyone with a mobile phone to quickly and easily explore, query, and learn about his or her air quality on the go. Ergo was done in collaboration with the U.S. Environmental Protection Agency (EPA) using their dataset based on fixed metropolitan air-quality measurement stations. Developed prior to today's smartphone and location-based mobile

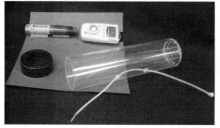 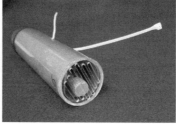 

Figure 10.1
Taxi-mounted tube with carbon monoxide, sulfur dioxide, and nitrogen dioxide sensors exposed (*left*) and packaged (*center*). Also, the student-worn setup containing similar air-quality sensors and GPS unit (*right*).

technology, Ergo was the first system of its kind to allow citizens to receive real-time air-quality data. Ergo delivered over 200,000 air-quality reports and generated a range of extremely positive feedback that included comments from people with respiratory problems. For example, several individuals reported on how the system improved their lifestyle and provided them with easy access with real-time geographically measured air-quality reports on their mobile phone. In fact, people began integrating the data they received from Ergo into planning their outdoor routes and activities across urban areas. Several years later in 2009, Ergo inspired the development of the EPA's and Bay Area Air Quality Management District's (BAAQMD) own EnviroFlash application for providing mobile-phone-based air-quality reports by AirNow.

Accra, Ghana: Air-Quality Sensing Field Study
This work was carried out in collaboration with Intel Research and R. J. Honicky.

In 2007 we initiated a more ambitious project in which we recruited taxi drivers and students in Accra, Ghana, to participate in a two-week study to collect air-quality data. We worked closely with local officials and NGOs in developing and deploying the study. Taxi drivers and students were provided with sensors for CO, SO_2, and NO_2, as well as a GPS unit (figure 10.1). A series of visualizations (figure 10.2) from the quantitative sensor data as well as qualitative interviews resulted in a series of design recommendations and significant behavioral changes in our participants to improve air quality. Perhaps the most surprising results from this study were not that air urban quality varies wildly over time and space, but that the participants recruited to collect these datasets begin to experience what we referred to as the "Prius effect." Just as Honda Prius automobile drivers, when shown real-time miles-per-gallon values, are influenced to alter their driving behavior as they attempt to "score" 100 mpg, our participants, exposed to real-time values for air quality, developed sophisticated strategies to minimize their exposure to poor air quality by altering their routes and times

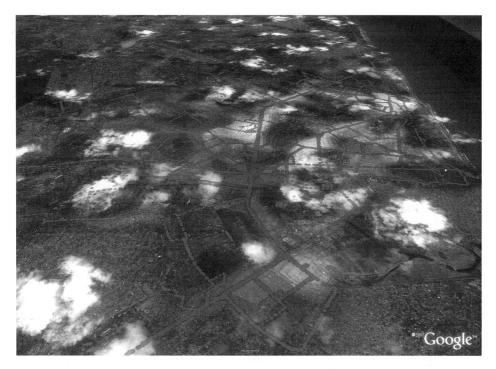

Figure 10.2
A heat-map visualization of carbon monoxide readings collected by citizens of Accra, Ghana rendered atop Google Earth. Intensity levels of carbon monoxide are shown as varying shades of gray.

of travel across the city of Accra (Paulos, Honicky, and Hooker 2009; Paulos, Honicky, and Goodman 2007).

Air-Quality Sensing with Mobile Phones

This work was carried out in collaboration with Intel Research, Allison Woodruff, Paul Aoki, Alan Mainwaring, Chris Myers, Sushmita Subramanian, and R. J. Honicky.

Informed by our studies, we designed, built, and integrated various air-quality sensors into a mobile phone. The resulting hardware combines carbon monoxide, nitrogen dioxide, ozone, temperature, and humidity sensors with Bluetooth wireless communication to the mobile phone (figure 10.3 *top*). This set of sensors can be attached to the mobile phone, worn, or carried in a purse or backpack and can measure gases strongly associated with air pollution—primarily from automobiles and diesel exhaust. We furthered our development of these mobile-phone-based platforms with the integration of air-quality sensing with Apple's iPhone through a direct connection (figure 10.3 *bottom*). Data is sampled, time and location stamped, and sent using SMS to a central server where it is shared publicly via a web-based interface with a standardized SQL database backend. This allows the public to query and use the data within the repository (figure 10.4). While a large range of research efforts in mobile sensing are focused on the system-level challenges of integrating such sensors and addressing hardware power issues, a much larger research challenge is clearly found in developing the social and sharing visualization tools to interact with these datasets, avoiding instigating a culture of fear, designing for doubt (Paulos 2009), using persuasive tactics (Cialdini 2007), and promoting real participatory campaigns for change.

A Vehicle for Research: Collecting Air-Quality Data Using Civic Infrastructure
This work was carried out in collaboration with Intel Research, Allison Woodruff, Paul Aoki, Alan Mainwaring, Chris Myers, Sushmita Subramanian, and R. J. Honicky.

We believe it is critical to the success of these citizen science efforts to not simply develop the technology components, but to collaborate with all parts of the environmental "ecosystem"—local and regional governments, public health NGOs, atmospheric scientists, activists, concerned citizens, and so on. We collaborated with the City of San Francisco, Office of the Mayor, Department of Public Works, and San Francisco Department of the Environment to integrate our air-quality sensing systems into the municipal fleet of street sweepers (figure 10.5 a–d) (Aoki et al. 2009). We collected street-by-street air-quality readings as the vehicles do their work. The street sweepers also offered us the opportunity to test and refine our system in a very challenging real-world environment. Using only a dozen street sweepers augmented with sensors to measure carbon monoxide (CO), nitrogen oxide (NO_x), ozone (O_3), temperature, relative humidity, and motion (3D accelerometer), we were able to collect sensor readings every few days from nearly every part of the city. We were also able to remotely calibrate the sensors each evening when the sweepers were all parked together in the yard. While this approach appears to move away from a citizen-collected view, we see this strategy as a more realistic future hybrid approach where "participation" in data collection is interpreted broadly as citizen, civic, and infrastructure. Such approaches are also great scaffolding techniques toward larger-scale public data collection.

InAir: Indoor Air Quality and Persuasive Technologies
This work was carried out in collaboration with Sunyoung Kim at Carnegie Mellon University.

In our previous studies we explored only gas sensing. In this study we designed and deployed a novel system integrated with an Apple iPhone for measuring and

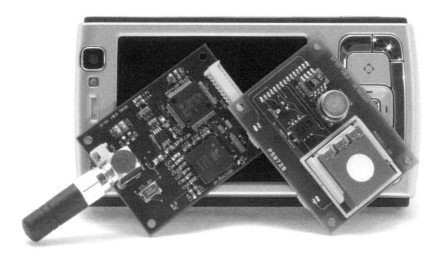

Figure 10.3
Two versions of air-quality measurement sensing integrated with mobile phones: Bluetooth (*top*) and attached (*bottom*).

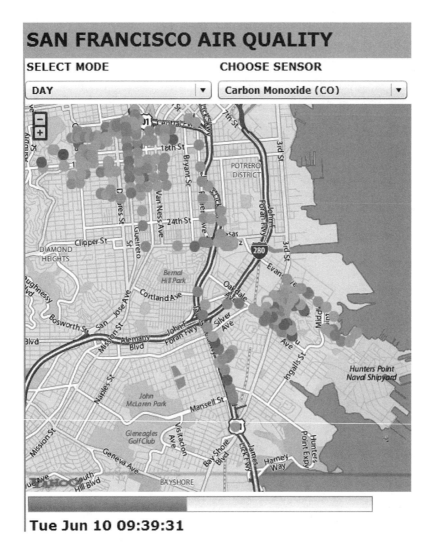

Figure 10.4
An interactive Flash-based visualization tool for exploring daily street-sweeper air-quality data.

Figure 10.5
The sensing platform mounted onto municipal street-sweeping vehicles.

visualizing current and historic hazardous particulate matter (figure 10.6). Perhaps more interestingly, we explore the concept of sharing measurements and visualizations of indoor air quality within one's social network as a persuasive technique. Through a four-week study of fourteen households as six groups, we found that this system, called inAir (Kim and Paulos 2009), (1) increased awareness of and reflection on air quality; (2) promoted behavioral changes that resulted in improved indoor air quality; and (3) demonstrated the persuasive power of sharing in further improving indoor air quality by fostering new social awareness, causing behavior changes, strengthening social bonds, and prompting collaborative efforts across social networks to improve human health and well-being (Kim and Paulos 2010, 2009). One unintended, surprising result was that one of our participants, after viewing her air-quality data compared with others, quit smoking! This is consistent with studies where it is shown that people are heavily influenced by the behaviors and actions they expect or know others to be performing (Cialdini 2007).

In the past several years, a growing body of scientific evidence has indicated that indoor air pollution in homes and other buildings can be worse than the outdoor air pollution in even the largest and most industrialized cities. For example, the California

Figure 10.6
InAir system standing on a living-room table.

Air Resources Board (2010) estimates that indoor air pollutant levels are 25 to 62 percent greater than outside levels, and the U.S. Environmental Protection Agency's (EPA) Total Exposure Assessment Methodology study revealed that levels of about a dozen common organic pollutants were found to be two to five times higher, and occasionally more than 100 times higher, inside homes than outside regardless of whether the homes were located in rural or highly industrial areas (U.S. Environmental Protection Agency 1987). What makes these numbers more significant is that we spend by far most of our daily lives indoors, working, eating, sleeping, and spending time with loved ones in enclosed environments. EPA statistics indicate that people in the United States spend 65 to 90 percent of their time indoors (U.S. Environmental Protection Agency 2004). Thus, for many people, the health risks may be greater due to exposure to air pollution indoors than outdoors. According to the World Health Organization (2002), indoor air pollution is the eighth most important risk factor for disease, responsible for 2.7 percent of the global burden of disease and 1.6 million deaths due to chronic respiratory disease per year.

From cooking, to cleaning, to chemical use, and even home printers (Schripp et al. 2008), numerous factors threaten to degrade indoor air quality. However, people are often completely unaware of these issues since air quality is difficult to sense, understand, and interpret. Three main factors contribute to people's misunderstanding of indoor air quality. First, people are not aware of how their various indoor activities affect the overall air quality of their environment. Second, it is very difficult with human perception to detect the changes in air quality since many air pollutants are invisible and impossible to detect with human senses. Last, existing indoor air-quality sensors (e.g., smoke detectors) report only binary data triggered by a threshold condition such as safe or unsafe. With the emergence of ubiquitous computing technologies in homes, offices, and schools there is an opportunity for such technologies to play a

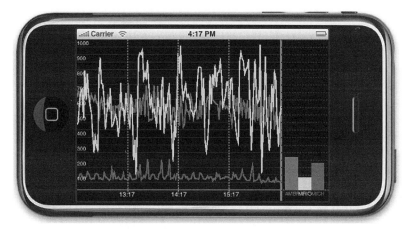

Figure 10.7
A detailed view of inAir visualization of user-shared air-quality readings over time on iPhone.

primary role in improving the quality of indoor environments by measuring, visualizing, and helping people better understand indoor air quality.

We designed and implemented *inAir*, a system to measure, visualize, and share indoor levels of particulate matter. For data visualization, the inAir screen is divided into two regions (see figure 10.7). The left side of the screen is used to render a line graph representing the particle count over four consecutive hours. The graph shows data not only for the local sensor but also data from other households in one's social network. The right side of the screen is used to visualize the current number of airborne particulates as bar charts. The bar charts update every fifteen seconds and show the most recent local measurement compared to others in your social network.

The ability to assess the numeric representation of indoor air quality increased awareness and knowledge about indoor air pollution and its relationship with indoor activities. Also, noticing changes in air quality led to reflection on possible causes of poor air quality and how to improve it. The ways participants speculated on the causes and solutions varied from personal reflection to talking to other residents to discussions with other participants. Participants reported discovering many influences on indoor air quality that they did not expect (e.g., running a dishwasher, motorcycles passing by, applying cleaning products on hot surfaces, the next-door neighbor moving out, and an upstairs neighbor's running on a treadmill). In summary, our analysis showed that inAir increased participants' opportunities to think about indoor air quality and health-related issues.

Throughout the design discussion sessions about data visualization in the poststudy interview, we found different preferences in design by different populations. Parents with young children valued simplicity and easy interpretation as the most important factors in order to teach children how to read the data. They commented on the current version of visualization as *scientific* and preferred alternative designs we presented such as a gauge, color map, or iconic virtual pet. Seniors valued aesthetics as one of the most important factors since it helped provide or fit into their home. This age group regarded the current version of visualization as *clinical*, preferring ambient bubble and abstract designs. Finally, younger participants such as students preferred the original visualization, the graph, describing it as simple and intuitive.

In our analysis we found that more engaging systems resulted in more awareness about the level of indoor air quality and its relationship to activities. Sharing also plays a significant role in maintaining engagement in the system by providing emotional, entertaining, and comparative features to users. Sharing was also an effective mechanism for triggering positive actions through social influence. Shared air-quality data played an important role in heightening understanding of the relative level of air quality across population groups. When the level deviated significantly from the norm, people collaborated to discover the reasons for the discrepancy. It appeared that this high variation was a primary motive in prompting solutions, discussing best methods, and drawing from mutual knowledge and experience. People were similarly concerned about other participants when they observed significantly worse air-quality readings than normal. Our analysis revealed that an increase in user awareness promoted direct changes in behavior when the sources of the problem were apparent and solvable. However, inAir also aroused feelings of powerlessness and concern, particularly when the source of the problem was unknown or no solutions were provided. This evidence argues for the incorporation of designs elements that provide feedback about not just poor air quality, but as important, its probable causes and proposed solution strategies.

Equally interesting were our findings around privacy. Overall, air-quality data was not regarded as private information that seemed inappropriate or awkward to share. Every participant in our study justified this response by explaining that they think air-quality data does not contain any personal information and thus they do not feel that sharing such data with anonymous people compromises privacy. While we find this result encouraging for future environmental data sharing, it is likely that participants did not reflect on the full range of privacy issues involved (e.g., tracking home occupancy, exposing "unclean" homes, etc.) and thus there is an increased obligation for the designers of such systems to make users more aware of these concerns.

Finally, while our system was designed to provide helpful information to improve domestic health and well-being, several people commented on how such a system also could place an extra burden on home life by presenting yet another thing to worry about (e.g., air quality and all the new complex issues with which they must now be concerned). However, unlike other types of public health hazards that are often beyond the control of an individual (e.g., nuclear power, outdoor air quality, pollen,

Figure 10.8
WearAir clothing for sensing and publicly expressing air quality.

groundwater chemicals, etc.), domestic air quality was considered by participants as a personal territory within their control and maintenance (Pope, Ezzati, and Dockery 2009). The desire to locate the cause of poor air quality, to learn proper methods of solving problems, and to improve the overall air quality was a major concern of participants.

In a related study, we developed a wearable garment, *WearAir* (figure 10.8) (Kim, Paulos, and Gross 2010), which measured and expressed air quality to the nearby public. This was a provocative example of delivering messages and viewpoints through clothing choice, even to those that may have little or no interest. We view this "electronic ecoclothing" prototype as a new genre of political, environmental, and health-conscious clothing intentionally designed to advertise one's viewpoint and engage others in topics of concern around the health, environment, and well-being. We have introduced the moniker "Spectacle Computing" to capture this novel strategy for increasing engagement and awareness of personal and societal concerns across public spaces and communities using a range of expressive technologies.

UpStream: Motivating Water Conservation with Low-Cost Sensing and Persuasive Displays

This work was carried out in collaboration with Stacey Kuznetsov at Carnegie Mellon University.

Moving beyond mobile-phone-based and air-quality sensing strategies, we focused on measuring the effectiveness of various persuasive displays on water conservation using low-cost sensing in public and private spaces (Kuznetsov and Paulos 2010c). We also wanted to extend the environmental awareness research design space beyond simply air quality. Water is our most precious and most rapidly declining natural resource, and one out of six people in the world does not have access to safe drinking water (1.1 billion people), over 2.5 billion lack adequate sanitation, and more than 5,000 deaths, many of them of children, are caused by water-related illnesses every day (Ki-moon 2009; World Health Organization 2009). These water issues are coupled with a range of environmental, political, and human heath factors, which affect food

Figure 10.9
Persuasive displays deployed in public faucets indicating current water consumption and daily
average with visual indicators.

supplies, industrial demands, and climate variations. These challenges are not confined to developing regions: water depletion affects many parts of the world, with
water levels receding as much as 300 feet in some areas during the last decade
(Galloway, Jones, and Ingebritsen 1999). Increased demand for freshwater leads to
aggressive pumping, resulting in reduced water flow in streams and lakes, land sub-
sistence (collapsing soil), and deteriorating water quality, not to mention greater costs
of obtaining freshwater due to its increased depth (U.S. Geological Survey 2003).

Our work aims to raise awareness and motivate water conservation through the
design, deployment, and evaluation of several in situ persuasive displays integrated
with low-cost water-flow sensors (figure 10.9). In the spirit of design research, our work
probes consumption as a whole and inspires curiosity about water practices outside
the facilities studied (dishwashing, lawn watering, laundry, etc.). A longer-term goal
of such work is to demonstrate how increased awareness can lead to large-scale personal and societal-level changes in other domains such as industrial practices and
agriculture.

Our sensing approach, which relies on an external microphone to measure water
flow, is inspired by prior work on microphone sensing to infer activities in the home
(Chetty, Tran, and Grinter 2008; Fogarty, Au, and Hudson 2006). In the spirit of do-
it-yourself (DIY) approaches, our sensor system, called *UpStream*, is inexpensive (under
$40) and easily replicated by nonexperts. Early *UpStream* prototypes were installed at
public faucets and a private (shared) shower (figure 10.9). These efforts were followed
by three-week-long deployments in four private showers with two display styles—
ambient and numeric (figure 10.10), showing individual and average water consumption. The numeric display presents current usage to the nearest tenth of a gallon, while
the ambient visualization presents this same information as a "traffic light" metaphor
for water usage.

Our studies revealed different behavioral outcomes in public spaces (bathrooms)
opposed to the semiprivate (shared showers) and private showers. Our playful design

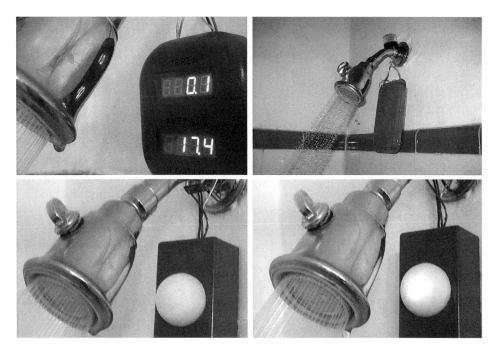

Figure 10.10
Numeric (*top*) and ambient (*bottom*) displays communicating water usage.

inspired curiosity about the interface, resulting in increased usage (novelty effects) in public bathrooms, while similar displays effectively decreased water usage in the private showers during the pilot study and long-term deployment. New people continuously accessed public displays and were able to explore the technology (cycle through all ambient lighting modes) without providing identifiable data. Conversely, private displays showed individual data to the same people, facilitating faster adoption. This tension between curiosity and anonymity in public spaces and identifiable usage and ownership in private settings highlights the importance of context for pervasive technology. Ambient displays, especially with clear positive or negative behavioral benchmarks, may encourage water conservation for long-term users who are familiar and accustomed to the technology in private settings. Moreover, curiosity and anonymity in public spaces can be leveraged to motivate public health and safer hand washing through interactive visualizations.

Our studies also expose the natural tension between abstract and literal output modalities for datasets designed to promote conservation. To encourage reflection, curiosity, and awareness, our initial designs intentionally chose ambient visual cues (color and graphs). However, while users asked for numeric data, our further exploration of the design space between the abstract and the literal suggests that information-rich numeric displays can in fact be less effective. Although literal displays offer greater detail, interpretation of this information requires attention and processing from users already engaged in activities (such as showering). Appropriate pacing is also crucial: the usage number rapidly advanced at every tenth of a gallon, which proved too fast and even stressful for some users who only occasionally glanced at the display. However, a display that updates too slowly may appear broken as users look to ensure some model of correct operation.

The peripheral use of our displays (i.e., occasional glancing) suggests that persuasive technologies must provide a clear, easily perceptible indication of good and/or bad behavior. Our ambient visualization communicated acceptable or excessive water usage through obvious light cues and proved effective for more participants than the numeric display. The advantage of numeric feedback, however, is that it invites participants to personally define acceptable ranges, inspiring analysis and curiosity about the impact of activities outside the shower. The persuasive "sweet spot" thus lies within a hybrid of this design territory where users can experience details of the data as well as view less distracting benchmarks for their usage. Future work can focus on exploring the range of these hybrid ambient-numeric output modalities and persuasive design landscapes.

Another design opportunity exists in the space of data sharing and displays that afford interperson comparisons. None of our participants considered their water usage data private, nor did they feel uncomfortable sharing it with others. Moreover, several people felt that seeing their friends' data would add incentives for lowering water usage through competition. In addition, one participant wanted to see the data of strangers (other people in the study) to gain perspective on personal usage compared to that of other people. Such comments motivate a design space that incorporates visual sharing of personal water usage across individuals and households.

Finally, we note that the numeric display was ultimately less popular and less effective, despite participants' initial preference and requests for the numeric modality. Thus, while user preferences can identify functional needs and help narrow design scope, actual design, construction, and in situ deployment of such technologies is vital to measuring and evaluating the ultimate impact and success of such persuasive systems.

Place-Based Public Environmental Sensing and Expression
This work was carried out in collaboration with Stacey Kuznetsov at Carnegie Mellon University.

Moving further beyond mobile-phone-based and even air and water sensing, we explore how the act of participatory sensing is not only a mechanism for data collection, visualization, and sharing, but also an approach for authoring, engaging, and activating individuals in a wide range of public spaces using movable, attachable environmental sensors (Kuznetsov and Paulos 2010a). We draw inspiration from existing public authoring tools such as SoundMites and LED Throwies (Seitinger, Perry, and Mitchell 2009) that enable users to leave interactive objects on public surfaces, which activate these spaces (Paulos et al. 2008) with mobile lights and audio. Returning to our citizen science theme, how will such new urban objects participate as public environmental sensors?

We propose a system of modular, low-cost, networked sensors that measure environmental factors such as air pollution, radiation, water quality, noise, and so on. Rather than belonging to a particular person or space, these sensors are designed to invite stakeholders—people occupying or passing through a space—to move and leave them in points of interest, thereby engaging with their environment. We scoped our study around four communities, and make the following assumptions about each: (1) *students* are a young demographic occupying spaces in and around universities, with interests that reflect similar educational backgrounds and lifestyles; (2) *parents* form an older group, characterized by personal and family interests in spaces that revolve around children (schools, playgrounds, etc.) as well as work (office, etc.) and friends (theaters, malls, etc.); (3) *bicyclists* traverse a wide range of urban spaces with vested interests in roads, parks, and traffic, among others; and (4) the *homeless* are a low-income, nomadic community, with sociopolitical perspectives that lead to unique appropriations of technology, often overlooked by mainstream HCI literature (Le Dantec and Edwards 2008). We hypothesize that each group embodies unique values and attachments to public spaces, and sensor placements will reveal community and individual needs. Moreover, we predict that willingness to share and act on sensor data will in part reflect participants' involvement in their particular community as well as their perceived role in public spaces.

We chose to abstract from specific chemicals, such as ozone and carbon monoxide, to make the study more intuitive and gain insights into the source of environmental concerns expressed by each community. We selected six factors, which most participants found to be comprehensive: exhaust (vehicle-related pollution), smog (industrial pollution), pathogens (bacteria, germs, etc.), noise, chemicals (cleaning products, pesticides, VOCs, etc.), and dust. We developed probe kits, each consisting of six mock environmental sensors with an acrylic half-sphere to simulate sensor input (figure 10.11). Magnets along the bottom of each probe enabled easy attachment to metal (nonhorizontal) surfaces. Given the challenges of implementing and deploying working sensing systems in the real world, we highlight the advantages of our approach, which leverages nonworking sensor probes. The use of probes (instead of real sensors) allowed us to engage with four diverse communities without the overhead of troubleshooting technical difficulties or the financial losses associated with damaged or stolen equipment. More importantly, this method enabled us to abstract from specific

Figure 10.11
Sensor probe placements by various community participants.

environmental data and explore broader concerns as voiced by each group. Rather than reacting to a particular sensor value, participants were invited to think about how factors such as germs, exhaust, and smog play into public spaces throughout their everyday lives. Our findings reveal a wide range of values, environmental concerns, and sensor appropriations across the four communities studied, and we now discuss community expressions and the motivations for collecting data.

Our findings show that sensing, even in the abstract form of nonworking probes, inspires people to reconsider and engage with public space. Some spaces afford similar questions across communities: parents, students, and the homeless all placed the pathogen probe in public bathrooms, and across all four communities, participants

attached exhaust and noise probes on bus stops or onto street poles at busy intersections. Other spaces, however, evoked different interpretations. A homeless participant
placed the noise probe on a trash can, while parents and students commonly saw this
as a site for pathogen sensing. While all four groups shop at grocery stores, only
parents decided to place a pathogen probe on store counters and shopping carts.
Sensor placement—as an act of demarcating a place to be sensed—shifted participants'
perceptions of spaces: they became more aware of dust at construction sites or germs
on door handles, ("I noticed more dust and stuff," "I started carrying more antibacte-
rial," etc.) This range of spatial affordances supports our initial presentation of participatory sensing as an approach for community-based activation of public surfaces.
Future systems can leverage human curiosity and spatial affordances in real-time
sensing applications that support community needs.

Our participants discussed "sensor data" as an artifact that can be shared, broadcast,
or articulated within and across communities. Parents wanted to discuss this information with their community and present it to other parents through school award
ceremonies, children's sporting events, school websites, and so on. Students saw the
data as an opportunity to negotiate dialogs with policymakers: they suggested ways
to present data directly to local officials and authorities. Meanwhile, homeless participants wanted to broadcast this information to the general public by making the
sensors more visible, or conveying the information through notes and flyers. The
homeless participants' uncertainty about how to contact authority figures, as well as
their disappointment in the government at large, suggests that they might hope to
leverage the general public's reaction to the data—rather than personal activism—as
a means of changing the environment. Perhaps by showing passengers that a bus
contains germs or by proving to pedestrians that exhaust levels are harmful, the homeless hope to incite the kind of public activism that they themselves do not feel empowered to take part in.

These findings suggest environmental data as a social currency: a potential for
parents to act together with other parents, for the homeless to speak to and incite action
from the general public, and for students to open a channel with policymakers. Future
systems could therefore present environmental data in modalities that allow for inter-
and cross-community sharing. Closer communities such as parents may prefer sharing
to take on the form of data exchange between members, which inspires bottom-up
activism that highlights their concerns. For students, new technologies could empower
direct communication between citizens and policymakers through mechanisms that
provide feedback, and for the homeless, interfaces might open opportunities to voice
personal concerns in ways that appeal to the broader public, who in turn can serve as
intermediaries between the homeless and civic government.

The act of placing sensors is a statement: the presence of a sensor expresses the
relationship between the citizen and the space. The intentional act of tagging an area

as a candidate for high exhaust, smog, or pathogen levels not only reflects participants' perception of space but is itself a political act. This action restructures the relationship between a specific environment and the public. Future work can leverage participatory sensing as an approach to projecting stakeholders' concerns into the public sphere, articulating their relationships with urban spaces, and potentially transforming these spaces to reflect the more preferable states of the world they desire. Rather than being mere instruments to gather input, sensors become an output modality just by virtue of their presence, revealing design opportunities for sensors as mediums of expression.

Citizen Séance: Ethics and the Dark Side

Although there a number of malicious citizen science scenarios, we describe a few that highlight fundamental problems such as data accuracy and human perception. First, is it even possible to design a neutral sensor? By our very choice of sensors and problem framing we have set up a natural bias in the system. For example, in our own work we present the technology as "pollution sensors" or even "air-quality sensors"— implying a good and bad scale. What if we instead called them "nutritious air sensors" and simply flipped the bias? Similarly, we may measure pollen where high counts are interpreted as bad since they often give rise to allergies and other adverse respiratory problems in humans. However, taken from nature's point of view, high pollen counts are indicative of improved pollination, healthy plants, available food sources for bees, and improved ecological life. We need to draw from ideas across this entire design space.

How will we deal with the malicious use of data such as reporting poor air-quality data from within a neighborhood to drive down housing prices? Even well-intended data can be unwelcome. Take for example the event that inspired *Life Inc.: How the World Became a Corporation and How to Take It Back*. The author, Rushkoff (2009), posted details about a mugging in his neighborhood on a web-based community message board to warn others. Rather than being thanked for his act of community "kindness," he was shamed by the community for publicly logging location data about the event and potentially driving down their home values.

Another concern comes when citizen science tools are adopted in society and are increasingly viewed as mechanisms to lodge complaints, gripe, and direct blame. Such systems will most certainly soon be ignored by those who can make change. We need to ensure that our designs avoid finger pointing and make sure everyone has some "skin in the game." We need to design such systems to allow creative solutions that do not always place the blame on a single person or organization.

Are the tools we are developing for citizen science unintentionally creating a culture of fear? Are we giving individuals accurate levels and details to make rational decisions about measured pollution levels, water quality, and other effects on human health?

It is critical that the designs promote optimism and encourage the development of new solutions rather than instilling fear and panic. Nevertheless, this issue is a real concern. We have observed anxiety in previous studies we have performed where individuals become aware of new health concerns after their involvement in citizen science. While increased awareness is an encouraging result of such persuasive interfaces for citizen science, we need to ensure they are in check with reality and modulated by a larger picture of life, health, happiness, and well-being.

Technology-driven citizen science tools, crowdsourcing, and new citizen models of participation are absolutely certain elements of our future culture. The challenge is to operationalize the problem-making techniques of design research to engage with these societal-level wicked problems, to ask the challenging questions now, to create the rewarding (as well as disturbing) experiences, and to become active architects of our future society and world.

Acknowledgments

The work in this chapter spans several years' research conducted at Intel Research, UC Berkeley, and the Living Environments Lab at Carnegie Mellon University. More important, none of these projects would have been possible without the efforts of many colleagues who played vital roles in developing this research. They include Allison Woodruff, Paul Aoki, Alan Mainwaring, Chris Myers, Sushmita Subramanian, R. J. Honicky, Ben Hooker, Ian Smith, and Elizabeth Goodman. Countless thanks are owed to these colleagues. These projects were also supported in part by funding from Intel Research, Carnegie Mellon University, and the Vira I. Heinz Endowment.

References

Anderson, D. P., J. Cobb, E. Korpela, M. Lebofsky, and D. Werthimer. 2002. SETI@ home: An experiment in public-resource computing. *Communications of the ACM* 45 (11): 56–61.

Aoki, P. M., R. J. Honicky, A. Mainwaring, C. Myers, E. Paulos, S. Subramanian, and A. Woodruff. 2009. A vehicle for research: Using street sweepers to explore the landscape of environmental community action. In Dan R. Olsen, Jr, Richard B. Arthur, Ken Hinckley, Meredith Ringel Morris, Scott Hudson, and Saul Greenberg, eds. *Proceedings of the 27th International Conference on Human Factors in Computing Systems*, Boston, 375–384. New York: ACM.

Beck, U., A. Giddens, and S. Lash. 1994. *Reflexive Modernization: Politics, Tradition, and Aesthetics in the Modern Social Order*. Stanford, CA: Stanford University Press.

Blevis, E. 2007. Sustainable interaction design: Invention & disposal, renewal & reuse. In Mary Beth Rosson and David Gilmore, eds. *Proceedings of the SIGCHI Conference on Human Factors in Computing Systems*, San Jose, CA, 503–512. New York: ACM.

Brossard, D., B. Lewenstein, and R. Bonney. 2005. Scientific knowledge and attitude change: The impact of a citizen science project. *International Journal of Science Education* 27 (9): 1099–1121.

Burke, J., D. Estrin, M. Hansen, A. Parker, N. Ramanathan, S. Reddy, and M. B. Srivastava. 2006. Participatory sensing. Paper presented at Workshop on the World Sensor Web at SenSys, Boulder, CO., October 31.

California Air Resources Board. 2010. http://www.arb.ca.gov.

Campbell, A. T., S. B. Eisenman, N. D. Lane, E. Miluzzo, R. Peterson, H. Lu, X. Zheng, M. Musolesi, K. Fodor, and G.-S. Ahn. 2008. People power—the rise of people-centric sensing. Special issue on mesh networks, *IEEE Internet Computing* 12, no. 4 (July-August): 12–21.

Chetty, M., D. Tran, and R. E. Grinter. 2008. Getting to green: Understanding resource consumption in the home. In Jakob E. Bardram and Marc Langheinrich, eds. *Proceedings of the 10th International Conference on Ubiquitous Computing*, Seoul, South Korea, 242–251. New York: ACM.

Cialdini, R. B. 2007. Descriptive social norms as underappreciated sources of social control. *Psychometrika* 72 (2): 263–268.

Corburn, J. 2005. *Street Science: Community Knowledge and Environmental Health Justice*. Cambridge, MA: MIT Press.

Costa, B. D., J. Schulte, and B. Singer. 2008. AIR. http://www.pm-air.net.

DiSalvo, C., K. Boehner, N. A. Knouf, and P. Sengers. 2009. Nourishing the ground for sustainable HCI: Considerations from ecologically engaged art. In Dan R. Olsen, Jr, Richard B. Arthur, Ken Hinckley, Meredith Ringel Morris, Scott Hudson, and Saul Greenberg, eds. *Proceedings of the 27th International Conference on Human Factors in Computing Systems*, Boston, 385–394. New York: ACM.

DiSalvo, C., P. Sengers, and H. Brynjarsdóttir. 2010. Mapping the landscape of sustainable HCI. In Elizabeth Mynatt, Geraldine Fitzpatrick, Scott Hudson, Keith Edwards, and Tom Rodden, eds. *Proceedings of the 28th International Conference on Human Factors in Computing Systems*, 1975–1984. New York: ACM.

Dourish, P. 2010. HCI and environmental sustainability: The politics of design and the design of politics.. In Olav W. Bertelsen and Peter Krogh, eds. *Proceedings of the 8th ACM Conference on Designing Interactive Systems,* Aarhus, Denmark, 1-10. New York: ACM.

European Union. 2004. Towards a thematic strategy on urban environment. COM 60. http://ec.europa.eu/environment/urban/pdf/com_2005_0718_en.p

Fogarty, J., C. Au, and S. E. Hudson. 2006. Sensing from the basement: A feasibility study of unobtrusive and low-cost home activity recognition. In Pierre Wellner, ed. *Proceedings of the 19th Annual ACM Symposium on User Interface Software and Technology*, Monterey, CA, 91-100. New York: ACM.

Foley-Fisher, Z., and C. Strohecker. 2005. *An Approach to the Presentation of Information from Multiple Sensors*. Technical Report MLE EL-TR2005-02. MIT Media Lab Europe.

Foth, M., C. Satchell, E. Paulos, T. Igoe, and C. Ratti. 2008. Pervasive persuasive technology and environmental sustainability. Workshop at the 6th International Conference on Pervasive Computing, Sydney, Australia, May 19.

Galloway, D. L., D. R. Jones, and S. E. Ingebritsen. 1999. *Land Subsidence in the United States: U.S. Geological Survey*. Circular 1182, p. 177.

Hooker, B., W. W. Gaver, A. Steed, and J. Bowers. 2007. The pollution e-sign. In Jay Hasbrouck, Tom Igoe, Jennifer Mankoff, and Allison Woodruff, eds. *Proceedings of the Workshop at the Ubiquitous Sustainability: Technologies for Green Values*, Innsbruck, Austria, September 16.

Irwin, A. 1995. *Citizen Science: A Study of People, Expertise, and Sustainable Development*. London: Routledge.

Jasanoff, S. 2003. Technologies of humility: Citizen participation in governing science. *Minerva* 41 (3): 223–244.

Jenkins, E. W. 1999. School science, citizenship and the public understanding of science. *International Journal of Science Education* 21 (7): 703–710.

Jeremijenko, N. 2005. Feral robotic dogs. http://www.nyu.edu/projects/xdesign/feralrobots/.

Kanjo, E., and P. Landshoff. 2007. Mobile phones to monitor pollution. IEEE Distributed Systems Online. *Urban Computing and Mobile Devices* 8 (7): 2.

Kim, S., and E. Paulos. 2009. InAir: Measuring and visualizing indoor air quality. In Sumi Helal, Hans Gellersen, and Sunny Consolvo, eds. *Proceedings of the 11th International Conference on Ubiquitous Computing,* Orlando. New York: ACM.

Kim, S., and E. Paulos. 2010. InAir: Sharing Indoor Air Quality Measurements and Visualizations. Atlanta: ACM SIGCHI.

Kim, S., E. Paulos, and M. Gross. 2010. WearAir: Expressive t-shirts for air quality sensing. In Marcelo Coelho, Jamie Zigelbaum, Hiroshi Ishii, Robert J. K. Jacob, Pattie Maes, and Thomas Pederson, eds. *Proceedings of the Fourth International Conference on Tangible, Embedded, and Embodied Interaction*, Cambridge, MA, 295–296. New York: ACM.

Ki-moon, Ban. 2009. Water is our most precious natural resource. Speech by United Nations Secretary-General Ban Ki-moon, March 22. UNIS/SGSM/100. http://www.unis.unvienna.org/unis/pressrels/2009/unissgsm100.html

Klonoff-Cohen, H., P. K. Lam, and A. Lewis. 2005. Outdoor carbon monoxide, nitrogen dioxide, and sudden infant death syndrome. *Archives of Disease in Childhood* 90:750–753.

Kuznetsov, S., and E. Paulos. 2010a. Participatory sensing in public spaces: Activating urban surfaces with sensor probes. In Olav W. Bertelsen and Peter Krogh, eds. *Proceedings of the 8th ACM Conference on Designing Interactive Systems*, Aarhus, Denmark. New York: ACM.

Kuznetsov, S., and E. Paulos. 2010b. Rise of the expert amateur: DIY projects, communities, and cultures. In Ebba Þóra Hvannberg, Marta Kristín Lárusdóttir, Ann Blandford, and Jan Gulliksen, eds. *Proceedings of the 6th Nordic Conference on Human-Computer Interaction: Extending Boundaries,* Reykjavík, Iceland. New York: ACM.

Kuznetsov, S., and E. Paulos. 2010c. UpStream: Motivating water conservation with low-cost water flow sensing and persuasive displays. In Elizabeth Mynatt, Geraldine Fitzpatrick, Scott Hudson, Keith Edwards, and Tom Rodden, eds. *Proceedings of the 28th international conference on Human factors in computing systems,* Atlanta: New York: ACM.

Laurel, B. 2003. *Design Research: Methods and Perspectives.* Cambridge, MA: MIT Press.

LeBaron, G. 2006. The 106th Christmas Bird Count. National Audubon Society.http://web4 .audubon.org/bird/cbc/pdf/AB_106_001-09w%20jump1002FINAL.pdf

Le Dantec, C. A., and W. K. Edwards. 2008. Designs on dignity: Perceptions of technology among the homeless. In Mary Czerwinski and Arnie Lund, eds. *Proceeding of the Twenty-sixth Annual SIGCHI Conference on Human Factors in Computing Systems,* Florence, Italy. New York: ACM.

McCray, W. P. 2008. *Keep Watching the Skies! The Story of Operation Moonwatch and the Dawn of the Space Age.* Princeton, NJ: Princeton University Press.

Meymaris, K., S. Henderson, P. Alaback, and K. Havens. 2008. *Project BudBurst: Citizen Science for All Seasons.* San Francisco, CA: American Geophysical Union.

Milicevic, M. 2007. Imaginary to dos: Three initiatives for personal environmental explorations. In Jay Hasbrouck, Tom Igoe, Jennifer Mankoff, and Allison Woodruff, eds. *Proceedings of the Workshop at the Ubiquitous Sustainability: Technologies for Green Values,* Innsbruck, Austria, September 16.

Milton, R., and A. Steed. 2007. Mapping carbon monoxide using GPS tracked sensors. *Environmental Monitoring and Assessment* 124:1–19.

Ostrom, E. 1990. *Governing the Commons: The Evolution of Institutions for Collective Action. Political Economy of Institutions and Decisions.* Cambridge: Cambridge University Press.

Paulos, E. 2009. Designing for doubt. Engaging Data: First International Forum on the Application and Management of Personal Electronic Information, October 12. MIT, Cambridge, MA.

Paulos, E., R. J. Honicky, and E. Goodman. 2007. Sensing atmosphere. In Carlo Ratti, Assaf Biderman, Alex (Sandy) Pentland, and David Lazer, eds. *Proceedings of the Workshop on Sensing on Everyday Mobile Phones in Support of Participatory Research,* Sydney, Australia. Cambridge, MA: Senseable City Lab.

Paulos, E., R. J. Honicky, and B. Hooker. 2009. Citizen science: Enabling participatory urbanism. In Marcus Foth, ed., *Handbook of Research on Urban Informatics: The Practice and Promise of the Real-Time City,* 414–436. Hershey, PA: IGI Global.

Paulos, E., T. Jenkins, A. Joki, and P. Vora. 2008. Objects of wonderment. In *Conference Proceedings Designing Interactive Systems,* Cape Town, South Africa. New York: ACM.

Petersen, J. C. 1984. *Citizen Participation in Science Policy*. Amherst, MA: University of Massachusetts Press.

Pope, C. A., III, M. Ezzati, and D. W. Dockery. 2009. Fine-particulate air pollution and life expectancy in the United States. *New England Journal of Medicine* 360 (4): 376.

Preece, W. H., F. J. Bramwell, C. W. Siemens, J. Hopkinson, F. A. Abel, and W. T. Kelvin. 1884. *The Practical Applications of Electricity: A Series of Lectures Delivered at the Institution of Civil Engineers, Session 1882–83*. London: The Institution.

Rittel, H. W. J., and M. M. Webber. 1973. Dilemmas in a general theory of planning. *Policy Sciences* 4 (2): 155–169.

Rittel, H. W. J., and M. M. Webber. 1974. Wicked problems. In N. Cross, D. Elliot, and R. Roy, eds., *Man-Made Futures: Readings in Society, Technology and Design*. London: Hutchinson Educational/Open University Press.

Rushkoff, D. 2009. *Life Inc.: How the World Became a Corporation and How to Take It Back*. New York: Random House.

Schripp, T. M., E. Wensing, T. Uhde, C. Salthammer, L. He, and L. Morawska. 2008. Evaluation of ultrafine particle emissions from laser printers using emission test chambers. *Environmental Science & Technology* 42 (12): 4338.

Seitinger, S., D. S. Perry, and W. J. Mitchell. 2009. Urban pixels: Painting the city with light. In Dan R. Olsen, Jr, Richard B. Arthur, Ken Hinckley, Meredith Ringel Morris, Scott Hudson, and Saul Greenberg, eds. *Proceedings of the 27th International Conference on Human Factors in Computing Systems*, Boston, 839–848. New York: ACM.

Social Tapestries. 2007. Snout. http://socialtapestries.net/snout.

U.S. Environmental Protection Agency. 1987. *The Total Exposure Assessment Methodology (TEAM) Study*. 600/S6-87/002. Washington, DC: U.S. Environmental Protection Agency.

U.S. Environmental Protection Agency. 2004. *Green Building Workgroup Building and Environment: A Statistical Summary*. Washington, DC: U.S. Environmental Protection Agency.

U.S Environmental Protection Agency. 2007. *CO: What Does It Come From?* Washington, DC: U.S. Environmental Protection Agency.

U.S. Geological Survey. 2003. *Ground Water Depletion across the Nation*. Fact Sheet 103-03. Washington, DC: U.S. Geological Survey.

Ward, D., K. Meymaris, S. Henderson, and R. Johnson. 2008. *The Great World Wide Star Count*. Washington, DC: American Geophysical Union.

Woodruff, A., J. Hasbrouck, and S. Augustin. 2008. A bright green perspective on sustainable choices. In Mary Czerwinski and Arnie Lund, eds. *Proceedings of the Twenty-sixth Annual SIGCHI Conference on Human Factors in Computing Systems*, 313–322, Florence, Italy, 313–322. New York: ACM.

Woodruff, A., and J. Mankoff. 2009. Environmental sustainability. *IEEE Pervasive Computing* 8, no. 1 (January): 18–21.

World Health Organization. 2002. *The World Health Report.* http://www.who.int/whr/2002/.

World Health Organization. 2006. *Fact Sheet No. 307: Asthma.* World Health Organization. http://www.who.int/mediacentre/factsheets/fs307/en/index.html.

World Health Organization. 2009. *Health through Safe Drinking Water and Basic Sanitation.* WHO Guidelines for Drinking-Water Quality. http://www.who.int/water_sanitation_health/dwq/guidelines.

III   Creative Engagement

Foreword

Gary Marsden

Because I am a computer scientist, it may seem strange that I have been asked to write the introduction to the book's section on creative engagement; computer scientists do not usually top the list of creative professions. However, the end goal of any software is to get users to engage (hopefully creatively) with computer hardware. At its core, computer science is about providing tools that are sufficiently flexible to let users express themselves how they wish, yet provide sufficient abstraction from the underlying hardware to prevent users from becoming baffled by needless complexities. The same design goals remain for creative engagement in urban environments.

The question is, can we, as designers, ensure that creativity will follow from the abstractions and systems we create? We want the users of these systems to invest something of themselves so that the result is beyond what we had initially anticipated. It almost seems paradoxical that we wish to design systems to be used in ways that we had not intended.

Through the chapters in this section, we start to see how we can encourage users to become more creative. For example, the use of audio, as a more visceral medium than visual stimulus, is reported in several of the chapters. Sometimes this takes the form of ambient noise, which has been shown to help immersion and sensations of presence in a virtual environment, as Jeni Paay and Jesper Kjeldskov suggest in chapter 14. In their work as well as in Sarah Barns's (chapter 11), explicit audio narrative is also used to highlight aspects of the environment that may be visually unexciting, but still hold interest for people in that environment. By "layering" audio on top of the physical environment, they introduce a new way of interpreting a physical environment that, as they show, engages people creatively. The reality of this "audio" layer can then be further enhanced through notions of priming (Nunez and Blake 2003) by providing users with a backstory or require them to Live Action Role Play (LARP) and wear the clothes of the fictional protagonists.

Andrew Wong and Richard Ling's chapter (chapter 15) explores how digital technology in the developing world can be used to "layer" information from the rest of the world onto the (sometimes) bleak experiences of youth living in Bangladesh. So rather than encouraging users to focus more deeply on their existing environment (as was the goal with the audio interventions), the mobile handset is allowing people to engage in possibilities beyond their current living conditions. While the mobile phone is no doubt changing the lives of people in the developing world, it is a device designed for the consumption of media. If we want to be engaged by those living in the developing world, we need to design technologies that allow those who only have access to a mobile handset to create and share their ideas digitally.

I find it ironic that all the chapters in this part of the book refer to mobile technology in one form or another. The original goals behind mobile computing were to allow us to communicate free from any physical constraint. I find it intriguing that much of the work here reports on how mobile technology allows us to become more engaged with our physical environment, rather than freeing us from it. It appears that building digital devices that can work across a doorway are more important than devices than can operate across a continent. Much of this book is a celebration of this fact, as we realize the importance of the physical environment and seek to use digital technology to enhance our relationship with it rather than using the technology to ignore it.

Chapter 12—by Hilary Davis, Peter Francis, Bjorn Nansen, and Frank Vetere—seeks to further embed the technology, not just within a physical but also a social context. What I find particularly exciting is the possibility of helping autism spectrum disorder (ASD) sufferers cope with the ambiguities of life by layering a pattern of navigation onto the physical environment.

Finally, the work of Christopher Kirwan and Sven Travis (chapter 13) inverts the ideas of other chapters and shows us that a given urban environment can be used in an abstract form to provide creative engagement in other domains. Using sensors and data feeds from an urban environment can serve as the inspiration for whimsical artworks through to providing critical overview information for disaster management scenarios.

In short, this section of the book challenges us as designers to think about what digital information we can and should layer onto a physical environment, and what effect it might have on the environment and the people living there. The effect that these systems have had in the lives of those who helped develop them also comes with a great responsibility when undertaking such an intervention. There is no doubt that this is inspiring and interesting work, but we should not lose sight of the responsibility we have to our users. What may be creative and engaging to us, may be irritating or even infuriating to those who have to live permanently with any given technology intervention. Humans cannot be creative and engaged all the time. For the sake of sanity, we must also explore how to build disengagement and passivity into our designs in order to release creativity.

Reference

Nunez, D., and E. Blake. 2003. Conceptual priming as a determinant of presence in virtual environments. In *Proceedings of the 2nd international conference on computer graphics, virtual reality, visualisation and interaction in Africa* (AFRIGRAPH '03), 101–108. New York, NY ACM.

11 Street Haunting: Sounding the Invisible City

Sarah Barns

I could tell you how many steps make up the streets rising like stairways, and the degree of the arcades' curves, and what kind of zinc scales cover the roofs; but I already know that this would be the same as telling you nothing. The city does not consist of this, but of relationships between the measurements of space and the events of its past.

—Italo Calvino, *Invisible Cities*, 1974

In Italo Calvino's *Invisible Cities* (1974), fluid assemblages of signs and images litter a subterranean landscape, marking the destinations to which Marco Polo has traveled.[1] Polo recounts these destinations to his emperor, Kublai Khan, without recourse to a map or a wayfaring guide; he offers little by way of their geography, or any sense of the spatial connections between each recalled location. Instead there are only fragments, the improbable exceptions of remembrance and experience. These "invisible cities" are all given names, women's names like Irene, Chloe, Raissa and Adelma. Irene, for example, "is the city visible when you lean out from the edge of the plateau at the hour when the lights come on" (p. 112). There are many cities, but in fact they are always the one: Venice. This is the Venice collapsed or hidden behind its contemporary, overexposed tourist facade, whose "invisibility" Calvino cultivates as the imaginative potentiality of everyday encounters with a familiar space. Of this Venice no general claims are made; instead, from the singularity of this one city are teased provisional cities that capture a mood, a memory, a fleeting gesture, or the tracery of a half-glimpsed pattern.

What might Calvino's peculiar treatment of urban spatiality offer to today's practitioners of urban computing? Boyer (1996b, 142) has noticed the way *Invisible Cities* represents a network "much like the matrix of a hypertext, in which the reader can select multiple routes and draw a variety of conclusions." Calvino, during the 1960s, was interested in how the combinatory complexities of cybernetics offered a new way of perceiving the world, as a series of discrete, divisible parts rather than being more continuous in form.[2] *Invisible Cities* can in this sense be understood as an attempt by Calvino to engage the narrative potentials of cybernetics' recombinatory logic, allowing for an imaginary projection of urban space to be shaped according to a set of algorithmic relationships. Here, as Calvino (1974, 164) recounts, places and experiences exchange their qualities of form, order, and distances, as they become variously assorted "like the letters in a name."

By introducing the quotient of experience—"the events of the past"—to his representation of the city, Calvino considered the application of this recombinatory logic not only to discrete spatial entities, but also to an intimately temporal sphere as well. But here, time is not continuous, rather it is experienced as discontinuous and elliptical. Just as there is no clear linear passage through the spatial environment of the city of Venice, so too there is no clear passage through its shifting temporalities, or the discrete stages and events of Marco Polo's journey. "All the future Berenices," he writes, "are already present in this instant" (p. 146). This is a temporality that figures like the experience of memory, in which recollections emerge without warning, as discrete, embodied moments that might flash up at any given time—such as, perhaps, when you lean out of a window in the early evening.

As he was attracted to the narrative potentials of cybernetics, Calvino also remained ambivalent about the implications of its abstracted mode of knowledge. As Boyer has observed, Kublai Khan had focused so narrowly on a chessboard of black and white squares that the game's meaning had eluded him, having simply become an abstract piece of wood (Boyer 1996b, 143). But when Marco Polo reminded him that this chessboard was "inlaid with two woods, ebony and maple," Khan's imagination took flight. Boyer suggests that in this way Calvino teaches us a lesson: we might reduce events to abstract patterns that facilitate the procedures of logical operations, or we can work to engender or revive imaginary projections—in this case, making words reveal the very tangible qualities of a given object—which in turn might allow for "the continued presence of the unfathomable, the invisible" (Boyer 1996b, 143).

This chapter retrieves Calvino's imaginative conception of invisible cities and considers its place within the contemporary, emergent terrain of urban computing. It explores how an enduring attraction to that which remains "invisible" within the contemporary city has historically inspired alternative, sometimes radical urban interventions, which have sought out different ways of knowing and experiencing cities, against the predominance of visual representations and abstracted schemas. These have inspired situated, embodied, and sensory accounts of urban spatial experience, which have resisted a tendency to rely on visual urban abstractions as a means to "improve" cities. Returning to the now well-told story of urban modernism's failure to realize its utopian project of urban social reform, the chapter revisits some imaginative conceptions of invisible cities, particularly as they emerged in response to the failures of twentieth-century urban modernism. It then moves on to discuss a specific project I have initiated, which has taken up some of these concerns and applied them to a mobile production project. This project, released in 2008 by the Australian

Broadcasting Corporation (ABC) as *Sydney Sidetracks*, has made extensive use of sound archives to generate different ways of "seeing" contemporary spaces in central Sydney, Australia. Sound has been used in this project in a way that foregrounds an embodied, experiential approach to navigating networked digital environments, working against the more dominant visual representational techniques of network mapping and data visualization. As it has offered a creative response to the potentials of mobile urban computing today, the *Sidetracks* project has also explored the potential for invisible cities to inspire different spatial practices within the emerging environments of urban computing.

"Forget Old Ways to Describe Cities": Picturing the Invisible in the Real-Time City

Today, the ability to graphically enhance our imaging of cities as multiscalar, networked environments offers profound potentials, introducing an array of new urban management and design techniques that make use of more detailed, real-time urban data.[3] Just as a shapeless dust cloud invaded the continents of *Invisible Cities*, today's real-time cities are underpinned by an information architecture of sensors and applications, whose databases express the mutating, multiscalar complexities of the material world. Embedded sensor networks reveal that which might otherwise be invisible to the naked eye; like coins rubbed over wax paper, they make visible a myriad of fluid, complex exchanges between material, social, and informational universes.

For many, this computational intensification of the material world retrieves hidden, hitherto banished possibilities, and can be put to disruptive uses (Foth 2009, 19). To Foth, practitioners of urban informatics can act as "urban anatomists," dissecting urban environments and infrastructure by "trying to microscopically uncover the connections and interrelations of city elements," seeking to "picture the invisible and . . . zoom into a fine-grained resolution of urban environments."[4] Peter Hall and Janet Abrams (2006, 12) have suggested "mapping has emerged in the information age as a means to make the complex accessible, the hidden visible, the unmappable mappable." The application of hyperlocal, multiscalar, and real-time mapping techniques, it is argued, presents opportunities to expose "hidden" or hitherto invisible relationships, including the relationships between center and periphery, power and influence (see Sassen 2008; Boyer 2006).

For Hill, there is the potential to avoid grand infrastructural interventions, which inevitably become "hardwired into the urban fabric" for subsequent generations, and to instead develop a more "iterative, responsive field of 'urban acupunctures.'"[5] Location-aware computing has also been seen to greatly expand the range of possibilities for artists, architects, and designers to "re-enchant the world," offering "a way of making visible all these hidden stories of place" (Crang and Graham 2007, 815; see also Shirvanee 2007). The embedding of microprocessors via sensor web networks in physical environments also enables the informational life worlds of millions of "users," human or otherwise, to be made visible, such that the needs not only of humans but also of natural environments can be revealed as diffuse, complex systems of interaction.

In many ways, the potentials associated with real-time mobile networks are predicated on the ability to make visible that which has hitherto remained unseen— whether the enhanced visibility of traffic flows, social usage patterns, environmental data, or those "hidden stories of place." But when considering the kinds of disruptive uses these visualization tools might be put to, toward enhanced modes of political and creative engagement, or improved techniques of urban management, we need also to remain mindful of their limitations. It helps to remember that today's real-time cities are not themselves "new," but emerge with their own historical geography of sorts. And this historical geography reminds us that there are limitations associated with relying too heavily on technologies of visual abstraction as a basis on which to create a politically reformist agenda for the city.

While today's computational capacity far outstrips that which has preceded it, nevertheless many contemporary claims made for the progression of new political, environmental, and societal reforms using networked urban computing devices echo earlier claims made "when old technologies were new" (Marvin 1988). Indeed, when current shifts toward enhanced speed, mobility, and information processing are placed in a historical perspective, we can see they are an intensification of processes that have a history as long as the modern, industrial city itself (Graham and Marvin 1996, 74; Townsend 2009; Mumford 1961). As Scott McQuire (2008, 4) has also noted, "the widening of the gap between ways of life primarily grounded in place, and emergent ways of life in which spatial experience is increasingly opened to events occurring elsewhere, has been a primary characteristic since industrial modernity." By connecting distant peoples and places, the establishment of train networks during the nineteenth century profoundly restructured people's understandings of everyday space and time, and was anticipated to provide the basis for a "universal bond" among hitherto disparate societies (Mattelart 2002, 179; Galloway 2008, 112). The installation of the first optical telegraph line in France in 1794 was likewise accorded an emancipatory capacity to "organize humans in one great family in pursuit of the same objective: the establishment of a concord that transcended social and national division" (Mattelart 2002, 180).

The introduction of wireless radio networks in the United States in 1912 was expected to bring "mutual understanding to all sections of the country, unifying our thoughts, ideals and purposes, making us a strong and well knit country" (Douglas 1986, 54). As Eric Gordon (2005, 252) writes, "unlike other elements of the urban environment, like crowds of people and the congestion of buildings that were increasingly associated with crime and danger in the popular press, the crowding of invisible messages on radio waves carried redemptive possibilities." Gordon suggests that radio's emergence as a popular medium brought the invisible to the forefront of everyday life and significantly altered how a city could be imagined: "It de-emphasised its centre and placed importance on the hubs surrounding it in a radial fashion" (p. 252).

Historical advances in the tools used to visualize urban space have likewise had a profound impact on claims to restructure and improve cities, from the first maps to the latest in satellite imagery (Townsend 2009, 20). The aerial perspective unleashed a wave of rethinking about urbanism, enabling the city to be revealed in the minutest of detail (Campanella 2001 in Townsend 2009, 22). New ways of visualizing urban space encouraged the reworking of cities as abstracted, unified entities, whose efficient reorganization would rid existing urban geographies of their unwanted, disorganized, unhealthy elements. As technologies of speed and motion altered the sense of proximity and distance, the accomplishment of more abstracted urban schemas encouraged highly utopian fantasies about the role of urban planning in reforming urban society. These presumed that the ills of urban society could be reformed through the development of new urban schemas; Geddes' Regionalism and Howard's Garden City concepts were each predicated on classificatory schemas for "the city" devised as an abstracted and generalizable form (Hall 1988; Welter 2002, 86).

"Where Did I Lose You, My Trampled Fantasies?"

Today, many of the modern urban visions inspired by new technologies of seeing are remembered as tragic (Buck-Morss 1991, 89; Pinder 2005, 46), particularly for their failure to account for the material production of spatiality, including the social relationships and economies of production that would give rise to specific urban formations.[6] During what Ed Soja (2000, 95) has called the "urban crisis" of the 1960s, the critique of urban modernism was particularly acute, as critics lamented the tendency to assume that urbanism's progressive potential lay in riding the waves of technological and economic development, and persistently ignoring specific social and historical contexts (see also Scott 2007, 24).

In 1961, for example, Jane Jacobs published *The Death and Life of Great American Cities*, now a classic urban planning textbook, in which she challenged the modernist urban designs of urban planning, which resorted to abstracted schemas or blueprints—"the dishonest mask of pretended order"—as a basis from which to represent, and renew, cities. In her straightforward prose, her evocative rendering of Greenwich street life, and her pointed emphasis on the importance of local, unplanned diversity to the city, Jacobs successfully unsettled the planning establishment despite her position as a relative outsider (Sennett 1970). To Jacobs "the city" was not a plan, a grid, or a highway network, it was a disorganized collection of haphazard incidents and accidental encounters between strangers. Jacobs later reflected that in writing *Death and*

Life, "learning and thinking about city streets and the trickiness of city parks launched me into an unexpected treasure hunt."[7] It was through daily intimate observation that she revealed the complexities of urban life in a way that many traditional planning designs, informed more by abstracted aerial views, did not tend to do.

In Europe of that year, there were different kinds of treasure hunts going on, which also sought alternate spatial representations of the city, though articulated as a more overtly radical program of action.[8] In 1961 Raoul Vaneigm (1961, 120) published "Comments against Urbanism" in the *Internationale Situationniste* in which he decried urbanism as "the most concrete and perfect fulfillment of nightmare" and noted the incredible dullness "in everything having to do with urbanism." That same year the French leader of the Situationists, Guy Debord, delivered via tape recorder a lecture on the "Prospects for Conscious Modifications of Everyday Life" that drew attention to the "scandalous poverty" of everyday life. Debord had been a part of the Lettrist International of the early 1950s, which had been devoting themselves to a certain kind of urban exploration—that of the *derive*. Drifting through the city for days, weeks, or months at a time, the group sought out what they called the city's "psychogeography," to find signs of what Chtcheglov called "forgotten desires"—images of play, eccentricity, secret rebellion, and creativity against the dominant practices of the city (Marcus 2002, 4). Through practices of psychogeography it was argued that the historical "absences" produced by urban planning could be retrieved.

These French Situationists sought to revive the spaces of the city not simply through the production of tracts, or books, or the radical redesign or representation of environments, but simply by wandering the city (*errant*) (Pinder 2005, 149). Their ideas were strongly influenced by the ideas of Henri Lefebvre, sometimes described as a Marxist phenomenologist, who, like Jane Jacobs, was critical of attempts to progress purely visual abstractions of the city in ways that were not grounded in the reality of everyday urban existence. In *The Right to the City*, Lefebvre (1996, 138) considered "planning as ideology," specifically urban ideology, which "formulates all the problems of society into questions of space and transposes all that comes from history and consciousness into spatial terms. He argued that such spatial terms, rationally ordered into circulatory patterns—for example, the city as a network of circulation and communications, or of information and decision making—present as "truth and total dogma," enabling the spatial planner, and the architect, to position themselves as "architect of the world, human image of God the Creator" (p. 137).

Against these tendencies, Lefebvre sought to reclaim space as not only conceptual but also experiential. Like Calvino, he drew on the resources of memory to challenge spatial abstractions, thinking of space and time together, by using auditory metaphors such as that of rhythm (Lefebvre 1994, ix). He also turned to writers such as Bachelard (1994, xxxv), whose spatial terrain was the poetic, eulogized space of the imagination, a topophilia of felicitous space, "the spaces we love and inhabit." To Bachelard, all "really inhabited space" contains a notion of home; as inhabited spaces, such sites become places of memory, anchoring the past in the present, and the present in the past.

Importantly for both Lefebvre and Bachelard, the activation of the resources of memory was not simply a recourse to nostalgia. Instead they turned to ideas about intimate, "everyday" spatiality as a means by which to retrieve hidden sources of possibility and progressive change, by articulating a phenomenology of experience from which the impulse for change might emerge. To Bachelard (1994, 57), "if we have retained an element of dream in our memories, if we have gone beyond merely assembling exact recollections, bit by bit the house that was lost in the midst of time will appear from out of the shadow." Like Calvino, Bachelard wanted to establish a way of thinking about space that included that which cannot be seen, taking into account the role of memory and imagination in shaping the way we experience space as an embodied encounter. Crang and Travlou (2001, 163) have more recently suggested that such tactics resemble less a theory of *representation* (as original, copy, simulation) than that of spatial *practices* associated with temporal folding and marking within a "memory topi," where the past features "literally and figuratively, [as] a presence."

In seeking out different ways of knowing and experiencing the city, the formation of these different spatial epistemologies challenged the primacy of abstracted visual schemas and their mobilization as a basis for urban reform. Against the backdrop of technological modernization, they maintained a place for invisible cities—cities of memory, of topophilia, of auditory reverberations, of psychogeographic ambiences or accidental treasure hunts—in order to disrupt the reliance on visual modes of representation in understanding, and in turn reforming, cities.

Such alternate spatial epistemologies are worth remembering when we consider the potentials of mobile urban computing in the real-time cities of today. Of course, the promises of today's real-time cities are very much predicated on the ability to disrupt these modernist, abstracted, urban views, through recourse to more contextually aware, embedded datascapes that are much better at capturing complex data. And yet, real-time mobile networks are not necessarily neutral in the way they activate "hidden" data. Crang and Graham (2007, 789) have expressed concern that embedded within the everyday life worlds of "sentient cities" is what they call a "politics of visibility," which relates to how technologies are made visible to us, and how we are made visible to them. They have suggested that an increasing saturation of urban spaces with "anticipatory technologies," which profile users in more and more sophisticated ways, may potentially pacify users by creating a sense of delegated agency. By linking imaginations and anticipations of future behavior(s) to categorical renderings from computerized memory, it may be that digital urbanists today "risk delegating whole sets of decisions and, along with that, the ethics and politics of those decisions, to invisible and sentient systems." They argue that as they become seamlessly integrated through mobile devices into local, urban environments, such practices may in fact "enact and organize global and transactional flows producing an ongoing geography of distanciated, technological performance" (p. 789).

Critical reflections like these remind us that urban computing does not simply activate the invisible, dormant potentialities of urban spaces. To argue this suggests that these spaces somehow exist as empty or neutral containers for action, and might otherwise remain stagnant and alienating places without the enhanced vitality of interaction characteristic of mobile networks. This instrumentalist treatment of urban spatiality unfortunately has much in common with the views of the urban modernists, though the geometrical forms may no longer be Euclidean. When practitioners of urban computing therefore claim the benefits associated with "picturing the invisible," it is worth remembering that to some, this may be, as Calvino suggested, "the same as telling you nothing."

Listening in to the (Invisible) Past within the Present: Archival Detours and Auditory Detournements

This chapter returns to the imagined spaces of invisible cities as the inspiration for an alternative way of engaging the creative and political potentials of urban computing today. As part of a recent mobile plot project, released by the ABC in 2008 as *Sydney Sidetracks*, I drew from these ideas as a way of exploring the spaces of central Sydney via mobile platform. This project reimagined the spaces of central Sydney as wireless geographies, filled not just with contemporary mobile usage data but historical wireless broadcasts as well, drawing on the ABC's sound archives recorded on location during different moments of a site's history. The project took what auditory traces remained of these historical moments and used them to frame a particular auditory encounter with the same sites today, digging the archives out of obscurity and making them available for digital download to mobile device. The invisibility of an auditory trace of the past was used here to frame a visual encounter with the present day. In this way, the *Sydney Sidetracks* project saw Calvino's narrative technique adopted as a tool for audio production using the mobile device, as the "measurements of space" were calibrated by the auditory traces associated with the "events of its past."

The project was not confined to its use of sound archives but also located extensive amounts of documentary film, television, and photographic archival material as well, which were featured as part of over fifty "points of interest" across central Sydney. Nevertheless its original focus was on making particular use of sound archives for a mobile listening experience, making use of the qualities of mobile listening in framing contemporary urban experience. To Michael Bull, the proliferation of mobile listening devices—mobile phones, iPhones, iPods, and so on—means that sound has become "a way of perceiving the world" (2007, 6), and means that mobile users today have overpowering resources to construct urban spaces to their liking (2004, 122). Bull is critical of the role of mobile devices in shaping a listener's experience of the city, and argues that listening to an iPod promotes an idealized or aestheticized experience of public spaces of the city that mimics the listener's desires, enabling mobile listeners to become enclosed in "pleasurable and privatized sound bubbles" (2004, 122). But the *Sidetracks* project also recognized that mobile devices not only distance people *from* their environments; they might also promote different ways of listening *to* urban spaces. The soundwalks of Janet Cardiff have, for example, overcoded the present city with memories of the past, enabling listeners to experience a space that is not quite of the now but is rather haunted by ghostly, technologically preserved or recalled presences. The UK artist group Proboscis developed Urban and Sonic Tapestries to encourage users to create their own recordings of their everyday habitats (see urban-tapestries.net). In Sydney the UK arts group Blast Theory introduced their Rider Spoke game into the Rocks in 2009, offering participants GPS-equipped bikes to explore and document the psyche of the city and its inhabitants, as riders search for undiscovered hiding places and record their own responses to the terrain.

The *Sidetracks* project was different from these mobile sound projects because instead of generating new recordings it excavated archival radio recordings as invisible substrata of the wireless city. Research toward this project was particularly focused on identifying sound traces that amplified how much had changed to the urban environment over time, making extensive use of recordings of buildings now demolished, raucous crowds now dispersed, and detailed, historic descriptions of places long gone, annihilated by the relentless modernization of Sydney during the decades of the 1960s and 1970s. The recordings identified included street recordings of the Builders' Labourers' Federation (B.L.F.) Green Bans protests as they held up development work around the Rocks and Woolloomoloo during 1973–1974; of Vietnam War protesters gathering outside the old Commonwealth Centre (now Chifley Square); and the muffled sounds of former Prime Minister Robert Menzies being heckled by communists at the now-demolished Sydney Stadium in 1948. The project also featured short audio compilations or "soundwalks" that contain collections of interviews and archival field recordings capturing changing streetscapes and locations. These include a recording of the auctioning and demolition of the Hotel Australia, the demolition of the Pyrmont Incinerator designed by Walter Burley-Griffin, and a collection of recordings about the decade-long construction of the Sydney Opera House at Bennelong Point, including the sounds of ships in Sydney Harbour the day of its opening in 1973 by Queen Elizabeth II.[9]

As a user experience, the "sidetrack" therefore offered a journey that charted locations and events mostly invisible to the naked eye. In this way, the project foregrounded a listening experience that might establish a certain kind of displacement: listening to a recorded event or lost site as it was originally documented in situ could on the one hand affect a sense of distance—being from another time and capturing what can no longer be seen—just as it revisited the event "here" as it "really happened." Rather than promoting a screen-based mobile-phone experience, *Sidetracks* therefore used the built environment as a spatial context or platform from which to excavate its invisible history, through the act of listening in to the traces of its recorded documentation.

Conclusion

To some, the idea of getting lost in cities presents a certain allure. To German sociologist Walter Benjamin, writing in the first decades of the last century, it was an aspiration. "Not to find oneself in a city may well be uninteresting and banal," he wrote, "it requires ignorance—nothing more. But to lose oneself in a city—as one loses oneself in a forest—that calls for quite a different schooling" (Benjamin [1932] 1999). Benjamin explored the metropolitan spaces of Paris and Berlin for their labyrinthine qualities, in which all kinds of lost dreams, hopes, and artifacts, often swept aside in accounts of modern development and Haussmann-like "disencumbering," might be unwittingly stumbled on. Like many of the writers and theorists discussed in this chapter, Benjamin's approach sought a kind of urban engagement that retrieved the hidden, invisible cities nestled in among the proliferating spaces of technological modernity.

As this chapter has discussed, throughout the twentieth century ideas about invisible cities have been recalled as a basis from which to explore different ways of understanding cities, which extend beyond the activation of advanced visualization techniques to encompass other senses and other spaces: poetic, imagined, or perhaps only half-recalled. Through the project *Sydney Sidetracks* I have explored how the excavation of historic wireless broadcasts might enable a way of listening in to a different historical terrain from that which might be "seen" within the city today. As a creative response to the potentialities of mobile-phone use today, it seeks to remind us that while the increasing computational intensification of urban space may radically enhance our capacity to "picture the invisible" and reveal that which has hitherto remained hidden from view, there remain other pathways, other spatial epistemologies, that confirm the enduring potency of what cannot be seen.

Notes

1. With respect to the title of this chapter, "Street Haunting" comes from Virginia Woolf's short story by the same name. See Woolf 2005.

2. Calvino discussed cybernetics in a 1967 talk called "Cybernetics and Ghosts." See Boyer 1996b, 142.

3. On the quote in the heading, see the project notes for "Mobile Landscape: Graz in Real-Time" by the SENSEable City Lab, http://senseable.mit.edu/graz/#city.

4. See the Workshop description for *Digital Cities 6: Concepts, Methods and Systems of Urban Informatics*, http://cct2009.ist.psu.edu/workshops.cfm.

5. See Hill's prediction for 2009 at Archinect online, http://tinyurl.com/yhpp2r3.

6. The quote in the heading is from Bachelard 1994, 57.

7. See the foreword to the Modern Library edition, 1993, http://www.walksf.org/essays/janejacobs.html.

8. Many critical responses to urbanization during the 1960s drew heavily on the writings of Marx and Engels, an intellectual tradition attuned to conditions of disorder, upheaval, discontinuity, and economic crisis if not directly concerned with cities (see Soja 2000, 97).

9. Individual audio recordings discussed in this chapter can be found at http://www .sitesandsounds.net.au or through *ABC Sydney Sidetracks* at http://www.abc.net.au/sidetracks, which offers access to recordings online or through a mobile application that can be downloaded directly to the phone. Note that the mobile application does not make use of GPS technology but rather includes all content in the phone application itself, to save users any potentially unpleasant data charges.

References

Bachelard, G. 1994. *The Poetics of Space*. Boston: Beacon Press.

Benjamin, W. [1932] 1999. A Berlin chronicle. In M. Jennings, ed., *Selected Writings*. Cambridge, MA: Harvard University Press.

Boyer, Christine M. 1996a. *The City of Collective Memory: The Historical Imagery and Its Architectural Entertainments*. Cambridge, MA: MIT Press.

Boyer, Christine M. 1996b. *Cyber Cites: Visual Perception in the Age of Electronic Communication*. New York: Architectural Press.

Boyer, Christine M. 2006. The urban question in the 21st century: Epistemological and spatial traumas. In A. Graafland and L. J. Kavanagh, eds., *Crossover: Architecture, Urbanism and Technology*, 312–332. Rotterdam: 010 Publishers.

Buck-Morss, S. 1991. *The Dialectics of Seeing: Walter Benjamin and the Arcades Project*. Chicago: University of Chicago Press.

Bull, M. 2004. *Sounding Out the City: Personal Stereos and the Management of Everyday Life*. Oxford: Berg.

Bull, M. 2007. *Sound Moves: iPod Culture and Urban Experience*. New York: Routledge.

Calvino, I. 1974. *Invisible Cities*. Trans. William Weaver. New York: Harcourt Brace Jovanovich.

Campanella, T. 2001 *Cities from the Sky: An Aerial Portrait of America*. New York: Princeton Architectural Press.

Crang, M., and S. Graham. 2007. Sentient cities: Ambient intelligence and the politics of urban space. *Information Communication and Society* 10 (6): 789–817.

Crang, M., and P. S. Travlou. 2001. The city and topologies of memory. *Environment and Planning, D: Society & Space* 19 (2): 161–177.

Douglas, S. 1986. Amateur operations and American broadcasting: Shaping the future of radio. In J. Korn, ed., *Imagining Tomorrow: History, Technology, and the American Future*, 35–37. Cambridge, MA: MIT Press.

Foth, M., ed. 2009. *Handbook of Research on Urban Informatics: The Practice and Promise of the Real-Time City*. Hershey, PA: IGI Global.

Galloway, A. 2008. A Brief History of the Future of Urban Computing and Locative Media. Unpublished doctoral dissertation. http://www.purselipsquarejaw.org/dissertation.html.

Gordon, E. 2005. Towards a networked urbanism: Hugh Ferris, Rockefeller Centre, and the "Invisible Empire of the Air." *Space and Culture* 8:247.

Graham, S., and S. Marvin. 1996. *Telecommunications and the City: Electronic Spaces, Urban Places*. New York: Routledge.

Hall, P. 1988. *Cities of Tomorrow: An Intellectual History of Urban Planning and Design in the Twentieth Century*. Oxford: Blackwell.

Hall, P., and J. Abrams, eds. 2006. *Else/where Mapping: New Cartographies of Networks and Territories*. Minneapolis: University of Minnesota Design Institute.

Jacobs, J. 1961. *The Death and Life of Great American Cities*. New York: Random House.

Jacobs, J. 1972 Foreword to the 1972 Modern Library edition of *Death and Life of American Cities*. Republished (no pagination) online at Walk San Francisco. http://www.walksf.org/essays/janejacobs.html.

Kunstler, J. 1993. *The Geography of Nowhere: The Rise and Decline of America's Man-Made Landscape*. New York: Touchstone Press.

Lefebvre, H. 1994. *Rhythmanalysis: Time, Space and Everyday Life*. Trans. London: Continuum.

Lefebvre, H. 1996. *Writings on Cities*. Trans. E. Kofman and E. Lebas. Oxford: Blackwell.

Marcus, G. 2002. The long walk of the Situationist International. In T. McDonough, ed., *Guy Debord and the Situationist International: Texts and Documents*, 1–25. Cambridge, MA: MIT Press.

Marvin, C. 1988. *When Old Technologies Were New: Thinking about Electric Communication in the Late Nineteenth Century*. New York: Oxford University Press.

Mattelart, A. 2002. Mapping modernity: Utopia and communication networks. In D. Cosgrove, ed., *Mapping*, 2nd ed., 169–192. London: Reaktion Books.

McQuire, S. 2008. *The Media City: Media Architecture and Urban Space*. London: Sage.

Mumford, L. 1961. *The City in History: Its Origins, Its Transformations and Its Prospects*. London: Penguin.

Pinder, D. 2005. *Visions of the City*. Edinburgh: Edinburgh University Press.

Sassen, S. 2008. New York City's two global geographies of talk. In C. Ratti, ed., *New York Talk Exchange: The Book*. New York: SA&P Press. http://senseable.mit.edu/nyte/publications.html.

Shirvanee, L. 2007. Social Viscosities: Mapping social performance in public space. *Digital Creativity* 18(3): 151–160.

Sennett, R. 1970. An urban anarchist. *New York Review of Books* 13, no. 12 (January 1, 1970).

Scott, F. 2007. *Architecture or Techno-utopia: Politics after Modernism*. Cambridge, MA: MIT Press.

Soja, E. 2000. *Postmetropolis: Critical Studies of Cities and Regions*. Oxford: Blackwell.

Townsend, A. 2009. Foreword. In M. Foth, ed., Handbook of research on urban informatics: the practice and promise of the real-time city. Information Science Reference. Hershey, PA: IGI Global.

Vaneigm, R. 1961. Comments against urbanism. In T. McDonough, ed., *Guy Debord and the Situationist International: Texts and Documents*, 119–129. Cambridge, MA: MIT Press.

Welter, V. M. 2002. *Biopolis: Patrick Geddes and the City of Life*. Cambridge, MA: MIT Press.

Woolf, V. 2005. *Street Haunting: A London Adventure*. London: Pocket Penguin.

12   Family Worlds: Technological Engagement for Families Negotiating Urban Traffic

Hilary Davis, Peter Francis, Bjorn Nansen, and Frank Vetere

This chapter considers the role that information and communication technologies, in particular mobile telephones, play in the negotiation and management of familial coordination and play in urban environments. The chapter draws on examples from our recent work and from the literature in order to explore the role of technology in familial life, in particular how families manage and synchronize their flexible schedules, dispersed activities, and the mobility of various members of the household in urban settings today. In addition, we explore the use of mobile-phone technology to support intergenerational play between grandparents and grandchildren. We describe the technologically supported efforts to collectively manage the routines of individual family members and support social connections over a distance as "urban traffic," or the mobility and movement of people and data across urban environments. We view urban traffic as a dynamic of networked coordination. This form of organization relates to the establishment and maintenance of distributed and aggregated relationships for both practical ends and emotional reassurance. Finally, we discuss some implications for the design of family-oriented technologies, arguing that designers of technology intending to support interaction between distributed family members generally—and in particular, between adults and children—should be cognizant of the work identified in this chapter. We suggest several important issues for those considering creating new applications to existing technologies, or the creation of new technological artifacts, that aim to support and encourage familial interaction for distributed familial members negotiating urban traffic.

Families and Technology

Families come in a variety of different forms, and they may contain myriad social relationships—child, parent, and grandparent—that span different generations. Each member of the family therefore may have different cognitive, social, and emotional capabilities—and these skills are continually developing and changing as children grow up and parents age and as the power dynamics between family members respond to these changes. Thus families are made up of a group of people who are not necessarily like-minded or working toward the same goals when using technology, but who have to negotiate and manage individual technology use within the framework of the family collectively. On occasion the differences in these goals can lead to tensions within the family group (see Shepherd, Arnold, and Gibbs 2006; Davis et al. 2008a), particularly when individual members use technologies in ways not considered in the best interests of the family unit, such as when a teenager uses MSN or Facebook when his parents believe that he is doing his homework or when a father surfs the net instead of spending time with his family.

There is a growing body of work that looks at the role of "mundane technologies"—that is, technologies and applications that are commonplace and that most people, including families, use such as mobile phones, texting, and e-mail (see for example, the special issue edited by Dourish et al. 2010)—and a burgeoning body of literature that addresses the pervasive nature of all types of technology in the home (Howard, Kjeldskov, and Skov 2007). However, there is little literature that specifically addresses the challenges families face when negotiating urban environments, aside from general discussions of specific social problems such as divorce, homelessness, domestic violence, overcrowding, and so on (see, e.g., Family Net Keys 2010). While not wishing to sideline this literature, we are interested in the everyday lived experience of families who work or live in urban environments. As such, this chapter discusses the role of technology—particularly mobile phones—in negotiating the minutiae of family life across and within urban environments. Specifically, we discuss how Mom and Dad use technology to stay in touch with home-based family members while they are commuting to work, and how families negotiate familial schedules while in different locations at different times. We are interested in how parents, in particular, use technologies to ensure that their children arrive wherever they need to be safely and at the right time. In essence, this chapter explores how families keep in touch using new technologies while ensuring (as much as possible) the safety of its various members, and while they are physically moving through different spaces and social situations in urban life.

These issues are particularly important given the current rapid growth of many Australian cities, and the perceived dangers that accompany this growth in urban contexts. Much of the work discussed here is drawn from our research conducted in Melbourne, Australia. While this city is not particularly large by international standards (with a population of approximately 4.8 million), we believe families living in similar urban contexts might also face many of the issues faced by families living in and around Melbourne.

This chapter seeks to unpack some of the difficulties families face and some of the technological-based strategies they use to negotiate different times/spaces and situations. We draw on our work from the Connected Homes and Intergenerational Play projects to highlight these issues. We then suggest a number of implications for the design of technology that might support families living in urban contexts.

New Technologies and the Distributed Family

Families today may be distributed both spatially and temporally—that is, although each individual is a member of the family unit as a whole, they are often separated from each other and engaged in different activities in different locations at the same time. For example, Dad might be at work in the city while Mom rests after working the night shift, the children are at school, and the teenager is studying overseas. Studies such as Litwak 1960 demonstrate that the phenomenon of the distributed, extended family and the impact of communication technologies on the maintenance of relationships predate the computer age. Litwak challenged the perception that the twentieth century had seen the nuclear family (a father, mother, and children under one roof) overtake the traditional extended family (three or more generations living in close proximity), contending that extended families survived geographic dispersion, enabled in large part by the increasing availability of communication technologies, principally the telephone. Today, the support for familial communication over distance has grown and has been supplemented by coordination tools such as shared calendars. What may have also changed are the nature of the relationships sought by family members, and how they are enacted.

Within family groups individual members might use the same technologies in different ways. For example, Mom and Dad might both use a smartphone; Mom uses it to keep in touch with colleagues at work, to send text messages to family and friends, to make shopping lists, and to entertain the kids. Dad uses his to search the Internet, update his calendar, and send e-mails. In addition, within family groups individual members use different technologies in different ways. For example, when commuting to work by train, Dad might respond to his e-mails via laptop, while Mom uses her smartphone to search the Internet.

These differences in usage reflect a range of issues, including access to technology, capability and speed of the technology, and personal preferences for types of technology (hardware and software) as well as the power dynamics within the family (e.g., Jack works full time so he has the better laptop). For many family members, such as teenage children, mobile phones may have a dual role, both representing freedom from parental control and serving as an instrument of control by parents. Mobile communication technologies are increasingly woven into the fabric of the urban family to the point where their presence is assumed. What is important here is not that family members are attracted to different technologies, or that in some families individual members use similar technologies, but that regardless of the technologies chosen, much of the usage is attributed to familial interaction or engagement. We go on to explore this further through a discussion of the specific challenges families face in urban environments and of some technologies they employ in meeting those challenges. The chapter then examines the role technology plays in familial life, primarily in terms of ensuring connection between distributed members, enabling families to manage routines and allowing individual members, particularly children, to negotiate urban traffic. Finally, we discuss some implications for the design of family-oriented technologies.

Familial Use of Technologies in Urban Contexts

There has been explosive growth in the use of social and mobile technologies among families to support communication, connectivity and coordination. A great deal of literature attests to both the communicative function and social meaning of these technologies, with research into family use of technologies covering a diverse range of practices and geographies—including leisure, work, the home, identity, and youth (e.g., Goggin and Hjorth 2009; Ling 2004; Livingstone 2002.). This literature reflects a growing body of research addressing questions of time and the possibilities and implications for coordinating more distributed routines and patterns of familial life (see, e.g., Daly 1996; Green 2002; Licoppe 2004; Nansen et al. 2009; Southerton 2003), which is not so much a question of technologies promoting individualization and "living together separately" (Livingstone 2002), but of utilizing media to organize collectively and to coordinate lives through networked collaborations. The use of mobile telephones has infiltrated the lives of people in Australia to such a degree that among eighteen- to thirty-nine-year-olds, 94 percent regularly use a mobile phone (Wajcman et al. 2007, 8), and many people possess more than one mobile phone at a time.

Studies of mobile phone use illustrate that much of this technology is used for social purposes such as engaging in what we might loosely term "social chatter" between groups of individuals who already know each other. In particular, a large study of mobile-phone use in Australia reports that logs of actual calls and SMS texts show that the predominant use of the mobile phone is for contacting family and friends; work-related reasons are far less important (Wajcman et al. 2007). These calls predominantly fall at the end of school hours and in the evening, highlighting the increasingly critical role technologies also play in supporting the maintenance of familial relationships and coordinating routines. However, mobile phones and other technologies are also being used to forge and maintain connections between people who are strangers, particularly for people who are living with social problems or other challenges such as cancer (Davis et al. 2008b).

Many technological devices have been specifically designed to assure parents of the health and well-being of their children and other family members. These range from external devices such as "nanny cameras" and GPS trackers to internal devices such as microchips for children (Shelley 2007). While uptake is reported to be slow, there appears to be a parental demand for technologies that communicate where their children are at any given time. More commonly, schools and other educational and social institutions are using mobile phones and other technologies to update and engage parents in their child's progress. For instance, reports indicates that over two-thirds of UK parents would like schools to use technologies such as text messaging and the Internet to communicate with them more frequently. However, currently only 8 percent of parents surveyed are kept informed using these methods (Becta 2009). Companies are now beginning to design applications that allow schools to send SMSs on issues such as attendance, exam schedules, fees, and so on (e.g., see Dreamteam 2009).

However, parents are not just concerned about the whereabouts of their children, and who they are spending time with, during school hours. Nor are they only concerned with the movements of the younger members of the family. For many families, a grandparent who is prone to wander due to Alzheimer's disease or dementia is a cause of concern, as is a parent who may be living with a disease such as type 1 diabetes. For many families the dangers inherent in an urban context—traffic, pollution, violence, disease, and terrorism (see Webb 2006)—may be far more obvious than those present in rural settings. A critical challenge faced by families traversing urban contexts in Australia today is how best to flexibly manage the dispersed activities and increased mobility of individual family members, which includes children, stepchildren, parents, grandparents, and other quasi-members such as pets.

Managing Familial Routines While Negotiating Urban Traffic

As part of a broader challenge to collective rhythms and traditional schedules today (e.g., Shove 2009), media technologies enable a whole raft of social and employment activities to be done from different locations and at different times, and to be conducted in a more ad hoc rather than formalized manner. Thus, media help to disrupt the sequential ordering of time, the clear division of space, and the established and structured routines that prevailed through most of the twentieth century. But the same technologies are also employed as practical resources to overcome and reorganize these conditions, thereby assisting in coordinating social and work activities.

In this context, individual and variable routines raise problems for the conduct and maintenance of family relationships in terms of coordinating and synchronizing the schedules of various household members. We have referred to this mobility as "urban traffic." This term has been used in its broader sense to refer to the passage of people along transportation routes—that is, the mobility of individual family members using a variety of means of transport such as car, rail, or tram—as well as to the conveyance of messages or data through a system of communication. In other words, we use "urban traffic" to imply both the mobility of individual family members through urban life and the technology they use while in transit to maintain familial connections, coordinate schedules, ensure the safety of individual members, and generally keep in touch. In this section we discuss the interplay of urban traffic with the coordinating, scheduling, or synchronizing of copresence in everyday life. Within this framework we call on the "lived experience" of commuters in the city. This lived experience should be familiar to us all, because it occurs on an everyday microlevel— for example, when Dad pulls over to the side of the road to answer his mobile phone; when high school student Kyle updates his Facebook status to "bored as a rock" while on the bus to school; when Mom on her way home from work texts "10 minutes away" to her children while waiting for the traffic lights to change; or Grandma, on her way into the city, takes a photograph of a train and sends it by MMS to her grandson's mobile phone. However, the relationship between families and urban traffic is not a singular one, as these examples might imply (mother to son, grandparent to grandson). Instead it is a dynamic relationship, which can encompass many family members, and as we will see, is emotive and value laden.

For some commuters, mobile and other technologies are managed and seamlessly integrated into an urban context. But for many families, the challenge of coordinating the routines, activities, events, and people within a family unit is complicated by the fact that individual family members' schedules may be unstructured, constantly subject to change, and thus unstable. This arrangement of traffic exposes the inadequacy or limitations of traditional or formalized scheduling strategies, or the shortcomings of only addressing personal organization. Instead, methods for coordinating family life demand addressing through negotiating and organizing one's schedule in relation to the schedules of others—for example, one parent's schedule in relation to her partner's schedule and to that of the individual children. This problem is exemplified in familial life through utilizing social and mobile media to weave together patterns, routines, and schedules of family members' activities as they take shape across domestic, suburban, and urban contexts of traffic. This traffic is particularly evident in relationships between parents and children in, for example, the use of technologies to coordinate parents attending or picking up children from extracurricular activities such as sporting events. We discuss children and urban traffic later in this chapter.

In the Connected Homes project (Arnold 2004), the coordination of family members occurred through the integration of people, devices, and applications. In particular, it involved the use of electronic groupware calendar systems such as the Apple iCal (Lord 2008; Salzman and Palen 2008), mobile 3G devices such as the iPhone, and family members maintaining a shared calendar, schedule, or diary and synchronizing their individual activities by entering their activity data from different locations while on the move. The following quotes give an account of how different families manage this activity: "We have a computer diary system to check what everyone is doing. It all goes in the diary . . . which goes to the Apple server somewhere before coming back here. Katie's work she inputs on her computer upstairs, which is connected to her dot Mac account . . . and mine's similarly for work appointments . . . a lot of it is specifically about managing time."

Many parents reported that they attended to these activities while commuting to and from work: "I know now I can sit on the train—tomorrow I am running a workshop at the MCG [Melbourne Cricket Ground] and I will get the train from Jolimont to Macleod—and on the way home I will knock off any email, any voicemail, I can check the Web on this [iPhone]. I can just get all that done in half an hour on the train, which means when I come home I am clear. And now I know what I check here [iPhone] and what I check there [desktop] is the same thing."

Other parents described the process whereby they integrated technologies (such as iPhones with home computers) in order to more smoothly manage familial schedules and appointments with them: "I've set up my home computer so I can upload from the phone to that so that I can coordinate . . . it's useful to be able to make an appointment when you are not on the computer, so that they don't clash. I use it for all sorts of reminders to myself—or appointments, sporting appointments. So I know the girls' hockey schedule between now and the end of the year is all in there, so I know what games we play and where."

This use of mobile technology is not atypical of mobile-phone use in Australia. It has been reported elsewhere that conveying information about the "timing of arrival at home" and "making arrangements to meet with other family members" are the major uses of the mobile phone for microcoordination. Among parents, arranging to deliver goods or children and "finding out where children are" are rated as important reasons for mobile-phone use (Wajcman et al. 2007). These findings echo those of Palen and Hughes (2007), who in their study of primary caregivers, found parents and others viewed their mobile phones as a means for staying connected or tethered across different kinds of situations. They also found that the age of children, and their involvement with other institutions beyond the family, affected how parents utilized their mobile phones. Their data showed that parents only relaxed their attention to their own mobile phones when in the company of their children.

Some participants in the Connected Homes project appropriated a range of technologies to support family coordination. The multiple convergent *and* divergent schedules of familial routines were synchronized via a server, which incorporated data entered from separate devices in real time to visually map and provide a comprehensive overview of the family's activities. This scheduling system was regularly maintained by all family members to better coordinate multiple and variable work patterns and to better manage both personal and shared activities. The success of the dynamic could not be attributed to a single device or application. Instead the interplay of individual family members' hardware and software, interacting, inputting, and accessing data about people's routines, enabled the synchronization to work. Thus, the appropriation and domestication of these technologies challenge the individual-izing and fragmenting picture often portrayed in the media and in certain strains of academic research. Multiple technologies are integrated in these family contexts to support the social purpose of familial coordination and synchronization.

These technical affordances, uses, and practices—of coordinating times and sched-ules via mobile and social media—suggest that not only are technologies used to support forms of microcoordination (Ling and Yttri 1999), but also forms of distrib-uted and shared coordination, called *networked coordination*. The term *microcoordination* refers to social coordination organized through flexible dynamics and ongoing nego-tiation and improvisation in transit and on the move—especially via mobile phones—which allow for incrementally adjusting or gradually modifying an impending meeting right up until the moment and place at which it occurs. In contrast, the dynamic of networked coordination identified here affords the establishment and maintenance of more distributed and aggregated relationships, such as familial relationships; it supports a greater variety of appointments and a more extended schedule of events (over days, weeks, and months), and finally it offers a more orderly form of coordina-tion by providing an overview of the families' schedule and movements (from any number of screens).

Such networked forms of coordination are becoming increasingly common across organizational, social, and familial contexts. They suggest flexible, negotiated, and unfolding arrangements, adaptable through collaboration between people and tech-nologies in networked relationships. These arrangements underscore the contrasting dynamics facilitated through mobile media: one involving individual and flexible arrangements, the other involving networked and collaborative arrangements. Both modes of coordination allow for a degree of fluidity in organizing copresence or syn-chronizing schedules. These alternative patterns of synchronization are clearly appli-cable to different social contexts, including both the more mundane social chatter and interaction between friends, and the pragmatics of purposeful organizational dynamics of families and family schedules.

Children and Urban Traffic

Parents today are concerned for their children's safety as they negotiate urban streets. Indeed, increased security is cited as the major reason for buying children a mobile phone in Australia, regardless of the gender of the child (Wajcman et al. 2007, 24). Parental concerns about the security of their children have had a major impact on the lives of children today. The numbers of Australian children walking and cycling for transport, which are already low in comparison to many other developed countries, have declined substantially in recent decades. For example, in Melbourne in 1970,

55.3 percent of young people walked to school or higher-education institutions, but this fell to 22.2 percent in 1994. In the same period, cycling to school declined from 7.5 to 3.9 percent and car travel increased from 14.3 to 55.3 percent. In the rest of Victoria over this time period, figures were less dramatic than these (Garrard 2009, 9). Children seem less likely to walk to school for a variety of reasons, including changes in school zoning restrictions preventing many children from attending their local school. In the United States it is reported that the main reason for a decline in children walking to school is parental fear of "stranger danger." This idea is refuted by anecdotal conversations from Melbourne parents, who argue that parents are more concerned that their child might be injured as a pedestrian walking to school (for a discussion between Melbourne and U.S. parents, see Simon 2009). It has been reported, however, that an Australian child is nearly twice as likely to be killed as a car *passenger* than as a pedestrian, and more than four times as likely to be killed as a car passenger than as a cyclist (Christie et al. 2004). The issue of why fewer children are walking to school is complex and largely outside the scope of this work. However, what is important here is that these concerns (however they play out in practice) provide a motivation for many parents to drive their children to school or to use technologies to keep in touch with them while they are in transit from home to school, or from home to distributed family members or elsewhere. We have explored this motivation in some of our previous work focusing on mobile technologies for parent-child relationships (Yarosh et al. 2009). What we know is that parental anxiety diminishes when their children carry a mobile phone. In practical terms this means that around 30 percent of parents would allow their teenage children to stay out late if they had a phone with them (Wajcman et al. 2007).

Familial Play and Urban Traffic

Mobile phones and other devices may also be appropriated for family-based activities other than the coordination of schedules or ensuring the safety of children while in transit. The value of grandparent interactions in families is widely recognized, yet despite this, the importance of intergenerational interactions remain underresearched, both generally (Ward 1999) and more specifically in terms of technology (Lindley, Harper, and Sellen 2009). In the Intergenerational Play project we provided geographically distributed grandparents and grandchildren with mobile phones for use while in transit and at home. The grandparents and grandchildren used the phones to take photographs and compose messages, which were then posted to a server or system known as the Collage (Vetere et al. 2009).

Both grandparents and grandchildren sent many photos from home as well as photographs taken while in transit. Many of the photographs and messages exchanged were related to moving in and through urban traffic. One boy, age four, sent more than a dozen photos of cars and trucks. These included toy trucks and cars that he had arranged at home, photographs of his father's trucks and other moving equipment parked in his backyard and at different work locations, and many random photographs of cars and trucks parked or moving on the road. He took many of these photos out the back window of his parents' car while in transit. His older brother tended to post photographs relating to particular events away from home. For example, he took the camera with him on Cub camp and posted many photographs of himself engaged in activities such as archery, camping, and so on.

The photographs and messages appeared on touch screens in the respective family homes, cascading in a perpetual loop. Photographs could then be manipulated (stopped, moved, rotated, enlarged) by simple motions on the touch screen. When one family member, such as the grandchild, manipulated the photograph, the other, like the grandparent, observed the action on a distant screen. This resulted in playful, dancelike behavior, as the grandparents and grandchildren negotiated how to orient and manipulate the photographs. The Intergenerational Play project served many purposes for these families. While the children's mobile-phone use was often negotiated with parents and others such as siblings and school authorities, the phones provided both independence from parents, and reassurance for parents and grandparents (i.e., the children were safe and enjoying themselves). Grandparents felt particularly reassured when their grandchildren were interacting with Collage, because they knew they were safely at home.

Discussion

This chapter highlights a range of roles that new technologies—in particular, mobile phones—play for families in urban environments. The stories are not really about communication over distance, because the distances were often relatively small. Nor were they simply about overcoming separation by time. Perhaps they are better defined by the causes of "separation"—the factors that gave rise to the need for mobile communication technologies.

We have shown that mobile phones are used in practical ways to support familial activity while families are in transit. Families use them to structure, coordinate, enforce, and promote familial routines; in essence they use them to help manage familial activity. Attendance to these tasks often takes place while individual family members—usually the parents—are moving through and into particular urbanized spaces such as in their daily commute to work. It is interesting to note that a large study of Australian mobile-phone activity found that only a small proportion of calls were work-related (16 percent). Mobile phones were used overwhelmingly for contacting family (48 percent) and friends (26 percent). Of calls to family, women were most likely to call their spouse or partner (18 percent), parents (12 percent), children (11 percent), and extended family members (11 percent) (Wajcman et al. 2007, 13).

We have also seen how emotional concerns are reflected in the use of mobile phones among families. The primary reason children carry a mobile phone is to provide a sense of reassurance of safety for their *parents*—an opportunity to be in contact with the child regardless of the time or their location. Children, however, will use the phones strategically—they will make decisions about which texts or calls to respond to, and which to ignore, depending on the situation. For example, some Melbourne high schools have a policy of only allowing mobile-phone use during school lunch breaks and after school, so students cannot call their parents back outside of these times. For parents, the role of mobile phones is to provide a sense of security; they help to alleviate anxiety about the location and nature of their children's activities, regardless of the gender of the child. Conversely, mobile-phone use, similar to the use of other new technologies such as the Internet, may also become a cause for concern for parents. They view their children as potentially vulnerable to unwanted attention from strangers (such as pedophiles online) as well as known acquaintances (e.g., in the form of cyberbullying or stalking). In addition, the invention of "where-am-I-apps" (e.g., mobile-phone tracking applications such as foursquare, http://foursquare.com/), and of other applications that use GPS tracking to pinpoint the user's physical location, has exacerbated the fears parents have for their children (Andrew 2010). There are concerns, too, that websites such as http://pleaserobme.com/, which purport to highlight the dangers of users sharing their physical location on social media such as Twitter and Facebook, are now potentially making the family vulnerable as strangers become aware that the home is unoccupied (Boorsbom, Groenveld, and van Amstel 2010).

Mobile phones are also used as a source of information by families, and are used by parents to provide vital up-to-the-minute prompts for their children: "Don't forget your cricket match after school," "Nan will pick you up today," and "The train is running late." Children may initiate as well as respond to these prompts when negotiating urban settings in order to provide reassurance to their parents, thus actively collaborating with other family members to ensure that their independence continues. Moreover, mobile phones and other new technologies may be instrumental in defining individual families. For example, there are accounts of people finding biological family members they never knew existed via social networking sites such as Facebook (e.g., see Charrison 2009), and others where family members have been excluded from being "friends" on Facebook and other social networking sites.

Implications for Design of Family-Oriented Technologies

We believe that designers of technology intending to support interaction between distributed family members—and in particular, between parents and their children—should be cognizant of the work identified in this chapter. We suggest several important issues for those considering creating new applications for existing technologies or designing new technological artifacts in order to support and encourage familial interaction for distributed familial members.

Recent work has highlighted some implications for the design of playful intergenerational technologies between grandparents and grandchildren (Davis et al., 2011, forthcoming). Some of the themes arising from that work are relevant to this chapter. Designers of new technologies that aim to support familial activity, particularly in an urban context, should be cognizant of the possible span of generations that fall within families. Families may include young children, teenagers, young adults, middle-aged parents, and older people. As such, if designers wish to support family interaction, their technologies should have an intergenerational appeal, and components of the technology should be applicable to young, middle-aged, and older users.

Furthermore, individual family members may play a variety of roles. A mother of young children may also be a stepmother to teenage children, a wife, a doctor, a daughter, and so on. New technologies that support individual family members in their various roles and that allow them to smoothly transition between these roles, particularly when they are moving through and within urban "traffic," are particularly valued.

Designers of familial technologies should recognize that families use mobile and social technologies for a variety of reasons and for a variety of activities. Many activities, such as sending a text message, may appear to be primarily instrumental. But in a family context they often have an underlying social purpose—for example, to build a family calendar to organize future familial activities, to support a child in negotiating urban traffic, or to alleviate anxiety in a parent. These roles may change depending on the characteristics of the members (age, gender, role), the grouping of the members (child to parent, parent to parent, parent to grandparent), the location of the interaction (at school, after football, on the commute home), and the social situation itself in which the family member is located. The difficulty for designers of familial technologies is that in designing for families they must also incorporate elements of design recommended for intergenerational exchanges. This is because families may include a spectrum of age groups and will encompass different physical, intellectual, and social characteristics. Even more problematic, if it is not to become redundant fairly quickly, designers of new technology must recognize that families evolve as children grow up and are allowed more independence and control over the technology (Davis et al. 2008a), and as parents and grandparents age.

Parents are concerned that their children's activities are safe, healthy, and interesting. New familial technologies should be designed so as to minimize any risk to families, particularly to younger or vulnerable users, while allowing them to engage in interactions that are exciting and interesting to both parties. This might help explain some of the success of the iPhone for families. It has been documented that many parents with iPhones regularly let children use their phones to download games and often use their phones at grocery stores to compare prices and check their grocery lists (Lardinois 2009). We have also seen how iPhones were used in the Connected Homes project to construct and share family calendars. In the United States an iPhone application has been developed to inform concerned parents about the whereabouts of sexual and other predators (Family Watchdog LLC 2009). These activities fall outside the traditional uses for a mobile phone.

However, smartphones should not be seen as the "solution" to the "problem" of organizing family coordination or scheduling. While these services enable parents and others to keep in touch over a distance, they also shape these very schedules. For example, the iPhone calendar allows scheduling in five-minute intervals and upward, and alerts users from five minutes to two days prior to an event. For parents, this means that they can schedule an increasing range and number of engagements for both themselves and their children. Indeed, considerable research laments that children's structured activities have increased while their free playtime has continued to decrease. It is argued that this is to the detriment of both promoting healthy development of children and promoting familial bonds (see, e.g., Ginsburg 2007). Thus, current social technologies may present both a problem and a solution for parents as their children traverse urban traffic. For example, while a text message may reassure a parent that their child is on the way home, the absence of a message can also create anxiety among parents. Technologies such as the swarm-phone application (Satchell 2003) can provide engaging up-to-date information about the location and activities of teenage children, while at the same time allowing those children freedom to construct the "story" of those activities. This type of technology would be particularly welcomed by families.

Finally, technologies that allow flexibility—so that they can be used in myriad ways for a variety of purposes—are more likely to capture and sustain the interest of families. This is particularly important in an urban context, where individual family members have to balance a variety of roles while facing the ongoing challenges of urban life, whether it be the daily commute, the busy office, the stresses of school, or an evening out. New technologies that allow children, parents, and other family members to support each other, while also recognizing the differences each party brings to the interaction, are particularly valued by families.

Conclusion

The family has been radically redefined since Litwak's 1960s, when the nuclear model gained acceptance as the norm. At that time it was asserted that communication technologies made it possible to maintain extensive family contact over distance. While mobile communication technologies have broadened this capability, they have done more. The level of coordination among family members could well be higher among the dual-income, calendar-sharing families in our stories; however, we have also recounted situations in which mobile phones can be used for nonpurposeful familial interaction such as intergenerational play. In addition, we can see that such coordination may serve to increase control by some family members or to aid in democratizing decision making, however these parameters are defined, negotiated, and played out among individual family members. Therefore, a potential exists for familial technologies to allow participation by family members who might otherwise experience social exclusion from the family unit, such as young children and older people..

Technologies can evoke mixed feelings for those who desire more face-to-face contact with their children or other family members. Yet mobile technologies that allow and maintain contact over distance offer greater freedom for all members of the family negotiating and traversing urban traffic.

References

Andrew, Keith. 2010. Four-Square: We are aware of privacy concerns—Location-based social app responds to media criticism. http://www.pocketgamer.biz/r/PG.Biz/Foursquare/news.asp?c=18604.

Arnold, Michael. 2004. The Connected Homes project: Probing the effects and affects of domesticated ICTs. In A. Bond, ed., *Artful Integration: Interweaving Media, Materials and Practices*, vol. 2 of *Proceedings of the Eighth Biennial Participatory Design Conference*. Toronto: Computer Professionals for Social Responsibility.

Becta. 2009. Parents want schools to text about child's progress. http://news.becta.org.uk/display.cfm?resID=38299.

Grueneveld, Frank, Barry Borsboom, and Boy van Amstel. 2010. Please rob me: Over sharing and location awareness. http://www.cdt.org/blogs/cdt/over-sharing-and-location-awareness.

Charrison, Emily. 2009. Matthew finds a family on Facebook. http://city-messenger.whereilive.com.au/news/story/online-to-find-a-family/.

Christie, Nicola, Elizabeth Towner, Sally Cairns, and Heather Ward. 2004. Children's road traffic safety: An international survey of policy and practice. *Road Safety Research Report No. 47*. London: Department for Transport.

Daly, Kerry. 1996. *Families and Time: Keeping Pace in a Hurried Culture*. London: Sage.

Davis, Hilary, Martin Gibbs, Michael Arnold, and Bjorn Nansen. 2008a. From exotic to mundane: Longitudinal reflections on parenting and technology in the connected family home. Proceedings of the workshop on Social Interactions and Mundane Technologies, 1-5 Cambridge, Lancaster University. November 20–21.

Davis, Hilary, Frank Vetere, Shawn Ashkanasy, Gavin Dyson, Penelope Schofield, Kate Thompson, Giselle Withers, and David Thomas. 2008b. Towards social connection for young people with cancer. In Proceedings of OZCHI 2008: Designing for Habitat and Habitus, Cairns, Australia, December 8–12, 319–322. Melbourne: ACM Press.

Davis, Hilary, Frank Vetere, Martin Gibbs, and Peter Francis. 2011. Come play with me: Designing technologies for intergenerational play. *Universal Access in the Information Society*. Forthcoming.

Dourish, Paul, Connor Graham, David Randall, and Mark Rouncefield. 2010. Special theme issue: "Social Interaction and Mundane Technologies." *Personal and Ubiquitous Computing* 14 (3): 171–180.

Dreamteam. 2009. "A novel initiative" school SMS system. http://www.dreamteam.co.in/gnewsview.php?newsid=-65.

Family Net Keys. 2010. http://www.aces.edu/urban/FamilyWebsite/topics.html.

Family Watchdog L. L. C. 2009. New iPhone app increases family safety, provides sex offender information. http://www.beststuff.com/fromthewire/audiovideo-news/new-iphone-app-increases-family-safety-provides-sex-offender-information.html.

Garrard, Jan. 2009. Active transport: Children and young people (an overview of recent evidence). *VicHealth Publication*. http://www.vichealth.vic.gov.au/en/Resource-Centre/Publications-and-Resources/Physical-Activity/Active-transport/Active-Transport-Children.aspx.

Ginsburg, Kenneth. 2007. The importance of play in promoting healthy child development and maintaining strong parent-child bonds. *Paediatrics* 119 (1): 182–191.

Goggin, Gerard, and Larissa Hjorth, eds. 2009. *Mobile Technologies: From Telecommunication to Media*. London: Routledge.

Green, Nicola. 2002. On the move: Technology, mobility, and the mediation of social time and space. *Information Society* 18 (44): 281–292.

Howard, Steven, Jesper Kjeldskov, and Mikael B. Skov 2007. Pervasive computing in the domestic space. Special issue of *Personal and Ubiquitous Computing* 11 (5): 329–414.

Lardinois, Frederic. 2009. How moms use their iPhones. http://www.readwriteweb.com/archives/iphone_moms_shopping_entertaining_kids.php.

Licoppe, Christian. 2004. "Connected" presence: The emergence of a new repertoire for managing social relationships in a changing communication technoscape. *Environment and Planning, D: Society & Space* 22 (1): 135–156.

Lindley, Sian. E., Richard Harper, and Abigail Sellen. 2009. Desiring to be in touch in a changing communications landscape: Attitudes of older adults. In *Proceedings of the 27th International Conference on Human Factors in Computing Systems*. Boston: ACM.

Ling, Richard. 2004. *The Mobile Connection: The Cell Phone's Impact on Society*. San Francisco: Morgan Kaufmann.

Ling, Richard. and Birgette Yttri, 1999. Nobody sits at home and waits for the telephone to ring: Micro and hyper-coordination through the use of the mobile phone. Report 30/99. Kjeller: Telenor Research and Development.

Litwak, Eugene. 1960. Geographical mobility and extended family cohesion. *American Sociological Review* 25:385–394.

Livingstone, Sonia. 2002. *Young People and New Media: Childhood and the Changing Media Environment.* London: Sage.

Lord, Christopher. 2008. Evolution of the electronic calendar: Introducing social calendaring. Southampton: University of Southampton. http://chrislord.net/files/paper.pdf.

Nansen, Bjorn, Michael Arnold, Martin Gibbs, and Hilary Davis. 2009. Domestic orchestration: Rhythms in the mediated home. *Time & Society* 18 (2/3): 181–207.

Palen, Leysia, and Amanda Hughes. 2007. When home base is not a place: Parents' use of mobile phones. *Personal and Ubiquitous Computing* 11:339–348.

Salzman, Marilyn, and Leysia Palen. 2008. *The Tools We Live By: A Description of Personal Support Media in Work Life.* Technical reports. Boulder: University of Colorado. http://www.cs.colorado .edu/department/pub lications/reports/marilyn_salzman.html.

Satchell, Christine. 2003. The swarm: Facilitating fluidity and control in young people's use of mobile phones. In Stephen Villier and Peta Wyeth, eds. Proceedings of OzCHI 2003 New Directions in Interaction: Information Environments, Media and Technology, November 26-28. Brisbane: University of Queensland.

Shelley, Tom. 2007. Micro-chipping children for their safety. http://rinf.com/alt-news/ surveillance-big-brother/microchipping-children-for-their-safety/1031/.

Shepherd, Chris, Michael Arnold, and Martin Gibbs. 2006. Parenting in the connected home. *Journal of Family Studies* 12 (2): 203–222.

Shove, Elizabeth. 2009. Everyday practice and the production and consumption of time. In Elizabeth Shove, Frank Trentmann, and Richard Wilk, eds., *Time, Consumption, and Everyday Life: Practice, Materiality, and Culture*, 17–34. New York: Berg.

Simon, Jonathan. 2009. My daughter does walk to school. http://prawfsblawg.blogs.com/ prawfsblawg/2009/09/my-daughter-does-walk-to-school.html.

Southerton, Dale. 2003. Squeezing time: Allocating practices, coordinating networks, and scheduling society. *Time & Society* 12 (1): 5–25.

Vetere, Frank, Hilary Davis, Martin Gibbs, and Steven Howard. 2009. The Magic Box and Collage: Responding to the challenge of distributed intergenerational play. *International Journal of Human-Computer Studies* 67 (2): 165–178.

Wajcman, Judy, Michael Bitman, Paul. Jones, Lynne Jonhnstone, and Jude Brown. 2007. *The Impact of the Mobile Phone on Work/Life Balance.* Preliminary report. Australian Research Council Linkage Project. Canberra, Australian National University.

Ward, Christopher R. 1999. The intergenerational field needs more ethnographic research. *Child and Youth Services* 20 (1/2): 7–23.

Webb, Joelle. 2006. Big city dangers. http://serendip.brynmawr.edu/biology/b103/f01/web3/webb.html.

Yarosh, Svetlana, Hilary Davis, Paulina Moditba, Mikael Skov, and Frank Vetere. 2009. Mobile technologies for parent/child relationships. In Allison Druin, ed., *Mobile Technology for Children: Designing for Interaction and Learning*, 289–310. San Francisco: Morgan Kaufmann.

13 Urban Media: New Complexities, New Possibilities—A Manifesto

Christopher Kirwan and Sven Travis

The purpose of this chapter is to introduce the emerging field of study our team at Parsons The New School for Design has termed "urban media"—media experimentation on an urban scale. We are interested in the bridge between theory and practice; the case studies presented here are based on real urban media projects produced or in production, intended to realize and test our theories. Recognizing the need for accuracy and completeness, we acknowledge that our conclusions are not yet fully substantiated or academically referenced. Hence we present this chapter as a kind of manifesto—a challenge to others to review our early-stage research and to then build on it with their own unique experience. The goal is to further this experiment with different approaches and outcomes.

Understanding Urban Media

Urban media may be seen both as a conceptual process and as an operating system whose mission is to capture and portray the dynamic interaction of the social (cultural), physical (environmental), and virtual (technological) dimensions of the city. Our goal is to stimulate interdisciplinary efforts in the fields of art and science toward the formation of a *collective intelligence*, a network capable of addressing the huge challenges facing not only our urban centers but also the entire planet.

Today we have the capacity to assess massive data streams in the analysis of human and environmental behavior in real time, to make accessible a visually integrated overlay of physical and cultural information that previously could not be expressed by any single media or communication mechanism.

This chapter outlines several case studies conducted at Parsons over the past ten years to provide examples of the potential use of urban media. Led by faculty members Christopher Kirwan and Sven Travis, these studies have focused on research projects in the major metropolitan centers of New York, Dubai, and Beijing.

The concept of urban media draws on key intellectual theories and applications introduced in the second half of the twentieth century by the gurus of urban planning, systems theory, cognitive studies, media, and sustainable design. We have included references to the work of several of these leaders in the following paragraphs.

In *Understanding Media*, Marshall McLuhan (1994) stipulated that each form of communication within the media spectrum has a unique frequency that conveys its inherent formal language. Using the same logic, the modern city can now be viewed as a form of media organism made possible by our ability to collect live data, to track movement and activities, and to stream this data through multitiered media channels to users in all sectors of the population. The current social media phenomenon is a pertinent example of the way this system could develop and operate.

In parallel with advances in informatics, cognitive science has broadened our understanding of human perception and intelligence, shedding new light on the many ways that people interact with their environment. Howard Gardner's "theory of multiple intelligences" from *Frames of Mind: The Theory of Multiple Intelligences* (1993) serves well to explain this fact and illustrates how individuals possess differing inherent capacities to structure and respond to information based on their mental makeup and experiential profiles. This theory is currently being applied with success in a variety of digitally centric arenas like the field of education, and it can be a useful resource in the presentation and analysis of research data such as economic trends, environmental factors, and patterns of human movement and consumption.

Physical forms, as well as historical, social, and economic structures are unique for each community; similarly, the ways that cities are understood, planned, and designed also contain a unique identity or DNA. In his influential book *Pattern Language* (1977), architect Christopher Alexander describes how the dynamic forces of urban life can be perceived as patterns that can be employed to establish the design criteria or program for the planning of structures at any scale—from a small structure to a larger city or metropolitan region.

In his book *The Image of the City* (1960), Kevin Lynch explores how people create mental maps of local conditions—including pathways, boundaries, districts, and historical landmarks—to navigate a particular city or region. In the case studies presented here, the first step was to document the special qualities or ethos of each city and to shape an "urban narrative" from the inherent activity patterns and culture and at the same time link the local culture to a broader context to encourage growth and change. The process of moving from the mental to the tangible—capturing these maps as data in some practical container that is accessible, searchable, and presentable—is fundamental to the production of the layers that can be used as *urban narratives*.

Urban Narratives

The case studies and subsequent on-site work in the three selected cities—New York, Dubai, and Beijing—differ significantly in the ways the urban media research and design process has been applied. In recognition of the unique character of each city as well as its links to the international community, we have adopted the term *glocal*, popularized by the expression *think globally and act locally* (Robertson 1995). Glocal describes our hybrid approach: the interface of global patterns and trends with local conditions—cultural, environmental, and technological.

We have presented our studies as narratives to stimulate new thinking on the role of temporality and the expansion of urban socioeconomic knowledge within a global ontological frame of reference. The three selected communities are at significantly different stages in their social evolution; this fact is perhaps more important than the extraordinary variety of their physical layouts and patterns of growth. New York, for example, has a more advanced sense of collective culture than that of the United Arab Emirates (UAE), which has three predominant and independent community identities, while Beijing has a unique combination of ancient history and the current Communist identity, along with an extreme division of class, wealth, and influence that is becoming increasingly apparent within the society.

In the last decade, our selected cities have experienced phenomenal growth across all sectors and have been at the center of powerful movements on the global stage. For brevity, we have compressed their descriptions into simplified frames of reference to define underlying themes for each case study.

New York supports a century-old infrastructure, mature economic markets, and an established identity as the city of diversity, innovation, finance, and the arts—the collective body. The project response has three iterations: the city as organic, living system; the city interface as individual perception filters; and the city as a collective consciousness network.

Dubai boasts a brand-new infrastructure (airport terminal, elevated people mover, roads, and bridges), and a contemporary culture that has evolved in a very short time frame into an assemblage of the traditional Arab host and a new multiethnic society. The project response describes the city identity as a media network reconnecting the fragments of its cultural legacy and its important landmarks/places.

Beijing, the final case study, is a work in progress. With a relatively new infrastructure and an ancient cultural legacy, Beijing is in the state of rediscovering and defining its identity between its glorious traditions, recent history of the cultural revolution, and the present period of rapid growth and economic prosperity. The project describes the city as frames: experiential frames of reference focused on art, culture, media, and technology as catalysts for growth and social progress.

Case Studies

Case Study 1: New York—The Organic Metropolis
The elongated shape of Manhattan Island, nestled between the East River on one side, the mainland of the Bronx, Queens, and Brooklyn on a second, and the Hudson River and New Jersey on a third, appears as some form of anatomical organ, a highly

stimulated erogenous zone nourished by the constant flow of energy all around it. This perhaps explains why this particular piece of land has been so productive in such a relatively short history. But it took the combination of the Native Americans, the Dutch, and the English to realize its value both strategically as a port of entry and as an unusual geographic habitat for generations of immigrants—each group shaping the island and the surrounding womb (New York metro region) in their own cultural manifestation. This unique combination of geographic and topological particularities and an unprecedented human migration has provided the creative fodder for endless representations of Manhattan, whether in films, photography, musical scores, texts, paintings, or new media experimentations. The physiological nature of the city— combining the metaphor of the city as an anatomical organ and the physical dimensions representing the natural flow of currents, wind, water, air, magnetic energy, human activities, and human-made systems—has been the subject of our research and the search for an appropriate virtual representation.

New York is truly a city of *multiple identities*, a special case whose sense of community is not based on a conventional geographic definition of place, but has evolved from earlier immigrant neighborhoods to become a city of communities defined by differing factors of identification and perception—each occupy a unique frequency on the collective urban bandwidth.

Here we present three projects related to New York. The first two, "Projec[tions]" and "Multiple Identities," were artistic media abstractions. The third, "New York City Action Alert Network," was a practical response to the pain and uncertainty we all faced after the 9/11 events. For the first two projects we created digital interactive maps of New York City to explore the city as a live organism—the maps incorporated streaming media content that captured both realistic and abstract media bytes throughout the city. Our focus was on the creation of narratives that would provide a content-rich representation of the living metropolis and structure these images into categories generated by the infrastructure systems underlying the city (Ascher 2007). These included circulation, reproduction, waste, and so on, which demonstrated how humans have formed cities and urban systems from the study of parallel structures in nature. It has been well documented that individuals have a natural tendency to form concepts of spatial and structural organization based on the metaphor of the mind–body, the inherent state of being human (Miele 2000). The New York City Action Alert Network project was an attempt to move the urban media concept into the pragmatic realm immediately following a major disaster.

Project 1: Organic Systems

For Projec[tions] (presented at Siggraph 1996), we developed a multiuser interactive installation representing the city as an ever-changing organism. The interactive map "projected" various immersive experiences of the city based on urban systems layers,

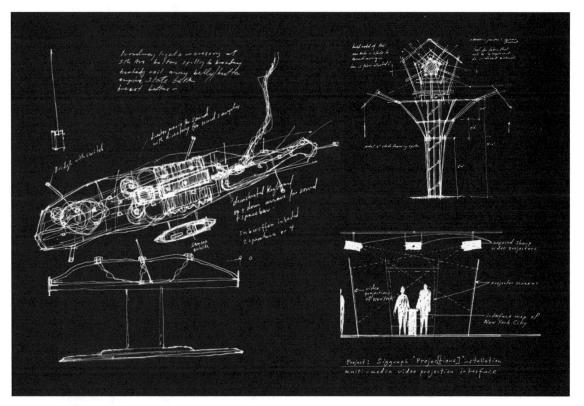

Figure 13.1

Projec[tions] anatomical installation—city:body

Faculty member Christopher Kirwan developed sketches for the Manhattan multiuser urban interface table and installation design. Collaborative studio semester-long project, Parsons School of Design, fall 1996, C. Kirwan, E. Lucero, S. Travis, faculty.

each layer translated through video content, still images, and sound (see figure 13.1). The installation allowed multiple users to interact with the map, with the surrounding installation environment, and with each other, creating a virtual simulation of the rich interactive multiplicities of the New York City urban experience. The interface design consisted of a large 3D anthropomorphic map of Manhattan with data input and output channeling through the map in the form of human biological systems. The touch interface was constructed as acupuncture needles forming the pressure points or chakra points from which the users could trigger multiple surround video and audio impressions—media bytes of the city (see figure 13.2).

This type of interactive mapping device is now in its second generation of development. It holds great promise for tourism and commercial interests and

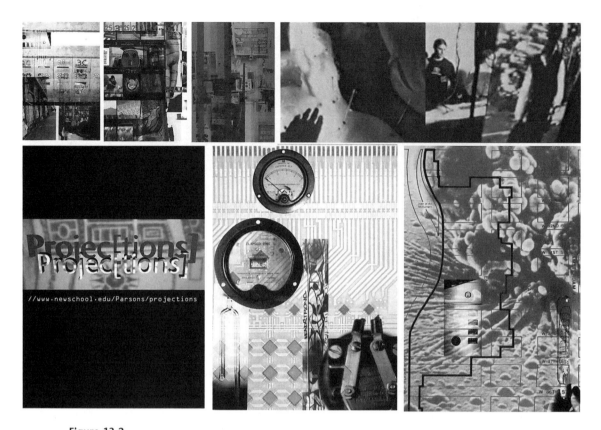

Figure 13.2

Projec[tions]: Urban interface media content

Development of macro-micro representations of urban systems based on human, environmental, and technological growth patterns. Collaborative studio semester-long project, Parsons School of Design, fall 1996, C. Kirwan, E. Lucero, S. Travis, faculty.

provides more useful content and improved access to those seeking to utilize urban resources.

Project 2: Individual Perception

Our interactive installation, Multiple Identities, presented at Siggraph 1997, was organized via individual perceptions of the city using virtual avatars as tour guides (elderly, commuter, homeless, student, rap artist, drag queen, child, and tourist) (see figure 13.3). The entire exhibition area was covered with soft material functioning as a screen for multiple projected images of people and places. Individual stations allowed individual users to select avatars and navigate the city by selecting various points of

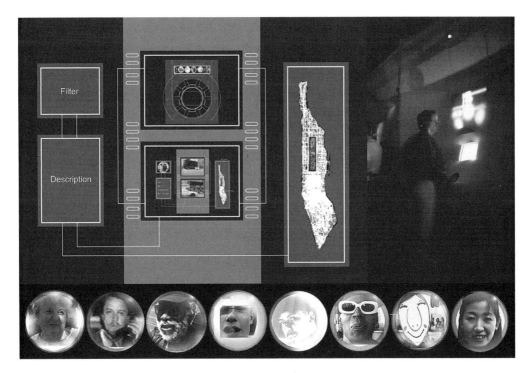

Figure 13.3
Multiple identities: Urban interface
New York City digital interface based on unique personal perspectives and filters. Projected instal-
lation presented at Siggraph 1997. Collaborative studio semester-long project, Parsons School of
Design, fall 1997, C. Kirwan, E. Lucero, S. Travis, faculty.

interest, each determined by the specific avatar's unique perspective of the city. In the
process of using the installation, we discovered that the resulting image of the city
became a composite of a random selection of human personality types, and visitor
reaction was diverted from the "real" content by the effect of the virtual simulation.
This unexpected outcome was revealing and has led us to incorporate more real-time
data into similar research projects.

Project 3: Collective Network

In 2002 the Parsons team helped to initiate the New York City Action Alert Network
(or NYCAAN)—a response to the 9/11 attack on New York City that was seen as a
major threat to the collective security of the nation (Steven 2002). Our efforts centered
on developing a social behavior systems approach, which was actually an early form
of social networking. As an alternative model to a one-to-many hierarchy or point of

control being used in many defense or security systems, our strategy was to place the responsibility in the hands of the citizens of New York City, with each citizen making up part of what would become a kind of collective consciousness and awareness. This model would more accurately measure civic behaviors and provide real-time data monitoring in contrast to the current system of reporting that has limited points of input and response.

Our first effort was to collect and map every possible source of data within the myriad of city/region information and media networks. This data was compiled by public, private, and individual sources, type and frequency of updates, and geographic location. We then constructed information layers by category—compiling singular and multiple information sources to better visualize emerging patterns and scenarios. Additionally, the system facilitated two-way communication via synchronous multi-modal communication channels with field operators collecting data on the ground where an event was taking place. The project *mediawall*, a large screen containing a real-time data visualization display of the multiple feeds, was proposed to be the main control center and located in the New York City mayor's office (see figure 13.4). Additional modular installations were to be based in various government agencies, which allowed both city employees and the public to access and monitor information.

A natural extension of the NYCAAN project would be to create a self-generating, collective intelligence network using principles developed by Norbert Wiener in his pioneering work *The Human Use of Human Beings: Cybernetics and Society* (1950). We see many important applications for such a system of collective intelligence in our cities. These applications can provide public-sector agencies with the capability to monitor, filter, and direct activity in the areas of public safety, health, environment, transportation, and energy. They can also furnish real-time information on glocal political, financial, and marketplace trends to private-sector business, industry, banking, and real estate organizations. Another current example of coordinated data collection and management is seen in the smart cities programs now being successfully employed in many communities (Incheon City—Smart Cities). In the near future, mayors, city councils, and planning boards will have access to well-equipped "situation rooms" (such as that developed by CNN) to assist them in making critical decisions in the compressed time frames now familiar to all in the twenty-first century.

Case Study 2: Dubai—City of Divergent Networks

Dubai is a linear city with no real center. Sheikh Zayed Road, running parallel to the coastline, provides the symbolic urban spine of the city and nation. At one time the city was focused around the traditional seaport village at Deira and the Creek, now only partially preserved as an archeological site and tourist destination (Al-Rustamani 1991). The Deira district has been slowly transformed into the old city that now houses the working class and Southeast Asian merchants, while continuing to be a very active

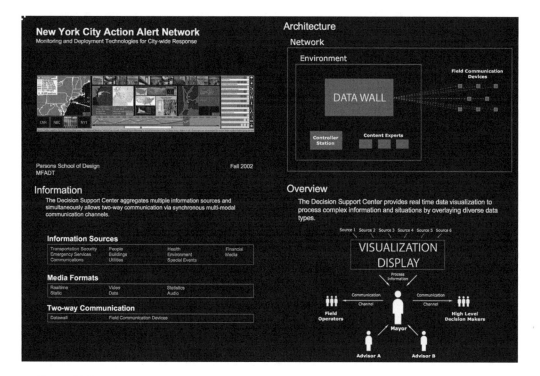

Figure 13.4
NYCAAN integrated real-time media and visualization platform
Project developed an integrated real-time information management and visualization platform
for the New York City mayor's office. Collaborative studio semester-long project, Parsons School
of Design, fall 2002, C. Kirwan, G. Petroff, S. Travis, faculty.

district full of authentic life and culture. As the city expands further north into the
desert and west toward Dubai's sister Emirate, Sharjah, and her big brother to the east,
Abu Dhabi, the city appears to have no distinguishable formal edges except for the
sea and coastline (Dubai Municipality). These geological boundaries play into the
landscape of the city, both seamlessly and as a planned afterthought. Dubai is a city
with many centers—a dispersed city and culture like the Bedouin nomads forming the
cultural backdrop of the new futuristic skyline.

Dubai has had an exceptional marketing strategy and has successfully created one
of the top branded cities in the world (Tosches 2006), with the trademarked luxury
lifestyle, tolerant society, and multicultural population exemplified by the bold advertising campaign in 2007 showing African warriors in a Dubai hypermarket dressed
in their traditional dress with grass skirts, spears, and face and body painting. While
the city brand has promoted diversity, the city's cultural population has remained

segregated into three main categories: the local Emirati, the South Asians, and the European expats (primarily dominated by the British, who have had significant cultural and political impact in the UAE and larger region). Social interaction occurs in the work environment, and English is widely spoken as the neutral language, yet the social and cultural lives of these three groups are independent largely due to differing cultural habits, religious differences, and language.

With unprecedented growth came the inflation of property values and a dramatically increased cost of living in Dubai. Early in 2008 many real estate and financial analysts began predicting that the property-market bubble would burst. This situation immediately had significant impact on growth and provided an opportunity for a new consciousness to occur, much to the approval of the local Emirati (Slackman 2008). In Dubai the Emirati represent only approximately 15 percent of the population, and they had often been critical of the speed of development and the deterioration of the cultural heritage and lifestyle of the indigenous Arab Bedouin tribes. Dubai represents a challenge: the need to find a balance between rapid growth and the preservation of cultural identity (Boussa 2000). It has to go back in time to go forward; the first step in that process is to build a bridge between the old and the new, to link the vibrant cultural heritage and the expansive new city with the goal of creating a new sense of collective identity. Our case study suggests ways that urban media and other new technologies might assist in that process (Kalay 2007).

Project Description

The opportunity to study culturally significant landmarks such as the archeological site in Deira—on the brink of extinction due to rapid urban development—led to the creation of a team of students and faculty from four universities[1] whose task was to explore multidisciplinary approaches such as urban planning, architectural preservation, new media, marketing, and branding in order to reengage these sites within the urban fabric (Warren 1982).

While each heritage site has its unique conditions and requires location-specific solutions, there is a compelling need to connect these sites within a comprehensive media strategy—one that positions the heritage areas within the cultural framework of the Emirates as a whole, yet retains the brand identities that reflect the uniqueness of each Emirate and individual heritage site. The government of Sharjah is proactive in building on this cultural base and has developed a strong arts and culture program with a well-designed brand identity and web presence—a solid foundation for extending the cultural network. Our study involves a review of the current branding and communication channels and how they can be developed further by the UAE, both on a national and local-community level via new technology and media strategies.

The design challenge is to develop an integrated multidimensional monitoring and promotion-based media platform and comprehensive branding system we have termed *urban interface*. The platform uses web-based software linking multiple location-based communication and data collection hardware modules. These modules incorporate live media streams that provide information generated at the specific locations, which include the activity of passersby and miscellaneous environmental data. This monitoring data is then combined with promotion media representing both preselected content and live broadcast media content that is representative of the heritage areas and their brand identities. Key assets of the heritage areas are their cultural underpinnings and existing content such as the traditional souk marketplace, courtyard dwellings, and cottage industry arts and crafts clusters. All of these sites provide culturally rich content in their own right, which can be co-opted into these desired media campaigns.

This fusion of real-time data streams and preselected media content is then promoted into the mainstream urban phenomenology; it is broadcast from the heritage areas into the central business districts and other commercial spaces in Dubai and the other Emirates via multiple media channels that include government websites, outdoor media venues, and kiosks. This site-specific media is overlaid, within the same media network, with other data such as information on flight arrivals and departures, information for tourists visiting an area, and promotion of the cultural brands—thus cross-selling the broader, urban data and UAE brand content with location-specific content, reinforcing the link between the cultural heritage sites and the mainstream environments in the UAE.

"UAE Urban Identities" is our effort to reconcile the dichotomies of the past and the future with the application of new media technologies (Butt, Bywater, and Paul 2008) to create an urban interface—a commercially viable monitoring and promotion system that is a dynamic fusion of interactive media, cultural content, advertisements, architectural installations, and urban networks. The project is now in the design and development phase with a planned exhibition and event at Cityscape Dubai, where it will present a contrasting image to the megadevelopment presentations usually seen at this important real estate development convention. Our exhibit will center on an interactive 3D map of the UAE that will highlight the key heritage sites in the UAE. Users will be able to explore media content projected on surrounding surfaces by interacting with touch-sensitive surfaces that trigger the content. A real-time data feed will be established at each of the heritage sites to demonstrate the live-data aspect of the urban interface (see figure 13.5).

Case Study 3: Beijing—The Radiating Metropolis

With the massive infrastructure development resulting from the 2008 Olympics, Beijing is now truly a cosmopolitan city, a fact often touted by the Chinese government as the modern rebirth of the People's Republic of China. Legend has it that Beijing started as a windblown seed landing on a vast field—which later became the

Figure 13.5

UAE urban identities installation

The proposed installation incorporates an interactive 3D map of the UAE linked to models and live feeds from UAE heritage sites. Collaboration with UAE, UK, and South Korean institutions, Parsons The New School for Design, spring 2009, C. Kirwan, S. Travis, faculty.

grounds of the Imperial Forbidden City. The modern city radiates from this point, forming a concentric urban plan, with uniform rings expanding into the surrounding mountains and touching the edge of the Great Wall of China (Huang 2004). The center ring, which is shared by Tiananmen Square, the Forbidden City, the People's Hall, and Mao's Mausoleum, is a vast and austere framework that effectively uses its spatial, cultural, and metaphysical power to transmit the Chinese Han Dynasty's existential philosophy. Indeed, Beijing stands tall in comparison with any major planned metropolis in the world (Paris, Madrid, or Rome), when considering city form as a manifestation of overwhelming national consciousness.

Unlike Rome and Paris at their core, Beijing is not walkable; it is a city of monumental scale and prominent circulation routes. Consequently, its urban space cannot be comprehended entirely from a pedestrian point of view (Robert 1998), leaving the observer to search for other forms of identification. Looking through the lens of

Communist Party symbolism, it is possible to experience an ancient and modern city, at once impressive and oppressive—a vast dichotomy that needs to be reconciled in relation to the overall Chinese identity and the implication of China's new global dominance. Herein lies a fascinating opportunity to create a new frame of reference: this is the future city, thrust on the world without warning.

China is rapidly embracing new technologies—the Internet and new media. While it cannot presently compete with its neighbors in Taiwan, South Korea, and Japan in terms of absorption, it has the muscle and massive market to have the global impact of a tsunami. The institutional resources of the government, universities, and private sector workforce are giving rise to a new generation of knowledge workers, as the country evolves from industrial manufacturing to the information age (Dahlman, Aubert 2001). This will result in China soon equaling the technological resources of the developed Western world. Yet two factors differentiate contemporary Chinese reality: first, the government has positioned itself as controller of the media/ technological superstructure, and second—unlike Taiwan, South Korea, and Japan— the society is becoming increasingly fragmented as the elites gain more wealth and access to information and the rural populations remain disconnected from main-stream media channels.

We believe new media can be a vital integrator, stitching the frayed edges of society back into the collective social fabric, rich in cultural substance and diverse narratives, to produce a multiethnic, multiclass, multiperspective, multimedia China. We do not see this occurring as a renegade response to the government, but instead brought about by the government at a scale never attempted before.

It is important here that we attempt to comment on the potential role of government in the urban media development process. Each of the three sections of this chapter present cities under differing forms of government control and approaches to urban planning: New York City—democratic, Dubai—monarchic, and Beijing— centrally controlled socialism. In the case of the 798 Art Zone (discussed in the following paragraphs), where the Beijing government has the final and irrevocable decision-making power, this involvement can have a direct impact on the viability and direction of the project, while the New York City government, for example, might have less influence.

Project Description

The purpose of this project is to utilize the unique identity and accessibility of the 798 Art Zone (Beijing's Dashanzi Art District) to create an open dialog via a dedicated broadband virtual pipeline, streaming media about urban culture, art, fashion, and technology between China and the United States. The 798 Art Zone (Zhu 2005) provides a geographic context and contained area in which to conduct the urban media experiment. Bursting with post–cultural revolution propaganda, contemporary art, scripted romance, and bits of remaining rebellion, 798 has quickly emerged as the New York City/SoHo of Beijing (798 originated when local Beijing artists sought cheap space outside the direct influence of the government) (R. Huang 2004). Now of little remaining interest to artists (passé in terms of relevance to the art world, because the cutting edge has moved to areas like Liquor Factory in the Jiuchang Art District), 798 is nonetheless presented to the public by the government as *the* arts district. Herein lies the experiment. Can this district, stripped of cultural meaning the moment it was embraced by the local government, be rejuvenated by the use of urban-scale new media?

In spring 2010, faculty and students from Parsons The New School for Design (New York) and Tsinghua University Academy of Arts and Design (Beijing) began a large-scale urban media experiment in the 798 Art Zone. The project, named "Beijing~New York FLOW," reflects the nature of the virtual extension of 798, to engage audiences in real time beyond the physical site-specific installation—before, during, and after the planned forty-eight-hour media happening on location there. The project goals are simple, yet ambitious, and can be broken into three basic propositions:

• Can a simple wireless urban media experiment be implemented, as a layer, on top of an existing urban development initiative?
• Will the public interact with such an experiment?
• Will the government engage the project, first by acknowledging (and approving) its existence, and later by taking advantage of its presence to augment the tourist offerings and economic growth of the district?

The project, under the lead of authors Kirwan and Travis, is being undertaken by the Center for Mobile Creativity and [SpyLab] at Parsons and the Laboratory for Media Art Research at Tsinghua and builds on two recent Beijing-based projects: "1000 Cell Phones" (2008) and "Streetwalk" (2009) (see links at the end of the chapter). The project will use three basic technologies: GPS, SMS, and scripted Flash visualization to engage pedestrians at 798. Tourists or gallery visitors will be greeted at one or more of the entrance gates to the 798 district with instructions for engaging with the project (Hawking et al. 2005).

If the public chooses to join, they will interact via SMS (GPS tagged) while they are in 798. They will be met by two additional media installations along the way (see figure 13.6): first, depending on where they are sending the SMS from, they will receive SMS messages about 798 history at their approximate location, and second, they will find information screens and projections in notable galleries and public spaces along the way, with some aspect of the public's presence in 798 scripted into the media presentation. Initially, media will probably be installed in some of the trendy landmarks that have transformed the industrial 798 district into its present commercial

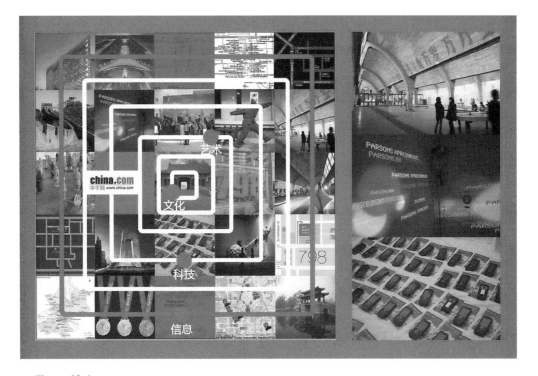

Figure 13.6

Beijing~New York FLOW conceptual media plan

This project proposes to create a new urban media installation in Beijing's 798 Art District combining mobile-phone interface and projections. It is a collaborative project with Tsinghua University and Parsons The New School for Design, spring 2010, C. Kirwan, S. Travis, faculty.

identity, including the Timezone 8 bookstore, Long March Space gallery, and Lord of Salt restaurant.

Technologies being used in the media installation include Nokia's Simple Context, an end-to-end system for data collection, storage, retrieval, and sharing (it was designed to help users, researchers, and developers more easily collect, organize, and work with large amounts of dynamic mobile, social, and sensor data), and SydeWynder, an SMS receiver and sender module written in Python for S60 phones (e.g., Nokia N80). It can automate the responses of messages and is used as a mobile application server in areas where setting up a traditional server may be difficult.

It is important to note that the presence of participating team members halfway around the world will allow for interesting human interaction and multimedia real-time communication. On a personal note, there was no such possibility for global exchange when Projec[tions], the first project mentioned in this chapter, was executed in the mid-1990s.

Conclusion

Urban centers worldwide are now facing dramatic changes and challenges in almost every arena: population, health and public safety, environment, information access, housing, employment, security, banking, government, and global economic competition. To effectively overcome these hurdles, cities are being re-presented and revitalized through many different strategies (Modernization and Regionalism 2006), including the regeneration of historic districts in Shanghai, government green-design policies in Berlin, and the rebranding of Las Vegas to call attention to its exceptional physical attractions—efforts in each case that were planned to capitalize on the unique consumer appeal of each destination.

The urban media concept can facilitate this renewal process by developing urban narratives that capture the inherent cultural, physiological, and informational characteristics of a city or region, employing various media to channel these assets into comprehensive, integrated, and active brand identities that reflect the city as a desirable place to live, work, play, and invest. We have attempted to demonstrate in our New York, Dubai, and Beijing case studies that the urban media process can be highly effective in accomplishing these objectives.

At this point in time, we view urban media as an evolving concept that has high promise for the future by bringing interdisciplinary teams together to meet these daunting challenges and explore new possibilities in our cities and our nations. We look forward to other urban media-teurs sharing their views and experiments in this emerging discipline—an intriguing mix of actual and virtual, practical and theoretical. At Parsons we seek collaboration around the world to engage these new realities, complexities, and opportunities.

Acknowledgments

We are pleased to acknowledge the many students and faculty at Parsons The New School for Design for contributions to and collaboration in the projects represented in this chapter. We would also like to acknowledge the participants in the UAE Urban Identities educational project and initiative, including Dr Samia Rab and students at the American University of Sharjah; Dr Aylin Orbasli, Jonathan Bassindale, and students at Oxford Brooks University; Sangmin Bae, KAIST; and Anna Batchelder and Nabeel Ahmad from Bon Education for their extensive work on the collaborative technology supporting this project; and participants in the Beijing Red Lenses projects, including Tsinghua University faculty and students. Thanks also to Newwork's professional team of urban planners, media designers, and real estate consultants for contributions to the applied research in the field of urban redevelopment. Finally, we thank Ernest E. Kirwan and Edward S. Grant, senior advisors and intellectual sounding boards for the ongoing research.

Note

1. Parsons The New School for Design (U.S.), the American University of Sharjah (UAE), Oxford Brooks University (UK), and KAIST University (South Korea).

References

Alexander, Christopher. 1977. *Pattern Language*. Oxford: Oxford University Press.

Al-Rustumani. 1991. *Dubai and Its Architectural Heritage*. Dubai: Al-Safeer.

Ascher, Kate. 2007. *The Works: Anatomy of a City*. New York: Penguin.

Boussa, Djamel. 2000. Why preserve the past? Paper presented at the Second Arab Gulf Conference, Al Ain, UAE.

Butt, Danny, Jon Bywater, and Nova Paul. 2008. *Place: Local Knowledge and New Media Practice*. City: Cambridge Scholars Publishing.

Chermayeff, Serge. 1964. *Community and Privacy*. New York: Doubleday Anchor Books.

Dahlman, Carl J., and Jean-Eric Aubert. 2001. *China and the Knowledge Economy: Seizing the 21st Century*. World Bank.

Dubai Municipality. Date. Dubai *Urban Area Structure Plan: 1993–2012*. Dubai: Dubai Municipality.

Gardner, Howard. 1993. *Frames of Mind: The Theory of Multiple Intelligences,* New York: Basic Books.

Hawking, Paul, Andrew Stein, John Zeleznikow, Pramod Sharma, Devon Nugent, Linda Dawson, and Sue Foster. 2005. Emerging Issues in Location Based Tourism Systems. International Conference on Mobile Business (ICMB'05), 75–81.

Huang, Rui, ed. 2004. *Beijing 798: Reflections on Art, Architecture and Society in China*. Hong Kong: Timezone 8 / Thinking Hands.

Huang, Yan. 2004. Urban spatial patterns and infrastructure in Beijing. *Land Lines*, October.

Incheon City, *Smart Cities*. Date. Government Agency, South Korea. http://Incheon.go.kr/.

Kalay, Yehuda E., Thomas Kvan, and Janice Affleck. 2007. *New Heritage: New Media and Cultural Heritage*. London: Routledge.

Lynch, Kevin. 1960. *The Image of the City*. Cambridge, MA: MIT Press.

Masdar Plan. 2008. *The Economist*, July.

McLuhan, Marshall. 1994. *Understanding Media*. Reprinted. Cambridge, MA: MIT Press.

Miele, Paola, Jacques Houis, and Mark Stafford, eds. 2000. *Being Human: The Technological Extensions of the Body*. Marsilio Publishers.

Modernization and Regionalism: Re-inventing the Urban Identity. 2006. Session at the International Conference of the United Nations Educational, Scientific and Cultural Organization, Mojib, Imran, October 18.

Robert, Michael. 1998. *Streetlife China*. Cambridge: Cambridge University Press.

Robertson, R. 1995. Glocalization: Time-space and homogeneity-heterogeneity. In M. Featherstone, S. Lash, and R. Robertson, eds., *Global Modernities*, 25–44. London: Sage.

Slackman, Michael. 2008. Emirates see fiscal crisis as chance to save culture. *New York Times*, November 12.

Steven L. Newman Real Estate Institute. 2002. Between Expedience and Deliberation: Decision-Making for Post-9/11 New York. Symposium.

Tosches, Nick. 2006. Dubai is the limit. *Vanity Fair*, June.

Warren, J. 1982. *Integrating Traditional Areas into the Modern Urban Fabric in Adaptive Reuse*: *Proceedings of Seminar 3, Designing in Islamic Cultures*. Cambridge, MA: MIT Laboratory of Architecture and Planning.

Zhu, Yan, with contributions by Yin Jinan and Li Jiangshu. 2005. *798: A Photographic Journal*. Hong Kong: Timezone 8.

Links: Active Projects, Parsons The New School for Design

Beijing~New York Flow. 2010. http://a.parsons.edu/~bjnyflow/info/.

1000 Cell Phones. 2008. http://dave.parsons.edu/projects/1000cellphones/index.html.

UAE Urban Identities. 2009. http://a.parsons.edu/~uae/info/.

Urban Design. 2010. http://www.newschool.edu/parsons/subpage.aspx?id=47350.

14 Bjørnetjeneste: Using the City as a Backdrop for Location-Based Interactive Narratives

Jeni Paay and Jesper Kjeldskov

with Jonatan R. Andersen, David Bahr, Pelle Hede, Kasper S. Hornbek, and Jan Jensen

Reality is everywhere. It is right there in our face when we wake up in the morning, and it continues to sneak up on us throughout our day, in the car, in our offices, in the tearoom, and at the dinner table. In recent years it has even invaded our TVs, not only through eternal streams of live news from wherever, but also through endlessly boring reality TV shows documenting minute-by-minute details of people's mundane lives. However, let's face it, most people cannot live by reality alone. Perhaps this is why so many spend quite a lot of effort (and money) on escaping reality. We day-dream, we tell stories, we go to the cinema, we rent a video, or we read or listen to a book. We immerse ourselves in imaginary worlds and stories as a way of escaping everyday life. We immerse ourselves in *fiction*.

Imagine if the city could tell us stories. Let us for a minute move away from the concept of mobile guides presenting their users with fact after fact related to their physical surroundings as they move through the city. Let us instead imagine that we could turn a city street into the stage on which a fictional story unfolds, and use the city as a physical backdrop for its narrative. Interactive stories taking place in the urban places we live in and move through. What kind of user experience would such a concept offer an urban citizen engaging with their physical surroundings? What would it be like if the city around us was digitally augmented not only with facts about people, places, and so on, but also with fiction? By taking an orthogonal view on the content of location-based services for use in the city, we propose a non-goal-directed user experience that weaves fiction into the immediate physical surroundings of people as they move through the city. We exemplify this view as we describe a concept location-based story conveyed though an urban environment, "Bjørnetjeneste," that was designed to create an experience that is immersive, thought provoking, emotionally engaging, fun, and frustrating—rather than providing functional utility.

In our recent research, we have been exploring the design, implementation, and user experience of context-aware and location-based mobile information services for urban dwellers, which "augment the city" with a digital layer of information about, for example, people, places, and the users' physical surroundings (Paay et al. 2009).

Common to our research has been that the systems and services explored have provided users with factual information about their environment that would otherwise be invisible. From this information people can then decide what to do while socializing out on the town—where to go, how to get there, what to do there, who to meet up with, and so on. In many ways, this matches most research and design being done within the area of mobile guides: catering to the "social butterflies" of the city (Foth, Gibbs, and Satchell 2009) by providing users on the move with facts about the social and physical reality in which they are situated.

However, why not let mobile guides provide people with fiction about their physical surroundings rather than facts alone? Inspired by this question, our research has explored the user experiences achieved by "augmenting the city with fiction" in a way that is playful, ambiguous (Gaver, Beaver, and Benford 2003), and opaque, rather than goal-oriented and transparent. This evokes some fundamental questions, because little is known about how people would engage with this type of creative content embedded in their physical surroundings. How can location-based mobile systems provide for people's desire for fictional content? How can we narrate engaging interactive stories in an urban environment, taking into consideration the user's location, movements over time, and perhaps even their social context? How does the interplay between stories, locations, and people function? What is the relationship between interactivity and narrative structure in this particular context? These are some of the many questions that inspire our current work, which encourages urban citizens to engage with their physical surroundings through embedded creative content, and thereby form engaged relationships with their urban environment. In this chapter we consider some of these issues on the basis of our experiences.

Related Work

Making interactive narratives and relating stories to locations are not new ideas on their own. However, combining the two into mobile systems that respond to the user's location and interactions in an urban environment is a relatively new phenomenon, with key references in the research literature dating only a few years back. In the following section we outline some of the related work in mobile location-based guides, games, and stories, as well as in interactive narratives.

Mobile Location-Based Guides, Games, and Stories

Early mobile city guides such as *Cyberguide* (Abowd et al. 1997), the Lancaster *GUIDE* (Cheverst et al. 2000), and *Hippie* (Gaver, Beaver, and Benford 2003) provided urban dwellers, visitors, and tourists with location-based experiences that included pertinent information and guidance about the urban environment around them. While they did not focus as such on narrative content, these systems still serve as useful references for understanding some of the basic interaction and technical issues related to the design and user experience of mobile systems for city contexts. Mobile games such as *Pirates*! (Bjork et al. 2001), *ARQuake* (Piekarski and Thomas 2003), *Mindwarping* (Starner et al. 2000), and *Can You See Me Now?* (Benford et al. 2006) represent a different genre of location-based applications targeted at people in cities. These systems offer important inspiration for alternative purposes of mobile technologies in urban environments, such as facilitating entertainment and engagement. In particular, *Can You See Me Now?*—with its engaging artistic experience of seamlessly connecting online players in a virtual world to play against real players in the actual city—demonstrates new forms of human interaction with computers and among players in the context of the city. Expanding on the creation of engaging gaming experiences in urban environments, others have actively incorporated story elements into their location-based games. *Backseat Playground* (Gustafsson et al. 2006) provides a narrated experience interweaving a crime mystery, visible physical elements of the environment, and gaming for children sitting in the backseat of a car while on a trip. *Uncle Roy All Around You* (Benford et al. 2004) is a programmed game that incorporates the surrounding city, live actors, and online and street players following a set of prescripted clues and story elements to find Uncle Roy's office.

Moving away from the gaming genre, the delivery of location-based stories using mobile technology includes systems such as *Urban Tapestries* (Jungnickel 2004), *Riot!* (Blythe et al. 2006), *Hopstory* (Nisi et al. 2004), and *Geist* (Malaka, Schneider, and Kretschmer 2004). *Urban Tapestries* is a collection of stories, histories, experiences, and events of a community linked to familiar and related locations. *Riot!* delivers authored episodes triggered by specific locations about a historical riot in and around Queen Square, where the installation operates. *Hopstory* allows visitors to enter a historic brewery to collect location-related video vignettes as they navigate the building, then to view their collected story at the end of the visit. *Geist* provides an augmented reality experience for visitors to the city of Heidelberg, which combines history and fiction to allow the viewer to experience how it felt to be in that city during the Thirty Years' War in the seventeenth century.

These mobile-guide, game, and story applications all illustrate systems that in different ways induce people to engage with the city around them. While we have not ourselves worked with mobile games, our research in urban informatics has involved both mobile-guide-type applications and, more recently, mobile interactive stories.

Anecdotally, many forms of evidence point to people's interest in fiction. Several bestselling novels have illustrated the appeal of blurring the boundaries between fact and fiction and suggest the importance of the "suspension of disbelief'" in storytelling. As one of many examples, The *Da Vinci Code* (Brown 2003) has sold over eighty million copies and has been translated into forty-four languages worldwide; it is the thirteenth bestselling book of all time and inspired a feature-length movie that was the second highest grossing movie of 2006 worldwide (Box Office Mojo 2009). The *Da Vinci Code* establishes its sense of intrigue from a clever interweaving of real places and things that we know to be historical facts with "believable" fictional stories involving these places and facts as central elements. Crime fiction becomes all the more evocative when it locates its scenes in places we are familiar with and invites us to believe that these events may have happened in those locations. For example, crime stories about a Melbourne baker by Melbourne writer Kerry Greenwood (2004, 2005, 2006) walk us through the streets of Melbourne, narrating possibilities of dark happenings that we are unaware might be occurring in the city we think we know so well. This technique is also employed in *Riot!*, *Hopstory*, and *Geist* (Blythe et al. 2006; Nisi et al. 2004; Malaka, Schneider, and Kretschmer 2004), described above.

At the same time, we have experienced a meteoric rise in the popularity of personal music players over the last decade, such as the Apple iPod and mobile phones with audio playback capabilities. While these were originally used primarily for listening to music while on the move, new types of digital audio content, such as podcasts and audiobooks, have emerged in the slipstream of these devices. The same has happened with digital video content for mobile devices. However, we have only seen the beginning of what is to come in the area of digital mobile media. As has been the case with other new media in modern history (e.g., printed books, theater, radio, movies, TV, the Internet, etc.), the use of new media initially imitates that of old and familiar ones (e.g., filming theater for playback in cinemas). Following a period of imitating the old and familiar, new genres emerge from experimentation with the new means of expression. For digital mobile media we are still in the imitation phase, but experimentation with, for example, location-based guides, games, and stories is contributing to the development of new genres and applications of this type of media that incorporate our urban surroundings in interactive stories. We have the desire for fiction and other kinds of appealing content, we have the context of the urban environment, and we have the digital devices and infrastructure to build such systems—but do we have the ability to integrate these in a meaningful and engaging manner?

Interactive Narratives

One issue that needs to be investigated further before smoothly functioning and engaging interactive location-based stories can be created is the relation between facilitating user interaction and ensuring narrative structure. A great deal of research has been done on the design and implementation of computer-based interactive narratives. One of the many challenges revealed by this research is the fundamentally conflicting relationship between interactivity and narrative structure (Galyean 1995; Skov 2002; Juul 2005). In traditional narratives the author has control over the storyline and sequence of events and the receiver takes the role of a noninteractive or

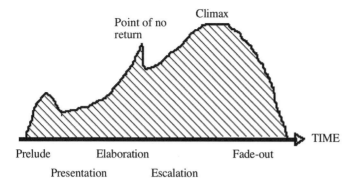

Figure 14.1
The Aristotelian curve of tension (from Skov and Andersen 2001).

spectator audience. This means that the author can make use of classical principles of storytelling such as creating a plot, building tension, introducing key characters at key times, deciding courses of action taken by each character, and so on. When a narrative is made interactive, by definition some of this control is lost. The more interactive a narrative becomes, the less control the author has over the storyline. Consequently, increasing interaction often results in reduced narrative quality.

At the same time, many interactive narratives exist that exhibit both user interaction and narrative structure. One of the ways to overcome the conflict between interaction and narrative structure is to limit interactivity so that it happens within certain boundaries of the storyline, and to combine this interactive freedom with narrative structures that force the reader through certain key scenes. In this way, one of the fundamental principles of classic storytelling, the Aristotelian curve of tension (see figure 14.1), can still be deployed to ensure an experience that captures the reader's imagination, provides context, builds momentum, crosses the point of no return, and ultimately escalates toward and beyond a climax.

In an interactive narrative built around the Aristotelian curve of tension, interactivity happens within the boundaries of the current phase or act of the story. The order of particular subplots may change and choices may be made that have influence later on, and certain subplots may be omitted and others included, but the overall storyline keeps progressing toward the next step on the curve in a timely manner. Many different variations of the points of no return may exist depending on the choices made, but ideally *a* point of no return is always reached within a certain time. The same goes for the climax and ending. Interactive narrative research forms a good foundation for how location-based stories might unfold that combine interactivity and storytelling structure.

Augmenting the City with Fiction

Inspired by the 2006 OZCHI (Australian Computer-Human Interaction) conference keynote presentation by Bill Gaver in Sydney, Australia, titled "Designing for Our (Sur) real Lives" (Gaver 2006), we decided to explore an orthogonal approach to our previous work on the design of location-based urban guide systems (Paay et al. 2009). Rather than augmenting the city with facts, we wanted to explore augmenting the city with *fiction*.

Augmenting the city with fiction through location-based mobile technology inherits the challenges of interactive narratives described above and adds these to the complexities of location-based services and urban informatics. In augmenting the city with fiction, narratives are linked to specific physical locations, and the user can interact with the storyline, among other mechanisms, just by moving through the urban environment. While allowing the user a large degree of freedom, key points in a narrative can be linked to specific locations, thus requiring the user to go to particular places as a part of the experience. Linking narratives to specific physical locations adds to the expressive devices available to the author by creating an opportunity to use features of the locations as a backdrop for their story (e.g., visuals, sounds, smells, buildings, typical people, etc.). At the same time, of course, the use of these features also potentially makes stories sensitive to the dynamics of physical space—for example, at different times of the day and across the seasons of the year. This in turn can also be regarded as a creative opportunity for storytelling.

To explore these interesting new challenges and opportunities for urban informatics, we set up a project in 2007 that involved a class of eighteen informatics students at Aalborg University's Department of Computer Science as a part of their fifth-semester project. The students were divided into three groups and given the overall assignment to sketch, design, and implement a mobile location-aware system that provided an interactive narrative using the physical surroundings of the city as a backdrop. From brainstorming on different story concepts, figure 14.2 shows some of the early sketches produced that explore fiction in the city.

From discussions of possible roles for technology, the sketches depicted in figure 14.3 show two different concepts for accessing the otherwise invisible digital layer of fiction in the city. Tangible physical artifacts such as a pair of binoculars take the viewer back in time, and the rearview mirror of a car shows virtual characters in the backseat.

Following the idea generation process, the student groups chose one particular concept to develop further and to then demonstrate through a functional prototype. The three prototype systems each explored a different storytelling genre—a murder mystery, science fiction, and film noir—and all three were successful in creating engaging user experiences. In the following section we focus on one of these three concepts, a film noir story titled "Bjørnetjeneste."

Figure 14.2
Design sketches for fictional content that explores urban environments or specific places in the city as backdrops.

Figure 14.3
Design sketches for "Time Binoculars" and "Ghost in the Rearview Mirror".

Bjørnetjeneste

The Danish term *bjørnetjeneste* can be translated literally as "bear favor." It stems from an eighteenth-century fable by the French poet Jean de La Fontaine about a bear that threw a massive stone at his master's head to wipe away a fly but instead ended up crushing his skull. Based on this story, a bear favor is a well-intentioned act that turns out to do more harm than good. However, about fifteen years ago, a survey revealed that many people in Denmark did in fact not know the correct meaning of the term. Half the population surveyed thought a bear favor was a bad thing (the correct interpretation), while the other half thought it was a good thing—a big favor. In reaction to this, the Danish Language Committee (the official regulatory body of the Danish language under the Danish Ministry of Culture) decided to officially change the meaning of the term to reflect *both* common understandings although they have diametrically opposed meanings (Politiken 2005). As a consequence, the term *bjørnetjeneste* is now totally ambiguous—and therefore in practice completely useless. The implication depends on the context and in reality needs to be accompanied by a description of the intended meaning. In this way, the very meaning of the term has become as dualistic as the concept it originally described! This peculiarity of the Danish language, along with thoughts about fate and conscience (figure 14.4), inspired the concept and storyline of the location-based interactive narrative called "Bjørnetjeneste." The story is about good and bad, about not always being able to tell the

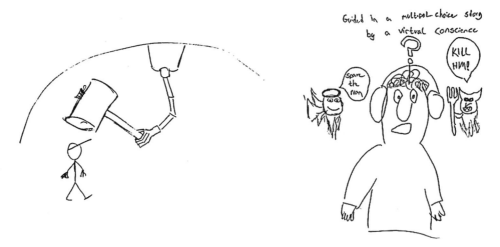

Figure 14.4
Early design sketches exploring fate and conscience that developed into the "Bjørnetjeneste" concept.

difference, and about sometimes making choices based on the best of intentions that turn out to have an unforeseen negative consequence.

During the experience of the story, the user (or rather "interactor"), acting on behalf of the main character, a postman, has to make a series of ethical choices according to their conscience as an urban citizen. However, no matter what choices are made along the way, they will only make the situation worse and eventually lead to the same film noir–type ending. Fate—unlike the meaning of words—cannot be changed, and the ending for the postman is inevitable.

The Bjørnetjeneste Prototype System

"Bjørnetjeneste" was designed to run on a lightweight tablet computer with a pair of headsets and a GPS. This form factor allowed the use of detailed graphics and stereo sound to convey the story in response to the user's location in the city. As the user moves through the city, they are presented with a series of photographs on the screen, taken from their current location, and then overlaid with animated 3D graphics of characters and objects from the story. Spoken narration, dialog, the thoughts of the main character, and the user's choices are delivered through the headset, and the user can respond through simple spoken commands (figure 14.5).

The graphics used to convey the story are designed to clearly stand out from the photograph in their style and color, thus creating a clear figure-ground boundary and

Figure 14.5
"Bjørnetjeneste" in use.

Figure 14.6
Photographs of physical surroundings overlaid with 3D graphics, creating a composite scene of fiction in the city.

drawing attention to the fictional elements overlaid on the urban environment (figure 14.6). The effect sought by mixing photographs and graphics as illustrated in figure 14.6 is one of augmented reality, but without the use of high-tech display equipment.

The secondary role of the tablet PC is to intermittently display the cover of the local newspaper as the interactive story unfolds. This is used to convey the updated effect of the user's actions on the fictional world that they are immersed in. As with the story of Marty McFly and Doc Brown in *Back to the Future* II and III (Zemeckis and Gale 1989, 1990), the headings and stories in the newspaper change content to reflect the implications of the actions taken by the postman (figure 14.7 left). Along with the tablet computer and headset, the user is given a series of physical props at the beginning of the story experience: a postman's jacket to wear and a postman's bag containing letters and parcels. These props play particular roles during the course of the story.

The Storyline

The storyline of "Bjørnetjeneste" follows a day in the life (or death) of a postman in Aalborg. The story requires the user to move physically through the city following a predefined path (unknown to them) between a series of key locations where the story unfolds (figure 14.7 right). During the story, the user is prompted for interaction that influences the choices made by the postman. There are seven main scenes in the story. In the following section, we describe three of these to give an impression of their

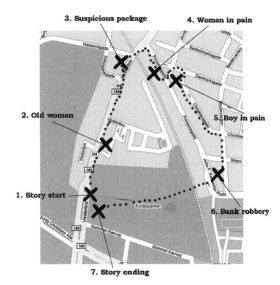

Figure 14.7
The dynamic newspaper (left) and the location of the seven scenes along a predefined route taking the user back to the starting point (right).

content and form. Common to all, the postman is put into situations where he has to make a choice between good and bad. Should he help a person appearing to be in need or should he just mind his own business? However, no matter what he does, his day just gets worse.

The Suicide

The story opens in the parking lot outside the tallest building in the city of Aalborg, Hotel White House. Here, the user is immersed in the character of "the postman." He is told that he has just committed suicide by jumping off the building, and on the screen he can see his own dead body in a pool of blood on the ground. He remembers that he is married and has a twelve-year-old son, and he feels that something terrible has happened, but he can't remember what. An old man then approaches him and says, "Well, that didn't go too well, did it? I have been talking to the grouchy man in the cellar about your fate, and we have decided to give you another chance." The old man hands him a newspaper, and when the postman looks up, the old man has disappeared. He looks at the paper again. The top story is about a postman who has died in a fall from a building. The police are uncertain if it was suicide or an accident, but they believe the incident may be related to a series of other events on the same day in the city center nearby. The postman's heart begins to pump faster and suddenly

Figure 14.8
Encounter with the old lady.

the old man appears next to him again. "So, are you up for the task of seeing if you can get things right this time, or should we just decide who gets your soul by flipping a coin?", the old man asks. The postman accepts the challenge, closes his eyes, and is taken back to earlier in the day when it all started. He is at the beginning of his normal route and starts walking down the main street to deliver his letters and packages.

The Old Lady
The first incident happens a block down the main road. Here the postman encounters an old lady who asks him to help her cross the street (figure 14.8). Two voices appear in his head (through the headset). One tells him not to waste his time on charity, while the other tells him that he should always help other people in need. The two voices continue to debate in his head, and the postman (the user) has to make a choice. The two choices, A and B, and their respective resulting storylines are described below.

A. The postman helps the lady across the street. As they reach the other side, they hear a strange noise from above. Then a large satellite dish plunges to the ground right in front of them. The old lady starts to look faint. She loosens her grip on the postman's arm and drops dead from a heart attack. The postman reaches for his newspaper; he sees a new story appear describing the death of an old woman apparently caused by the reckless act of a postman walking her to an area on the sidewalk where workers were installing heavy equipment on the roof of a city building.
B. The postman ignores the old woman and walks on. She starts yelling at him and bystanders show their disapproval, calling him selfish and not civic-minded. The postman runs away from the scene. As he turns the corner his attention is drawn to his newspaper. On the front page a story appears describing the death of an old lady

Figure 14.9
Pleasure or pain?

who was run over by a bus while crossing the street. The bus driver didn't see her. "If only someone had helped her cross the street," the bus driver is quoted as saying. "People only think about themselves these days."

Woman in Pain

The postman is shaken but continues on his delivery route. As he turns the corner he hears a woman's screams coming from one of the buildings. Once again voices appear in his head. One urges him to be responsible and go to the woman's rescue. The other voice tells him to just ignore the screams and deliver the mail to the building. The postman must make a choice between these two courses of action.

A. The postman decides to rescue the woman. He goes to the apartment where the screams are coming from and opens the door. He enters a dark hallway with lights at the end. He walks to the end and pushes the half-open door. Inside he sees a woman, naked and chained to the ceiling. Behind her is a man, naked from the waist up, with a black leather mask covering his face and holding a whip (figure 14.9). The woman looks at the postman and yells, "Get out you pervert!" The man with the whip joins in: "Hey, I know you, you're the local postman. I always knew you were a bit of a pervert. I'll tell everyone that you go around spying on other people's private business. Now get out!" The postman runs to the front door, embarrassed by the voices in his head that are laughing at him.

B. The postman chooses to ignore the screams. He approaches the building, quietly slips the letters into the mailbox, and hurries away. The screams continue but he ignores them. "Its probably just the TV," he thinks, but the voices in his head remind him about his newspaper. He pulls it out and takes a look. The front page shows a gruesome story about a murdered woman. The address is the same as on the letters he has just delivered and the picture shows the front door he has just been standing at. The postman feels sick and wonders if he should contact the police, but the voices in his head remind him that there is no time for remorse or guilt—if he wants to save his own soul.

The story continues like this and leads the postman through increasingly tragic episodes, eventually resulting in the death of his son and four other children in a shooting near the Hotel White House. After this, the postman finds himself back in the parking lot outside the hotel where the story began.

The End

Fuelled by distress, the postman enters the public elevator in the Hotel White House and heads for the observation deck on the top floor. As he reaches the top floor, he is met by the old man from earlier in the day. The old man shakes his head and says, "Well, that didn't go too well either did it? The guy upstairs is really pissed off at me for playing this trick on you, but I guess that's why they call me a devil. Now, go ahead and finish it off. Let me see you jump again. You have certainly got every reason in the world." Voices start inside the postman's head: one begging him to walk away, the other agreeing with the old man that the postman's fate is the concrete parking lot sixteen stories down. For one last time, the postman (the user) has to make a choice.

A. The postman decides to jump. He walks to the edge, pauses, then takes one big step forward and plunges to his death. The old man laughs and says, "I always knew you would jump. They always do."
B. The postman decides to live. He moves toward the elevator, but as he walks along the edge of the building he is caught by a gust of wind and swept off the building. He plunges to his death. The old man laughs and says, "You really thought you had a choice didn't you? They all do."

As the user exits the building on the ground floor, an old man approaches him and says, "Well, that didn't go too well did it? I've been talking to the grouchy man in the cellar about your fate and we've decided to give you another chance." The user can then go through the story again and try to alter the outcome. But as *we* know, the fate of the postman cannot be changed.

User-Experience Test Screenings

The user experience of "Bjørnetjeneste" was examined through a small number of studies on location in the city center of Aalborg. The user-experience studies did not

Figure 14.10
Test screening 1 with a paper-based storyboard.

focus specifically on the usability of the concept or system, but on people's responses to it. Hence, these studies deliberately took the form of "test screenings" of a movie or TV show in order to gauge audience reaction (Cousins 2004) rather than that of user-based evaluations of a computer system. Consistent with the type of focus for a test screening, we were interested in people's responses to the general concept of embedding fiction in an urban environment and wanted to see how people engaged with the urban environment throughout the experience. We were also interested in their opinions about the experience of the "Bjørnetjeneste" story as an example of fiction in the city; we were curious about the interplay between the physical backdrop of the city and the fictional content when embedded in this setting through graphics and sound.

The "screenings" of "Bjørnetjeneste" took place at two different points in the design process. The first screening (with five people) took place after the basic storyline and concept had been conceived, but before any functional prototype was created. In place of the tablet PC, this screening made use of a paper prototype of the system with sketched content and dialog read by a person (figure 14.10). The screening focused on the overall concept and storyline, and led to some changes to both.

Figure 14.11
Test screening 2 with a functional prototype on a laptop computer (wrapped in plastic because of the rain).

The second screening made use of a functional prototype system with interactive graphics and digital audio (figure 14.11). This enabled the user to experience the photographs augmented with 3D graphics, as well as the spoken narration, dialog, and especially the stereophonic "voices in the head" envisioned for the concept.

Test screenings took place both at the university as walkthroughs (five people) and on location walking through the city center of Aalborg (three people). Responses were collected through note taking during the screening and postscreening feedback interviews.

Discussion

The purpose of "Bjørnetjeneste" was not to create a "useful" user experience in the traditional sense of the term, but rather to create an urban experience that builds a relationship between the user and their city, aimed at regular denizens rather than tourists. It plays with the user's sense of community and social conscience, and the goal is to make it an immersive, thought-provoking, emotionally engaging, fun, and frustrating experience.

The two test screenings of "Bjørnetjeneste" provided feedback on the overall concept, the story, and the functional prototype. Because it was not a full-scale or formal evaluation, we will refrain from drawing definitive conclusions and generalizations. Instead, we will merely present and discuss some of the qualitative feedback we gathered.

The first test screening focused on the overall concept and storyline and led to modifications of both. Getting this feedback at an early stage was valuable, because it would have been time consuming to make these changes to the overall concept and storyline later in the process. The initial test screenings confirmed that the concept was interesting and that the basic storyline made sense and built tension over time regardless of what choices the user made. It was also confirmed that the narrative felt interactive despite the relatively simple set of choices and the relatively fixed structure hidden beneath the surface. However, it was also found that the storyline itself had to be simplified to ensure that it made sense and built tension regardless of what paths were chosen by the user. Because the initial story appeared a bit too much like a game with right and wrong answers, the choices presented to the user were made harder and the outcomes more ambiguous. Adding to this effect, and in line with the concept of film noir, it was decided that the story should end with the death of the postman regardless. This outcome took the experience further away from a game in which the user has to "save" the main character. Finally, the originally envisioned use of physical props was reduced due to the practicalities involved with carrying and handling them as well as the tablet PC. The remaining props were the postman's jacket, the mysterious parcel, and a mobile phone.

The following feedback emerged during the second test screening with the prototype system on a PC tablet, headphones, and props that took place in the streets of Aalborg. Participants found the whole experience—wearing an actual Danish Post outfit and carrying an actual mailbag—very immersive. Because this was the outfit of actual postmen, rather than a fancy dress costume, there were no concerns about feeling as if they were on show or looked silly. In fact, they quickly assumed the anonymity of postmen walking around our cities even though they were carrying a tablet PC because postmen are often encumbered by various bags, packages, and letters.

As we have found with other *fiction in the city* systems that we have evaluated in situ (Paay et al. 2008), the storyline woven around familiar and not-so-familiar parts of the city gives people a new perspective on their urban environment. They discover new aspects of their city or take time to look at the detail on the upper floors of buildings that they would normally just walk past with their eyes at street level. When they imagine stories that might conceivably be happening behind those facades, they begin to consider the lives of those around them and so forge a kind of relationship with other urban dwellers—even though they remain strangers. One participant began to think about the lives of real people that passed her during the test-screening session, and even imagined her own storylines, beyond that of the system, that interwove the strangers passing her into the experience of the system. With "Bjørnetjeneste" in particular, the fact that participants are challenged to make ethical choices about fictional people conceivably in their immediate environment makes them start to develop a sense of responsibility for the well-being (or not) of those around them. By making these choices for the fictional characters, they accept whatever the fictional social and environmental consequences of those choices might be, and they are forced to examine their own belief systems during the course of interaction with the system. This made the whole experience quite emotionally engaging and challenging for some of the participants whose only prior experience with this kind of situation was in gaming, seated safely in their rooms in front of a PC where their choices had no connection to real-world situations.

In some parts of the storyline sounds were delivered through the postman's headphones that related story scenes taking place behind closed doors. These were particularly poignant for the participants, because the suspension of disbelief was heightened in this situation. As far as your senses were concerned, there was a real person involved in a serious situation behind the door you were facing who needed your assistance in some way—do you help them or not? This decision became much more realistic for the participants because they were right there, facing a very real door in a ordinary everyday environment, hearing dialog or sounds that they would indeed find troubling if it was not part of our interactive experience.

As with all artistic endeavors delivered in the genre of "noir," the aim is to give the consumer an experience that is disturbing, subversive, funny, and poetic. Design noir is based on the premise that "Beneath the glossy surface of official design lurks a dark and strange world driven by real human needs" (Dunne and Raby 2001, 6). "Bjørnetjeneste" delivered an array of such experiences to our test participants. Some of the choices that had to be made were all the more disturbing when the newspaper confirmed that something terrible had happened in the wake of their interference or complacency in the situations in which they were asked to intervene. Some responded by desperately trying to make things right—others responded by purposefully (and subversively) trying to get a dramatic newspaper report as a result of their actions. Either way, the outcomes were "black." This produced both elements of fun in the experience and elements of frustration. For us, the reward was finding that using this system in the city was an evocative experience, which climaxed at the end where a final decision leads to the inevitable, and poetic, ending that is merely another beginning.

Conclusion

What would it be like if the city around us was digitally augmented with fiction? What kinds of user experience could this provide urban citizens engaging with their community and their physical surroundings, while making ethical choices, through location-based fiction? These are the questions we have explored in this chapter. We have presented a case for anchoring fiction in people's physical surroundings, using this as a backdrop for interactive narratives and responding to people's movements through the city. We have argued that this new genre of mobile digital content needs to be developed through experimentation with the new means of expression afforded by these media. We have described how we have done such experimentation through the development of three exploratory interactive narratives for urban dwellers in Aalborg. Our specific use of the digital mobile media for augmenting the city with fiction is illustrated through the "Bjørnetjeneste" concept and prototype system, which we have described here in some detail, both in terms of user-experience design and in terms of the specific interactive narrative developed and explored.

"Bjørnetjeneste" and our other urban-fiction systems were designed to create an experience that is immersive, thought provoking, emotionally engaging, physical, fun, and frustrating—rather than providing functional utility. From the responses gained through our test screenings of these systems, we are sure that we did not create something with functional utility in the traditional usability sense of the term. We did, however, create something that people engaged with emotionally, that provoked them, and that they found both fun and frustrating at times. In that sense, we have succeeded in what we set out to do. However, the story does not end here. The concept and design study of "Bjørnetjeneste" only indicates that this is a relevant and viable area for urban informatics, and that some subjective value can be created for urban citizens engaging with the city around them through the creation of interactive location-based narratives. It is not in any way complete in terms of how the basic concept of augmenting the city with fiction could be explored, and how urban citizens can engage with people and the city through fiction. Further studies are needed to explore other genres of location-based interactive narratives, different types and levels of user interaction, different narrative structures, and different technologies. Professional writers should create the story content, and systems should be created to reach a large cohort of people in order to facilitate user-experience studies with more people and over longer time periods.

Finally, we think it would be interesting to develop and explore application frameworks for the creation and distribution of user-generated story content that enable actively engaged urban citizens to participate in the media content creation side and weave dynamic storylines based on who they are, who they are with, and where they are in the city.

Acknowledgments

We would like to thank all the students in the INF3 semester of 2007 for their enthusiasm with the project theme of "Fiction in the City." We also thank all the test-screening participants, especially Jørgen Riber Christensen.

References

Abowd, G., C. Atkeson, J. Hong, S. Long, R. Kooper, and M. Pinkerton. 1997. Cyberguide: A mobile context-aware tour guide. *Wireless Networks* 3:421–433.

Benford, S., A. Crabtree, M. Flintham, A. Drozd, R. Anastasia, M. Paxton, N. Tandavanitj, M. Adams, and J. Row-Farr. 2006. Can you see me now? *ACM Transactions on Computer-Human Interaction, TOCHI* 13 (1): 100–133.

Benford, S., W. Seager, M. Flintham, R. Anastasia, D. Rowland, J. Humble, D. Stanton, et al. 2004. The error of our ways: The experience of self-reported position in a location-based game. In N. Davies, E. Mynatt, and I. Siio, eds. *Proceedings of Ubicomp 2004*, 70–87. London: Springer.

Bjork, S., J. Falk, R. Hansson, and P. Ljungstrand. 2001. Pirates! Using the physical world as a game board. In M. Hirose, ed. *Proceedings of Interact 2001*. Amsterdam: IOS Press.

Blythe, M., J. Reid, P. Wright, and E. Geelhoed. 2006. Interdisciplinary criticism: Analysing the experience of riot! A location-sensitive digital narrative. *Behaviour & Information Technology* 25 (2): 127–139.

Box Office Mojo. 2009. http://boxofficemojo.com/yearly/chart/?view2=worldwide&yr=2006.

Brown, D. 2003. *The Da Vinci Code*. London: Bantam Books.

Cheverst, K., N. Davies, K. Mitchell, A. Friday, and C. Efstratiou. 2000. Developing a context-aware electronic tourist guide: Some issues and experiences. In T. Tumer, G. Szwillus, M. Czerwinski, F. Peterno, and S. Pemberton, eds. *Proceedings of CHI 2000*, 17–24. New York: ACM Press.

Cousins, M. 2004. *The Story of Film: A Worldwide History of Film from the Host of the BBC's* Scene by Scene. New York: Da Capo Press.

Dunne, A., and F. Raby. 2001. *Design Noir: The Secret Life of Electronic Objects*. Basel: Birkhauser.

Foth, M., M. Gibbs, and C. Satchell. 2009. From Social Butterfly to Urban Citizen. HCSNet Workshop on Social and Mobile Technology to Support Civic Engagement, July 13–14, Queensland University of Technology, Brisbane, Queensland. http://eprints.qut.edu.au/31085/.

Galyean, T. A. 1995. Narrative Guidance of Interactivity. Unpublished doctoral dissertation, MIT.

Gaver, W. 2006. Designing for our (sur)real lives. In J. Kjeldskov and J. Paay, eds. *Proceedings of OZCHI 2006*, Sydney, Australia, 5. Sydney: ACM and CHISIG Australia.

Gaver, W., J. Beaver, and S. Benford. 2003. Ambiguity as a resource for design. In G. Cockton and P. Korhonen, eds. *Proceedings of CHI 2003*, 233–240. New York: ACM Press.

Greenwood, K. 2004. *Earthly Delights*. Melbourne: Allen & Unwin.

Greenwood, K. 2005. *Heavenly Pleasures*. Melbourne: Allen & Unwin.

Greenwood, K. 2006. *Devil's Food*. Melbourne: Allen & Unwin.

Gustafsson, A., J. Bichard, L. Brunnberg, O. Juhlin, and M. Combetto. 2006. Believable environments—Generating interactive storytelling in vast location-based pervasive games. In H. Ishii, N. Lee, S. Natkin, and K. Tsushima, eds. *Proceedings of ACE 06,* no. 24. New York: ACM Press.

Jungnickel, K. 2004. Urban tapestries: Sensing the city and other stories. *Proboscis "Cultural Snapshot"* 1–10.

Juul, J. 2005. *Half-Real: Video Games between Real Rules and Fictional Worlds*. Cambridge, MA: MIT Press.

Malaka, R., K. Schneider, and U. Kretschmer. 2004. Stage-Based Augmented Edutainment. *Lecture Notes in Computer Science* 3031:54–65.

Nisi, V., A. Wood, G. Davenport, and I. Oakley. 2004. Hopstory: An interactive, location-based narrative distributed in space and time. In *Proceedings of TIDSE 2004*, 132–141. Berlin: Springer.

Paay, J., J. Kjeldskov, A. Christensen, A. Ibsen, D. Jensen, G. Nielsen, and R. Vutborg. 2008. Location-based storytelling in the urban environment. In F. Vetere, C. Graham, C. Satchell, eds. *Proceedings of OZCHI 2008,* Cairns, Australia, 122–129. Sydney: ACM and CHISIG Australia.

Paay, J., J. Kjeldskov, S. Howard, and B. Dave. 2009. Out on the town: A socio-physical approach to the design of a context aware urban guide. *Transactions on Computer-Human Interaction, TOCHI* 16 (2): 7–34.

Piekarski, W., and B. H. Thomas. 2003. ARQuake—modifications and hardware for outdoor augmented reality gaming. In *Proceedings of 4th Australian Linux Conference*, Perth, Australia.

Politiken. 2005. *Politikens Nudansk Ordos* (the official Danish dictionary). 19th ed. Copenhagen: Politikens Forlag.

Skov, M. B. 2002. Design of Interactive Narratives: Concepts, Methods, and Architectures. Unpublished doctoral dissertation, Aalborg University Computer Science Department, Aalborg, Denmark.

Skov, M. B., and P. B. Andersen. 2001. Designing interactive narratives. In F. Nack, ed. *Proceedings of the First International Conference on Computational Semiotics in Games and New Media, COSIGN 2001*, Amsterdam, 69–75. Amsterdam: CWI.

Starner, T., B. Liege, B. Singletary, and J. Pair. 2000. MIND-WARPING: Towards creating a compelling collaborative augmented reality game. In H. Lieberman, ed. *Proceedings of IUI 2000*, 256–259. New York: ACM Press.

Zemeckis, R., and B. Gale. 1989. *Back to the Future Part II*. Universal Pictures. http://www.imdb.com/title/tt0096874/.

Zemeckis, R., and B. Gale. 1990. *Back to the Future Part III*. Universal Pictures. http://www.imdb.com/title/tt0099088/.

15 Mobile Interactions as Social Machines: Poor Urban Youth at Play in Bangladesh

Andrew Wong and Richard Ling

On the surface, mobile interactions are about a sender and receiver communicating through their phones. Over time, our mobile needs become our habit and our mobile habit is becoming part of our social lives. Why are we becoming so obsessed with mobile use? How have we become social animals fueled by this mobile use? We theorize that mobile interactions are an evolving social machine that involves a sheer amount of overt and covert mobile use in the engagement and production of meaning. The ever-growing number of users and complexity of mobile usage increase the emergence of new mobile interactions, and subsequently influence the production and consumption of local social behavior. Our case study focuses on the growing mobile use of poor urban youth (PUY) in Bangladesh, and we center our discussion on how the PUYs' mobile-use behavior is structured based on covert mobile behavior and external influences.

The functional interpretation of mobile use is about space and time compression between two or more individuals—communication without the need for physical encounter. A common theme in this discussion is the issue of coordination between users. The social interpretation of mobile use is about the dynamic, layered interactions between two or more individuals (Ling and Yttri 2002; Agar 2003; Taylor and Harper 2003). As in most technology adoption and domestication, we first adopt a technology in the name of utility and the benefits it will bring. It fits well into our daily life; it will motivate us to further embrace it as a convenient tool (Silverstone and Haddon 1998; Silverstone, Hirsch, and Morley 1999; Silverstone 2005). In the mobile-use context, users are likely to purchase a mobile phone and mobile subscription service for the immediate purpose of making calls or texting. Over time, they gain familiarity with mobile use and gain confidence vis-à-vis the patterning of mobile use in accordance with their lifestyle and surrounding social context.

As part of our ongoing research work on mobile use in developing countries, we have studied mobile use by the poor and more often the poorest of the poor. Our initial hypothesis is that the economic threshold for the poor is much higher; therefore they either share the mobile phone or go to a public calling office (a staffed mobile-phone booth) to make or receive a call for a few cents (Roldan, Helmersen, and Wong 2007). In this context, a poor person who can afford his or her own mobile phone would be very sensitive to the cost of use, even down to the level of seconds per call (Anderson 2006; Zainudeen, Samarajiva, and Abeysuriya 2006;). However, we have witnessed something much more profound. While the issue of practical utility of mobile use is central, we have observed that the attraction of the mobile use is not only about getting things done more efficiently via mobile, but also about the influence of social interactions on the use of mobile phones.

The purpose of the chapter is twofold: first, to help develop a general theoretical framework that examines social interactions surrounding mobile use, and second, to attempt to answer these questions: Why are Bangladeshi PUYs becoming obsessive mobile users? How are the social lives of PUYs fueled by mobile use? The results of our study should be of interest to both scholars and practitioners because they shed light on how mobile communication influences social interactions, and perhaps most importantly, because our analysis provides insight into the future evolution of mobile interactions by employing a metaphoric description of mobile interactions as a social machine.[1]

Mobile-Use Holding Power

The Growth of Mobile Use in Developing Countries

Despite the mobile phone's growth in the number of subscribers and its success as an everyday communication tool on a worldwide scale, it remains an emerging technology in developing countries and among the poor (Donner 2008). This chapter places special emphasis on the social role that communication tools play in the lives of poor urban youth, especially in Bangladesh, which ranks among the world's least developed countries. Relative to other information and communication technologies (ICTs), mobile phones hold the edge in both ownership rate and degree of centrality in owners' everyday lives. The International Telecom Union's (2008) work on the global information society shows the importance of mobile phones. The subscription statistics show that 92 out of 100 persons in developed countries have a mobile-phone subscription. They also show that 33 per 100 in developing countries and only 10 per 100 persons in the least developed countries have a mobile phone. When compared with Internet access, the mobile phone differentiates itself as the leading ICT tool for communication and interaction purposes. In the case of the Internet, there are only 24 users per 100 persons in developed countries, 4 per 100 in developing countries, and 0.2 per 100 in the least developed countries.[2] Macrostatistics aside, if we explore at the micro level—that is, individual and group level—we can add another layer of understanding to the statistical material. This microlevel is discussed in the next few paragraphs.

Urban Environments and Local Community Needs in Bangladesh

Bangladesh is a country with a population of 159 million. Half the population is considered literate.[3] As in many parts of the developing world, there is a massive, ongoing migration toward the cities, leading to a drastic rise in poverty among unskilled urban workers. Many have difficulty finding a job in the first few months after their arrival, which means they are left performing low-wage, odd jobs for as long as a year. One of the key reasons for this is that they are not able to match their skill set with the requirements of the city's employers. Many live in slums and squatter situations with low living standards; they also have limited access to economic and social systems like schooling and government welfare. More than 50 percent of the population is less than thirty-five years old due to age-selective rural-urban migration. There are several push factors to migrate to urban areas such as overpopulation in rural areas, constant floods and other natural disasters, river erosion, growing landlessness, and exploitation by the rural elites and moneylenders. In contrast, what attracts people to the urban centers are employment opportunities in the informal sectors (e.g., rickshaw puller, odd jobber, etc.), a better social life, and the opportunity for entertainment in the city. There is also relative freedom for women in urban areas.

In our study of mobile-phone use by the poor, we explore the needs and aspirations of the local community as a springboard to better understand mobile use among the PUYs. Furthermore, identifying local needs gives us insights into possible mobile interactions that might be relevant for the PUYs. Based on our study of the PUYs, broad categories of interactions pertain to information, communication, entertainment, and livelihood. Information needs could include knowing the condition and whereabouts of family members and friends, news, and updates on natural calamities and disaster relief. Other reasons include having access to information on basic services such as health, making bill and tax payments, and being able to take advantage of both formal and informal educational opportunities. The communication needs often involve getting in touch with family members, relatives, and friends. Workers and businesspeople need to contact colleagues, customers, and suppliers, as well as to make outbound international calls and calls across districts in Bangladesh. Other work needs involve sourcing for supplies, checking prices, communicating with customers, knowing what goods to sell and where to sell them, advertising, transferring money, and simultaneous communication with three or more people in the form of a group chat for business networking. People also need mobile phones during critical periods, as in personal emergencies and natural disasters, as well as to exchange greetings on special occasions like festivals, birthdays, and other family occasions. Access to music, exchanging pictures of family members, chatting with family, friends, and neighbors, and obtaining information on celebrities, sports stars, and movies fulfill many entertainment needs.

Mobile Interactions as Social Machines

It is important to understand the social aspects of PUYs' mobile interactions as a whole and to grasp the continuing social impact of the phones through the lens of urban interactions. According to Townsend (2000), mobile communication systems are essentially a form of urban metabolism. They have fundamentally rewritten the spatial and temporal constraints of human communication in work, family, recreational, and entertainment contexts. Beyond this there is the need for a systems approach, in the sense of "social informatics" of mobile interaction. This approach is necessary to be able to foresee and make sense of future mobile use (Kling 1999). Holistically, PUYs' mobile interactions must be studied as an entity in their own right to make sure they are captured accurately. According to Kling (1999), "A serviceable working conception of 'social informatics' is that it identifies a body of research that examines the social aspects of computerization." The same would apply to mobile use.

On the other hand, mobile use is different from many previously studied social systems. First, it is usually a personal technology. Second, the adoption of mobile devices is growing at a faster rate than other communication tools, and it is spreading more equally and broadly among the world's population. Human social interaction is now, in nearly in every sense, linked to mobile use, because of the central role mobile phones have acquired in transmitting the human voice or text across distance, as information disseminator, and as entertainer (Bell 2005; Cairncross 1997; Horst and Miller 2006; Wong 2007). Therefore, the notion of mobile interactions as social machines (as discussed later) is in part the result of the vast and decentralized use of the phones. Moreover, aligning our conceptual frame with the idea of "mobile interaction as social machine" will allow us to better understand human communicative and interactive behavior, and in particular, urban interactions over time. The last phrase is especially important, because the social-interactional perspective informs us about interactive behavior unfolding over time. Bakeman and Gottman (1986) argue that through a sequential view, researchers are best able to clarify the dynamic nature of social interaction. The rise of mobile communication makes it possible to test ideas along these lines.

Methodology

In this chapter we draw on three mobile-use case studies, carried out by the first author, that focus on poor households and individuals in three large cities in Bangladesh—Dhaka, Chittagong, and Sylhet—between 2006 and 2008. The data documents the lives of the PUYs and their use of the mobile phone in different contexts. In the context of this work, the PUYs are defined by several characteristics: a dependent, typically living in an urban household with less than 7,000 Takas (US$102) per month, aged between twelve and twenty-five years, and mostly still in school and college or working odd jobs.

Research design, according to Pelto (1970, 331), "involves combining the essential elements of investigation into an effective problem-solving sequence." This chapter relies on interviews with individuals carried out by the first author, observations, and interpretative analysis. We relied on local interpreters for the purpose of translating language and any particular local/cultural particularities. The material provides new mobile-use insights as a result of the fieldwork interviews and long hours of observation (i.e., deep hanging out) at social places such as cricket fields, local libraries, sidewalks, and teashops, among other places, in an effort to show that the sociocultural and economic situation of the PUYs can be understood from their point of view. The analysis of this research draws on work across mobile information and communication that was framed by three key genres of mobile-phone use: (1) solely for entertainment purposes, (2) as a means to create a larger network, and (3) being creative to maximize per-minute airtime usage by means of SIM switching and coded missed calls. These three genres of use arose from the data analysis and represent a way of describing different degrees of usage sophistication and intention for social communication.

A selection of thirty-two individuals was drawn from the three ethnographic studies mentioned above. The breakdown of participants by city is fourteen in Dhaka, seven in Sylhet, and eleven in Chittagong.[4] These sites and the thirty-two individuals were selected due to their residency in the three major cities in Bangladesh with differing cultural, socioeconomic, and familial influences (i.e., influences from family members who had spent time overseas).

Findings

Social Patterns of Mobile Interactions

In this section we discuss the more salient mobile interactions among the PUYs. In order to offer content and rich context, we do not intend to generalize each social pattern that emerged from mobile use. Rather we are selective and analyze those social patterns that are most salient based on observations in the field. As such, we will discuss three different social patterns that have emerged from mobile-use interactions to challenge our thinking about the impact of the present mobile interactions in Bangladesh, and how the interactions will evolve over time.

While the material provides a wide variety of insights, we will discuss the three prominent mobile interaction themes that emerged from the data. These findings emerged as we engaged in making sense of our informants' feedback and their views on their phone usage. These three themes can be conceptualized as referring to social interactions via mobile use. First, the *in-group connects* relate the performance of overt and covert mobile and social behavior. Second, the *mesh connects* describe the coalescing of local and global culture. Finally, the *collective action connect* explains the process in which group social behavior is being molded through actions taken as a group.

In-Group Connects

In-group connects play out via the mobile phone in different ways. In-group interaction can take place when there are chance encounters among mobile users. In these cases, the PUYs do a mix of mobile maneuvering. That is, they listen to one another's ringtones and radios, compare and comment on phone features, and pass on the shared phones. In this context the in-group interaction became a type of local ritual (Ling 2008a; Taylor 2005).

Aside from these physical meetings ,it is also interesting to note that there were two forms of in-group virtual interactions (i.e., no physical meeting). These include coded missed calls and SIM-switching practices. Missed calls are a system of dialing another person and then hanging up before they answer, and are used extensively in the developing world as a type of free signaling system (Donner 2007;Geirbo and Helmersen 2007). The caller and recipient have to have a prearranged agreement regarding the meaning of the call. A missed call might mean that one partner is finished working and is free to meet, or that he or she needs to be picked up, and so forth. In addition, we observed that some groups develop a type of lexicon for missed calls. For instance, in the city of Chittagong (a port city situated southeast of Bangladesh), we observed that the youth have predefined signaling systems—for example, one missed call (I am near your house), two missed calls (I am with my parents), three missed calls (I am not able to get out of the house), and so on. The missed calls made at different times of day add another layer of sophistication to their localized behavior. In the morning school period, young people may have different missed-call signaling protocols, such as one missed call (this is a boring class), two missed calls (let's get together after school), or three missed calls (there is an exciting plan after school).

Some of the same types of interactions can be seen in the case of SIM switching. This is a practice where a person may have several different SIM cards containing subscriptions to different operators. People use different SIM cards to avoid interconnectivity charges across operators. If both the sender and the receiver are "on net" or with the same operator, it is cheaper to call or text with that operator. SIM cards can also be switched in and out of a handset depending on which operator has coverage in a certain area or which operator has inexpensive tariffs at a particular time of day. In this context, the missed call is a way to signal to a friend that they should, for example, switch the SIM card in their phone to another operator so that they can benefit from cheaper rates for a call.

While on the surface there is a motivation to save money by using missed calls and SIM switching, there are also strong underlying social and entertainment factors. At the social level, the missed calls (especially those missed calls that boys make to girls) are used in the broader project of getting to know another person. Such contact-seeking behavior is motivated by the need to socialize amid cultural restrictions on male/female premarital relationships in Bangladesh. The entertainment factor is also another pull factor. When such behavior is normalized, it becomes a socially acceptable form of entertainment. This is different from the entertainment experience that teens in developed countries are accustomed to. Such side entertainment can include competition with friends as well as strangers in sending the greatest number of missed calls. It can also just be a form of killing time—for example, when callers signal to another party not to pick up the call because they just want to listen to the ringback tones.

The following quotes illustrate the homogeneity that exists among the views of interviewees, and their pride about the creative use of mobile services in SIM switching and missed calls. Here is a young, married female on her perception about the daily need for missed calls:

After my husband comes back from the office at 5:30 p.m. he gives me a missed call because we live on the 5th floor and when he reaches the ground floor he gives a missed call to signal me to throw the gate keys down.

A male commented on his opportunistic approach toward a missed call:

One day I received several missed calls. When I called back, I found it was a girl. I was about to react, but decided against it. Then she asked my name, which I refused to give. For the next 10 minutes we went on arguing but afterwards we became friends.

A youth discussed his daily cycling between different mobile operators to get the best deal:

Tk1.96 per minute. Again there is a Tk89 call charge. Covers most. Also I used to have a Banglalink SIM with 0191 number, but the one I use I get 55 minutes free talk time. I recharge it for Tk300 and still now get 55 minutes free. So I use mostly Banglalink.

These in-group social interactions represent a type of communication between two individuals that is hyperlocalized. At certain times it happens one to one, and at other times, between one individual and a multiple of three to four individuals (who happen to share a mobile phone) (see figure. 15.1). Due to this hyperlocalization, coded behaviors and practices exist as a reflection of their need to personalize their attitude, mood, and attachment to a cause or personality. Here, a mobile phone plays the role of relationship builder with a strong emphasis on private life.

Mesh Connect

The in-group connects—that is, interaction with close family and friends—are by far the most central uses of mobile communication (Ling 2008a). In addition, there are

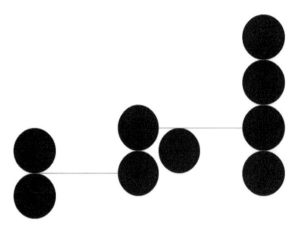

Figure 15.1
In-group connect.

some types of broader social networking via sites such as Facebook, Orkut, and Twitter. At no time in history have youth around the world been able to share a common social platform and interact so easily with others. While the vast majority of calls, texts, and missed calls are local, mobile use—especially mobile Internet use—is not bounded locally.

We call this *mesh connects* to represent the growing trend in which youth mesh their local culture with that of broader, global cultural trends (see Fig. 15.2). In the context of Bangladeshi youth, they model their behavior on or aspire to connect with the cultural centers in India (Bollywood) and the Western countries (for example, the United States for its music and movie influences).

We observed a growing trend toward mobile use permeating the PUYs' contemporary lifestyle. The role mobile phones play here is as an activator with a strong emphasis on public life that meshes with a broader, global outlook. PUYs' wholehearted tendency to accept and enjoy interacting with the world beyond their national borders is clear. A PUY explicitly stated his ambition to interact more with others:

I love the fact that there are a lot of people outside of Bangladesh who I can share my culture with, and they too are interested in me. That makes me happy. I will continue to instant message on my mobile with my friends from overseas as long as I can afford to.

We believe that mobile use will not only quicken the spread of cross-cultural influences, but will also increase the chance of creating pockets of global cultures. Via mobile phone, PUYs have the opportunity to connect socially, yet virtually, on a global scale. Many of the PUYs interviewed in this project connected to the Internet via their small-screen mobile or via a mobile tethered to a personal computer. We noted statements like this:

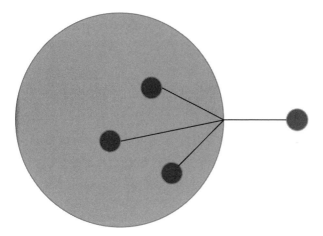

Figure 15.2
Mesh connect.

Given the chance to mingle and chat with friends far, far away is great, and sharing different experiences gives us a brand-new way to think about this world, and more importantly we learn how things like freedom, fashion, and so on are perceived.

These statements strike us as an important indication that the PUYs are moving along a path that builds their confidence in spreading their culture and also accepting culture beyond their country's borders.

Collective Action Connect

The widely distributed mobile use across Bangladesh has a large impact on the way the society communicates and interacts with others. However, there is a secondary, more tightly integrative role for mobile use. The observation data shows that the PUYs used their mobile phones to carry out specific type of activities. We also observed that the traditional psychographic makeup such as age or gender is less of an influence on this type of social interaction. We termed this *collective action connect*, due to the fact that the demographic makeup of the group is less important than usual when thinking about group cohesiveness. What is more important is some form of collective action such as a movie group, cricket buddies, or a weekend getaway gang. These types of collective interactions create a form of social obligation and influence among the individuals in the group to progressively move their social activities into tighter connections (see figure 15.3). For instance, the movie group may increase their mobile use to share information about a movie, coordinate movie timing, or discuss a moving rating. This collective action behavior depends on the fact that the PUYs actively seek to connect with each other. They may also develop a sense of the general dynamics

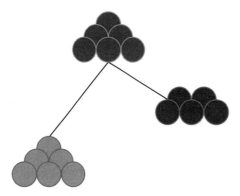

Figure 15.3
Collective action connect.

of the group. They might know that there will usually be friends at a particular location or at a particular type of event. The mobile phone has become a central tool in
this process.

Anchoring their views on mobile-phone experiences, the respondents linked economic and social factors to justify their collective actions. A youth recounts his fun
experiences in trying out features in the mobile phone he shares:

Yeah . . . most of my friends are pretty much like me. We encourage each other to try out new
things.

A young woman highlights the positive influence of her close-knit group on her social
life:

I really do enjoy how close we are when we are participating in creating a music club among
ourselves. We have more music on our mobile phone, and most important of all, it brings us
closer together.

A teen in Dhaka shares his views about transforming his mobile into a social calendar
to coordinate his group's passion for cricket:

This mobile thing is really great. When I first have it, I am just using it for calling my friends.
It turned out that I can use it for more than that, although I don't have a very nice phone
[showing his monochrome-screen phone]. I don't have a good calendar in my phone, but I can
use SMS to keep track of our activity.

Discussion

This ethnographic study is exploratory in nature. That said, it allows us to sense
certain behavioral outcomes of the mobile interactions. Other researchers have also

provided material to which we can apply the themes of in-group, mesh, and collective action connect and bring fresh perspectives to the discussion of mobile interactions. For example, Donner and Gitau (2009) discuss the local use of Internet-enabled services called MXit (a downloadable South African Mobile IM Social Network Service). Similarly, as with the earlier discussion of SIM switching and missed calls, MXit requires collective action among a number of people in the local settings to make this service successful. There is a need for a critical mass of users before the service can be seen as useful and appealing. Donner and Gitau elaborate that the main appeal of the MXit service is that MXit chats have replaced many phone conversations and SMS messages with a person's friends. Thus, it is a cost-saving alternative for the user. In turn, the "expert" on MXit will often become the mentor to help others configure and download so that more people can use the service to interact. This is an example of in-group connect, whereby on the surface, users adopt and use the service for the purpose of cost saving. However, if only one or two users in a local setting use the service, it becomes unappealing; a critical mass of users is necessary before the service can become functional as a shared platform for communication.

Another interesting case by Paragas (2005) discusses the internationalization of mobile use in the Filipino diaspora for the purpose of communicating with relatives and friends back home. According to Paragas, there is an interesting mix of social and economic issues at play whenever the global (overseas Filipinos) connect with the local (in-country Filipinos). For example, Filipinos in Japan apparently rarely use texting since there is a cultural sense in Japan that texting is immature and used by kids. Accordingly, they adapt to their new environment. This adaptive nature is an essential blending-in process, reflecting what we have called mesh connects. In Paragas' case study, the overseas Filipinos modeled the cultural values of the Japanese in order to live harmoniously with their Japanese colleagues.

There are two immediate points of significance here for researchers and practitioners alike who would like to better understand the particularities of mobile use from the social-machine perspective. First, if we attempt to understand mobile use, we should view it through a creative social-expression lens because the creative social expressions of mobile use, such as the experiences of using a mobile service or application, build on each other. For example, in the case of missed calls, the social expression of coded missed calls developed over time with a localized missed-call "language" distinguished by time of day, gender, group activities, and so on. Could it be these creative social expressions such as missed calls can be extrapolated toward the creation of formal services—that is, chargeable mobile services? Product-development managers and marketers should take a closer look at these social expressions not just for the purpose of understanding a consumer behavioral shift, but also possibly to establish a profitable venture if they can analyze, create, and then deliver a business model that provides appealing customer relationships, understands the right target segment, and offers a simple channel for such social expressions.

Previously we theorized and applied the model of in-group, mesh, and collective action connects to describe the ever-growing numbers and increasing complexity of mobile use among the PUYs. The consequence of this increasing usage is the creation of various types of mobile interactions, which is our second significant point. We observed that some of the mobile interactions are more common among the PUYs, but others have not been adopted. Is it possible for us to differentiate the "winners" from the "losers"? We first link this question closely to the Darwinian theory of evolution, which may suggest that the "winners" are those most open to functional flexibility (e.g., missed calls can replace a short voice call or act as a coded message in a close-knit group). Second, these interactions could be a substitute for nonmobile practices (e.g., the coded missed calls replace the need for voice to communicate certain actions or hard-to-express feelings). Third, and more importantly, the mobile interactions that contribute most to increased group spirit seem especially likely to be adopted and to survive. For example, in a group of close friends, and due to the addictive nature of the missed calls, it will naturally pull the group closer to develop more coded missed calls. ("Coded" means missed calls can be like a Morse code: for example, three missed calls means "I will be there in three minutes.) As a result, this will generate more mobile interaction usage.

The Impact of Mobile Use on Social Life

We posed two questions earlier in the chapter: Why are we becoming so obsessed with mobile use? And how have we become social animals fueled by mobile use? We attempt to answer the first question by describing the PUYs' different mobile interactions. The in-group and mesh connect illustrate two different kinds of mobile interactions. At one end of the scale, the localized nature of the in-group connect exemplifies the need to be closer to someone for caring, nurturing, loving, and so on. At the opposite end of the scale, the globalized nature of the mesh connect represents the need to be connected to a wider society. The collective action connect helps to illustrate the common values and actions among the PUYs. Thus, our assertion is that the very nature of the mobile phone allows the phone to recreate new instances of mobile usage. They are flexible and scalable (can be shared and can be extended in use for other purposes such as missed calls or radio), ubiquitous (owned or shared by the mass population), and affordable (less than a month's pay for the poor).

The second question touches on the power of mobile phones as a catalyst for social change. We hypothesize that as the PUYs increasingly depend on the mobile phone for social interactions, their dependency, or more appropriately interdependency, on others is becoming stronger. We further hypothesize that PUYs' theories about how to live as young adults and how the mobiles blend into their lives will continue to change and adapt to new environments. Will their views change as a consequence of their lived experiences with the mobile use that is a dominant feature in their life? We think so. Cases illustrated in this chapter, as well as support from a swath of studies, suggest that mobile use has far greater influence than we had previously realized (Rivière 2005; Ito 2005; Ikeda 2002; Srivastava 2005; Özcan and Koçak 2003; Solis 2007). As a social machine, the mobile phone appears to be adaptable to different social contexts. For instance, it is adapted as a coordination tool for a group cricket activity or as an entertainment tool for sharing music via Bluetooth. As a social machine, the mobile phone appears to be increasingly addictive. For instance, the PUYs can use the mobile to communicate in many different ways: through SMS, voice, missed calls, or sending music tones as a communication medium (e.g., love songs that represent one's feelings).

Conclusion

In this chapter, we have approached the relationship between mobile and social inter-actions from the social-machine perspective. This perspective allows us (or forces us to a certain extent) to be sensitized to how the PUYs' social life is intertwined with the lives of others, and to realize how mobile-phone use directly (or indirectly) forces the PUYs to not only change their behavior but to reassess their relationships with others. The principal purpose of discussing mobile use as social machine is to elucidate the social contextual perspective of mobile use from an individual and group stand-point. The central tenet of this chapter is that mobile interaction is evolving alongside societal changes. There are observable models of mobile interactions, and by truly understanding the different mobile interaction models, we can portray with greater detail the social interactions triggered by mobile use or influenced by social factors.

Acknowledgments

Many thanks to the team members at the Telenor Research and Innovation Center Asia Pacific for their fieldwork and active interactions over the past two years of study-ing poor youth in Bangladesh.

Notes

1. In separate work, the mobile phone is described as a social fact in the Durkheimian sense of the word. For the purposes of this chapter we will use the idea of the social machine (Ling 2008b).

2. There is a unit-of-analysis issue here in that the mobile phone tends to be a personal device, where often the Internet is a household device.

3. Based on an analysis of those aged fifteen and older.

4. The difference in the number of participants in each city was due to availability and suitability.

References

Agar, Jon. 2003. *Constant Touch: A Global History of the Mobile Phone*. Cambridge: Icon Books.

Anderson, Jamie L. 2006. A structured approach for bringing mobile telecommunications to the world's poor. *Electronic Journal of Information Systems in Developing Countries* 27 (2): 1–9.

Bakeman, R., and J. M. Gottman. 1986. *Observing Interaction: An Introduction to Sequential Analysis*. Cambridge: Cambridge University Press.

Bell, G. 2005. The age of the thumb: A cultural reading of mobile technologies from Asia. In P. Glotz, S. Bertschi, and C. Locke, eds., *Thumb Culture: The Meaning of Mobile Phones for Society*, 67–88. Bielefeld, Germany: Transcript Verlag.

Cairncross, F. 1997. *The Death of Distance: How the Communications Revolution Will Change Our Lives*. Boston: Harvard University Business School Press.

Donner, J. 2007. The rules of beeping: Exchanging messages using missed calls on mobile phones in sub-Saharan Africa. *Journal of Computer-Mediated Communication* 13 (1): 1–22.

Donner, J. 2008. Research approaches to mobile use in the developing world: A review of the literature. *Information Society* 24 (3): 140–159.

Donner, J., and S. Gitau. 2009. New paths: Exploring mobile-only and mobile-primary Internet use in South Africa. Paper presented at the Workshop on Africa Perspectives on the Role of Mobile Technologies in Fostering Social Development, Cape Town, April 15, 2009.

Geirbo, H. C., and P. Helmersen. 2007. *Missed Call: Messaging for the Masses*. A study of missed call signaling behavior in Dhaka. Internal Telenor R&I publication. Fornebu: Telenor R&I.

Horst, H., and D. Miller. 2006. *The Cell Phone: An Anthropology of Communication*. Oxford: Berg.

Ikeda, K. 2002. Patterns of a mobile phone use: A social psychological viewpoint. In *The Information Society and Youth: Report of the Fourth National Survey on "The Information Society and Youth,"* 287–301. Cabinet Office of Japan.

International Telecom Union. 2008. *The Global Information Society: A Statistical View*. New York: United Nations.

Ito, M. 2005. Mobile phones, Japanese youth, and the re-placement of social contact. In R. Ling and P. E. Pedersen, eds., *Mobile Communications: Re-negotiation of the Social Sphere*, 131–148. London: Springer.

Kling, R. 1999. What is social informatics and why does it matter? *D-Lib Magazine* 5 (1). http://www.dlib.org:80/dlib/january99/kling/01kling.html.

Ling, R. 2008a. *New Tech, New Ties: How Mobile Communication Is Reshaping Social Cohesion*. Cambridge, MA: MIT Press.

Ling, R. 2008b. The "unboothed" phone: Goffman and the use of mobile communication. Paper presented at the Media and the Change of Everyday Life Conference, Erfurt, Germany.

Ling, R., and B. Yttri. 2002. Hyper-coordination via mobile phones in Norway. In J. E. Katz and M. Aakhus, eds., *Perpetual Contact: Mobile Communication, Private Talk, Public Performance*, 139–169. Cambridge: Cambridge University Press.

Özcan, Y. Z., and A. Koçak. 2003. Research note: A need or a status symbol? Use of cellular telephones in Turkey. *European Journal of Communication* 18:241–254.

Paragas, Fernando. 2005. Migrant mobiles: Cellular telephony, transnational spaces, and the Filipino Diaspora. In K. Nyíri, ed., *A Sense of Place: The Global and the Local In Mobile Communication*, 241–249. Vienna: Passagen Verlag.

Pelto, P. J. 1970. *Anthropological Research: The Structure of Inquiry*. Cambridge: Cambridge University Press.

Rivière, C. 2005. Mobile camera phones: A new form of "being together" in daily interpersonal communications. In R. Ling and P. E. Pedersen, eds., *Mobile Communications: Re-negotiation of the Social Sphere*, 167–185. London: Springer.

Roldan, G., P. Helmersen, and A. Wong. 2007. *Connecting the Unconnected: Examining Local Needs, Exploring Service Opportunities in Bangladesh*. Telenor research paper. Cyberjaya: Telenor Research and Innovation Center Asia Pacific.

Silverstone, R., ed. 2005. *Media, Technology and Everyday Life in Europe: From Information to Communication*. Aldershot: Ashgate.

Silverstone, R., and L. Haddon. 1998. Design and the domestication of information and communication technologies: Technical change and everyday life. In R. Silverstone and R. Mansell, eds., *Communication by Design: The Politics of Information and Communication Technologies*, 44–74. Oxford: Oxford University Press.

Silverstone, R., E. Hirsch, and D. Morley. 1999. Information and communication technologies and the moral economy of the household. In R. Silverstone and E. Hirsch, eds., *Consuming Technologies: Media and Information in Domestic Spaces*, 15–31. London: Routledge.

Solis, R. J. C. 2007. Mobile romance: Exploring a new landscape for courtship in the Philippines. In Gerard Goggin and Larissa Hjorth, eds., *Mobile Media: Proceedings of an International Conference on Social and Cultural Aspects of Mobile Phones, Media, and Wireless Technologies*, 75–84. Sydney: University of Sydney.

Srivastava, L. 2005. Mobile phones and the evolution of social behavior. *Behaviour & Information Technology* 24:111–129.

Taylor, A. 2005. Phone-talk and local forms of subversion. In Rich Ling and Per Pedersen, eds., *Mobile Communications: The Re-negotiation of the Social Sphere*, 85–92. London: Springer.

Taylor, Alex, and Richard Harper. 2003. The gift of the gab?: A design oriented sociology of young people's use of mobiles. *Computer Supported Cooperative Work* 12:267–296.

Townsend, A. M. 2000. Life in the real time city: Mobile telephones and urban metabolism. *Journal of Urban Technology* 7 (2): 85–104.

Wong, A. 2007. The local ingenuity: Maximizing livelihood through improvising current communication access technology. In *Ethnographic Praxis in Industry Conference Proceedings* 2007 (1): 104–114. Washington, DC: American Anthropological Association.

Zainudeen, A., R. Samarajiva, and A. Abeysuriya. 2006. *Telecom Use on a Shoestring: Strategic Use of Telecom Services by the Financially Constrained in South Asia*. Colombo: LIRNEasia.

IV Technologies of Engagement

Foreword

Atau Tanaka

"The most profound technologies are those that disappear. They weave themselves into the fabric of everyday life until they are indistinguishable from it." It is with this well-known quote that the late Mark Weiser (1991) set out the challenges for ubiquitous computing in 1991. In the time since, technology and society have in many ways lived up to Weiser's predictions—there seems to be a seamless integration of omnipresent information services into our everyday lives.

In the twenty years since the publication of the influential *Computer for the 21st Century*, engineers have produced enabling technologies, and society has taken up, assimilated, and even misused these fruits of technological progress. Researchers in the field have occupied the space between the laboratory and the real world, designing the technologies to be developed or imagining scenarios for their use.

We will look back on this period as one where the research emphasis shifted from a technological focus to a societal one. Throughout this time, researchers in the field sought to validate their experiments in situ or "in the wild." In the late 1990s, ubiquitous mobile services were prototyped in Japan using laptops with mobile network access via Personal Handy-phone System (PHS) modems, which at the time advanced from 32 kbps bandwidth to 128 kbps throughput. Many of the initial concepts for mobile media sharing systems like Media Lab Europe's TuNA were implemented on personal digital assistants (PDAs) of the day with early 802.11b wireless data cards. Consumer devices, in a very ad hoc way, slowly started to have the form factors and capabilities imagined by researchers. Palmtop computers such as the Sony Vaio U series met limited commercial success yet became standard research platforms. Hardware technology was being productized more quickly than network infrastructures and provided the compelling services that would ultimately drive usage.

It is important to recall this progress, not just for purposes of techno-nostalgia, but to remind us of the basic challenges that have been addressed. With massive 3G/HSPA takeup, and increasingly sophisticated smart mobile devices, ubiquitous technologies have not only arrived, but have, in Mark Weiser's terms, disappeared into everyday life. But where does this leave research, and the fundamental questions that have driven the field? Does research disappear in the same way that the technology does? Technology may become dispersed into the real world, but core issues of use, usability, and innovation do not just go away. On the contrary, conducting research in an area that is an integral part of mainstream culture requires foresight to continue to evolve technologies in ways that are meaningful for human use, rigor to challenge assumptions, and flexibility to remain open to unexpected uses. The rich interaction between technology, commerce, and social use makes for a permanently moving target.

In chapter 18, Timo Ojala et al. deploy urban computing technologies in the wild, testing technologies in real-world settings. These contexts create specific demands that require thoughtful engineering, providing not just well-engineered technology, but also systems called horizontal resources—engaging, nonhierarchical access for a community and its citizens.

With Germaine Halegoua in chapter 17, we move from Scandinavia to Korea and extend the scope of work across public and private sectors. Ubiquitous computing enables cities from the ground up to become living laboratories; Halegoua considers not only the end user's needs, but also the relationships between public and private sectors in the partnerships forged in order to deploy ubiquitous services. She identifies in the space between business and user, culturally driven product offering that reflect Eastern sensibilities that have an export potential.

In chapter 19, Francisco C. Pereira et al. explore information processing technologies to enhance the social usefulness of user-generated content. By using natural language text analysis on tags that describe uploaded photos and videos of tourist destinations, they contextualize the experience of a broad range of visitors. The crowd becomes not just a source of information, but also sensors of experience articulating lines of desire and creating a virtual city that describes the real city. This creates forms of implicit engagement that approach topics discussed in part II of this book.

In chapter 20, Laurianne Sitbon et al. use similar information processing technologies to facilitate the formation of virtual communities through forms of what they term "opinion mining." Semantic profiles that characterize common interest are created through a hybrid of collaborative filtering and content-based approaches. They propose an approach that does not rest on a count of who is "for" or "against" an opinion, but instead note an expressive vector that indicates interest—and indeed engagement—in issues that create identity in a community.

In chapter 16, Ava Fatah gen. Schieck et al. take the question of identity and go back out to the real world to study the potential of technology to mediate and project identity. In their field trials they observe and measure the reaction of people to the public display of identity communicated via their mobile phones. In a two-stage experiment, they first observe how users project their personal identities by creating a publicly visible Bluetooth device name for their mobile phone. In a follow-up study they project the presence of people in public space by displaying device names in a café and in a nightclub. This provocative way of peeling back layers of privacy to gauge user response looks at how technology mediates sociality, and how common protocols such as Bluetooth channel identity and create forms of social representation.

Reference

Weiser, Mark. 1991. *The Computer for the 21st Century*. Scientific American Special Issue on Communications, Computers, and Networks, September. http://www.ubiq.com/hypertext/weiser/SciAmDraft3.html

16 Sensing, Projecting, and Interpreting Digital Identity through Bluetooth: From Anonymous Encounters to Social Engagement

Ava Fatah gen. Schieck, Freya Palmer, Alan Penn, and Eamonn O'Neill

The public arena offers a "stage" for interactions on which people negotiate boundaries of a social and cultural nature. With the advent of mobile and pervasive computing, technologies such as public screens and wireless network access points are becoming embedded in the fabric of the city, while other technologies such as more personal displays, GPS, and Bluetooth are becoming embedded in many consumer goods and artifacts, notably the increasingly ubiquitous mobile phone. The introduction of these technologies may modify existing social practices and stimulate new social behaviors, as well as creating new stages on which people can play out their engagements and project identities mediated by the new media technologies. How do technologies such as the mobile phone support people in mediating and projecting identities? What happens when people are made aware of their digital identity and presence in the public space? Will this stimulate different types of social interaction? To address these issues this chapter presents findings from two complementary studies that form part of our ongoing efforts to develop, apply, and refine methods for understanding pervasive systems as an integral facet of the city. The studies aimed to investigate people's perceptions of Bluetooth names in the city of Bath in (1) a laboratory setting in which we studied the perception and interpretation of Bluetooth names without other confounding stimuli; and (2) a field-based intervention in two urban settings exploring people's perceptions of and responses to the display of Bluetooth names in real social settings.

In an urban environment augmented by mobile and pervasive computing systems the interaction space depends on the characteristics of the particular technologies, the architecture in which they are embedded or through which they move, and the particular activities in which people are engaged. Technologically mediated interaction spaces come in various forms, including visual, auditory, or wireless. Wireless interaction spaces may be static, as in "WiFi hotspots," or mobile as in the interaction spaces created by technologies such as Bluetooth. The Bluetooth chipset on a mobile phone creates a short-range wireless interaction space surrounding the phone and its user. As the user moves, this interaction space comes into contact with various other features of the digital landscape such as services beamed from an interactive poster or Bluetooth phones belonging to friends, colleagues, and strangers. Bluetooth proximity detection has been applied in a number of projects, often to infer digital encounter by detecting nearby devices and, by further inference, the people who carry them. This has been applied to social networks, groups, and "familiar strangers" (Eagle and Pentland 2006; Nicolai et al. 2006; Paulos and Goodman 2004). It has also been applied in a number of settings to make urban areas easier to navigate—to walk around and to be appreciated by pedestrians (Heisser et al. 2006).

Bluetooth also allows users to project some aspects of their identity through their mobile phones. For instance, the Mobitip project (Rudström, Höök, and Svensson 2005) reported that in 2004 a surprisingly high percentage of people's phones were discoverable by Bluetooth in Kista, Sweden, and that some users had changed the default Bluetooth names of their phones to interesting alternatives. A study conducted as part of the Cityware project put such Bluetooth naming practices in their social, physical, and intentional context (Kindberg and Jones 2007).

In the research reported in this chapter we focus on the wireless interaction spaces generated by mobile Bluetooth devices—which overwhelmingly means Bluetooth-enabled mobile phones—carried by people in the city. We examine technologically mediated social behavior, how it supports the projection of identity, and how this identity is perceived and interpreted by others. In the next section, we provide a brief overview of factors that influence the construction of identity. We then present the concepts underlying a digital encounter and describe the two studies. We go on to outline our findings on people's perceptions of others' Bluetooth names and reactions to the public display of their own and others' Bluetooth names. We conclude by summarizing our ongoing work.

Space, Place, and Identity

The built environment plays a critical role in the construction and reflection of social behaviors. Urban spatial morphology not only reflects and expresses social patterns, but can also play a part in generating these patterns, providing a platform for rich and diverse social encounters (Hillier and Hanson 1984). Architectural spaces have values attached and as such convey cultural meaning and frame behavior. Additionally, the presence of others within architectural space affects our behavior and perception of such space. One might say that architectural places have embedded understandings, conventions, and protocols regarding appropriate behavior (Harrison and Dourish 1996). In this sense, space implies the area for (inter)action, whereas place infers socially understood boundaries and sociocultural values (i.e., uses and norms) that shape interaction and are constructed over time (Canter 1977, 1997). This dynamic interplay of place and interaction inevitably shapes how identity is communicated; it changes the context of communication and how it is "suitable" or even possible to do so. As a result, space and place play a potentially significant part in the construction and communication, as well as our experience and understanding, of identity.

"Identity" encapsulates the essence of a given object or being. When referring to people, identity inevitably involves embodied activity (Budgeon 2003) and thus interaction between physical and social-psychological factors. Work within social psychology, and particularly more critical schools, has reflected this (e.g., Goffman 1959). Critical approaches emphasize processes of dynamic construction by which individuals, groups, and society define these concepts and themselves. Identity, rather than being a relatively fixed and static entity within the individual (as implied by traditional psychology), is ascribed according to our own and others' discourse (Gergen 2002). This in turn shapes how we view the world and ourselves (Burr 2003). Social identity thus involves perception and interpretation, as well as projection. Identity (and associated values and meanings) is dynamically constructed through the communication and discourse of social interaction and maintained through relationships and social networks (De Fina, Schiffrin, and Bamberg 2006; Thoits and Virshup 1997). People's physical nature, behavior, and social interactions are colored by the interaction of the individual's and the wider society's understanding of such matters (Burr 2003).

Processes of interaction, notably banal discourse (e.g., everyday communication and conversation), can be considered critical in the construction of identity (see Potter and Edwards 2001 for a comprehensive discussion). However, more implicit uses of, and interactions with, objects in constructing identity have also been well documented (e.g., Csikszentmihalyi and Rochberg Halton 1981; Dittmar 1992). In this context, digital communication artifacts are especially interesting because they enable additional dynamics of interaction. As with interactions between the user and object, communication devices mediate interaction with other people (both locally and remotely) implicitly, through the construction and argumentation of discourse (Fortunati 2005), and explicitly through direct communication.

Computer-based communication systems and "online identity" have been widely discussed (e.g., Bargh and McKenna 2004; Turkle 1995). However, technologically mediated identity is perhaps most salient in relation to mobile technology. The mobile phone, in particular, has become intrinsically linked to our everyday lives, both physically and sociofunctionally. It has taken a step beyond enabling the "presence of absence" by providing a reminder of another person (Gergen 2002); rather it enables the relatively novel possibility of being reachable almost anywhere by anyone at any time.

This pervasiveness is possible because of the mobility of such devices, but they are not just portable; they are personal. We no longer contact the location; instead we contact the person (Ling 2004). In this sense, the device is an extension of its owner and serves as a reminder of the individual's connectedness (Ling and Yttri 2002), reinforcing a sense of social identity.

Much literature that discusses communication technologies addresses their role in remote communication, often focusing on its disembodied nature (e.g., Turkle 1995). However, as noted, aspects of mobile technologies are much more embodied. Mobile wireless interaction spaces created by technologies such as Bluetooth typically move with their users as they carry their devices through the city. As a feature of the Bluetooth protocol, a degree of anonymity is associated with Bluetooth contact and communication. However, given the need for proximity, Bluetooth lies somewhere between wholly embodied face-to-face conversation and the wholly disembodied medium of Internet chat between remote strangers (Kindberg and Jones 2007).

The close coupling of mobile communication device and owner means that a Bluetooth name becomes a pseudonym used in contacting the individual, and represents the person rather than just their device. Thus, the customized Bluetooth name becomes a mode by which the individual communicates her "digital social identity." It enables the device to be identifiable to in-group members (e.g., friends) as belonging to its owner, without it becoming obvious to others who it is (Kindberg and Jones 2007); therefore, social identity is communicated and reinforced. Users appropriate the way in which Bluetooth operates as a "partially embodied" medium to project their digital identity, which makes it a unique paradigm of socially and physically embedded communication.

In the next section we describe (1) a lab-based study in which we investigated people's perceptions of Bluetooth names, sensed and recorded in the city of Bath, and (2) a field-based intervention study in which we sensed and publicly displayed in real time the Bluetooth names of nearby devices in two public areas in Bath.

The Studies

Lab-Based Study: Interpreted Identity—Categorizing Bluetooth Names

Between 2005 and 2009 approximately twelve static Bluetooth sensors were operational in the city of Bath (O'Neill et al. 2006). Each sensor continuously searched for discoverable Bluetooth devices (i.e., those with Bluetooth switched "on" and "visible") passing within range of the sensor, recording both the unique Bluetooth ID (often, if erroneously, referred to as MAC address) and Bluetooth name. The dataset used here consisted of 35,144 unique Bluetooth names recorded over three years. While names may be chosen and projected by users for a variety of reasons from illicit to benevolent (e.g., Friedman and Resnick 2001; McCarthy 2007), the study reported here investigated how people exposed to the names perceived and interpreted them as instances of technologically mediated social identity.

An open card-sort methodology was used to uncover mental models of Bluetooth name interpretation since the method enables participants to categorize names and attribute these groupings with labels and descriptions they consider appropriate (Hinkle 2008).[1] Two independent studies were conducted using the same card-sorting methodology but different sorting criteria. The first study asked participants to sort the Bluetooth names into groups according to any criteria of similarity they deemed appropriate. The second study asked participants to sort the names into groups they regarded as similar in terms of social identity (similarity of the people the name belongs to or describes). The first grouping exercise provided a general mental model of Bluetooth names, whereas the second explicitly addressed social identity as expressed through the Bluetooth names. It was thus possible to compare the social-identity groupings with the general groupings to show how explicit or implicit social identity is as a factor in Bluetooth name interpretation.

Multivariate hierarchical cluster analysis was used to analyze participants' Bluetooth name categorizations. Relatively clear cutoff points between the resulting metacategories of Bluetooth names could be observed. These distinctions became particularly evident when participants' rationales for their card groupings were also considered, providing qualitative support and a level of contextual understanding to these metacategories.

Participants' group labels formed the titles of the emergent metacategories of Bluetooth names through assessing the frequency with which each group label was attributed to each name and therefore to each category of names. In doing so, we were able to gain some understanding of *how* participants conceptualized the names as similar. Due to similarity between the metacategory titles, these were collapsed to form a summary of *types* of Bluetooth names (table 16.1).

Several themes emerged when addressing the types of names and associated interpretations. The perceived "tone" in which names were written was often used to characterize the type of person behind the name. For example, names regarded as fun, playful, jokey, serious, threatening, and so on were often regarded as belonging to people possessing corresponding personality traits, or wishing to be perceived as such. This interpretating was often extrapolated to offer additional inferred detail about the "character" of the name's owner.

Anonymity and the degree to which the name revealed a "real" name or information about the person's "character" were repeatedly mentioned. Participants distinguished between nicknames that they perceived the owner was called in "real life" and were likely to have been *attributed to* her, and those that were likely to have been *made up by* the owner. The latter were often regarded as being for use in contexts where anonymity was expected or valued, such as online chatrooms. However, participants also suggested that users making up their own pseudonyms were likely to be doing so

Table 16.1

The "types" of Bluetooth names established from the collapsed metacategories and a summary of the associated interpretations of these. (Descriptive explanations of the social identity associated with each of these kinds of names were generated from the collated participants' rationales.)

Type of name	Subtype of name		Description
Device names	Default model		Default device model numbers / randomly chosen, or at least hidden meaning. Indescript people who do not want to be noticed.
	Person's ownership		Identify themselves through association with something (likely to be a device), almost boastful about ownership/association.
People's "real" names	Full/formal name (or first name with initial), no embellishment		Full/formal name (or first name with an initial) with no embellishment. Average, ordinary people.
	First name		"Normal," "stable" people with no reason to hide/want to be recognized and are happy for people to know it is them. Likely to be serious with less imagination.
Nicknames	Based on "real" name	Abbreviation of "real," formal name	Not really trying to stand out, do not say much about their personality or interests, etc., but make a little effort to identify themselves by adding an initial, etc., or by making it more playful. Gregarious, fun people.
		Symbols added / spelled with symbols	As with "First name" group, but embellishments are just to make the names recognizable as being unique (i.e., could be quite a common name), or possibly to draw attention to it. Interpreted as playful in manner. But often confuses people as to the meaning (interpreted as "random"). Likely to be quite a young person, perceived as most likely to be female.
		Name contained within phrase	Likely to be a nickname made up/used by others, based on the person's name. The person is likely to be trying to be creative/funny or to brag. They are happy to broadcast nicknames that describe something of themselves/how they wish to be seen by others. Often interpreted as playful. But the name is not always perceived as revealing much about them as a person.
	Descriptive	Pet names	Nicknames used in "real life" by others.
		Aliases	Nicknames made up by the person, usually likened to online context. Not actually called this by anyone but anonymously reveals something of the person—they want to tell people this is what they are like/they wish to be "mysterious but unique." Likened to a username. Likely to be concerned with privacy, but lighthearted, fun, friendly people possibly trying to be funny/brag (but sometimes self-deprecating).

Table 16.1
(continued)

Type of name	Subtype of name	Description
Dynamic messages	Attention-seeking / declarative messages	Likely to include e-mail address to reflect their awareness others may want to contact them/ encourage contact in this way. Trying to communicate without necessarily revealing themselves overtly.
	Expressive statements	Saying something about how they feel, or expressing an opinion, rather than necessarily identifying or describing themselves. Possibly also to reflect how they would like to be seen, but is likely to come across as "random." Not obvious who or what the name is communicating, but it appears to communicate a message to the reader to provoke a response.

specifically to project a particular "image" of themselves. Participants often placed the names within a context where this kind of name would be "appropriate for its imagined owner," meeting expected norms of anonymity, tone, and so on. The denotation of ownership/belonging and the context within which a name would be used were often referred to as contributing factors in making social-identity-related judgments. Some participants explicitly suggested that when some users chose to use a "real nickname" they were referencing a shared group experience and/or projecting an identity by which they had become known within a specific in-group. By using this as their name, they are reinforcing their ties to this social group while remaining anonymous to others (see Kindberg and Jones 2007).

Bluetooth names were interpreted similarly in both card-sorting studies, producing similar categorization labels. However, rationales given for label choice varied between the studies. The social-identity-based card sort elicited more explanation in terms of the kinds of people who participants perceived would use such a name and the reasons they thought someone might do so—that is, interpretations of the social identities projected by these names. This indicates that social identity was a salient factor when interpreting names in situations where the physical owner of the name was not present to provide further information regarding its actual meaning.

In summary, participants appeared to exhibit an awareness of the potential Bluetooth names have as a medium for communicating social identity. Further, they interpreted the names in terms of social identity and perceived that others used them as a medium for projecting social identity. While interpretation of the kinds of people represented by given Bluetooth names is likely to vary between individuals based on subjective schemata, our results illustrate that factors likely to lead people to make such social-identity-related judgments are essentially similar. Therefore, although individual interpretations in themselves may vary, the information sought in order to interpret and construct social identity in this way is similar.

Field-Based Intervention Study: Increasing the Embodiedness of Bluetooth Names

The laboratory study isolated Bluetooth names as the sole method of communication and stimulus for interpretation, deliberately removing other means of making social-identity judgments. However, as discussed above, the interpretation of identity is a reflexive and dynamic social activity shaped by the dynamic interplay of place and social interactions. To explore this active relationship between Bluetooth names, digital identity, and social participation, moving from anonymous encounter to social engagement, we investigated people's perceptions of and reactions to Bluetooth names in a field-based intervention study in two real urban social settings.

In our previous work we have explored digital interactions in the city and noted the importance of two key human capacities: consciousness of communication and intention of interaction (Fatah gen. Schieck, Kostakos, and Penn 2010). We highlighted how technology can be appropriated for shared interactions that support conscious or unconscious social communication. In any given situation people can be conscious or unconscious of the communications taking place and can carry out interactions intentionally or unintentionally (table 16.2).

During an encounter the state of each of the two parties may be different. Conscious-intentional encounters are those that a person initiates—for instance, seeing a

Table 16.2

Aspects of technologically mediated encounter: Users may be conscious or unconscious of the communication and interactions can be intentional or nonintentional.

| | | Intention of interaction | |
		Intentional	Nonintentional
Awareness of communication	Conscious	Goal oriented: (particular) Talk to a friend	Circumstantial: (nonparticular) Friend talks to me
	Unconscious	(particular) Broadcast	Ambient: (nonparticular) Copresence

friend on the street and shouting to get her attention. Similarly, a person using her mobile phone to call a friend or send a photograph to a nearby person using Bluetooth can initiate such encounters. Conscious-nonintentional encounters are situations where a person is aware of the communication taking place but does not intentionally want to interact. Examples of this are when a person is spoken to on the street or is the recipient of an unsolicited Bluetooth message in a café. There are other interesting aspects of encounters that one could consider; however, we suggest that the combination of consciousness and intention becomes particularly interesting with the introduction of technology to augment encounters.

We explored these aspects of technologically mediated encounters in an intervention-based field study at two sites in Bath: in a café during daytime and in a nightclub during the evening. Our aim was to identify people's interaction forms and possible changes in Bluetooth names triggered by our intervention (Fatah gen. Schieck, Penn, and O'Neill 2008). Discoverable Bluetooth devices were sensed using a computer that constantly recorded their Bluetooth IDs and Bluetooth names within a 10-meter range. Bluetooth names were detected and projected in real time on a surface in the location. In the nightclub, the projection surface was large and central in front of the main entrance to the space so it could be seen clearly when people entered. In the café, however, there was no dedicated projection area. The projection surface was on the wall next to the entrance but in a less prominent location with brighter ambient lighting. People were therefore not as instantly aware of it when they entered the space as they were in the nightclub (figure 16.1).

Whenever a device was discovered, its Bluetooth name was projected on the surface and a tentacle appeared around it. As an attempt to attract people's attention to what

Figure 16.1
Sensing and revealing the digital identity in a club (*left*) and a café in Bath (*right*).

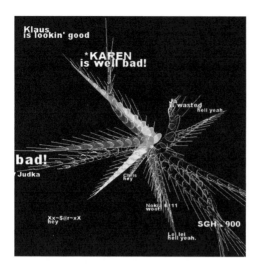

Figure 16.2
Bluetooth names are linked to a randomly selected "tag." With several names appearing along with several tags, the visualization became a dynamic representation of an evolving social network.

was projected on the screen, a "tag" was attached to each name (e.g., an expression or a social description such as *Hey!* or *is looking good!*). Every Bluetooth name was coupled to an arbitrarily selected tag. Thus, the visual representation was not limited to the presentation of the Bluetooth name assigned to a device by its user but was rather an attempt to trigger reactions by creating a dialog between the people present and the display's content. Once a Bluetooth device was no longer detected as present, the tag faded away and disappeared from the projection surface, so the projection represented Bluetooth devices—and by inference their owners—that were present at the same time in the same place (figure 16.2).

This intervention was coupled with "snapshot" observations: during the sessions a human observer recorded people's positions, behaviors, and movements through space, as well as the time of these activities. Interactions with the projection surface and the projected information were captured. In addition, various interactions with other people in the area were observed and recorded by two researchers using a still camera and a digital video camera. Finally, changes in the Bluetooth names displayed on the projection surface were tracked over time and analyzed. These observations were subsequently compared with the data recorded by our onsite Bluetooth sensors. Following the sessions, a number of participants were asked to complete questionnaires. Twenty-five questionnaires were collected, ten at the nightclub and fifteen at the café.

Figure 16.3
In the club, various social interactions were triggered. Some people started changing their Bluetooth name.

Our approach in the field setting involved a range of methods from interpretative-ethnographic to experimental. Assigning the "tag" to the Bluetooth names triggered mixed reactions by the observers. Questionnaires showed that people varied in how comfortable they were with the projection (in the café, more uneasy; in the club, more comfortable). During the projection we felt that the casual atmosphere at the nightclub made people more receptive to the projection, unlike the café, where people's reactions were more reserved and the social interaction was very limited. It seemed that having the projection of Bluetooth names in such a space was unexpected and to some extent regarded as intrusive. In the nightclub when people were faced with the visualization of Bluetooth names of other people present in the physical space, various social interactions were triggered (figure 16.3).

Most people found the process playful and entertaining; they kept changing their Bluetooth names and waited to see the result on the display. For instance, in table 16.3, we can see that *Davey-G* changed his (or her?) name twice, from *Davey-G* into *Everyone wants lonsdale!* and then into *Pete has ten inches?* Some people used the projection as an interactive message board. For instance, *Optimus prime* turned her/his Bluetooth name into *Hi camera lady*, referring to our researcher, who was capturing the interactions with her camera. Altering the device's name may therefore suggest an intention for social interaction with the observer through this medium.

Table 16.3

The projection of the digital identity though the Bluetooth names at the club

Time sessions	No. of people at the club	Scanned Bluetooth names		Tags
22.00–22.15	25	Hello beautiful!		Is looking good
		Davey-G		Woot!
		Jodie		Hey
		Jx		ROCKS!
		W880		Is bitchin'!
		JawaDeman		
		Scarlet x x		
		Man Mountain		
		Kuva!		
		Gorgeous		
		D*ck Willie C* x		
		Princess		
		2 unknown		
22.15–22.30	38	Pleb Nokia 6300		Smelly
		S*X APPEAL BUT DEPERATE PLZ		Is well bad
		Gem		—
		Abel		Is wasted
		Lonsdale is GAY		
		Optimus Prime		
22.30–22.45	45	Everyone wants Lonsdale!	(from Davey-G)	
		Jodie		
		Get ur spade out!		
		Rob N Roll		
		Hey camera lady . . .	(from Optimus Prime)	
		Pete has ten inches?		
		Jesson is Gay	(from Davey-G)	
		Newman is a s*x pest	(from Gem)	
		Likes To L*ck		
		BP 4232-MBPRO-4	(from D*ck Willie C* x)	
		Jo wants to sh*g Dom		
		Rob N F**kin Roll		
		I unknown	(from Lonsdale is GAY) (from Rob N Roll)	
22.45–23.00	42	Helphire are shite		Woot!
		Mcraith wants jesson		Hey
		I want c*ck!		Is well bad
		Tjeres only one!		—
		2 unknown		Is shaking it good
				—

The Bluetooth- and display-mediated conversation between *Davey-G* and *Pete* demonstrates a different kind of socially meaningful engagement, facilitated by the novel interaction space created by our sensing and projection of Bluetooth names. The user took advantage of the degree of personal anonymity but very public display afforded by this medium. Everybody in the club could see the display but there would have been doubt in the minds of all those, apart from close friends, as to the identity of *Davey-G* and *Pete*. One could potentially read from the tone of the interchange, presumably its intended message, that these users had a sense of humor and were outgoing. By using the projected Bluetooth display, they took advantage of the novel form of embodiedness provided by our shifting Bluetooth from its usual, and itself novel, partially embodied form to a more embodied—but still anonymous to those outside the in-group—medium for social engagement.

The questionnaire responses indicated that people who were broadcasting Bluetooth names were mainly between twenty-one and twenty-five years old. Older people tended to suggest that they did not know the technology well and were not inclined to use it. In response to the question "How do you feel about your name being made public and interacted with?" eight people were comfortable and two responded negatively. These two reacted in an extreme way and expressed their anger about this type of "surveillance" and the way technology was projecting their "personal information." Our findings indicated that a few people were critical about the exposure of what they regarded as their personal data and our approach in provoking interaction with their digital identity, but most people wanted to participate through playful interactions.

A number of factors may have influenced people's responses, which encouraged different and sometimes ambivalent reactions. Some factors are related to the individual—age, knowledge, and use of digital media. Other factors are related to the space itself, activities in that space, and the projection, such as the projection location and its relation to the main space, clarity, and the projection time and duration.

Conclusion and Ongoing Work

In this chapter we have described an investigation of people's perceptions of and reactions to Bluetooth names in a lab-based study and a field-based intervention study. The lab study investigated the interpretation of Bluetooth names without other stimuli confounding these perceptions. Hence, the Bluetooth names themselves were the sole method of communication and stimulus for interpretation of the social identity of the name's owner. The study illustrated that there are individual differences in the way that people interpret Bluetooth names. This is unsurprising because participants were from varied backgrounds and unlikely to share the same perspectives. However, the study also found commonality in the factors on which these social identity judgments were based, even if the judgments themselves differed. Where the details of individuals' interpretations differed, participants still tended to seek the same types of information to provide salient social identity "clues" on which to base their interpretations of the identities behind Bluetooth names.

The lab-based study focused on the interpretation of Bluetooth names in isolation but, as discussed earlier, the interpretation of identity is not a one-way process but rather a reflexive and dynamic social activity. Therefore, we also investigated people's perceptions of and responses to Bluetooth names in two real urban social settings. Here, people were able to interact and react more naturally, so it was possible to observe identity processes more holistically and in context.

Our preliminary findings suggest that by altering the relation between consciousness of communication and the intention of interaction, technology can be appropriated to support emergent behavior. This may help throw light on the complex relationship between the digital space and public space in general, and the way that this relationship is mediated by and mediates people's relationships to each other. Our approach offered a "digital stage" that facilitated and encouraged different types of social interactions. Presenting people with a visualization of their unconscious-intentional (or unintentional) projection of their digital identity and sharing it with others made people aware of the influence it can have on others and provided them with an incentive to change the way they engage with others.

As part of our ongoing work we are addressing a number of issues that came up in our studies. Specifically, we are exploring how digital encounters can augment the experience of public space. In this respect a particularly important insight comes from the observed effects of publicly "tagging" a digital identity with an additional phrase. It seems that this was understood by the viewers as giving the installation a personality or at least suggesting that there was human agency involved in the piece that encouraged a conversational form of interaction. We suspect that in order for public display and use of these technologies to be engaging, the viewer needs to be able to construct a meaningful social relationship. The engagement with "camera girl" provides one example of this, as the user connects the presence and behavior of the display with the presence and activity of the person observing and recording the event.

Our intervention in visually and publicly displaying the Bluetooth names shifted Bluetooth from its usual partially embodied status, although still not to the extent of explicitly associating a given Bluetooth name with an identifiable person. This study demonstrated that the projection of one's partially embodied digital identity, making it part of the physical environment, can trigger various types of interactions not only in an unintentional form but also as a conscious-intentional projection of identity. Further research is needed in order to evaluate the degree to which this approach might provide a motivation to change the way people communicate and engage with others in various settings. We need to examine in greater detail which factors influence people's perceptions and behavior and how they do so in relation to their urban spatial context.

Acknowledgments

We would like to acknowledge the efforts of Kaiti Papapavlou, Adi Ahmad, and Olivier Ottevaere of the MSc Adaptive Architecture and Computation 2007–2008 cohort. We thank Vassilis Kostakos, Alasdair Turner, and Tim Kindberg for their valuable contributions. The research presented in this chapter was partially funded by the UK Engineering and Physical Sciences Research Council project *Cityware: Urban Design and Pervasive Systems* (Grant EP/C547683/1), www.cityware.org.uk.

Note

1. The number of names provided challenges in presenting this information to participants for grouping and labeling. Five separate sets of fifty names were extracted randomly from the complete set. Fifty participants were asked to categorize these sets. The two different card-sorting exercises used independent participants but the same five sets of fifty names, to avoid repetition bias but allow comparison between card sorts. Participants were recruited from a combination of cohort members associated with the Cityware project and a general opportunity sample. The Cityware cohort comprised members of the public selected to represent a wide demographic range (Jay and Stanton Fraser 2008). The varied demographic range was used to reduce sampling bias.

References

Bargh, J., and K. McKenna. 2004. The Internet and social life. *Annual Review of Psychology* 55 (February): 573–590.

Budgeon, S. 2003. Identity as an embodied event. *Body & Society* 9 (1): 35–55.

Burr, V. 2003. *Social Constructionism*. 2nd ed. London: Routledge.

Canter, D. 1977. *The Psychology of Place*. London: Architectural Press.

Canter, D. 1997. The facets of place. In G. T. Moore and R. W. Marans, eds., *Advances in Environment, Behavior and Design, 4: Towards an Integration of Theory, Methods, Research and Utilization*, 109–148. New York: Plenum Press.

Csikszentmihalyi, M., and E. Rochberg Halton. 1981. *The Meaning of Things: Domestic Symbols and the Self*. Cambridge: Cambridge University Press.

De Fina, A., D. Schiffrin, and M. Bamberg, eds. 2006. *Discourse and Identity*. Studies in Interactional Sociolinguistics XX. Cambridge: Cambridge University Press.

Dittmar, H. 1992. *The Social Psychology of Material Possessions: To Have Is To Be*. Hertfordshire: Harvester Wheatsheaf/New York: St. Martin's Press.

Eagle, N., and A. Pentland. 2006. Reality mining: Sensing complex social systems. *Personal and Ubiquitous Computing* 10:255–268.

Fatah gen. Schieck, A., V. Kostakos, and A. Penn. 2010. Exploring the digital encounters in the public arena. In K. S. Willis, G. Roussos, K. Chorianopoulos, and M. Struppek, eds., *Shared Encounters*, 179–195. London: Springer Verlag.

Fatah gen. Schieck, A., A. Penn, and E. O'Neill. 2008. Mapping, sensing and visualising the digital co-presence in the public arena. In H. J. P. Timmermans and B. de Vries, eds., *Design Decision Support Systems in Architecture and Urban Planning*, 38–58. Leende, NL. (CD Rom).

Fortunati, L. 2005. Mobile telephone and the presentation of self. In R. Ling and P. E. Pedersen, eds., *Mobile Communications: Re-negotiation of the Social Sphere*, 203–218. London: Springer Verlag.

Friedman, E., and P. Resnick. 2001. The social cost of cheap pseudonyms. *Journal of Economics & Management Strategy* 10 (2): 173–199.

Gergen, K. 2002. The challenge of absent presence. In J. Katz and M. Aakhus, eds., *Perpetual Contact: Mobile Communication, Private Talk, Public Performance*, 227–241. Cambridge: Cambridge University Press.

Goffman, E. 1959. *The Presentation of the Self in Everyday Life*. New York: Doubleday Anchor.

Harrison, H., and P. Dourish. 1996. Re-place-ing space: The roles of place and space in collaborative systems. In Computer-Supported Cooperated Work *CSCW 1996*, November 16–20, 67–76. New York, NY: ACM Press.

Heisser, M., S. Klapdor, M. Maron, and S. Schaefer. 2006. Way finding, routing and getting information with mobile, Internet or stationary information system. *Spatial Metro ICT Workshop Report*, April 26. Koblenz, Germany.

Hillier, B., and J. Hanson. 1984. *The Social Logic of Space*. Cambridge: Cambridge University Press.

Hinkle, V. 2008. Card-sorting: What you need to know about analyzing and interpreting card sorting results. *Usability News* 10 (2). http://www.surl.org/usabilitynews/102/cardsort.asp.

Jay, T., and D. Stanton Fraser. 2008. The role of a cohort in the design and evaluation of pervasive systems. In 7th ACM Conference on Designing Interactive Systems (DIS 2008), 31–39. Cape Town, South Africa.

Kindberg, T., and T. Jones. 2007. Merolyn the phone: A study of Bluetooth naming practices. In J. Krumm, G. D. Abowd, A. Seneviratne, T.Strang, eds, 9th International Conference Proceedings on Ubiquitous Computing. Lecture Notes in Computer Science–335. Innsbruck: Springer.

Ling, R. 2004. *The Mobile Connection: The Cell Phone's Impact on Society*. San Francisco: Morgan Kaufmann.

Ling, R., and B. Yttri. 2002. Hyper-coordination via mobile phones in Norway. In J. E. Kaatz and M. Aakhus, eds., *Perpetual Contact: Mobile Communication, Private Talk, Public Performance*, 139–169. Cambridge: Cambridge University Press.

McCarthy, J. F. 2007. The challenges of recommending digital selves in physical space. In J. A. Konstan, J. Riedl, B.Smyth, eds, Proceedings of the 2007 ACM conference on Recommender systems *RecSys 2007*, Minneapolis, October 19–20, 185–186.

Nicolai, T., E. Yoneki, N. Behrens, and H. Kenn. 2006. Exploring social context with the wireless rope. In R. Meersman, Z. Tari, P. Herrero, eds. , On the Move to Meaningful Internet Systems. OTM Workshops, LNCS, vol. 4277, 874–888. Heidelberg: Springer Verlag.

O'Neill, E., V. Kostakos, T. Kindberg, A. Fatah gen. Schieck, A. Penn, D. Stanton Fraser, and T. Jones. 2006. Instrumenting the city: Developing methods for observing and understanding the digital cityscape. In P. Dourish, A. Friday, eds., 8th International Conference, UbiComp 2006, Orange County, CA.

Paulos, E., and E. Goodman. 2004. The familiar stranger: Anxiety, comfort, and play in public places. In E. Dykstra-Erickson, M. Tscheligi, eds., Proceedings of the 2004 Conference on Human Factors in Computing Systems, *CHI 2004*. Vienna, ACM.

Potter, J., and D. Edwards. 2001. Discursive social psychology. In W. P. Robinson and H. Giles, eds., *The New Handbook of Language and Social Psychology*, 103–118. London: Wiley.

Rudström, Å., K. Höök, and M. Svensson. 2005. Social positioning: Designing the seams between social, physical and digital space. In *Proceedings of the 1st International Conference on Online Communities and Social Computing, HCII 2005*, Las Vegas, 24–27.

Thoits, P., and L. Virshup. 1997. Me's and we's: Forms and functions of social identity. In R. Ashmore and L. Jussim, eds., *Self and Identity: Fundamental Issues*, 106–133. Oxford: Oxford University Press.

Turkle, S. 1995. *Life on the Screen: Identity in the Age of the Internet*. New York: Simon and Schuster.

17   The Policy and Export of Ubiquitous Place: Investigating South Korean U-Cities

Germaine Halegoua

By 2015, South Korea will house two "ubiquitous cities" or U-cities, one of which, New Songdo, will be considered the largest in the world, erected entirely from the ground up. The 1,376-acre project is located approximately 40 miles from downtown Seoul, and less than a three-hour flight from Shanghai, Tokyo, and Hong Kong. Though several news outlets refer to New Songdo as an extrusion of Seoul, the capital city is slated to house its own ubiquitous district, the Digital Media City (DMC). According to English language popular press outlets, official press releases, and trade journal reports, these ubiquitous cities promise to serve as major information technology hubs for East Asia. Since their public announcement in 2004, the cities were slated to showcase pervasive computing and locative media projects, responsive environments, wireless technologies, radio frequency identification and quick-response coding projects, as well as housing telecommunications research-and-development headquarters. The Digital Media City will function as an industrial park and showroom for the information and communication technology and service industries (Seoul Metropolitan Government 2009). New Songdo City, in nearby Incheon, is being constructed as a magnet for foreign direct investment and a living laboratory within which to test ubiquitous computing technologies. As the director of the Persuasive Technology Lab at Stanford University noted five years ago, "New Songdo sounds like it will be one big Petri dish for understanding how people want to use technology" (O'Connell 2005, para. 17). New Songdo developers repeatedly suggested that once inhabited, the city will exemplify a digital way of life, referred to as "U-life" (O'Connell 2005, para. 8). At present, U-life is yet to be seen in a form other than an eponymous liaison organization between the development company and IT firms. Managers of Songdo U-Life, the organizational committee that exists to manage the IT end of the New Songdo development, hope that whatever the social and technological manifestation of "U-life," it will be native to South Korea, profitable, and exportable.

The New Songdo developers (Gale International and POSCO), planners (Kohn Pedersen Fox), IT consultants (Songdo U-Life), and government officials (particularly Mayor Ahn Sang-soo of Incheon) involved in the U-city project publicly emphasize that although New Songdo will incorporate prominent architectural elements from around the world, the city will emphasize local practices, Korean culture, and style. However, the Korean government has been discussing the possibility of exporting the Incheon U-city model to overseas governments. Media outlets report that the New Songdo developers have signed contracts with the Algerian government to develop a U-city in Buinan, also being built on vacated land (Ha-won 2007; Ministry of Foreign Affairs and Trade 2010). My interviews conducted with developers of the New Songdo project confirmed the desire to develop a profitable business model for the U-city, which included the strategy of exportation. The tensions and seeming contradictions among the emphasis on local particularities in design, the specific role of the U-cities within the Korean social context, and the strategy of global exportation raise critical questions about the potential success of a U-city exportation model.

The Korean U-cities, particularly New Songdo, represent a novel case through which to investigate design and development strategies that attempt to harness and define ubiquitous computing while circulating discourses about networked technologies and urban spaces for global attraction, profit, and export. The case studies of Korean U-cities provide a unique opportunity to investigate the social shaping of technology and the social production of place. While this sort of investigation seems premature due to the present lack of residents and technologies in New Songdo, the sociotechnical imaginary of the U-city is ripe for investigation (Jasanoff, Kim, 2009). Through government press releases, promotional literature, site visits, popular press, trade journals, and interviews with representatives from Gale International, Songdo U-Life, and Kohn Pedersen Fox, I assess how the implementation of ubiquitous computing is simultaneously imagined with the urban built environment. One of the central questions of this chapter is: What do planners and developers hope the incorporation of ubiquitous and pervasive computing opportunities will do for the resident/visitor's experience of the city and their interpersonal interactions? This question was posed to representatives from Gale International and Kohn Pedersen Fox, which included Songdo U-Life's IT Director (Jeong Wha Huh), Gale International's Executive Vice President and Project Manager (David Moore), and KPF's Senior AP for New Songdo (Richard Nemeth). The answers to questions concerning the role of ubiquitous computing in relation to spatial experience, quality of life, civic engagement, and interpersonal interaction revealed that the union of urban place and ubiquitous computing envisioned for New Songdo has more to do with policy formation and amenity provision than with civic engagement and creative interaction. In this case, the incorporation of ubiquitous computing technologies is viewed as a commodity to raise rents, move units, and "sell" a city on the global market.

Scholarly work on Korean U-cities has just recently received attention in a variety of disciplines (Choi 2010; Hill 2010; Kim 2010; Mortice 2008; Segel et al. 2005; Shin 2009; Townsend 2007). Several of these studies pay attention to the larger social context within which the U-cities are being constructed. Much of this literature builds on scholarly considerations of the position of East Asian cities and urban corridors within processes of globalization (Choe 1998; Kohli 1999; Lo and Yeung, 1996; Olds 2001; Olds and Yeung, 2004; Radovic 2008; Sassen 2001; Sassen 2002), as well as the role of IT services and industries in the formation of Asian global cities (Heitzman 2004; Park and Choi, 2005; Rimmer 1998). However, in the case of New Songdo in particular, developers attempt to position the U-city in relationship to a national context and national culture as well (Gale International 2004; Gale International 2008). Gale International and KPF have publicly claimed that the design and development of New Songdo are intended to mesh with the Korean context. The following section will take a brief look at some of the specific social, cultural, and industrial contexts of South Korean urban culture and electronics industries in order to explain the pertinence and promise of U-cities in South Korea. This section is intended to illuminate some reasons why these U-cities might distinctly suit South Korea. Subsequent sections begin to consider some of the problems the developers might face in exporting New Songdo as a U-city model abroad.

Korean Social Context and U-Cities

Design
The design of New Songdo is recognized by KPF as a hybrid, or "synergy city." This hybridization comes from two main programming agendas. The space of the city as described by senior architects at KPF has been programmed as a collage or aggregation of successful design and planning elements from other global cities. However, while the architecture of the city incorporates iconic building and planning styles from around the world, it is also recognized as explicitly incorporating design elements referenced as "Korean typology and Korean ecology." Korean typology and ecology refer to shapes and patterns of parks and open spaces that reference the Korean landscape (Onishi 2006). Representatives from both Gale and KPF stated that over the course of several meetings the designers had to justify their design choices to government officials as viable and sound. Richard Nemeth, Senior Associate Principal at KPF, noted that some of the controversial designs included plans to build a "tent city" with buildings of various heights and sizes and increasing the number of pedestrian walkways, along with other programming features that would render the city more walkable (Nemeth 2009). The planners and architects of New Songdo tend to operate under the assumption that urban Korean landscapes consist of "multilane thoroughfares and large buildings on small plots of land, which don't support a vibrant street life" (Cortese 2007, para. 17). The planning for a "tent city," green spaces, canals, and walkable environments are design efforts aimed to counteract negatively perceived aspects of the local urban character, and provide the corporate city with a

"well-balanced diet" and increased "quality of life" (Nemeth 2009). However, the density typically associated with a Korean urban landscape is considered a value to be maintained. KPF's master plan exhibits density in conjunction with an effort to program a sustainable urban environment.

Hybridization or mixing of urban purpose (and to some extent design and culture) is not unheard of in South Korean cities. In debates and analyses of the Korean Wave, Seoul in particular has been noted as an anchoring point, or salient node in the Asian distribution of Western cultural products. Seoul serves as a filter through which Western products and media pass in order to be reinterpreted, remixed, and made palatable to Asian audiences (Onishi 2006). In this sense, South Korean cities are already hybridized. Functioning as an industrial park for Seoul, the architecture of the Digital Media City adheres to the notion that Seoul is indeed a regional sieve for Western culture. The district towers over the more traditional Korean neighborhood adjacent to it, touting glass skyscrapers and digital displays on the sides of buildings that visually promote the national telecommunication and technology firms head-quartered there.

Compared to the Digital Media City in Seoul, New Songdo's culture may be difficult to identify as immediately local. Unlike the DMC, New Songdo is yet to be fully con-structed and repopulated (even the fishermen and their families that previously resided near the city have been displaced). While Korean culture might ultimately become evident in New Songdo, the international business district at present resembles a cosmopolitan hub intended to attract international money and international talent with a design and urban plan that are vaguely familiar to transnational business elites. Currently, residential units in Block 125, which houses the "First World" building, have been sold. There are already prospective buyers lined up to purchase housing in the "North Canal" row-housing blocks that will be on the market by the end of 2009. From the perspective of David Moore, Executive VP at Gale International, the initial wave of expected residents are wealthy Korean nationals. He profiles these residents as doctors attracted to the new hospital, or upscale Korean families attracted to the international schools. Ironically, current ownership regulations for New Songdo limit the benefits that foreigners and foreign companies can reap from the project. Though New Songdo has been zoned within Incheon Free Economic Zone (IFEZ), a zone estab-lished in 2001 to attract direct foreign investment and transnational headquarters, legal preference has been given to Korean nationals in regard to residential and com-mercial purchasing (Moore 2009). At present, almost negating the purpose of "the zone," no foreign headquarters have migrated to New Songdo.

Technology and Industry

A dominant culture of broadband and networked consumer technology use prevails in Seoul's everyday urban life. Public places designated for technology use and media consumption, such as Internet cafés, PC bangs (or rooms), and DVD bangs, line Seoul's sidewalks (see Choi, Foth, and Heam 2009). Phone and laptop use on subways and streets, public competitions of StarCraft, an overload of visual information in public spaces, and DMB (digital multimedia broadcast) toting smart mobs are present in a variety of accounts and observations of daily practices in Seoul. It can be argued that a specifically Korean culture of computing and digital media consumption exists in this urban environment, one that involves public access to computing opportunities and hyperconnectivity through mobile devices. Anthony Townsend (2007), a consultant on the Digital Media City project in Seoul, notes that factors such as high levels of broadband and fiber optic penetration, mobile technology use, a general embrace and culture of computing and gaming, and maintenance and attendance of specialized public spaces for networked communication all unite in order to compose something that resembles a Korean computing culture. In investigating social networking practices in Seoul, Jaz Choi (2010) presents Seoul as a densely populated urban center, a city of screens, *bangs*, and broadband. One could also argue that this present media culture, coupled with government policies encouraging IT industry augmentation, as well as the country's historic reliance on electronics and technology sectors helps to breed a particularly Korean sociotechnical imaginary of the future of computing and the future of urban space as well.

Some scholars and journalists have suggested that in Korean cities there is less expectation of privacy, and consequently less value placed on containing the spread of or limiting the interconnectivity and accessibility of personal information (Kim 2004). Prominent Korean architect Minsuk Cho (2009) has noted that some of his projects are influenced by the lack of privacy a typical Korean family member is able to attain within the space of the city as well as within the single-family home. These culturally specific logics of privacy and publicity may resonate within the U-city technological services and architectural style, however the hybridity of urban form and accommodation of international residents may complicate these loose boundaries of public and private spheres.

The role of the Korean government in establishing technical standards, deeming national telecommunications infrastructure a policy priority, and maintaining control over the electronics industry should be considered in discussion of U-cities promotion and construction as well. The industrial logic and organization of the electronics *chaebols* (transnational, family-controlled conglomerates), particularly Samsung and LG, should also be evaluated as a local specificity that shapes the construction and need for U-cities within the nation-state. As H. Lee (1995) has noted, the Korean electronics industry has cultivated a specialization in mass-produced consumer electronics that operates under the logic of economies of scale. While this creates certain benefits in profit margin, this production strategy also creates challenges for expansion into global markets and technology services. Through their strategic cultivation and dependence on mass-produced consumer electronics, these companies have failed to develop adequate R&D and testing grounds needed for the development of luxury, niche electronic products and next-generation services. This is a key challenge for chaebols like Samsung and LG to overcome. The cultivation of U-cities, then, can also be analyzed as spaces carved out as test sites for prototypes and pilot studies of networked services. The cities not only yield technological cachet and a means to attract foreign investment and talent through the promise of ubiquitous computing, but also fill an essential void in the current structure of the electronics industry. Technology providers and developers for New Songdo speculate that many technologies implemented in this space will undoubtedly fail. However, the services and technologies that function and yield high adoption rates within this urban environment may help transform Korea's electronics industry.

New Songdo as Ubiquitous City

A large part of the popular understanding of ubiquitous computing is derived from research projects and personnel at Xerox PARC in the 1980s. Mark Weiser's often-cited article, "The Computer for the 21st Century" (1991, 94), notes that the "most profound technologies" are ones that "weave themselves into the fabric of everyday life," that virtually disappear but are context aware. In this article and subsequent articles and interviews, Weiser presented ubiquitous computing as technology that caters to social relations and habit, technologies that are embedded within the built environment, but that are meant to be simultaneously engaged with and ignored. As Anne Galloway (2004, 388) explains, ubiquitous computing technologies are currently represented as "mobile, wearable, distributed, and context-aware computing applications" that rely on information about physical location and user identity and that may combine virtual and physical objects and environments. While technology designers' and everyday users' understandings of ubiquitous computing are consistently evolving, there is a general perception of ubiquitous computing (or ubicomp) as technologies that correspond with the aforementioned descriptions.

The technologies currently being implemented in New Songdo and the Digital Media City seem to diverge from, more than mesh with, descriptions and imaginations of ubiquitous computing. Additionally, some technologies and technological infrastructures already exist in other Korean urban and suburban areas outside of New Songdo. The fiber optic infrastructure of the U-cities is already laid and in service, along with WiBro and Digital Multimedia Broadcasting (DMB) capabilities. Millions of South Koreans already subscribe to these services and take advantage of this infrastructure in other cities on a daily basis. At the time of my research, the exact technologies and services that will ultimately fill residences and offices and line city streets in New Songdo and DMC are yet to be wholly implemented and/or designed. Consequently, the uses and practices that will accompany these technologies are yet to be seen. Additionally, of equal importance to an understanding of ubiquitous computing is the sociocultural context and the physical locations in which these technologies are being embedded and used. However, these social contexts and physical locations are also yet to be established.

At present, some of the technologies and digital projects that have been suggested include:

• "Green" technologies such as a centralized pneumatic tubing systems for waste management; charging stations for electric vehicles; smartcard-activated bicycle rental stations; RFID sensors on recycling bins to credit users for their deposits; water recycling systems for buildings. All buildings will be LEED certified and equipped with "intelligent building systems."

• "HomeNet" systems that include information and data collection systems that overlay residential, medical, government, and commercial data; homes, offices, and public and commercial spaces equipped with embedded computers and computing opportunities; smartcards or other mobile information storage devices for residents that will serve as a universal interface for various activities. The city will also be blanketed with CCTV.

• Sentient objects and RFID sensors/transmitters throughout households, workspaces, and places of leisure. Suggested projects have been floors that sense a fall and call for help, as well as objects that "know" where they came from and relay commercial information about their production (O'Connell 2005). Responsive environments have been discussed, too, including intelligent streetlighting and efficient management and regulation of municipal infrastructure.

• "U-services" that focus on home, office, education, street, retail, transportation, healthcare, entertainment, security, and environmental activities and spaces. U-culture focuses on "application services" that network, converge, and relay information in real time between the aforementioned sectors of society (Huh 2009a). U-community focuses on outfitting these spaces with networking and computing infrastructure and opportunities, providing residents with sensing and smartcard technology. U-IT focuses on wireless and broadband infrastructures for mobile and dynamic platforms of media and information consumption; one feature will be a New Songdo City U-Life web portal that recently went live (Huh 2009b). The web portal provides access to local information about transportation and navigation, and will soon allow residents to share information about the experience of living in New Songdo.

• Urban design projects like the Media Board and Digital Odometer were proposed for the Digital Media City. The Media Board incorporates digital signage on building facades to be used for announcements, for events, and by artists. The Digital Odometer is a visualization of information being generated by the DMC. The DMC will also house "E-Boards," or public kiosks, where pedestrians can access bus schedules in real time, traffic and neighborhood maps, weather information, and live TV, and can participate in Internet shopping, chat, and e-mail. During the summer of 2009, prototypes of these DMC technologies were on display in the DMC Gallery in Sangam, at the base of what is slated to be the "Digital Media Street."

Jeong Wha Huh, the IT Director for Songdo U-Life, mentioned the potential to forge community through media while describing the expected use of the web portal. Huh noted that providing residents with an online space in order to share experiences is also a potential way to foster interaction. This aspect of the portal seems similar to social networking and Web 2.0 sites currently in use around the world, and was the sole instance when a connection between communication and community formation was mentioned.

The first networked service currently being tested in one of the residential blocks of New Songdo, and areas of Incheon directly bordering New Songdo, is a healthcare service. The u-Healthcare system outfits household members with mobile, networked devices that can monitor biosigns like weight and blood pressure. Data are collected and transmitted in a constant stream to a central database. Nurses and doctors can assess the information and respond if there is an abnormality in the data, or initiate an emergency call (Huh 2009a). Huh noted that u-Healthcare system users were reluctant to use the free service, and surmised that residents might grow disenchanted and discontinue service once developers require them to pay for u-Healthcare. In regard to users' hesitation to adopt u-Healthcare, Huh suggested that the target audience for the service was too limited, and the product too specialized. Additionally, this service is not unique to New Songdo; currently LG CNS offers a similar portable monitoring system called the "Touch Doctor," which is now on the market.

All of my respondents tended to agree that the purpose of technology within the space of New Songdo is to improve residents' "quality of life," provide increased convenience, and ensure better maintenance and efficiency of city and facility services. Gale International, KPF spokespeople, and promotional materials tend to focus on a general promise that living in New Songdo will be an improved or "safer," "more enjoyable," or "better" way to live. Richard Nemeth (2009) of Kohn Pedersen Fox, when questioned about the attraction of New Songdo, rhetorically answered: "Why would I want to be here rather than New York?" In response to his own question, Nemeth explained that New Songdo would provide its residents with comfort, a livable hub for business in Asia, a unique cosmopolitan culture, a safe space for families, and access to elite education systems. New Songdo, he insisted, was programmed to be all of these things (Nemeth 2009). The ubiquitous technology was understood as an aid in establishing these conditions, but was simultaneously secondary. What these technologies might look like, or the activities or knowledge they might encourage, were not the designer's primary concerns.

M. Curtin's (2004, 205) notion of "media capitals" seems to be directly applicable to the development of these ubiquitous cities. Curtin describes media capitals as "sites of mediation where complex forces and flows interact." These capitals are control and command centers of media production and distribution, and "meeting places where local specificity arises out of migration, interaction and exchange." The ubiquitous cities are sociotechnical imaginaries that anchor the global flows of information, talent, and resources within local space. The cities represent designated places from which a unique composite of digital culture (U-life) is expected to arise. The culture and exchanges of the U-cities, then, are expected to add a "specific logic of [their] own" to the infrastructure and activities involved. If only temporarily, these cities have the potential to become new media centers—media capitals governed more by the market and the drive toward innovation than by the Korean state.

Information and communication technology development and implementation, and even the title of "U-city," can be read as elements of place promotion (Kim 2010). Harnessing the rhetoric and discourses of information technology and ubiquitous computing is a strategic effort to foster attraction and investment in the global arena. To cultivate an urban space as a media capital would be to gain cachet and visibility as a global player or node in a particular type of global network. Unlike the urban environments identified by Curtin, the singularity of New Songdo and Seoul as media capitals would lie in the specialization of these cities as places of new media *consumption* as well as production, experimentation, and distribution. Seoul may already be viewed as a media capital based on the city's coordination of computing hardware and consumer electronics. However, Korean cultural policy is currently refocusing industry activities toward the development and exportation of web-based digital products such as games and mobile services. As regional and global networks of IT production shift in similar directions, Korea aims to be included in these networks, with the country's U-cities as capitals of production and consumption, and emblematic of what the implementation of ubicomp in a large-scale urban form actually signifies. Additionally, the strategy of harnessing the term *ubiquitous computing* might not be solely about place promotion but about the production of place as well. Currently, a main attribute that grounds the elaborate construction site that is New Songdo, and renders it unique and with a specific logic of its own, is that it is a U-city. In this case, the harnessing of ubiquitous computing as a concept (even before it is developed and implemented) can be read as an act of place-making, of constructing this abstract space as a more rooted, bounded place through the formation and harnessing of technology and technology discourses.

Exportation of Urban Form

With the rise of *Hallyu*, or the Korean Wave, cultural products originating in Korea have been circulating in high demand regionally and globally. Korea has exerted a newfound dominance in cultural products such as cuisine, pop music, television dramas, films, video games, and fashion. Regional consumers' perceptions of South Korea as a filter or sieve for Western culture and cultural products may aid the exportation of the country's own cultural goods. Global media products are bought on the international market and localized using Korean actors, language, fashion, cultural norms, settings, style, and sensibilities. The hybridized cultural products are then transported regionally for profit. Youth audiences often associate Korean goods and services with cosmopolitanism, wealth, modernity, and an openness typically associated with the United States (Onishi 2006). The idea that Korean lifestyles and products echo the West but retain "Asianness" in some fashion has been considered attractive to consumers in South and East Asia in particular.

An argument can be made for the retention of these connotations in the conceptualization and representation of the U-cities. The U-cities can augment the catalog of circulating *Hallyu* products, because the cities themselves are also "products" for export. The intended export of ubiquitous computing IT and the ubiquitous city model is not entirely surprising. Coupled with biotechnology and "cultural technology" (or the technologies that produce cultural products like television, film, animation, video games, music), information technology was listed as a goal for export by the Korean Culture and Content Agency (KOCCA) and its "Export Strategy Team" in 2001 (Shim 2008).

In most cases, successful urban development or urban megaprojects often generate funds through consulting fees or contracting clients. The project architects achieve fame by creating a new paradigm of planning and design, garnering attention in textbooks, the popular and trade press, or exhibitions. An often-cited example is the development spurred by the Barcelona 1992 Olympics. In this noteworthy case, event-driven construction and urban renewal projects brought the city and its architects acclaim and profit in marketing their successful urban management and urban regeneration model to other locales. In the case of New Songdo the goal has been to create, a priori, an *exportable* urban model, yet the question remains as to what exactly is being exported.

In October 2007 the Korean Ministry of Construction and Transportation announced that the Korean government would begin exporting the "U-city design," specifically "its ability to solve existing transportation and environmental problems and significantly improve education, medical and high-tech services" (Ministry of Construction and Transportation 2007). The Korean government has also reported that representatives from Algeria commissioned five Korean construction companies in 2007 to complete the satellite city of Buinan (30 kilometers south of Algiers) by 2011 (Ministry of Construction and Transportation 2007). As of January 2010, approximately twenty-five Korean construction firms had entered the Algerian market (Ministry of Foreign Affairs and Trade 2010). Journalists from popular and trade publications have noted the continued effort by Korea-based IT firms like SK C&C, one of the largest Korean telecommunications companies, to export their services and products to Central Asia, attempting to fashion a regional IT *Hallyu*. At present, the initial wave of Korean IT exports to Central Asia focuses on infrastructure and software designed to make paradigmatic urban networks more efficient. Networks used for the transport of people and goods, such as transportation and postal systems, are being streamlined for efficiency through SK technology in particular (Roe 2009).

Although Seoul can be used as a model for "the rapid deployment of broadband," Townsend clearly notes how paradoxical it would be to replicate this model in a disparate location. He concludes that "broadband networks and applications have generally worked themselves into or mimicked existing urban culture, not radically transformed it" (Townsend 2007, 409). The implementation of IT infrastructure is viewed as intentionally indigenous, in that this infrastructure must cater to a local culture in order to be incorporated and potentially transformed by it. Similarly, Richard Nemeth at KPF concedes that information technology in New Songdo is meant to enhance lifestyle, not generate it (Nemeth 2009). How the pervasive broadband networks and networked practices will mesh with a nascent, nearly nonexistent urban culture in New Songdo is a prognostication at best, because cranes and unfinished buildings will dominate the landscape until 2015 at least.

However, New Songdo's model may be globally exportable for precisely the reason that there is no urban culture to mesh with or mimic as of yet. Instead, there exists only a model with an intended purpose. According to this logic, the construction in Buinan, Algeria, is *extraterritorial*, similar to a location used for "runaway production" in film—a place where local, identifiable specificities are erased or substituted with the particularities of another (i.e., when Toronto is dressed up as New York to save costs) (Easterling 2007). In searching for service providers and "killer applications" for U-city services and technologies in New Songdo, it is evident that the players involved are fueled by potential profit as much as they are motivated by policy initiatives and beneficial zoning regulations. Respondents from Gale International and Songdo U-life noted that the consortium is experimenting with profitable business models for U-city services and technologies, even though the technologies themselves are still under development and have not been tested by users in an urban environment.

David Moore noted during an interview that foreign governments find New Songdo's private/public relations and funding models particularly attractive. The model employed is that a private developer like Gale International finances the construction of the U-city from the outset. In general, the role of the government becomes cooperation through tax subsidies, beneficial zoning laws, and public promotion and support. Moore suggested that this type of private/public partnership is attractive to developing countries, naming several officials from neighboring countries (including Vietnam, Cambodia, China) who have expressed interest in the New Songdo model. Jeong Wha Huh noted that exportation of the New Songdo U-city model will most likely consist of Songdo's IT infrastructure design and implementation, coupled with selected U-services that will be packaged for sale.

The imminent goal of exporting the U-city infrastructure, business model, and U-services may explain the disassociation of visions of ubiquitous computing from user experiences of place and community in this project. While Kim (2010) accurately identifies ubiquitous computing as a significant element of place promotion for New Songdo, it is also important to interrogate visions of intended technology use in the city. How, if at all, are these technologies intended to enrich one's experience of place? Green facilities systems that recycle water and conserve resources, healthcare systems that monitor biosigns, and convergence of data on smartcards may qualify as ubiquitous computing, but none of these exhibit a tendency toward creative engagement with technology or the city. The exclusion of place and local particularities in the development of technologies for New Songdo provides flexibility and portability, streamlining this model for exportation. The manner in which ubicomp is utilized for place promotion in representations of New Songdo caters specifically to the context of South Korea; once these technologies are embedded in an environment outside of South Korea, the use of ubiquitous technologies in the promotion of place will undoubtedly change.

Civic Engagement and the U-City

As previously mentioned, the computing and networking opportunities in New Songdo keep community engagement and creative interaction at bay. Additionally, the term *ubiquitous* may not even apply to these technologies. A focus on data convergence, efficiency, and facilities management promotes a superficial interaction with the urban places in which these technologies are embedded. Along with ubiquitous computing, New Songdo executives and planners emphasized "quality-of-life projects" as an asset of Songdo. These projects include a central park, international schools, a shopping mall, a convention center, and a Jack Nicklaus golf course. Interviewees referred to the ubiquitous technology slated for New Songdo as the sixth quality-of-life project. The IT projects currently under discussion, however, read like amenities in a real estate brochure—regulating water recycling, enhancing security systems, and providing network infrastructure. When questioned whether technology and "quality of life" included community and creative engagement with other residents or the place-based experience of New Songdo, the visionaries in charge of programming and planning the city and its technologies were unable to answer this question directly. None of the participants interviewed during the summer of 2009 had explicit ideas about what ubiquitous technology could do for an individual's enrichment or understanding of the place in which they live or the people they live among. While some of the technologies imagined for New Songdo can arguably be said to improve spatial relations in terms of safety and efficiency (with respect to traffic, parking, and security, for example), there is minimal feedback between the city and the citizens. For the planners, developers, and IT consultants questioned, the sociotechnical imagination of ubicomp in New Songdo resembles an overall effort to establish convenience, safety, and efficiency, as well as the appearance of luxury and familiarity for the transnational dweller.

It is possible that the actual use of ubicomp in New Songdo will not reflect the intended use. It is also possible that the slated technologies for the U-city will not remain the same, or will be regenerated as the city grows. As Dr. Jong Sung Hwang— director of the National Information Society Agency (NIA)—suggested that the U-city will be developed in three stages: "real-time data gathering; context-awareness (in processing the gathered data to provide the optimum solution within the given context); and finally, autonomy in its operation, turning the city into an intelligent and autonomous network system" (Choi 2010, sec. 4.3, para. 1). The technologies currently under discussion and development may indeed represent the first stage, indicating that more context-aware, or community-oriented, technologies can be expected in the future.

In its current form, New Songdo fulfills policy initiatives of technology development and exportation but tends to disregard the citizens in its construction. Future residents are considered as pilot groups for new technologies or potential niche markets for particular products and services. Applicable to this case is Dong Hee Shin's (2009) query in his article on the Korean U-city initiatives: "Why have the public become marginalized in the development of the U-city?" Although he does not address New Songdo in particular, Shin notes: "The public in the U-city case was not in the positions that influence or give input in the design. In other words, they are structurally marginalized by the government's officials" (p. 524). It is not solely government officials that have marginalized the decision-making power of the public in the case of New Songdo; the appropriation of the concept of ubiquitous technologies by private development companies has guided this future vision of computing in Korea as well. While Korea can be considered one of the frontiers of ubiquitous computing development and its execution in urban environments, scholars must be careful to consider exactly what this means. As the New Songdo case exhibits, Korea may also be the frontier for the appropriation and manipulation of the concept of ubiquitous technology for the generation of profit in the global market. As the development of ubicomp applications proliferate, the fashion in which these technologies and the implementation of these computing opportunities within urban form are being explained as ubiquitous computing in New Songdo can be read as a *Korean* model of ubiquitous computing. This understanding of what ubicomp actually is and how it functions within urban space is what is being built alongside tangible edifices and prototypes in New Songdo.

As Shin (2009) suggests, the Korean U-cities have a tinge of technological determinism involved in their conception. Arguing that the "push" model of introducing technologies, coupled with the underlying attitude that the presence of technology alone will create a U-city, he expresses a technological determinist perspective. However, none of my respondents seemed to believe that technology alone would transform society, nor did they regard ubiquitous computing as a causal factor in anything related to society's evolution or revolution. Instead, ubicomp was viewed as an amenity of neoliberal society—an impetus for residential and commercial real estate sales, and as a potential foundation for an export and lucrative business model.

KPF has taken great measures to make New Songdo walkable, open, and pedestrian, as well as to include gathering places. Interviewees report that the architects have steadfastly supported their designs despite disapproval from Korean officials and planning boards. It is paradoxical that ubicomp for New Songdo is not being imagined in a fashion similar to its built environment. In programming the city, residents are viewed as producers of place, and the built environment provides residents with ample opportunities to perform this role. It is possible, therefore, to interpret the architects' efforts as a desire to cultivate a "place of encounters" or a "place of the unexpected," a place of interactions and exchanges both commercial and never for profit (Lefebvre 1996). Although most technologies have yet to be prototyped, the technologies actively discussed and tested lack this emphasis on the organization of space as a place of urban and community engagement and encounters. The technologies envisioned to fill the city tend to hail residents as consumers instead of producers. The opportunities for residents to act as information and communication producers are currently limited to the web portal, to identifying information they may provide for smartcards, and to the biosigns they involuntarily produce.

Conclusion

A research question taken up by cultural geographers of media production in regard to the clustering of specialized industries and activities has been: Why this place and not another? This question should also be asked about the development of the Korean U-cities: Why Seoul and Incheon and not some other place? Of New Songdo, we may further ask: Does it have to be this place? Why can it not be another place instead? On its completion, New Songdo may be viewed as a form of digital media capital. The authority primarily gained by New Songdo in the global arena may be as a place of experimentation and innovation rather than a place in which media products are directly produced. If viewed as a media capital in the making, New Songdo has the potential to become a control and command center not only of services, but of digital innovation and new media consumption as well.

Spaces such as Silicon Valley in the United States, Bangalore in India, and the Multimedia Super Corridor in Kuala Lumpur have attracted the attention of media, urban studies, and technology studies researchers who read these spaces as innovative locations of production. Research on spaces of technological consumption has been less prominent (i.e., studies of cybercafés, computer labs, arcades, corporate buildings, and households). U-cities offer a unique opportunity to examine new media practice and consumption at the level of the urban street and everyday life. In U-cities, virtual activities may not be confined to four-walled spaces, neither the room nor the screen, but are located in physically walkable environments. The major initiative in New Songdo and the Digital Media City is to construct urban digital hubs that are public, interactive, profitable, and filled with design ideas that coincide with pedestrian and business needs. However, as this study has shown, pedestrian and business needs are interpreted through a lens of potential profit, not always as actual everyday practices and needs. Recognizing the relationships between various individuals and communities—their exchanges, interactions, and conflicts—is imperative to understanding how a city works. To "improve" an urban space, to augment the comfort, efficiency, safety, and "quality of life" of a city, designers should also consider how the citizens and residents have actively produced, experienced, and re-produced their space and place. New Songdo is a unique opportunity to examine the social shaping of technology in this respect. When technologies are selected and implemented, the city should undoubtedly be examined again from this perspective.

Once we consider the various roles and types of technologies slated for the U-city, we can also consider circumstances or situations in which these paradigms can be packaged for export in a similar fashion as Hallyu products. While Korea is regionally understood as a filter for Western cultural products, the goal of the U-city seems to be to construct other places as filters through which U-city design must pass in order to be palatable locally. What is successful about the harnessing of discourse about ubiquitous computing technologies and the use of ubicomp for place promotion in New Songdo is how the imagination of U-cities meshes with the Korean urban context. Place-based specificities like computing culture, industry logics and shortcomings, the aesthetics of density, benevolent policy formation, and aggregations of talent all influence the ways in which New Songdo can be promoted abroad and to the Korean public as a rational "investment in the future" (McNeill 2009).

The city as a category has been investigated as a series of "electronic spaces" with prefixes such as wired, digital, or smart. Through these studies, scholars have dealt with the reality that cities are never *completely* digital, electronic, or wired, that there are always spaces that are not linked within the network. In the case of the U-cities in Seoul and Incheon, this duality of with and without is not evident. These urban environments are places in which wireless and virtual networks are not being implemented in the "right spaces" in the "right ways," but indiscriminately every-where. Even before traditional markers of place are established in this U-city—the urban form completed, the streets and buildings inhabited, or an indigenous or digital culture formed—the ubiquity of networked technologies is being used to produce *place* out of seemingly abstract *space*. The use of ubicomp (as a rhetorical concept and a technical application) in New Songdo is not only a strategy of global development but also a way to socially produce the city as a place with a specific logic of its own. The imaginative prospects of ubiquitous technology and its imminent presence (as opposed to how the technology is used, or the communities that will engage with it) are being harnessed to produce New Songdo as a rooted, bounded, distinct place. The intentional carving out and clearing of large areas of geographic space for the promotion of digital culture and technology implementation, especially when attempted with public/private partnerships, is relatively novel and worthy of further analysis. As the U-cities and districts develop and gain inhabitants, the power relations and development conflicts between these networked spaces and the places that border them should not be ignored.

Understanding the U-city as a place of social engagement and community exchange as well as a profit-making model might similarly meet the goals of the Gale Corporation, IT industries, the Korean government, and their partners. The encouragement of a prolonged and enriched relationship between residents and place can potentially be accomplished through the use of ubicomp. Incorporation of technology in this manner may also attract investment, industry, and talent to the area. Currently, this participatory image of the ubiquitous city is not overtly prominent in the Korean sociotechnical imaginary of New Songdo. This is unfortunate since the encouragement of community and urban engagement through technology might benefit the people gathering in the walkable streets, sending their children to elite international schools, and living in the efficient facilities, safe environments, and high-tech buildings as well.

References

Cho, Minsuk. 2009. Interview. Seoul, July.

Choe, Sang-Chuel. 1998. Urban corridors in Pacific Asia. In Fue-chen Lo and Yue-man Yeung, eds., *Globalization and the World of Large Cities*, 155–173. Tokyo: United Nations Press.

Choi, Jaz Hee-jeong. 2010. The city is connections: Urban social networking in Seoul. Paper presented at MindTrek '08: Proceedings of the 12th International Conference on Entertainment and Media in the Ubiquitous Era, Tampere, Finland, October 6-9, 2008.

Choi, J. H.-J., M. Foth and G. Hearn. 2009. Site specific mobility and connection in Korea: bangs (rooms) between public and private spaces. Technology in Society 31 (2): 133–138.

Cortese, A. 2007. An Asian hub in the making. *New York Times*, December 30. http://www
.nytimes.com/2007/12/30/realestate/commercial/30sqft.html?ref=commercial&pagewanted=all

Curtin, Michael. 2004. Media capitals: Cultural geographies of global TV. In Lynn Spigel and Jan
Olsson, eds., *Television After TV: Essays on a Medium in Transition*, 270–302. Durham, NC: Duke
University Press.

Easterling, Keller. 2007. The zone. In Christine de Baan, Joachim Declerck, and Veronique
Patteeuw, eds., *Visionary Power: Producing the Contemporary City*. Rotterdam: NAi Publishers.

Gale International. *Songdo IBD*. http://www.songdo.com/.

Gale International and KPF. 2008. *New Songdo Green City*. New York: KPF Associates PC.

Gale International, POSCO E&C, KPF. 2004. *New Songdo City*. New York: KPF Associates PC.

Galloway, Anne. 2004. Intimations of everyday life: Ubiquitous computing and the city. *Cultural
Studies* 18 (2/3): 384–408.

Ha-won, Jung. 2007. In a first, Seoul plans to build entire town in a foreign country. Korea
Joongang Daily, January 15. http://joongangdaily.joins.com/article/view.asp?aid=2871374.

Heitzman, James. 2004. *Network City: Planning the Information Society in Bangalore*. New Dehli:
Oxford University Press.

Hill, Dan. 2010. Notes on New Songdo City. Or, what does your Seoul look like (part 1). *City of
Sound* blog, January 10. http://www.cityofsound.com/blog/2010/01/notes-on-new-songdo-city.
html.

Huh, Jeong-Wha. 2009a. PowerPoint presented at ICCEM Conference, Jeju, Korea, May 27–30.

Huh, Jeong Wha. 2009b. U-Life. Incheon, Interview. July.

Jasanoff, Sheila, and Sang-Hyun Kim. 2009. Containing the atom: Sociotechnical imaginaries
and nuclear power in the United States and South Korea. *Minerva*. 47:119–146.

Kim, Chigon. 2010. Place promotion and symbolic characterization of New Songdo City, South
Korea. *Cities* (London) 27:13–19.

Kim, Mun-Cho. 2004. Surveillance technology, privacy and social control: With reference to the
case of the electronic national identification card in South Korea. *International Sociology* 19 (2):
193–213.

Kohli, Atul. 1999. Where do high growth economies come from? The Japanese lineage of Korea's
"developmental state." In Meredith Woo-Cumings, ed., *The Developmental State*. Ithaca, NY:
Cornell University Press.

Lee, H. 1995. Globalization, FDI, and Korean competitive strategies of Korean electronic companies. In Nomura Research Institute and Institute of Southeast Asian Studies, eds., *The New Wave
of Foreign Direct Investment in Asia*. Farnham: Ashgate Publishing.

Lefebvre, Henri. 1996. *Writings on Cities*. Cambridge: Blackwell.

Lo, Fu-chen and Yue-man Yeung. 1996. *Emerging World Cities in Pacific Asia.* Tokyo: United Nations University Press.

McNeill, David. 2009. On land reclaimed from the sea, South Korea is building a new city that aims to banish the problems of the modern world. *The Independent*, June 24.

Ministry of Construction and Transportation. 2007. Korea to export new city design. Government press release, October 16. http://www.kdi.re.kr/kdi_eng/highlights/govern_view.jsp?no=1950&page=4&rowcnt=10.

Ministry of Foreign Affairs and Trade. 2010. Korea-Algeria leaders congratulate 20th diplomatic anniversary. Government press release, January 18. http://korea.net/detail.do?guid=43780.

Moore, David. 2009. Interview.

Mortice, Z. 2008. New Songdo City looks back at the New World for older urban models. *AIArchitect*, July 25. http://info.aia.org/aiarchitect/thisweek08/0725/0725d_songdo.cfm.

Nemeth, Richard. 2009. Kohn Pedersen Fox. Interview. New York, July.

O'Connell, P. 2005. Korea's high-tech utopia, where everything is observed. *New York Times*, October 5.

Olds, Kris. 2001. *Globalization and Urban Change: Capital, Culture and Pacific Rim Mega-Projects.* Oxford: Oxford University Press.

Olds, Kris, and Henry Wai-Chung Yeung. 2004. Pathways to global city formation: A view from the developmental city-state of Singapore. *Review of International Political Economy* 11 (3): 489–521.

Onishi, N. 2006. China's youth look to Seoul for inspiration. *New York Times*, January 2.

Park, S., Ji-Sun Choi, P. W. Daniels, K. C. Ho, and T. A. Hutton. 2005. IT service industries and the transformation of Seoul. In P. W. Daniels et al., eds., *Service Industries and Asia-Pacific Cities.* New York: Routledge.

Radovic, Darko. 2008. The world city hypothesis revisited: Export and import of urbanity is a dangerous business. In Mike Jenks, Daniel Kozak, and Pattaranan Takkanon, eds., *World Cities and Urban Form: Fragmented, Polycentric, Sustainable?* London: Routledge.

Rimmer, P. 1998. Transport and telecommunications among world cities. In F. Lo and Yue-man Yeung, eds., *Globalization and the World of Large Cities.* New York: United Nations University Press.

Roe, Sam. 2009. E-government export key to national ICT development. *Korea IT Times*, September 9.

Sassen, Saskia. 2001. *The Global City: New York, London, Tokyo.* Princeton, NJ: Princeton University Press.

Sassen, Saskia. 2002. Locating cities on global circuits. In Saskia Sassen, ed., *Global Networks, Linked Cities.* New York: Routledge.

Segel, Arthur I., Brandon Blaser, Gerardo Garza, Albert Kim, John Richard, and Andrew M. Murphy. 2005. *New Songdo City HBS Case Study No. 206-019*. Cambridge, MA: Harvard Business School.

Seoul Metropolitan Government. 2009. *Digital Media City: Gateway to Tomorrow*. Seoul: Seoul Metropolitan Government.

Shim, Doobo. 2008. The growth of Korean cultural industries and the Korean wave. In Chua Beng Huat and Koichi Iwabuchi, eds., *East Asian Pop Culture: Analyzing the Korean Wave*. Hong Kong: Hong Kong University Press.

Shin, Dong-Hee. 2009. Ubiquitous city: Urban technologies, urban infrastructure and urban informatics. *Journal of Information Science* 35 (5): 515–526.

Townsend, Anthony. 2007. Seoul: Birth of a broadband metropolis. *Environment and Planning, B: Planning & Design* 34:396–413.

Weiser, Mark. 1991. The computer for the 21st century. *Scientific American* 265 (3): 94–104.

18 Engaging Citizens and Community with the UBI Hotspots

Timo Ojala, Hannu Kukka, Tommi Heikkinen, Tomas Lindén, Marko Jurmu, Simo Hosio, and Fabio Kruger

The vision of modern urban landscapes is currently undergoing what might be considered the most radical change since the advent of computing. New technological innovations introduced in the very fabric of urban space allow for a deeper connection between the city and its inhabitants, making the hidden layers of social, economic, and political processes, tensions, and flows both transparent and visible in ways that were never possible before (Paay and Kjeldskov 2008; Townsend 2009). However, despite the potential for enriching the experience of the city for its inhabitants through this new technology, we have yet to discover the "killer" applications that would really bring the experience of the city to the next level. Researchers in different fields have begun the search from different starting points, often framing the urban environment as fraught with difficulties and problems to overcome with the new technology (Bassoli et al. 2007).

We argue that the lack of lasting and visible results (in terms of applications) in urban informatics is partly due to the lack of open computing infrastructure in the public space. Successful public spaces are mixtures of activities and applications, which purposefully combine physical and virtual spaces. They link places and context, consciously avoiding the "anything, anytime, anywhere" paradigm. Doing this in practice requires permanent local infrastructure, which for business reasons is often deployed as closed verticals. We wish to challenge this with an open computing infrastructure, which is provided as a "horizontal" resource to the whole community.

Suchman (1987) ushered in a new design ideology of creating an awareness of use situated in the context within which it would occur. This concept is particularly relevant for real-world ubiquitous computing systems that are culturally situated in the city and cannot be reliably assessed with lab studies detached from the real-world context. Infrastructure and time are needed to establish the required technical and cultural readiness and the critical mass of users, before a ubiquitous computing system can be evaluated as "(un)successful" (Greenberg and Buxton 2008). Prior work has devoted considerable effort to addressing the problems of integrating technology in urban environments, be it from a technical, design, or methodological perspective

(Brown et al. 2009; Jay and Stanton 2008; O'Hara, Glancy, and Robertshaw 2008; Paay and Kjeldskov 2008; Pinch 2003; Redhead and Brereton 2006; Satchell et al. 2008). Our goal is to conduct longitudinal, real-world case studies of system usage by extending the notion of conducting "research in the wild" by turning the city into a laboratory. In doing so, we hope to achieve a contextualized and deeply embedded approach to the design of urban ubiquitous technologies (O'Neill et al. 2006).

We have launched an ambitious project to create an experimental public laboratory for studying urban computing (Kindberg, Chalmers, and Paulos 2007) in an authentic setting in downtown Oulu, Finland, with diverse real users and with sufficient scale and time span. The laboratory is based on a citywide pervasive computing infrastructure, which comprises different types of wireless networks, large public displays, and other resources (Ojala et al. 2010a). The infrastructure is provided as an open horizontal resource to the whole community to stimulate the development of services intended to make downtown Oulu a better place for people. A key component of our laboratory is a novel concept called a UBI hotspot (later just hotspot) that we have deployed for 24/7 availability to the general public.

UBI Hotspots

Motivation

In our long-term vision the urban space is populated with hotspots, which provide rich interaction between the physical, virtual, and social spaces. Our hotspot (figure 18.1) is effectively a large public display embedded with associated computing resources. We do not offer our hotspots as solutions to specific (research) problems in downtown Oulu, which undoubtedly would survive just fine without the hotspots. Instead, we promote our hotspots as "heavyweight" urban probes (Paulos and Jenkins 2005) and research enablers.

A probe is an instrument that allows measurement of an unknown, in the hope of producing useful and interesting data. In our case the unknown is the urban landscape, where new technology is emerging and where complex social roles of the urban communities, people's movement and traces through cities, and people's interactions with place and public artifacts intersect. An urban probe is a direct constructive intervention into the urban landscape made to alter or disrupt the usage, actions, or flow within the urban space. An urban probe must be an artifact that does not blend into the landscape, but is provocative enough to elicit direct reaction and promote immediate discussion about its presence. By assessing the reaction and interaction of people and place with the new artifact, we hope to learn more about the urban landscape (Paulos and Jenkins 2005).

Our hotspots enable in situ urban computing research with real users and with sufficient scale and time span. The hotspots are effectively versatile computing

Figure 18.1
Outdoor UBI hotspot in downtown Oulu.

platforms that facilitate provisioning of a diverse range of services to the general public in authentic urban settings. By deploying a number of hotspots for a sufficiently long time, we wish to establish the technical and cultural readiness and the critical mass of users needed for determining whether these kinds of computing infrastructure and services would be useful additions to the urban landscape.

Ideally, the hotspots will provide insights into the complex relationships between the infrastructure of the city and the people that use it; the nature of the space the technology occupies; the interests of other state stakeholders such as local government and the media; and even the role of nature itself, which interferes with the hotspots when it snows!

User Study

In June 2008 we kicked off the design of the hotspots with a brainstorming day organized to give different stakeholders an opportunity to contribute to the initial design. The day consisted of two half-day sessions, so that the morning session focused on

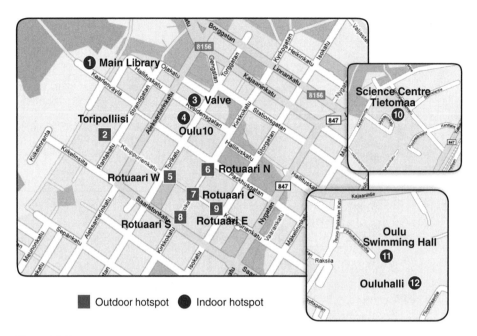

Figure 18.2
Locations of the UBI hotspots around downtown Oulu.

wireless sensor networks (with twenty-one participants from seven organizations) and the afternoon session on large public displays (thirty-one participants from twelve organizations). Both sessions featured an introduction to the research program followed by stimulating presentations, demos, and brainstorming with the "double-teaming" method. Participants in both sessions were asked to double-team ideas about useful applications that utilized either sensor networks, public displays, or both, in an urban environment. Each team then presented their ideas to other participants for feedback and discussion (figure 18.3).

Overall, the outcome of the workshop was positive. Participants expressed enthusiasm while brainstorming potential services, and suggestions ranged from the ordinary such as location-based gaming, friend finding, public transportation information, and so on, to the artistic—mapping "experience layers" of people in the city using radio stations and different types of sensor trails and presenting these as an "experience map" on public displays. Really innovative ideas were also introduced, such as a "weather mirror," which included stationing a semitranslucent mirror in front of a public display and augmenting the users' reflection with animated weather information.

In September 2008 we conducted a user study around downtown Oulu to obtain a better understanding of user needs that could be satisfied with our hotspots. Our

Figure 18.3
Participants presenting their ideas in the workshop.

researchers conducted in situ interviews equipped with a mock-up display, build from a framed whiteboard rigged on a wheeled base (figure 18.4). We asked people to describe their information needs and service ideas, and offered them a chance to interact with the mock-up display by drawing their suggestions for useful services on the whiteboard. We also solicited suggestions on locations where these types of displays would be useful. The interviews were videotaped and researchers gathered field notes and photographs.

During the course of the two-day study we conducted seventy-four free-form interviews in four central locations, which we had identified as potential hotspot locations in collaboration with the city officials who, naturally, had to approve the locations of these highly visible additions to the urban space. Overall, the feedback received from people was positive, and the need for this type of public infrastructure was recognized. The types of services most often proposed included public transportation timetables (by far the most common), municipal and commercial services, current and upcoming events in Oulu, news headlines, microweather forecasts, free parking spaces in the downtown area, and the status of queues at taxi stops.

We also employed storytelling as an informal way of identifying user needs and giving our community a chance to actively participate in the innovation process. In the main local newspaper, we published a long article that outlined the concept of the upcoming hotspots and our vision of "ubiquitous Oulu" in the year 2020. The article challenged the citizens to write their own stories of what everyday life would be like in downtown Oulu in the year 2020. As a model we wrote a set of our own "Oulu 2020" stories, which were published on the project website. However, even though a raffle with handsome prizes was arranged to entice citizens to write stories, the final outcome was rather disappointing. We received only eight stories, describing innovations ranging from smart home systems to context-aware wrist computers, and at the other extreme, a holographic guide dog.

Around the UBI hotspot, some mixture of karaoke and dance-gaming appeared to be starting up. Young people and tourists seemed attracted to the installation like virtual flies to electronic honey.—Ville (translated by the authors)

Deployment

We installed a network of twelve hotspots at pivotal outdoor and indoor locations around downtown Oulu (figure 18.2) in 2009. The five outdoor hotspots (5–9) cover the entrances and the center of the pivotal walking street area at the heart of the city, while the sixth (2) was placed at the main entrance to the market area. The indoor hotspots were placed in popular public buildings. Valve (3) is the youth and culture center, and Oulu10 (4) is the main municipal service center of the city. Hotspots 1–11 were installed between late May and early July 2009 and hotspot 12 in early November (Ojala et al. 2010b).

The hotspot has two different versions for outdoor and indoor use. While the portable indoor version has one LCD panel controlled by an industrial-grade PC, the permanently installed outdoor version is double-sided with two LCD panels back to back and separate control PCs for each panel. The LCD panels and other components are housed in a weatherproof aluminum casing with heating and cooling systems. The visible component of the hotspot is the 57-inch landscape LCD panel with full HD resolution. The panel is protected by a 6 mm hardened safety glass. Behind the glass is a projected capacitive touch-screen foil. A loudspeaker is implemented by a transducer that transforms the front cover into a loudspeaker. A NFC/RFID reader is attached behind a plastic window at the front of the case and two cameras are integrated into the top frame of the case. Bluetooth and WLAN access points are placed inside the hotspot and their antennas are integrated into the roof of the casing.

In terms of software our goal has been a cost-efficient implementation utilizing existing open-source and Internet components. The modular software architecture of the hotspots is designed to allow each hotspot to function individually based on its

Figure 18.4
Researchers conducting in situ interviews in downtown Oulu with a mock-up display.

proximity context. At the same time the hotspots are also networked in a loosely coupled fashion via an event-based communication overlay, which allows the hotspots to publish and subscribe to events related to their context. This design allows application distribution on multiple levels, from reliance on one hotspot to the utilization of multiple, physically separated hotspots simultaneously.

Services

The specification of the service portfolio of the first version of the hotspot was multiplexed from the findings of the user study, the availability of internal and external resources, and our research interests (Ojala et al. 2010b). We included a wide range of services to learn which services are (not) used in a highly public setting and why (not). In addition to the information services requested by people during the initial study phase, we also wanted to include other services that would address issues such as playfulness and entertainment, and that would arouse the users' curiosity so they would want to explore the information environment more fully (Erdelez 1997).

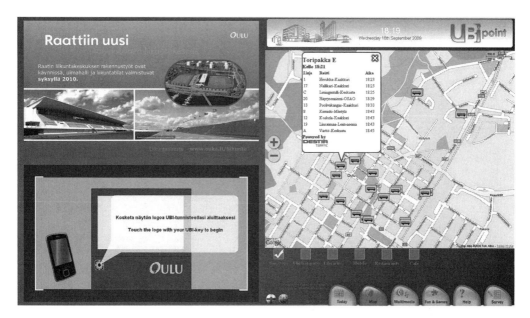

Figure 18.5
UBI hotspot in interactive mode.

In the current interaction model the hotspot alternates between a passive broadcast mode and an interactive mode (figure 18.5). The transition to the interactive mode is triggered when a user touches the touch screen or presents a so-called UBI key to the RFID reader, or when a face is detected from the video feed of the two overhead cameras.

In the broadcast mode the whole screen is allocated to a digital signage service called the UBI channel, which features a playlist of image/video "spots" that are configurable on a per-hotspot basis. In particular, the cultural organizations of the city have embraced the opportunity to advertise their upcoming events and exhibitions in the UBI channel.

During the transition to the interactive mode, the UBI channel is smoothly squeezed into the upper-left-hand part of the screen and two additional virtual screens are created, one assigned for a touch-screen portal called UBI portal and another assigned for mobile services. The end of the interaction is determined by a timeout since the last interaction or face-detection event, after which the display returns to the passive broadcast mode.

The UBI portal has a two-level page (service) hierarchy, where the first-level pages are, in brief, Oulu Today (topical news and events in Oulu); Map (a map-based service directory with real-time bus schedules, restaurants, hotels, shops, etc.), Multimedia (image and video galleries including user-uploaded files); Fun and Games (games and social networking); Survey (a questionnaire for gathering research data); and Help. The UBI portal also includes several mobile services that combine a personal mobile device (private UI) and the LCD panel of a hotspot (public UI) into a distributed user interface (Hosio et al. 2010). To launch these services the user has to present her personal UBI key (RFID tag) coupled with her personal mobile device to the RFID reader of the hotspot. For instance, one of the services allowed downloading different types of information to the mobile device over a no-cost Bluetooth connection (Kakka et al. 2009), thus adding information to the personal information collection (Bovey 1996).

Usage Analysis

Because our installation of twelve hotspots is available on a 24/7 basis in the public space, they are subject to continuous use and scrutiny by the general public. To collect quantitative data on the usage of the hotspots, we have been logging every interaction event since July 17, 2009. Further, to collect qualitative data, we executed a three-month field trial from June to August 2009. The field trial was coordinated from a field trial office operated by a customer service team of six students who were also on call at the hotspots; they advised people on the use of the hotspots, collected observations, and conducted in situ interviews. In August we organized so-called UBI walks, where the general public was welcome to join a guided tour of the hotspots led by a member of the customer service team. After a slow start the UBI walks became surprisingly popular.

We tried to recruit people as identified test users, which effectively required them to come to our field trial office to collect their personal UBI key that was paired with their personal mobile phone. Regrettably, we managed to sign up only eighty test users during the field trial. Consequently, the usage of the mobile services that required the UBI key remained rather minimal. A number of factors contributed to this dismal outcome. First, we have to keep in mind that the services of the UBI portal could be used anonymously without the UBI key. We underestimated the logistical challenge of distributing UBI keys to the general public. Our mobile client software required a particular modern smartphone platform, which has not yet acquired large-scale market distribution. Further, the perceived usefulness of our mobile services was apparently poor.

The graph in figure 18.6 shows the number of daily sessions involving usage of the UBI portal for the 199-day period from July 17, 2009, to January 31, 2010. We observe a weekly cycle in the usage of the outdoor hotspots with peaks on Saturdays, when people went downtown to shop. We also see a decreasing trend in the number of sessions toward January, which might be explained by the arctic conditions in Oulu

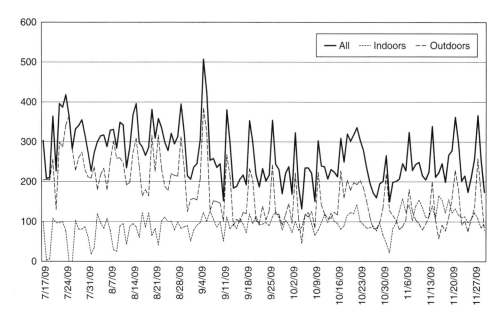

Figure 18.6
Daily number of sessions involving use of UBI portal.

during the winter months. The capacitive touch screens work poorly with gloves on; using the outdoor hotspots without gloves in the freezing cold winter temperatures is not an attractive option.

Table 18.1 provides UBI-portal usage statistics for four selected hotspots during the 199-day period, together with average statistics for indoor, outdoor, and all hotspots. The average number of days with sessions involving use of the UBI portal were well below 199, because one hotspot was installed in late November, some locations of the indoor hotspots were closed on weekends and official holidays, and some hotspots were out of order due to the occasional broken touch screens. We see that hotspots attracted short sessions; the average session involved 184 seconds of browsing time with 4.0 selections of the first-level services. Comparing the usage of indoor hotspots 4 and 11 highlights the importance of the location of a hotspot. While hotspot 4 (located at the clinical and businesslike entrance to the main municipal service center) recorded only 2.4 sessions per day, hotspot 11 (located at the entrance to the main swimming hall) recorded 49.4 sessions per day—that is, twenty times more. The contrast was even more striking in the average total daily browsing times of the two hotspots, 310 and 12,638 seconds, respectively. The swimming hall proved to be a favorable location for the hotspot, because the patrons have spare time while waiting for their training shift to start, for a friend to arrive or to come out of the locker room,

Table 18.1

Usage statistics of selected hotspots and averages of indoor, outdoor, and all hotspots. A and B correspond to the two panels of an outdoor hotspot.

	Indoor hotspots			Outdoor hotspots					All hotspots
	4	11	average	2A	2B	9A	9B	average	
Days with UBI-portal sessions	126	190	140	195	185	195	193	166	157
UBI-portal sessions per day	2.4	49.4	17.0	17.9	21.1	10.6	13.2	12.6	14.0
Times 1st-level services were accessed per session	2.6	6.7	5.4	3.3	3.8	2.9	2.8	3.1	4.0
Map (%)	18	17	17	17	18	16	17	18	18
Oulu Today (%)	26	16	17	24	26	21	22	22	20
Multimedia (%)	21	18	17	20	19	19	20	19	18
Fun and Games (%)	15	35	34	25	23	32	30	28	31
Survey (%)	16	7	7	7	8	7	6	7	7
Help (%)	4	7	7	6	6	6	5	6	6
Browsing time per session (s)	174	298	250	180	204	138	113	142	184
Map (%)	48	23	26	31	36	34	34	34	30
Oulu Today (%)	12	6	7	10	12	7	8	9	8
Multimedia (%)	20	12	12	16	16	14	16	16	14
Fun and Games (%)	15	55	51	38	29	40	38	36	44
Survey (%)	3	3	3	4	4	3	3	4	3
Help (%)	2	1	1	2	1	1	1	1	1

or for their ride home. Similarly, outdoor hotspot 2 in the market area had a larger number of longer sessions than the other five outdoor hotspots in the pedestrian zone at the heart of the Oulu. This reflects the fact that while people are busy running errands in the downtown area, they are in a much more leisurely mood in the market area, which leaves them with more time to interact with the hotspot.

We see that Fun and Games was the most popular service category, with 31 percent share of the clicks and 44 percent of the browsing time overall. It includes two particularly popular services, the traditional Hangman game and UbiPostcard. Hangman contributed a whopping 39 percent of the browsing time for the hotspot at the swimming hall; we sometimes observed kids queuing up in large numbers to play. In the hotspot at the municipal service center, Hangman's share of the browsing time was only 6.7 percent, whereas Map contributed 48 percent. UbiPostcard is a very simple social networking application that allows users to take a photo of themselves using the integrated cameras in the hotspots and to then e-mail the photo with a textual annotation to a friend. A total of 4,884 postcards were sent during the 199-day period—40 percent of them from hotspots 2 and 11, discussed above. The popularity of this service shows that social networking is valuable to people in an urban context.

The qualitative data came from the questionnaires submitted via the survey page in the UBI portal, the interviews conducted during the three-month field trial, and observations. The questionnaire consisted of two demographic attributes (gender and age range) and eight statements randomly drawn from a set of thirty-one statements. The thirty-one statements were grouped into eight categories addressing different aspects of Nielsen's system acceptance model (Nielsen 1993) (social acceptability, reliability, usefulness, learnability, efficiency, memorability, errors, and satisfaction), so that one random question from each category was included in a particular questionnaire. A respondent was supposed to assess each statement on 5-point Likert scale. The submission of an incomplete questionnaire was allowed.

In all, 927 questionnaires were submitted via the hotspots during the forty-six-day data collection period. We discarded 216 questionnaires that did not contain any answers (155) or had assessed less than four statements (61). In table 18.2 we briefly summarize statistics for a few selected statements by reporting the number of respondents and the percentage of them agreeing (4 or 5) and disagreeing (1or 2) with the statement. Answer 3 is considered to be *neutral* or *no opinion*. While inconclusive, these statements serve as anecdotal evidence for respondents' attitudes toward accepting the hotspots as a useful addition to the downtown area of Oulu.

The members of the customer service team conducted both free-form and semistructured interviews with people who had used a hotspot. Eighty-one semistructured interviews were recorded with audio recorders and transcribed for later reference. The free-form interviews were not recorded, because they were in situ conversations on the street. During the interviews we asked people to give their opinion on the usability

Table 18.2

Selected statistics from the questionnaires submitted via the UBI portal

Statement	N	Agree (%)	Disagree (%)
Using UBI hotspot in a public space feels natural	62	63	21
UBI hotspots fit in downtown Oulu	75	61	24
UBI hotspots make downtown Oulu a more interesting place	124	52	26
In my opinion UBI hotspots are useful	228	47	36
I got useful information from the UBI hotspot	216	44	37
The services in the UBI hotspot have boosted my daily activities	194	25	57
I found the needed information from the UBI hotspot quickly	138	41	36
I will use UBI hotspots again in the future	125	66	22

and usefulness of the hotspots, and especially the different services provided through them.

Findings from the interview data identify the Map service as the most useful information service and, interestingly, Fun and Games as the least important service. People especially appreciated the real-time bus schedule, often naming it their number one favorite of all the services. A search feature that would pinpoint addresses and routes was often requested and will be implemented in the near future.

I think the services available here are useful. Bus schedules, weather, and news are interesting when I'm downtown. The map service was especially good; now I won't have to call home and ask them to Google where something or other is. An address-search function would be good to have.—Hanna, 25, female

People readily agreed that the large form factor of the hotspots makes finding and reading information easier when compared to using a mobile phone for the same task. People also agreed that the hotspots are apparent in the cityscape, but without being overly distracting.

This is a welcome innovation. I think it was time people started taking their eyes off their mobile phone. . . . Information has to be available where you can see it; people's lives revolve around their mobiles too much.—Maria, 23, female

When thinking about the typical research questions related to large public displays, the challenge of enticing the user to interact with the hotspot was very apparent. A number of well-educated citizens reported having had no idea that they could actually touch the hotspot. One mechanism included to persuade people to interact with the hotspot was a spot in the UBI-channel playlist that invited people to touch the display. We did not collect extensive observation data that would allow rigorous assessment of display blindness (Huang et al. 2008; Müller et al. 2009). However, this was implicit in the comments of local residents, many of whom had regarded the hotspot by default as some advertising scheme or tourist information kiosk. The "honeypot" phenomenon (Brignull and Rogers 2003; Holleis et al. 2007) was very apparent. Many times when a member of our field trial team started fiddling with a lonely hotspot, citizens promptly started gathering around, obviously encouraged by someone else using the hotspot and curious about what could be done with this peculiar artifact.

Discussion

We have provided a snapshot of our ambitious and expensive attempt at introducing visible and hopefully lasting change in the digital fabric of downtown Oulu. While we have successfully engaged the city government, which was mandatory in order to have any chance of succeeding, engaging individual citizens has proven much more challenging. All anonymous users fiddling with the hotspots make a great contribution to our research, but we still would want to recruit as many identified test users as possible, because they would facilitate a more holistic and longitudinal exploration (Huang, Koster, and Borchers 2008).

We have seen that the location of a hotspot plays a very important role in the overall usage of the hotspot and in the usage of individual services. Our hotspots seem to attract relatively short opportunistic interaction, where context, user-created content, social networking, and amusement play a big role. These observations should serve as useful guidelines in designing the locations of upcoming hotspots.

The hotspots have now been operational for two years, and we have collected massive amounts of data on their usage, user acceptance, and overall value to the community. This chapter, however, discusses only data gathered from the first version of the hotspot, as fitting two years' worth of data into a single chapter is nearly impossible. Moreover, given all the data, it is still early to draw any final conclusions on the actual impact of the hotspots. Given the early feedback and usage, we are cautiously optimistic. However, we are still far from rigorously proving our abstract hypothesis of "making the urban space a better place for people" with the hotspots and the services provided by them. This is fundamentally difficult because there are no universally accepted metrics for evaluating this kind of a real-world deployment. While usability evaluation has established itself as the de facto yardstick in mainstream lab studies, it is not sufficient for assessing real-world systems (Greenberg and Buxton 2008). Building on previous efforts (Jay and Stanton 2008; Kostakos et al. 2009; Scholtz and Consolvo 2004), the research community should engage in a serious attempt at developing and adopting metrics for evaluating real-world deployments. We have launched a research initiative to do just this, and we hope to able to contribute a framework that the whole research community can adopt as a tool for evaluating such real-world systems. Another unproven aspect is scalability: to what extent would our ongoing deployment in a small downtown of a city of about 140,000 people scale up to a really large urban space?

We have learned a number of lessons from our project. First, it is important to balance traditional academic research with development, public service, and commercial use—inevitable aspects of our work. Second, sustainability is also crucial, because every infrastructure deployment is subject to a review of its economic and technological sustainability. Many academic infrastructure projects have failed because they did not have a long-term financial basis for covering maintenance and further development. While public sources have covered the capital expenditure for our hotspots, we do not have public funding for operational expenses. To cover the costs we are selling a portion of the capacity of the hotspots for commercial use, which is proving challenging and imposes obvious limitations on research use. Technological sustainability refers to the expected lifetime of the current infrastructure and the expensive renewal of outdated infrastructure in the future. Third, high-quality engineering is essential. Deploying and maintaining a large-scale distributed system that the user community expects to be available 24/7 in a city center has proven to be a totally different ballgame than presenting a one-shot demo to our sponsors or conducting an evaluation in the controlled environment of our usability lab. Fourth, urban planning requires considerable attention. Priorities include conforming to the formal requirements of the city administration, the "battle" for the urban space with other things such as bicycles and snow, and the prevention of vandalism after installation. Fifth, we have learned important lessons about the public scrutiny by the general public and the local media, which has been very ill-tempered at times in our case, suggesting a need to invest more in media management in the future.

We acknowledge the fact that the first version of the hotspot was by no means a "complete" product, but just a beginning. We launched the second version of our hotspot software June 1, 2010, and are currently gathering extensive user data on the use and acceptance of this iteration. Version 2.0 includes a new service selection menu; a subtle interaction mode for enticing people to approach the display and become active participants; a set of new services and improvements to existing services, including the much-requested navigation feature to the map service; a possibility to integrate user accounts with existing social media services such as Facebook; and many other upgrades. The underlying software architecture was also completely redone, making the hotspots much easier to maintain and update remotely. We will launch the third version in June 2011, again addressing issues and requirements gathered from the user community.

We have initiated a number of activities to make our hotspots available to the whole community. Students design new services for the hotspots as part of their coursework. Other research projects are welcome to deploy their own applications in the hotspots. Businesses can purchase rights to offer commercial services there. We executed a national "UBI Challenge" in 2010, which challenged both individuals and organizations to innovate and implement novel services for the hotspots, and the best proposals were supported with grants. The selected three finalists developed and deployed their services on top of the hotspots, and we are currently in the progress of gathering data on their usage.

As a follow-up, we have announced an international "UBI Challenge," prepared with a number of leading researchers, which invites the international research community to show what they are able to do in conjunction with our urban computing testbed. The challenge will be executed during summer 2011, with the finalists deploying their services and gathering data from July to August 2011.

References

Bassoli, A., J. Brewer, K. Martin, P. Dourish, and S. Mainwaring. 2007. Underground aesthetics: Rethinking urban computing. *IEEE Pervasive Computing* 6 (3): 39–45.

Bovey, J. D. 1996. Event-based personal retrieval. *Journal of Information Science* 22 (5): 357–366.

Brignull, H., and Y. Rogers. 2003. Enticing people to interact with public displays in public spaces. *Proceedings of INTERACT 2003,* Zurich, Switzerland, 17–24. Amsterdam: IOS Press.

Brown, B., K. O'Hara, T. Kindberg, and A. Williams. 2009. Crowd computer interaction. In Proceedings of the 27th international conference on Human factors in computing systems, Boston. New York: ACM.

Erdelez, S. 1996. Information encountering: A conceptual framework for accidental information discovery. In *Proceedings of the International Conference on Information Seeking in Context 1996 (ISIC 1996),* Tampere, Finland, 412–421. London: Taylor Graham Publishing.

Greenberg, S., and B. Buxton. 2008. Usability evaluation considered harmful (some of the time). In Mary Czerwinski, Arnie Lund, and Desney Tan, eds. *Proceedings of the Twenty-Sixth Annual SIGCHI Conference on Human Factors in Computing Systems,* Florence, Italy, 111–120. New York: ACM.

Holleis, P., E. Rukzio, F. Otto, and A. Schmidt. 2007. Privacy and curiosity in mobile interactions with public displays. In Peter Fröhlich, Rainer Simon, Lynne Baillie, Joi L. Roberts, Roderick Murray-Smith, Matt Jones, and Rahul Nair, eds. *Proceedings of the CHI 2007 Workshop on Mobile Spatial Interaction,* San Jose, CA. New York: ACM.

Hosio, S., M. Jurmu, H. Kukka, J. Riekki, and T. Ojala. 2010. Supporting distributed private and public user interfaces in urban environments. In Angela Dalton and Roy Want, eds. *Proceedings of the Eleventh Workshop on Mobile Computing Systems & Applications,* Annapolis, MD, 25–30. New York: ACM.

Huang, E. M., A. Koster, and J. Borchers. 2008. Overcoming assumptions and uncovering practices: When does the public really look at public displays? In Jadwiga Indulska, Donald J.

Patterson, Tom Rodden, and Max Ott, eds. *Proceedings of the 6th International Conference Pervasive Computing*, Sydney, Australia, May 19–22. Berlin: Springer.

Jay, T., and Fraser D. Stanton. 2008. The role of a cohort in the design and evaluation of pervasive systems. In Johann van der Schijff and Gary Marsden, eds. *Proceedings of the Conference on Designing Interactive Systems 2008 ,* Cape Town, South Africa, 31–39. New York: ACM.

Kindberg, T., M. Chalmers, and E. Paulos. 2007. Guest editors' "Introduction: Urban Computing." *IEEE Pervasive Computing* 6 (3): 18–20.

Kostakos, V., T. Nicolai, E. Yoneki, E. O'Neill, H. Kenn, and J. Crowcroft. 2009. Understanding and measuring the urban pervasive infrastructure. *Personal and Ubiquitous Computing* 13 (5): 355–364.

Kukka, H., F. Kruger, and T. Ojala. 2009. BlueInfo: Open architecture for deploying web services in WPAN hotspots. In Ernesto Damiani, ed. *Proceedings of 2009 IEEE International Conference on Web Services*, Los Angeles, 984–991. New York: IEEE.

Müller, J., D. Wilmsmann, J. Exeler, M. Buzeck, A. Schmidt, T. Jay, and A. Krüger. 2009. Display blindness: The effect of expectations towards digital signage. In Hideyuki Tokuda, Michael Beigl, Adrian Friday, A. J. Bernheim Brush, and Yoshito Tobe, eds. *Proceedings of the Pervasive Computing 7th International Conference, Nara, Japan, May 11–14.1.* Berlin: Springer Verlag.

Nielsen, J. 1993. *Usability Engineering.* San Francisco: Morgan Kaufman.

O'Hara, K., M. Glancy, and S. Robertshaw. 2008. Understanding collective play in an urban screen game. In Bo Begole and David W. McDonald, eds. *Proceedings of CSCW 08.* San Diego. New York: ACM.

Ojala, T., K. Kukka, T. Heikkinen, T. Lindén, M. Jurmu, F. Kruger, S. Sasin, S. Hosio, and P. Närhi. 2010a. Open urban computing testbed. In Thomas Magedanz, Anastasius Gavras,Nguyen Huu Thanh, and Jeff Chase, eds. *Proceedings of the 6th International Conference on Testbeds and Research Infrastructures for the Development of Networks & Communities*, Berlin, 1277–1288. Berlin: Springer Verlag.

Ojala, T., H. Kukka, T. Lindén, T. Heikkinen, M. Jurmu, S. Hosio, and F. Kruger. 2010b. UBI-hotspot 1.0: Large-scale long-term deployment of interactive public displays in a city center. In *Proceedings of the 5th International Conference on Internet and Web Applications and Services (ICIW 2010)*, Barcelona, 285–294. New York: IEEE.

O'Neill, E., V. Kostakos, Tim Kindberg, A. Fatah gen. Schieck, A. Penn, D. Stanton Fraser, and T. Jones. 2006. Instrumenting the city: Developing methods for observing and understanding the digital cityscape. In Crista Lopes, Paul Dourish, and Adrian Friday, eds. *Proceedings of the 8th International Conference on Ubiquitous Computing,* Orange County, CA, 315–332. Berlin: Springer.

Paay, J., and J. Kjeldskov. 2008. Understanding situated social interactions: A case study of public places in the city. *Computer Supported Cooperative Work* 17 (2–3): 275–290.

Paulos, E., and T. Jenkins. 2005. Urban probes: Encountering our emerging urban atmospheres. In Wendy Kellogg and Shumin Zhai, eds. *Proceedings of CHI 2005*, Portland, OR, 341–350. New York: ACM.

Pinch, T., ed. 2003. *Non-Users Also Matter: The Construction of Users and Non_Users of the Internet*, 67–79. Cambridge, MA: MIT Press.

Redhead, F., and M. Brereton. 2006. A qualitative analysis of local community communications. In *Proceedings of OzCHI 06*. Sydney, NSW: CHISIG.

Satchell, C., M. Foth, G. Hearn, and R. Schroeter. 2008. Suburban nostalgia: The community building potential of urban screens. In *OZCHI: Australasian Human-Computer Interaction Conference,* December 8–12, Cairns.

Scholtz, J., and S. Consolvo. 2004. Toward a framework for evaluating ubiquitous computing applications. *IEEE Pervasive Computing* 3 (2): 82–88.

Suchman, L. 1987. *Plans and Situated Actions: The Problem of Human-Machine Communication*. New York: Cambridge University Press.

Townsend, A. 2009. Foreword. In M. Foth, ed., *The Handbook of Research on Urban Informatics: The Practice and Promise of the Real-Time City*. Hershey, PA: IGI Global.

19 Crowdsensing in the Web: Analyzing the Citizen Experience in the Urban Space

Francisco C. Pereira, Andrea Vaccari, Fabien Giardin, Carnaven Chiu, and Carlo Ratti

The midsized and large cities of the twenty-first century lead a "double life," because they exist in both in the physical and the digital worlds. Although these worlds do not physically share the same spatial or temporal dimensions, the anonymous citizen constantly projects the physical world onto the digital world. Websites such as Flickr, Twitter, Facebook, and Wikipedia are repositories of what citizens sense in the city and include reports or announcements of events and descriptions of space.

In this chapter, we analyze the pulse of a city using publicly available user-generated web data. We describe the technical and methodological processes followed and present three case studies that illustrate their potential.

Introduction

The growing popularity of online platforms based on user-generated content is gradually creating a digital world that mirrors the physical world. For almost every city in the world, a parallel digital version exists, spread across different platforms and systems. Such "digital cities" are as rich in diversity and content as their physical counterparts. Furthermore, much of the content is actively generated and updated by residents, tourists, and organizations, in many cases at a quasi-real-time rate. This dynamic creates a historically unprecedented level of intensity to the experience of life in the city. With a common smartphone, a citizen can find and communicate with other individuals, learn of the nearest events at a given time and place, generate content, seek guidance, or report problems, among other capabilities.

For these reasons, the potential impact of an individual's actions in the digital age is often overrated because of this unprecedented apparent social and technological power. An individual's behavior, however, rarely deviates significantly from that of the crowd—jointly with peers, his or her behavior *builds* the crowd (Rheingold 2002). The crowd uploads pictures of *popular* events, sends tweets in real time about new happenings, creates and updates pages on Wikipedia about the city, and responds with opinions and hits on the *best* content. These acts of communication generate different kinds of data that provide unique views on how people experience and view the city.

The crowd therefore becomes a distributed network of sensors that allows us to understand the dynamic patterns of the city and the experiences of its citizens at a quasi-real-time rate, hence the term *crowdsensing.*

In this chapter, we review several types of online data sources related to cities and present techniques available to collect and mine these sources. We then present three case studies that explore what crowdsensing can tell us about how people experience a city. This comprehensive presentation aims to offer the reader insights into the possible applications of crowdsensing in diverse fields and contexts. We focus particularly on collectively built and shared content—content that generates a high level of public interest, or *buzz* (Currid and Williams 2009), during a certain period of time. We describe each case comprehensively to convey the main concepts and results. We invite the interested reader to analyze the suggested literature in more detail.

In the first case study, the *Eyes of the World,* we estimate the attractiveness and popularity of places and events based on the density of user-generated data, in particular the photographs uploaded by Flickr users with tags including information on their location and time in addition to a description. We summarize the results of two experiments in Rome and New York City, employing information visualization to ground and evaluate urban strategies. In the second case study, *My Architect*, we take the idea of exploring the density of user-generated data a step further, using these data to benchmark "iconic architecture." In this context, the measurement of buzz is correlated to the popularity of an aesthetic, helping to evaluate the success of architects in promoting the image of a city.

In the third and final case study, *Semantics and the City,* we analyze the textual descriptions of points of interest (POIs) and events found on the web, both on individual homepages and on encyclopedic platforms such as Wikipedia. This analysis is carried out with the application of *information extraction* (IE) and *natural language processing* (NLP) techniques that extract the most important concepts found in freely flowing text. From these concepts, we generate an augmented view of the meaning of space, both from a dynamic perspective (based on events), and a static perspective (based on homepages or Wikipedia).

Collecting and Mining Buzz

The Internet is extremely rich in content on the spatiotemporal and semantic dimensions of cities. This wealth of information is generated by the interactions of users with wireless and online services that enable us to develop new methods for collecting and analyzing data related to the social dynamics of the city (O'Neill et al. 2006). The integration of content spread over many websites and services could build new metrics for describing the spatial distribution and temporal evolution of the built environment

(Kostakos et al. 2008). Additionally, the distributed presence of personal devices creates a vast sensor network that could reveal collective behaviors with unprecedented details (Goodchild 2007; Zook et al. 2004; Budhathoki, Bruce, and Nedovic-Budic 2008; Eagle and Pentland 2006). As table 19.1 illustrates, these *digital footprints* present an opportunity in urban and tourism studies to build more efficient ways to collect aggregate information about visitors' activities.

Two of the case studies presented in this chapter focus on the information hidden in every photograph uploaded on the Flickr website. People using the Flickr service to share and organize photographs also have the option to add geographic attributes. When a photograph is anchored to a physical location, Flickr assigns longitude and latitude values together with an accuracy attribute derived from the zoom level of the map in use to position the photographs. Therefore, photographs positioned on a map when the user zooms in to the street level receive a higher accuracy estimate than those positioned when the user zooms out to the map view. The system also adds metadata embedded by the camera into the image using the *Exchangeable Image File Format* (EXIF) information, thus completing the spatiotemporal information.

In the *Eyes of the World* and *My Architect,* we develop an application that retrieves Flickr photographs with specific types of digital information such as georeferences and matching tags. To understand and rank the buzz of user-generated content within the scope of architecture, custom text-filtering software was used to monitor and ensure the quality of the Flickr photos we collected. Data were primarily categorized and filtered textually in English.

These two projects illustrate the wide applicability of user-generated content in the study of urban processes. This dataset allows for the study of mobility and tourism on many different scales, from within the city to between cities or even countries. Connections between different areas of the city become salient (e.g., which tourist hotspots are visited by people from a similar origin), and insights are revealed into how cities are interpreted (e.g., which locations are considered more or less important and what is captured by the eyes of the people who are there).

The *Semantics and the City* project takes a broad approach and considers a wide range of websites. The initial seed is a *point of interest* (POI) or an event, such as a concert or theater performance. Given its location and title, we conduct a search for the best set of pages associated with the POI or event, and then perform a sequence of natural language analyses: *part-of-speech tagging, noun phrase chunking, named entity recognition*, and *WordNet concept extraction*, using available NLP tools (Toutanova et al. 2003; Ramshaw and Marcus 1995; Finkel, Grenager, and Manning 2005; Fellbaum 1998). A list of words representing each POI or event is thus extracted. The last step consists of applying *information retrieval* techniques to rank those words in relative importance, more specifically *term frequency times inverse document frequency* (TF IDF). For each document, this measure balances the popularity of certain words with respect to all documents for that POI against the frequency of those words in that specific

Table 19.1
Data capture techniques with their main strength and weakness in the context of tourism and urbanism studies.

Data capture	Strength	Weakness	Example of application
Land-use and census data	Applicable to many scales and over long time period.	Infrastructure and service based, static view of urban dynamics.	Estimate the tourism intensity of an area.
Manual surveys	Capture high-level information such as motivations and reasons for staying in specific areas.	Very costly and applies to limited time periods.	Capture the motivation for visiting and length of stay.
Near-field communication	Precise real-time mobility data.	Costly infrastructure deployment.	Describe the social and spatial characteristics of space (Kostakos et al. 2008).
GPS logs	Precise mobility data.	Does not scale well if deployed for the purpose of a survey alone. Limited in time and participants.	Cluster tourist routes (Asakura and Iryob 2007).
Cellphone (device-based)	Timely mobility data, potentially augmented with in situ survey.	Does not scale well if deployed for the purpose of a survey alone. Limited in time and participants.	Context-aware experience sampling to capture the experience in situ (Froehlich et al. 2006).
Cellphone (aggregated network–based)	Use existing infrastructure to provide real-time density and mobility data, covering multiple geographic scales (neighborhood, city, country).	Reveal large-scale phenomena but do not explain the reasons.	Real-time traffic detection (Yim 2003).
User-generated content	Exploit publicly available data with no need for deployment or preexisting infrastructure.	Credibility of information and no systematic coverage.	Reveal flows of photographers (Girardin et al. 2008).

document. For example, given two terms that appear once in a POI word list (e.g., *menu* and *Indian cuisine*), the one that appears in many documents relating to that POI (e.g., *menu*) in restaurant POIs gets a lower TF IDF value than one that appears only in a few documents (e.g., *Indian cuisine*), because the latter is more informative. Frequency inside the document can influence this balance—for example, if *menu* appears much more often than *Indian cuisine*, it will become more important. The final outcome is a ranked list of words for each POI or event. As expected, this list is very dependent on the initial search; therefore, we divide our approach into a number of perspectives that consist essentially of a preselection of search spaces. In the Wikipedia perspective, we only search on Wikipedia.org; in the events perspective, we search on upcoming.org and specific study-area sites, such as calendar.boston.com, while in the Open Web perspective we use the Yahoo!Search API to perform an unbounded search.

The *Eyes of the World*: Visualizing Buzz as it Comes Online

Visitors to a city have many ways of leaving voluntary or involuntary electronic trails: prior to their visits, tourists generate server log entries when they consult digital maps (Fischer 2007) or travel websites (Wöber 2007); during their visit, they leave traces on wireless networks (Ahas et al. 2007) whenever they use their mobile phones or credit cards (Houée and Barbier 2008); and after their visit they may contribute reviews (Mummidi and Krumm 2008) and photographs (Crandall et al. 2009) online. In this section we present analyses and visualizations of photographs left by visitors on Flickr.

The explicit character of photograph geotagging and manual disclosure to the world generates many dimensions of interest. Positioning a photo on a map is an act of communication that embodies the locations, times, and experiences that an individual considers to be relevant to himself or herself and of interest to others. Our results clearly show that Flickr users have a tendency to point out the highlights of their visit to a city while skipping over the lowlights.

Previous research has also shown that cellular networks in urban areas are efficient tools to study both individuals (González, Hidalgo, and Barabási 2008) and crowds (Ratti et al. 2006) due to their pervasive coverage and the widespread usage of cellular phones. For example, the analysis of mobile data (see Yim 2003) can generate information about traffic conditions in real time. Cellular network signals can also be correlated (albeit with limited success) to the actual presence of vehicles and pedestrians in the city (Sevtsuk and Ratti 2007). In a case study of tourism dynamics in Estonia, Ahas et al. prove that the sampling and analysis of passive mobile positioning data is a promising resource for tourism research and management.

In the case study of Rome (Girardin et al. 2008), we illustrate the potential of user-generated electronic trails based on the sequences of photographs to reveal the presence and movement of visitors in a city. Our analysis allows us to identify the areas that attract the greatest attention such as the Coliseum and the main train station next to the Piazza della Repubblica, as well as the temporal signature of these places— that is, the level of congestion with respect to the time of day and day of the week.

The study of digital footprints also reveals *desire lines* embodied in the paths of those traveling throughout the city. We first reveal the most active areas through spatial clustering of the data and then aggregate individual paths to generate lines capturing the sequential preferences of visitors. This process produces multiple directed graphs that allow us to compute the number of sites visited by season, the most visited hotspots, and so forth.

For instance, figure 19.1 illustrates the main paths taken by photographers between points of interest in the city. Significantly, the 753 visiting Italian photographers (top) are active across many areas of the city, while the 675 American visitors stay on a narrow desire line between the Vatican, the Forum, and the Coliseum. One cannot conclude that American visitors only explore these areas of Rome, but rather that they concentrate on these points of interest when relaying their experience of the city.

In a follow-up case study in New York City (Girardin et al. 2009), we exploit the spatiotemporal characteristics of buzz to inform local authorities about the success of the "New York City Waterfalls," a public art project consisting of four human-made waterfalls rising from the New York Harbor in the East River from June 26 to October 13, 2008. The waterfalls were intended to attract residents and visitors to the city's waterfront with the goal of stimulating social and economic activity.

Given the large investment in the temporary installation, its organizers wished to assess the economic impact of the event. Traditional methods such as people counts and surveys, which produce accurate estimates only for confined areas, failed to capture the dynamics of the open spaces around the waterfront. Our analysis of geo-referenced photographs, on the contrary, helped to quantify the influence of the public art exhibition on the attractiveness and popularity of various vantage points in proximity to the event.

We conceptualized the level of attractiveness and popularity as properties of a well-defined place that could vary in intensity. We then used indicators inspired by economic analysis and network theory to measure the attractiveness of the main points of interest around the waterfalls based on their relative strength, and the evolution of the popularity of the waterfront based on its centrality in the network of points of interest.

Table 19.2 shows the variations of the *comparative relative strength* indicator based on the presence of photographers during the summers (June to October) of 2006, 2007, and 2008. It reveals a positive growth in the waterfront's attractiveness of 8.2 percent in the summer of 2007 and 20.7 percent in the summer of 2008 with respect to other areas of interest in New York City, such as Times Square and Central Park. It should be noted that the maximum growth in attractiveness, 29.9 percent, observed during

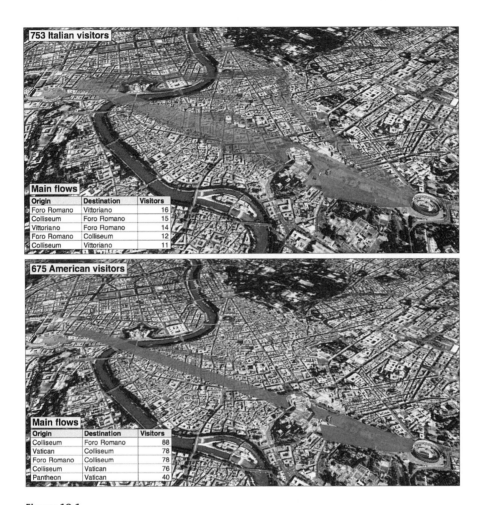

753 Italian visitors

Main flows

Origin	Destination	Visitors
Foro Romano	Vittoriano	16
Colliseum	Foro Romano	15
Vittoriano	Foro Romano	14
Foro Romano	Colliseum	12
Colliseum	Vittoriano	11

675 American visitors

Main flows

Origin	Destination	Visitors
Colliseum	Foro Romano	88
Vatican	Colliseum	78
Foro Romano	Colliseum	78
Colliseum	Vatican	76
Pantheon	Vatican	40

Figure 19.1
Geovisualization of main paths taken by photographers between points of interest in Rome.
Significantly, (*top*) the 753 visiting Italian photographers are active across many areas of the city,
whereas (*bottom*) the 675 American visitors stay on a narrow path between the Vatican, Forum,
and Coliseum. (Different scales apply to each geovisualization.)

Table 19.2
Variation of CRS indicators from 2006 to 2008

	Photographers 2006	Photographers 2007	Photographers 2008	CRS 2006	CRS 2007	CRS 2008	2006 to 2007	2007 to 2008
Central Park	1874	2619	1537	0.111	0.101	0.100	−0.091	−0.008
Chelsea	1146	1790	1125	0.068	0.069	0.073	0.015	0.062
East Village	652	971	606	0.038	0.037	0.039	−0.031	0.054
WTC site	564	775	374	0.032	0.029	0.024	−0.075	−0.184
Time Square	1227	1883	1026	0.073	0.072	0.067	−0.002	−0.079
Vantage Points	538	896	640	0.032	0.034	0.041	0.082	0.207

the summer of 2008, was recorded in DUMBO, Brooklyn: this was likely supported by the increased presence of photographers, elicited by the waterfalls, at the proximate vantage points of Pier 1 and Main Street Park.

We assess the popularity of an area of interest by studying its ties to other areas in the city. The stronger the ties, and as it becomes part of a popular route, the more frequently an area is accessed. This is measured by applying network analysis techniques to study the connectivity of a network in which the nodes represent areas of interest and the edges represent flows of people between them. Figure 19.2 illustrates the flows estimated by analyzing Flickr photos in conjunction with the reported location where and when the photos were taken.

These aggregate, spatiotemporal records lead to a novel perspective on different aspects of mobility and travel. Although the results are still fairly coarse, we clearly show the potential for geographically referenced digital footprints to reveal patterns of mobility and preference among different visitor groups.

We also analyze the flows of visitors between several points of interest in Lower Manhattan to track the evolution of the centrality of the waterfront area in comparison to other points of interest. Mapping this new type of digital footprint analysis shows the capacity of an event to drive people to less explored parts of a city over time, information that can be highly valuable for urban design and tourism studies.

Ranking Buzz: A Case Study in Architecture

The intimate relationship between photography and architecture has been well documented since the early days of photography (Robinson and Herschman 1988).

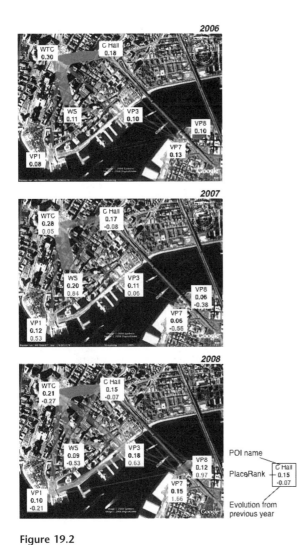

Figure 19.2
Evolution of the flows of photographers in proximity to the exhibit based on the analysis of photos generated in June–October 2006, June–October 2007, and June–August 15 in 2008. In 2008, when Waterfalls opened, VP3, VP6, and VP7 massively increase their PlaceRank.

Photographs reflect on the built world in which we live and generate awareness of its visual qualities, allowing us to make connections and observations that would not have been obvious otherwise. A collection of photographs of a particular place tells a story of the way it is designed to be experienced. Flickr provides vast amounts of this type of data, particularly for places that are of substantial interest, including the most important architectural sites.

My Architect offers a global view of the presence and work of a selection of the world's greatest architects. Designed under the same principles and built from a very similar set of components as the *Eyes of the World*, it serves as an extension of this project but focuses solely on architecture. The public creates narratives based on their activities from which we are able to extract a general opinion of these spaces.

My Architect visualizes the formation of iconic architecture and "starchitect" culture. Through this visualization, we highlight the clusters of the physical presence of each architect and showcase their most famous works through stunning photographs captured by anonymous photographers around the world. This project also features a ranking of the architects based on the size of their online photograph collection. This ranking deviates from the media's measure in that it is not simply representing which buildings are photographed the most; it is instead an examination of pop architecture culture formalized via peer-to-peer information sharing online. This bottom-up approach to conveying information related to architecture contrasts with the traditional top-down approach in which communication media and other third parties measure the success of architectural practice and professions.

For this case study, we develop several filtering methods to extract desired photographs for evaluation that are from a large collection in the Flickr database. We begin with gathering a list of approximately three hundred living architects from around the world, using information from various online platforms including Wikipedia and the most popular blogs and sites related to architecture. We then establish the preliminary scope for this project by retrieving the total number of available photographs on Flickr for each of the architects included in this list. From this initial search, the top hundred architects were selected for further analysis based on the frequency of photographs of their work. The following paragraphs introduce the procedures we used to further control and refine the quality of the search results, and furthermore analyze the user-generated tags that are associated with the Flickr photographs.

Using simply the names of the architects creates unreliable search queries, because they are not unique to those specific individuals (e.g., Smith). Therefore, to ensure that the photographs returned from the search are relevant to architecture, we compile a list of the most popular words with which Flickr users tag photographs related to architecture, including, among others, *exterior, interior, architecture, building, windows, doors, facade, design, architect, designer, skyscraper, museum, outdoor, tower, house, contemporary,* and *modern*. All available tags retrieved for each photograph are matched

Figure 19.3
Scanning for top architects.

against these words, and the selection is narrowed to those photographs overlapping most strongly with the list. Using a filter script to check for matches between the lists, we extract photographs that contain a minimum of one match. The top fifty architects in the world are selected based on the size of the photograph collection filtered through this process.

We design two distinct visualizations to exhibit the data collected. The first one (figure 19.3) introduces the overall concept of the project to the audience. A "crowd detector" scans across the global map, revealing the names of architects as it scans over the geographic area where each architect contributes or is photographed the most in relation to the rest of his or her work. The size and color of each architect's name correspond to the frequency with which his or her projects are photographed. The second visualization (figure 19.4) focuses on displaying the data for each individual architect. A line scans across the screen and generates a particular heat map for the selected architect while presenting the Flickr photographs to viewers.

The analysis and mapping of these data reveal the global points of architectural interests and how they contribute to the level of tourist activity. They also expose how

Figure 19.4
A sequence of four snapshots. Notice the sweep line crossing from west to east, leaving a trace of photos.

architectural landmarks and the role of starchitects contribute to shaping urban activity and aesthetics. The image of a place or city reveals the dynamic aspect of how people utilize the photographic medium to explore architecture and the architectural experience.

Understanding Buzz: Natural Language Text Analysis of User-Generated Content

Our main goal in *Semantics and the City* is to understand the meaning of space in static and dynamic terms—that is, what exists and what happens in a particular space. Coupled with other types of data from the city such as mobile-phone usage and GPS traces, we can extract relationships between space and mobility in the city. For example, understanding that a specific place has recurrent congestion due to its point of interest (POI) profile and events—for example, a sports stadium and important games or rock concerts—would facilitate the development of a traffic prediction model. Other examples concern the sociological relationship between space and mobility: people who go to family concerts also go to interactive museums; people from specific neighborhoods prefer sports events or musical concerts, and so on.

As described in the above section, given a POI or event, we apply a sequence of steps that use natural language processing, information retrieval, and information extraction techniques to obtain a list of words that correspond to the "meaning" of that place. The first decisive step is the choice of the document search space. We call each choice a perspective, because it reflects the type of knowledge embedded:

Wikipedia   This perspective relies on encyclopedic information. Although the accuracy of its content may vary, Wikipedia contains over three million pages created and maintained on a crowdsource basis. Given a POI, we consider two different analyses: documents corresponding to the type(s) of the POI (red wiki perspective) and documents with the same or a similar title to the name of the POI (yellow wiki perspective).

Events   This perspective is based on analyzing events occurring at a given place. For a specific study area, we manually search for the website(s) that cover the largest number of public events. The minimum information on each event normally contains details on the time and location in addition to a small description. For a given location or venue, we analyze the descriptions of the events, and furthermore, for each of the most relevant words, search on Wikipedia for related documents. For example, the description of an event containing the words *Bach, Partita, Handel*, and *Vivaldi* could lead to terms in Wikipedia such as *baroque* or *concerto grosso*, which were not referred to in the original text.

Open Web   This is the unconstrained perspective. It simply uses the Yahoo!Search API to find pages on a POI. This perspective possesses the highest potential because it can obtain the "official" homepages; it is also the most challenging because there is no a priori control to exclude noise or secondary information.

We initially considered the Flickr perspective. For the POIs and events in our database, however, the top words obtained from Flickr typically focus on geographic information, which becomes redundant (e.g., photos of the Brooklyn Bridge are mostly tagged as "Brooklyn," "Bridge," "Manhattan," "New York," etc.). There are also many nongeographic tags, but these are extremely varied according to the individual and therefore become submerged under the geographic tags because they appear with a lower frequency. Only in POIs with a strong aesthetic component such as architectural monuments, visual arts museums, and so on, will such data be more relevant, because descriptive words become more common (e.g., *baroque, cubist,* etc.), as we can see in *My Architect*.

In any of the perspectives, the choice of the "ideal" set of words concerning an event or place ordered by relevance is ultimately a subjective task. What we obtain is either the result of a consensus (Wikipedia) or the union of individual contributions (events, Open Web), and the process we apply is ultimately based on statistical analysis. We therefore claim to obtain a valid set of words that accurately represents the way places and events are referred to by the crowd in all of these perspectives, as opposed to an ideal single set of words. As an example, while the words *fat, unhealthy,* and *capitalism* are associated with many fast food chains, they are rarely used on Wikipedia and the homepages of the chains. This justifies the exploration of other perspectives including crowd opinion and sentiment analysis.

From our collection of a large set of POIs from Boston, New York, and San Francisco, we begin the computationally time-consuming extraction of words that results in what we term "enrichment." The average time for the analysis of a POI from the Open Web perspective is approximately 108 seconds; analysis from the red and yellow wiki

Table 19.3
Summary of statistics

	New York	Boston	San Francisco	Overall
Yahoo!	183144	64133	94466	251839
YellowPages	7694	12878	—	21333
Boston Calendar	13999	2867	9497	26364
OpenWeb	757	2020	—	2896
Red Wiki	69011	20309	—	90210
Yellow Wiki	4400	1928	—	6330
Events	—	7591	—	—
Enriched Events	—	3827	—	—

requires 57 and 31 seconds, respectively; and analysis from the events perspective takes 30 seconds on average. The Open Web is the most time consuming, because it searches the entire web. In the events perspective, the system already contains the initial text descriptions for the events, and its subsequent steps are similar to those involved in the yellow wiki perspective, hence the similarity in time requirements. In table 19.3, we present the overall statistics.

We obtain a total of 77,558 different words, of which 9,746 (12.6 percent) are also identified in WordNet, a lexical database for the English language. An analysis of these concepts was performed on the average information content (IC) (Resnik 1995), which reflects the balance of s of a concept on a scale of 0 to 17. The average we obtain is 16.313395 (st. dev. = 1.7263386), indicating that the concepts the words illustrate are very specific. This level of specificity can, however, pose risks. If the concepts prove to be generic as opposed to very specific, the probability of being accurate with respect to the place is much higher. Table 19.4 includes excerpts from results illustrating both the strengths and weaknesses of the approach.

Taking into account the top five words in each case, the experiments show that the median of correct words[1] is four in both the Wikipedia and events perspectives and two in the Open Web perspective. More specifically, the red wiki perspective most reliably ensures correctness, because it sacrifices the specificity of each POI for the analysis of its category and then typically yields correct results. The yellow wiki and Open Web perspectives prove to be the best for extracting exact information on a specific place. The former is preferable when the POI exists on Wikipedia, while the latter is the only alternative option. Finally, the events perspective is unique in that it brings information about what happens in the place rather than how the place is defined on the web.

This work is currently being applied in two different analyses: (1) the correlation of cellphone usage with event types and semantics, and (2) the identification of

Table 19.4
Excerpt of results

Name	Categories	Terms
Red Wiki		
Bowdoin Square Exxon	Gas stations	pumps, gasoline, fuel dispenser, filling station, gasoline stand
Harvard Market	Grocery stores	groceries, retailing, food, vegetables, products
Kim Depole Design Incorporated	Interior design	office space, architects, private residence, code, decoration
Yellow Wiki		
Victoria's Secret	Clothing, Womens clothing	Victoria, wear, limited brands, top model, fashion models
Boston Police Department	Law enforcement	Massachusetts, law enforcement agency, correction, investigation, responsibility
TD Garden	Entertainment venues	Boston Celtics, arena, Boston Blazers, naming rights, National Lacrosse League
Events		
Nature Trail and Cranberry Bog	Nature	Pond, falls, streams, currents, winter
The Haunted House	Theater	Orpheum, journey, spirit, tale, surprises
Salem Farmers' Market	Farmers' markets	Cultures, consumption, carbohydrate, food safety, gastronomy
Open Web		
Envirotech Incorporated	Waste and environmental consulting	Industrial services, asbestos management, mildew removal, asbestos removal, residential services
Grasshopper	Telecommunications	Boston telecommunications, Gary, communication services, Boston Business Directory, telephone communications
Cambridge Savings Bank	Banks	Houston, reading room, Allston, Senior Commercial Loan and Business Development, federally chartered

attendees' origins according to event types and semantics. In the first case, we focus again on the waterfalls area during the same period described above and search for causality relations between the semantics of events and cellphone activity. The hypothesis is that, for example, an event that involves the concept "films" or "cinema" would have less activity than one that involves "family" or "sports." We partition areas using cellphone coverage maps and cluster event venues according to those areas. We then choose events isolated in time with respect to their area to avoid ambiguities with concurrent events, extract their words and categories, and compare cellphone activity with similar periods for the same area. When "activity," the number of calls received or sent, is higher or lower than typical cellphone activity by more than one or two standard deviations, we classify the event as having high/very high or low/very low activity, respectively. We next run associative machine learning algorithms (the a priori algorithm) to understand nominal correlations between the two datasets. In table 19.5, we show the top twelve rules obtained. In general, the results confirm our hypothesis, but further experimentation is needed to reach more confident conclusions.

Table 19.5

Top 20 association rules considering all attributes (S/C=support/confidence)

Precondition	Activity	S/C
category=Music time=afternoon	normal	35/35
category=Performing/Visual Arts day=weekday	normal	25/25
category=Other day=weekend	normal	25/25
category=Commercial day=weekday	high	15/15
category=Commercial time=morning	high	15/15
category=Festivals	high	10/10
category=Education time=morning	normal	10/10
category=Performing/Visual Arts day=weekend	high	10/10
category=Performing/Visual Arts time=night	normal	10/10
category=Education day=weekend time=afternoon	normal	10/10
word=request	normal	6/6
category=Sports	normal	5/5
time=dawn	very high	5/5
category=Education time=night	high	5/5
category=Media day=weekday	very low	5/5
category=Media time=morning	normal	5/5
category=Commercial day=weekend	normal	5/5
category=Commercial time=afternoon	normal	5/5
category=Social time=night	normal	5/5
day=weekend time=morning	normal	5/5

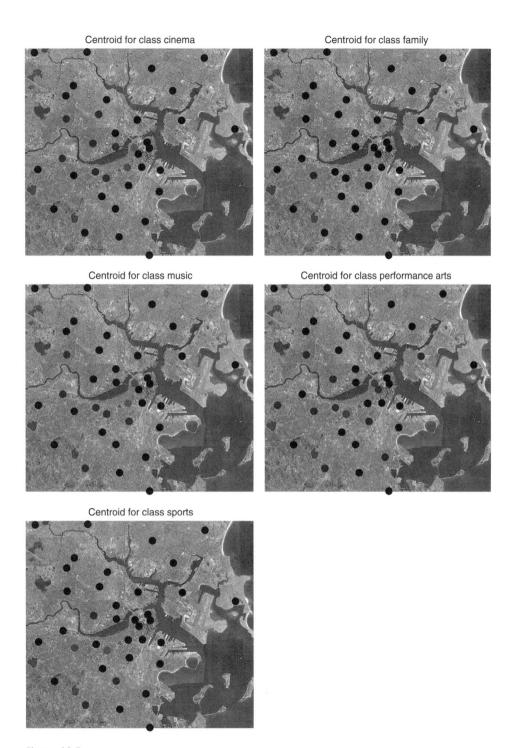

Figure 19.5
Spatial visualization of clusters centroids. The circles correspond to zip-code areas with values greater than zero. The shade from light (low) to dark (high) is proportional to the values.

To explore the nature of events, we analyze the correlations between large events and attendees' origins in Boston. Using over one million anonymized cellphone user traces triangulated to obtain general location (zip code), we obtain the origins for a sample of attendees at each of the selected events. For example, for "Shakespeare on the Common," a large outdoor theater event on Boston Common, we identify that 11 percent of attendees came from the immediate neighborhood, followed by 16 percent in the bordering areas, and so on. From the categories of events not concurrent in space and time, we built a neural network classifier that predicts event types given origin distributions with accuracy ranging from 60 to 90 percent (Calabrese et al. 2010). In figure 19.5 we summarize the overall clustering results of origin distributions for each event type.

Conclusions

As with any dataset, user-generated data yields incomplete conclusions. The subjective nature of this type of data facilitates an understanding of the experience of a city based on the preferences and values of residents and visitors. Instead of being the result of intentional contributions, user-generated data is a form of *implicit engagement*; digital content is a contribution to the city itself, and social networks are now part of the experience of the city. The collection and analysis of these data enable the development of new urban indicators useful to evaluate urban strategies.

In all of the works mentioned, we face the challenge of validating this pervasive, user-generated content. Indeed, our data processing techniques try to account for the inconsistent quality of user-generated data, which can substantially impede our ability to generate accurate information. For instance, the timestamps extracted from the camera-generated EXIF metadata do not necessarily match the real time when a photo was taken because the user may not have set the clock on their camera to the local time, or even to the time from their area of origin. User-generated data points can also be apparently idiosyncratic and, for instance, indicate not the point where the photo was taken but the location of the photographed object.

Strong concerns also arise in the validation of semantics obtained from online texts. The ambiguous and subjective nature of information hinders the identification of a ground truth; the decision on whether a word is related to a context on a qualitative scale, however, should be attainable. In our case, care was taken to rank words correctly by applying TF IDF, then using extended stop word lists[2] to filter out format words such as *http*, and finally analyzing self-consistency. For example, a clustering analysis shows that each category of POI attracts a different set of words. A field survey analyzing the results beyond the laboratory is a necessary next step to this project.

Finally, another important limitation of these approaches is the bias toward "loud" crowds and events—that is, those that due to the nature and character of their crowd lead to more Flickr photos or textual contributions on the web, because their attendees tend to be more technologically savvy. Any application of these analyses should heed this bias.

These shortcomings currently limit the usability of digital footprints for city management and decision making. Visualizations produced from these datasets, however, are already offering new tools to communicate different features of activity in urban areas. Along with interactive software, visualization is a useful tool for many actors in the city such as researchers, practitioners, service providers, and local authorities to discuss how to interpret data and put information in context. For example, an area with strong calling activity and weak photographic activity could be primarily commercial; one with weak calling activity and weak photographic activity could be residential; one with strong calling activity and strong photographic activity could be friendly toward tourist- and leisure-related activities. Similarly, an outdoor area with strong attractiveness indicators even during adverse weather conditions suggests that it is critical for visitors; an indoor area with weak attractiveness indicators during adverse weather conditions indicates that it may not be easily accessible.

Virtual cities are growing. Everyday more people become new residents who increasingly use more websites and devices. While the virtual city may never merge into the physical one, it will gradually reflect reality more accurately and become an even more powerful resource to understand the cities in which we live and the cities we would like to visit.

Acknowledgments

We are extremely grateful to our colleague Caitlin Zacharias for her valuable comments and her expert editorial guidance. We also acknowledge generous support from the members of the SENSEable City Lab Consortium, Volkswagen of America, the AT&T Foundation, Airsage, and the MIT-Portugal Program.

Note

1. For determining *correctness* for each sample we examined whether the words were specifically related to a POI or event or if they were unrelated—for example, whether "laundry service" refers to a place for laundry as opposed to Shakira's pop music album—and if the information the words refer to was too general.

2. Stop word lists are a specific type of list that contains words that have little semantic meaning, such as articles, "as" "and" "or," HTTP codes, tags, and so on.

References

Ahas, R., A. Aasa, S. Silm, and M. Tiru. 2007. Mobile positioning data in tourism studies and monitoring: Case study in Tartu, Estonia. In Marianna Sigala, L. Mich and J. Murphy, eds.,

Information and Communication Technologies in Tourism 2007, 119–128. Ljubljana, Slovenia. Vienna: Springer.

Asakura, Y., and T. Iryob. 2007. Analysis of tourist behaviour based on the tracking data collected using a mobile communication instrument. *Transportation Research, Part A: Policy and Practice* 41 (7): 684–690.

Budhathoki, N., B. Bruce, and Z. Nedovic-Budic. 2008. Reconceptualizing the role of the user of spatial data infrastructure. *GeoJournal* 72 (3): 149–160.

Calabrese, F., C. Pereira, L. Liu, G. Lorenzo, and C. Ratti. 2010. The geography of taste: Analyzing cell-phone mobility and social events. In Patrik Floréen, Antonio Krüger, and Mirjana Spasojevic, eds. *Proceedings of the 8th International Conference on Pervasive Computing.* 22–37. Heidelberg: Springer.

Crandall, D. J., L. Backstrom, D. Huttenlocher, and J. Kleinberg. 2009. Mapping the world's photos. In *Proceedings of the 18th international conference on the World Wide Web*, 761–770. New York: ACM.

Currid, E., and S. Williams. 2009. The geography of buzz: Art, culture and the social milieu in Los Angeles and New York. *Journal of Economic Geography.*

Eagle, N., and A. S. Pentland. 2006. Reality mining: Sensing complex social systems. *Personal and Ubiquitous Computing* 10 (4): 255–268.

Fellbaum, C. 1998. *WordNet: An Electronic Lexical Database* . Cambridge, MA: MIT Press.

Finkel, J. R., T. Grenager, and C. Manning. 2005. Incorporating non-local information into information extraction systems by Gibbs sampling. In *Proceedings of the 43rd Annual Meeting on Association for Computational Linguistics* (ACL '05), 363–370. Stroudsburg, PA: ACL.

Fisher, D. 2007. Hotmap: Looking at geographic attention. *IEEE Transactions on Visualization and Computer Graphics* 13 (6): 1184–1191.

Froehlich, J., M. Y. Chen, I. E. Smith, and F. Potter. 2006. Voting with your feet: An investigative study of the relationship between place visit behavior and preference. In P. Dourish and A. Friday, eds., *Ubicomp: Lecture Notes in Computer Science*, 333–350. Berlin: Springer.

Girardin, F., F. Calabrese, F. Dal Fiore, C. Ratti, and J. Blat. 2008. Digital footprinting: Uncovering tourists with user-generated content. *IEEE Pervasive Computing* 7 (4): 36–43.

Girardin, F., A. Vaccari, A. Gerber, A. Biderman, and C. Ratti. 2009. Quantifying urban attractiveness from the distribution and density of digital footprints. *International Journal of Spatial Data Infrastructure Research* 4:175–200.

González, M. C., C. A. Hidalgo, and A.-L. Barabási. 2008. Understanding individual human mobility patterns. *Nature* 453 (7196): 779–782.

Goodchild, M. F. 2007. Citizens as voluntary sensors: Spatial data infrastructure in the world of Web 2.0. *International Journal of Spatial Data Infrastructures Research* 2:24–32.

Houée, M., and C. Barbier. 2008. Estimating foreign visitors flows from motorways toll management system. Paper presented at the 8th International Conference on Survey Methods in Transport: Harmonisation and Data Comparability, Annecy, France, May 25–31.

Kostakos, V., T. Nicolai, E. Yoneki, E. O'Neill, H. Kenn, and J. Crowcroft. 2008. Understanding and measuring the urban pervasive infrastructure. *Personal and Ubiquitous Computing* 13 (5): 355–364.

Mummidi, L. N., and J. Krumm. 2008. Discovering points of interest from users' map annotations. *GeoJournal* 72(3): 215–227.

O'Neill, E., V. Kostakos, T. Kindberg., A. F. gen. Schieck, A. Penn, D. S. Fraser, and T. Jones. 2006. Instrumenting the city: Developing methods for observing and understanding the digital cityscape. In P. Dourish and A. Friday, eds. *Ubicomp: Lecture Notes in Computer Science*, 315–332. Berlin: Springer.

Ramshaw, L., and M. Marcus. 1995. Text chunking using transformation-based learning. Paper presented at *The 3rd Workshop on Very Large Corpora: WVLC-1995*.

Ratti, C., R. M. Pulselli, S. Williams, and D. Frenchman. 2006. Mobile landscapes: Using location data from cell-phones for urban analysis. *Environment and Planning, B: Planning & Design* 33 (5): 727–748.

Resnik, P. 1995. Using information content to evaluate semantic similarity in a taxonomy. In *Proceedings of the International Joint Conference on Artificial Intelligence (IJCAI'95)*, 448–453. San Francisco, CA: Morgan Kaufmann.

Rheingold, H. 2002. *Smart Mobs: The Next Social Revolution*. New York: Basic Books.

Robinson, C., and J. Herschman. 1988. *Architecture Transformed: A History of the Photography of Buildings from 1839 to the Present*. Cambridge, MA: MIT Press.

Sevtsuk, A., and C. Ratti. 2007. Mobile surveys. In J. Van Schaick and S. C. Van Der Spek, eds. *Urbanism of Track,* 103–119. Del;ft: Delft University Press.

Toutanova, K., D. Klein, and C. Manning C. 2003. Feature-rich part-of-speech tagging with a cyclic dependency network. In *Proceedings of the 2003 Conference of the North American Chapter of the Association for Computational Linguistics on Human Language Technology—Volume 1,* 173–180. Stroudsburg, PA: ACL.

Wöber, K. 2007. Similarities in information search of city break travelers - a web usage mining exercise. In Marianna Sigala, L. Mich, and J. Murphy, eds., *Information and Communication Technologies in Tourism 2007,* 119–128, Ljubljana, Slovenia: Springer Vienna.

Yim, Y. 2003. *The State of Cellular Probes*. Technical report. Institute of Transportation Studies, UC Berkeley.

Zook, M., M. Dodge, Y. Aoyama, and A. Townsend. 2004. New digital geographies: Information, communication, and place. In S. Brunn, S. Cutter, and J. W. Harrington, eds. *Geography and Technology* 155–176. Dordrecht, Netherlands: Kluwer Academic Publishers.

20 Empowering Urban Communities through Social Commonalities

Laurianne Sitbon, Peter Bruza, Renato Iannella, and Sarath Indrakanti

In this chapter, we explore the technological challenges and solutions in creating sound communities based on shared interests across social networks. The creation of a new online community presupposes that the system has access to some knowledge about the users of the networks. However, each user may restrict part of their information to some systems or to some users. In an ideal world, the barriers between the social network services available online would disappear and users would be able to manage the availability of their data. We present a path to this ideal world involving interoperability and profile management. The quality of a suggestion to build a community is inherent in the quality of a connection between two of its members. If this connection is suggested by an automatic system, then its quality is in turn inherent to the quality of the abstract representation of the user. We outline a new paradigm for representing users that succeeds where current recommendation systems tend to fail. The approach we propose is based on semantic spaces and allows for representation of user topics of interest along with the opinions they hold about these topics. The representation of opinions is investigated here as a special case of the representation of social context and commonalities observable through public comments left by users on news websites. We suggest that making more effective comparisons between people requires a better understanding of the social processes at play when people express various kinds of opinions.

The formation of communities is an important empowerment process that can lead to an improvement in the health status of an individual or group (Laverack 2006). Social network services and social media are important enablers in the process by allowing citizen participation in e-deliberations (Maciel, Roque, and Garcia 2009). Research on communities shows that the key factors in the success of online communities include

- *Anonymity* Discretionary levels of identity disclosure (from showing all personal information to showing none)
- *Identity persistence* A member's ability to learn the history of other members

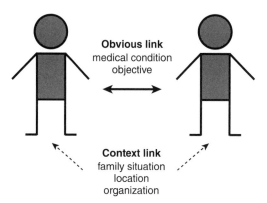

Figure 20.1
Connecting urban communities with commonalities.

• *Trust building* Building trust among the members through member directories, photographs and video clips, commenting features and recommender systems, and matching profiles
• *Clear identification of operators* "Member profiles, transparency of providers" (Iriberri and Leroy 2009)

The development of a successful community identity is subject to "a shared emotional connection in time and space and is an affective component based upon opportunities to share experience and resolve events, through the development of bonds of trust and understanding arising from mutual cooperation" (Puddifoot 1995, 357–370). In the specific case of virtual communities, "the direct link between offline interaction and posting activity suggests that offline meetings strengthen solidarity and intimacy among community members, encouraging them to be more active in posting content online and requiring more time and mental resources than the simple viewing of existing content" (Koh et al. 2007, 68–73).

Currently, many virtual communities are created around a particular goal and never catch on, for various reasons. Host organizations also form communities to foster mutual support among people in similar situations (e.g., medical) without taking personal factors into account. In our vision of the future (figure 20.1), underlying context links such as similar family situation, passions, locations, and factors that may not be disclosed in the defined network, can be used in order to enhance the quality and efficiency of the relationship created.

In this chapter we discuss how semantic profiles of online users can be utilized to effectively bring people from urban locations together to form communities with commonalities between people. We propose a semantic profile framework that matches user opinions using semantic spaces. This framework also allows users to create appropriate privacy safeguards with their profiles.

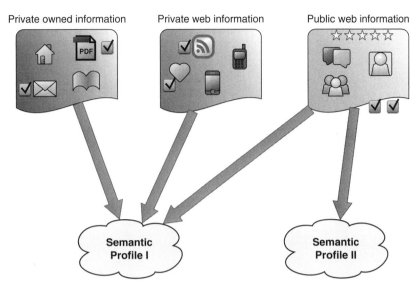

Figure 20.2
Selection of various sources of information to build different semantic profiles.

In the following pages, we first discuss the semantic profiles of users, including the sources of user profile information and the role of the "partial profile." We then describe the recommendation approach. Finally, we propose the semantic space approach to match user opinions, thereby providing a basis for urban communities with commonalities.

Semantic Profiles

Sources of User Profile Information

Various sources of information can be used to build a semantic profile of a person (see figure 20.2). They include (1) private owned information, (2) private web information, and (3) public web information.

Private owned information includes

- Documents
- Web pages visited
- E-mails

Among other things, private web information includes

- Status on social networking sites (Facebook, Twitter)
- Queries, such as mobile queries

The better-known forms of public web information are

- Blog posts
- Comments on blog posts
- Comments on social networking sites
- Messages in discussion forums
- E-mails in mailing lists
- Rating of items on websites allowing reviews (online shopping, bookmarking, etc.)

To effectively gain access to these three types of user information to build someone's semantic profile, we need a novel framework that encompasses interoperability. In this chapter we assume that such a framework exists, but a detailed description of it is beyond the scope of the chapter.

In the next section, we describe the notion of "partial profile."

Partial Profiles

In the digital world many web users manage different social and professional network accounts and utilize them in different ways depending on the digital context. For example, Facebook has more friendly chats, whereas LinkedIn has more professional discussions. Maintaining these online profiles is cumbersome and time consuming for the typical web user. This is also an impediment for new social networks to attract new members simply because of the effort involved in creating and maintaining "yet another profile" and reestablishing all the aspects of a user's profile in a new context. The scalability and noninteroperability of social networks seriously fragment the global digital world. Also, "multiple user profiles and multi-level access controls can help users manage their online identities, without unintended leakage between corporate and social personas" (DiMicicco and Milen 2007, 383–386).

So, when the physical world meets the digital world, what users really need is the opportunity to create and control their own single profile and, more importantly, the ability to determine the aspects of the profile that they will expose to different social networks, as illustrated by figure 20.3. This gives the user a feeling of centralized control, even though the data could be distributed, by empowering them to decide how their information should be viewed and contextualized by different services.

Open standards for interoperable partial profiles are the enabling technology; they will allow more social networks to give web users the necessary control of their own profiles. These standards will allow them to decide which service providers they will share which partial profiles with. It will make it easier to move profiles to other service providers, and it will make the service providers compete for the attention of web users, which improves value-added services. Technical issues, such as profile synchronization, can also be addressed with the clearer management of profile sources.

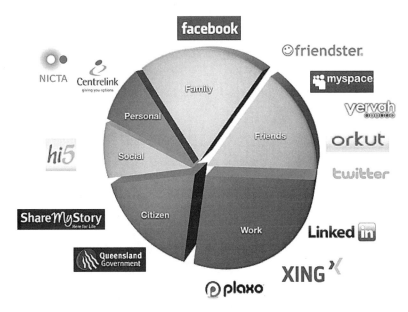

Figure 20.3
Shares of a profile across various applications.

With the user in charge of access to their partial profiles, privacy then becomes somewhat easier to control. As their own "data custodian," the user can decide which service providers can access their personal details via exposing one (or more) partial profiles to that provider. This is an explicit act; the user makes the decision to share the information and can just as easily retract it.

Displaying Semantic Profiles When Suggesting Connections between People

From a user point of view, allowing a system to access a range of textual data to create an automatic profile is very different from allowing any user to access their textual data. Hence the question of how to justify a connection established between two users based on their semantic profile is really challenging.

The first and easiest approach is to not provide any justification and only show public profiles when people are not yet connected. This is what is currently done in most social networks for "people recommendations." A second option consists of investigating levels of "publicness" and trying to classify sources of information about the user according to the level of privacy associated with them. A third approach would offer a partial view of the recommended user according to the matching areas only. This could be presented as a summary (user X thinks that topic A is B), as a comparative summary (user X and you have the same opinion about topic X), or as a comprehensive view of the supportive text (a summary or a set of keywords).

A user study would allow for a better understanding of how much information users are willing to provide to potential connections and how much they want to see about potential connections. It is largely assumed that the context influences the sensitivity of displayed data.

Having the semantic profile framework in place, we now propose mechanisms to connect people based on their profiles.

Recommendation Approach

The Link Approaches

Existing social and professional networks such as Facebook and LinkedIn currently suggest that users make connections to other users they might already know. The principles behind this prospective matching are mainly a matter of increasing the density of already-dense regions of the network surrounding the user. The main features in use are

- People connected to several connections
- People connected to connections into a similar group

These approaches focus on reconnecting the user with people they might already know. Liben-Nowell and Kleinberg (2007) evaluate several link-prediction approaches and conclude that the nearest neighbors are the most promising ones.

Recommender Systems

Recommender systems have been heavily investigated, starting with filtering systems for news and now extending to movie recommendations, product recommendations, and suggestions for friends. Montaner, López, and De La Rosa (2003) present a detailed investigation of how recommender systems create user profiles, how they update these profiles, and how they use the profiles for comparison with items that include the profiles of other users.

All these systems employ multidimensional representations of users and products to establish some degree of similarity. The most commonly used similarity measure in multidimensional environments is the cosine similarity inherited from information retrieval (Salton et al. 1975). For an element (user or product) A represented by a vector of n dimensions $\{a_1, a_2, \ldots an\}$ where the ai are the values of each dimension for the element, and an element (user or product) B represented by a vector of n *dimensions* $\{b_1, b_2, \ldots bn\}$, the cosine similarity sim is calculated according to the equation in figure 20.4.

The representation of the elements in a set of dimensions can be put together in a matrix. Matrix reduction approaches such as Singular Value Decomposition can extract latent semantics and significantly reduce the number of dimensions looked at

$$sim = \frac{\sum_i a_i.b_i}{\sqrt{\sum_i a_i^2}\sqrt{\sum_i b_i^2}}$$

Figure 20.4
Calculation of the cosine similarity sim.

(Landauer and Dumais 1997). If one considers representing a user by the books they have purchased at a bookstore, the dimensions would then be all the books available in the bookstore, which would be really high before reduction.

There are three main classes of algorithms for recommendation: collaborative filtering, content-based filtering, and hybrid methods. Collaborative filtering usually represents ratings made by the user over a set of items. The similarity is then calculated directly or through matrix reduction methods to recommend items chosen by similar users. This is mainly applied for the recommendation of purchases. Content-based approaches use the features of the items highly ranked by a user to try to find similar items. These features can originate from the text associated with the item or a range of discrete data such as classification or release date for movies. The features become the dimensions of each user as well as the dimensions of the item. Thus users and item can be directly compared in terms of similarity. As the name suggests, hybrid approaches combine elements of both collaborative and content-based approaches in the one system. They use a vote by both collaborative and content-based approaches, decompose the content elements of the items in the collaborative representation, or incorporate collaborative features in the content representation of the items.

How Recommender Systems Could Be Improved

Recommender systems can be improved in many ways, as suggested in Adomavicius and Tuzhilin 2005. As a starting point, their paper suggests a "comprehensive understanding of users and items" as the first avenue for improvement. Following from this, recommender systems can build a "cognitive profile," which really boils down to a picture of what topics the user shows an interest in. Such approaches could connect the user with *people they might want to know*. Jung and Euzenat (2007) suggest that the use of several levels of connections at the same time would be most beneficial. Chen et al. (2009) present an experiment run on an enterprise social network where users are offered links coming from either links analysis or content analysis.

People who share similar interests can be found based on topical criteria in both collaborative and content-based approaches, such as

- People who are in similar discussion groups
- People who write about the same topics

Yet people can share some topics in totally opposite ways: the same topical interest that might suggest that people could like each other is exactly the reason why they are more likely to dislike each other. Imagine two persons writing with passion and commenting on the details of Barack Obama's campaign during the U.S. elections in 2008. One might say that the campaign was great and communicative, while the other might think it only involved advertising and was stupid. In this context a system could match those two because they both use very similar and important names, and various locations visited. However, the messages surrounding those facts are completely different and therefore a source of disagreement. To complicate matters, some users might specifically seek a confrontation with people who think differently than they do.

The opinions expressed by a user about a topic can also be seen as a context in which this topic is relevant to the user. Since a given user may hold one opinion for each topic they are interested in, the system would need as many descriptions of context as there are topics.

In a pilot study we created artificial user profiles for each participant, which included a similar and an opposite profile in order to estimate how a standard "bag-of-words" approach would behave. To this end we selected five topics from the website procon.org. The chosen topics fell into very different categories (politics, heath, environment, etc.). Each topic Ti was divided into at least twenty subtopics Sx for which there was a listing of pro and con arguments, at least three of each. For each topic Ti we created ten testing environments as follows. First, a base profile was created by concatenation of a pro argument from a subtopic $TiSx$, a con argument from another subtopic $TiSx+1$, and a pro argument from a subtopic of another topic $TjSz$. Then, two similar profiles were created with the other pro/con arguments in the same topics/subtopics, and two opposite profiles were created with the opposite pro/con arguments of the same topics/subtopics. Finally, ninety-six random profiles were created out of three arguments taken randomly from all topics but Ti and all subtopics but $TjSz$. An index was then created with the search engine Lucene for all hundred profiles except the base profile, and a search was performed using the base profile as a query. In total, fifty base profiles were used for experimentation and for each of them there were two similar profiles found and two opposite profiles not found out of a hundred profiles. Given the small number of similar profiles, we only focused on the recall values, the percentage of similar and opposite profiles found among the first two search results (which corresponds roughly to the number of suggestions that users are usually offered with recommender systems) and among the first ten search results (which corresponds to the number of results users examine when they do a search). It was found overall that 64 percent of the similar profiles were retrieved in first or second position, but also that 28 percent of the opposite profiles were found in such positions. The recall at rank 10 was 85 percent for both similar and opposite profiles. These very high recall values are to be expected since the topics were chosen from very different categories. The relatively high rate of opposite profiles found at rank 2 was also to be expected since the system does not differentiate pro and con sentiments associated with the arguments.

This analysis led us to explore models that allow for a spatial (matrix) representation of users instead of a linear (vector) representation.

Semantic Space Approach

We have established in the previous section that in order to recommend people, the systems should build semantic profiles based on texts written, read, or commented on by a user. We also noted that topics of interest are only part of the semantics gathered by the text manipulated by the users and that opinions about these topics are also important.

What's in an Opinion?

"Opinion mining" has interested a growing number of researchers, and they are exploring various aspects of this process (Pang and Lee 2008). The most common tasks they are addressing relate to automatic rating and detection of opinionated terms. Rating involves a binary position of the opinion, which is generally positive/negative/neutral. The presence of opinionated terms is explored in information retrieval through blogs and summarization as a means to explore opinions expressed about a particular subject on the web.

Researchers have investigated the connection between topic and polarity and proposed ways to represent it. Brooke and Hurst (2009) argue that a domain ontology contains words specifically positive or negative for particular topics and that these can be encoded in the ontology. Mei et al. (2007) suggest including priors corresponding to polarity to the topic probability distribution in a topic model, thus separating the positive, negative, and neutral aspects of the topics identified. This approach presupposes a corpus of examples to be used to learn the prior values. Both these approaches require prior knowledge (examples, ontologies) and hence can be seen as domain specific. They also focus only on the polarity aspects of expressed opinions.

However, as Wiebe et al. (2003) show, the notion of opinion goes far beyond a positive/negative distinction; it can have more to do with the terms surrounding the central terms of a specific topic. The notion of opinion is then seen as perspectives expressed around one topic, as illustrated by figure 20.5. The rating of a particular topic with positive or negative terms is only one way to express an opinion. A single mention of a topic by a user should be regarded as an implicit sign that the user finds this topic interesting. A confrontation pitting one user against another on two sides

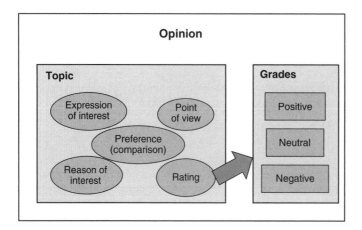

Figure 20.5
Possible contents of an expressed opinion.

of a single topic never mentioned (e.g., camera versus video recorder, DVD versus cinema, etc.) would reveal two opinions without necessarily rating the opposite one as negative with words. An opinion can also simply be a point of view on an event that could involve many adjectives but no rating (this would be marked as "neutral" by previous systems—what does a "neutral" opinion mean?).

The reason for a user's interest is also very important, because two users can have a positive opinion about the same topic for completely different reasons. For example, two users might love California, but one for the wineries and the other for the beaches. Some of the following examples show how very different opinions can be expressed on some subjects without using positive/negative opinion terms.

Example 1   A loves cooking. She likes making pies and various stews. However, she never uses spices since she cannot digest them very well. B loves cooking. He likes making pies and various stews. However, he is a vegetarian and loves using spices. C loves eating. She particularly likes gratins and pizzas. However, she is a vegetarian and cultivates spices.

In example 1, A and B are interested in very similar topics. They can even have a great overlap in recipes. Yet there is little chance that they would want to interact, since they are interested in radically different aspects of the topic. This is not expressed in the text as positive/negative words since none of them would mention the aspect of the others that they do not like. The interests of B and C seem rather different. However, these persons share a strong positive opinion of spicy vegetarian food and might be happy to exchange ideas with each other.

Semantic Spaces to Distinguish Sides

The terms used in cooking will be very similar—utensils and a lot of ingredients. But the terms associated with those common topics can be expected to be radically different. Similarly, if we consider graduated opinion terms as in politics, for example, the terms associated with the main common entities (names and places) are the clues that will help establish if the users agree with each other.

Current approaches for comparing people are those used to compare documents. They are based on "bag-of-words" approaches where each person/document is represented as a set of the terms that can be associated with them. These terms can be provided explicitly as a list of interests or mined automatically from text. In the latter, weights can be allocated to each word in the set, thus forming a vector in the space of terms describing potential interests of all users. Users can then be compared by measuring the angle formed by their representative bag-of-words vector (*cosine similarity measure*; see figure 20.4). However, these approaches do not account for the relationships between the terms, because they are all treated individually.

Approaches utilizing semantic spaces are based on the idea that the way the words interact in a text is as important as the words themselves. The construction of a semantic space is based on a co-occurrence matrix where distance between terms or their presence together in a text window is reported. If the users are represented with the semantic space of their written text instead of bag-of-words vectors as is currently done, those subtleties are going to be determinant in the computation of the similarity between the users.

Figure 20.6 illustrates how matrix representations highlight some nuances that bag-of-words approaches do not. This virtual example is based on user A talking positively about Washington and the United States and negatively about President Obama, and user B talking positively about Obama and the United States but negatively about Washington. The bag-of-words representation leads to two very similar profiles, whereas the matrix representation highlights the differences that can be seen between the users, especially about Obama.

Semantic spaces can also be a reduced representation of this matrix. Many mathematical reduction approaches exist. Nonnegative matrix factorization (NMF) has the advantage of offering a reduction with only positive factors, which can then be interpreted (Lee and Seung 1999). In this case the reduced representation could correspond to the topics the users agree on and the topics they disagree on if opinion words can be identified.

One of the advantages of semantic spaces is that they provide a distance score that can be easily combined with other sources of evidence to match people. These sources of evidence include network density and structured information such as groups and locations. In a further perspective, semantic spaces could also be constructed around

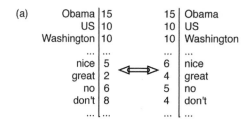

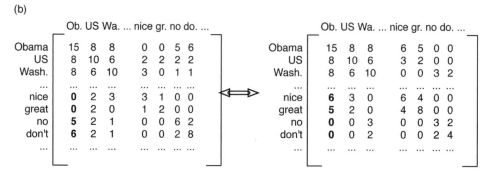

Figure 20.6
Bag-of-words (*a*) versus matrix (*b*) representations.

a specific topic to provide the users' rating, but this is not what we want to do here. We are only interested in matching people with similar opinions on similar topics.

Comparing Semantic Profiles

While comparisons of texts by topic have been thoroughly studied in information retrieval, and many approaches have been proposed based on keyword comparison, the issue of how to compare opinions on a topic is more complex. In particular, being interested in a topic (e.g., reading about it) does not necessarily mean similarity with other users interested in that same topic; opinions may in fact diverge.

Figures 20.7 through 20.9 illustrate the example of a user A being successively compared with three other users B, C, and D, according to a profile based on comments A, B, C, and D made on common news stories. The first story is about a dingo killing cattle in a village. The second story is about a participant in a cooking show. The third story is about yet another highway accident. User B disagrees with A on the first story, agrees with A on the second story, and agrees with A on the third story. User C agrees with A on the first story, disagrees with A on the second story, and agrees with A on the third story. User D agrees with A on the first story but does not express an opinion about the second and third stories. The disagreement on the first story what do you expect they have to eat, if you want to protect your animals all you have to do is put up an electric fence around the paddock you want to protect. Once the Dingo has been zapped i'll bet they wont return to get another jolt of electricity. "I know" that's how we keep our 4 beautiful Dingoes in, and others OU

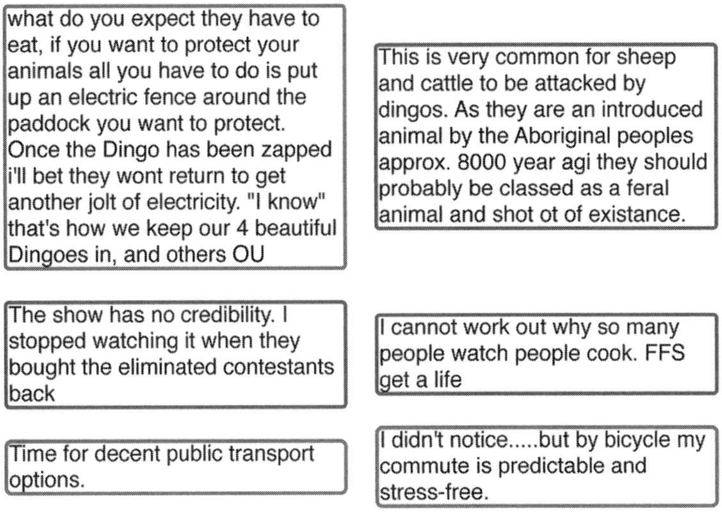

This is very common for sheep and cattle to be attacked by dingos. As they are an introduced animal by the Aboriginal peoples approx. 8000 year agi they should probably be classed as a feral animal and shot ot of existance.

The show has no credibility. I stopped watching it when they bought the eliminated contestants back

I cannot work out why so many people watch people cook. FFS get a life

Time for decent public transport options.

I didn't notice.....but by bicycle my commute is predictable and stress-free.

Figure 20.7
Opinions of user A vs. opinions of user B on a set of three articles.

what do you expect they have to eat, if you want to protect your animals all you have to do is put up an electric fence around the paddock you want to protect. Once the Dingo has been zapped i'll bet they wont return to get another jolt of electricity. "I know" that's how we keep our 4 beautiful Dingoes in, and others OU

What is the danger. If the dingoes are behind a 2m high fence, how will they get at children. If people are so worried about willd life they should think twice before they go to live near the bush. They can always build a big fence between them and the dingoes, or stay in town and have to put up with neighbours dogs.

The show has no credibility. I stopped watching it when they bought the eliminated contestants back

Good luck to each contestant! It has been great watching from the beginning, how they have excelled in each episode. I know I have enjoyed learning more about food & presentation. I hope they go forward in the future!

Time for decent public transport options.

I didn't notice.....but by bicycle my commute is predictable and stress-free.

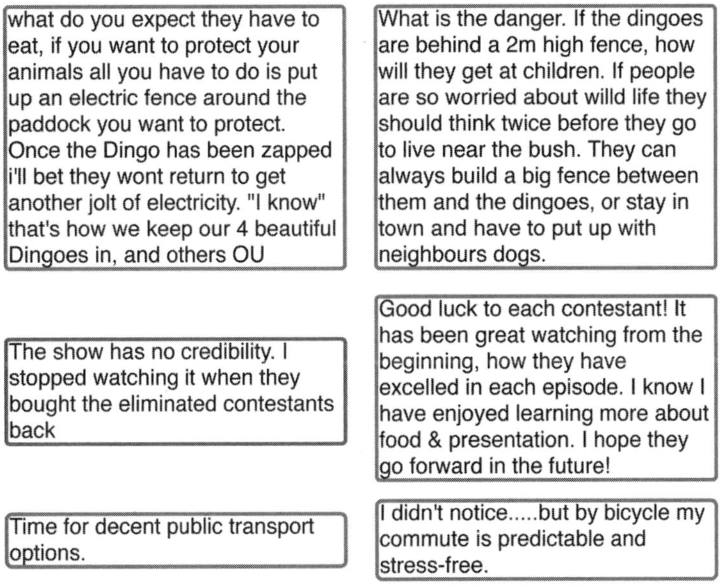

Figure 20.8
Opinions of user A vs. opinions of user C on a set of three articles.

what do you expect they have to eat, if you want to protect your animals all you have to do is put up an electric fence around the paddock you want to protect. Once the Dingo has been zapped i'll bet they wont return to get another jolt of electricity. "I know" that's how we keep our 4 beautiful Dingoes in, and others OU

What is the danger. If the dingoes are behind a 2m high fence, how will they get at children. If people are so worried about willd life they should think twice before they go to live near the bush. They can always build a big fence between them and the dingoes, or stay in town and have to put up with neighbours dogs.

The show has no credibility. I stopped watching it when they bought the eliminated contestants back

Time for decent public transport options.

Figure 20.9
Opinions of user A vs. opinions of user D on a set of three articles.

centers around whether dingoes should be protected or killed, whereas the differences of opinion on the second story have to do with enjoying a TV show or considering it stupid.

It is not obvious from this example which of users B, C, and D is "closest" to user A. This section presents the challenges to be solved through collaboration among researchers from various disciplines in order to establish the best means of comparing users as a basis for establishing meaningful communities.

A first pilot study should survey users and try to understand the criteria they use for comparing people based on a snapshot of their opinions. In particular, we need to better understand how much of a role disagreement actually plays. The other necessary topic for investigation is whether user A would better match someone who has the same opinions on all shared topics of interest but has fewer shared interests (such as user D) than someone who shares more interests but disagrees more (such as users B and C).

Measure

A standard way to compare matrices would be to compute an average of Euclidean distances or cosine similarities between all the columns and raw vectors. By doing this with the semantic space embedding opinions, there is a fair risk of smoothing all comparisons and ending up with all users being mostly similar. Methods inspired from

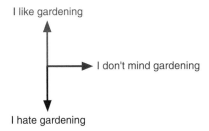

Figure 20.10
The third polarity in opinion expression: Proposition 1.

face recognition such as linear discriminant analysis and other techniques (Chunyan, Savvides, and Kumar 2006) can also be considered.

Subspace distances have been successfully used for comparing semantic spaces in document retrieval tasks (Zuccon, Azzopardi, and Van Rijsbergen 2009). The main intuition behind the subspace distance is that the meaning of a set of documents is decomposed into several subsets. The subspace distance offers the ability to compare sets of documents including coherent subsets. This translates into user representations by considering the subsets to be the different topics about which the users are expressing opinions.

Polarities and Similarities

Although opinions held about a topic can be regarded as a special case of context, they actually pose a new problem in terms of comparison. Indeed, because many contexts tend to be only more or less distant from one another, opinions can be opposite or independent (distant) from each other. In that sense, the polarities expressed via sentiments disrupt the way similarity is usually dealt with. The use of negative values is not allowed in classical models of information retrieval (such as the vector space model or probabilistic models).

A disturbing question with polarities pertains to the representation of the neutral position when comparisons between opposites are being made. Figure 20.10 shows an intuitive space representation of three opinions—positive, negative, and neutral. The positive and negative have to be represented on the same axis since they express some opposition. The neutral position has been represented here as orthogonal, but this is probably not its correct place since it is related to both the positive and negative positions. Thus it should stand somewhere in between on the same axis.

Another approach would involve adding a second dimension only for the polarity, as suggested in figure 20.11. The drawback to this representation is that then opposite opinions are orthogonal and would be considered at the same level as an unrelated topic. However, this approach counters the intuition that it might be worse to disagree

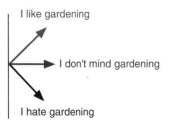

I like gardening

I don't mind gardening

I hate gardening

Figure 20.11
The third polarity in opinion expression: Proposition 2.

on some important topic than to be interested in different topics. The representation of polarities in a semantic space is still an open problem that is crucial to solve in order to take opinions into account in a comparison process.

Weighting Disagreement

Some topics are more sensitive than others when it comes to disagreement; differences of opinion can represent a wall between users, even creating hard feelings among friends. There is no easy known way to identify the topics on which agreement is most crucial. The approaches we envision to determine the importance of agreement on a topic are as follows:

• Identify topics where users express disagreement through analysis of forum discussions and comments.
• Rank the level of disagreement according to the volume of opposing comments and to the emotional vocabulary used (this implies a better knowledge of emotional terminology).
• Estimate the amount of disagreement around the topic across already-connected users in a network.

Another important consideration in weighting disagreement is temporality. The weighting should take into account the evolution of the user's opinions (because people can evolve) as well as the importance of the disagreement at a certain time; some contentious subjects may not be as debatable after new facts come into play.

Conclusion

Although the literature from the social sciences suggests that social commonalities are important to the success of a community, it is difficult to measure such commonalities. In this chapter we have identified opinions on topics as one example of critical social commonalities that can be extracted from free text information provided by a user, which then allows for the construction of a user profile without additional effort being required from this user. The potential for creating comprehensive semantic profiles based on such user data implies and ensures that privacy zones are only part of an interoperable generated profile of interests but not displayed to other users.

We also offer a framework for representing a user's interests in the context of their opinions about each of these interests. This framework uses a matrix representation of a user that is a semantic space where the dimensions are the terms employed by the user. Although this framework efficiently maintains the contextual information about the interests, its use for measuring a link between two users relies on a better understanding of the social processes acceptable for comparing people and their opinions. Subspace distances can be used to measure the distance between two semantic spaces, but it remains unclear what should be considered similar and what should be considered distant in an environment where opinions can be identical, unrelated, or opposite, and where some topics may be more important than others.

Finally, we have established a roadmap for research on both profile standards and semantic space. Addressing the challenges in both areas will provide greater understanding of social commonalities—knowledge that in turn can provide a path toward empowering urban communities.

References

Adomavicius, G., and A. Tuzhilin. 2005. Toward the next generation of recommender systems: A survey of the state-of-the-art and possible extensions. *IEEE Transactions on Knowledge and Data Engineering* 17 (6): 734–749.

Brooke, J., and M. Hurst. 2009. Patterns in the stream: Exploring the interaction of polarity, topic and discourse in a large opinion corpus. In *Proceedings of the First International CIKM Workshop on Topic-Sentiment Analysis for Mass Opinion Measurement*, Hong Kong, 1–8. New York: ACM.

Chen, J., W. Geyer, C. Dugan, M. Muller, and I. Guy. 2009. "Make new friends, but keep the old"—recommending people on social networking sites. In *Proceeding of CHI 2009*, Boston, 201–210. New York: ACM.

Chunyan, X., M. Savvides, and B. Kumar. 2006. Comparison of feature space methods for face recognition. In *Proceedings of Computer Vision and Pattern Recognition Workshop*, Carnegie Mellon University, 46. IEEE.

DiMicicco, J., and D. Milen. 2007. Identity management: Multiple presentations of self in Facebook. In *Proceedings of the 2007 International ACM Conference on Supporting Group Work*, Florida, 383–386. New York: ACM.

Iriberri, A., and G. Leroy. 2009. A life-cycle perspective on online community success. *ACM Computing Surveys* 41 (2): 1–29.

Jung, J. J., and J. Euzenat. 2007. Towards semantic social networks. In *Proceedings of the European Semantic Web Conference*, Innsbruck, Austria, 267–280. Berlin: Springer Verlag.

Koh, J., Y.-G. Kim, B. Butler, and G.-W. Bock. 2007. Encouraging participation in virtual communities. *Communications of the ACM* 50 (2): 68–73.

Landauer, T., and S. T. Dumais. 1997. A solution to Plato's problem: The latent semantic analysis theory of acquisition induction and representation of knowledge. *Psychological Review* 104 (2): 211–240.

Laverack, G. 2006. Improving health outcomes through community empowerment: A review of the literature. *Journal of Health, Population, and Nutrition* 24 (1): 113–133.

Lee, D. D., and H. S. Seung. 1999. Learning the parts of objects by non-negative matrix factorization. *Nature* 401:788–791.

Liben-Nowell, D., and J. Kleinberg. 2007. The link prediction problem for social networks. *Journal of the American Society for Information Science and Technology* 58 (7): 1019–1031.

Maciel, C., L. Roque, and A. C. B. Garcia. 2009. Democratic citizenship community: A social network to promote e-deliberative process. In *Proceedings of the 10th International Digital Government Research Conference*, Puebla, Mexico, 25–34. Digital Government Society of North America.

Mei, Q., X. Ling, M. Wondra, H. Su, and C. Zhai. 2007. Topic sentiment mixture: Modeling facets and opinions in weblogs. In *Proceedings of the Word Wide Web Conference, Banff, Alberta, Canada*, 171–180. New York: The Association for Computing Machinery.

Montaner, M., B. López , and J. L. De La Rosa. 2003. A taxonomy of recommender agents on the Internet. *Artificial Intelligence Review* 19:285–330.

Pang, B., and L. Lee. 2008. Opinion mining and sentiment analysis. *Foundations and Trends in Information Retrieval* 2 (1–2): 1–135.

Puddifoot, J. E. 1995. Dimensions of community identity. *Journal of Community & Applied Social Psychology* 5:357–370.

Salton, G., A. Wing, and C. S. Yang. 1975. A vector space model for automatic indexing. *Communications of the ACM* 18 (11): 613–620.

Wiebe, J., E. Breck, C. Buckley, C. Cardie, P. Davis, B. Fraser, D. Litman, et al. 2003. Recognizing and organizing opinions expressed in the world press. In *Working Notes—New Directions in Question Answering*, AAAI Spring Symposium Series, Stanford University, 12–19. Palo Alto, CA: Stanford University.

Zuccon, G., L. A. Azzopardi, and C. van Rijsbergen. 2009. Semantic spaces: Measuring the distance between different subspaces. In *Proceedings of the 3rd International Symposium on Quantum Interaction*, Saarbrucken, Germany, 225–236. Berlin: Springer Verlag.

V Design Engagement

Foreword

Mark Blythe

Sitting on the Train with Our Backs to the Engine

In *The Napoleon of Notting Hill,* G. K. Chesterton imagines a future where political leaders are chosen not by election but by lottery. This might seem like an attractive idea at a time when voting means choosing between the lesser of two (or two and a half) evils. Current frustration with two-party systems of democracy is such that it was recently neatly parodied in the cartoon *South Park*: the eighth graders are forced to choose for their school mascot either "a giant douche" or "a turd sandwich." When Stan refuses to vote for either he is berated for failing to take part in the democratic process. For Chesterton a national lottery where the winner was crowned king was already preferable to the politics of his time. But he also knew that the prediction that it would one day come to pass was probably wrong. He described a game that humanity likes to play called "cheat the prophet." Here everyone listens very attentively and respectfully to what the clever people have to say about what is going to happen, and then they promptly go away and do something entirely different. For Chesterton the game gets harder to play in the twentieth century when there are so many prophets and prophesies that sooner or later one of them is bound to be right. He describes the twentieth-century prophets' method as Noticing something that is certainly happening in their own time and then imagining that it is going to happen much more in the future (Chesterton 1904). Another great writer of science fiction, C. S. Lewis (2000), likened the process to sitting on a train with your back to the engine and trying to guess what you are going to see based only on what has already flashed by. Sometimes there are clues: this mountain range will not be passed for quite a long while. But sometimes there is no warning at all: the hills and trees suddenly become a rocky coastline and a sea roaring by. Each of the following chapters is concerned with the future of designing for engagement, and there are good guesses on what is to come in each of them.

Our guesses about the future are not only informed by what is happening now but to whom it is happening. We are much more likely to notice the things that are happening to us as we use our iPads than what is happening to the Chinese workers who make them in conditions where suicide seems like a career move (Wagner 2010). Over a decade ago, Alan Cooper (1999) noted the tendency of computer programmers to design machines for people who are either like them or the person sitting next to them. He pointed out that the number of people in the world who think like computer programmers is surprisingly small and suggested the use of personas to give a broader idea of the user. Personas—though successful—were in turn criticized as being two dimensional and stereotypical, and a range of additional approaches were developed in studies of human–computer interaction. Alan Newell et al. (2006) employed actors who got to know older people so that they could play them in design workshop improvisations. Ann Light developed theatrical personas through the use of props (Light et al. 2009) and Lene Nielsen worked with professional writers to create more compelling characterizations. Pastiche has also been used to create personas and situations of use; scenarios for new surveillance technologies look very different in idylls such as the English villages of Miss Marple and in the dystopian nightmares of Burgess's *Clockwork Orange* or Orwell's *1984* (Blythe, Wright, and Monk 2004). In chapter 24, Marcus Foth et al. present the use of dramatic personas to inform the development of residential apartment designs. During design workshops with residents, researchers make character notes; these are then turned into pastiches of Elias Canetti's short stories to produce three-dimensional characters. When considering civic engagement it is easy to forget that societies are made up of people with very different and competing priorities. Such methods keep individuals in sight as we look at crowds.

In chapter 23, Laura Forlano imagines what an open-source city might look like as she describes a series of design interventions from a project aptly titled *Breakout!* Perhaps the most striking illustration of the city as a workplace is in the description of a workshop organized for a conference in Japan. Douglas Adams once remarked that no language has ever developed the phrase "as beautiful as an airport" and the same is true of conference centers. Rather than sit in their conference center and discuss notions of wireless work, the participants were taken out into the city in order to carry out a "flash mob ethnography." An interdisciplinary group of computer scientists, interaction designers, and social scientists visits a shop. They take photos and notes and are scolded by the staff. For the moment the shop is their workplace. In another intervention a line of chalk is drawn on the pavement to divide the city from a temporary office. As an ethnographer Forlano makes ingenious use of Twitter to share field notes with her colleagues. Such experiments blur the boundaries of work and public spaces, which is perhaps an extension of the notion of a flat rather than a hierarchical organization. The boss is no longer the boss but also your Facebook friend. The café is no longer just the café but also your hot desk. Public space becomes, at least potentially, corporate space. Here then is the disturbing possibility of a new enclosure of common land, a digital enclosure of physical space.

In chapter 21, Michael Arnold presents a concept design that attempts to resist utilitarian and mercantile notions of civic engagement. The work is part of a long history of public installations that attempt to connect different publics across the world. He points out that over thirty years ago the *Hole in Space* first provided a video link between a center for performing arts in New York and a department store in Los Angeles. When people first saw this technology they waved at one another, blew kisses and tried to start up conversations. Later the *Hole in the Earth* linked the Netherlands and Indonesia through screens in the pavement that passersby peered down to wave at distant strangers. In 2008 the "Telectroscope" was presented to the city of London as a marvel of Victorian engineering using mirrors and a tunnel under the Atlantic to link the capital of Great Britain to New York. This time people queued up and paid to wave, blow kisses, and try and start up conversations. If Michael Arnold gets his way (and some funding), there will be a similar portal linking a Greek precinct of Melbourne to its sister city of Thessaloniki. What people will do with the portal is to be left deliberately open. Perhaps there will be waving, kissing, and attempts at conversation, but there may also be a further awareness of the extent to which we are all now part of a global public.

A global perspective is precisely what informs Carl DiSalvo and Jonathan Lukens's concern with the nonhuman in design in chapter 22. The way that we study our relationship with technology has shifted dramatically over the last sixty years. The earliest uses for studies of people using machines were military. The focus was later expanded toward making workplaces more efficient. In Scandinavia, traditions of participatory design were explicitly political: when new technologies were developed for workplaces, it was a point of principle that trade unions should be involved. In American traditions of user-centered design the focus was on the individual users of the new technology rather than the class of people affected by it. This focus on the individual over the group was maintained as the home became a site of inquiry. In recent years there have been increasingly urgent calls for a wider focus. Here DiSalvo and Lukens build on Actor Network Theory (ANT) to consider nonhuman actors in sociotechnical systems. They point out that an ANT of fishing would consider the scallops being fished as well as the fisherman pulling them out of the sea. It is becoming increasingly clear that the environmental impact of our sociotechnical systems must be of greater concern than user experience, which necessitates a radical shift of priorities. DiSalvo and Lukens advocate nonanthropocentric systems that decenter the human in the design process; to illustrate they describe a study where participants were given sensors to measure noise in the city. The participants saw the city divorced form their affective and experiential sense of it—the sound of a bus going up a hill was no louder than the sound of children playing. For DiSalvo and Lukens such work challenges the boundary between agency and identity and between environment and actor.

In the twenty-first century it has become more important than ever to understand how the activities of the current generations are going to affect the next. Playing Chesterton's "guess the future game" is increasingly a matter of survival. For the philosopher Slavoj Zizek (2010, x), we are currently living through the end times: "The global capitalist system is approaching an apocalyptic zero point. Its 'four riders of the apocalypse' are comprised by the ecological crisis, the consequences of the biogenetic revolution, imbalances within the system itself (problems with intellectual property; forthcoming struggles over raw materials, food and water) and the explosive growth of social divisions and exclusions."

We are reaching material limits in terms of the extent to which it is possible to exploit natural resources and maintain the social and political relations of previous ages. But this is not necessarily a cause for dismay. Zizek (2010, x) claims that our "social consciousness" is currently going through the five stages of grief articulated in popular psychology: denial, anger, bargaining, depression, and finally acceptance. When we have accepted the traumatic truth we will no longer see the situation as a threat but the chance of a new beginning. Now more than ever it is necessary to have a global conception of civic engagement. Perhaps sometime soon there will be an iPad application that provides a portal to the factory in China where it was made. Perhaps we will wave, blow kisses, or join them in their struggle against the forces of Apple. Perhaps trauma and despair will provide the opportunity for the kinds of new beginning that Zizek imagines. However, nothing is flashing by in our current landscape to suggest this, but we are after all traveling with our back to the engine.

References

Blythe, M. A., P. C. Wright, and A. F. Monk. 2004. Little brother: Could and should wearable computing technologies be applied to reducing older people's fear of crime. *Springer Journal of Personal and Ubiquitous Computing* 8 (6): 402–415.

Chesterton, G. K. 1904. *The Napoleon of Notting Hill*. Salt Lake City, UT: Project Gutenberg Press.

Cooper, A. L. 1999. *The Inmates Are Running the Asylum: Why High-Tech Products Drive Us Crazy and How to Restore the Sanity*. Indianapolis: Sams.

Lewis, C. S. 2000. *Essay Collection and Other Short Pieces*. London: HarperCollins.

Light, A., G. Simpson, L. Weaver, and P. G. Healey. 2009. Geezers, turbines, fantasy personas: Making the everyday into the future. Paper presented at the Conference on Creativity and Cognition, Berkeley, CA, October 26–30, 39–48. New York: ACM.

Newell, A. F., M. E. Morgan, P. Gregor, and A. Carmichael. 2006. Theatre as an intermediary between users and CHI designers. In *CHI '06,*extended abstracts on Human Factors in Computing Systems, 111–117. New York: ACM.

Wagner, W. 2010. iPad factory in the firing line: Worker suicides have electronics maker uneasy in China. *Spiegel Online*, July 29. http://www.spiegel.de/international/business/0,1518,697296,00 .html.

Zizek, S. 2010. *Living in the End Times*. London: Verso.

21   A Streetscape Portal

Michael Arnold

In this chapter I describe a proposal to place relatively simple communication technologies in public places, to create an "always-on," real-time visual and aural connection through which individuals and the publics of each place may communicate, play, and perform with one another and for one another, in whatever ways emerge, for indeterminate purposes.

Rather than carrying art, entertainment products, news, advertising, or private communications as such, and rather than implementing networked mobility or new modes of personalization, the project seeks to enliven public space, draw attention to place in a global context, and provide spectacle to create publics in public places through communicating the improvised social interactions of people in the same place to another place.

After describing the concept and its three suggested modes of operation, the chapter discusses the project's underlying concerns with forms of spontaneous sociality, the construction of a public present to itself, the significance of public space and of play and performance in the public sphere, and the importance of seeing "my place" and "your place" in the same context. The discussion concludes with a comparison of the proposed system to four others that in different ways share similar concerns—the Hole in Space and the Hole in Earth, Lozano-Hemmer's Body Movies, i3's Satellite, and the Telectroscope.

All of these projects share important concerns. They are all concerned with play, spontaneity, and improvisation as a means by which people might interact. They are all concerned with encouraging interaction among strangers. They are all concerned with creating a local spectacle and thus a local public. They are all concerned with public performances in public places that invigorate these public places. In these ways they all propose to use contemporary technologies to create displays in support of local community and urban life.

Background

Urban displays—whether statues of the good and the great, public art, decorative flower beds, flash mob performances, or contemporary public screens—have the capacity to gather individuals and construct a public; provoke interaction among strangers; bring people into relation with their past, with the moment, and with the future; and position people clearly in place. Whether these capacities are realized in any particular instance is of course another matter. Contemporary urban displays are either strictly commercial, such as advertising displayed alone, or hybrid creations, where advertising is interleaved with media products such as sports. Those who view these displays are constructed as consumers of material products, services, or cultural products. The observation that the urban environment is saturated with commercial imagery needs little elaboration. If not commercial, urban displays tend to be earnest, even to the point of being humorless, and provide for content that is self-consciously useful, worthy, historical, educative, or artistic. Monuments, for example, are an ancient form of community display, and almost every town in Australia boasts a bronze statue of a soldier standing atop a generally long list of the slain. Only three villages in England (the "Blessed Three") are without a World War I memorial. Other public displays go more to community status than community spirit, sometimes to the point of being pretentious—a new estate's baroque entrance gates, grandiose fountains, and the like. Educative displays are also popular and many communities have permanent displays of historical photographs or documents, local flora, fauna, geology, and other indigenous cultural material. Public artworks such as murals and sculptures have long been a popular way to provide a focal point for community identity and spirit, though the choice of particular works is invariably controversial because for some, public art is by definition a waste of public money, or more ironically, because the commissioning authority has erased anything that might be of interest in the art in a quest to avoid controversy.

In this chapter I argue that public displays to support community and urban life do not necessarily have to carry video art or artistic imagery, or historical content, public-interest information, community news, educational material, or other content that might be described as self-consciously worthy—much less commercial entertainment, sports, news, or advertising—but instead, might simply enable people to be in one another's presence, to engage with one another, to play with one another.

To provide an example of this, an installation is proposed that places large-format communication portals in public places, linking the people and the life of one place to the people and life of another.

Described in a sentence, a Streetscape Portal displays on the walls of lanes, an "always-on," real-time, one-to-one scale, visual and aural connection between one place and another through which individuals and the publics of each place may

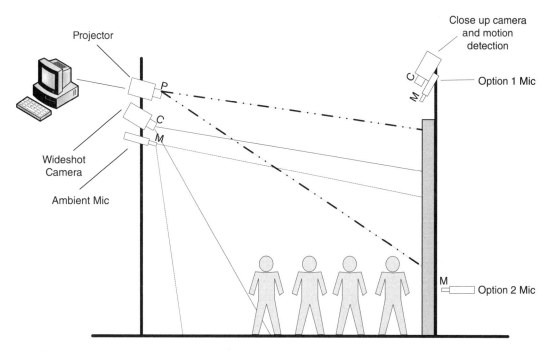

Figure 21.1

A portal. Illustration by Peter Benda.

observe, communicate, play, and perform with one another and for one another. To achieve this, the Streetscape Portal deploys daylight-capable projectors focused at street level on a prepared wall, motion-sensitive digital cameras capable of taking in either the streetscape or a closer focus on an individual, as well as speakers and microphones, all linked via broadband to a matching Streetscape Portal somewhere else in the world.

The project thus places a relatively simple communication system in public places, as an ambient aspect of the streetscape, and simply leaves it in public hands for whatever performance might arise. Rather than carrying entertainment product, advertising, sporting events, or news (as does the BBC's "Public Space Broadcasting" initiative, for example), and rather than carrying dispersed individuated and personal media content (as do mobile media in public places), the Streetscape Portals seek to redeploy what are now ubiquitous technologies to the public sphere, for whatever indeterminate purposes emerge, through use. In this sense the Streetscape Portal takes up the call to provide communication infrastructure for embodied action and bodily encounters between people (Dourish and Bell 2007), to be populated as the public sees fit.

The Streetscape Portal

The most significant potential of the portal is, in a sense, potentiality itself. That is, the portal is pretty much a media in search of a message, a tabula rasa, or contentless infrastructure, and its uses and its point of being are by no means fixed; they are emergent in use, and are thus not clearly defined (which may be why it has not yet attracted funding!). However, three modes of operation and the performances mediated by those modes are easy to describe, and from there it is not a great leap to a discussion of its implications for public space, the public sphere, and the construction of publics.

The three modes of the proposed sociotechnology—personal copresence, public copresence, and place in local and global terms—are as follows.

Interpersonal Copresence

Spontaneous and playful use of the portal at an individual level is triggered when a person happens to occupy a "hotspot" in, say, Melbourne, and a person also occupies a hotspot in, say, Tianjin. *Me*, a person who just happens to be standing in the hotspot in Melbourne, will see the image of *You*, a stranger from another Place, on the screen (or rather, the prepared wall). The situation is of course mirrored in Tianjin. The portal's motion-sensitive cameras recognize that the hotspots are occupied and then will focus a camera and microphone on the occupants. Hotspots may be marked, by say a one-meter-diameter brass ring inlaid into the surface of the footpath (reminiscent of Victorian-era time machines), or may be unmarked, to be stumbled upon.

You and *Me* may have been reading Sennett and might recognize that it is important to politely ignore one another, or alternatively, we may well wave to each other, blow a kiss, mirror-dance, make a rude gesture, or try to strike up a conversation. The sensation of communicating in real time with a complete stranger from another land, due only to happenstance, using body language, gesture, and voice, is a potentially powerful experience for the participants, and at the same time makes for engaging street theater for local observers in the lanes and streets of each place.

Half-whacked people may well emerge from city clubs, pubs, and bars and make their way to a portal for a bit of crude banter. Some people will go out of their way to be racially abusive, and "flashers" may well be attracted to the potential of exposing themselves to an international audience. The Fallon Gong in Melbourne will no doubt pose a challenge to authorities in Tianjin. Australian Socceroos supporters will no doubt challenge their counterparts in Milan and Thessaloniki. But such is the nature of a public sphere, and such is the nature of the public, and it is in our interest that risks are taken and these spheres exist and are accessible. While the ordinary law of the land constrains people's behavior on the street in the usual way, the portal itself offers no further constraint and resists the many myths about the inherent irrationality and antisociability of the "madding crowd" (Goffman 1963, 1971; Schweingruber and Wohlstein 2005).

The "blank screen" described thus far in the chapter, populated only by passersby, may or may not constitute a focal point powerful enough to seduce and hold our *neo-flâneurs* and convert them into personal communicants and public interlocutors. That is, it may not be enough to provide a camera, a microphone, and a screen to communicate *with*, without also providing something immediate and to hand to communicate *about*. To further stimulate communication it may thus be fun to augment the system. For example, *You* and *Me* might be provided with a "virtual balloon" sitting in the corner of the projected image. In Wii-like fashion we might use an arm motion to hit the virtual balloon into the air, and we might set about cooperating to keep it in the air. We have something between us to play with and to communicate about. Although the portals are not intended to present the works of interactive media artists, and indeed, the concept counterindicates this use, the portals are nevertheless consistent with the artistic project, which is to transfer subjective and intersubjective lifeworlds to the public domain. Inventive interactive game designers will no doubt come up with all sorts of hijinks when given large format live images, motion-sensitive cameras, Internet connections, computers, and fifty or more participants on each side of the world.

But my own view is that such fun and games may be a distraction from the simple presence of the Other. A significant feature of the Streetscape Portal is that it is not framed as an artwork or as a gaming environment. Rather, the intention is for it to become translucent—a portal that connects people and urban environments without calling attention to itself as something special. Ideally, the streetscape of one place takes its place seamlessly as part of the streetscape of another place. The two are melded together rather than each being framed as an exhibit for the other.

As knowledge of the portal becomes available, *You* and *Me* may also like to use it in strategic ways by making preplanned arrangements to catch up with friends or family. By meeting through the portal, tourists, backpackers, conference delegates, and businesspeople can "videoconference" with one another, transmitting both voice and image in real time.

And so the portal is intersubjective, but it is also public. While the communication between *You* and *Me* may be one-to-one and interpersonal, the *neo-flâneurs* and denizens of the lanes in each city will witness their fellow citizens in their successful or less successful attempts at communicating. We are watching people communicating, we are watching people watching people, and we are watching people watching people communicating. Personal copresence simultaneously creates copresent publics who are drawn to witnessing the live action, and at the same time the screen action. The portal's work in the simultaneous construction of multiple parallel publics, some here, some there, some watching the screen, and others watching the communicants, some of whom are here and some of whom are there, provides a potentially rich field for the exploration of the construction of a public, the multilevel reflexive nature of interaction, and the nature of public spectacle.

I am present to you through the portal, but I am also present to those who witness my presence to you, both here and there. Those who witness my presence to you here, also witness the presence of those who are witnessing your presence there. So individuals become community ambassadors of a sort, speaking for themselves, but in a sense also speaking for those observing, both here and there. Those who are here may of course intervene in the speaker's efforts at any time. Observers will bear witness to personal interaction, and may join in personal interaction, and this public witnessing of intimacy may well be in part heartwarming, in part amusing, but always interesting.

Public Copresence

If the hotspots are not occupied, or in parallel with the action on the hotspots, the portal presents a second mode of operation. In this second mode, the camera and microphones focus on a broader area of the street—say 10 to 15 meters in length. In this mode the portal takes in whole numbers of people as they go about their daily business, and displays this 10- to 15-meter streetscape on a prepared wall in another city on a one-to-one scale. The sights and sounds of daily life in the lane, in this place, in this community, are captured and communicated as life occurs within the focal area.

Our architecture and theirs, our streetscape and theirs, our time of day and theirs, our fashion and theirs, our faces and theirs, our pace of life and theirs, our sounds and colors and theirs, are each available to the other as it happens, where it happens, in situ. Our streetscape becomes part of theirs and theirs part of ours. The citizens of the streets and lanes in these different communities thus see themselves in numbers, in the context of urban life, and in the context provided by their counterparts from across the world. Global and local comparisons and contrasts become evident by glancing from the street to the wall. "There" is also "here." All the sights and sounds of street life generated by the many people who just happen to be passing through the portal at that time are captured and made available in real time, across the world. In the absence of framing, the sights and sounds of the Other are ambient—part of the urban furniture.

But used more strategically, groups of locals may choose to use the portal in planned ways. Organized groups of people may gather at the portal to celebrate sporting, cultural, or other performances; planned events by musicians, artists, interest groups, school groups, and what have you, may be narrowcast from one city's public places to another. The potential for organized political or religious interaction and intervention is also evident.

Place

The communication portals are "glocal"—an ugly but useful term in this context. The portals use Internet protocols to transmit video and sound from place to place around the globe and are in that sense global. But importantly they are also clearly local. In the context of globalism they speak of place (Blij 2008), and in the context of interconnection they speak of difference (Tuan 1995). Video and sound are not transmitted from anywhere to anywhere or everywhere, but from one carefully chosen point to another. As envisaged, the portals link a particular Place to another particular Place to operationalize the performance of historical, cultural, and community links between those places. For example, in my home town of Melbourne, Australia, one may well imagine such links being established between Lt. Bourke St. (Melbourne's "Chinatown") and a street in Melbourne's sister city, Tianjin, or between Lt. Lonsdale St. (a Greek precinct) and a street in Thessaloniki (also a sister city). Global links between this Place and that Place may thus reinforce that which is local about a Place, as the local and the exotic, the familiar and the strange, the material and the image, are all intertwined and invited to interact in one Place, in real time. But then again, the portal may also be deployed in quite different circumstances. In Belfast, for example, where a concrete wall separates Orange and Green precincts and materializes an intention that the communities not interact, the portal might be deployed. A portal that links long-standing enemies may do more harm than good if it provides a touchpoint for the expression of rage and violence. Yet over time it may also normalize the Other, as the Other's virtual presence becomes a mundane presence in daily life.

Perspective

To further reinforce a notion of place, the portal may pull back from close-ups and midrange shots of the here-and-now and take a wider, more distanced, "bird's-eye" perspective of the city, its communities, and its urban and historical surroundings. The portal may intermittently cut from the default mode where copresence at the personal and streetscape level is mediated, and direct to an "Archive" mode in which the life of this Place is recontextualized in space and time.

In Archive mode, prepared file images and sounds of the cities and its people are presented. These comprise combinations of panoramic images of the cities' urban landscapes, cartographic images of the cities, historical images of the cities, and prepared soundscapes and montages of the cities and their peoples. The *neo-flâneur* and the interlocutor are distanced from the immediate experience of life in the city by exposure to its history and geographic context; by crosscutting from one city to the other, comparison and contrast between the cities, between the communities that inhabit the cities, and between past and present are invited.

By shifting the focus in this way to a different scale in space, and to a different point in time, the life of the street becomes part of a larger phenomenon and is seen in the context of all of the city's streets, in the context of other cities, and in the context of history.

Place is important in our global networks even though the spaces between places are becoming less so. The global mobilization of communication systems, corporations, individuals, armies, communities, products, religions, diseases, foods, cultural commodities, pollutants, technologies, and values is an experience that is materialized and performed in daily life here, and there, and this other place, and over there as well. That is to say, globalism is an unevenly distributed network of relations that is local at every point. And it is the localization of the global (everything is potentially in every place as a local resource) and the globalization of the local (everything in every place is potentially a global resource) that energize globalization's promises and threats—the promise of mutually supportive synergies operationalized through interaction on a global scale. The threats posed by the contemporary imperial conquistadors—bent on maximizing the exploitation of people and places under frictionless conditions—remain.

Of course the portals are on the side of the natives, not the conquistadors, and the battle is not over.

Discussion

Public space has been granted a position at the center of civil society—literally so, in the case of the Agora (à la Arendt), the Athenian Pynx (à la Sennett), the coffeehouse (à la Habermas), or the town hall (à la Tocqueville), and figuratively so, in the case of the provision of communicative space for public information exchange, discourse, and contestation (Castells 1996). Through most of human history these public spaces have been more or less clearly marked in the urban environment. Architectural forms such as stone-paved town squares, grand train stations, market squares, meeting halls, the intersections of roads, village greens, amphitheaters, porticoes, the forecourts of churches, village wells, shaded benches, and local pubs defined a space as a public place, and mediated the activities that transpired in that place. In the context of this discussion, the most important activity mediated by the use of these places is the construction of publics present to one another, and the exchange of information, conversation, and debate among those publics. It provides a social and geographic space where such discourse might occur, and importantly, it provides a space in which a public might be known to itself as a public—as a collective that recognizes itself as sharing a common present and possible future. In his 1901 article "Making the Crowd Beautiful," American essayist Gerald Stanley Lee (1901) put forth a highly charged polemic in favor of progress, mechanization, and democracy, all of which is exhibited in the spirit of the "aestheticised crowd" (Raynsford 1996). The role of public space for these purposes has thus provided important infrastructure in the history of democratic action and in the development of the notion of a community and a civil society, and arguably, contemporary communication technologies also provide important contexts for the conduct of public life. In this context, interventions like the Streetscape Portal can make a further contribution to this important urban infrastructure. Quoting Star (1999), Dourish and Bell (2007) point to nine properties of public infrastructure, each of which is materialized in the portal. The portal is "embedded" in architectural and social arrangements of the street; its uses are transparent; its reach extends beyond a single site; its use is communal; it is linked to conventions of practice; it embodies standards; it is dependent on an installed base; it is visible in breakdown; and it is positioned incrementally.

The decline of public infrastructure, public space, and the public sphere is often noted, and important characteristics of our current social condition are said to be attributable to its fragmentation and fall (Sennett 1974; Putman 1995; Bauman 2000; Graham and Marvin 2001; Mitchell 2003). In the twentieth century, the rising power of the state posed a threat to the notion of the individual, yet in the twenty-first century, the rising power of individualism and privatization has posed a threat to the public (Archer 1997; Sheller and Urry 2003). Certainly, in the last fifty years and more, public space (and public service, public duty, the public sector, public interest, public opinion, etc.) have come under sustained attack from both the left and the right on grounds of legitimacy, relevance, and efficiency (Kumar 1992). The Habermasian notion of the public sphere continues to be assaulted not only on these grounds, but also by new technologies—through the erasure of clear boundaries between public and private domains and by the interbreeding of the private and the public evident in the ambiguous position of mobile phones, shopping malls, webcams, social networking systems, or talk shows. The public invasion of private space (TV, radio, and Internet in the lounge room), and the private colonization of public space (privatization in all its forms), now frame activity that is at once commercial, and social, and private, and public, and personal, and political—such is the ambiguous, shifting field on which we play out our relations with the current lifeworld.

Is Facebook a public or private space? When I am alone in my car, am I in private? Is our water or electricity a public or private asset? When I use my mobile to make a call on the street, is that a private act or a public act? When I watch TV in my lounge room, am I alone, or are we alone together? When I listen to my iPod on the train, am I in a private place?

Contemporary media and geographic spaces that allow for the promiscuous intermingling of that which was public and that which was private have an effect not just on public space and the public sphere, but also on the notion of the public present to itself as a collective. That is, these new hybrid spaces have the active and conscious effect of dispersing the crowd and dissolving the manifestation of a public sphere (Smithsimon 2008). Of course, people are often present together in large numbers—at the shopping mall, on the streets, on the Internet, on the phone, in front of the TV—but we are copresent individuals, not present to ourselves and to others as a public, as a collective—as was "the polis" revered by historians of democracy, or as was "the mob" feared by the privileged—first present to itself, and then to its enemies. The polis and the mob is each conscious of its collective character, a consciousness not present in the shopping mall or in front of a television show.

There is a lack of clarity about the public interest and individual interests (in the political domain), public assets and private property (in the economic domain), and public duty and private subjectivities (in the ideological domain). This has a centrifugal effect on publics like communities, which might now be better regarded as an aggregate of individuals with coinciding subjectivities, rather than a collective with a distinct ontology and ongoing solidarity.

The Streetscape Portal seeks to address some of these concerns. It presents itself and it performs as public infrastructure, not as a private asset. It gathers up a self-defined public at either end of the portal that is present to itself as a public through collocation and interaction. It does not impose a particular performance or purpose and its use is an emergent property of its publics. It is ambient, and thus normalizes public interaction rather than rarefying it as an art installation or spectacle. It exposes interactions to public scrutiny, mores, and etiquette, either in the breech or in the abeyance, and thus takes a step back from the "tyranny of intimacy." It presents one public and its place in the context of another public and their place. Like the *flâneur* of Benjamin's *Arcades Project* (1999), the *neo-flâneurs* gathering at the portal are invited to make meaning from the presence of publics in public places and of the cultural and social insights thereby made legible.

Public space for action in the public sphere is difficult to identify in contemporary society, and the publics (as opposed to the individuals) that might inhabit such public spaces are equally difficult to identify.

Other Examples

While public space in the towns and cities was once demarcated only in bricks and mortar, the contemporary city also marks its public spaces electronically (McQuire 2006). For example, the BBC's "Public Space Broadcasting" initiative has installed large screens in city squares across five cities with a further fifteen planned over the next five years; the primary aim is to screen BBC news, information, and sporting events, and to screen alternative content such as experimental film and video (McQuire, Papastergiadis, and Cubitt 2008). McQuire, Papastergiadis, and Cubitt have also identified new public-screen initiatives in Berlin, Amsterdam, Melbourne, and Seoul, and the public screens of Times Square, Tokyo, Hong Kong, and other cities are well known. Contemporary public spaces are thus marked as such by electronic "monuments" on both a grand scale (Piccadilly Circus) and a small scale (almost any bus stop). Public places—grand and humble—now display advertising, sporting events, performance art, and news bulletins. These electronic spectacles are integral to the definition, function, and ambience of public spaces.

A key difference between these screens and the Streetscape Portal is that the latter is not framed as spectacle and does not interpolate the *neo-flâneur* as audience. The screens that help define contemporary cities are gigantic and elevated, literally and figuratively standing above their public. The intention is to use size, position, and spectacular content to overwhelm. In contrast, the Streetscape Portal is life-sized, is not elevated, is not framed in any way, and is meant to recede and take its place as part of the life of the street rather than dominating the street.

In addition to being marked out by these media of spectacle, display, and dissemination, public spaces are also marked out by electronic media that surveil and police the publics that gather in these spaces, neatly closing the loop on the public that is both the source and the target of information flows. The London "Ring of Steel" is the premier example of an ambiguous public-private city center defined by a wall of electronic surveillance, an initiative since taken up by Manhattan and no doubt by other cities, and reproduced on smaller scales in "gated communities" all over the world.

By positioning electronic displays within public spaces, and positioning surveillance cordons within and around the perimeters, electronic media have provided definition and focus to the space, and help create the publics that inhabit those spaces in large numbers for routine sociocommercial activity. Electronic media also provide a compelling reason to come to a public space on special occasions, and anyone who has watched a major international sporting event on a public screen rather than at home can attest to the vibrancy of the experience.

The portal described here gestures to these issues, albeit in small ways. The portal confuses the logic of virtual reality and virtual environments, which typically represent physical objects and geographic topographies within digital spaces by presenting digital representations within physical spaces (Dourish and Bell 2007). The portal suggests that personal copresence, public copresence, the construction of a public present to itself and of publics present to one another, the emphasis on place, and links between place, and the communication of all of this across the world, can contribute to the public sphere and to public life in the city.

To the best of my knowledge no Streetscape Portals are in existence, and indeed, this fact in itself attests to the challenges of engaging urban media as public infrastructure. However, these same themes of emergent cooperative action among the publics of public spaces also run strongly through other work, which, crucially I think, is understood as "art." A sample of this work is discussed below.[1]

Figure 21.2
Kit Galloway and Sherrie Rabinowitz, "Hole in Space," 1980. http://www.medienkunstnetz.de/works/hole-in-space/.

"Hole in Space" and "Hole in the Earth"

One of the earliest examples of a "Streetscape Portal" was the Hole in Space project, created and produced by Kit Galloway and Sherrie Rabinowitz in 1980. For three days the Hole in Space linked the Lincoln Center for the Performing Arts in New York City and a department store located in Los Angeles. In Elaine Ho's description, people "tell jokes, sing songs, and begin chatting-up strangers ('Where you goin' baby?' 'I'm right here with you!'). The sculpture gives form to a social space that is at once displaced and intimate. People are enthusiastic to make contact with others in a much more uninhibited manner than could be found in the normal urban environs of New York or LA. They wave and scream into the camera, and the protective layer shielding city dwellers dissolves into an unabashed fascination with the other" (see http://catalogue.montevideo.nl/art_play.php?id=931).

Designed and built by Maki Ueda in 2004, the "Hole in the Earth" was a similar installation that was to link Rotterdam, in the Netherlands, with Bandung, in Indonesia, using small screens, cameras, and microphones set into the pavement.

Body Movies

Rafael Lozano-Hemmer's "Body Movies" is a performance art installation where members of the public are the performers and the installation consists of a very large prepared wall in a public place, very bright spotlights, and a series of projected images of local people. As he originally envisaged the installation, the projected portraits would be washed out by the bright spotlights until revealed by the shadows of passersby. The performance of the public was thus thought to be concerned with the

Figure 21.3
"Hole in the Earth." Images courtesy of Maki Ueda, obtained from http://www.ueda.nl/earth/index.html.

Figure 21.4
Lozano-Hemmer's "Body Movies." Image courtesy of Karine Charbonneau.

revelation of the portraits. But the more interesting aspect of the installation in action had little to do with revealing portraits and a lot to do with spontaneous and cooperative shadow play the public engaged in among themselves. The shadows cast by the spotlights varied in size from 2 to 30 meters—depending on the person's distance from the wall—and up to fifty or so people were able to play with their shadows collectively and individually.

Shadow-puppet "giants" play with shadow-puppet "dolls," shadow animals chase one another, and so on. People in public places, who may well be strangers to one another, are relating to one another in ways that are both playful and considered; people are aware of themselves as a plurality, as well as of their embodied individuality.

The claim for public good that is implicit in the portal project, and I think in Lozano-Hemmer's work, is in part a response to a symmetrical set of social harms associated with the parlous state of public space and public infrastructure for people to be present to one another as subjects and as a public. Playing together in public places, through infrastructure such as that described, is one way of doing this.

The Satellite

A third example is a concept that arose at the "i3 Summer School 2001" at the Interactive Institute in Ivrea, Italy, where designing new interactive technologies for communities was the core theme (Battarbee et al. 2002). One such technology was the "Satellite," a concept for a communication system with two input-output devices that look like large soccer balls. Each is placed in a different part of the city, whereupon

Figure 21.5
A sketch of the Satellite. Image courtesy of Katja Battarbee, reproduced from Battarbee et al. 2002, p.242.

Figure 21.6
The London end of the Telectroscope. Photographed by the author.

one communicates sound from its location to the other, which reciprocally communicates vision from that place back to the first. One node of the system can thus hear but not see, and the other can see but not hear.

The Satellite concept deliberately intervenes in communication modalities to create an asymmetry and thus awaken curiosity. Body Movies is also interventionist in its dramatic construction of shadows.

The Telectroscope

The Telectroscope is a portal that was installed between London's South Bank and Brooklyn, New York, and was in use from late May to early June 2008. The installation was designed by the artist Paul St George and was sponsored by Tiscali, a British telecommunications company. The conceptual and physical "framing" of the Telectroscope is very appealing. The story is told of St George's inheritance of a long-forgotten tunnel that was dug under the Atlantic by his great-grandfather, Alexander Stanhope St George, inventor of the Telectroscope. Through the placement of mirrors throughout the tunnel Alexander enabled the people of New York and the people of London to see and hear one another, predating teleconferencing by more than a century. The story is reinforced by the physical framing of the portal—a well-constructed Jules Verne–like device that marks the tunnel mouth and frames the screens physically and as a narrative.

People were charged one pound to use "the tunnel" for a minute or so and waited in the queue for over an hour to do so. According to the attendant this is typical, and many people did not doubt the truth of the "tunnel under the Atlantic" story. Their use of the tunnel was as anticipated for "Me and You" interaction—people wave to each other, blow a kiss, mirror-dance, make rude gestures, and try to strike up a conversation.

My own attitude to framing the performance of the system in this elaborate way is ambivalent. The tunnel story is very appealing, and the fact that many people are prepared to believe it attests to its appeal. The physical construction is artful and suits the story very well. On the other hand, the fact that the action is framed at all removes it from the streetscape and contextualizes it as something different—in this case, a commercial, retro-sci-fi entertainment. (Many sculptors have a similarly antagonistic attitude to the plinth—a structure that frames the sculpture and thus decontextualizes it and marks it as alien.) Rather than allowing "there" to be a part of "here," the Telectroscope's elaborate framing removes and separates the action from the street and deliberately contextualizes it as unordinary. To hear the story of this mighty Victorian-era feat of engineering and derring-do, to see the magnificent brass-and-iron tunnel mouth, to queue for the system, to pay to use the system, to be positioned in front of the frame for a defined period—all this contextualizes the experience as a self-conscious entertainment rather than a part of daily life on the street.

The portal described at the outset of the chapter is much less interventionist in that, for the most part, it simply transmits sound and vision in a straightforward way, projected against a wall as part of the streetscape. This minimalist approach seeks to hide the technological component of the sociotechnical to focus on the social interaction facilitated by unadorned image and sound, whereas Body Movies, the Satellite, and the Telectroscope all draw attention to the sociotechnical machinery and associated performance as an artistic or entertainment artifact. Clearly, though, all four concepts share important concerns. They are all concerned with play, spontaneity, and improvisation as a means by which people might interact. They are all concerned to encourage interaction among strangers. They are all concerned to create a local spectacle and thus a local public. They are all concerned with public interaction and performance in public places. In these ways they all propose to use contemporary technologies in novel ways.

Conclusion

Screens—both fixed and mobile—are proliferating in private spaces as well as in public spaces. A screen experience is present in the lounge room, the stadium, the theater, the office, the streetscape, and in the hand. Maybe we *have* become the cursors of our screens (Holmes 1997). We experience the outdoors through car windshields (or windscreens), we remember through photo screens, we amuse ourselves through gaming screens, we do our work through computer screens, we announce ourselves through social networking screens, we know the world through TV screens, and we talk to our friends through handheld screens. These screens are the public sphere (DeLuca and Peeples 2002), but common characteristics of these screens also include the individuation of the screened experience, and the commercialization of the service and the spectacle.

Our own screens enable us to be together, but also to the point, they enable us to be alone together. We are alone together watching the Sopranos and we are social on Facebook, but not together. We are not truly alone—for we alone are not alone, together we are all alone—and this is better than simply being alone. But this form of togetherness is vicarious rather than visceral, and makes for an attenuated sociality.

In contrast, the sociality mediated by the shared public-private spectacle of the cinema screen, live concert, or football stadium provides for a being-together of a different order. We are not alone, and we are not just together in not being alone, we are together to one another. We constitute a public to one another, sharing not just the spectacle that brings us together, but also sharing the gravity and momentum of common presence, and the energy of feedback and feedforward loops that operate within that self-conscious copresence. The portal intends to create infrastructure for such a public sociality—a shared presence present to us all, albeit on a small scale.

Where the portal differs from the cinema, the football, and most other public screens and spectacles is that commercial or artistic content is not the catalyst for the creation of public sociality. The catalyst is the simple presence of the public per se, the presence of the street, the crowd, and the life. The public interest is in one another—in the personal copresence of *You* and *Me*, and a public copresence of Others, and not in a contrived spectacle that delivers a public.

The portal can and should take a place as common public infrastructure, and as public infrastructure the portal opens up a new aspect of the public sphere to be put to whatever purpose the public desires—as an open-access, unmoderated channel of playful, personal, social, and cultural exchange between cities and their peoples.

Acknowledgments

Thanks to Peter Benda for his work on technical specifications, and to those who attended the Prato Community Informatics Conference, where an earlier version of this chapter was presented.

Note

1. For many other examples of urban screens used in different modes, see http://www .urbanscreens.org/.

References

Archer, K. 1997. The limits to the imagineered city: Sociospatial polarization in Orlando. *Economic Geography* 73 (3): 322–336.

Battarbee, K., N. Baerten, M. Hinfelaar, P. Irvine, S. Loeber, A. Munro, and T. Pederson, 2002. Pools and satellites—intimacy in the city. In Designing Interactive Systems. Proceedings of the 4th Conference on Designing Interactive Systems: Processes, Practices, Methods, and Techniques. New York: ACM.

Bauman, Z. 2000. *Liquid Modernity*. Cambridge, UK: Polity Press.

Benjamin, W. 1999. *The Arcades Project*. Cambridge, MA: Belknap Press.

Blij, H. D. 2008. *The Power of Place: Geography, Destiny, and Globalization's Rough Landscape*. Oxford: Oxford University Press.

Castells, M. 1996. *The Rise of the Network Society*. Cambridge, MA: Blackwell.

DeLuca, K. M., and J. Peeples. 2002. From public sphere to public screen: Democracy, activism, and the "violence" of Seattle. *Critical Studies in Media Communication* 19 (2): 125–151.

Dourish, P., and G. Bell. 2007. The infrastructure of experience and the experience of infrastructure: Meaning and structure in everyday encounters with space. *Environment and Planning, B: Planning & Design* 34 (3): 414–430.

Goffman, E. 1963. *Behavior in Public Places: Notes on the Social Organization of Gatherings*. New York: Free Press.

Goffman, E. 1971. *Relations in Public: Microstudies of the Public Order*. New York: Basic Books.

Graham, S., and S. Marvin. 2001. *Splintering Urbanism: Networked Infrastructures, Technological Mobilities and the Urban Condition*. New York: Routledge.

Holmes, D., ed. 1997. *Virtual Politics: Identity and Community in Cyberspace*. London: Sage.

Kumar, K. 1992. New theories of industrial society. In P. Brown and H. Lauder, eds., *Education for Economic Survival: From Fordism to Post-fordism?* London: Routledge.

Lee, G. S. 1901. Making the crowd beautiful. *Atlantic Monthly* 87:243.

McQuire, S. 2006. The politics of public space in the media city. *First Monday*, special issue #4: Urban screens—Discovering the potential of outdoor screens for urban society. http://www.firstmonday.org/issues/special11_2/mcquire/index.html.

McQuire, S., N. Papastergiadis, and S. Cubitt. 2008.Public screens and the transformation of public space. *Refractory: A Journal of Entertainment Media* 12.

Mitchell, D. 2003. *The Right to the City: Social Justice and the Fight for Public Space*. New York: Guilford Press.

Putman, R. 1995. Bowling alone: America's declining social capital. *Journal of Democracy* 6:65–78.

Raynsford, A. 1996. Swarm of the metropolis: Passenger circulation at Grand Central Terminal and the ideology of the crowd aesthetic. *Journal of Architectural Education* 50 (1): 2–14.

Schweingruber, D., and R. T. Wohlstein. 2005. The madding crowd goes to school: Myths about crowds in introductory sociology textbooks. *Teaching Sociology* 33 (2): 136–153.

Sennett, R. 1974. *The Fall of Public Man.* Cambridge: Cambridge University Press.

Sheller, M., and J. Urry. 2003. Mobile transformations of "public" and "private" life. *Theory, Culture & Society* 20 (3): 107–125.

Smithsimon, G. 2008. Dispersing the crowd: Bonus plazas and the creation of public space. *Urban Affairs Review* 43 (3): 325–351.

Star, S. L. 1999. The ethnography of infrastructure. *American Behavioral Scientist* 43:377–391.

Tuan, Y.-F. 1995. Island selves: Human disconnectedness in a world of interdependence. *Geographical Review* 85 (2): 229–239.

22 Nonanthropocentrism and the Nonhuman in Design: Possibilities for Designing New Forms of Engagement with and through Technology

Carl DiSalvo and Jonathan Lukens

Over the past several decades, scholarship in science and technology studies and in philosophy has increasingly drawn attention to the ways a variety of things other than humans exert influence in the construction and maintenance of action and experience. These nonhumans include animals, the built environment, and objects of all kinds, including all manner of technical objects such as software, hardware, protocols, and networks. Although there are substantially different perspectives and methods within this work, it shares a common feature: a shift away from an anthropocentric perspective that privileges the individual human actor. This shift has resulted in what we can characterize as a nonanthropocentric perspective, which considers the human a single factor in a larger system of relations and interactions between humans and nonhumans alike. What is important in these relations and interactions is not a categorical quality of any one factor (e.g., whether it is alive or not), but rather how the capabilities and limitations of all of the factors work in concert or against one another in a given scenario—establishing, delegating, and reconfiguring capacities for action and experience.

While nonanthropocentric perspectives, and the nonhumans that populate them, seem to be moving toward a more prominent role in the humanities and social sciences, human-centeredness continues to reign in design. On the surface, these two perspectives seem to confound one another. By definition, nonanthropocentric perspectives decenter the human. We can certainly imagine that a shift away from an anthropocentric perspective has implications for design and design research, but what exactly do nonanthropocentric approaches to design really mean, and why would one want to decenter the human in design?

Nonanthropocentric approaches to design do not negate the human. Rather, they attempt to better account for nonhumans in design in order to better understand, describe, critique, or intervene in a given scenario. That is, the human in a nonanthropocentric approach does not disappear: it becomes one entity among many entities, all of which are granted legitimacy in a kind of radical pluralism among objects and things, human and otherwise. In shifting away from a centering, and thus privileging, of human activities and desires, nonanthropocentric design broadens the conditions and issues of design and design research. At the very least, it reveals new opportunities for and experiences of design, particularly in regard to designing new forms of engagement with and through technology. Furthermore, it has the potential to realign perspectives in design practice and research in significant ways.

In this chapter we explore these opportunities, experiences, and realignments, providing an introduction to the ideas and issues of nonanthropocentrism and the nonhuman in design. We begin by providing a brief introduction to two theoretical roots for this exploration. We then trace nonanthropocentrism and directed attention to the nonhuman through a series of contemporary design projects and discourses, highlighting generative and interpretive themes for design practice and research. Finally, we discuss decentering as an experiential component of nonanthropocentrism, drawing from our own research activities of designing creative community technology programs.

Theoretical Roots of Nonanthropocentrism and the Nonhuman

Ideas of nonanthropocentrism, and, by extension, the nonhuman, can be found throughout a range of disciplines and subjects. Indeed, the consideration of nonhumans splinters positions in fundamental domains such as religion and philosophy. For example, the centrality of the human in the Judeo-Christian tradition can be contrasted with the pluralistic cosmology of Buddhism. Recently, "Object Oriented Ontology" has emerged as an association of philosophical positions that share a common goal of divorcing philosophy from anthropocentrism and considering objects as entities in their own right without requiring recourse to human use, perception, or meaning making. In this chapter we will draw selectively from Manuel DeLanda's reconstruction of Gilles Deleuze and Félix Guattari's writing on nonhuman expressivities, and from Actor-Network Theory (ANT). Because the former comes from the humanities and the latter from science and technology studies, when taken together, they provide diverse grounding for inquiries into nonanthropocentrism and the nonhuman in design.

Expressivities and Affordances in Deleuze, Guattari, and DeLanda

Getting over ourselves, getting over the myth of our position at the top of a *scala naturae*, can begin with the consideration of nonhuman expressivities—with the capacity for expression by things that we may not usually consider as having the agency to express themselves. DeLanda's work, which draws on Deleuze and Guattari's remarks on nonhuman expressivity as well as Gibson's (1977) theory of affordances, provides a starting place. DeLanda's reconstruction of Deleuze and Guattari abandons the elements of their experimental style that some may view as superficially similar to "post-modern" texts (DeLanda 2002, 3). His work provides examples that are relevant to urban design and architecture. For instance, DeLanda calls attention to Frei Otto's work, in which we can see the nonhuman revealed in the use of soap film as a mechanism for computing and designing the optimal surface tension of human-made structures (DeLanda 2007a, 18–23).

In addition, DeLanda claims that artists should not lose their ability to be moved by the majesty of the natural world, something we may experience in viewing the Grand Canyon, the Alps, cloud formations, or other expressions of geological or biological systems. This reconnection with the sublime requires us to imagine ourselves at a point before our differentiation from other forms of life. Further, like Deleuze and Guattari, DeLanda reminds us that even inorganic matter is capable of expression. For example, a crystal expresses itself through its refraction of light and its form (DeLanda 2007c). Most importantly, Deleuze and Guattari (1987, 316–344) argue that art began with the migration from genetically determined to externally determined expressivities. For instance, consider a male Bowerbird's construction of a mating nest versus the composition of its plumage: while it cannot alter its appearance, it can produce a variety of possible structures. Its plumage, in a way, exists a priori, while the structures it is capable of building do not. As such, less brightly colored birds can compensate for their physical inadequacies through more elaborate constructions (DeLanda 2006, 122–123). DeLanda's as well as Deleuze and Guattari's perspectives move us beyond the human as the singular or preeminent frame of reference and thus are useful for grounding inquiries into nonanthropocentrism and the nonhuman in design. Corollary perspectives can also be located in science and technology studies, specifically in Actor-Network Theory, which provides us with another approach toward decentering the human and exploring nonanthropocentric approaches to design.

Actor-Network Theory

Actor-Network Theory (ANT) is one of several constructs in science and technology studies that have brought the nonhuman to the fore. Initially developed by Michel Callon, Bruno Latour, and John Law, ANT describes the relations between heterogeneous networks of humans and nonhumans. In particular, ANT works to describe the roles and effects of nonhumans in the construction and maintenance of facts, knowledge, and practices. At its core, ANT is an approach to science and technology studies that allows for the introduction of objects and things into sociological discourse in a radical new way. In producing descriptions of science and technology, Callon, Latour, and Law (among others) found the traditional sociological methods too limiting (Latour 1992). According to Latour, such methods privilege a human "social" world devoid of (and certainly not bound to) objects. Against this tradition, ANT makes the rhetorical move of granting symmetry to human and nonhuman actors in networks of relations.

ANT is a nonanthropocentric perspective in that it decenters the human from being the sole cause of action. Instead, ANT posits a network of relations in which the human is but one among many forces. Latour (1999, 181) outlines this perspective when he states: "The prime mover of an action becomes a new, distributed, and nested set of practices whose sum may be possible to add up but only if we respect the mediating role of all the actants [inclusive of nonhuman actors] mobilized in the series." Thus, from an ANT perspective, nonhumans have a vital role in the constitution of any condition or experience. To thoroughly describe and rigorously analyze those conditions or experiences requires that we include nonhumans as real forces and actors (or actants, to use ANT terminology). For example, in his article "Some Elements of a Sociology of Translation: Domestication of the Scallops and the Fishermen of St. Brieuc Bay," Callon (1986) discusses the harvesting of scallops and the various forces that interact to comprise successful fishing. Strikingly, he calls out the scallops themselves as actors in this process, participating (or not, as the case may be) in the endeavor. Similarly, in his historical discussion of Portuguese shipping, John Law (1986) has outlined the actor network at play in enabling oceanic navigation. This network includes skilled navigators, engineers, an astrolabe, and the Pole Star—all necessary to and potentially symmetrical in the composition of the network needed to enable global sea trade.

The move to grant symmetry to the nonhuman has generated significant debate about the nature of agency and the empirical validity and usefulness of Actor-Network Theory in certain sectors of the social sciences. In our argument it is not necessary to purchase ANT wholesale as a metaphysical position. It is enough to consider how ANT frames "action" as something that is made possible and taken up by both humans and nonhumans in the environment, and as something that redescribes agency as a quality not restricted to humans alone.

Nonanthropocentrism in Design

Throughout DeLanda's work and within ANT, the human is repeatedly decentered in order to make room for an understanding of the qualities and roles of nonhumans and to redescribe "the social" as a space of complex exchanges and relations between people and things. Within contemporary design practice and discourse we can also find emerging examples of nonanthropocentric approaches and directed attention to the nonhuman. In what follows we provide such examples, highlighting the themes of exploring the space of design possibilities, considering material agency, appropriating nonhuman form, investigating nonhuman senses, and designing for nonhumans. These examples are purposefully disparate, chosen with the intention of demonstrating the possibilities and effects of nonanthropocentrism across a range of design practices and forms.

As previously stated, a nonanthropocentric perspective can provide new opportunities for, and experiences of, design. Perhaps the most obvious and direct way it does so is through the generation of ideas: it enables a new exploration of the space of design possibilities that exists at the interface of environments, animals, and materials. In this way, a nonanthropocentric perspective and a serious consideration of the nonhuman can inform not only a search through a space of possible solutions—something that is already a part of the design process—but also the population of that space of choices (DeLanda 2001). Thus, a nonanthropocentric perspective can generate concepts for design that may be overlooked or veiled in a typical human-centered approach.

We can begin this exploration of the space of design possibilities in terms of an extension of Gibson's theory of affordances. As is familiar to many in design, Gibson (1977, 79) defined an affordance as "a combination of physical properties of the environment that is uniquely suited to a given animal—to his nutritive system or his action system or his locomotor system." As is commonly held, then, the space of possibilities and limitations within any design context includes all of the affordances in an environment. But moving outside of human and animal actors, we can also consider plants, rocks, and minerals (i.e., a particular soil composition or geological niche affords a different pattern of growth), as well as nonorganic actors such as infrastructure, buildings, and of course technical objects, as providing affordances and acting in concert with the affordances provided by all of the others. By cataloging and considering the affordances of the multiplicity of actors in the environment—and, by way of ANT, extending the role of "actor" to all of the entities in the environment, both human and nonhuman—we can imagine, and design for and with, a much broader range of action.

Extending the discussion of material affordances, a nonanthropocentric perspective can also affect design through a consideration of material agency. By material agency, what is usually meant is not the attribution of intentionality to materials, but acknowledgment of how humans and materials interact relationally. Moreover, this relational interaction is rarely a totalizing control or mastery of the material by the human, but rather a productive entanglement, in which it is hard to discern the distinctions that have historically framed discussions of structure versus agency (e.g., Giddens 1984). As Lambros Malafouris describes in "At the Potter's Wheel: An Argument for Material Agency" (2008), materials do more than react to human force, they become imbricated in the totality of the action or endeavor. In describing the making of a vessel, Malafouris states that "the physical resource, be that of clay, wheel, water or instrument, is not simply used by the potter's body following the command of the potter's brain. The physical resources are fully integrated into the functioning and movement of the agent" (p. 32). In considering material agency, then, a nonanthropocentric approach reminds us that in design we are in constant dialog with the nonhuman through our materials.

When considering material agency, it is important to remember that actors interact with other actors regardless of our preexisting ideas of agency. For example, the DNA of a particular plant may not *want* or *will* itself to make copies of itself. We do not think of plants as entities that have desires. Yet fruit is produced that affords us sustenance, and more directly, that affords the plant the ability to distribute its genetic material. As DeLanda (2007b) reminds us, "Capacities are relational: a capacity to affect always goes with a capacity to be affected. This is why a given distribution of opportunities and risks depends both on an environment's materiality as well as on the behavioral capacities of an animal."

Finally, in terms of providing new opportunities for and experiences of design, a nonanthropocentric perspective can also include the investigation and appropriation of nonhuman form. Biomimetic architecture is an obvious example. In the introduction to his book *Digital-Botanic Architecture*, Dollens (2005, 16) explains that

Biomimetic investigation can be used to produce architectural and design prototypes where morphological qualities of a plant, say leaf overlap, or asymmetric harmonic proportion (Fibonacci phyllotaxis) can be applied to the shape and function of potential architectural structures and surfaces while maintaining a linked consideration of the new material properties intended to bring the structure into being as a bio animate environmental participant and sensor.

Here we find that leaving the realm of the human and entering into a consideration of the morphology of plants provides the designer with new forms to investigate.

Extending the exploration and use of nonhuman forms, nonhuman senses can also be investigated and appropriated. The *Animal Superpowers* project—a collaboration between students Chris Woebken and Kenichi Okada of the Design Interactions program at the Royal College of Art and students at the Oxford Said Business School— includes designs and prototypes for a line of sensory-enhancing toys (Woebken and Okada 2008). These designs include an ant costume, which comes with hand-mounted microscope antennas to see the world from the perspective of an ant as you crawl along the ground; a bird costume that provides the wearer with a physical sense of magnetic fields; a giraffe costume that changes the wearer's voice; elephant shoes that which receive vibrations from other nearby "elephants"; and a helmet that provides children with spatial vision similar to that of an electric eel. These designs not only demonstrate a consideration of the nonhuman, but also attempt to allow a human user direct visible or tangible experience of a nonhuman perspective.

A nonanthropocentric approach can also realign perspectives in both design practice and scholarship in significant ways. One noteworthy example comes from environmental ethics, which considers and then designs for the nonhuman as a client or interactor. Nonanthropocentric design may provide a rubric for otherwise subjective design analyses, particularly in regard to environmental issues and their aesthetic and political dimensions. As Craig Delancey notes in his essay "Architecture Can Save the World: Building and Environmental Ethics," while we may share a sense of aesthetics and utopian leanings, these are ultimately indecisive criteria. Delancey (2004, 148) states that "even though you and I both know a strip mall is not a piece of utopia, we are not going to have any hard criterion from this claim alone that will enable us to respond to the strip mall developer when he tells us he makes strip malls because they are, as he sees it, a little piece of utopia." Delancey continues to discuss different forms of environmental ethical theory, breaking them into the anthropocentric, which views everything in terms of its utility to human beings (i.e., I should prevent global warming because I don't want to drown), and two subcategories of the nonanthropo-centric. These are biocentric individualism, the belief that all living things deserve some moral respect, and the ecological ethic, the belief that ecosystems deserve moral respect as wholes.

Furthermore, modern history is replete with examples of urban planning, architec-ture, and industrial design projects that have had significant negative ecological effects. From the perspective of environmental ethics, it is important to attend to nonhumans in order to avoid decision making, planning, and design that serve human interests at the expense of other species. For example, considerable research suggests that urban sprawl has been detrimental to wildlife by causing habitat loss through fragmentation and generalization, ultimately decreasing the diversity of the biomass (e.g., Benfield, Raimi, and Chen 1999). The effects of digital environment corollaries such as electromagnetic fields on plants and animals in and around the city are still unknown.

Not surprisingly, nonhumans figure prominently in many ecological discourses. For example, in the discourses of deep ecology, anthropocentrism is often considered a cause of our contemporary ecological crisis (e.g., Plumwood 1993; Routley 1980). A move toward more astute recognition of nonhumans and the interplay between humans and nonhumans would be, from that perspective, a move toward a more sustainable society and future. Shifting from a human-centered to a nonanthropocen-tric approach and granting legitimacy, if not equivalency, to plants, animals, and other biomass, would draw heightened attention to the need to understand and account for the systemic effects of design across species and throughout the environment.

Drawing from issues of environmental ethics, we can also consider cases of design for nonhumans. For example, Delancey (2004, 155) suggests possibilities of design for nonhuman "nondomesticated" organisms:

For what is perhaps the first time in architectural practice, environmental ethics may provide the motivation for building that serves not humans, but other nondomesticated organisms. There is some precedent to this, perhaps, but it is wholly marginal: the birdhouse is an obvious example. Larger-scale projects include salmon runs built into dams and other river obstructions, and artificial reefs. These projects, which are largely for human benefit, provide a glimpse into possibilities for nature-restoring architecture, including architecture that does not directly serve any human interests.

This idea extends notions of environmental remediation and casts nonhumans as the potential subjects of design—users of a very different sort. From this, we can imagine a range of endeavors, from the design of goods and services for animals and plants, new forms of engagements with nonhumans, to more interventionist measures such as the design of barricades and hostile landscapes, which protectively thwart our interaction with the environment.

One example of designing for nonhumans is Natalie Jeremijenko's (2007) project *OOZ*: an attempt to design and develop spaces in which humans and willing animal participants interact. Because animals are intended to participate in these interactions by choice, the sites of these interactions have to be designed to attract and accommodate them. This raises the nonanthropocentric design consideration of evaluating the quality of the life of an animal. To that end, Jeremijenko lists several design goals for these sites of interaction that include providing shelter, food, species-specific comforts and conveniences, and technologies that animals can master. Interspecies interaction at these sites is intended to be reciprocal—for example, "the light switch in the preliminary beaver home would be operable by both the beavers and the humans, such that humans may turn the light on to better observe the beaver, however the beaver could turn it off again, or vice versa" (Jeremijenko 2007). This allows conditioning, traditionally performed on animals by humans, to be performed on humans by animals as well.

In contrast, consider another example of modifying an environment to assist a nonhuman. *The Naked Garden* is a nonanthropocentric design of a robotic system made to interact with natural environments (Stangeland and Kropf 2008). Created by architects Stangeland and Kropf for the 2008 Manifesta biennale, *The Naked Garden* uses a robot to construct and maintain a conducive living environment for microorganisms in an abandoned factory. For this installation, the architects programmed an industrial robot arm to engrave channels into the wall of the factory. The designs of these channels were based off of known patterns of fungi growth. Removing the outermost layer of the wall along these patterns allowed the elements (water, light, and air) to enter into the structure of the building, supporting the growth and spread of fungi throughout the factory. *The Naked Garden* has similarities to other uses of robotics that tend to the natural environment. But unlike the projects such as Ken Goldberg and Joseph Santarromana's well-known *Telegarden* (1996), which ultimately functions for the experience and pleasure of the human viewer or interactor, or farming robots that engage in labor in service of our needs, *The Naked Garden* serves no immediate instrumental objective for people. While the system would not come to be without human design, it exists, in concept, to serve the purposes of the fungi. It thus illustrates a decidedly nonanthropocentric approach to design: one that does not negate the human, but emphasizes a network of relations between entities, in which human capabilities, actions, and desires are present and exerted, but are not taken uncritically as the focus or driving purpose.

The Experience of Decentering

So far our discussion has highlighted various themes and instances of nonanthropo-centrism in design. These can be taken as suggestive of the generative and interpretive capacities of nonanthropocentrism to the practice of design and design research. But nonanthropocentrism can operate in another manner as well—it can be experiential. More precisely, the decentering of the human perspective can be an experiential component of a designed encounter with the world. Suggestions of this are present in the *Animal Superpowers* project, in which technologies are employed to provide users with a simulated experience of being an animal. In our own research activities of designing creative community technology programs, we found evidence of critical moments, or incidents, of decentering. In these incidents, participants were thwarted by their initial framing of technology from a human-centered perspective. Consequently, they were challenged, if only briefly, to alter their perspective, interpretations, and actions in order to better understand and take into account the qualities and forces of the non-human in shaping their knowledge and action.

In the following section, we describe two such critical incidents, which highlight the experience of decentering as a productive occurrence in community engagements with technology. These incidents are drawn from our research conducted as part of the City As Learning Lab (CaLL) project: an interdisciplinary research project that investigates the use of robotics (and by extension sensing) as a subject and medium. Through CaLL we have worked with multiple urban communities, youth groups, and cultural institutions in two cities in the United States (Atlanta and Pittsburgh). Although each CaLL project is distinct as shaped by the communities we partner with, they share a speculative approach to design and strive to foster critical engagements and creative expression with technology as a means for fostering technological fluency (DiSalvo et al. 2008).

Seeing the City

In the spring of 2009 we conducted a two-day robotic arts workshop with teenage youth through the Boys and Girls Club Youth Art Connection program in Atlanta. In the workshop the youth were tasked with creating a minidocumentary on urban infrastructure from a robot's perspective. The activity was designed to simultaneously introduce the youth to the topics of infrastructure and the capabilities and limitations of robots, and to allow them to begin to explore the use of robotics for creative ends.

The "robot" the youth used was a remote-controlled truck on which we mounted a small wireless camera. The camera transmitted a video signal to a laptop, which saved the video to its hard drive. The challenge for the students was to capture video footage of items on a list of infrastructural elements. These would later be edited into a final video. The youth set out in groups of five to seven in search of items on the list. Within each group, one student would hold the laptop while another would control the robot, and they took turns in each of these roles.

With certain infrastructural items from the list, the activity turned out to be more of a challenge than we had expected. But, as such, it was a fortuitous challenge that served to reinforce one of our desired goals: to have the youth begin to understand the robot's perspective of the city, and how its perspective of the city was different from theirs. A salient example of this challenge was the task of documenting traffic lights (provided as an example of transportation infrastructure). As the youth approached an intersection with a traffic light, they excitedly pointed it out to one another. The youth controlling the robot positioned it near the traffic light and asked the youth with the laptop to begin recording, which they did, only to quickly point out that they could not see the traffic light through the video stream. At first this caused some consternation among the youth because the traffic light was "right there" and the robot was "right near it." The youth quickly realized, however, that the camera on the robot did not have the same point of view they did. Through experimentation they discovered that for the traffic light to be in the camera's view, the robot needed to be almost half a block away. To capture the traffic light with the robot's camera required the youth to set aside their previously unquestioned perceptions of what was in view, and to conceptualize the perception and point of view of the robot. Although a simple example and problem, it was a significant learning experience for the youth.

The experience of decentering was encountered again and reinforced later in the workshop when the youth reviewed the video footage captured by the robot. Throughout their foray into downtown, the youth had captured video of infrastructural items such as the traffic light in the example above, as well as recorded video as they navigated sidewalks, curbs, parking lots, and street crossings (see figure 22.1). On review, the youth were invariably surprised by the video footage. Because the robot moved at a fairly quick pace and the camera angle was low to the ground, the scenes captured were both visually chaotic and ambiguous.

When seen out of sequence, it was often unclear precisely where the robot was at any given moment. Moments of locational awareness came when the robot collided with an object, and the view of that object combined with the jolt as the robot bounced back and the camera captured a fleeting broader field of vision, providing a short-lived spatial grounding for the youth. Once again, in order to make sense of the images they were viewing, the youth were challenged to consider the robot's perception of the city and attempt to develop ways of identifying spatial markers that aligned

Figure 22.1
Downtown Atlanta as seen from the perspective of the robot.

with the perspective of the robot. This experience was all the more decentering because the youth were intimately familiar with this locale—they walked along these streets regularly, and yet, in the captured video, the streets appeared unfamiliar.

Sensing the City

In the summers of 2007 and 2008 we conducted a series of participatory sensing workshops with community groups in Pittsburgh. The participants ranged in age, though most were middle-aged adults. Almost all of them used information technology on a regular basis for work and for everyday tasks (word processing and spreadsheets; texting and surfing the Internet for pleasure), but only one (out of approximately three dozen) had any prior experience with environmental sensing technologies. As a starting activity in this program, participants were given CO, CO_2, and sound sensors and sent on neighborhood scavenger hunts. During these scavenger hunts participants were tasked with taking readings of places with various experiential qualities, such as places they found pleasant or unpleasant, noisy or quiet, relaxing or stressful. They were also tasked with finding the highest and lowest readings in the neighborhood— that is, the place with the highest sound levels or the lowest CO_2.

As participants set out in groups with their sensors, they sought out their favorite and least favorite places in the neighborhood, and, not surprisingly, tended toward extreme environments with the expectation of gathering interesting readings. For example, they sought out and measured sewers, gardens, building HVAC systems, alleyways, front porches, playgrounds, and portable toilets (see figure 22.2). But, in using the sensors to gather readings, they were often surprised by the measurements they did, and, just as often, did not, gather. The portable toilet is a case in point.

Figure 22.2
Participants sensing portable toilets.

In the heat of the summer, a portable toilet placed in a park can be an unpleasant space that prompts visceral reactions to its smell and context. This unpleasantness, however, did not register on the sensors given to the participants. The inside of the portable toilet registered no difference in CO or CO_2. From the perspective of the sensor it was a space no different from a participant's own front porch.

Similarly, the readings from the sound sensors sometimes caused confusion. Participants sought to measure loud sounds, but came to realize that the sounds were not as loud as they thought, and that unpleasant sounds were not necessarily any louder than sounds they found pleasant. For example, the sound of a bus driving up a hill did not register as any louder than the sound of children playing at the playground. Such experiences caused a kind of productive dissonance between the capabilities of the sensors and the lived experience of the participants. Moreover, participants discovered new qualities of the environment detected by the sensors of which they had been previously unaware. For instance, by reaching into sewer grates, participants discovered that the interior of these spaces were often quite loud, registering sound levels on the sensors that were not so perceptible from the their usual vantage of walking along the sidewalk above. In discussions of these experiences, the participants came to better understand that sensors operate on the material environment, not the affective environment of experience and memory. To gather extremes in readings or novel readings, participants had to look at the environment anew, divorced from their emotional and experiential associations, with a consideration of the material, though often unseen, constitution of spaces.

Both of these examples of critical incidents serve to highlight the experience of decentering through which participants encounter how nonhuman qualities and forces shape knowledge and action. Moreover, these experiences of decentering were productive because they prompted a new, and arguably greater, understanding of the given technological objects, the specific (urban) environments, and the relations between those factors. In doing so, they also prompted the participants to reconceptualize their place within these networks of factors and adjust their activities accordingly. As such, these experiences suggest opportunities for the design of future community engagements, which might take the nonhuman and nonanthropocentrism as more explicit themes.

Conclusion

A nonanthropocentric perspective allows us to see and understand the environment and technology in new ways; it opens up new possibilities and requirements for design. In effect, it works to decenter the human, at least momentarily, from its presumed position of prominence in contemporary design. It is, however, difficult to argue for the importance, or existence, of a strong nonanthropocentric perspective because many arguments advocating for particular areas or methods of study define importance in purely human terms. Things are deemed important because they benefit us, collectively or individually, as humans. Paradoxically, many arguments for a nonanthropocentric perspective rest entirely on the benefit to the human of adopting such a perspective. In this way, the human is not negated, because frequently, as witnessed in our examples, a nonanthropocentric perspective often is a means to an end of some human benefit.

Beyond simply framing nonanthropocentricism as a novel means to human ends, we can also explore a more challenging discussion of the nonhuman—one that asks us to abandon some of our familiar notions of agency, of identity, and of the boundaries between actor and environment. This momentary overcoming of anthropocentrism requires us to imagine the world anew and involves imagining movement outside of our own patterns, outside of things like being bipedal. It involves imagining perception outside of binocular vision—outside of the placement of our eyes at the tops of our heads and our ability to rotate our necks. It involves imagining the perception of wavelengths outside of those visible and audible to us. It involves imagining devices other than the opposable thumb. It involves the recognition that our perceptions of causality, history, morals, and agency all too often assume that they are reciprocated in kind by agents incapable of reciprocation. Ultimately, it involves our overcoming the narrative fallacies and rationalizations that we use to place ourselves at the top of a chain, and instead placing ourselves in a web in which the components are impossible to isolate from the whole.

Adopting a nonanthropocentric perspective in design—whether as a deliberate exercise in generating new design ideas, taking new approaches to the study of

technical systems, addressing environmental ethics, designing for a nonhuman interactor, or as we detail in our case studies, occurring as an unintended result of engagements with the city—provides an opportunity to consider how things other than
humans figure into action and experience and move us beyond an uncritical privileging of human activities and desires. Through the nonanthropocentric, we can strive
toward a new understanding of the interdependence of living and nonliving technical
and biological systems, which opens a broad expanse of possibilities for the design
and study of new forms of engagement with and through technology.

References

Benfield, F. K., M. D. Raimi, and D. D. T. Chen. 1999. *Once There Were Greenfields: How Urban
Sprawl Is Undermining America's Environment, Economy, and Social Fabric*. New York: Natural
Resources Defense Council.

Callon, Michel. 1986. Some elements of a sociology of translation: Domestication of the scallops
and the fishermen of St Brieuc Bay. In John Law, ed., *Power, Action and Belief: A New Sociology of
Knowledge*, 196–233. London: Routledge & Kegan Paul.

Delancey, Craig. 2004. Architecture can save the world: Building and environmental ethics.
Philosophical Forum 35 (2): 147–159.

DeLanda, Manuel. 2001. Deleuze and the use of the genetic algorithm in architecture. Presented
at *Between Bladerunner and Mickey Mouse: New Architecture in Los Angeles*, exhibition, Madrid,
04-22.04.01. http://www.cddc.vt.edu/host/delanda/pages/algorithm.htm.

DeLanda, Manuel. 2002. *Intensive Science and Virtual Philosophy*. New York: Continuum Books.

DeLanda, Manuel. 2006. Material expressivity. *Domus* 893:122–123. http://lebbeuswoods
.wordpress.com/2009/01/05/manuel-delanda-matters-4/.

DeLanda, Manuel. 2007a. Material elegance. *Architectural Design* 77 (1): 18–23.

DeLanda, Manuel. 2007b. Opportunities and risks. *Domus* 901:86–87. http://lebbeuswoods
.wordpress.com/2009/01/30/manuel-DeLanda-opportunities-and-risks/.

DeLanda, Manuel. 2007c. The philosophy of Gilles Deleuze. Lecture at European Graduate School
Communication Studies Department, Saas-Fee, Switzerland, June 30, 2007. http://www.youtube.
com/watch?v=zqisvKSuA70.

Deleuze, Gilles, and Felix Guattari. 1987. *A Thousand Plateaus*. Trans. Brian Massumi. Minneapolis: University of Minnesota Press.

DiSalvo, C., D. Holstius, I. Nourbakhsh, A. Akin, and M. Louw. 2008. The Neighborhood
Networks Project: A case study of critical engagements and creative expression through participa-
tory design. In *PDC '08: Proceedings of the ACM Participatory Design Conference*, 41–50. New York:
ACM Press.

Dollens, Dennis. 2005. *Digital-Botanic Architecture*. Santa Fe: Site Books.

Gibson, James J. 1977. The Theory of Affordances. In Robert Shaw and John Bransford, eds., *Perceiving, Knowing, and Acting: Toward an Ecological Psychology*, 67–82. New York: Wiley.

Giddens, Anthony. 1984. *The Constitution of Society*. Cambridge: Polity Press.

Goldberg, K., and J. Santarromana. 1996. *Telegarden* online project documentation. http://www.usc.edu/dept/garden/.

Jeremijenko, Natalie. 2007. *OOZ* online project documentation. http://www.nyu.edu/projects/xdesign/ooz/ooz_intro.html.

Latour, Bruno. 1992. Where are the missing masses? The sociology of a few mundane artifacts. In Wiebe E. Bijker and John Law, eds., *Shaping Technology/Building Society: Studies in Sociotechnical Change*, 225–258. Cambridge, MA: MIT Press.

Latour, Bruno. 1999. *Pandora's Hope: An Essay on The Reality of Science Studies*. Cambridge, MA: Harvard University Press.

Law, John. 1986. On the methods of long distance control: Vessels, navigation, and the Portuguese route to India. In John Law, ed., *Power, Action and Belief: A New Sociology of Knowledge*, 243–263. London: Routledge.

Malafouris, Lambros. 2008. At the potter's wheel: An argument for material agency. In Carl Knappett and Lambros Malafouris, eds., *Material Agency*, 19–36. New York: Springer.

Plumwood, Val. 1993. *Feminism and the Mastery of Nature*. London: Routledge.

Routley, Richard. 1980. Human chauvinism and environmental ethics. In D. S. Mannison, M. McRobbie, and R. Routley, eds., *Environmental Philosophy*, 96–189. Canberra: ANU Research School of Social Sciences.

Stangeland, R., and S. Kropf. 2008. *The Naked Garden* online project documentation. http://www.hha.no/work.

Woebken, C., and K. Okada. 2008. *Animal Superpowers* online project documentation. http://www.woebken.net/animalsuperpowers.htm.

23 Building the Open-Source City: Changing Work Environments for Collaboration and Innovation

Laura Forlano

For much of the last century, the professional and work lives of white-collar office dwellers have revolved around the specialization of knowledge, the focus on individual accomplishments, and the discipline of sitting at a single desk in an office cubicle for eight or more hours a day. However, these ways of living and working are increasingly challenged by the need to solve complex problems that require interdisciplinary knowledge and cross-disciplinary approaches, which call for more collaborative teamwork and allow for increased mobility across a variety of work settings and spaces. The Internet, along with laptops and mobile phones, has enabled emergent forms of production that harness and engage the contributions of many citizens across distributed geographies. Perhaps the most notable of these emergent forms is that of the success of open-source software such as Linux and the online dictionary Wikipedia, which are based on peer production. These examples emphasize a movement away from proprietary forms of intellectual property toward knowledge sharing and collaboration as an important mode of engagement with ideas and people.

While the early decades of the Internet emphasized the transformation of online economies of digital goods such as music and software, we are just beginning to understand how information and communication technologies might allow for the emergence of sharing models with respect to physical goods such as cars, clothes, and books in local economies. For example, Zipcar has enabled a more flexible and affordable way to get access to transportation without the cost of owning a car, and coworking communities have created shared spaces where citizens can work side by side with likeminded colleagues. How might we conceive of sharing physical spaces such as offices or residential spaces in ways that are economical and environmentally beneficial as well as enabling more interdisciplinary collaboration among ad hoc groups? Or, to put this another way, how can citizens be engaged in the creation of an open-source city? What knowledge, skills, and competencies are necessary in order to facilitate these emergent forms of collaboration and peer production in urban areas? While this chapter focuses primarily on work activities, it should be noted that these questions are also relevant for other kinds of citizen participation, urban dwelling, and collective action, which are the focus of a number of digital tools and applications such as Groundcrew,[1] a mobile coordination tool for assembling local "action networks," and FixMyStreet, a web-based tool for reporting, viewing, and discussing local problems.[2]

This chapter considers the application of peer-production models from the realms of software and online collaborative knowledge work to new domains such as design, architecture, and urban planning. While design work is considered collaborative by its very nature, designers have not engaged as readily with the open-source community and open-source modes of production in part because the majority of the tools used by designers, such as Adobe Photoshop and InDesign, are still proprietary (Zer-Aviv 2010). Through the primary lens of science and technology studies and design, this chapter analyzes *Breakout! Escape from the Office*, a yearlong collaborative design project about mobile work that was featured in the Architecture League of New York's Toward the Sentient City[3] exhibition in fall 2009. Specifically, this project used parks and public spaces in urban settings as a platform for the organization of interdisciplinary, collaborative, and mobile work among relative strangers. To better explore the potential of peer production in new sectors and settings, this chapter describes three of the main *Breakout!* session formats, which were held over the course of the monthlong event: Coworking in Public Spaces, Designing the Mobile Office, and Flash Mob Ethnography sessions.[4]

As a member of the *Breakout!* team, my role was to conduct ethnographic observation as well as participate in the research process and events on which this chapter is based. My involvement included attending all of the team's planning and design meetings, which took place on a monthly basis over the course of the year, as well as expanding the project to Europe through a partnership with Citilab Cornellà, a media lab and incubator about twenty minutes from Barcelona, Spain. I also contributed by applying concepts of peer production and mobile work to my own field though the creation of a series of Flash Mob Ethnography events that brought together interdisciplinary groups for ad hoc fieldwork in urban settings (discussed at the end of the chapter). Designers often conduct ethnographic research at the early stages of the human-centered design process, which makes it an interesting method in which to apply concepts of peer production.

Theoretical Background

In recent years, scholars in science and technology studies (STS) have begun to turn to analysis of architecture, design, and the built environment. In particular, in the tradition of STS, many studies approach the architecture studio as a kind of scientific laboratory in which they analyze the social construction (Bijker, Hughes, and Pinch 1987; Pinch and Bijker 1984) of "technologies" such as buildings, models, prototypes, and floor plans. In accordance with Actor-Network Theory (Latour 2005), these technologies are then discussed in terms of their position in a network of human and nonhuman actors. In addition, their affordances (Gibson 1977; Norman 1990) and constraints are discussed in tandem with the narratives about their sociocultural, economic, political, and environmental shaping. For example, Yaneva (2005) gives a useful account of how STS can be used to understand the work of architects in her description of the work of Rem Koolhaas's Office for Metropolitan Architecture. From this perspective, STS offers a useful lens through which to view the *Breakout!* project and, in particular, its complex arrangement of citizens, technologies, and spaces, which require an understanding of sociotechnical approaches that are common in STS.

Building on a theoretical grounding in STS, it is useful to add a methodological understanding from design research since this forms the basis of the *Breakout!* collaborative research process. Currently, there is great interest in "design thinking" (Brown 2008; Buchanan 1992), which is characterized by human-centered, iterative, interdisciplinary, systems thinking, and long-range approaches to innovation in the private sector and universities alike. Design methods include ethnography and qualitative research (Flores 1993; Leonard and Rayport 1997; Plowman 2003); brainstorming (Kelley 2001); sensemaking (Dervin 1992; Weick 1995; Weick, Sutcliffe, and Obstfeld 2005); visualization, mapping, and prototyping (Roam 2008); scenario planning (Wilkinson 1995); positioning (Ries and Trout 1993); and personas (Cooper 1999; Don and Petrick 2003; Kelley 2005). This work has yielded important results in universities as well as design consultancies—for example, IDEO, Doblin, frog design, and design-oriented groups within multinational technology companies such as the Intel People and Practices group and IBM Social Computing group. In addition, design has moved from the aesthetics of graphics and usability of interfaces to the creation of services (Penin and Tonkinwise, forthcoming), the spaces and structuring of organizations, and the transformation of society through projects focused on sustainability (Elkington 1997; Hawken, Lovins, and Lovins 1999; McDonough and Braungart 2002; Savitz and Weber 2006; Tonkinwise 2009a, 2009b) and innovation. These two orientations—STS and design research—help orient the *Breakout!* project discussed in this chapter.

As inspiration for the *Breakout!* project itself, concepts from research on architecture, innovation, and organizational behavior have proved illustrative. For example, DEGW founder Frank Duffy's *Work and the City* (2008) gives a useful overview of the history of office arrangements and argues for the dramatic reorganization of cities by enhanced, semipermeable, and shared spaces for the purpose of environmental sustainability. While we might trace the evolution of the corporate office from Taylorist forms of the early twentieth century, which enabled surveillance, to the cubicle farms of the 1980s, and open offices of the current era, we do not yet have a "floorplan" for the mobile office. Duffy's vision for the future of work is interesting—the application of modes of peer production to the field of architecture and urban planning through space sharing—but it cannot be implemented without significant changes in laws and regulations that govern the zoning of cities. On a more microscale, scholars have discussed how the Internet and information communication technologies have transformed spaces and places with the introduction of concepts such as "media spaces" (Couldry and McCarthy 2004), the "spaces of flows" and the "space of place" (Castells 1996), "non-places" (Augé 1995), and "third places" (Oldenburg 1989).

"Innovation spaces" (Allen and Henn 2006; Moultrie et al. 2007) have also been the subject of design and business literature, with examples found in corporate offices such as Google, Bloomberg, and BMW, to name just a few. This illustrates how spatial arrangements coevolve along with changes in methods, processes, and ways of working, which raises the question of the processes that might emerge from the introduction of mobile work across various settings and spaces. Another relevant question is whether mobile work is an intrusion on other forms of interaction and citizen engagement in public spaces or whether the opposite might be true—specifically, the erosion of strictly commercial and proprietary modes of production.

As traditional work activities supported by mobile and wireless technologies spill out of corporate headquarters, and the economic recession puts significant pressure on corporate footprints, there is a need to rethink the other kinds of spaces that we inhabit on a daily basis in order to support different kinds of activities other than those related to work. Mobile work represents a radical break from how knowledge, collaboration, and the bodily experience of work have been organized; this juncture offers possibilities as well as constraints. For example, mobility affords the ability to encounter new communities, ideas, and places while at the same time shifting the burden of many common aspects of day-to-day work onto the employee themselves. These include finding outlets for daily interaction, motivating oneself, monitoring productivity, gaining access to connectivity and knowledge, and searching for suitable places to work. In fact, scholars have argued that new media workers in the creative industries share a precariousness of working conditions with low-level workers in other sectors (Ross 2008), and this applies to mobile workers, many of whom are in media, telecommunications, and technology fields. While many of these needs have become apparent with the shift toward virtual organizations, mobile work offers a new set of challenges since the methods, processes, spaces, and infrastructure are lacking.

Peer production and the sharing economy (Bauwens 2009; Benkler 2006) and, in particular, blogs and Wikipedia, have challenged the nature of specialized knowledge. For example, projects like the "University of the People" and the "Public School for Architecture" have begun to offer peer-produced courses supported by networks of volunteers. While some fear the devaluing and deskilling of professions that require specialized expertise, others have explored the benefits of informal learning ecologies and communities of practice, which are believed to be important in education and innovation (Lave and Wenger 1991; Wenger 1998; Wenger, McDermott, and Snyder 2002). These informal settings are integral to the *Breakout!* concept since the project aims to reorganize citizens in parks and public spaces for the purposes of ad hoc collaboration.

A final source of inspiration for the *Breakout!* concept is literature on innovation (Drucker 2002), entrepreneurship, and organizational behavior. Specifically, lead users (Von Hippel 1978, 2005), user entrepreneurs (Tripsas and Shah 2007), and social entrepreneurs (Dees 2001) are important for the innovation of new products and services. We might also apply these concepts to the creation of emergent forms of organizing. Unlike telework (Gillespie and Richardson 2000; Nilles1997), which was predicated on the notion that people would work largely from home, mobile work builds on the existence of virtual and distributed organizations and expands work activities into new settings and environments such as cafés, parks, public spaces, and coworking communities. In particular, *Breakout!* considers mobile work to be an emergent form that has implications for future work scenarios and settings. As a result, nomadic workers can be viewed as lead users of these emergent modes of working, which are supported by a wide range of mobile and wireless technologies. My earlier work (Forlano 2008) described how mobile workers appropriated semipublic spaces like cafés as temporary incubators to get feedback on their work from passersby. Building on the experiences of lead users, *Breakout!* incorporates concepts of organizing diversity (Girard and Stark 2002) and weak ties (Uzzi and Dunlap 2005), which have been found to enhance the innovation potential of traditional firms, in order to facilitate mobile work events that combine interdisciplinary groups and allow for the formation of new weak ties.

Breakout! Escape from the Office

The project *Breakout! Escape from the Office* began in June 2008 as a grant proposal to the Architectural League of New York's Toward the Sentient City exhibition. According to the proposal, *Breakout!* "returns creative work back to the streets of New York. Using coworking as a model, and injecting lightweight versions of essential office infrastructure into urban public spaces, BREAKOUT! seeks to explore new and productive niches for collaborative knowledge work outside of traditional office buildings" (Townsend et al. 2008). Coworking is a way of sharing the costs of physical office space while providing the opportunities to participate in a community of likeminded others, although, for the most part, members do not actually work together. The name was appropriate, given the topic of the proposal: the project emerged in part out of discussions held by key team members at several meetings in August 2008 at Gramstand, a former East Village coffee shop that at the time was popular in the New York coworking scene as the location of a group known as CooperBricolage or "CooBric" (Dickert and Bacigalupo 2008).

CooBric, organized by Sanford Dickert and Tony Bacigalupo, was one of the first coworking communities in New York. "Coworking is a movement to create cafe-like community/collaboration spaces for developers, writers and independents," according to the Coworking Community Blog (2009). During our early planning meetings, we met "coworkers," signified by the green-and-black stickers on their laptops, and witnessed the informal interaction, knowledge sharing, and swapping of job leads and opportunities among CooBric members. As the interest and community around CooBric and coworking grew, the group founded a new space of its own, New Work City, which opened in November 2008. Over the past five years, coworking communities such as New Work City have been growing at a rapid rate in countries around the world, as indicated by a large online directory of resources, spaces,[5] and materials documenting the coworking model (Centre for Social Innovation 2010). Coworking members emphasize the importance of being in a community of likeminded others where they can exchange ideas. Furthermore, in the technology field, coworking communities rely on social media such as Twitter to gain awareness of each other's activities and interests. As a result, Twitter formed a critical part of the technology infrastructure for the *Breakout!* project for the purposes of coordination, collaboration, and documentation.[6]

Building on the experience of coworking communities, *Breakout!* sought to stage mobile work and coworking activities in public spaces in order to reintegrate these practices into everyday life with a belief in the potential to spur creative thinking, build new networks, and take advantage of New York's natural demographic diversity. Citizens and passersby were believed to be both participants and observers in an ongoing experiment in mobile work and peer production. By considering factors such as the interplay between people, places, and technologies, the team believed that it was possible to improve individual experiences and group interactions as well as to create new modes of collaboration and innovation. For example, organizational diversity (expertise, demographics, work style), trust, weak social network ties and heterogeneity, and informal face-to-face interactions are considered to play an important role in the exchange and communication of new ideas.

Breakout! attempted to amplify the emergent practice of mobile work through curated events, yet in other ways, it was reminiscent of an earlier era of New York's history in which vendors in the garment industry sold their wares from carts on the streets of the Lower East Side. Thus, rather than viewing mobile work as a new phenomenon, it is important to recognize its historical precedent as well as how the introduction of mobile and wireless technology enables new opportunities and constraints. According to the *Breakout!* project description,

Offices are becoming obsolete as we move towards a knowledge-based economy. Work is being transformed by new technologies and practices of mobility. . . . While the office is on its way to becoming a kind of vestigial organ, new forms for organizing knowledge work are evolving. . . . BREAKOUT! therefore seeks to create a new architecture for the creative city by appropriating public spaces for the collaborative knowledge work that drives the city. (Townsend et al. 2008)

The project responds to the considerable socioeconomic and technological transformations that are occurring in society. These transformations encompass the increased ranks of freelance, self-employed, and independent workers, including include entrepreneurs (Horowitz et al. 2005); the growth of virtual organizations, telecommuting, and remote working arrangements; the ubiquity of technologies that support mobility; and the economic crisis, which requires lower capital costs (such as money spent on real estate and office footprints) while seeking out more creative, collaborative, and innovative modes of working. The project was initially conceived of as having architectural and technological components such as a physical intervention and a technology platform. However, since the project was fundamentally about reorganizing people in new ways, it was recognized that demonstrating, facilitating, and describing new formats for engagement were critical to the success of the project.

In October 2008, after the proposal was accepted by the League as one of the five projects that would be featured in the Toward the Sentient City exhibition, the team began a series of bimonthly planning meetings held at DEGW, a design consultancy founded by Frank Duffy, in New York's financial district. As Tish Shute (2009) writes, "[The exhibition] *Toward the Sentient City* brought 'architects and urban designers into a conversation that until now has been limited largely to technologists,' and created an extraordinary opportunity to investigate distributed architectures of participation of what we might call the 'outernet.'" The "outernet" refers to "smart things" and the "internet of things," as everyday objects, spaces, and artifacts quickly get tagged, geolocated, and connected to the Internet (International Telecommunication Union 2005). Specifically, while the Internet has been conceived of primarily as an online, virtual, and digital space for the past several decades, a growing range of technologies are enabling the Internet to be connected to physical and material objects linked to information available online. For example, it is now possible to take a picture on an iPhone and have its location information included in the digital file, which can then locate the photo on an online map. Interestingly, many of the projects featured in the exhibit did just that—by linking up plants, garbage, fish, and inanimate objects. From this perspective, *Breakout!* was considerably more low-tech and human-centered; it focused on the places, people, and interface needed to facilitate mobile work.

After a yearlong design research process that involved planning, prototyping, and testing, *Breakout!* was featured at the Toward the Sentient City exhibition in mid-September 2009. The exhibit consisted of photographs, design research, architectural concepts, wireframe images of the technology platform, a DVD of over 300 images of mobile work from around the world taken over the past five years, and a "mobile office kit." In addition to the gallery installation, over thirty *Breakout!* "sessions" were held in New York and the Barcelona area during the following month. The events ranged from two to twenty participants and were documented through Twitter feeds and notes as well as over 1,000 photographs and videos.

While the team envisioned over ten possible organizational formats for *Breakout!* sessions, the majority of sessions were dedicated to facilitating either coworking or collaboration focused on a specific task. Specifically, coworking sessions were intended to test out new environments for work including parks, public atria, and city-to-city WiFi-enabled buses to form links among heterogeneous networks. Collaboration sessions focused on a group activity such as brainstorming, prototyping, coding, or writing, and acknowledged that each of these activities presented different levels of participation and engagement. For example, while brainstorming requires the greatest number of inputs from all participants, coding or writing can be done simultaneously sitting side by side with less interaction while still having the possibility of producing a joint result. There were two collaboration tracks during the monthlong event. One was a set of three sessions on the future of mobile work and another was a set of three sessions titled "Flash Mob Ethnography." The collaboration sessions sought to apply peer-production processes to new domains of work beyond software programming and online content, including design, architecture, and urban planning as well as specific design methods such as ethnographic research.

Discussion

Over the course of the monthlong event, the *Breakout!* team held a variety of coworking, design, and research sessions in parks and public spaces throughout New York. What follows is a detailed description of these activities along with a discussion of the opportunities, constraints, and implications for the future of mobile work. While the coworking events were relatively open, the other two formats were focused on specific design research activities that had to be accomplished collaboratively. As a result, these formats offered greater promise for the application of peer production to the work of designers than open-ended events in which collaboration was expected to emerge spontaneously through digital and face-to-face interactions.

Coworking in Public Spaces

The day after the opening of the Toward the Sentient City exhibition (figure 23.1), I met Anthony Townsend, an urban planner and collaborator on Breakout!, for lunch at French Roast, a European bistro on Eleventh Street and Sixth Avenue adjacent to Jefferson Market Garden, the location of one of our first official *Breakout!* sessions, which took place later that afternoon. The garden was empty when we entered, a quiet

Figure 23.1
Breakout! Escape from the Office on display at Toward the Sentient City exhibit at the Architectural League of New York in September 2009.

respite from the busy Sixth Avenue traffic; we had selected it as an ideal spot for a short meeting on one of the two-person benches. Once the WiFi was up and running, we logged into the *Breakout!* platform in order to signify that we had begun the session and to document the session in 140-character "field notes" using Twitter. The WiFi was enabled by a small, portable unit, which was connected to the Internet through a 3G cellular connection. Once the unit was turned on, it was possible to join the open WiFi network, which did not require passwords or logins. However, while the technological infrastructure was relatively easy to set up, the network was sometimes slow and unreliable. In addition, since the team had only two units and a set amount of bandwidth, it was not possible to hold multiple events simultaneously.

During the two-hour session, Townsend gave me a short tutorial on how to use Prezi, an open and dynamic presentation software designed by Kitchen Budapest, a research and innovation lab sponsored by Magyar Telecom, the Hungarian telecommunications company. In contrast to commonly used presentation software packages such as PowerPoint or Keynote, Prezi—quickly becoming popular among tech-savvy presenters—is notable for its ability to dynamically rearrange text and images in a nonlinear format using a free-form spatial metaphor.[7] For example, rather than viewing a chronological set of slides, which range from one to fifty, Prezi displays slides as arrangements of text, images, and graphs that are splayed out on a desktop. In this way, users are able to draw a different pathway from text to image to text every time they give a presentation without the actual reorganization of the slides.

When the glare of the sun reflecting on our laptop screens became problematic, I opened a mushroom-colored Muji-brand umbrella from the *Breakout!* Mobile Office Kit. Since the kit was on display at the League's exhibition, each of the over thirty objects—such as Moleskine notebooks, Bose noise-cancellation headphones, Post-it Notes, a Nalgene water bottle, and a portable Joe Coffee mug—had been highly curated and selected to communicate the aesthetics, social needs, and challenges of mobile work (e.g., the need for shade to prevent glare on a laptop screen). As anticipated during the planning stages of the project, glare became a constant obstacle to bringing screen-based work activities outdoors. This challenge suggests a need for designs of public spaces that allow for greater protection from the sun in order to support mobile work activities as well as the need for screen technologies that work well in outdoor settings (for example, Amazon's Kindle).

After about forty-five minutes, I moved to another bench in a well-shaded area of the garden where our colleague, Antonina Simeti, was sitting. As we were talking, along came a gaggle of five-year-olds with large red magnifying glasses. I recorded this on the *Breakout!* platform with the following note from my iPhone:

Kids with magnifying glasses looking at plants in the garden, a nice change of pace:) 1:09 PM Sep 18th, 2009 from Twitterrific

By using Twitter as a means of taking short ethnographic field notes, I sought to invent new methods of documentation while at the same time participating in emergent modes of mobile work. In the garden the children scurried along with delight at seeing the plants close up. Seeing them full of excitement and wonder was inspiring and spontaneous in exactly the way that *Breakout!* had intended. Later that afternoon, the *Breakout!* team headed to Tompkins Square Park where the Urballoon (Gomez de Llarena 2009), a new media art project, was being showcased as part of the Conflux 2009 festival. The Urballoon, a large inflated balloon, suspends a projector in midair and connects to the Internet wirelessly (in this case, with a WiFi connection provided by the *Breakout!* team) to allow for the display of text messages and photos on the ground below. While we were waiting for the balloon to rise, Townsend attempted to have a conference call in the southwest corner of the park on Seventh Street and Avenue A. He wrote:

Anthony T.: after 3 years of trying, I'm just about ready to give up trying to find a quiet public place for a call in Manhattan.

In addition to glare, sound and background noise present obstacles to working outdoors. While we included a range of devices such as noise-canceling headphones and iPhone earbuds in the Mobile Office Kit, these technologies are not particularly useful for collaborative activities or phone conversations. This suggests a need for public-space designs that offer protection against noise problems in cities in order to allow for these spaces to become more usable.

The following afternoon, a Saturday, I hopped in a yellow cab across Fourteenth Street in order to participate in a coworking session on a small stretch of concrete in the Meatpacking District. The *Breakout!* team was converging to experiment with iPhone applications for tethering (using your mobile phone provider as an Internet connection for your laptop), a potentially valuable application for mobile work. When I arrived, there was a white chalk line that demarcated the *Breakout!* team's "OFFICE" from the rest of the "CITY" (figure 23.2). A woman with a laptop had moved her table closer to those staked out by the *Breakout!* team in order to be in the "office" space, and another woman borrowed my black extra fine Pilot Rolling Ball Pen while she studied for graduate school entrance exams. While the borrowing of a pen may hardly seems significant, it is a relatively uncommon interaction in the public spaces of New York, which suggests that our simple chalk-design intervention had signaled our willingness to engage passersby.

At 1:58 p.m., I announced via Twitter on the *Breakout!* platform that I was "sitting in the sun outside the 14th St. Apple Store"; thirty minutes later, I had "5 e-mails down, 46 more to go." Meanwhile, after switching from the *Breakout!* WiFi network to the nearby open Apple Store network, Townsend had learned that the company was blocking the file needed for tethering from their network in order to appease AT&T, the wireless carrier for the iPhone since its introduction in June 2007. AT&T prohibits tethering since this is a service that they would like customers to pay a monthly fee to use. While not completely surprising, this realization illustrates another obstacle for mobile work, specifically, the lack of widespread open WiFi networks in cafés, parks, and other public spaces. Yes, the Apple Store's network is open but the fact that it imposes political restrictions on the kinds of files that can be uploaded and downloaded is a cause for concern (Forlano 2009). This example suggests that, in many ways, cities are not conducive for mobile work in that the required physical and technical architecture is not available or is provided by commercial actors with restrictions on the place, duration, and kind of use allowed. Furthermore, while individuals can subscribe to their own plans to access communication and the Internet, cities do not consider telecommunications infrastructure to be a public good that has the potential to support a range of work and leisure activities.

Figure 23.2
A line of white chalk marking the boundary between the office and the city in a *Breakout!* coworking event held in the Meatpacking District in New York in September 2009.

Toward the end of the session, I overheard a group of forty-something women sitting at an adjacent table commenting on the role of social network sites. While the *Breakout!* team sat engaged in downloading, updating, and Tweeting, I documented this comment on my Twitter feed:

"I don't use that Facebook, Twitter . . . What is it good for?" says stylish Asian woman sitting at the next table at The Triangle. 3:12 PM Sep 19th, 2009 from Twitterrific

This question illustrates the considerable gap in technology use that exists across demographic categories; it highlights the limitations of the *Breakout!* platform's current interface, which relies on interoperability with Twitter for updates. In order to register to attend events on the *Breakout!* platform, it was necessary to provide a Twitter login name. This was an obstacle to broader citizen participation in the *Breakout!* events because while Twitter is heavily used by early adopters of social media such as technologists active in coworking communities, it is not being used by mainstream populations. To serve wider demographic groups, future versions of the interface will need to support text messaging as well as other social media applications such as Flickr, Facebook, and LinkedIn. In particular, Facebook has been adopted much more widely than Twitter, and thus if the *Breakout!* platform had been interoperable with Facebook's login, it might have been possible to engage a wider range of participants. This illustrates how technologists often disregard the needs of average users due to assumptions that people will easily adopt new social media platforms, or the assumption that if people are not using the latest platform, they are not worth including or communicating with. In fact, even among the *Breakout!* team, there were team members that had not used Twitter prior to the events, which resulted in a learning curve about the purpose, norms, and modes of communication on this platform. In addition, international events held by Citilab did not use the *Breakout!* platform for similar reasons since adoption of Twitter among the local community was low and the platform's registration process was in English rather than Spanish.

The coworking events invited participants to work independently, side by side, but there was little focused collaboration. While it was possible to accomplish one's own work and occasionally interact with strangers in an ad hoc manner, it was difficult to attract passersby. Still, these sessions challenged the team to think more carefully about the environmental and infrastructural constraints on mobile work—sun, noise, and available seating and connectivity. Rather than disrupting the urban environments with a work agenda, it was relatively easy to assimilate into public settings since laptops and mobile devices are increasingly common artifacts for both work and leisure activities. In contrast to coworking communities, which offer membership and participation in a likeminded group over more sustained time periods, short coworking events in public spaces did not seem to offer similar opportunities for access to diverse groups of people and ideas. In short, the lack of focused collaboration in these sessions was a drawback to citizen engagement and participation.

Future of Mobile Work

A second type of session that occurred during *Breakout!* was design-oriented sessions about the future of mobile work. Led by Antonina Simeti of the design consultancy DEGW, the initial session took place on Tuesday, September 24, at noon in the 60 Wall Street atrium, a public atrium in the Deutsche Bank building in the financial district. Unlike the venues for some of the other events, the atrium is extremely quiet, protected from the sun, and offers free WiFi (with the support of the Downtown Alliance, a business improvement district). The event brought corporate human resources professionals in charge of planning mobility solutions for their companies together with founders from coworking communities and the *Breakout!* team. By day, the atrium is filled with a mix of lunching finance professionals seated at small individual tables and a resident homeless population, many complete with their own netbooks, which they plug into clandestine outlets around the perimeter of the space. Taken to its extreme, the hybrid nature of the appropriation of the space by both mobile workers and homeless residents suggests a dystopian future in which people have neither offices nor homes but are employed as low-wage virtual workers. This scenario resembles Rivera's 2008 film *Sleep Dealer*, which posits a world of Mexican construction workers that build luxury condominiums in California from factories in Tiajuana where they are plugged into the Internet.

Previous research (Forlano 2008) illustrated the 60 Wall Street atrium's utility as a mobile workplace for high-technology workers that were often dispatched to client sites, in part due to its proximity to public transportation with the subway trains just underneath. Another mobile worker that participated in *Breakout!* disclosed that she liked to work on the subway itself because it was a place that she could focus on doing usability testing on small mobile devices. Similar to the ethnographic process of going "into the field" (Plowman 2003), corporate professionals participating in the discussion were able to get a glimpse of the possibilities of public spaces for mobile work.

A few weeks later, on a breezy fall Tuesday in October, the team held a Designing the Mobile Office event at the Shake Shack, a hamburger joint in Madison Square Park on Broadway and Twenty-Third Street. The session was well attended with over seventeen designers, architects, technologists, and social scientists participating. After a round of introductions and some initial discussions, the group broke into three teams for more intensive design charrettes or short, collaborative sessions focused on problem solving.[8] One of the features of the park that made it ideal for this activity was the plentiful presence of movable chairs (Whyte 2000), making it possible for the groups to dynamically reorganize themselves. Following an hourlong brainstorming and sketching session, several of the groups recombined in order to present their work (figure 23.3). Yellow tracing paper, known as "onion skin" among architects, designers, and urban planners, was wrapped around trees and affixed on green folding tables for display as the mobile-office concepts were introduced.

In contrast to the coworking events, the Future of Mobile Work events attracted the attention of passersby and onlookers—some briefly glanced while one even stopped to watch the presentations. The collaborative nature—for example, seeing small clusters of people working together at makeshift drafting tables with a colorful assortment of pens, Post-It Notes, and paper—was a significant factor in attracting the attention of passersby. However, at the same time, citizens did not seem to feel that they were invited or allowed to participate in the ongoing activities. The guarded nature of New Yorkers, their tendency to be in a hurry, rushing from place to place, and their relatively infrequent interactions in public spaces are perhaps to blame for the difficulty in engaging them more explicitly in the activities.

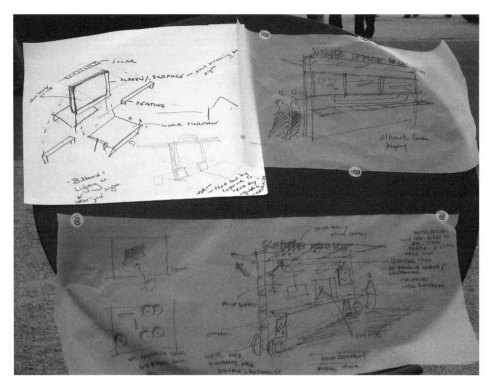

Figure 23.3
Architectural sketches and drawings on display on a park table in Madison Square Park during a *Breakout!* "Designing the Mobile Office" event in September 2009.

Flash Mob Ethnography

The Flash Mob Ethnography sessions were conceived of as a way to introduce more collaborative forms of data collection, analysis, and writing to the practice of ethnographic fieldwork by bringing together interdisciplinary groups in ad hoc sessions for short, focused exercises on specific themes around the impact of the economic recession on the built environment in the Union Square area.[9] While these sessions were deliberately curated and organized weeks in advance (requiring that participants sign up on the online *Breakout!* platform with their Twitter name, the term *flash mob* describes the fleeting and ad hoc nature of the collaborative sessions as well as their openness to citizen engagement, as in Rheingold's *Smart Mobs* (2003). While ethnographic research is a skill that takes many years to learn, I did not want the seriousness of formal academic research to prevent people from participating. Thus, the use of the term is an attempt to popularize the practice of ethnographic research and integrate the possibility of working together in groups rather than in isolation, as ethnography is typically conducted in academia.

During the first session, three teams set out to conduct research on the evidence of the economic crisis in the Union Square area in New York. For the most part, I was the only person that knew all of the participants in these sessions, which spontaneously combined professional and academic anthropologists, filmmakers, interaction designers, design students, and activists. About forty-five minutes were set aside at the beginning and end of the research for introductions and wrap-up, and the remaining hour and a half was dedicated to photographing, mapping, and observing. Each team had at least one person with advanced skills in ethnographic research; in addition, one person focused on picture taking, one on sketching, and another on note-taking. A total of about twelve people participated in the session. Each team was responsible for negotiating and deciding how to divide the work among the team members as well as setting the tone of the observation, which included how much they communicated to each other throughout their fieldwork. Some groups communicated constantly about their observations and worked closely together, while others worked more independently and then discussed their observations together with the larger group at the end of the session. This raises the question of how tightly coupled collaborators must be in order to consider their work generative rather than merely the coordinated sum of many parts.

Following our session, one corporate anthropologist noted, "Too much of my work is proprietary; I wanted to learn more about how designers practice ethnography." This signals the understanding that, by coming into a public space and participating in a free event, it is possible to share knowledge and skills in a way that might not be possible within secured corporate offices, which require that all research be proprietary. There is value in introducing peer production to the practice of ethnographic fieldwork through the organization of mobile, ad hoc collaborative sessions among interdisciplinary teams.

In the second session, Flash Mob Coding and Analysis, which was held approximately two weeks later on Columbus Day, as the Italian American parade marched down Fifth Avenue, about eight participants met at the Sony Public Atrium in midtown Manhattan to code and analyze the over 250 photos taken during the earlier session. The groups coded the photos by sorting them into piles based on themes. A number of interesting themes emerged from the research—advertising campaigns that echoed narratives about the recession, the use of empty storefronts as pop-up shops and campaign headquarters, the swift takeover of many bank branches by Chase, and the disruption of the traditional economy with the introduction of digital content such as music and books. For example, Virgin Records, one of Union Square's most recognizable landmarks, had closed, yet the majority of young people in the area could be seen with white Apple iPod earbuds protruding from their pockets, purses, and persons (figure 23.4).

During the final session, exactly five days after the coding session, a small group of three gathered first at The New School and then at a café before moving to a Parsons

Figure 23.4
The boarded-up Virgin Megastore as documented during a *Breakout!* "Flash Mob Ethnography" event in Union Square in October 2009.

The New School for Design studio space where we held a Flash Mob Writing Sprint.[10] We first reflected about the experience of participating in the Flash Mob Ethnography sessions before outlining and writing a short article. All three of us had laptops but we were unable to connect them to the Internet, since only I had a valid login and password for The New School's wireless network. The absence of connectivity disrupted the collaborative writing process because we had planned to write the article simultaneously using Google Docs. Yet we all worked individually on our contributions to the article, and within an hour, we succeeded in writing a 1,000-word blog post. Rather than having a meeting to discuss the article or coordinating the writing of the article electronically, it was refreshing that we could accomplish the writing of the article in a single session.

While these sessions did not succeed in engaging a wider group of citizens in the events for reasons similar to those explored in the previous two sections, the collaborative nature of the events was important to the process. For the most part, participants enjoyed taking some time in the middle of a busy workday to meet new people from a wide range of professions, explore a part of the city that they may not be as familiar with, and work together on short but interesting activities that challenged their observational and documentary skills. In addition, results from the Flash Mob Ethnography sessions indicated that these types of ethnographies have great potential as a pedagogical tool in a variety of settings, including universities, conferences, workshops, as well as prisons. Since being deployed as part of *Breakout!* in fall 2009, it has been run as a standalone event in a graduate-level qualitative methods course at Cornell University, in an introductory anthropology course in a prison in upstate New York, at a Values in Design workshop at New York University, and at the annual professional ethnography conference, EPIC 2010, in Tokyo.

Conclusion

The specialization of knowledge, the focus on individual skills, and the lack of physical mobility have dominated our working lives for the last century. However, we are currently living in an age that requires exposure to diverse ways of thinking, demands the ability to work in collaborative teams, and allows for greater physical mobility—supported by a range of portable technologies such as laptops and cellphones. *Breakout!* is a design intervention, conducted in New York in the fall of 2009, following a yearlong collaborative research process that experimented with the conditions for mobile work as well as the opportunities for interdisciplinary linkages and collaborations in public settings.

This chapter has discussed the merits of citizen engagement and participation in three types of sessions that focused on coworking, designing the future of mobile work, and flash mob ethnography. There were a number of specific environmental and infrastructural challenges to the events, such as sun, connectivity, noise, and sitting space, which continue to make mobile work activities difficult. While the *Breakout!* project attempted to address these obstacles, much work still has to be done to identify workable solutions to these problems. Furthermore, there is a need for technological platforms that can enable interactions between copresent strangers. The *Breakout!* platform's major challenge was that it relied solely on Twitter for registration and participation. Regarding collaboration, on the whole, events that incorporated explicit opportunities for strangers to work together were more successful than those that merely curated their copresence. While it was difficult to engage passersby for a number of reasons, events that included specific collaborative tasks as well as material signals and artifacts such as chalk lines, colored Post-It Notes, tracing paper, and other physical symbols caught a greater amount of attention than those in which participation was expected to emerge organically and spontaneously. While peer production in software collaboration and online content has the benefit of drawing resources from interested citizens around the world, the application of peer production among strangers in offline public spaces such as design charrettes and ethnographic fieldwork requires different modes of engagement, communication tools, and strategies.

In summary, *Breakout!* experimented with the technologies, settings, and formats for mobile work with the goal of creating design-driven interventions that support discovery, collaboration, and innovation. As a wide variety of work activities move outside of traditional institutions, whether due to economic pressures, individual initiatives, or emergent forms of organizing, it is vital that managers, designers, and technologists alike begin to plan for and support these activities. At present, mobile workers are forced to sustain much of the burden of interaction, motivation, and monitoring while at the same time experimenting with various types of connectivity and searching for suitable places to work. Rather than leaving these responsibilities to mobile workers, organizations would do well to support them more fully in order to gain exposure to emergent modes of organizing. As such, we may view mobile workers as a new constituency with shared experiences and needs but for which there is not yet clear leadership or an agenda. Greater experimentation with these mobile forms in tandem with concepts of peer production is needed for the creation of ad hoc citizen engagement that may form the basis of the creation of the open-source city.

Acknowledgments

I would like to thank Jelena Karanovic, Ingrid Erickson, and Christina Dunbar-Hester for their generous and helpful feedback on an earlier version of this chapter in addition to the book's anonymous reviewers, who greatly helped to strengthen the ideas presented.

Notes

1. For more information, see http://www.groundcrew.us.

2. For further details, see http:www.fixmystreet.com.

3. For an overview of projects, activities, and events included in the exhibition, see http://www.sentientcity.net and http://www.situatedtechnologies.net/?q=node/89.

4. For a detailed discussion of the conceptual basis of the project, see Townsend, Forlano, and Simeti 2011.

5. See http://coworking.pbworks.com/Directory.

6. Follow @breakoutnow and team members @anthonymobile, @laura4lano, @danaspiegel, and @asimeti on Twitter in order to read documentation of the events between August and October 2009.

7. For an example, see Anthony Townsend's presentation about *Breakout!*, which was created with Prezi, at http://prezi.com/n2g1oi4eabh-/breakout-escape-from-the-office/.

8. See the Wikipedia definition: http://en.wikipedia.org/wiki/Charrette.

9. The Flash Mob Ethnography sessions were in part inspired by a Values in Design workshop held in August 2008 at Santa Clara University, in which Susan Leigh Star advocated for more sharing of insights between qualitative researchers in order to compare the findings from individual cases. Since it is often difficult to build theories based on analyzing a single case, Star recommended that researchers work in groups to identify themes across many different cases that might lead to theory building.

These sessions were also preceded by a conference workshop on Pervasive Shopping held at the 2009 Pervasive Computing conference in Nara, Japan. At the workshop, led by Yasmine Abbas, Shin'ichi Konomi, and Jie-Eun Hwang, rather than reading prepared conference papers, the participants formed interdisciplinary teams for the ethnographic study of Japanese convenience stores. Each team at the workshop included a social scientist, a computer scientist, and an architect or interaction designer; at least one spoke Japanese. Each team was assigned a specific chain of convenience stores to research, document, and report on to the group. We were assigned the task of conversing with the staff in the convenience store and assembling a meal using only ingredients from the store. In two hours, we had taken hundreds of photos (and repeatedly gotten scolded by the staff), diagrammed the layout of the Circle K and prepared our lunch of *oyako-don* (translated as "parent and child on rice," consisting of chicken and omelet over rice). At the end of the workshop, we presented the findings of our research and went to a traditional Japanese *izakaya* for dinner. Having flown halfway around the world and taken a five-hour train trip to get to Nara, I was pleased with the use of the collaborative workshop to generate new data and findings, instead of the usual paper presentations with their passive, captive audiences. Rather than speaking in a hypothetical and speculative way about the integration of ubiquitous computing into everyday shopping experiences, we were able to give concrete and vivid examples of how such technologies might improve and hinder the interactions that unfolded over the counter at a typical Lawson, a large chain of Japanese convenience stores similar to 7-Eleven that can be found throughout the country.

Finally, these sessions were based on my own reflections about the solitary nature of social science research (dissertation projects in particular) and my own interest in incorporating design research techniques that foster collaboration (Brown 2008; Roam 2008). While big science projects are notable for their need to bring large teams, budgets, and networks together in order to pursue distributed, collaborative research, this is not common in qualitative social science. At the Consortium for the Science of Socio-technical Systems (CSST) Summer Research Institute at Blue Mountain Lake in the Adirondacks in June 2009, a group of qualitative researchers interested in the developing world discussed the possibility of organizing large networks of ethnographers around the world to come together virtually to pursue common research questions that they could pursue in their local field sites. Such a network was proposed in lieu of the customary but expensive method by which large corporations such as Microsoft, Intel, IBM, and Nokia essentially parachute a team of researchers into Brazil, Uganda, or Vietnam for two weeks of intensive ethnographic research, which is often supported by a team of local experts. The proposal for a network of researchers would aim to achieve rigorous results while decreasing the time, cost, and carbon footprint of the project. In addition, the purpose of such a network is to bring a diverse set of findings together to answer specific research questions with data from around the world.

10. I first encountered the writing-sprint methodology at a community wireless conference in London in October 2005. A group of hackers were writing a book, *Wireless Networking in the Developing World*, the bulk of which they produced in two weeks, and in about six months the resource was available as a free download that was later translated into several languages.

References

Allen, Thomas J., and Gunter Henn. 2006. *The Organization and Architecture of Innovation: Managing the Flow of Technology*. Chicago: Butterworth-Heinemann.

Augé, Marc. 1995. *Non-Places: Introduction to an Anthropology of Supermodernity*. New York: Verso.

Bauwens, Michael. 2009. Co-creation and the new industrial paradigm of peer production. *Fibreculture* 14. http://fourteen.fibreculturejournal.org/fcj-097-co-creation-and-the-new-industrial-paradigm-of-peer-production/.

Benkler, Y. 2006. *The Wealth of Networks: How Social Production Transforms Markets and Freedom*. New Haven, CT: Yale University Press.

Bijker, Wiebe E., Thomas P. Hughes, and Trevor Pinch. 1987. *The Social Construction of Technological Systems*. Cambridge, MA: MIT Press.

Brown, Tim. 2008. Design thinking. *Harvard Business Review*. 86 (6): 84–93.

Buchanan, Richard. **Year.** Wicked problems in design thinking. *Design Issues* 8 (2): 5–21.

Castells, Manuel. 1996. *The Rise of the Network Society*. Malden, MA: Blackwell.

Centre for Social Innovation. 2010. *Emergence: The Story of the Centre for Social Innovation*. Toronto: Centre for Social Innovation.

Cooper, Alan. 1999. *The Inmates Are Running the Asylum*. Indianapolis, IN: Sams.

Couldry, N., and A. McCarthy. 2004. *Mediaspace: Place, Scale and Culture in a Media Age*. London: Routledge.

Coworking Community Blog. 2009. http://blog.coworking.info/.

Dees, J., Gregory. 2001. The meaning of social entrepreneurship. *http://www.caseatduke.org/documents/dees_sedef.pdf*.

Dervin, B. 1992. From the mind's eye of the user: The sense-making qualitative-quantitative methodology. In J. Glazier and R. Powell, eds., *Qualitative Research in Information Management*, 61–84. Englewood, CO: Libraries Unlimited.

Dickert, Sanford, and Tony Bacigalupo. 2008. Cooperbricolage. http://coobric.com/.

Don, Abbe, and Jeff Petrick. 2003. User requirements: By any means necessary. In Brenda Laurel, ed., *Design Research: Methods and Perspectives*. Cambridge, MA: MIT Press.

Drucker, Peter F. 2002. The discipline of innovation. *Harvard Business Review.* 80 (8): 95–103.

Duffy, Frank. 2008. *Work and the City*. London: Black Dog Publishing.

Elkington, J. 1997. *Cannibals with Forks: The Triple Bottom Line of the 21st Century*. Oxford: Capstone Publishing.

Flores, Fernando. 1993. Innovation by listening carefully to customers. *Long Range Planning* 26 (3): 95–102.

Forlano, Laura. 2008. When Code Meets Place: Collaboration and Innovation at Wifi Hotspots. New York: Graduate School of Arts and Sciences, Columbia University.

Forlano, Laura. 2009. The invisible politics of the public airwaves. NYCwireless. http://www. nycwireless.net/2009/10/the-invisible-politics-of-the-public-airwaves.

Gibson, J. J. 1997. The theory of affordances. In R. Shaw and J. Bransford, eds., *Perceiving, Acting, and Knowing*, 67–82. New York: Wiley.

Gillespie, A., and R. Richardson.2000. Teleworking and the City: Myths of Workplace Transcendence and Travel Reduction."In James O. Wheeler, Yuko Aoyama, and Barney Warf, eds. *Cities in the Telecommunications Age: The Fracturing of Geographies*, 228–245. New York: Routledge.

Girard, M., and D. Stark. 2002. Distributing intelligence and organizing diversity in new media projects. *Environment & Planning, A* 34 (11): 1927–1949.

Gomez de Llarena, J. Carlos. 2009. Urballoon.Com. Accessed on October 1, 2009.

Hawken, P., A. Lovins, and L. H. Lovins. 1999. *Natural Capitalism: Creating the Next Industrial Revolution*. Boston: Little, Brown.

Horowitz, Sara, Stephanie Buchanan, Monica Alexandris, Michel Anteby, Naomi Rothman, Stefanie Syman, and Leyla Vural. 2005. *The Rise of the Freelance Class: A New Constituency of Workers Building a Social Safety Net*. New York: Freelancers Union.

International Telecommunication Union. 2005. *The Internet of Things*. Geneva: International Telecommunication Union.

Kelley, Tom. 2001. *The Art of Innovation*. New York: Broadway Business.

Kelley, Tom. 2005. *The Ten Faces of Innovation*. New York: Broadway Books.

Latour, B. 2005. *Reassembling the Social: An Introduction to Actor-Network-Theory*. Oxford: Oxford University Press.

Lave, Jean, and Etienne Wenger. 1991. *Situated Learning: Legitimate Peripheral Participation*. Cambridge: Cambridge University Press.

Leonard, Dorothy, and Jeffrey F. Rayport. 1997. Sparking innovation through empathic design. *Harvard Business Review* 75 (6): 102–113.

McDonough, W., and M. Braungart. 2002. *Cradle to Cradle: Remaking the Way We Make Things.* New York: North Point Press.

Moultrie, James, Mikael Nilsson, Marcel Dissel, Udo-Ernst Haner, Sebastiaan Janssen, and Remko Van Der Lugt. 2007. Innovation spaces: Towards a framework for understanding the role of the physical environment in innovation. *Creativity and Innovation Management* 16 (1): 53–65.

Nilles, Jack M. 1997. Telework: Enabling distributed organizations. *Information Systems Management* 14 (4): 7–14.

Norman, Donald A. 1990. *The Design of Everyday Things.* New York: Doubleday.

Oldenburg, R. 1989. *The Great Good Place: Cafés, Coffee Shops, Community Centers, Beauty Parlors, General Stores, Bars, Hangouts and How They Get You through the Day.* New York: Paragon House.

Penin, Lara, and Cameron Tonkinwise. Forthcoming. The politics and theater of service design. *Journal of Design Research.*

Pinch, T. J., and Wiebe E. Bijker. 1984. The social construction of facts and artefacts: Or how the sociology of science and the sociology of technology might benefit each other. *Social Studies of Science* 14 (3): 399–441.

Plowman, Tim. 2003. Ethnography and critical design practice. In Brenda Laurel, ed., *Design Research: Methods and Perspectives.* Cambridge, MA: MIT Press.

Rheingold, Howard. 2003. *Smart Mobs.* Cambridge, MA: Perseus Books Group.

Ries, Al, and Jack Trout. 1993. *Positioning: The Battle for Your Mind.* New York: Warner Books.

Roam, Dan. 2008. *The Back of the Napkin.* New York: Portfolio Hardcover.

Ross, Andrew. 2008. The new geography of work: Power to the precarious? *Theory, Culture & Society* 25 (7–8): 31–49.

Savitz, A., and K. Weber. 2006. *The Triple Bottom Line: How Today's Best-Run Companies Are Achieving Economic, Social, and Environmental Success—and How You Can Too.* San Francisco: Jossey-Bass.

Shute, Tish. *Response to toward the Sentient City.* New York: Architectural League of New York. http://www.sentientcity.net/exhibit/?p=672.

Tonkinwise, Cameron. 2009a. Sustainability is not a humanism: A review essay of Allan Stoekl's Bataille's Peak. *Design Philosophy Papers*, no. 1.

Tonkinwise, Cameron. 2009b. Weeding the city of unsustainable cooling: The unsystematic nature of systemic unsustainability, or, many designs rather than massive design. In Lisa Tilder and Beth Blostein, eds., *Design Ecologies: Sustainable Potentials in Architecture.* Princeton, NJ: Princeton Architectural Press.

Townsend, A., L. Forlano, and A. Simeti. 2011. Breakout! Escape from the Office: Situating knowledge work in sentient public spaces. In M. Shepard, ed., *Sentient City*. Cambridge, MA: MIT Press.

Townsend, Anthony, Georgia Borden, Laura Forlano, Dana Spiegel, Tony Bacigalupo, Dennis Crowley, and Sean Savage. 2008. Breakout! Escape from the Office. Proposal submitted to The Architecture League of New York.

Tripsas, Mary, and Sonali K. Shah. 2007. *The Accidental Entrepreneur: The Emergent and Collective Process of User Entrepreneurship*. Harvard Business School Entrepreneurial Management Working Paper No. 04-054.

Uzzi, Brian, and Shannon Dunlap. 2005. How to build your network. *Harvard Business Review* 83 (12): 53–60.

Von Hippel, E. 1978. Users as innovators. *Technology Review* 80 (3): 31–39.

Von Hippel, E. 2005. *Democratizing Innovation*. Cambridge, MA: MIT Press.

Weick, K. 1995. *Sensemaking in Organizations*. Thousand Oaks, CA: Sage.

Weick, K., K. M. Sutcliffe, and D. Obstfeld. 2005. Organizing and the process of sensemaking. *Organization Science* 16 (4): 409–421.

Wenger, Etienne. 1998. *Communities of Practice: Learning, Meaning and Identity*. Cambridge: Cambridge University Press.

Wenger, Etienne, Richard McDermott, and William Snyder. 2002. *Cultivating Communities of Practice: A Guide to Managing Knowledge*. Cambridge, MA: Harvard Business School Press.

Whyte, William H. 2000. *The Social Life of Small Urban Spaces*. Washington, DC: Conservation Foundation.

Wilkinson, Lawrence. 1995. *Scenarios: The Future of the Future*. WIRED. http://www.wired.com/wired/scenarios/build.html.

Yaneva, Albena. 2005. Scaling up and down: Extraction trails in architectural design. *Social Studies of Science* 35 (6): 867–894.

Zer-Aviv, Mushon. 2010. The case for open-source design: Can design by committee work? *Smashing Magazine*, September 1. http://www.smashingmagazine.com/2010/09/01/the-case-for-open-source-design-can-design-by-committee-work/.

Dramatic Character Development Personas to Tailor Apartment Designs for Different Residential Lifestyles

Marcus Foth, Christine Satchell, Mark Bilandzic, Greg Hearn, and Danielle Shelton

with Fiona Crawford

Urban planning plays a key role in shaping the physical and digital city environments we inhabit, as well as the transition spaces in between. The analyses informing many urban planning approaches tend to focus heavily on quantitative data such as population reports, surveys, census data, demographic tables and figures, and other statistics. This data is critical for understanding what is happening in urban environments and to inform decision making with demographic forecasts and future projections of building sites. However, it is difficult to have a definitive understanding of why something is happening, why a certain trend is occurring, or why there are nuances between two otherwise similar localities within the same city. Quantitative data does not easily articulate the lived experiences of residents, as Odendaal (2006, 36) points out:

The multicultural diversity of cities, the need to understand differing ways of life, . . . and insurgent planning processes where people take their own initiatives with regards to governance, will reveal a diversity of urban experiences. . . . The access to this information is not necessarily through reports and documents, but may have to be gained through oral histories, story-telling, and poetry.

Moreover, the future-oriented nature of design makes meaningful projection of residential experiences essential in the urban planning process. Following this line of thought, we appropriated and extended human-centered design methods—particularly persona development that leads into scenario-based design strategies—to suit the context of urban planning. The personas are grounded in rich data gathered from performance-based workshops that utilize dramatic character development activities and creative exercises.

In this research study, we employed and appropriated a technique first made popular by Cooper (1999) that by now has been well established in human–computer interaction design, but is still relatively unknown in many types of urban planning practices: design personas (figure 24.1). Personas are a tool used by interaction designers that enable them to capture the nuances of user behaviors in a rich series of user archetypes (Cooper 1999). While traditionally employed in order to design

Figure 24.1
A set of staff and client personas developed by CISCO (Nieters, Ivaturi, and Ahmed 2007).

"user-friendly" digital technologies, we find personas are proving to be helpful for analyzing residential user behavior and their relationship to domestic spaces (Satchell et al. 2008).

The benefit of personas is that by providing a snapshot of the unique social and cultural practices of the different urban user groups, a clearer understanding of the end user emerges. When engaging personas as a design tool we found it crucial to avoid utilizing them in a manner that constructs flimsy approximations of user archetypes that convey bland user needs with no clear design problems that can be addressed. Lene Nielsen (2002) rightly argues against personas that are barely more than stereotypes. The personas must have the integrity needed to inform a design that will meet the actual needs of real people. To address these issues, our personas and consequent "use scenarios" are grounded in the empirical data from character development workshops that engage participants in a process of what Howard et al. (2002) call "acting out." By allowing the participants to become performers in focus groups and workshop sessions, it is hoped that what will be uncovered will extend beyond the skeletal bones of their actions to reveal the contextual meanings behind the actions.

The use of social media for engagement has been crucial at three significant points of the methodology of this research: first, during the *recruitment* phase, to find new workshop participants whose diverse demographic and sociocultural profiles complemented the pool of people who attended the conventional consultation events; second, during the *data gathering and analysis* phase, to utilize social networking profile pages as a conceptual scaffold that allowed us to highlight the limitations and gaps in our data set; and third, during the *scenario development* phase, as a means to publish, communicate, and interact the resulting creative works that are depicting future design scenarios with a wider community of residents. In this chapter, we will discuss

Figure 24.2
3D aerial view of the development site.

our use of social media to amplify the reach of our design engagement. We first introduce the contextual background of our case-study site. We then report on the workshop method, engagement of study participants, and the data analysis. Three examples
of the resulting design personas and potential use scenarios are given to illustrate the
outcomes of our research work. We conclude by articulating how they can be used in
the urban planning process.

The Case-Study Site

The study was undertaken for a master-planned development site in Brisbane, Australia, for a new mixed-use precinct (residential, commercial, recreational, and retail) on
17.4 hectares of former industrial land adjacent to the Brisbane River (figure 24.2).
The site is located 2 km from the CBD and 8 km from the airport. Our research team
collaborated with one of three separate construction companies that are independently developing their portions of the site guided by an integrated master plan. The
current version of the master plan sets a target of 1,200 new dwelling units and 2,200
residents for the site. Construction of road infrastructure and the first set of buildings

were completed at the end of 2010, with further development work underway throughout 2011 and 2012.

The range of apartments to be built may be divided according to occupancy type: rental, owner-occupied, investment, and initial property sales price: up to AU$500,000 (entry level); up to AU$800,000 (midrange); AU$800,000 and above (high end). Each segment can be grouped into further subsegments that are based on a mix of demographics and generational or occupational patterns—for example, baby boomers, early-career lawyers, and so on. These *market segments* provide a method that is well established in the business operations of our partner organization for identifying potential groups of buyers and matching them with an appropriate residential product from an existing range—that is, one-, two-, and three-bedroom apartments as well as studios. However, market segmentation per se is neither helpful in guiding the design of the products themselves, nor with engaging the future residents of the site to participate in the design process. Comparing market segments with personas, Brechin (2002) points out that "market segmentation provides a quantitative breakdown of the market, while personas provide a qualitative analysis of user behavior"—in our case: residential user behavior.

Having established a proud reputation of using new and unconventional means to attract new residents, our partner organization invited us to work with them on challenging the status quo and expanding the relative homogeneous design spectrum for residential apartments. Similar to the automobile industry that introduces different editions for each model of car ("Sport," "Elegance," "Eco," etc.), we were interested in finding new ways to personalize and customize the experience of living in a master-planned community site by tailoring a range of apartment designs that suit different residential lifestyles. Cowper (2009) found that despite living in a flat with the same size and layout, many residents customize their space according to personal tastes and individuality. Cowper's photographs "show a wealth of approaches to home-making and decoration, even when contained in the same architectural shell." The approach we take here allows for the customization to start not just after residents move in, but right at the beginning of the urban planning and design process itself. This approach seeks to not only help our partner organization better understand the needs and desires of their customers beyond a mere market segmentation, it also helps them distinguish themselves from the competition by being able to offer an innovative and unique residential product portfolio. This notion further expands previous work in the United Kingdom on architectural mass customization and tailored urban environments (Steele 2006). Our approach also contributes to creating a range of design scenarios with different—both positive/desirable and negative/unwanted (Nathan et al. 2008; Nathan, Klasnja, and Friedman 2007)—future predictions of what a building is used for and by whom, which may change over time after the construction process is completed. A "scenario-buffered" building (Brand 1997) has a better chance of being able to adapt to future usages that may differ from its original intention.

Our partner carried out community consultation and information sessions in late 2007 that were attended by 179 individuals. The sessions provided an opportunity to inform the local community about the proposed 2008 version of the master plan and obtain feedback prior to the landholders lodging separate applications for Preliminary Approval of their portions of the site in 2008. The Preliminary Approval specifies core components of the development such as land use, public realm, building envelopes, view corridors, access and transport, and sustainability initiatives. The consultation report summarizes and then analyzes the oral feedback collected during the information sessions as well as written submissions received from community members.

Although the report provides useful information that significantly guided the Preliminary Approval process, our observations throughout this phase gave rise to several concerns typical for this kind of consultation (Foth 2006) that inspired the development of our methodological approach: Are the communication strategies deployed suitable for all personality types found within the community, or is there a chance that some members of the community will be intimidated by the format, put off due to time constraints and other commitments, and thus will their voices remain unheard? Will previously unheard community voices remain unheard because quantitative analysis strategies are not fine-grained enough to recognize nuances among marginalized voices? Members of the same social clusters and their immediate surroundings sometimes show a homogeneous set of opinions and attitudes. Yet, how do we also recognize and consider the less well-represented, but perhaps crucial and ethical, points of view? How can we ensure that the urban planning process is ongoing and inclusive and engages the community at large—reaching members that are not actively participating in conventional consultation methods? Does the consultation process try to elicit tacit knowledge from community members by allowing them to act and reflect in their natural work and living environment instead of reporting on their action outside of it? In other words, how can the phenomenological and experiential domain be incorporated into the urban design process?

Workshop Method

Rationale

The development of personas that are authentic and useful to the design process requires them to be grounded in rich empirical data. Rather than conducting conventional focus groups, we were guided by Markova et al. (2007), who propose a more organic process of focus-group data analysis, and who draw on Mikhail Bakhtin's notion of "dialogism" to find new ways of interpreting focus-group responses and behaviors. The model that they suggest encourages the researcher to explore not just the individual and his or her mind or behavior, but also the interdependence between the self and others. Markova et al. (2007, 46) speak of socially shared knowledge as "by its nature characterized by tensions, contradictions, vagueness and ambiguities as well as by regularities and recurrent themes that are often exhibited in focus-group data." This dynamic is also true of the interactions through which social knowledge is shared—that is, conversations, experiences, memories, arguments, and so on. This call for awareness of the liminal, the subtextual, and the tacit things about ourselves that we know but do not readily tell (Polanyi 1966; Rust 2004) provides the perfect building blocks for a more emotionally aware and empathetic style of focus-group research, which encourages the participant to engage emotionally and, most importantly, personally with the subject matter. It is at this point that the significance and applicability of dramatic character-analysis techniques becomes apparent.

Theater- and drama-inspired techniques have been explored in human-computer interaction before (Laurel 1991; Howard et al. 2002; Jacucci et al. 2005; Jacucci and Kuutti 2002; Kortbek 2008; Macaulay et al. 2006; Newell et al. 2006). As Laurel (1991, xii) asked early on, "When we look toward what is known about the nature of interaction, why not turn to those who manage it best—to those from the world of drama, of the stage, of the theatre?" Actors, playwrights, screenwriters, and directors strive to create characters and performances steeped in the "real"—to infuse and fuel the capacity for belief in the world their characters inhabit (Benedetti 2008). In the same way, in this study we have strived to draw material from living models and not from stereotypes (Stanislavski 1980) through the adoption of dramatic and creative writing methodologies and their adaptation to the context of urban planning and design.

If for the purposes of this research we were to replace the concept of "actor" with "end user," we can begin to see our role as researchers align with that of the director. The director/researcher guides the actor carefully through their discovery of themselves so that the "audience" (or in this analogy, the commercial partner) is able to connect and empathize with the end user on a level that surpasses just discovering their needs. This process paves the way for an understanding of why those needs exist, and how and why they differ from user to user. The goal is to design products and services that are not only sensitive to the changing needs of the user, but that respond to a sense of intimacy—a sense of the designer knowing the end user and considering them personally when executing their design. This engenders a personal connection not just between designer and end user, but also between end user and product.

The study explored how the use of dramatic development techniques such as the *Stanislavski System* and the *Meisner Technique* create "character-focused groups" or workshops. Actors employ these dramatic systems and techniques to develop characters that can, and do, react to events and emotions in ways dictated by the character's life story, individual personality, and tendencies and neuroses. Many of these traits will be different from those of the actor playing the character, but they are no less real to the actor and to the observing "audience." As was Stanislavski's aim for his actors, the focus of our research methodology is to delve deeper into the participants' understanding of themselves; to glean the motivation that lies beneath their design statements, comments, and ideas; and to understand and appreciate not just the object of a design or user needs, but the rationale. To understand motive in performance is to be capable of depicting a character that resonates with the audience, even if that character is embedded in an environment alien to the audience, such as a science fiction film or a period play. Exploration of the motive helps us as researchers learn the participants' underlying—and sometimes tacitly held—reasons for their wants and needs, which ultimately helps us know how to fill those needs through design.

The success of these "character-focused groups" is reliant on two important elements. First, established drama techniques and exercises such as the *magic if*[1] should be interpreted to suit the researcher's problem statement. In our research we aim to know the motives of our participants' residential and lifestyle choices. Second, character analysis and dramatic direction are crucial skills required to draw out further detail and encourage participants to deeply explore the reasons behind their comments and statements as well as assisting the subtextual character analysis of resulting data.

Our goal for the character-focus groups is not to masquerade as a drama workshop, or to ask the participants to perform anything that does not reflect their authentic knowledge or behavior. Instead, we encourage participants to be as naturally themselves as possible, and to consciously strive for comfort and acceptance in the context of the workshop.

Recruitment

As a way to complement the pool of people who usually participate in the conventional consultation events organized by our industry partners, we employed a viral approach comprising various online channels to solicit participation in an online survey tool (Dillman 2007; Goldsmith 2002). A short questionnaire was created as an initial screening instrument asking for basic demographic information and to allow survey participants to express their interest in participating in a follow-up workshop. The survey invitation was disseminated on various popular social media sites such as MySpace, Facebook, and electronic mailing lists. The advantages of this approach included low cost, ease of use, large volume of diverse recipients, as well as the ability to target local networks to reach prospective study participants local to Brisbane.

Approach

We conducted three workshops that ran for approximately two hours each, and workshop sizes were between five and ten participants. The workshop facilitator attempted to win the participants' trust and confidence through relating, empathizing, and giving the participant a voice and a platform from which to orate. By providing the right questions, the participants were willing to talk about themselves. For example, Participant A hoped for greenery and gardening in their apartment complex. This response may be what the corporate partner wants to know, but we wanted much more detail in order to develop a related persona, so we asked: Do they cook? Do they garden? Do they simply garden to cook or for relaxation? Why does gardening relax them? What do they like about plants? How does a garden make them feel? How do they feel when they stand in the bush or a forest? How could they achieve that same feeling in a small apartment garden? The workshop facilitator always maintained respect by giving the participants the opportunity to decline to answer any of our questions. Even their reluctance to answer certain questions could tell us more about their character than if they had answered. All of these responses helped us navigate the process and decipher what the next question or action should be.

We made sure that the workshops did not come across as data-elicitation sessions. Our data gathering was embedded in the more dramatically structured exercises such as "Step It Out." Here, participants were asked to walk us through or describe (depending on the comfort of the participant with standing and "performing" in front of the group) their movements through their apartment on their return home from work every day. Participants were also asked to either use chalk to draw a rough floor plan of their apartment's layout on the floor of the workshop space, or crayons to draw on paper (figure 24.3). One participant began by saying:

I open the door, walk in and put down my bag/briefcase then go to the kitchen.

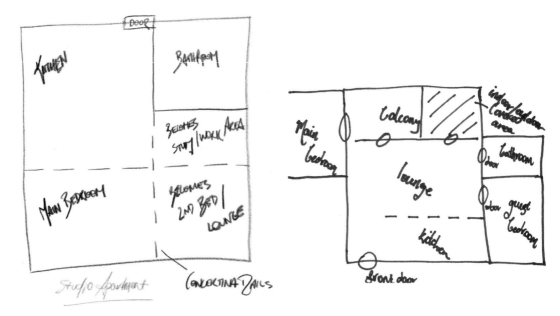

Figure 24.3
Floor-plan drawings created by participants during one of the workshop activities.

At this point the participant was stopped by the workshop facilitator and asked to describe in detail exactly what they placed their bag on, what it looked like, where it sat in relation to the rest of the room, what the bag itself looked like, and so on. The participant was then asked to proceed.

I go to the kitchen and put on the kettle.

They were stopped again and asked to describe where the kettle was, what was around it, and what they could see through their window and in their space. At this point, the participant was also asked to comment on their emotional state and how the environment and surroundings affected this emotional state. Gradually the participants became familiar and comfortable with the concept of exploring the emotional and personal aspects of their living environment, not only its appearance and physical elements. This in turn had a positive impact on the quality and density of information as well as the sense of camaraderie and sharing cultivated between the participants and the workshop facilitator.

During these workshops we applied drama techniques to reinterpret the inquiries of the researchers and the partner organization into more organic performance-based processes. For instance, our partner organization wanted to know about floor-plan size, but the average person may not know how to answer that question, so we looked for the element that lies at the core of the question: How do they use the space they already have (not how much space apartment dwellers need)? How do they feel about it? From their responses, we were able to analyze the data and develop design personas steeped in the lived experiences of the participants that could then help inform residential design solutions.

Data Analysis—Part 1: Design Personas

Inserting emotional replies into the research process paves the way for multilevel communication and data analysis—spoken and subtextual. For example, a participant may laughingly talk about spending as little time in their bathroom as possible because it feels as though the walls are closing in on them when they are there. Another participant may mention that their mirror is so poorly lit or positioned that they hate to look at themselves. We know, through the application of dramatic character analysis, that these participants are not only telling us things about their use of space, but also their emotional responses and their individuality. These are preliminary clues toward our persona development, which gathers momentum as the workshop progresses.

As a way to provide an interim scaffold for our collaborative data gathering, analysis, and persona development work in progress, we created Facebook profile pages (figure 24.4). These pages served as a central communication device and boundary object (Star and Griesemer 1989) between the workshop participants, facilitators/

Character Profile (RENTER One Bedroom 300-450k)

Mei Yao

Networks:	Queensland Tech.
	Gasworks Newstead
Sex:	Female
Relationship Status:	In a relationship.
Birthday:	April 4, 1989 (19)
Home Town:	Shanghai, China
Occupation:	Student

About Me:

For Breakfast:
Coffee! ...COFFEE!!!

For Lunch:
Fruit is good. Very portable.

For Dinner:
Whatever my boyfriend or his
housemates are cooking.

In the morning:
I sleep.

In the evening:
I listen to music, hang with friends or
my boyfriend or...ugh...do uni work.

On the weekend:
Dance, dance, dance!!

To exercise:
Dance, dance, dance!!

Information

Contact Info
Current Town: Brisbane, Australia
Personal Info
Interests: Myspace, Facebook, Surf the Channel,
                       Clubbing in the valley, Music Festivals
                       (Summerfield Daze, Splendor),
                       Photography, Hunting for vintage stuff
                       (Paddington, The Valley), Clothes
                       (Bessie Head, Fallow).

Favourite Music: Presets, Cut Copy, MGMT, Hot Chip, Block
                       Party.

Favourite Movies: Garden State, Mean Girls, Sunshine, The
                       Notebook.

Favourite TV Shows: Gossip Girl, Weeds, The Mighty Boosh, The
                       OC, Friends, Greys Anatomy.

Favourite Books: Harry Potter, A Million Little Pieces, A Walk
                       To Remember, Twilight.

Favourite Quotes: "This is my friend Jazz Funk."
                       Howard Moon, Mighty Boosh

                       ""The best love is the kind that awakens the
                       soul and makes us reach for more, that
                       plants a fire in our hearts and brings
                       peace to our minds, and that's what
                       you've given me. That's what I hope to
                       give to you forever."
                       Nicholas Sparks, The Notebook.

Figure 24.4

A Facebook-themed social media profile page as an early draft of a design data scaffold.

researchers, and the stakeholders at our partner organization. In the beginning these social media profile pages were purposefully flat and bland, because we tried to base them on the familiar market segmentations with which our partner organization was comfortable. However, as more detailed and nuanced data emerged from our workshops and analyses, we revised and enriched these profiles to move away from simple approximations of market archetypes toward behavioral user profiles that clearly addressed specific design needs.

For the purposes of our research, concepts used by our study participants were distilled into a set of categories that guided us toward the type of information retrieval necessary for useful design outcomes (Cole et al. 2005). These categories acted as boundary markers between which we were able to establish the factors that influence our participants' design needs, desires, requirements, and ideas. They were cross-tabulated with spatial design categories such as kitchen, bedroom, living/lounge, storage, car park, outdoors, as well as contextual and situational findings concerning lifestyle choices and social preferences. A short definition of each category follows:

• *History* Any event—good or bad, major or minor—that the participant has experienced and feels has affected the development of who they are.
• *Psychology* Participants' likes, dislikes, desires, dreams, fears, anxieties, or phobias.
• *Sociology* Socioeconomic factors influencing participants' social behaviors, opinions, convictions, and goals.
• *Environment* The impact of the participants' current environmental status and how that has influenced their current design needs. For example, a participant currently living in a studio apartment with little to no storage space will have different design priorities from one who currently resides in a larger space with better provisions. This category is also used to explore the impact of family members or pets living with participants, and therefore possibly influencing their design ideas.
• *Physiology* The participants' age, physicality, and any resultant needs and their impact on design and lifestyle needs. For example, an older apartment resident who suffers from a mild disability will have different priorities from those of a wheelchair-bound individual or a fitness enthusiast.

To get a better understanding of personas in our research, we applied character analysis to the audio/video recordings and the written field notes of each workshop. This was a process of repeated observation and analysis. We watched the participants when they spoke and when they did not, and we observed how they interacted with each other. Once we finished taking notes, we analyzed the data for commonalities and differences. From this data, we developed personas that embodied the dominant needs, desires, and emotional responses of the participants. We identified six personas, each with one or more clear user needs:

- *The Nomad* transitory, fast-paced lifestyle, uses the home as a base to conquer the urban environment
- *The Home Decorator* never satisfied with a given interior design, would love a "Swatch watch"–style apartment with changeable wristbands in different colors
- *The Gardener* lots of potted plants and greenery, ecologically conscious lifestyle, would prefer to live outdoors, surrounded by nature
- *The Flatmate* shares his or her accommodation with other tenants
- *The Converter* reconfiguration of spaces for different and unanticipated purposes such as on-site business or themed parties
- *The Bachelor* loves automation and a carefree environment requiring as little home maintenance as possible

In keeping with Nielsen (2002), we found it useful to get help from a professional writer to create rich and compelling personas. We engaged a colleague from the creative writing department of our institution in the data-analysis phase and discussed the results with her in detail. She was asked to write 1,000-word character sketches or "pastiches" for each persona (Blythe 2004) in a style similar to the "Fifty Characters" by Elias Canetti (1979). What follows are short passages from three of the sketches.

The Gardener

The Gardener defies the lonely-old-lady-with-cat stereotype.

She's happy—very happy—and far from alone.

She doesn't need a man and she's not missing company—she's missing hobbies, which feed her soul.

Having aspired to and achieved a house and marriage, the Gardener was never built for apartment living. But her circumstances have changed, and although the move was unfortunate and unplanned, she has been surprised at just how much she likes apartment dwelling. Her main regret is the loss of her garden, which was both a functional food producer and meditative sanctuary.

She's investigated and invested in indoor-dwelling plants and has crammed many full sunlight–requiring plants on her balcony. But shallow pots stationed on a concrete base aren't quite the same as tilling the earth with her hands, and while better than nothing, they're no substitute for the real thing.

Almost as though speaking aloud her own frustrations, her otherwise lovely downstairs neighbours occasionally grumble about the drips and grit that descend. All the pots are in trays—matching or make-do such as foil cooking trays—and she takes care not to over water, but it's a fine line. Rain, in particular, pays no attention to neighbourly harmony.

But her neighbours understand—even encourage—her green thumb. Both she and they are keenly aware that potted plants dominate her balcony and living space, while theirs are full of concrete and the occasional clothes-drying horse. She absolutely itches to conduct some late-night guerrilla pot-planting, and truth be told, her neighbours would be amenable to it as long as they could enjoy the greenery without having green thumbs.

The Nomad

The Nomad passes through his apartment as he would a hotel room.

Externally focused, he inhabits a suburb, not an apartment.

He's impulsive, active, gregarious, and fun.

The Nomad's keys and wallet are disgorged with a clatter onto the marble kitchen bench when he arrives home, and stay there until he pockets them again on his way out.

And it's never long before he leaves. The apartment is his telephone box—he ducks in to change and then heads out to take on the world. In fact, his neighbors could just about count to ten to measure the time between his entering his front door and exiting it again.

The Nomad circles his apartment, never straying too far from it. But he doesn't see this as a connection to home—he sees it as a practical set-up that allows him to return from work or the gym and shower, change, and go out again. It's the location of the apartment rather than the apartment itself to which he's attached. Walking distance to cafés and clubs is crucial—the Nomad might not be home much, but he's not a suburb-dwelling, commuting kind of man.

The Home Decorator

The ongoing Home Decorator considers a "look" temporary and is, subsequently, only temporarily satisfied with the look chosen. She is on a permanent decorating treadmill, characterised by the words "it would be perfect if only . . ." Her fridge is a blank canvas and goal board, the magnets semi-permanently holding magazine and catalogue-derived ideas and ideals in place as she determines their suitability for her living space. But, like shopping and to-do lists, they are discarded and forgotten once they have served their function.

She both occupies and observes a space. Bowerbird-like and discerning, she absorbs decoration ideas from films, magazines, cafés, art galleries, and friends' homes, and slots them Lego-like into her apartment. She actively surveys, catalogues, and mentally rearranges her friends', families', and neighbors' apartments with Bewitched-style efficiency and ease. In fact, she is so skilled at conducting small talk while surveying and virtually rearranging an apartment that her hosts are none the wiser.

The Home Decorator dresses her apartment as she would herself. More Posh Spice than Martha Stewart, she wishes to assemble, layer, and change her apartment as she does elements of an outfit. What suits her during the day or particular season is not what suits her the next; she, not unreasonably, expects her apartment space to grow and change with her and to accommodate her current interests.

The Home Decorator is not a homemaker but she likes to make her home. And, like working towards the perfect body, her apartment is a work in progress. Her never-ending stream of ideas doesn't allow her to settle, and while she definitively knows what she wants in one moment, her desires are equally as concrete but completely contrary in the next. She loves the mismatched wooden dining chairs that she's collected over the years from relatives, garage sales, markets, and even roadside collections. She thrives on the hunt for that perfect item to complement and complete the look, particularly if it's on sale or comes with its own back-story. And while she isn't afraid of commitment, she is afraid of relinquishing control, of being stifled or stuck with something so large, so expensive, and so difficult to change as an entire apartment.

Despite her decorating frustrations, the Home Decorator relishes the challenge and will continue to refine and reinvent her "permanently under construction" apartment. She is honing her craft with each refurbishment and is certain that with each new look her "it would be perfect if only . . ." will be transformed to "it's perfect." Yet both she and we know that she's not yet ready to step off the ongoing home decoration treadmill—she simply needs more inventive design solutions to facilitate her desires.

Data Analysis—Part 2: Use Scenarios

A rich pool of data provided the basis for developing a set of useful personas grounded in empirical research. To bring to life the findings from the focus group and character development workshops, we drew on techniques from Scenario Based Design (Carroll 2000). This type of design uses our emerging series of design personas and frames them within scenarios to provide a narrative depicting a future-use case. Not only does this technique provide a rich description of user needs grounded in in-depth research, it also reduces the chance for "conceptual drift" for those who implement the designs. In a multidisciplinary project such as this, the use of scenarios will enhance the interaction between members of the user-centered design team and become what Star and Griesemer (1989) call a "boundary object"—that is, an artifact that allows different parties to relate to the object through their own contexts.

Three potential use scenarios generated from our personas are presented below.

The Gardener Use Scenario

A "digital" window that virtually looks outside through the house into nature scenery.

It's Friday morning and Julie just got up. She goes to the kitchen and has muesli with fresh fruit and yogurt, as well as a ginger honey tea. If Julie could, she would spend the whole day outside in the local parks or her own garden, or live in an apartment building with an extensive garden on every balcony (figure 24.5). Nature gives her a sense of freedom. She has put some plants in her home office as well, but only the digital window gives her back what she misses from downstairs. As she switches the digital window display to the "garden" mode, the screen becomes a hole in the wall, a window that displays her flowers gently moving in the wind as if she was sitting downstairs, in the middle of her garden. She enjoys the nice atmosphere of being outside, yet she can use the office facilities. Two small yellow-blinking dots highlight two particular plants in the digital window. Their sensors have sent a signal that the water level is low. After an hour, Julie takes a break from work and goes downstairs to water them.

The Nomad Use Scenario

The Nomad's apartment is the equivalent to what's called a "hot desk" at work—accommodation that is "permanently temporary" (figure 24.6). In the Nomad's case,

Figure 24.5
Heavily gardened apartment balconies in Paraisópolis Favela, Morumbi, São Paulo, Brazil. Photo copyright 2005 Tuca Vieira. Used with permission.

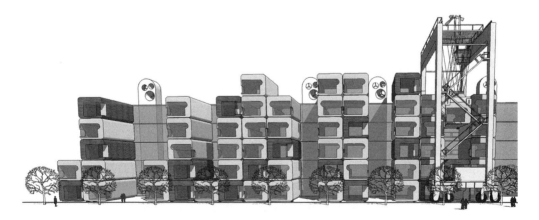

Figure 24.6
Corb 2.0 by Andrew Maynard Architects. Lots of automation, little maintenance, tiny or no kitchen, optimized for people on the move. In fact, the apartment is the equivalent of a "hot desk" at work . . . you can use anyone, anywhere, and maybe you want to be on top today, rather than on floor 7? City views today, river views tomorrow? Sketch copyright 2007 Andrew Maynard Architects http://www.andrewmaynard.com.au/corb.pdf. Used with permission.

the social network surface mirror functions as a fixed part of the infrastructure; it provides a stable connection to loved ones in his otherwise busy, spontaneous, and constantly changing physical environment.

Jeremy is a Nomad. He is constantly on the move, and he regards his apartment as a check-in/check-out hotspot rather than a warm and cozy home. He hates knick-knacks and mainly uses his apartment to sleep, shower, and change. It's 7 a.m., and Jeremy just got up in his one-bedroom apartment. As usual, he has hit the snooze button of his iPhone three times before getting up. He has exactly thirty minutes to catch the river ferry to work. As part of his daily routine, he puts on the kettle to make an instant coffee while he gets dressed. Equipped with hot coffee, he goes to the bathroom to get ready. The display behind the mirror illuminates as he turns on the lights in the bathroom (cf. "Dynamo" by Izadi, Fitzpatrick, Rodden, Brignull, Rogers, and Lindley 2005). A message from his girlfriend's phone appears on the mirror: "Good morning honey! Thanks for dinner yesterday, was yummy! :-)." In addition, sixteen of his Skype contacts turn green, including his mom, who always complains that he never rings back. He double-taps on her name. After a couple of rings she picks up, and her live image appears in the top-left corner of his bathroom mirror. While he brushes his teeth, combs his hair, and glances over an article in the latest issue of *GQ*, he listens to the latest family updates and reports what he had for dinner last night. After ten minutes they send each other hugs and kisses and hang up. Before Jeremy leaves the bathroom, he sees a Facebook status message popping up in the bottom-left corner of the mirror. Peter has just updated his status to: "What a crappy evening!" On his way out, he calls Peter to check what went wrong with his date yesterday.

The Decorator Use Scenario

The Home Decorator scenario employs a "Swatch-style" apartment design with inter-changeable or reversible panels and light displays (figures 24.7 and 24.8). Their content and colors can be changed easily. The interface is optimized to be changed quickly in order to create new looks.

Ana is a typical Home Decorator person. She likes to decorate and constantly change the style in and of her apartment. In fact, she treats the apartment as part of her personality, using the furnishings to express herself. She just came back from shopping and unpacked the new red carpet in the living room. The red of the carpet fits very well with the white leather sofa she bought last week, but it does not really match the purple of the digital frame picture in the living room. Ana likes to adjust the pictures according to her mood and interior furnishings. The interface is optimized to change and create new looks easily. She uses the display's search menu and browses through pictures by her favorite painter that would go well with the new carpet. She picks a green modern art oil painting. Satisfied with her interior setting, she opens the menu for the outside wall display. Because her in-laws are invited for a family dinner,

Figure 24.7
Customize your apartment just like you would your watch with interchangeable or reversible panels. Everything is optimized to be changed easily to create a new look.

she picks a rather conservative design and turns on the timer mode. At 7 p.m., right after dusk, the outside walls of the house start reflecting an attractive but rather discreet rainforest pattern.

Summary

Our set of six personas was well received by the partner organization. Set out as an exploratory design research project, our partner found the richness of the descriptions of different residential lifestyles useful to rethink some of the underlying assumptions of the master-planned community development approach that is inherently quite top-level and homogeneous. Additionally, the sales department appreciated the personas as a way to diversify and tailor their marketing approach beyond the rigid boundaries of the market-segmentation exercise. Aside from the benefits to our partner organization, there were also clear benefits of our approach for residents. Rather than

Figure 24.8
Interactive LED light installations provide different color light and allow you to personalize your space, both inside and outside, similar to this example at the Kelvin Grove Urban Village in Brisbane, Australia.

being merely consulted on preconceived urban planning ideas, the engagement with study participants through our workshop approach gave rise to a far richer and more nuanced view of different urban residential lifestyles. This process helps designers and architects better understand the communicative ecology and sociocultural microcosm of residents that may unfold in the tectonic structures, which are the central design elements of such master plans. An authentic appreciation of these dynamics may result in more livable residential and community spaces.

There are also constraints and limitations, some of which point to the need for additional work in the future. The number of participants and workshop events was limited, as were the personas that we were able to distill and develop using the time and budget given. A more diverse representation of residential lifestyles could have been developed if we had the chance to include more study participants and run additional workshops. Some metaquestions that arose during the data analysis suggested that additional workshop exercises—potentially including architects and urban designers—could be useful to focus less on the individual cases of people buying and inhabiting apartments and more on the sociality of living in an apartment complex or a master-planned community site. Further, only longitudinal studies could draw out changes in user behaviors and shifts in residential lifestyles to enable designers to see future changing needs.

Conclusion and Future Work

With the assistance from various student cohorts in the Creative Industries Faculty at QUT, our next phase of study will continue this experimentation at the nexus of character and persona development. We intend to use our set of personas as the basis for a cast of characters that inform further creative and performance-based activities. Just as Ann Light and colleagues (2009) employ storytelling and creative works to illustrate and reflect on new methods for engaging people in technology design, we hope to explore creative expression through three types of media outlets: creative writing and storytelling, short films, and online social media. A cohort of creative writing students will be asked to develop short pieces of narrative that use some or all of the personas as characters in their storyline. The setting of the story will be represented through historical records, or alternatively, the students will use a future-oriented setting within a science fiction genre. A group of film and TV students will also produce short films or minidocumentaries, and a cohort of communication design students will be asked to produce a web environment (e.g., game or online detective story) surrounding the characters and the site.

These creative works will be published locally using not only social media channels such as YouTube and Facebook, but also innovative mobile technology applications that move from an "anytime/anywhere" to a "here and now" paradigm such as our *Mobile Narratives* prototype trialed in a parallel study (Wiesner and Foth 2009). These dissemination strategies will be conducted in conjunction with the marketing plan of our partner organization. This creative output will not only raise the profile of the development site, but will also allow members of local neighborhood communities to read, review, continue, remix, and expand these works with their own stories. We are hoping that such an approach, following a long tail and user-generated content paradigm (Anderson 2006), will engage a diverse and more holistic section of the local community to express their views in creative ways. Furthermore, we hope that by continuing this work across multiple platforms, the new development site will become a part of the imagined and experienced local community history and memory even before the site's development is completed.

With the majority of the world's population now living in cities and urban environments, including urban slums (UNFPA 2007), urban planning as a discipline is more significant than ever in influencing and shaping our present and future habitat. The more people are affected by planning and design decisions, the more imperative it is to explore new ways to encourage a wider, more inclusive, and more diverse section of society to have a voice and participate in urban planning processes. Another key challenge is to integrate the solutions-based expert knowledge of town planners and residential designers with the domain and habitat-based knowledge of the people (their histories, experiences, and stories) living in urban environments (Hearn et al. 2009).

By reappropriating social media–enriched persona and scenario-based design approaches for use in the context of urban planning, we reached new insights that are different from and complementary to those usually captured by conventional community engagement strategies. We employed group activities and exercises adopted from drama and character development workshops to broaden the scope and quality of participation, which included performances and socioemotional responses from participants.

Our study suggests that we can find new ways of developing, recording, and publishing qualitative data as community stories to capture "lived experience," especially the experience of place. These accounts are at the heart of our study's community engagement strategy for urban planning. A well-theorized narrative approach is relatively novel in community engagement, but it enables traction both with the idiosyncratic experiences of community members and the planning and designing of frameworks and models. A narrative is "inter-subjective as well as communicative, since the plot renders meaning to specific experiences or logical deductions. It is also a powerful means of communicating an argument" (Guhathakurta 2001, 4). Moreover, community narratives shift the interests of design and planning processes toward pluralistic and subjective perceptions of space and its use, emphasizing the fundamental relationships between space and sociocultural processes (Kallus 2001). Sophisticated forms of representation and communication can also be used for decision support systems and multimedia to make pragmatic urban modeling tools for public forums (Guhathakurta 2001). In effect, such approaches construct "stories" of the past and project possible futures of a region to affect the evolution of an urban environment.

Acknowledgments

This research was supported under the Australian Research Council's Linkage Projects funding scheme (LP0882274). Marcus Foth is the recipient of a Smart Futures Fellowship supported by the Queensland State Government and National ICT Australia. The authors would like to thank our study participants and our partner organizations—FKP, the Sunshine Coast Regional Council, and Noosa District State High School—for supporting this research project. We also thank Helen Klaebe, Bhishna Bajracharya, Kerry Mallan, Ariella Van Luyn, Martin Gibbs, Michael Twidale, Mark Blythe, and the audiences at HCSNet Summerfest, University of New South Wales, Sydney (December 4–5, 2008); the Centre for HCI Design, City University London (June 5, 2009); and the CSIRO ICT Centre, Hobart (December 1, 2009). Thanks also to the anonymous reviewers who provided valuable comments on earlier versions of this chapter. Special thanks to Fiona Crawford for working with us on the data analysis and writing the six design personas in the style of Elias Canetti.

Note

1. Stanislavski made a critical distinction between being creative and being "actorish," between genuine emotion and an actor's emotion, between imaginatively feeling one's way into a situation and producing a facsimile of an emotion or representation of an emotion: "Truth of emotions, feelings that seem true in the hypothetical circumstances, that is what our minds require of a dramatic author. . . . For the actor [the circumstances] are actual, they are set." Stanislavski, quoted in Benedetti 2008, 50). "The actor, then, accepts the author's fiction as fact and by this capacity for make-believe, by using the *magic 'if'*, he creates an alternative reality, which is the world of the play." (Benedetti 2008, 50).

The *magic if* is a "headspace" in which actors place themselves in order to accurately experience the necessary emotional and physical responses their character will make during performance. An actor imagines how, if they were actually placed in the moment that the play is asking them to recreate, they would respond/react/feel/move during that moment.

References

Anderson, C. 2006. *The Long Tail: Why the Future of Business Is Selling Less of More.* New York: Hyperion.

Benedetti, J. 2008. *Stanislavski: An Introduction.* 4th ed. London: Methuen Drama.

Blythe, M. 2004. Pastiche scenarios. *Interactions* 11 (5): 51–53.

Brand, S. 1997. *How Buildings Learn: What Happens After They're Built.* Rev. ed. London: Phoenix Illustrated.

Brechin, E. 2002. Reconciling market segments and personas. http://www.cooper.com/journal/2002/03/reconciling_market_segments_an.html.

Canetti, E. 1979. *Earwitness: Fifty Characters.* New York: Seabury Press.

Carroll, J. M., ed. 2000. *Making Use: Scenario-Based Design of Human-Computer Interactions.* Cambridge, MA: MIT Press.

Cole, R., S. Purao, M. Rossi, and M. K. Sein. 2005. Being proactive: Where action research meets design research. In *Proceedings of ICIS'05*, Las Vegas, December 11–14, 325–336.

Cooper, A. 1999. *The Inmates Are Running the Asylum.* Indianapolis, IN: Sams.

Cowper, M. 2009. *Ethelburga Tower: At Home in a High-Rise.* (Photographic exhibition.) London: Geffrye Museum.

Dillman, D. A. 2007. *Mail and Internet Surveys: The Tailored Design Method.* 3rd ed. Hoboken, NJ: Wiley.

Foth, M. 2006. Network action research. *Action Research* 4 (2): 205–226.

Goldsmith, R. 2002. *Viral Marketing.* London: Pearson Education.

Guhathakurta, S. 2001. Urban modeling as storytelling: Using simulation as a narrative. *UCL Centre for Advanced Spatial Analysis—Working Paper Series*, London. September 1.

Hearn, G., J. Tacchi, M. Foth, and J. Lennie. 2009. *Action Research and New Media: Concepts, Methods, and Cases.* Cresskill, NJ: Hampton Press.

Howard, S., J. Carroll, J. Murphy, and J. Peck. 2002. Using "endowed props" in scenario-based design. In Olav W. Bertelsen, Susanne Bødker, and Kari Kuutti, eds. *Proceedings of NordiCHI'02*, Aarhus, Denmark, October 19–23, 1–10. New York: ACM.

Izadi, S., G. Fitzpatrick, T. Rodden, H. Brignull, Y. Rogers, and S. Lindley. 2005. The iterative design and study of a large display for shared and sociable spaces. In Richard Anderson, Brian Blau, and John Zapolski, eds. *Proceedings of DUX'05*, San Francisco, November 3–5. New York: American Institute of Graphic Arts.

Jacucci, C., G. Jacucci, I. Wagner, and T. Psik. 2005. A manifesto for the performative development of ubiquitous media. In Olav W. Bertelsen, Niels Olof Bouvin, Peter G. Krogh, and Morten Kyng, eds. *Proceedings of the 4th Decennial Conference on Critical Computing: Between Sense and Sensibility*, Aarhus, Denmark, August 20–24, 19–28. New York: ACM.

Jacucci, G., and K. Kuutti. 2002. Everyday life as a stage in creating and performing scenarios for wireless devices. *Personal and Ubiquitous Computing* 6 (4): 299–306.

Kallus, R. 2001. From abstract to concrete: Subjective reading of urban space. *Journal of Urban Design* 6 (2): 129–150.

Kortbek, K. J. 2008. Interaction design for public spaces. In Abdulmotaleb EL Saddik, Son Vuong, Carsten Griwodz, K. Selcuk Candan, and Alejandro Jaimes. *Proceedings of the 16th ACM International Conference on Multimedia*, Vancouver, Canada, October 26–31, 1031–1034. New York: ACM.

Laurel, B. 1991. *Computers as Theatre.* Reading, MA: Addison-Wesley.

Light, A., G. Simpson, L. Weaver, and P. G. T. Healey. 2009. Geezers, turbines, fantasy personas: Making the everyday into the future. In Nick Bryan-Kinns, Mark D. Gross, Hilary Johnson, Jack Ox, and Ron Wakkary, eds. *Proceedings of the 7th ACM Conference on Creativity and Cognition*, Berkeley, October 27–30, 39–48. New York: ACM.

Macaulay, C., G. Jacucci, S. O'Neill, T. Kankaineen, and M. Simpson. 2006. The emerging roles of performance within HCI and interaction design. *Interacting with Computers* 18 (5): 942–955.

Markova, I., P. Linell, M. Grossen, and A. Salazar-Orvig. 2007. *Dialogue in Focus Groups: Exploring Socially Shared Knowledge*. London: Equinox.

Nathan, L. P., B. Friedman, P. V. Klasnja, S. K. Kane, and J. K. Miller. 2008. Envisioning systemic effects on persons and society throughout interactive system design. In Johann van der Schijff and Gary Marsden, eds. *Proceedings of DIS'08*, Cape Town, South Africa, February 25–27, 1–10. New York: ACM.

Nathan, L. P., P. V. Klasnja, and B. Friedman. 2007. Value scenarios: A technique for envisioning systemic effects of new technologies. In Gary Olson and Robin Jeffries, eds. *Proceedings of CHI'08*, San Jose, CA, April 28–May 3, 2585–2590. New York: ACM.

Newell, A. F., M. E. Morgan, P. Gregor, and A. Carmichael. 2006. Theatre as an intermediary between users and CHI designers. In extended abstracts *CHI '06*, Montreal, Canada, April 22–27, 111–116. New York: ACM.

Nielsen, L. 2002. From user to character: An investigation into user-descriptions in scenarios. In Bill Verplank, Alistair Sutcliffe, Wendy Mackay, Jonathan Amowitz, and William Gaver, eds. *Proceedings of DIS'02*, London, June 25–28, 99–104. New York: ACM.

Nieters, J. E., S. Ivaturi, and I. Ahmed. 2007. Making personas memorable. In Mary Beth Rosson and David Gilmore, eds. *Proceedings of CHI'07*, San Jose, CA, April 28–May 3, 1817–1824. New York: ACM.

Odendaal, N. 2006. Towards the digital city in South Africa: Issues and constraints. *Journal of Urban Technology* 13 (3): 29–48.

O'Hara, K., M. Glancy, and S. Robertshaw. 2008. Understanding collective play in an urban screen game. In *Proceedings of CSCW'08,* San Diego, CA, November 8–12.

Pinch, T. Y., ed. *How Users Matter: The Co-construction of Users and Technology*. Cambridge, MA: MIT Press.

Polanyi, M. 1966. *The Tacit Dimension*. Gloucester, MA: Peter Smith.

Rust, C. 2004. Design enquiry: Tacit knowledge and invention in science. *Design Issues* 20 (4): 76–85.

Satchell, C., M. Foth, G. Hearn, and R. Schroeter. 2008. Suburban nostalgia: The community building potential of urban screens. In F. Vetere, C. Graham, and C. Satchell, eds. *Proceedings of OzCHI'08*, Cairns, Australia, December 8–12, 243–246. New York: ACM.

Stanislavski, K. 1980. *An Actor Prepares*. London: Eyre Methuen.

Star, S. L., and J. R. Griesemer. 1989. Institutional ecology, "translations," and boundary objects: Amateurs and professionals in Berkeley's Museum of Vertebrate Zoology, 1907–39. *Social Studies of Science* 19 (3): 387–420.

Steele, B. D., ed. 2006. *Negotiate My Boundary! Mass-Customisation and Responsive Environments*. Basel, Switzerland: Birkhäuser.

UNFPA. 2007. *State of World Population 2007: Unleashing the Potential of Urban Growth*. New York: United Nations Population Fund.

Wiesner, K., and M. Foth. 2009. Unleashing creative writers: Situated engagement with mobile narratives. In J. Kjeldskov, J. Paay, and S. Viller, eds. *Proceedings of OzCHI'09*, Melbourne, Australia, November 23–27, 373–376. New York: ACM.

Epilogue: The City as Information Organism

Judith Donath

The contributions to this book speak of cities filled with sensors, measuring physical conditions (chapters 7, 10, 17) and social interactions (chapters 16, 19, 20). The chapters speak of complex urban ecosystems, where the stakeholders are activists (chapters 6, 8), animals (chapter 22), gardeners (chapters 5, 9), apartment dwellers (chapter 24), and teenagers (chapters 12, 15). They speak of a rapidly evolving world in which information flows with unprecedented speed, where citizens are always connected, and where vast amounts of data about people and their environment is collected and analyzed.

Ubiquitous technologies—sensors and mobile communication devices—are bringing about a cultural revolution that was relatively unheralded. William Gibson's 1985 science fiction classic, *Neuromancer*, gave us a vivid popular image of the future, a world where bioengineered people with superhuman strength and vision fought virtual battles in brilliantly visualized cyberspaces—but they also needed to search hotel lobbies for pay phones to make a call (Gibson 2000). It has been a quiet but transformative revolution. Quiet, because it has been a revolution of incremental changes brought about through more efficient garden watering (chapter 9) and flexible work environments (chapter 23). Transformative, because it has turned the city, where there was once a clear distinction between infrastructure and inhabitant, into an integrated hybrid, an information organism (chapters 3, 13, 17).

This new city has eyes and ears, it can smell and feel. Its camera eyes are everywhere: in the convenience store, on the utility pole, and as part of the phone that nearly everyone carries. The camera eyes watch the cars at the stoplight, at the toll booth, and as they go over the bridge and through the tunnel. The city feels the weight of the cars on its traffic-monitoring sensors. It smells carbon, oxygen, and other compounds that float by in the air. It smells the bags of travelers at train stations. Its other senses collect abstract data. It knows where people spend money and where they get into cabs and what they are dying from in hospitals. It is the city of the twenty-first century, sentient and senseable (chapters 17, 19).

The sensory system of the urban organism is still embryonic. There are sensors here and there, but the city is far from having a comprehensive skin of them. Most of the time I walk in the city undetected. But in twenty-five years, we might find the idea of going anywhere, doing anything, without creating some sort of data trail to be a quaintly old-fashioned, and perhaps a disturbingly unmoored, way of being.

Sense organs are one part of an intelligent system. Far more significant is the nervous system that interprets their signals and then acts based on this incoming data. The human sensory system is rather mediocre: cats, dogs, bats, and rats all outdo us in perception of sound, smell, and light. We humans excel at interpreting what we see and at communicating about it to each other.

The nervous system of the city, too, is in the early stages of development. Aside from an occasional kiosk (chapters 18, 21), there is little in our cityscape that reveals the constant current of data flowing through the air (chapter 16). And even at our monitors, we are just beginning to be able to see, hear, and understand the patterns of information flow (chapters 11, 14, 19). Every day, though, sees new data becoming available, new connections being made. The synapses of the urban consciousness are being stitched together.

The urban nervous system is growing in the vast data centers that gather sensor data, find patterns, and make predictions about weather, earthquakes, traffic, crime, and next year's favorite shoe colors. It grows in the social network sites where millions of people post their passing thoughts to create a massive stream-of-consciousness recording of what the collective mind is thinking, a collective mind that, like many of us, lurches from pondering weighty issues—concern about the environment, political prisoners, the future of privacy—to the utterly mundane—an obscure celebrity's divorce problems, a meal just eaten, irritation at a coworker. The nascent urban nervous system comes together in Google searches and social networks (chapter 2), via growing habits of staying in touch (chapters 12, 15).

Marvin Minsky's *Society of Mind* lays out a conceptual model of the human mind as composed of numerous specialized agents each of which has evolved to perform a specific task. Their interaction creates what we experience as consciousness, though each individual agent may have only limited intelligence and communicative ability. Minsky's agents are metaphorical (though agentlike systems may turn out to be a fundamental part of cognition (Ruppin 2002)), but in the city-as-sentient-being model, they are literal: autonomous humans, animals, and other systems.

When we think of the city as sentient and senseable, we think of it, for all its unnatural smoke, buildings, and toxins, as an organism, an organic city. It is a powerful metaphor, the city as organism, for it raises difficult and provocative questions. What is its brain? What are its proximate goals? And what is its ultimate goal?

An animal's senses connect to its brain, its central nervous system. Its senses help it achieve its goals, they help it find food, find mates, and avoid danger. Ultimately, they help its genes survive. That is the ultimate goal, the path of evolutionary success. But the animal (human or not) does not think about evolutionary success, but rather of is immediate—that is, proximate—goals. The cat yowling on the fence is not thinking about curling up with some kittens in a few months, and certainly not about how its genes will be passed on to them.

Like other advanced organisms, the city has a complex nervous system. Its thousands of eyes feed their images into many processing units. Our understanding of how it functions as an organism depends on what we think of as its brain. For the brain of the new city is not just made of sensors and connections; most importantly, it is made of the people who live there, from deeply engaged activists and officials to disaffected dwellers.

The government is a key element of the city brain. Many of the senses—traffic cams, crime cams, environmental sensors—feed directly to it. As it needs and wishes to, it can scan through social networks, credit card records, and tourists' videos. What motivates this urban mind?

One view is that it wants to gather resources and grow. We, the inhabitants of the city, evolved at a time when sustenance was difficult and maximizing caloric intake a useful strategy. Today we have Weight Watchers and aspartame and gastric-bypass surgery to fend off the obesity that comes with having a vast appetite in a time of abundance. There is a parallel urban evolution. In the early days of cities, growth was essential and often difficult. The Greek city-states that give us much of our conceptual models and words for urban life—the agora, the polis—were tiny compared even to smallish contemporary cities. An appetite for growth and laws that support it was essential for keeping a town alive during times when decline was a greater threat than unsustainable expansion (Davis 1955; Ferguson 2008). Today we have sprawling, smoggy, traffic-snarled megalopolises (Mumford 1997): cities that are overspilling their jeans and splitting their seams, while gorging on rivers and chewing on mountainsides.

Overconsumption is a difficult habit to break for individuals or societies. When the goal is growth, we end up with the voracious city, offering jobs, cheap labor, and cheap homes, while devouring the surrounding resources. We can posit other goals, too. When the goal is power for the government, we get the authoritarian city whose many sensor eyes face inward on its citizens, watching their moves and refusing them exit visas. If it is sustainability, we get the green city with its small homes and bicycles, carbon sensors, and pedometers. These can coexist, and of course the government is only one part of the city mind. Networks of activists working to change how we live, as well as more informal groups of people socializing or working together, all shape the direction the city takes.

Power, resources, and growth are proximate goals. These vivid desires—hunger for food, for revenue—may be satisfied with rich, chocolaty cheesecake or a new factory or oil well, but they may in the end be at odds with the ultimate goal.

For the biological organism, the ultimate goal is passing on genes. *Goal* is not really the right word here, for evolution is a process, not a design. Genes that are expressed as features that help their host survive and reproduce will, through that process, be passed on, while features that hinder genetic continuity will fade away. When conditions changed slowly, this evolutionary process ensured that the organism's tastes led to beneficial behaviors. With the unprecedentedly rapid change that advanced human civilizations produce, preferences that change only at evolutionary rates—over many generations—now often poorly match contemporary conditions.

Returning to the city, we can posit continued existence as its ultimate goal. This gives us a humanistic interpretation of the evolutionary/organismic metaphor of the city in which the people are analogous to genes. What they create together is a culture, embodied in a particular urban setting, but the essence of survival is not the big organism, the city, but the individual humans who comprise it. It is a view that encompasses the way bits of one city or culture become embedded in another as people migrate, and as culture flows through radio waves and Internet connections.

While these may seem like abstract and academic distinctions, they have real impact on our policies. Think of New Orleans. What does it mean to save New Orleans, for it to continue to exist? Do we rebuild the physical embodiment of New Orleans, its distinctive architecture and neighborhoods, but again in its precarious location? Or do we invest in the people who had inhabited it, help them rebuild, recreate, and start fresh elsewhere?

Both the city and the people within it are changing rapidly as they adjust to massive infusions of information. With each snapshot that is posted online, each shoe that is rated, each carbon molecule counted, and each car flying through its EZpass gate, the collective knowledge of and for our community grows. But we do not yet have a very clear view of what kind of future it holds. The humans in this world are becoming increasingly knowledgeable and thus powerful. Twenty years ago there was no web. It is hard now to imagine what it was like to not have millions of facts and pictures and song lyrics immediately available, sorted and indexed not through any deliberate schema, but through the mapping of the emergent organization of the knowledge itself. Twenty years from now we will look back and be amused at how little information was available to us at this time. What will that future knowledge be? Perhaps it will be far more detail about individuals: generations are growing up whose parents publicly posted their sonograms, their first steps, and their toddler tantrums. It is a cliché to say that privacy is going away—the truth is more complex than that—but certainly a tremendous amount of detail will be recorded about all of us. Today, it seems rather suspicious if someone claims to be an expert if there is little record of him or her online. We expect any vaguely public figure to have a significant digital persona; without it, one seems to be a fraud. As more data becomes available about everyone and people grow increasingly accustomed to updating (or having some device that seamlessly, effortlessly updates) the world about their thoughts, location, most recent meal, and so on, it will seem increasingly strange not to have a detailed digital history.

Understanding, and shaping, the purpose for which this data is collected is profoundly important. At best, it is the glue holding society together. We humans are not solitary creatures; we evolved as social animals, and keeping track of each other, knowing who has contributed her proper share and who has shirked, is one of the fundamental abilities that makes society possible (Dunbar 2003). As we face a future of decreasing resources, the city that intelligently helps its citizens to move beyond a desire for growth and consumption will ultimately thrive (chapters 1, 4). An autocratic and oppressive regime can use the same information to feed its thirst for power at a terrible cost to its inhabitants. The decisions made today, from laws about data and privacy to system architectures and transparency as the nascent city nervous system takes shape, will help determine which of these cities we are likely to live in.

References

Davis, Kingsley. 1955. The origin and growth of urbanization in the world. *American Journal of Sociology* 60 (5): 429–437.

Dunbar, Robin I. M. 2003. The social brain: Mind, language, and society in evolutionary perspective. *Annual Review of Anthropology* 32:163–181.

Ferguson, N. 2008. *The Ascent of Money: A Financial History of the World*. New York: Penguin.

Gibson, W. 2000. *Neuromancer*. New York: Ace Trade.

Minsky, M. 1988. *The Society of Mind*. New York: Simon and Schuster.

Mumford, L. 1997. *The Culture of Cities*. London: Routledge.

Ruppin, E. 2002. Evolutionary autonomous agents: A neuroscience perspective. *Nature Reviews Neuroscience* 3 (2): 132–141.

Editor Biographies

Marcus Foth   Associate Professor Marcus Foth is Principal Research Fellow with the Institute for Creative Industries and Innovation, Queensland University of Technology (QUT), Brisbane, Australia. Professor Foth's research explores human-computer interaction design and development at the intersection of people, place, and technology with a focus on urban informatics, locative media, and mobile applications. He is the founder and director of the Urban Informatics Research Lab.

He received a QUT Vice-Chancellor's Research Fellowship (2009–2011) and a Smart Futures Fellowship from the Queensland State Government (2009–2011), cosponsored by National ICT Australia (NICTA), to explore how ubiquitous computing can be employed to bring real-time environmental data into the homes and hands of Queensland residents.

Foth was awarded the inaugural Australian Business Foundation Research Fellowship on Innovation and Cultural Industries 2010, sponsored by the Aurora Foundation. He was an ARC Australian Postdoctoral Fellow (2006–2008), and a 2007 Visiting Fellow at the Oxford Internet Institute, University of Oxford, UK.

The high quality of his research work has attracted over $2M in national competitive grants and industry funding since 2006. Professor Foth has published over eighty articles in journals, edited books, and conference proceedings. He is the editor of the *Handbook of Research on Urban Informatics* (IGI, 2009), and coauthor of *Action Research and New Media: Concepts, Methods and Cases* (Hampton Press, 2009). He was the conference chair of OZCHI 2009 in Melbourne, and the 5th International Conference on Communities and Technologies 2011 in Brisbane. http://www.urbaninformatics.net/

Laura Forlano   Laura Forlano is a writer, researcher, and consultant based in New York City. Currently, she is a Postdoctoral Associate in the Interaction Design Lab in the Departments of Communication and Information Science at Cornell University. Forlano's research is on the role of information technology in supporting open innovation networks in urban environments, with a specific emphasis on the use of mobile, wireless, and ubiquitous computing technologies to support collaboration. Her current project "Design Collaborations as Sociotechnical Systems," which is funded by the National Science Foundation, is an international comparative study that focuses on the role of technology in supporting networks of designers in New York, Barcelona, and Brisbane. Forlano received a 2011–2012 Fulbright grant to study social innovation networks in Toronto. Her research has been funded by the National Science Foundation, the Social Science Research Council, Microsoft Research, the Urban Communication Foundation and the American Council on Germany. Her research and writing has been published in peer-reviewed journals including *The Information Society*, *Journal of Community Informatics*, *IEEE Pervasive Computing*, *Design Issues*, and *Science and Public Policy*. She has published chapters for books including editor Mark Shepard's *Sentient City: Ubiquitous Computing, Architecture, and the Future of Urban Space* (MIT Press 2011) and The Architecture League of New York's Situated Technologies pamphlet series and is a regular contributor to their *Urban Omnibus* blog. Forlano received her Ph.D. in Communications from Columbia University in 2008. Her dissertation, "When Code Meets Place: Collaboration and Innovation at WiFi Hotspots," explores the intersection between organizations, technology (in particular, mobile and wireless technology) and the role of place in communication, collaboration, and innovation.

In 2008–2009, while a Kauffman Fellow in Law at the Information Society Project at Yale Law School, Forlano was part of a collaborative project "Breakout! Escape from the Office" that was included in The Architecture League of New York's *Toward the Sentient City* exhibition. Since 2007, Forlano has been an Adjunct Faculty member in the Design and Management department at Parsons and the Graduate Programs in International Affairs and Media Studies at The New School where she teaches courses on Innovation, Technology, and the City; New Media and Global Affairs; Service Design; and Design and Everyday Experience. She has also been active in research on public policy issues related to telecommunications and information technology. In 2011, she coauthored with Alison Powell a study "From the Digital Divide to Digital Excellence: *Global Best Practices for Municipal and Community Wireless Networks,*" for the New America Foundation. Forlano served on the Federal Communication Commission's Consumer Advisory Panel from 2005 to 2007. She serves as a board member of NYCwireless and the New York City Computer Human Interaction Association. Forlano received a Master's in International Affairs from Columbia University, a Diploma in International Relations from The Johns Hopkins University, and a Bachelor's in Asian Studies from Skidmore College. She studied at Sophia University in Tokyo, Japan from 1993 to 1994. Forlano speaks Japanese and has studied French, Spanish, Italian, and German. Forlano's blog can be found at www.lauraforlano.org.

Christine Satchell Christine Satchell, PhD, is a Senior Research Fellow with the Urban Informatics Research Lab at Queensland University of Technology, and an Honorary

Research Fellow with the Interaction Design Group at The University of Melbourne. Her research is dedicated to understanding the social and cultural nuances of everyday user behavior in order to inform the design of new technology. Integral to this is the development of a methodological approach that embeds cultural theory within Human-Computer Interaction.

She has published over thirty peer-reviewed book chapters, journal articles, and conference papers, and her work is frequently disseminated in public forums including keynote addresses and has been covered extensively by the media including *New Scientist, Wired Magazine,* and blogs such as Gizmodo.

Currently, she is focusing on the relationship between constellations of technologies including mobile devices, social networking sites, sensors, and shared displays in urban environments. Christine is dedicated to her chosen field of HCI and was Technical Program Co-Chair for the Twentieth Anniversary of *OZCHI 2008* and the Co-Chair for *Horizon CSCW* in China 2011. She is just completing her first science fiction novel called *Fast Net.*

Martin Gibbs   Martin Gibbs is a Senior Lecturer and member of the Interaction Design Group in the Department of Information Systems at The University of Melbourne. He completed his PhD in Science and Technology Studies (STS) in the Department of History and Philosophy of Science, The University of Melbourne, in 2000. Since 2003 his research has been located at the disciplinary intersection between STS and Human-Computer Interaction and has focused on how people use a variety of interactive technologies such as video games, community networks, and mobile phones for convivial and sociable purposes in a variety of situations.

His research has investigated the use of information and communication technologies in the home and in neighborhood communities. This work has examined issues such as technological opportunities to support domestic intimacy between marriage partners and to supporting playful engagement between grandparents and grandchildren. He has examined, through the Australian Research Council supported "Connected Homes" project, the material practices, temporal rhythms, and spatial configurations associated with information and communication technologies in the home and how these technologies connect people with friends and family, as well as the local neighborhood and other communities. His current research is extending these concerns with time, space, and material practice to consider engagement, presence and the body in collaborative virtual environments such as online multiplayer games and in emerging online practices associated with death, grief, and mourning.

Author Biographies

Michael Arnold Michael Arnold is a Senior Lecturer in the History and Philosophy of Science program, School of Philosophy, Anthropology and Social Inquiry, at the University of Melbourne, Australia. Arnold's ongoing research interests lie at the intersection of contemporary technologies and our society and culture. His current research projects examine (1) the appropriation of broadband technologies in domestic environments; (2) the varied appropriation of social networking systems across six Asia-Pacific sites; (3) the implications of ICTs for communities of various kinds; (4) the social implications of electronic patient health records; and (5) assessing the social return on ICT investments in the Third Sector. Arnold may be contacted at mvarnold@unimelb.edu.au.

Sarah Barns Sarah Barns is a researcher and producer with a background that includes interactive media production and strategic policy and planning across areas including telecommunications, broadcasting, and creative industries. Her dissertation, "The Death and Life of the Real Time City," is nearing completion through the University of Technology, Sydney (UTS). The mobile project "Sydney Sidetracks," which she conceived of, researched, and produced, was released in November 2008 as the ABC's first location-based mobile content offering, and can be viewed at http://abc.net.au/sidetracks. Elements of the ABC's sound archives drawn on for this project are in the process of being re-released under Creative Commons licenses through the ABC's social media website Pool (see http://pool.org.au). Specific sound excerpts referred to in her book chapter can also be accessed at http://sitesandsounds.net.au.

Mark Bilandzic Mark has completed his undergraduate and graduate degree in Media Computer Science at Ludwig-Maximilians-Universität in Munich, University of California Berkeley, and Queensland University of Technology in Brisbane. He has gathered work experience on various product development projects at Siemens/Croatia, Infosys Technologies/India, Computershare, and the Center for Digital Technology and Management (CDTM) Germany.Mark's focus is on human-computer interaction, mobile and ubiquitous computing, and ambient displays.When he is not working on his PhD, Mark is all about sports, especially playing soccer, tennis, running, and mountainbiking. He enjoys backpacking, reading,and listening to Croatian music. He just got a new DSLR and aims to become a better photographer.

Eli Blevis   Eli Blevis is an Associate Professor of Informatics in the Human-Computer Interaction Design program of the School of Informatics and Computing at Indiana University, Bloomington. His primary area of research, and the one for which he is best known, is sustainable interaction design. This area of research and his core expertise are situated within the confluence of human-computer interaction from the standpoint of the computing and cognitive sciences, and design as it reflects design criticism and the practice of critical design. His research also engages design theory, digital photography, and studio-based learning.

Mark Blythe   Mark Blythe is Professor of Interdisciplinary Design at Northumbria University. He is an ethnographer with a background in cultural studies. Recent work with Goldsmith's Interaction Research Studio has involved residents of a care home and a group of cloistered nuns. Like many academics he writes biographies of himself in the third person like Caesar.

Peter Bruza   Peter Bruza's research spans the fields of quantum mechanics (QM) and cognitive science, with a strong connection to applied logic and information processing and retrieval. Bruza was a pioneer in applied logic for information retrieval via his PhD dissertation in 1993. Since then he has made theoretical contributions to information retrieval and applied logic—for example, by developing an inductive theory for information retrieval evaluation, and operational models replicating human abductive reasoning to drive semiautomated scientific discovery. In the last five years, Bruza has been pioneering a line of research into subsymbolic reasoning using semantic space models, which are models emerging from cognitive science. In recognition of this groundbreaking work he was appointed to the editorial board of the *Journal of Applied Logic* (Elsevier) in the area of "human reasoning." More recently he has explored the intriguing connection between computational models and QM. He is pioneering a new field, Quantum Interaction, which aims to study QM outside of physics and utilize it in areas such as cognition, economics, artificial intelligence, and information retrieval.

Martin Brynskov   Martin Brynskov, PhD (computer science/HCI), is assistant professor in interaction technologies at the Department of Information and Media Studies at Aarhus University in Denmark. He is also director of the Civic Communication group at the Center for Digital Urban Living, a Danish national research center. Working closely together with journalists, media organizations, municipalities, artists, and industrial partners, he investigates the consequences of digitization and explores new forms of mediation within a variety of domains, with special focus on the role of social interaction and interfaces. The research is mostly carried out as interventions and experiments in the wild, deploying prototypes and semipermanent interactive systems. He was the project leader of Aarhus by Light, and he has been involved in the development of numerous other projects and products based on social interaction mediated by technology, working together with public institutions and industrial partners, including LEGO Company and Bang & Olufsen. During his doctoral work at the Center for Interactive Spaces, he developed tools for social construction for children using mobile and pervasive media based on the notion of "digital habitats." He also holds an MA in information studies and classical Greek.

Carnaven Chiu Carnaven Chiu holds an MS degree from the Department of Architecture, MIT, with a concentration in Design and Computation. She received her Bachelor of Architecture degree from Carnegie Mellon University and practiced architecture in New York City and Taipei shortly thereafter. Chiu is currently a research fellow at the SENSEable City Laboratory. Her work at the lab includes the study of utilizing and exploiting the potentials of user-generated online visual metadata as well as the design and development of unique visualizations that offer collaborative inquiry into the fundamentals of architectural design and experience through visual representation and textual description.

Jaz Hee-jeong Choi Jaz Hee-jeong Choi is an ARC Australian Postdoctoral Fellow (Industry) at the Institute for Creative Industries and Innovation, QUT. Her research interests are in playful technology, particularly the ways various forms of playful interaction are designed, developed, and integrated in different cultural contexts. Her doctoral research introduced a new conceptual approach to urban sustainability that recognizes "play" as the core of transformative interactions in cities as technosocial networks. Her current research explores designing and developing playful ubiquitous technologies to cultivate sustainable food culture in urban environments. She has collaborated with leading international researchers and published in books and journals across various disciplines. Her website is at www.nicemustard.com.

Hilary Davis Hilary Davis is a Senior Research Fellow in the Department of Information Systems at the University of Melbourne. Her research interests include the role of technology in mediating social relationships between distributed family members, and in particular between children and adults. Her current work focuses on technological support for people living with serious illnesses, such as diabetes and cancer. With a background in social science research, Davis is particularly oriented toward the application of ethnographic techniques in complex and sensitive settings.

Fiorella De Cindio Fiorella De Cindio is Associate Professor in the Department of Informatics and Communication of the Università degli Studi di Milano, where she teaches courses on Programming Languages, Distributed Systems Design, Software

Engineering, and Virtual Communities. Her research is twofold. On the one hand, it focuses on languages and methods for the analysis, design, and implementation of distributed systems, paying special attention to user involvement in the system development process (participatory design). On the other hand, her research focuses on the design and implementation of social interactive computer systems as well as their deployment in real-life settings. Within this framework, she has dedicated special attention to promoting civic participation and deliberation at the urban level, and to the development of software tools for supporting them. In both fields, she has invariably coupled research with field experience. To manage this integrated approach, she launched the Civic Informatics Laboratory (LIC) in 1994, which she still heads, and set up the Milan Community Network (RCM), which is now an autonomous body, namely a participatory foundation, of which she is president. Because of her activity in the community, the Milan Municipality presented De Cindio with the Ambrogino d'Oro, the municipality's highest award to citizens who have contributed to the city development, in December 2001.

Martijn de Waal   Martijn de Waal is a writer, researcher, and curator based in Amsterdam. His specialization is the relation between technology, media, culture, and society. Together with Michiel de Lange, he founded TheMobilecity.nl, an international platform focusing on mobile and locative media, urban culture, and identity. Under the auspices of the Mobile City he organized conferences on these themes in Rotterdam with the Netherlands Architecture Institute, and in Shanghai during the World Expo 2010. He is also part of the New Media, Public Sphere and Urban Culture research project, supervised by Rene Boomekens at the Department of Practical Philosophy at the University of Groningen. In 2009 de Waal was a visiting scholar at the MIT Medialab and the Center for Future Civic Media. In 2007 he took part in the Internationale Biennale of Urbanism and Architecture in Shenzhen, China. Over the years he has contributed to several volumes on urban culture and media culture, including the catalog for the International Architecture Biennale Rotterdam in 2007 as well as the MediaCity book published by the Bauhaus University Press in 2008. He is also involved in the Dynamic City Foundation and has contributed to its main publication, *The Chinese Dream*, edited by Neville Mars and Adrian Hornsby. For more, see www .themobilecity.nl or www.martijndewaal.nl.

Carl DiSalvo   Carl DiSalvo is an Assistant Professor in the School of Literature, Communication, and Culture at the Georgia Institute of Technology, where he directs the Public Design Workshop. He received a PhD in Design from Carnegie Mellon University in 2006 and was a postdoctoral fellow at Carnegie Mellon with joint appointments in the Studio for Creative Inquiry and the Center for Arts in Society in 2006–2007. DiSalvo's work draws together the humanities, science and technology studies, and interaction design to increase public engagement with technology and analyze the social and political uses and issues of contemporary technology. His interdisciplinary research has been published in *Design Issues* and in venues such as the ACM Conference on Human Factors in Computing Systems (CHI) and the Participatory Design Conference.

Judith Donath Judith Donath synthesizes knowledge from fields such as urban design, evolutionary biology, and cognitive science to build innovative interfaces for online communities and virtual identities. A Harvard Berkman Faculty Fellow and formerly director of the Sociable Media Group at the MIT Media Lab, she is known internationally for her writing on identity, interface design, and social communication. She created several of the earliest social applications for the web, including the original postcard service and the first interactive juried art show. Her work with the Sociable Media Group has been shown in museums and galleries worldwide, and was recently the subject of a major exhibition at the MIT Museum. Her current research focuses on understanding the social economics underlying communication, both face to face and online. This work bring a fresh understanding of the meaning embodied in everyday phenomena, such as fashion, faces, gifts, and so on—and it provides a strong foundation for designing engaging social environments that promote cooperation and trust. She has two books in progress, one on the design of sociable media and one that explores how we signal identity in both mediated and face-to-face interactions. She received her doctoral and master's degrees in Media Arts and Sciences from MIT, her bachelor's degree in History from Yale University, and has worked professionally as a designer and builder of educational software and experimental media.

Paul Dourish Paul Dourish is a Professor of Informatics in the Donald Bren School of Information and Computer Sciences at UC Irvine, with courtesy appointments in Computer Science and Anthropology. He teaches in the Informatics program and in the interdisciplinary graduate program in Arts Computation and Engineering. His primary research interests lie at the intersection of computer science and social science; he draws liberally on material from computer science, science and technology studies, cultural studies, humanities, and social sciences in order to understand information technology as a site of social and cultural production. In 2008, he was elected to the CHI Academy in recognition of his contributions to human-computer interaction. Before coming to UCI, he was a Senior Member of Research Staff in the Computer Science Laboratory of Xerox PARC; he has also held research positions at Apple Computer and at Rank Xerox EuroPARC. He holds a PhD in Computer Science from University College, London, and a BSc (Hons) in Artificial Intelligence and Computer Science from the University of Edinburgh. He is the author of *Where the Action Is: The Foundations of Embodied Interaction* (MIT Press, 2001), which explores how phenomenological accounts of action can provide an alternative to traditional cognitive analysis for understanding the embodied experience of interactive and computational systems. His new book, in collaboration with Genevieve Bell, is currently in press; it is tentatively titled *Divining a Digital Future: Mess and Mythology in Ubiquitous Computing.*

Ava Fatah gen. Schieck   Ava Fatah gen. Schieck is an architect, researcher and educator. She is a Lecturer in Digital Interaction in the MSc Adaptive Architecture and Computation program at The Bartlett, UCL. Her research is concerned with the design, implementation, and evaluation of mixed-reality, location-based, and responsive experiences that explore embodied and performative interactions mediated through technology. She was the UCL lead academic on the "SCREAM" project funded by the Urban Buzz knowledge exchange program, looking at critical design issues related to the implementation of large public screens in urban space. One of her contributions to the field has been published in the *Urban Screens Reader*, the first book to focus entirely on the topic of urban screens and media facades and offer rich resources of key texts. With expertise in arhiture and digital interaction in VR, AR, MR, and Ubiquitous Computing spanning both the building scale (architecture) and the urban scale (urban design), she has lectured internationally and published extensively on public space and its transformation and acquisition through new media and pervasive technologies.

Laura Forlano   Laura Forlano is a Postdoctoral Associate at the Interaction Design Lab in the Department of Communication at Cornell University. Her current research examines the ways designers collaborate on sustainability and social innovation projects. In 2008–2009, she was Kauffman Fellow in Law at the Information Society Project at Yale Law School. Forlano received her PhD in Communications from Columbia University in 2008. Her dissertation, "When Code Meets Place: Collaboration and Innovation at WiFi Hotspots," explores the intersection between organizations, technology (in particular, mobile and wireless technology), and the role of place in communication, collaboration, and innovation. Forlano is an Adjunct Faculty member in the Design and Management Department at Parsons and in the Graduate Program in Media Studies at The New School, where she teaches courses on Innovation, Design, and Everyday Experience; New Media and Global Affairs; and Technology and the City. She serves as a board member of NYCwireless and the New York City Computer-Human Interaction Association. Forlano received a Master's in International Affairs from Columbia University, a Diploma in International Relations from Johns Hopkins University, and a Bachelor's in Asian Studies from Skidmore College.

Peter Francis   Peter Francis is a lecturer in Information Systems at Victoria University, Melbourne. His research interests include health information systems adoption and strategy, as well as domestic technology design. His current work focuses on the modeling of complex support settings for people with cognitive disorders.

Jonas Fritsch   Jonas Fritsch is a PhD fellow at the Department of Information and Media Studies at Aarhus University, affiliated closely with the Center for Digital Urban Living (DUL), where he is primarily engaged in projects in the areas of civic communication and media facades. The subject of his dissertation work revolves around developing affect theory as a theoretical foundation for conceptualizing experience-oriented design of experimental urban interfaces and interactions. The theoretical foundation is continuously tested in practical design projects carried in the realm of DUL and elsewhere. He has been visiting researcher at the Workshop in Radical Empiricism (directed by Brian Massumi) at the University of Montreal and the SenseLab (directed by Erin Manning) at Concordia University, Montreal, where he has been engaged in theory building and activist urban projects on the verge of interactive art and design. He is still a member of the SenseLab and part of the editorial collective of Inflexions (www.inflexions.org). He holds an MA in information studies with a supplementary degree in aesthetics and communication from la Nouvelle Sorbonne, Paris, and has professional experience with interaction design as well.

Gillian Fuller   Fuller + Harley are an interdisciplinary research-production team who fuse new media theory and practice in a variety of formats. For the past five years, they have been working on a multimodal project that analyses the flows and network spaces of contemporary airports. Gillian Fuller, who trained as a semiotician and now specializes in new media geographies and mobile cultures, has worked in public radio, museums, and now academia. She has published in journals such as *Borderlands*, *Fibre-Culture*, and *Social Semiotics* and has contributed chapters to many international texts around topics of mobilities; airport cultures; and politics, biometrics, and biopower. She is coediting a forthcoming book, *Stillness in a Mobile World*, for the International Library of Sociology Series (Routledge). Fuller is a researcher at the University of New South Wales, Sydney. For more, visit aviopolis.com, stereopresence.net, and transitsemiotics.org.

Fabien Giardin   Fabien Girardin is a researcher and engineer at Lift lab, a research agency he cofounded. He is fascinated by the interplay between urban infrastructures, ubiquitous technologies, and people practices. His research mixes qualitative observations with quantitative data analysis to gain insights from the integration and appropriation of technologies in urban environments. Subsequently, he exploits the gained knowledge with engineering techniques to foresee and prototype ideas and solutions for designers, urban service providers, city planners, and decision makers. Giardin holds a PhD in Computer Science and Digital Communications from Universitat Pompeu Fabra in Barcelona, Spain. Along his academic journey, he was also affiliated with the SENSEable City Lab at MIT, leading the development of analysis methods of real-time and historical aggregated spatiotemporal records to improve the understanding of different aspects of human mobility and urban attractiveness.

Germaine Halegoua   Germaine Halegoua is a PhD candidate in the Media & Cultural Studies program in the Department of Communication Arts at the University of Wisconsin at Madison. Her dissertation, "New Mediated Spaces and the Urban Environment," explores the relationships between cities on the one hand and new media technologies and practices on the other. She specializes in the analysis of ubiquitous computing and public culture, mediated spatial relations in the urban environment, and the cultural geography of media. The fieldwork for this chapter was made possible through grants from the Robert F. & Jean E. Holtz Center for Science and Technology Studies, and the University of Wisconsin at Madison.

Ross Harley   Ross Harley is an artist and writer whose media work has been exhibited in venues such as at the Pompidou Centre, New York MoMA, Ars Electronica, and the Sydney Opera House. His writing has appeared in *Art + Text, Convergence, Screen, Rolling Stone*, and *The Australian*. His recent work, *Aviopolis: A Book about Airports* (with Gillian Fuller) was published by Black Dog Publishing, London, in 2005. He is a researcher at the University of New South Wales, Sydney. For further information, visit aviopolis. com, stereopresence.net, and transitsemiotics.org.

Greg Hearn   Greg Hearn is Research Professor in the Creative Industries Faculty at QUT. His work focuses on policy development and R&D for new services in the creative industries. He has over two decades of experience in managing large research and evaluation projects. He is one of Australia's foremost thinkers on social and economic frameworks for assessing creative services and in 2005 was a member of the Prime Minister's Working Party on the Role of Creativity in the Innovation Economy. He has authored or coauthored over twenty major research reports and books, including *Public Policy in Knowledge-Based Economies* (Edward Elgar, 2003), *The Knowledge Economy Handbook* (Edward Elgar, 2005), and *Knowledge Policy: Challenges for the 21st Century* (Edward Elgar, 2008). Hearn was one of the architects of the Creative Benchmarker project, a collaboration with the Queensland Department of Tourism Regional Development and Industry to evaluate economic performance of the Queensland creative sector (http://www.benchmarker.org.au/). He has more than thirty years experience in qualitative methods, which has included supervising more than fifteen higher degrees utilizing qualitative methodology. He has also won more $4 million worth of national competitive grants investigating services in the creative industries.

Tommi Heikkinen   Tommi Heikkinen is a researcher in the UrBan Interactions (UBI) research program and a doctoral candidate in the Department of Electrical and Information Engineering at the University of Oulu, Finland, where he obtained his MSc degree in 2003.

Tad Hirsch   Tad Hirsch is a design researcher with Intel Labs' Social Insights Research group, where he leads a team of designers, engineers, and social scientists that studies technology and cultural practice. He is currently working on technologies to support sustainable agriculture and public participation in environmental policymaking. Hirsch was a member of the Rhode Island School of Design's Digital Media faculty from 2006 to 2008, and has taught courses in art, design, and engineering at Carnegie Mellon University, MIT, and the University of Oregon. He holds PhD and MSc degrees in Media Arts and Sciences from MIT, and an MDes in Interaction Design from CMU. His dissertation, examining technology innovation by political activists, was completed in 2008 under the direction of William J. Mitchell in the Smart Cities group at the MIT Media Lab. Hirsch is also a founding member of the Institute for Applied Autonomy, an art/technology/activism collective that has been operating since 1998. His work has been included in festivals and exhibited in museums and galleries throughout Europe and America, including the Zentrum für Kunst und Medientechnologie Karlsruhe, Ars Electronica, the New Museum, the Aldridge Museum of Contemporary Art, and MassMoca. He has been the recipient of several prestigious awards and commissions, including an Award of Distinction at Prix Ars Electronica 2000 and Rhizome Net Art Commissions in 2002 and 2006.

Simo Hosio   Simo Hosio is a researcher in the UrBan Interactions (UBI) research program and a doctoral candidate in the Department of Electrical and Information Engineering at the University of Oulu, Finland, where he obtained his MSc degree in 2009.

Renato Iannella   Renato Iannella is a Principal Scientist at the National ICT Australia (NICTA) research laboratory, where he leads the Web Science research activity. His research covers technologies and standards in Internet information modeling and architectures, rights management, and policy-oriented web infrastructures. Renato has extensive experience in setting standards for Internet, web, and mobile technologies and was a former member of the World Wide Web Consortium (W3C) Advisory Board. He is also an Adjunct Professor at the Queensland University of Technology, Visiting Professor at the University of Hong Kong, and Adjunct Associate Professor at the University of Queensland, and was previously the Chief Scientist at LiveEvents Wireless, IPR Systems, and Principal Research Scientist at the Distributed Systems Technology Centre (DSTC).

Sarath Indrakanti   Sarath Indrakanti is a Research Scientist at the NICTA's Brisbane research laboratory. He is part of the team involved in the Social and Professional Interoperable Networks (SPIN) research activity. His research primarily covers information and distributed systems security, including SOA security, identity and access management, and Web 2.0 security. Indrakanti also holds an Adjunct Lecturer position at the University of Queensland. He holds a PhD in computer science from the Macquarie University.

Kurt Iveson   Kurt Iveson is Senior Lecturer in Urban Geography at the University of Sydney. He is primarily interested in the question of how social justice can be achieved in cities. Within this broad context, his previous research has focused on two main areas. First, he has examined the significance of the urban public realm for citizenship and democracy. Second, he has explored how urban planning might work better to achieve social justice in cities. He is author of *Publics and the City* (Blackwell, 2007) and coauthor (with Ruth Fincher) of *Planning and Diversity in the City: Redistribution, Recognition and Encounter* (Palgrave, 2008).

Marko Jurmu   Marko Jurmu is a researcher in the UrBan Interactions (UBI) research program and a doctoral candidate in the Department of Electrical and Information Engineering at the University of Oulu, Finland, where he obtained his MSc degree in 2007.

Sunyoung Kim   Sunyoung Kim is a PhD student in the Human-Computer Interaction Institute at Carnegie Mellon University. Previously, she received her master's degree in Human-Computer Interaction from the Georgia Institute of Technology. Kim is also a member of the Aware Home Research Initiative and the Ubiquitous Computing Research Group at the Georgia Institute of Technology. Her research interests fall under the umbrella of ubiquitous computing, mobile technology, and pervasive computing. Currently, her research focuses on the creation and use of technologies that contribute toward improving human well-being and environmental sustainability. Kim has also worked as an interaction designer and strategic planner at Samsung in the areas of Internet media, mobile-device interfaces, and the Ubiquitous Appliance for Apartment Complex in South Korea. She received her bachelor's degree in Architecture and Interior Design at Yonsei University, Korea.

Christopher Kirwan   Christopher Kirwan is a multidisciplinary consultant and educator with expertise combining urban planning, architecture, and media. Currently based in Beijing, he is working on a number of large real estate development and media projects while teaching a graduate-level research course at Parsons The New School for Design in collaboration with Tsinghua University. During the past decade, as creative partner in a thirty-person New York/Dubai consulting firm, he directed master planning projects in the New York/New Jersey area and in several Middle East countries. In all his projects, Kirwan strives to employ an integrated process, combining design innovation, financial profitability, environmental sustainability, and social well-being with an emphasis on new media, branding, and marketing. Earlier in his career, he worked in several renowned international design offices, including Sottsass Associati in Milan, Fitch in London, and Machado & Silvetti Architects in Boston. Since 1996, he has been adjunct professor at Parsons, visiting faculty at the Harvard Graduate School of Design, and guest lecturer in many international schools and conferences. He received his undergraduate degrees in Architecture and Fine Arts from

Rhode Island School of Design and carried out graduate studies at the MIT Center for Advanced Visual Studies. His permanent residence with his wife and daughter is in Manhattan.

Jesper Kjeldskov Jesper Kjeldskov is Associate Professor of Computer Science at Aalborg University in Denmark, Honorary Fellow at the University of Melbourne, and an Honorary Associate of the IDHuP Lab at the University of Technology, Sydney. Kjeldskov has a cross-disciplinary background spanning the humanities, social sciences, and computer science. He has published widely in the area of human-computer interaction and recently led a User Experience Research group in Australia. His main research focus is interaction design and evaluation of mobile systems of devices. Within this area he has recently completed a large Danish Technical Research Council–funded project exploring the theoretical concept of indexicality for describing and understanding the user experience of context awareness.

Fabio Kruger Fabio Kruger is a research assistant in the UrBan Interactions (UBI) research program, which he joined as an Erasmus exchange student in 2008 from the Politecnico di Milano in Italy, where he is currently pursuing the MSc degree.

Hannu Kukka Hannu Kukka is a PhD student in the department of Electrical and Information Engineering at the University of Oulu, Finland, and also the project manager of the UrBan Interactions (UBI) research program. He got his MSc degree from the Department of Information Processing Science at the University of Oulu in 2006. Kukka's research interests include studies in ubiquitous computing in urban environments, specifically dealing with how new computing resources and services can aid people in finding relevant in-situ information while in a public urban setting. Contact him at hannu.kukka@ee.oulu.fi.

Stacey Kuznetsov Stacey Kuznetsov is a PhD student in the Human-Computer Interaction Institute at Carnegie Mellon University. Her current research explores low-cost, do-it-yourself (DIY) technologies in the context of political discourse, street art, and other grassroots public expressions. Previously, she received a BA from New York University, with a dual degree in Philosophy and Computer Science. She then worked as a software engineer with Google's search quality team in New York City. Her prior projects span the domains of computer science, social science, information extraction, and computational archeology.

Tomas Lindén Tomas Lindén is a researcher in the UrBan Interactions (UBI) research program and a doctoral candidate in the Department of Electrical and Information Engineering at the University of Oulu, Finland. He obtained his MSc degree at the Helsinki University of Technology in 2005.

Richard Ling Richard Ling (PhD, University of Colorado, 1984) is a professor at the IT University of Copenhagen and a researcher at Telenor's research institute in Norway.

He has also been the Pohs Visiting Professor of Communication Studies at the University of Michigan. He now holds an adjunct position in that department. He is the author of the book *New Tech, New Ties: How Mobile Communication Is Reshaping Social Cohesion* (MIT). He is also the author of *The Mobile Connection* (Morgan Kaufmann) and, along with Jonathan Donner, he has written *Mobile Phones and Mobile Communication*. He has been recognized as an outstanding scholar by Rutgers University, received the 2009 Erving Goffman Award from the Media Ecology Association, and received the Telenor Research Award in 2009. He has been interviewed in many European and U.S. periodicals, including the *New York Times*, *The Economist*, and *Wired*. For more, visit http://richardling.com/ (see also http://mobilesociety.ning.com/).

Jonathan Lukens Jonathan Lukens studies under the auspices of the Public Design Workshop in Georgia Tech's school of Literature, Communication, and Culture. His work there is informed by his service as the director of operations for the *Reconstruction Report*—a project of the Design Trust for Public Space, facilitating public input into the redevelopment of Lower Manhattan after the events of 9/11. His thinking has also been shaped by his work as a project manager for a collaborative studio at Parsons Center for New Design that investigated issues surrounding land mines and unexploded ordnance. Before joining the Public Design Workshop, Lukens was an Assistant Professor of Graphic Design at Georgia State University, and taught at the Art Institute of Atlanta and at Parsons School of Design.

Gary Marsden Gary Marsden is a professor in the Computer Science Department at the University of Cape Town. His research interests are in Mobile Interaction Design and ICT for Development. He has coauthored a book with Matt Jones titled *Mobile Interaction Design*, published in 2006. He is currently director of the UCT ICT4D Research Centre and the UCT–Hasso Plattner Research School. He won the 2007 ACM SIGCHI Social Responsiveness award for his research in using mobile technology in the developing world. Despite all of this, he still cannot use all the features on his mobile phone.

Bjorn Nansen Bjorn Nansen is a Research Fellow in the McCaughey Centre at the University of Melbourne. His current research involves media sociologies of broadband in the home and ICT use in the contexts of familial life. He is interested in the critical theory and social study of human-technology relations; is completing his PhD dissertation in the School of Culture and Communication at the University of Melbourne on the temporal rhythms of sociotechnical practice; and has published a number of articles that consider the technological mediation of time, the body, and the everyday.

Timo Ojala Timo Ojala is Professor of Computer Engineering at the Computer Science and Engineering Laboratory and the Director of the MediaTeam Oulu research group at the University of Oulu, Finland. He is the scientific director of the UrBan Interactions (UBI) research program, which is the driving force behind the concept of the Open Ubiquitous Oulu. His research interests range from distributed systems to ubiquitous computing, with special emphasis on experimental urban computing research in a real-world setting. He has authored over 100 international scientific papers. He is the cofounder and the chair of the steering committee of the International Conference on Mobile and Ubiquitous Multimedia (MUM). He obtained his MSc and DrTech degrees from the Department of Electrical and Information Engineering at the University of Oulu in 1992 and 1997, respectively.

Eamonn O'Neill Eamonn O'Neill holds a PhD in Computer Science from the University of London. He is a Reader in Human-Computer Interaction in the Department of Computer Science at the University of Bath and a Royal Society Industry Fellow with Vodafone Group R&D, researching social networks and intelligent mobile services. He led the Cityware project that took a multidisciplinary approach to understanding and designing urban pervasive computing systems. He brings a human-computer interaction perspective to research on mobile and pervasive computing, taking into account a range of technical, social, and other factors in developing fundamental theory, principles, design tools, and methods. His interests include understanding, designing, building, and evaluating complex interactive systems involving multiple people and multiple technologies. His research is particularly focused on the relationships between mobile and pervasive technologies, the urban built environment, and people. He is also interested in making pervasive systems context-aware. Here, O'Neill is developing the fundamental theory for context-aware systems and reflecting this in working architectures and applications. He also investigates how pervasive computing can enhance and support people's creativity. His earlier PhD research on participatory design won the British Computer Society's Distinguished Dissertation Award.

Jeni Paay Jeni Paay is Assistant Professor of Computer Science at Aalborg University in Denmark and a Visiting Fellow of the IDHuP Lab at University of Technology, Sydney. Paay has a cross-disciplinary background spanning architecture, computer science, and interaction design, and has published widely in the area of human-computer interaction. Prior to this she was Lead Interaction Designer on the "Blended Interaction Spaces" project with CSIRO Australia, and has worked within the overall research theme of "Augmenting the City with Fiction."

Freya Palmer Freya Palmer is a researcher at the University of Bath, where her work focuses on the social use of technology, particularly in the communication of identity. She has always been interested in the study of people's everyday interactions—particularly those with, or mediated by, designed objects. She is interested in how and why people use social and communication technologies. Her main area of interest, however, is in how such aspects relate to our individual and social identities. These interests have been reflected in previous work addressing how groups with differing areas of expertise view everyday objects, the communication of individual and group identity within online social networks, and that of her PhD research—the use of mobile and pervasive technology in communicating social identity. In investigating the latter, she has worked closely with the Cityware research project in conducting fieldwork addressing interactions with pervasive technology as well as in analyzing their substantial dataset of Bluetooth names. Palmer has a BSc (Hons) in Psychology and MSc in Human Communication and Computing from the University of Bath, where she is currently in the final year of her PhD in Computer Science.

Eric Paulos   Eric Paulos is the Director of the Living Environments Lab and an Associate Professor in the Human-Computer Interaction Institute with courtesy faculty appointments in the Robotics Institute in the School of Computer Science and in the Entertainment Technology Center at Carnegie Mellon University. Previously, Paulos was Senior Research Scientist at Intel Research in Berkeley, California, where he founded the Urban Atmospheres research group—challenged to employ innovative methods to explore urban life and the future fabric of emerging technologies across public urban landscapes. His areas of expertise span a deep body of research territory in urban computing, sustainability, green design, environmental awareness, social telepresence, robotics, physical computing, interaction design, persuasive technologies, and intimate media. Paulos is a leading figure in the field of urban computing, having coined the term in 2004, and is a regular contributor, editorial board member, and reviewer for numerous professional journals and conferences. He received his PhD in Electrical Engineering and Computer Science from UC Berkeley, where he helped launch a new robotics industry by developing some of the first Internet tele-operated robots, including Space Browsing helium-filled blimps and Personal Roving Presence devices (PRoPs).

Jon M. Pearce   Jon M. Pearce in a senior lecturer in the Department of Information Systems at the University of Melbourne. His research focuses on engagement and interactivity, in both educational and noneducational contexts. His current research interests weave together strands from interactivity, multimedia, engagement, learning, and flow; his domains of interest are education and sustainability, particularly in a social networking context. Pearce's current development and research projects include the design and development of an automated peer review system to support teaching, an interactive system to support people in the efficient use of water in their gardens, and a novel online system to help people explore choices based on their personal preferences.

Alan Penn   Alan Penn is an architect, Dean of the Bartlett Faculty of the Built Environment, Professor of Architectural and Urban Computing, founding director of Space

Syntax Ltd (a UCL knowledge-transfer spinout), and Director of the VR Centre for the Built Environment at UCL. His research spans the fields of architecture, planning, and computing. He investigates the way the design of space relates to the ways people move through and use it, and the way these behaviors and the social interactions they produce are related, including to their use of new digital technologies. He is the UCL PI of the EPSRC WINES Cityware project. He was the founding chair of the RIBA's Research and Innovation Committee, serving in that role until 2006. He is chair of the Architecture & the Built Environment sub-panel 30 for the UK National Research Assessment Exercise 2008, and is a member of its main panel. He is also lead academic on the £5m Urban Buzz: Building Sustainable Communities knowledge exchange program, which is promoting more sustainable forms of urban development and intensification in London and the greater South East Region of the United Kingdom.

Cristian Peraboni Cristian Peraboni received his PhD in Computer Science at the Università degli Studi di Milano in 2009 and his MSc in Computer Science in 2005 at the same university. Currently he holds a research fellowship at the Department of Informatics and Communications of the Università degli Studi di Milano, with a project titled "Social Interactive Systems: Concepts, Environments, and Design Methods." His work has led to invitations to participate in several research projects in the e-participation arena. In particular, in the "e21 for the Development of Digital Citizenship in Agenda 21" project, he collaborated in the design and implementation of the openDCN software environment and its deliberative tools. openDCN is currently used for running several e-participation and e-deliberation initiatives (for an updated list of the openDCN instances, see http://www.opendcn.org). Peraboni is member of the Civic Informatics Laboratory (LIC), which set up the Milan Community Network and has managed it since 1994. His research interests include social interactive systems, digital habitats, virtual communities, e-participation, e-deliberation, online social networks, folksonomies, and knowledge management.

Francisco C. Pereira Francisco C. Pereira is an Assistant Professor at Faculdade de Ciências e Tecnologia da Universidade de Coimbra (FCTUC), Portugal, Department of Informatics Engineering (DEI). His main research field is artificial intelligence, with a focus on ubiquitous computing for the urban environment, particularly the transport systems. He has been collaborating with DUSP, MIT, in investigating applications of AI to urban contexts. With the SENSEable City Lab, Pereira is involved in Fusion of Mobility Data with Semantics and Behaviour Modeling for an Intelligent Route Planner (the AUDI project). He is also the leader of the iTEAM project, a collaboration between MIT and three Portuguese universities. He wrote the book *Creativity and AI: A Conceptual Blending Approach* (published by Mouton de Gruyter in 2007) as a result of his doctoral research. He has coauthored over fifty peer-reviewed publications, including many journal articles and book chapters.

Carlo Ratti   An architect and engineer, Carlo Ratti practices architecture in Turin and teaches at MIT, where he directs the SENSEable City Laboratory, a new research initiative in the Department of Urban Studies and Planning. Ratti's work has been exhibited in leading museums worldwide, including the Kunsthaus Graz (2005), Venice Biennale (2004, 2006, and 2008), MoMA (2008), and Design Museum Barcelona (2009). He has coauthored over 100 scientific publications and holds several patents. His Digital Water Pavilion at the World Expo 2008 was hailed by *Time* Magazine as one of the "Best Inventions of the Year." He was named Queensland's 2009 Innovator in Residence, cited as one of *Esquire* Magazine's 2008 Best & Brightest, and included in *Blueprint* Magazine's list of twenty people who would change the world of design in 2010. Ratti graduated with an MSc in civil structural engineering from both the Politecnico di Torino, Italy, and the Ecole Nationale des Ponts et Chaussées in Paris. He later received an MPhil and a PhD in Architecture from the University of Cambridge.

Yvonne Rogers   Yvonne Rogers is a professor of Human-Computer Interaction at University College London and director of UCLIC. Prior to that she was professor at the Open University (UK), Indiana University (US), and Sussex University (UK). She has also been a visiting professor at Stanford, Apple, Queensland University, and UCSD. Her research focuses on augmenting and extending everyday learning and work activities with a diversity of interactive and novel technologies. Central to her work is a critical stance toward theory and conceptual frameworks. She was one of the principal investigators on the UK Equator project (2002–2007), where she pioneered and experimented with ubiquitous learning. She has published widely, beginning with her PhD work on graphical interfaces and extending to her most recent work on public visualizations and behavioral change. She is one of the coauthors of the bestselling textbook *Interaction Design: Beyond Human-Computer Interaction* (3rd edition) and *Being Human: Human-Computer Interaction in the Year 2020.*

Phoebe Sengers   Phoebe Sengers is an associate professor of Information Science and Science & Technology Studies at Cornell University. Her work integrates human-computer interaction with cultural studies of technology. She analyzes IT in the context of North American consumer culture and the rise of efficiency, productivity, and faith in technoscience as hegemonic cultural values. She uses insights from this cultural analysis of IT to identify and rethink the assumptions underlying technologies, to build new applications for computing, and to develop new techniques for designing and evaluating technologies. She is currently engaged in a long-term design-ethnographic and historical study of sociotechnological change in the small, traditional fishing community of Change Islands, Newfoundland. Prior to coming to Cornell, she worked at the Media Arts Research Studies group at the German National Computer Science Research Center (GMD) in Bonn and was a Fulbright Scholar at the

Center for Art and Media Technology (ZKM) in Karlsruhe, Germany. She holds a self-defined interdisciplinary PhD in Artificial Intelligence and Cultural Theory from Carnegie Mellon University.

Danielle Shelton   Danielle Shelton has bachelor's degrees in Acting as well as Film & Television Production. She has been the recipient of numerous awards for both her performing and film making, including the QNFA award for Best Producer and Best Film along with several Australian Cinematographers Society Gold awards. In research, Shelton is fascinated by character and personality. In her creative practice she seeks to apply character development and analysis techniques to social and workplace behavioral patterns in an attempt to influence positive change in attitudes and relationships. She teaches drama at Queensland University of Technology.

Laurianne Sitbon   Laurianne Sitbon was awarded a PhD from the University of Avignon, France, in 2007 and now holds a postdoctoral position at the University of Queensland in Australia. Her research is centered around the contextual aspects of information retrieval in a wide understanding of context that ranges from special user needs during the search process to better representations of contextual meaning via distributional approaches. She has been involved at various levels in reviewing and organizing major journals and conferences in the field of information retrieval (TKDE, *Information Retrieval Journal*, SIGIR, ECIR, ICTIR).

Wally Smith   Wally Smith is a senior lecturer in Information Systems at the University of Melbourne. He is interested in the social and persuasive aspects of technology. Recent work includes an investigation of the role of commercial technology demonstrations ("Theatre of Use: A Frame Analysis of IT Demonstrations," in the *Social Studies of Science*) and a study of the nineteenth-century origins of the smart house in stage conjuring ("The Magic of Machines in the House," with Hannah Lewi, in the *Journal of Architecture*).

Atau Tanaka   Atau Tanaka holds the Chair of Digital Media at Newcastle University. He holds degrees from Harvard University and Stanford University's CCRMA. He has worked at IRCAM in Paris and as Artistic Ambassador for Apple France. In 2001 he was the first artist to become a researcher at Sony Computer Science Laboratory Paris. Tanaka's work bridges the fields of interactive media and computer music. He holds a patent on musical control interfaces using physiological biosignals. He seeks to harness collective musical creativity in mobile environments, seeking out the continued place of the artist in democratized digital forms. His work has received awards from Ars Electronica, Fondation Langlois, and the Fraunhofer Institute and has been funded by Research Councils UK (AHRC, EPSRC), the French National Research Agency (ANR), and the Japanese Ministry of Telecommunications. He has been mentor at NESTA and is currently the director of Culture Lab.

Sven Travis Sven Travis is a designer, an artist, and a skier, in addition to serving as Associate Professor of Media Design and Dean of the School of Art, Media, and Technology at Parsons. He has taught and administered at Parsons for more than twenty years. He is founder, chair, and on the faculty of the Parsons Design & Technology Department. He has served as a faculty member in the Parsons Product Design Department (Textile Design), as Parsons Director of Advanced Computing, as chair of the Parsons Digital Design Department (which he founded), as director of the Parsons Center for New Design, and as New School Associate Provost for Technology R&D. Travis spearheads several ongoing research initiatives, including Parsons/Tsinghua/ Tongji Media Arts Lab (New York/Beijing/Shanghai), [SpyLab] (illicit international data collection, provision, and manifestation), the Salted/Unsalted project (virtual-physical fabrication), the Fred Group (digitally generated textile printing and design), and Crazy Baldhead (neural network and fuzzy logic programming applied to interactive media). Travis was raised in Wisconsin and is a lifelong fan of the Green Bay Packers. He was educated at the Rhode Island School of Design and New York Polytechnic University. He is married with two children, and is a proud resident of Williamsburg, Brooklyn.

Andrea Vaccari Andrea Vaccari investigates people's lifestyle and sentiment through their interaction with digital technologies, pervasive systems, and the built environment. His projects focus on the study of mobility, tourism, and the distribution and evolution of activities and opinions to provide new tools to innovate and anticipate the effects of such innovations. Vaccari has collaborated with the MIT and the Santa Fe Institute. At the SENSEable City Lab, he focused on the study of interactions between people, their digital traces, and the city. His work has been exhibited at the Museum of Modern Art in New York City and the Design Museum in Barcelona, Spain, and featured in the *New York Times* and *Time* Magazine. Vaccari holds an MS degree in Computer Engineering from Politecnico di Milano, Italy. He also holds an MS degree in Computer Science from the University of Illinois at Chicago, where he is completing the PhD program.

Frank Vetere Frank Vetere has a PhD in Human-Computer Interaction (HCI) and leads the Interaction Design Group at the University of Melbourne. He researches the use of emerging ICTs for the purpose of understanding and designing useful, usable, and satisfying technology. He has over eighty scholarly articles and conference papers to his credit. He has been awarded research support from Nokia, Novell, Smart Internet Technologies CRC, and the Australian Research Council.

Andrew Wong Andrew Wong is a Senior Research Scientist at the Telenor Research and Innovation Centre Asia Pacific (TRICAP), part of Telenor's Corporate Development Division. His research focuses on the role of information and communication technologies in developing countries, mainly in Telenor's Asia business-unit footprint. In addition, he conducts research on the use of formal and informal financial services by the unbanked and unserved, mainly in Bangladesh, Pakistan, Thailand, and India. Prior to joining the Telenor Group, Wong worked with the International Data Corporation (IDC), an advisory and market intelligence firm with headquarters in Boston. He holds a doctorate in Management from Multimedia University (Malaysia) and a master's in Business Administration from Cardiff University (United Kingdom). E-Mail: Andrew.wong@telenor.com.

Index